◾CURRENCIES AND SYMBOLS◾

Country	Currency	Symbol	Country	Currency	Symbol
Liechtenstein	Franc	SFr	Senegal	CFA Franc	CFAF
Luxembourg	Franc	LF	Singapore	Dollar	S$
Macau	Pataca	MOP	So. Africa	Rand	R
Malaŵi	Kwacha	MK	S.W. Africa/	Rand (S. Afr.)	R
Malaysia	Ringgit	M$	Namibia		
Malta	Lira	Lm	Soviet Union	Rouble	Rb
Mauritius	Rupee	Rs	Spain	Peseta	Ptas.
Mexico	Peso	Ps	Sweden	Krona	SEK
Morocco	Dirham	DH	Switzerland	Franc	SFr
Netherlands	Guilder	Dfl, Fl or Fls	Taiwan	Dollar	NT$
Netherlands	Guilder	NAf	Thailand	Baht	Bht or Bt
Antilles			Transkei	Rand (S. Afr.)	R
New Zealand	Dollar	NZ$	Trinidad and	Dollar	TT$
Nigeria	Naira	₦	Tobago		
Norway	Krone	NOK	Turkey	Lira	TL
Oman	Rial	RO	United Arab	Dirham	DH or UD
Pakistan	Rupee	PRs	Emirates		
Panama	Balboa	B/.	United	Pound	£
Papua New	Kina	K	Kingdom		
Guinea			Uruguay	New Peso	N$ or N$U
Paraguay	Guarani	₲	Vanuatu	Vatu	VT
Peru	Inti	I/.	Venda	Rand (S. Afr.)	R
Philippines	Peso	₱	Venezuela	Bolivar	Bs.
Portugal	Escudo	Esc	Western Samoa	Tala	WST
Puerto Rico	Dollar (U.S.)	$	Zaire	Zaire	Z
Qatar	Riyal	QR	Zambia	Kwacha	K or ZK
Saudi Arabia	Riyal	SR	Zimbabwe	Dollar	Z$

Multinational Financial Management

Multinational Financial Management

■ FOURTH EDITION ■

Alan C. Shapiro
University of Southern California

■ Allyn and Bacon ■
Boston   London   Sydney   Toronto

Series editor: Rich Wohl
Series editorial assistant: Cheryl Ten Eick
Cover administrator: Linda Dickinson
Manufacturing buyer: Megan Cochran
Text design: Sylvia Dovner, Technical Texts
Editorial production service: Betty O'Bryant, Technical Texts

Copyright © 1992, 1989, 1986, 1982 by Allyn and Bacon
A Division of Simon and Schuster
160 Gould Street, Needham Heights, Massachusetts 02194

Library of Congress Cataloging-in-Publication Data
Shapiro, Alan C.
   Multinational financial management / Alan C. Shapiro. — 4th ed.
     p. cm.
   Includes bibliographical references and index.
   ISBN 0-205-13230-8
   1. International business enterprises—Finance.   I. Title. HG4027.5.S47 1991
658.15'99—dc20   91-19533
                                                  CIP

Printed in the United States of America
10 9 8 7 6 5 4 3 2   96 95 94 93 92

To my parents, Hyman and Lily Shapiro
—for their encouragement, support, and love

◾ CONTENTS ◾

26   The International Debt Crisis and Country Risk Analysis   671

▪PREFACE▪

Approach

As the multinational corporation becomes the norm rather than the exception, the need to internationalize the tools of financial analysis is apparent. The primary objective of this fourth edition of *Multinational Financial Management,* as has been the objective of the first three editions, is to provide a conceptual framework within which the key financial decisions of the multinational firm can be analyzed. Analytical techniques are relied on to translate the often vague rules of thumb used by international financial executives into specific decision criteria. Numerous examples, both numerical and institutional, illustrate the application of these concepts and techniques. In addition, the theoretical framework provided by the concept of market efficiency is used to determine which decisions are worth worrying about. This is particularly useful in the case of foreign exchange risk management where much of the available evidence suggests that currency forecasting to reduce hedging costs may be of limited value. On the other hand, astute tax management is especially useful for the multinational firm, and so the relevant tax factors are integrated with all the key decision areas throughout the book.

All the traditional areas of corporate finance are explored, including working capital management, capital budgeting, and cost of capital and financial structure. However, this is done from the perspective of a multinational corporation, concentrating on those decision elements that are rarely, if ever, encountered by purely domestic firms. These elements include multiple currencies with frequent exchange rate changes and varying rates of inflation, differing tax systems, multiple money markets, exchange controls, segmented capital markets, and political risks such as nationalization or expropriation.

Throughout the book, I have tried to demystify multinational financial management by treating it as a natural and logical extension of the principles learned in the foundations course in financial management. Thus, it builds on and extends the valuation framework provided by domestic corporate finance to account for dimensions unique to international finance.

The emphasis throughout this book is on taking advantage of being multinational. Too often companies focus on the threats and risks inherent in going beyond the home country rather than on the opportunities that are available to multinational firms. These opportunities include the ability to obtain a greater degree of international diversification than security purchases alone can provide as well as the ability to arbitrage between imperfect capital markets, thereby obtaining funds at a lower cost than could a purely domestic firm.

Multinational Financial Management offers a variety of real-life examples that demonstrate the use of financial analysis and reasoning in solving international financial problems. These examples have been culled from the thousands of illustrations of corporate practice that I have collected over the years from business periodicals and consulting assignments. By incorporating the best of these examples in the text, students can see the value of examining decision problems with the aid of a solid theoretical foundation. Seemingly disparate facts and events can then be interpreted as specific manifestations of more general financial principles.

Audience

The fourth edition of *Multinational Financial Management* is suitable for use by the same audiences as was the first three editions—in international financial management courses on both the graduate and undergraduate levels and in a number of bank management and other executive development programs worldwide.

Multinational Financial Management presumes a knowledge of basic corporate finance, economics, and algebra. It assumes no prior knowledge of international economics or international finance, however, and is therefore self-contained in that respect.

Features of the Fourth Edition

The fourth edition of *Multinational Financial Management* has been thoroughly revised and updated. It includes numerous new questions and problems for virtually all chapters and three new chapters: one on currency futures and options, a second on international portfolio investment, and a third on country risk analysis in international banking. It has also been reorganized. In particular, the chapter on the foreign exchange market has been split into two chapters (Chapter 2 on the spot and forward interbank foreign exchange market and Chapter 3 on currency futures and options) and moved to the front of the book, Chapter 7 on currency forecasting has been consolidated with the new Chapter 7 on parity conditions, and Chapters 8–10 on currency risk management have been rearranged so that chapters on currency risk measurement and management are now in sequence. In addition, the discussion of interest rate parity has now been moved to Chapter 2 on the foreign exchange market, where it seems to be a more natural fit.

Multinational Financial Management, fourth edition, also contains a good deal of new material. This edition discusses the effects on international financial markets and international business strategy of Europe 1992, the fall of communism in Eastern Europe, German reunification, new regulations in international banking, and the change toward market-oriented economic systems around the world. MFM also contains new material on put-call option interest rate parity; the theory of exchange rate overshooting; the theory of the optimum currency area; how inventory considerations affect the production location decision; comparing the cost of capital in the United States and Japan; how the Japanese financial system helps to reduce the costs of financial distress; country risk analysis for nonbanks; and the effects on Europe 1992 on international banking strategies.

This book also includes many more charts and illustrations of corporate practice that are designed to highlight specific techniques or teaching points. Again, the emphasis is on reinforcing and making more relevant the concepts developed in the body of each chapter. To make the text more suitable as a teaching vehicle, I have added numerous questions and problems at the backs of the chapters, most of which are based on up-to-date information and real-life situations.

Many readers also will be interested in the differences between the fourth edition of *Multinational Financial Management* (MFM) and the first edition of my other book on the same topic. The basic differences between the books are that relative to *Foundations of Multinational Financial Management,* the fourth edition of MFM contains more technical material; it has more examples, illustrations, questions, problems, and short cases; and it includes a chapter on cost of capital for multinational firms.

Pedagogy

In order to make this book more accessible to people with less analytical backgrounds, the second edition extracted most of the more technical material from the various chapters and placed it in appendixes following the chapters. This policy still stands. The extracted material can be skipped over without interfering with the flow of the course.

The first two sections of the book have been rewritten because this material provides the foundation for studying international financial management and because this is where most people seem to get bogged down. I continue to focus on the distinction between nominal and real values. This has been accomplished now by including many more examples and problems that illustrate the principles being taught.

The pedagogical thrust of the book is greatly enhanced by including the following learning and teaching aids:

1. *Focus on Corporate Practice.* Throughout the text, there are numerous real-world examples and vignettes that provide actual applications of financial concepts and theories. They show students that the issues, tools, and techniques discussed in the book are being applied to day-to-day financial decision making.

2. *Extensive Use of Examples and Illustrations.* Numerous short illustrations and examples of specific concepts and techniques are scattered throughout the body of most chapters.

3. *Lengthier Illustrations of Corporate Practice.* There are seven longer illustrations of actual company practices, at the end of key chapters, that are designed to demonstrate different aspects of international financial management.

4. *Questions and Problems.* There are hundreds of end-of-chapter realistic questions and problems that offer practice in applying the concepts and theories being taught. Many of these questions and problems relate to actual situations and companies.

5. *Glossary.* The back of the book contains a Glossary that defines all the key terms appearing in the text.

6. *Supplements.* A complete set of ancillary materials is available for qualified adopters of *Multinational Financial Management* to supplement the text. These include

   - An Instructor's Manual containing detailed solutions to the end-of-chapter questions and problems and tips for teaching each chapter

- A Testbank containing over 530 additional questions and problems suitable for use in multiple choice exams
- Lotus 1–2–3 Templates designed to solve a wide variety of international financial management problems
- A Study Guide containing detailed chapter outlines and a number of solved questions and problems

Thanks

Following the principles of continuous product improvement, my philosophy has been to constantly upgrade the basic product, strengthening a feature here, adding a new feature there, while keeping the basic message of the book intact. In this process, I have been greatly aided by the suggestions of numerous people along the way.

This edition has benefited from helpful comments by the following reviewers:

James C. Baker, Kent State University
Donald T. Buck, Southern Connecticut State University
Jay Choi, Temple University
D. Ghosh, Rider College
Janice Wickstead Jadlow, Oklahoma State University
Steve Johnson, University of Texas at El Paso
Boyden E. Lee, New Mexico State University
Marc Lars Lipson, Boston University
Dick Marcus, University of Wisconsin–Milwaukee
D. Mehta, Georgia State
William N. Pugh, Auburn University
Bruce Seifert, Old Dominion University
Steve B. Wyatt, University of Cincinnati

I remain indebted to the academic reviewers of the first three editions of *Multinational Financial Management*. They include

Charles Anderson, Long Island University
Robert Aubey, University of Wisconsin-Madison
Robert Boatler, Texas Christian University
Donald T. Buck, Southern Connecticut State University
C. Fred DeKay, Seattle University
William R. Folks, Jr., University of South Carolina
Roger Huang, Vanderbilt University
Laurent Jacque, University of Minnesota
Chong Lee, University of the Pacific
Donald R. Lessard, Massachusetts Institute of Technology
Ike Mathur, Southern Illinois University at Carbondale
John Mitchell, Central Michigan University
Tarun Mukherjee, University of New Orleans
S. Ghon Rhee, University of Rhode Island
Keith Taylor, Utah State University

Kashi N. Tiwari, Nicholls State University
Oscar Varela, University of New Orleans

My family, especially my wife, Diane, as well as my mother and three brothers, has provided me (once again) with continual support and encouragement during the writing of this book. I appreciate the (usual) cheerfulness with which Diane and my children, Tom and Kathryn, endured the many hours I spent writing this text.

A.C.S.
Pacific Palisades

PART I

Environment of International Financial Management

1

Introduction: Multinational Enterprise and Multinational Financial Management

What is prudence in the conduct of every private family can scarce be folly in that of a great kingdom. If a foreign country can supply us with a commodity cheaper than we ourselves can make it, better buy it of them with some part of the produce of our own industry employed in a way in which we have some advantage.

—Adam Smith (1776)—

■ International business activity is not new. The transfer of goods and services across national borders has been taking place for thousands of years, antedating even Joseph's advice to the rulers of Egypt to establish that nation as the granary of the Middle East. Since the end of World War II, however, international business has undergone a revolution out of which has emerged what is probably the most important economic phenomenon of the latter half of the twentieth century: the multinational corporation (MNC).

■ 1.1 ■
THE RISE OF THE MULTINATIONAL CORPORATION

The *multinational corporation* is a company engaged in producing and selling goods or services in more than one country. It ordinarily consists of a parent company located in the home country and at least five or six foreign subsidiaries, typically with a high degree of strategic interaction among the units. Some MNCs have upwards of 100 foreign subsidiaries scattered around the world.

Based in part on the development of modern communications and transportation technologies, the rise of the multinational corporation was unanticipated by the classical theory of international trade as first developed by Adam Smith and David Ricardo. According to this theory, which rests on the *doctrine of comparative advantage*, each nation should

3

specialize in the production and export of those goods that it can produce with highest relative efficiency and import those goods that other nations can produce relatively more efficiently.

Underlying this theory is the assumption that goods and services can move internationally, but that factors of production such as capital, labor, and land are relatively immobile. Furthermore, the theory deals only with trade in commodities—that is, undifferentiated products; it ignores the roles of uncertainty, economies of scale, and technology in international trade and is static rather than dynamic. For all these defects, however, it is a valuable theory and still provides a well-reasoned theoretical foundation for free-trade arguments. But the growth of the MNC can be understood only by relaxing the traditional assumptions of classical trade theory.

Classical trade theory implicitly assumes that countries differ enough from one another in terms of resource endowments and economic skills for these differences to be at the center of any analysis of corporate competitiveness. Differences among individual corporate strategies are considered to be of only secondary importance; a company's citizenship is the key determinant of international success in the world of Adam Smith and David Ricardo.

However, this theory is increasingly irrelevant to the analysis of the countries presently at the core of the world economy—the United States, Japan, Western Europe, and, to an increasing extent, the most successful East Asian countries. Within this advanced and highly integrated core economy, differences among corporations are becoming more important than aggregate differences among countries. Furthermore, the increasing capacity of even small companies to operate in a global perspective makes the old analytical framework even more obsolete.

Not only are the "core nations" more homogeneous than before in terms of living standards, lifestyles, and economic organization, but their factors of production tend to move more rapidly in search of higher returns. Natural resources have lost much of their previous role in national specialization as advanced, knowledge-intensive societies move rapidly into the age of artificial materials and genetic engineering. Capital moves around the world in massive amounts at the speed of light; increasingly, corporations raise capital simultaneously in several major markets. Labor skills and labor wages in these countries can no longer be considered fundamentally different; many of the students enrolled in American graduate schools are foreign, while training has become a key dimension of many joint ventures between international corporations. Technology and "know-how" are also close to becoming a global pool. Trends in protection of intellectual property and export controls clearly have less impact than the massive development of the means to communicate, duplicate, store, and reproduce information.

Against this background, the ability of corporations of all sizes to use these globally available factors of production is a far bigger factor in international competitiveness than broad macroeconomic differences among countries. Contrary to the postulates of Smith and Ricardo, the very existence of the multinational enterprise is based on the international mobility of certain factors of production. Capital raised in London on the Eurodollar market may be used by a Swiss-based pharmaceutical firm to finance the acquisition of German equipment by a subsidiary in Brazil. A single Barbie doll is made in 10 countries—designed in the United States, with parts and clothing from Japan, Korea, Italy, and Taiwan, and assembled in Mexico.

It is the globally coordinated allocation of resources by a single centralized management that differentiates the multinational enterprise from other firms engaged in international business. MNCs make decisions about market-entry strategy; ownership of foreign operations; and production, marketing, and financial activities with an eye to what is best for the corporation as a whole. The true multinational corporation emphasizes group performance rather than the performance of its individual parts.

■ ——

ILLUSTRATION

General Electric Globalizes Its Medical Systems Business. A critical element of General Electric's global strategy is to be first or second in the world in a business or to get out. For example, in 1987, GE swapped its RCA consumer electronics division for Thomson CGR, the medical equipment business of Thomson SA of France, to strengthen its own medical unit. Together with GE Medical Systems Asia (GEMSA) in Japan, CGR makes GE No. 1 in the world market for X-ray, CAT scan, magnetic resonance, ultrasound, and other diagnostic imaging devices, ahead of Siemens (Germany), Philips (Netherlands), and Toshiba (Japan). With this purchase, GE Medical Systems' foreign sales rose from 13% in 1985 to 45% in 1988.

GE's production is also globalized, with each unit exclusively responsible for equipment in which it is the volume leader. Hence, GE Medical Systems now makes the high end of its CAT scanners and magnetic resonance equipment near Milwaukee (its headquarters) and the low end in Japan. The middle market is supplied by General Electric CGR S.A. in France. Engineering skills pass horizontally from the United States to Japan to France and back again. Each subsidiary supplies the marketing skills to its own home market. ——————————————————— ■

Evolution of the Multinational Corporation

Every year, *Fortune* publishes a list of the ten most-admired U.S. corporations. Year in and year out, most of these firms are largely multinational in philosophy and operations. In contrast, the least-admired tend to be national firms with much smaller proportions of assets, sales, or profits derived from foreign operations. Although multinationality and economic efficiency do not necessarily go hand in hand, international business is clearly of great importance to a growing number of U.S. and non-U.S. firms. The list of large American firms that receive 50% or more of their revenues and profits from abroad and have a sizable fraction of their assets abroad as well reads like a *Who's Who:* IBM, Gillette, NCR, Dow Chemical, Colgate-Palmolive, Xerox, and Hewlett-Packard. Coca-Cola earns more money selling soda in Japan than it does in the United States.

Industries differ greatly in the extent to which foreign operations are of importance to them. For example, the oil companies and banks are far more heavily involved overseas than are packaged food companies and automakers. Even within industries, companies differ markedly in their commitment to international business. For example, in 1989 Exxon had about 56% of its assets, 73% of its sales, and 97% of its profits abroad. The corresponding figures for Atlantic Richfield are 19%, 18%, and 6%.

Appendix 1A provides further evidence of the growing internationalization of American business. It presents data on the size and scope of overseas investment by U.S. firms and U.S. investment by foreign firms. The numbers involved are in the hundreds of billions of dollars. Moreover, these investments have grown steadily over time. A brief taxonomy of the MNC and its evolution is given in the sections that follow.

Raw-Materials Seekers.   Raw-materials seekers were the earliest multinationals, the villains of international business. They are the firms—the British, Dutch, and French East India Companies, the Hudson's Bay Trading Company, and the Union Miniere Haut-Katanga—that first grew under the protective mantle of the British, Dutch, French, and Belgian colonial empires. Their aim was to exploit the raw materials that could be found overseas. The modern-day counterparts of these firms, the multinational oil and mining companies, were the first to make large foreign investments, beginning during the early years of the twentieth century. Hence, large oil companies such as British Petroleum and Standard Oil were among the first true multinationals; hard-mineral companies such as International Nickel, Anaconda Copper, and Kennecott Copper were also early investors abroad.

Market Seekers.   The market seeker is the archetype of the modern multinational firm that goes overseas to produce and sell in foreign markets. Examples include IBM, Volkswagen, and Unilever. Although there are some early examples of market-seeking MNCs (for example, Colt Firearms, Singer, Coca-Cola, N.V. Philips, and Imperial Chemicals), the bulk of *foreign direct investment,* which is the acquisition abroad of physical assets such as plant and equipment, took place after World War II. This investment was primarily a one-way flow—from the United States to Western Europe—until the early 1960s. At that point, the phenomenon of *reverse foreign investment* began, primarily with West European firms acquiring American firms. More recently, Japanese firms have begun investing in the United States and Western Europe, largely in response to perceived or actual restrictions on their exports to these markets.

Cost Minimizers.   Cost minimizers is a fairly recent category of firms doing business internationally. These firms seek out and invest in lower-cost production sites overseas (for example, Hong Kong, Taiwan, and Ireland) to remain cost competitive both at home and abroad. Many of these firms are in the electronics industry. Examples include Texas Instruments, Atari, and Zenith.

■ 1.2 ■
THE PROCESS OF OVERSEAS EXPANSION

Studies of corporate expansion overseas indicate that firms become multinational by degree, with foreign direct investment being a late step in a process that begins with exports. For most companies, the *globalization* process does not occur through conscious design, at least in the early stages. It is the unplanned result of a series of corporate responses to a variety of threats and opportunities appearing at random abroad. From a broader perspective, however, the globalization of firms is the inevitable outcome of the competitive strivings of members of oligopolistic industries. Each member tries to both create and exploit monopolistic product and factor advantages internationally while simultaneously attempting to reduce the competitive threats posed by other industry members.

To meet these challenges, companies gradually increase their commitment to international business, developing strategies that are progressively more elaborate and sophisticated. The sequence normally involves exporting, setting up a foreign sales subsidiary, securing licensing agreements, and eventually establishing foreign production. This evolutionary approach to overseas expansion is a risk-minimizing response to operating in a highly uncertain foreign environment. By internationalizing in phases, a firm can gradually move from a relatively low risk-low return, export-oriented strategy to a higher risk-higher return strategy emphasizing international production. In effect, the firm is investing in information, learning enough at each stage to significantly improve its chances for success at the next stage. Exhibit 1.1 depicts the usual sequence of overseas expansion.

Exporting

Firms facing highly uncertain demand abroad will typically begin by exporting to a foreign market. The advantages of exporting are significant: Capital requirements and start-up costs are minimal, risk is low, and profits are immediate. Furthermore, this initial step provides the opportunity to learn about present and future supply and demand conditions, competition, channels of distribution, payment conventions, financial institutions, and financial techniques. Building on prior successes, companies then expand their marketing organizations abroad, switching from using export agents and other intermediaries to dealing directly with foreign agents and distributors. As increased communication with customers reduces uncertainty, the firm might set up its own sales subsidiary and new service facilities, such as a warehouse, with these marketing activities culminating in the control of its own distribution system.

Overseas Production

There is a major drawback to exporting: an inability to realize the full sales potential of a product. By manufacturing abroad, a company can more easily keep abreast of market developments, adapt its products and production schedules to changing local tastes and conditions, fill orders faster, and provide more comprehensive after-sales service. Many

■ **EXHIBIT 1.1**   Typical Foreign Expansion Sequence

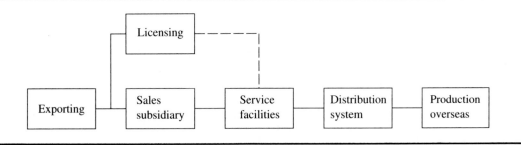

companies also set up R&D facilities along with their foreign operations; they aim to pick the best brains, wherever they are. The results help companies to keep track of the competition and to design new products. For example, the Japanese subsidiary of Loctite, a U.S. maker of engineering adhesives, came up with several new applications for sealants in the electronics industry.

Setting up local production facilities also shows a greater commitment to the local market, which typically brings added sales, and provides increased assurance of supply stability. Certainty of supply is particularly important for firms that produce intermediate goods for sale to other companies. A case in point is SKF, the Swedish ball bearing manufacturer. SKF was forced to manufacture in the United States to guarantee that its product, a crucial component in military equipment, would be available when needed. The Pentagon would not permit its suppliers of military hardware to be dependent on imported ball bearings, because imports could be halted in wartime and are always subject to the vagaries of ocean shipping.

Thus, most firms selling in foreign markets eventually find themselves forced to manufacture abroad. Foreign production covers a wide spectrum of activities from repairing, packaging, and finishing to processing, assembly, and full manufacture. Firms typically begin with the simpler stages—for example, packaging and assembly—and progressively integrate their manufacturing activities backward—for example, production of components and subassemblies.

Because the optimal entry strategy can change over time, a firm must continually monitor and evaluate the factors that bear on the effectiveness of its current entry strategy. New information and market perceptions change the risk-return trade-off for a given entry strategy, leading to a sequence of preferred entry modes, each adapted on the basis of prior experience to sustain and strengthen the firm's market position over time.

Associated with a firm's decision to produce abroad is the question of whether to *create* its own affiliates or *acquire* going concerns. A major advantage of an acquisition is the capacity to effect a speedy transfer overseas of highly developed but underutilized parent skills, such as a novel production technology. Often the local firm also provides a ready-made marketing network. This is especially important if the parent is a late entrant to the market. Many firms have used the acquisition approach to gain knowledge about the local market or a particular technology. The disadvantage, of course, is the cost of buying an ongoing company. In general, the larger and more experienced a firm becomes the less frequently it uses acquisitions to expand overseas. Smaller and relatively less experienced firms often turn to acquisitions.

Regardless of its preferences, a firm interested in expanding overseas may not have the option of acquiring a local operation. Michelin, the French manufacturer of radial tires, set up its own facilities in the United States because its tires are built on specially designed equipment; taking over an existing operation would have been out of the question.[1] Similarly, companies moving into developing countries often find they are forced to begin from the ground up because their line of business has no local counterpart.

---

[1]Once that equipment became widespread in the industry, Michelin was able to expand through acquisition (which it did, in 1989, when it acquired Uniroyal-Goodrich).

Licensing

An alternative, and at times a precursor, to setting up production facilities abroad is to *license* a local firm to manufacture the company's products in return for royalties and other forms of payment. The principal advantages of licensing are the minimal investment required, faster market-entry time, and fewer financial and legal risks involved. But the corresponding cash flow is also relatively low, and there may be problems in maintaining product quality standards. The licensor may also face difficulty controlling exports by the foreign licensee, particularly when, as in Japan, the host government refuses to sanction restrictive clauses on sales to foreign markets. Thus, a licensing agreement may lead to the establishment of a competitor in third-country markets, with a consequent loss of future revenues to the licensing firm. The foreign licensee may also become such a strong competitor that the licensing firm will have difficulty entering the market when the agreement expires, leading to a further loss of potential profits.

For some firms, licensing alone is the preferred method of penetrating foreign markets. Other firms with diversified innovative product lines follow a strategy of trading technology for both equity in foreign joint ventures and royalty payments.

A Behavioral Definition of the Multinational Corporation

Regardless of the foreign entry or global expansion strategy pursued, the true multinational corporation is characterized more by its state of mind than by the size and worldwide dispersion of its assets. Rather than confine its search to domestic plant sites, the multinational firm asks, Where in the world should we build that plant? Similarly, multinational marketing management seeks global, not domestic, market segments to penetrate, while multinational financial management does not limit its search for capital or investment opportunities to any single national financial market. Hence, the essential element that distinguishes the true multinational is its commitment to seeking out, undertaking, and integrating manufacturing, marketing, R&D, and financing opportunities on a global, not domestic, basis. For example, IBM's superconductivity project was pioneered in Switzerland by a German scientist and a Swiss scientist, both of whom recently shared a Nobel Prize in Physics for their work on this project.

A necessary complement to the integration of worldwide operations is flexibility, adaptability, and quickness. Indeed, speed has become one of the critical competitive weapons in the fight for world market share. The ability to develop, make, and distribute products or services quickly enables companies to capture customers who demand constant innovation and rapid, flexible response. Exhibit 1.2 illustrates the combination of globally integrated activities and rapid response times of The Limited, a 3,200-store clothing chain headquartered in Columbus, Ohio.

Another critical aspect of competitiveness in this new world is focus. *Focus* means figuring out, and building on, what a company does best. This typically involves divesting unrelated business activities and seeking attractive investment opportunities in the core business.

■ **EXHIBIT 1.2**   How The Limited Cuts the Fashion Cycle to 60 Days

From point-of-sale computers, daily reports on what is selling well flow into headquarters of The Limited in Columbus, Ohio.

To restock, the company sends orders by satellite to plants in the U.S., Hong Kong, South Korea, Singapore, and Sri Lanka.

The goods are hustled back to Columbus from Hong Kong aboard a chartered Boeing 747 that makes four flights a week.

At a highly automated distribution center in Columbus, apparel is sorted, priced, and prepared for shipment—all within 48 hours.

By truck and plane, the apparel moves out to The Limited's 3,200 stores, including Express and Victoria's Secret outlets.

Within 60 days of the order, the apparel goes on sale. Most competitors still place orders six months or more in advance.

SOURCE: *FORTUNE*, September 26, 1988, p. 56. Chart by Renee Klein, *FORTUNE*, © 1988 Time, Inc. All rights reserved.

■

ILLUSTRATION

Arco Chemical Develops a Worldwide Strategy. In the 1980s, Arco Chemical shed its less successful product lines. At one point, revenue shrank from $3.5 billion annually to $1.5 billion. But by stripping down to its most competitive lines of business, Arco can better respond to the world political and economic events it is constantly buffeted by. Around the world it can now take advantage of its technological edge within its narrow niche—mostly intermediate chemicals and fuel additives. This strategy has paid off: Arco has over 33% of its $2.6 billion in sales from abroad, and makes about half of its new investment outside the United States. And it claims half the global market for the chemicals it sells.

Arco went global because it had to. The company's engineering resins are sold to the auto industry. In the past, that meant selling exclusively to Detroit's Big Three in the U.S. market. Today, Arco sells to Nissan, Toyota, Honda, Peugeot, Renault, and Volkswagen in Japan, the United States, and Europe. And it deals with Ford and General Motors in the United States and Europe. Arco must be able to deliver a product anywhere in the world or else lose the business.

Global operations have also meant, however, that Arco Chemical faces increasingly stiff competition from abroad, in addition to its traditional U.S. competitors such as Dow Chemical. European companies have been expanding operations in America and Japanese competitors are also beginning to attack Arco's business lines. For example, Japan's Asahi Glass has begun a fierce price-cutting campaign in both Asia and Europe on products in which Arco Chemical is strong.

In response, Arco has set up production facilities around the world and entered into joint ventures and strategic alliances. It counterattacked Asahi Glass by trying to steal one of Asahi's biggest customers in Japan. Arco's joint-venture partner, Sumitomo Chemical, supplied competitive intelligence, and its knowledge of the Japanese market has been instrumental in launching the counterattack.

■

In this world-oriented corporation, a person's passport is not the criterion for promotion. Nor is a firm's citizenship a critical determinant of its success. Success depends on a new breed of businessperson: the global manager.

The Global Manager

In a world in which change is the rule and not the exception, the key to international competitiveness is the ability of management to adjust to change and volatility at an ever faster rate. In the words of General Electric Chairman Jack Welch, "I'm not here to predict the world. I'm here to be sure I've got a company that is strong enough to respond to whatever happens."[2]

The rapid pace of change means that the new global manager needs detailed knowledge of his or her own operation. The global manager must know how to make the product, where the raw materials and parts come from, how they get there, the alternatives, where the funds come from, and what their changing relative value does to his or her bottom line. He or she must also understand the political and economic choices facing key nations and how these choices will affect the outcomes of his or her decisions.

In making decisions for the global company, managers search their array of plants in various nations for the most cost-effective mix of supplies, components, transport, and funds. All this is done with the constant awareness that the choices change and have to be made again and again.

The problem of constant change disturbs some managers. It always has. But today's global managers have to anticipate it, understand it, deal with it, and turn it to their company's advantage. The payoff to thinking globally is a quality of decision making that enhances the firm's prospects for survival, growth, and profitability in the evolving world economy.

Political and Labor Union Concerns About Global Competition

Politicians and labor leaders, unlike corporate leaders, usually take a more parochial view of global investment flows. Many instinctively denounce local corporations that invest abroad as job "exporters," even though most welcome foreign investors in their own countries as job creators. However, a growing number of U.S. citizens today view the current

---

[2]Quoted in Ronald Henkoff, "How to Plan for 1995," *Fortune,* December 31, 1990, p. 70.

tide of American asset sales to foreign companies as a dangerous assault on U.S. sovereignty. They are unaware, for example, that foreign-owned companies account for more than 20% of industrial production in Germany and more than 50% in Canada without either of these countries appearing to have experienced the slightest loss of sovereignty.

Indeed, in an ever more integrated global economy, the ability of any nation's industries to gain or protect world market share—the ultimate gauge of their ability to produce jobs—will increasingly be determined by the efficiency with which companies manage their overseas expansion. Ford and IBM, for example, would be generating less U.S.-based employment today had they not been able earlier to invest abroad—both by "outsourcing" the production of parts to low-wage countries such as Mexico and by establishing assembly plants and R&D centers in Europe and Japan.

The growing irrelevance of borders for corporations will force policymakers to rethink old approaches to regulation. For example, corporate mergers that would once have been barred as anticompetitive might make sense if the true measure of a company's market share is global rather than national.

International economic integration also reduces the freedom of governments to determine their own economic policy. If a government tries to raise tax rates on business, for example, it is increasingly easy for business to shift production abroad. Similarly, nations that fail to invest in their physical and intellectual infrastructure—roads, bridges, R&D, education—will likely lose entrepreneurs and jobs to those that do. In short, economic integration is forcing governments, as well as companies, to compete.

The stresses caused by global competition have stirred up protectionists and given rise to new concerns about the consequences of free trade. For example, the recent U.S.-Canada trade agreement, which ends tariff barriers by the year 2000, has caused major disruption to Canada's manufacturing industry. Plants are closing, mergers are proliferating, and both domestic and multinational companies are adjusting their operations to the new continental market. As the following illustration of the U.S. auto industry indicates, companies and unions are quite rational in fearing the effects of foreign competition. It disrupts established industry patterns and limits the wages and benefits of workers.

So it is all the more encouraging that political leaders keep trying to stretch borders. The world's long march toward a global economy should accelerate considerably in the next few years if the U.S.-Canada free-trade pact and the European Community's drive to create a truly common market by 1992 proceed as planned. The greater integration of national economies is likely to continue despite the stresses it causes as politicians worldwide increasingly come to realize that they either accept this integration or watch their nation fall behind.

■ ——

ILLUSTRATION

Japanese Competition Affects the American Auto Industry.   Japanese competition has steadily eroded the influence of the Big Three U.S. automakers in the auto industry. During the 1980s, Japanese auto companies raised their U.S. market share 8 points, to 28%, versus 65% for Detroit and 5% for Europe. The future looks even bleaker for Detroit: Japanese car companies now win some 46% of buyers under age 45. If these buyers stay loyal to the Japanese as they age, Japan's market share will rise much further.

The tough Japanese competition is a big factor in the sales and profit crunch that has hit the Big Three. GM, Ford, and Chrysler have responded by shutting down U.S. plants and acting to curb labor costs. Thus, Japanese competition limits the wages and benefits that United Auto Workers union members can earn, as well as the prices that U.S. companies can charge for their cars. One solution, which allows both the Big Three and the UAW to avoid making hard choices—sales volume versus profit margin, and jobs versus wages—is political: Limit Japanese competition through quotas, tariffs, and other protectionist devices, and thereby limit its effects on the U.S. auto industry. Unfortunately, American consumers get stuck with the tab for this apparent free lunch in the form of higher car prices and less choice.

■ 1.3 ■
MULTINATIONAL FINANCIAL MANAGEMENT: THEORY AND PRACTICE

Although all functional areas can benefit from a global perspective, this book concentrates on developing financial policies that are appropriate for the multinational firm. The main objective of multinational financial management is to maximize shareholder wealth as measured by share price. Although an institution as complex as the multinational corporation cannot be said to have a single, unambiguous will, the principle of shareholder wealth maximization provides a rational guide to financial decision making. However, other financial goals that reflect the relative autonomy of management and external pressures will also be examined here.

The Multinational Financial System

From a financial management standpoint, one of the distinguishing characteristics of the multinational corporation, in contrast to a collection of independent national firms dealing at arm's length with one another, is its ability to move money and profits among its affiliated companies through internal transfer mechanisms. These mechanisms include transfer prices on goods and services traded internally, intercompany loans, dividend payments, leading (speeding up) and lagging (slowing down) intercompany payments, and fee and royalty charges. They lead to patterns of profits and movements of funds that would be impossible in the world of Adam Smith.

Financial transactions within the MNC result from the internal transfer of goods, services, technology, and capital. These product and factor flows range from intermediate and finished goods to less tangible items such as management skills, trademarks, and patents. Those transactions not liquidated immediately give rise to some type of financial claim, such as royalties for the use of a patent or accounts receivable for goods sold on credit. In addition, capital investments lead to future flows of dividends and interest and principal repayments. Exhibit 1.3 depicts some of the myriad financial linkages possible in the MNC.

■ **EXHIBIT 1.3**   The Multinational Corporate Financial System

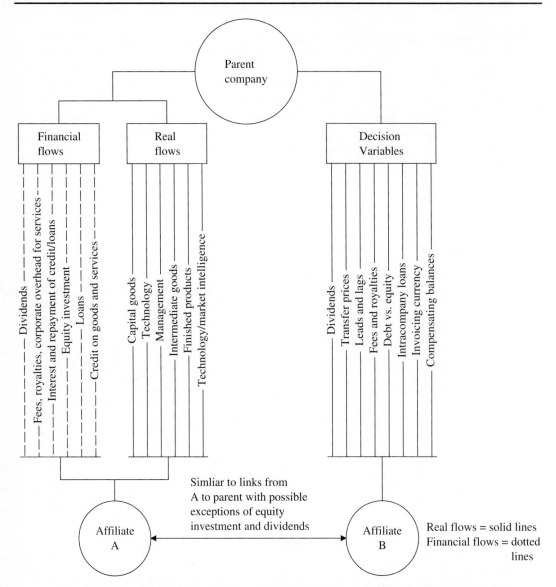

SOURCE: Adapted from Figure 1 in Donald R. Lessard, "Transfer Prices, Taxes, and Financial Markets: Implications of Internal Financial Transfers Within the Multinational Firm," in Robert G. Hawkins, ed., *The Economic Effects of Multinatioal Corporations* (Greenwich, Conn.: JAI Press, 1979), by permission of the author and the publisher.

Although all of the links portrayed in Exhibit 1.3 can and do exist among independent firms, the MNC has greater control over the mode and timing of these financial transfers.[3]

Mode of Transfer.   The MNC has considerable freedom in selecting the *financial channels* through which funds, allocated profits, or both are moved. For example, patents and trademarks can be sold outright or transferred in return for a contractual stream of royalty payments. Similarly, the MNC can move profits and cash from one unit to another by adjusting *transfer prices* on intercompany sales and purchases of goods and services. With regard to *investment flows,* capital can be sent overseas as debt with at least some choice of interest rate, currency of denomination, and repayment schedule, or as equity with returns in the form of dividends. Multinational firms can use these various channels, singly or in combination, to transfer funds internationally, depending on the specific circumstances encountered. Furthermore, within the limits of various national laws and with regard to the relations between a foreign affiliate and its host government, these flows may be more advantageous than those that would result from dealings with independent firms.

Timing Flexibility.   Some of the internally generated financial claims require a fixed payment schedule; others can be accelerated or delayed. This *leading and lagging* is most often applied to *interaffiliate trade credit* where a change in open account terms, say from 90 to 180 days, can involve massive shifts in liquidity. (Some nations have regulations about the repatriation of the proceeds of export sales. Thus, there is typically not complete freedom to move funds by leading and lagging.) In addition, the timing of fee and royalty payments may be modified when all parties to the agreement are related. Even if the contract cannot be altered once the parties have agreed, the MNC generally has latitude when the terms are initially established.

In the absence of *exchange controls*—government regulations that restrict the transfer of funds to nonresidents—firms have the greatest amount of flexibility in the timing of equity claims. The earnings of a foreign affiliate can be retained or used to pay dividends that in turn can be deferred or paid in advance.

Despite the frequent presence of governmental regulations or limiting contractual arrangements, most MNCs have some flexibility as to the timing of fund flows. This latitude is enhanced by the MNC's ability to control the timing of many of the underlying real transactions. For instance, shipping schedules can be altered so that one unit carries additional inventory for a sister affiliate.

Value.   By shifting profits from high-tax to lower-tax nations, the MNC can reduce its global tax payments. Similarly, the MNC's ability to transfer funds among its several units may allow it to circumvent currency controls and other regulations and to tap previously inaccessible investment and financing opportunities. However, since most of the gains derive

---

[3]See Donald R. Lessard, "Transfer Prices, Taxes, and Financial Markets: Implications of Internal Financial Transfers Within the Multinational Firm," in *The Economic Effects of Multinational Corporations,* Robert G. Hawkins, ed. (Greenwich, Conn.: JAI Press, 1979); and David P. Rutenberg, "Maneuvering Liquid Assets in a Multinational Company," *Management Science,* June 1970, pp. B–671–684. This section draws extensively from Lessard's article.

from the MNC's skill at taking advantage of openings in tax laws or regulatory barriers, governments do not always appreciate the MNC's capabilities and global profit-maximizing behavior. Thus, controversy has accompanied the international orientation of the multinational corporation.

Criticisms of the Multinational Corporation

Critics of the MNC liken its behavior to that of an octopus with tentacles extended, squeezing the nations of the world to satisfy the apparently insatiable appetite of its center. Its defenders claim that only by linking activities globally can world output be maximized. According to this view, greater profits from overseas activities are the just reward for providing the world with new products, technologies, and know-how.

Because its focus is on multinational financial management, this book does not deal directly with this controversy. It concentrates instead on the development of analytical approaches to deal with the major environmental problems and decisions involving overseas investment and financing. In carrying out these financial policies, though, conflicts with nation-states will inevitably arise.

A classic case is that of General Motors-Holden's Ltd. The General Motors wholly owned Australian affiliate was founded in 1926 with an initial equity investment of A\$3.5 million. The earnings were reinvested until 1954, at which time the first dividend, for A\$9.2 million, was paid to the parent company in Detroit. This amount seemed reasonable to GM management, considering the 28 years of foregoing dividends, but the Australian press and politicians denounced a dividend equal to over 260% of GM's original equity investment as economic exploitation and imperialism.[4]

More recently, Brazil, facing one of its periodic balance-of-payments crisis, chose to impose stringent controls on the removal of profits by MNCs, thereby affecting the financial operations of such firms as Volkswagen and Scott Paper. In addition, companies operating in countries as diverse as Canada and Chile, Italy and India, and the United States and Uruguay have faced various political risks, including price controls and confiscation of local operations. This book will examine the modification of financial policies in line with national objectives in an effort to reduce such risks and minimize the costs of the adjustments.

This text also considers the links between financial management and other functional areas. After all, the analysis of investment projects is dependent on sales forecasts and cost estimates, and the dispersal of production and marketing activities affects a firm's ability to flow funds internationally as well as its vulnerability to expropriation.

Functions of Financial Management

Financial management is traditionally separated into two basic functions: the acquisition of funds and the investment of these funds. The first function, also known as the *financing decision,* involves generating funds from internal sources or from sources external to the firm at the lowest long-run cost possible. The *investment decision* is concerned with

---

[4]Reported in, among other places, Sidney M. Robbins and Robert B. Stobaugh, *Money in the Multinational Enterprise* (New York: Basic Books, 1973), p. 59.

the allocation of funds over time in such a way that shareholder wealth is maximized. Many of the concerns and activities of multinational financial management, however, cannot be categorized so neatly.

Internal corporate fund flows such as loan repayments are often undertaken to access funds that are already owned, at least in theory, by the MNC. Other flows such as dividend payments may take place to reduce taxes or currency risk. Capital structure and other financing decisions are frequently motivated by a desire to reduce investment risks as well as financing costs. Furthermore, exchange risk management involves both the financing decision and the investment decision. Throughout this book, therefore, the interaction between financing and investment decisions will be stressed because it is the right combination of these decisions that will maximize the value of the firm to its shareholders.

Theme

Financial executives in multinational corporations face many factors that have no domestic counterparts. These factors include exchange and inflation risks; international differences in tax rates; multiple money markets, often with limited access; currency controls; and political risks, such as sudden and creeping expropriation.

When examining the unique characteristics of multinational financial management, it is understandable that companies normally emphasize the additional political and economic risks faced when going abroad. However, a broader perspective is necessary if firms are to take advantage of being multinational.

The ability to move people, money, and material on a global basis enables the multinational corporation to be more than the sum of its parts. By having operations in different countries, the MNC can access segmented capital markets to lower its overall cost of capital, shift profits to lower its taxes, and take advantage of *international diversification* of markets and production sites to reduce the riskiness of its earnings. Multinationals have taken the old adage of "don't put all your eggs in one basket" to its logical conclusion.

Operating globally confers other advantages as well: It increases the bargaining power of multinational firms when they negotiate investment agreements and operating conditions with foreign governments and labor unions; it gives MNCs continuous access to information on the newest process technologies available overseas and the latest research and development activities of their foreign competitors; and it helps them to diversify their funding sources by giving them expanded access to the world's capital markets.

In summary, this book emphasizes the many opportunities associated with being multinational without neglecting the corresponding risks. To properly analyze and balance these international risks and rewards, we must use the lessons to be learned from domestic corporate finance.

Relationship to Domestic Financial Management

In recent years there has been an abundance of new research in the area of international corporate finance. The major thrust of this work has been to apply the methodology and logic of financial economics to the study of key international financial decisions. Critical problem areas, such as foreign exchange risk management and foreign investment analysis, have benefited from the insights provided by *financial economics*—a discipline that emphasizes the use of economic analysis to understand the basic workings of financial markets, particularly the measurement and pricing of risk and the intertemporal allocation of funds.

By focusing on the behavior of financial markets and their participants, rather than on how to solve specific problems, we can derive fundamental principles of valuation and develop from them superior approaches to financial management—much as a better understanding of the basic laws of physics leads to better-designed and -functioning products. We can also better gauge the validity of existing approaches to financial decision making by seeing whether their underlying assumptions are consistent with our knowledge of financial markets and valuation principles.

Three concepts arising in financial economics have proved to be of particular importance in developing a theoretical foundation for international corporate finance: arbitrage, market efficiency, and capital asset pricing. We will rely on these concepts throughout the remainder of this book. Brief descriptions follow.

Arbitrage.   *Arbitrage* has traditionally been defined as the purchase of securities or commodities on one market for immediate resale on another in order to profit from a price discrepancy. However, in recent years arbitrage has been used to describe a broader range of activities. *Tax arbitrage,* for example, involves the shifting of gains or losses from one tax jurisdiction to another in order to profit from differences in tax rates. In a broader context, *risk arbitrage,* or speculation, describes the process that leads to equality of risk-adjusted returns on different securities, unless market imperfections that hinder this adjustment process exist. In fact, it is the process of arbitrage that ensures market efficiency.

Market Efficiency.   An *efficient market* is one in which the prices of traded securities readily incorporate new information. Numerous studies of U.S. and foreign capital markets have shown that traded securities are correctly priced in that trading rules based on past prices or publicly available information cannot consistently lead to profits (after adjusting for transactions costs) in excess of those due solely to risk taking.

The predictive power of markets lies in their ability to collect in one place a mass of individual judgments from around the world. These judgments are based on current information. If the trend of future policies changes, people will revise their expectations, and prices will change to incorporate the new information.

Capital Asset Pricing.   *Capital asset pricing* refers to the way in which securities are valued in line with their anticipated risks and returns. Because risk is such an integral element of international financial decisions, this book briefly summarizes the results of over two decades of study on the pricing of risk in capital markets. The outcome of this research has been to posit a specific relationship between risk (measured by return variability) and required asset returns, now formalized in the *capital asset pricing model* (CAPM).

The CAPM assumes that the total variability of an asset's returns can be attributed to two sources: (1) market-wide influences that affect all assets to some extent, such as the state of the economy, and (2) other risks that are specific to a given firm, such as a strike. The former type of risk is usually termed *systematic* or *nondiversifiable risk,* and the latter, *unsystematic* or *diversifiable risk.* It can be shown that unsystematic risk is largely irrelevant to the highly diversified holder of securities because the effects of such disturbances cancel out, on average, in the portfolio. On the other hand, no matter how well diversified a stock portfolio is, systematic risk, by definition, cannot be eliminated, and thus the investor must be compensated for bearing this risk. This distinction between systematic risk and unsystematic risk provides the theoretical foundation for the study of risk in the multinational corporation and is referred to throughout the book.

The Importance of Total Risk

Although the message of the CAPM is that only the systematic component of risk will be rewarded with a risk premium, this does not mean that *total risk*—the combination of systematic and unsystematic risk—is unimportant to the value of the firm. In addition to the effect of systematic risk on the appropriate discount rate, total risk may have a negative impact on the firm's *expected* cash flows.[5]

The inverse relation between risk and expected cash flows arises because financial distress, which is more likely to occur for firms with high total risk, can impose costs on customers, suppliers, and employees and, thereby, affect their willingness to commit themselves to relationships with the firm. For example, potential customers will be nervous about purchasing a product that they might have difficulty getting serviced if the firm goes out of business. Similarly, a firm struggling to survive is unlikely to find suppliers willing to provide it with specially developed products or services, except at a higher-than-usual price. The uncertainty created by volatile earnings and cash flows may also hinder management's ability to take a long view of the firm's prospects and make the most of its opportunities.

To summarize, total risk is likely to adversely affect a firm's value by leading to lower sales and higher costs. Consequently, any action taken by a firm that decreases its total risk will improve its sales and cost outlooks, thereby increasing its expected cash flows.

These considerations justify the range of corporate hedging activities that multinational firms engage in to reduce total risk. This text will focus on those risks that appear to be more international in nature, including inflation risk, exchange risk, and political risk. As we will see, however, appearances can be deceiving because these risks also affect firms that do business in only one country. Moreover, international diversification may actually allow firms to reduce the total risk they face. Much of the general market risk facing a company is related to the cyclical nature of the domestic economy of the home country. Operating in several nations whose economic cycles are not perfectly in phase should reduce the variability of the firm's earnings. Thus, even though the riskiness of operating in any one foreign country may be greater than the risk of operating in the United States (or other home country), diversification can eliminate much of that risk.

---

[5]The effect of total risk on cash flows is discussed in Alan C. Shapiro and Sheridan Titman, "An Integrated Approach to Corporate Risk Management," *Midland Corporate Finance Journal,* Summer 1985, pp. 41–56.

The Global Financial Marketplace

Market efficiency has been greatly facilitated by the marriage of computers and telecommunications. The resulting electronic infrastructure melds the world into one global market for ideas, data, and capital, all moving at almost the speed of light to any part of the planet. Today there are more than 200,000 computer screens in hundreds of trading rooms, in dozens of nations, that light up to display an unending flow of news. It takes about two minutes between the time a president, a prime minister, or a central banker makes a statement and the time traders buy or sell currency, stocks, and bonds according to their evaluation of that policy's effect on the market.

The result is a continuing global referendum on a nation's economic policies, which is the final determinant of the value of its currency. Just as we learn from TV the winner of a presidential election weeks before the electoral college even assembles, so also we learn instantly from the foreign exchange market what the world thinks of our announced economic policies even before they are implemented. In a way, the financial market is a form of economic free speech. Although many politicians don't like what it is saying, the market presents judgments that are clear-eyed and hard-nosed. It knows that there are no miracle drugs that can replace sound fiscal and monetary policies. Thus, cosmetic political fixes will exacerbate, not alleviate, a falling currency.

The Role of the Financial Executive in an Efficient Market

The basic insight into financial management we can gain from recent empirical research in financial economics is the following: *Attempts to increase the value of a firm by purely financial measures or accounting manipulations are unlikely to succeed unless there are capital market imperfections or asymmetries in tax regulations.*

Rather than downgrading the role of the financial executive, the net result of these research findings has been to focus attention on those areas and circumstances in which financial decisions can have a measurable impact. The key areas are capital budgeting, working capital management, and tax management. The circumstances to be aware of include capital market imperfections, primarily caused by government regulations, and asymmetries in the tax treatment of different types and sources of revenues and costs.

The value of good financial management is enhanced in the international arena because of the much greater likelihood of market imperfections and multiple tax rates. In addition, the greater complexity of international operations is likely to increase the payoffs from a knowledgeable and sophisticated approach to internationalizing the traditional areas of financial management.

■ 1.4 ■
OUTLINE OF THIS BOOK

This book is divided into six parts. These parts are

- Part I: Environment of International Financial Management
- Part II: Foreign Exchange Risk Management

- Part III: Multinational Working Capital Management
- Part IV: Foreign Investment Analysis
- Part V: Financing Foreign Operations
- Part VI: International Banking

The following sections briefly discuss these parts and their chapters.

Environment of International Financial Management

Part I examines the environment in which international financial decisions are made. Chapter 2 describes the foreign exchange market and how it functions, while Chapter 3 describes foreign currency futures and options contracts. Chapter 4 discusses the basic factors that affect currency values. It also explains the basics of central bank intervention in foreign exchange markets, including the economic and political motivations for such intervention. Chapter 5 describes the international monetary system and shows how the choice of system affects the determination of exchange rates. Chapter 6 analyzes the balance of payments and the links between national economies, while Chapter 7 is a crucial chapter because it introduces three of the key equilibrium relationships—between inflation rates, interest rates, and exchange rates—in international finance that form the basis for much of the analysis in the remainder of the text.

Foreign Exchange Risk Management

Part II discusses foreign exchange risk management, a traditional area of concern that is receiving even more attention today. Chapter 8 discusses the likely impact of an exchange rate change on a firm (its exposure) from an accounting perspective, while Chapter 9 analyzes the costs and benefits of alternative financial techniques to hedge against these exchange risks. Chapter 10 examines exposure from an economic perspective. As part of the analysis of economic exposure, the relationship between inflation and currency changes and its implications for corporate cash flows is recognized. Chapter 11 develops marketing, logistic, and financial policies to cope with the competitive consequences of currency changes.

Multinational Working Capital Management

Part III examines working capital management in the multinational corporation. Chapter 12 deals with current liability management, presenting the alternative short-term financing techniques available and showing how to evaluate their relative costs. The subject of trade financing is covered in Chapter 13. Chapter 14 discusses current asset management in the MNC, including the management of cash, inventory, and receivables. Chapter 15 describes the mechanisms available to the MNC to shift funds and profits among its various units, while considering the tax and other consequences of these maneuvers. The aim of these maneuvers is to create an integrated global financial planning system.

Foreign Investment Analysis

Part IV analyzes the foreign investment decision process. Chapter 16 begins by discussing the nature and consequences of international portfolio investing—the purchase of foreign stocks and bonds. In Chapter 17 the strategy of foreign direct investment is discussed, including an analysis of the motivations for going abroad and those factors that have contributed to business success overseas. Chapter 18 presents techniques for evaluating foreign investment proposals, emphasizing how to adjust cash flows for the various political and economic risks encountered abroad, such as inflation, currency fluctuations, and expropriations. Chapter 19 seeks to determine the cost-of-capital figure(s) that MNCs should use in evaluating foreign investments. Chapter 20 discusses the measurement and management of political risks. It identifies political risk and then shows how companies can control these risks by appropriately structuring the initial investment and by making suitable modifications to subsequent operating decisions. This part concludes with Chapter 21's discussion of international tax planning. It points out which decisions are affected by tax regulations and how those decisions can be structured to reduce taxes paid to the world.

Financing Foreign Operations

Part V focuses on laying out and evaluating the medium- and long-term financing options facing the multinational firm, then developing a financial package that is tailored to the firm's specific operating environment. Chapter 22 describes the alternative external medium- and long-term debt financing options available to the multinational corporation. These options include an outline of the international capital markets; namely, the Eurocurrency and Eurobond markets. Chapter 23 discusses special financing vehicles available to the MNC, including currency swaps, international leasing, and debt-equity swaps. In conclusion, Chapter 24 presents a three-stage framework for designing a global financing strategy.

International Banking

Part VI contains two chapters dealing with international banking. Chapter 25 discusses the development and expansion of international banking activities and the international debt crisis. Finally, Chapter 26 shows how to analyze country risk—the credit risk on loans to a foreign nation—a topic of great concern these days.

■ QUESTIONS ■

1. a. What are the various categories of multinational firms?

    b. What is the motivation for international expansion of firms within each category?

2. a. How does foreign competition limit the prices that domestic companies can charge and the wages and benefits that workers can demand?

    b. What political solutions can help companies and unions avoid the limitations imposed by foreign competition?

    c. Who pays for these political solutions? Explain.

3.   **a.** What is the internal financial transfer system of the multinational firm?

    b. What are its distinguishing characteristics?

    c. What are the different modes of internal fund transfers available to the MNC?

4. How does the internal financial transfer system add value to the multinational firm?

5.   **a.** Why do companies generally follow a sequential strategy in moving overseas?

    b. What are the pluses and minuses of exporting? Licensing? Foreign production?

6. What is an efficient market?

7. In seeking to predict tomorrow's exchange rate, are you better off knowing today's exchange rate or the exchange rates for the past 100 days?

8.   **a.** What is the capital asset pricing model?

    b. What is the basic message of the CAPM?

    c. How might a multinational firm use the CAPM?

9. Why might setting up production facilities abroad lead to expanded sales in the local market?

10.   **a.** Are multinational firms riskier than purely domestic firms?

    b. What data would you need to address this question?

    c. Is there any reason to believe that MNCs may be less risky than purely domestic firms? Explain.

11. In what ways do financial markets grade government economic policies?

12.   **a.** How might total risk affect a firm's production costs and its ability to sell? Give some examples of firms in financial distress that saw their sales drop.

    b. What is the relation between the effects of total risk on a firm's sales and costs and its desire to hedge foreign exchange risk?

■ Appendix 1A ■
SIZE AND SCOPE OF MULTINATIONAL CORPORATIONS ABROAD

This appendix presents data on direct foreign investment by U.S. firms and on the U.S. investment position of foreign firms. It also discusses some recent changes in the overall U.S. foreign investment position.

■ 1A.1 ■ U.S. DIRECT INVESTMENT ABROAD

Exhibit 1A.1 shows the foreign direct investment positions of U.S. firms, broken down by major areas of the world, for the years 1979–1989. The *foreign direct investment position* is defined as the book value of the equity in, and net loans outstanding to, foreign businesses in which Americans own or control, directly or indirectly, at least 10% of the voting securities. The data reveal the strong preference exhibited by U.S. firms for investment in developed countries; the fraction of U.S. direct investment going to developed countries has remained at a stable 73%–75% of the total. Canada alone accounts for just under 20% of total U.S. direct investments abroad. Slightly less than 25% of U.S. foreign direct investment goes to the *less-developed countries* (LDCs) of Latin America, Africa, the Middle East, Asia,

■ **EXHIBIT 1A.1**   U.S. Direct Investment Abroad by Major Regions, 1979–1989

| | **Billions of U.S. Dollars** | | | | | | | | | | |
	1979	**1980**	**1981**	**1982**	**1983**	**1984**	**1985**	**1986**	**1987**	**1988**	**1989**
Developed Countries											
Canada	41	45	47	46	48	47	47	51	58	63	67
Twelve Common Market countries	66	78	81	78	79	70	81	99	120	131	150
Other Europe	17	19	21	22	24	22	24	22	26	26	27
Japan	6	6	7	7	8	8	9	12	15	18	19
Australia, New Zealand, and South Africa	10	11	12	12	12	11	10	12	13	15	16
Total	139	158	167	164	170	157	172	196	232	253	279
Developing Countries											
Latin America	35	39	39	33	30	25	28	37	45	51	61
Africa	3	4	4	5	5	4	4	4	5	4	4
Middle East	−1	2	2	2	3	5	5	5	5	4	4
Asia and Pacific	7	9	11	12	13	15	15	15	17	19	21
Total	45	53	56	52	51	49	53	61	72	78	91
International	4	4	5	5	6	5	5	5	5	3	4
Total All Countries	188	215	228	222	226	211	230	262	309	334	373
	Percent of Total										
	1979	**1980**	**1981**	**1982**	**1983**	**1984**	**1985**	**1986**	**1987**	**1988**	**1989**
Developed Countries											
Canada	22	21	21	21	22	22	20	19	19	19	18
Twelve Common Market countries	35	36	36	35	35	33	35	38	39	39	40
Other Europe	9	9	9	10	11	10	10	8	8	8	7
Japan	3	3	3	3	4	4	4	5	5	5	5
Australia, New Zealand, and South Africa	5	5	5	5	5	5	4	5	4	4	4
Total	74	73	73	74	75	74	75	75	75	76	75
Developing Countries											
Latin America	19	18	17	15	13	12	12	14	15	15	16
Africa	2	2	2	2	2	2	2	2	2	1	1
Middle East	−1	1	1	1	1	2	2	2	2	1	1
Asia and Pacific	4	4	5	5	6	7	7	6	6	6	6
Total	24	25	25	23	23	23	23	23	23	23	24
International	2	2	2	2	3	2	2	2	2	1	1
Total All Countries	100	100	100	100	100	100	100	100	100	100	100

NOTE: The numbers may not sum exactly because of rounding errors.

SOURCE: *Survey of Current Business*, U.S. Department of Commerce, various issues.

and the Pacific, with the remainder being investments in foreign affiliates with operations spanning more than one country.

Despite the overall stability of the investment breakdowns, the regional shares have varied over time. Most noticeably, direct investment in Latin America declined substantially in absolute and percentage terms beginning in 1982. This decline coincided with the Latin American debt crisis and reflects both the poorer economic prospects of these countries and the additional constraints imposed on MNCs' ability to repatriate profits from their Latin American units. As Latin American prospects have improved in recent years so has the flow of direct investment.

The basic generalization we can draw from the data is that American investment flows to those nations with the largest economies and best economic prospects. The most striking departure from this generalization is Japan. Although the Japanese economy is the second largest in the non-Communist world, and one of the most dynamic, U.S. direct investment in Japan is now about 5%. This is less even than U.S. direct investment in the Netherlands and about one-fourth of such investment in Great Britain. This is strong evidence of the strong barriers, both formal and informal, to American direct investment in Japan.

The pattern of U.S. foreign direct investment is also noteworthy for what it doesn't indicate. Despite claims by U.S. labor unions, overseas investment by American multinationals does not appear to be driven solely by the search for low-cost manufacture; U.S. investment in Mexico fell 17% between 1980 and 1987, despite the growth of low-cost, labor-intensive maquiladora factories on the American border.

Exhibit 1A.2 shows the U.S. direct foreign investment position cross-classified by industrial sector and region of the world at the end of 1989. The industrial sectors are petroleum, manufacturing, and other (mining, trade, banking and finance, and other industries).

■ **EXHIBIT 1A.2**   U.S. Direct Investment Abroad by Industrial Sector and Region, 1989 (U.S. $ Billions)

	Petroleum		Manufacturing		Other		Total	
	Amount	Percent	Amount	Percent	Amount	Percent	Amount	Percent
Developed Countries								
Canada	11	16	32	48	24	36	67	100
Europe	22	14	71	45	64	41	157	100
Other	7	19	16	44	13	36	36	100
Total	40	14	126	45	113	41	279	100
Developing Countries								
Latin America	5	8	21	34	35	57	61	100
Other	10	34	8	28	11	38	29	100
Total	15	16	29	32	46	51	91	100
International	3	75	1	25	1	25	4	100
All Countries	58	16	156	42	160	43	373	100

SOURCE: *Survey of Current Business*, U.S. Department of Commerce, August 1990, p. 56.

Manufacturing is the most important sector, accounting for 42% of total foreign direct investment by U.S. companies. Far behind is petroleum, at 16%. Although the data are not presented here, the three most important manufacturing industries in terms of foreign direct investment are chemicals, nonelectrical equipment, and transportation equipment.

Rates of Return on U.S. Direct Investment Abroad

The U.S. Department of Commerce calculates the rate of return on U.S. foreign direct investments annually. These data are contained in Exhibit 1A.3 for the years 1988 and 1989. The rate of return is estimated as net income (including interest income) divided by the average of the beginning and end-of-year direct investment position. There are several biases in these data, however. Because assets are carried at historical costs instead of their current values, the return on investment is overstated. On the other hand, the estimate of income excludes fees and royalties. Inclusion of fees and royalties would have increased income by 30% in 1988 and by about 25% in 1989. These biases downgrade the estimated return on foreign investment. Moreover, these estimates are not adjusted for varying debt ratios or risk.

Historically direct investment in LDCs, particularly in Latin America, has been relatively unprofitable as compared with similar investments in developed countries. That fact helps account for the diminishing share of investment directed towards LDCs during most

■ **EXHIBIT 1A.3**   Rates of Return on U.S. Direct Investment Abroad, 1988–1989 (Percent)

	1988	1989		1988	1989
Developed Countries			**Developing Countries**		
Canada	12.1	10.6	Latin America	8.9	14.2
Petroleum	5.0	4.2	Petroleum	7.5	12.5
Manufacturing	14.0	13.9	Manufacturing	18.0	18.5
Other	13.4	9.5	Other	3.1	11.8
Europe	17.5	16.2	Other	23.4	23.3
Petroleum	16.8	18.6	Petroleum	17.9	25.4
Manufacturing	20.0	18.6	Manufacturing	32.0	24.3
Other	14.8	12.9	Other	23.8	20.5
Other	16.5	14.4	Developing Countries—All	13.9	17.2
Petroleum	18.9	8.7	Petroleum	14.4	21.2
Manufacturing	17.5	17.8	Manufacturing	21.8	20.0
Other	13.7	13.3	Other	8.4	14.0
Developed Countries—All	16.0	14.6	**All Countries**	15.4	15.2
Petroleum	13.8	12.9	Petroleum	13.4	14.6
Manufacturing	18.2	17.3	Manufacturing	18.8	17.8
Other	14.4	12.2	Other	12.7	12.7

SOURCE: *Survey of Current Business*, U. S. Department of Commerce, August 1990, p. 44.

of the 1980s. However, the data in Exhibit 1A.3 show that this situation is now changing, with returns from LDCs on a par with those from developed countries. Petroleum investments have historically earned higher returns overseas than manufacturing investments. This is no longer true and is probably accounted for by the sharp drop in oil prices in recent years.

Capital Expenditures by Majority-Owned Foreign Affiliates of U.S. Companies, 1977–1990

Exhibit 1A.4 shows the annual amount of capital expenditures made by majority-owned foreign affiliates of U.S. companies between the years 1977 and 1990 by area and industry (data for 1990 are estimated). Capital expenditures include all expenditures made to acquire, add to, or improve property, plant, and equipment and that are charged to a capital account. The resulting figure understates the amounts invested overseas because it does not include investments in research and development or additions to working capital.

The drop in overseas investment in the early 1980s reflects the severity of the worldwide recession. In general, the growth of foreign direct investment by U.S. companies has slowed

■ **EXHIBIT 1A.4**   Capital Expenditures by Majority-Owned Foreign Affiliates of U.S. Companies, 1977–1990

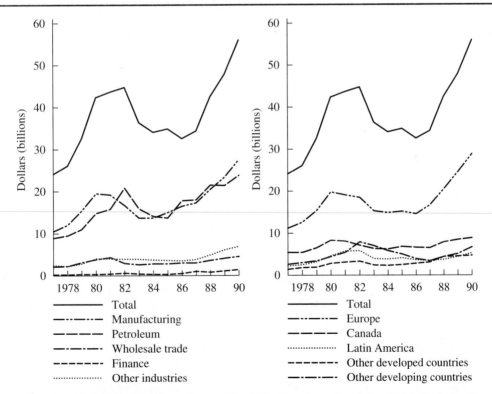

SOURCE: U.S. Department of Commerce, *Survey of Current Business,* September 1984, p. 23; March 1985, p. 24; March 1987, p. 26; September 1987, p. 26; September 1990, p. 30.

substantially since the 1970s. However, it has picked up again in the late 1980s as world economic growth strengthened. Although petroleum and manufacturing investments have historically run neck and neck in importance from one year to the next, recent investments in manufacturing have consistently outpaced those in petroleum. This reflects the lower returns from petroleum investments, a casualty of the fall in oil prices.

New investment is primarily concentrated in Europe and Canada, with Latin America in third place. The slowdown in new investment in Canada in the early 1980s reflects both the world recession and the increasingly nationalistic posture of the Trudeau government. The replacement of the Trudeau government in 1984 by a more conservative one that seems to welcome foreign corporate investors appears to have reversed that trend. The effects of the debt crisis are evident in the steep decline in Latin American investments following 1982. Conversely, the promise of Europe 1992—an integrated market of 320 million wealthy consumers—has led to a dramatic rise in European investments by U.S. multinationals. By 1990, Europe accounted for over two-thirds of U.S. overseas manufacturing investment.

■ 1A.2 ■ FOREIGN DIRECT INVESTMENT IN THE UNITED STATES

The United States itself is an increasingly attractive source of foreign direct investment prospects. Foreigners now own Firestone Tire & Rubber, Rockefeller Center, Columbia Pictures, MCA/Universal, TV Guide, A&P, 20th Century Fox, Brooks Brothers, CBS Records, RCA, Pillsbury, MGM/UA, and about 30% of all office space in downtown Los Angeles. Exhibit 1A.5 shows that the foreign direct investment position in the United States grew by 22% in 1989—to $401 billion—compared with 21% in 1988 and 23% in 1987. From 1983 through 1986, growth in foreign direct investment in the United States averaged 15% annually. In the four years before 1982, the average annual growth rate was 30%. The pickup in foreign direct investment in the United States, after the slowdown during the mid-1980s, has coincided with a lower dollar, leading to the charge that foreigners have been buying American assets on the cheap. Of course, the foreigners also get a dollar earnings stream that is worth less in their currencies.

The importance of foreign investment in the United States is indicated by a few facts: Four of America's six major record concerns are now foreign-owned; Goodyear is the last major American-owned tire manufacturer; by 1993, Japanese auto companies will be able to build more than two million cars a year in their U.S. plants (see Exhibit 1A.6 for a list of these plants), over 25% of the total in a typical sales year; four of Hollywood's largest film companies are now foreign-owned; and of the 21 companies manufacturing televisions in the United States, Zenith is the only American-owned one.

European corporate parents account for 65% of the year-end 1989 foreign investment position. Canadian and Japanese parents accounted for another 8% and 17%, respectively. By industry of the U.S. affiliates, 40% of the position was in manufacturing, 14% in wholesale trade, 9% in petroleum, and 37% in other industries, mainly real estate, banking, and insurance.

Two countries—the United Kingdom and Japan—accounted for over 45% of the increase in foreign direct investment in the United States. Busy as the Japanese are, the data reveal that they are by no means the biggest U.S. shoppers. That prize goes to the British,

■ **EXHIBIT 1A.5**   Foreign Direct Investment in the United States, 1989 (U.S. $ Billions)

By Country	Total End 1988	1989 Inflow	Increase (%)	Total End 1989	Percent of Total FDI
United Kingdom	$102	$17	17%	$119	30%
Netherlands	49	11	24	60	15
Japan	53	16	31	70	17
Canada	27	4	15	32	8
West Germany	24	4	17	28	7
Switzerland	16	3	19	19	5
Netherlands Antilles	11	—	—	11	3
France	11	5	45	16	4
Other	36	12	33	48	12
Total	$329	$72	22%	$401	100%

By Industry	Amount	Percent of Total
Manufacturing	$160	40%
Wholesale trade	55	14
Petroleum	35	9
Real estate	36	9
Insurance	23	6
Banking	20	5
Retail trade	15	4
Finance	11	3
Mining	7	2
Other	37	9
Total	$401	100%

NOTE: Numbers are inconsistent due to rounding

whose companies invested $17 billion in 1989, with the largest increases in manufacturing and wholesale trade. Japanese parents increased their U.S. position by $16 billion, with the largest increases coming in manufacturing and real estate. The Dutch, who were bypassed in 1987 by the Japanese as the second largest foreign direct investors in the United States, invested $11 billion in 1989.

Although not displayed here, a striking aspect of the returns on U.S. investments earned by foreign companies is how low they are, 3.8% overall (2.1% for the Japanese) in 1989. Apparently, foreign firms are willing to invest large sums in the United States, earning only marginal returns compared with what could be earned in Treasury bills or other riskless instruments.

Motives for Foreign Direct Investment in the United States

Investment by foreign multinationals in the United States can be attributed to many of the same factors that propelled U.S. firms abroad: the size and growth potential of the market, the fear of future protectionism (especially true for Japanese firms), the desire to compete

■ **EXHIBIT 1A.6**   Japanese-Owned or Joint Venture Auto Plants in the United States

Year Completed	Company	Location	Annual Production Capacity
1982	Honda Motor Co.	Marysville, Ohio	360,000
1983	Nissan Motor Co.	Smyrna, Tennessee	250,000*
1984	Toyota-General Motors	Fremont, California	240,000
1987	Mazda Motor Co.	Flat Rock, Michigan	240,000
1988	Mitsubishi-Chrysler	Normal, Illinois	240,000
1988	Toyota Motor Co.	Georgetown, Kentucky	218,000
1989	Subaru-Isuzu	Lafayette, Indiana	120,000*
1989	Honda Motor Co.	East Liberty, Ohio	150,000
1992	Nissan Motor Co.	Smyrna, Tennessee	190,000
1993	Toyota Motor Co.	Georgetown, Kentucky	200,000
		Total planned capacity by 1993	2,208,000

*Includes light trucks

with and learn from rivals on their home ground, and lower relative production costs in some industries. Foreign firms may also seek access to new technology and operations that complement existing product lines in order to improve their global market positions. The positive aspects of foreign direct investment in the United States are that it often brings technology, spurs competition, and provides access to foreign markets.

■ **1A.3** ■ **THE NET INTERNATIONAL WEALTH OF THE UNITED STATES**

The preceding sections concentrated on direct investment abroad. However, direct investment is only one part of capital flows. Even more important is the flow of portfolio investment and bank lending overseas. The net of U.S. investment abroad and foreign investment domestically makes up the net international wealth of the United States. In 1981, the net U.S. international wealth peaked at $141 billion. Beginning in 1982, net U.S. international wealth began a long-term decline. Sometime during 1985, the continued decline in net international wealth turned negative. Exhibit 1A.7 depicts the changing net international wealth position of the United States from 1970 through 1990. The negative net international wealth position of the United States reached –$576 billion by the end of 1990.

Historical Perspective

The United States was a net debtor to the rest of the world until World War I. In the early stages of its industrial development, the United States depended heavily on foreign capital; in building up its industries, it "mortgaged" part of its wealth to foreigners. In 1900, for example, when the total wealth of the United States, including land and reproducible assets, was an estimated $88 billion, net liabilities to foreigners were $2.5 billion; these

■ **EXHIBIT 1A.7**   International Investment Position of The United States, 1970–1990

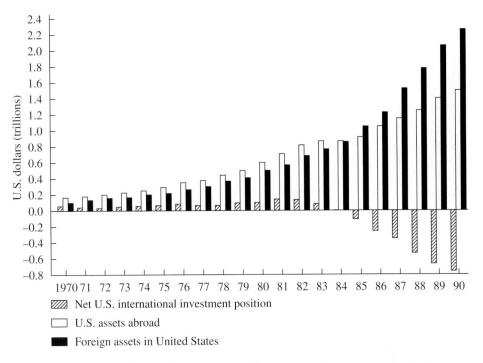

Net U.S. international investment position

U.S. assets abroad

Foreign assets in United States

SOURCE: Based on data from *Survey of Current Business*, U.S. Department of Commerce, various issues.

liabilities far exceeded U.S. claims on foreigners. On the eve of World War I, total foreign investment in the United States amounted to $7.2 billion—nearly twice the $3.7 billion Americans had invested abroad. The effects of the war reversed this situation: By the end of 1919, U.S. claims on foreigners exceeded foreign claims on the United States by $3.7 billion.

Net U.S. international wealth continued to increase throughout the 1920s, and by 1930, it reached a peak of about $9 billion. During the depression-ridden 1930s, the value of U.S. assets abroad declined, while the flight of capital from war-threatened Europe to the United States increased total foreign claims on the United States. These factors contributed to a slightly negative net U.S. foreign investment position.

The Post–World War II Period

Following the end of World War II, U.S. wealth abroad increased dramatically, first as a result of the vast flow of aid-related credits provided by the U.S. government to war-devastated countries; then later as U.S. companies sharply expanded their investment in foreign countries. By 1970 the U.S. international investment position showed a surplus of some $60 billion.

During the 1970s, the basic trend in the net U.S. international investment position was sharply upward. Between 1971 and 1979, U.S. foreign assets rose from about $165 billion to $510 billion, and foreign assets in the U.S. rose from $107 billion to $416 billion. These capital flows boosted the net U.S. international wealth position to $94 billion by 1980, as shown in Exhibit 1A.4.

The 1980s

From 1980 through 1986, U.S. foreign assets rose at an average annual rate of 11%, bringing total U.S. assets abroad to $1.068 trillion. At the same time, however, U.S. liabilities to foreigners were rising at an annual rate of 18%. In 1985, the inevitable consequence of these trends finally occurred: The United States became a net international debtor, reverting to the position it was in at the turn of the century. This decline in net international wealth reflects the large trade deficits the United States has been running in recent years. The trade deficits in turn result from basic shifts in savings and investment behavior in the United States and abroad. Chapter 6 discusses these factors at length.

The Consequences

The consequences of a reduction in a nation's net international wealth depend on the nature of the foreign capital inflows that cause the erosion. If the capital inflows finance new investments that enhance the nation's productive capacity, they are self-financing in that they will eventually generate the necessary resources for their repayment. But if the investment flows finance current consumption, their repayment will eventually reduce the nation's standard of living below where it would have been in the absence of such inflows. The need to reduce future living standards to pay back foreign debts is the problem facing many of the debtor Latin American nations.

In the case of the United States, a good portion of the inflows seem to have been of the "productive" variety. But a growing share of capital inflows, particularly since 1982, might be classified as "consumption" in nature. If so, the erosion of net U.S. international wealth, traceable to the U.S. federal budget deficits (see Chapter 6), will inflict new burdens on the U.S. economy in the future.

■ BIBLIOGRAPHY ■

Eaker, Mark R. "Teaching International Finance: An Economist's Perspective." *Journal of Financial and Quantitative Analysis,* November 1977, pp. 607–608.

Folks, William R., Jr. "Integrating International Finance into a Unified Business Program." *Journal of Financial and Quantitative Analysis,* November 1977, pp. 599–600.

Lessard, Donald R. "Transfer Prices, Taxes, and Financial Markets: Implications of International Financial Transfers within the Multinational Firm." In *The Economic Effects of Multinational Corporations.* Robert G. Hawkins, ed. Greenwich, Conn.: JAI Press, 1979.

∎ 2 ∎

The Foreign Exchange Market

The Spaniards coming into the West Indies, had many commodities of the country which they needed, brought unto them by the inhabitants, to who when they offered them money, goodly pieces of gold coin, the Indians, taking the money, would put it into their mouths, and spit it out to the Spaniards again, signifying that they could not eat it, or make use of it, and therefore would not part with their commodities for money, unless they had such other commodities as would serve their use.

—Edward Leigh (1671)—

∎ The volume of international transactions has grown enormously since the end of World War II. U.S. exports of goods and services now account for about 10% of gross national product, or over $500 billion annually. For both Canada and Great Britain, this figure exceeds 25%. Imports are about the same size. Similarly, annual capital flows involving hundreds of billions of dollars occur between the United States and other nations. International trade and investment of this magnitude would not be possible without the ability to buy and sell foreign currencies. Currencies must be bought and sold because the U.S. dollar is not the acceptable means of payment in most other countries. Investors, tourists, exporters, and importers must exchange dollars for foreign currencies, and vice versa.

The trading of currencies takes place in foreign exchange markets whose primary function is to facilitate international trade and investment. Knowledge of the operation and mechanics of these markets, therefore, is important for any fundamental understanding of international financial management. The purpose of this chapter is to provide this information. It discusses the organization of the most important foreign exchange market—the interbank market—including the spot market, the market in which currencies are traded for immediate delivery, and the forward market, in which currencies are traded for future delivery. It also describes the links between the spot and forward markets. Chapter 3 examines the currency futures and options markets.

■ 2.1 ■

ORGANIZATION OF THE FOREIGN EXCHANGE MARKET

If there were a single international currency, there would be no need for a foreign exchange market. As it is, in any international transaction, at least one party is dealing in a foreign currency. The purpose of the *foreign exchange market* is to permit transfers of purchasing power denominated in one currency to another—that is, to trade one currency for another currency. For example, a Japanese exporter sells automobiles to a U.S. dealer for dollars, and a U.S. manufacturer sells machine tools to a Japanese company for yen. Ultimately, however, the U.S. company will likely be interested in receiving dollars, whereas the Japanese exporter will want yen. Similarly, an American investor in Swiss-franc-denominated bonds must convert dollars into francs, and Swiss purchasers of U.S. Treasury bills require dollars to complete these transactions. Because it would be inconvenient, to say the least, for individual buyers and sellers of foreign exchange to seek out one another, a foreign exchange market has developed to act as an intermediary.

Most currency transactions are channeled through the worldwide *interbank market,* the wholesale market in which major banks trade with one another. This market is normally referred to as *the* foreign exchange market. In the *spot market,* currencies are traded for immediate delivery, which is actually within two business days after the transaction has been concluded. In the *forward market,* contracts are made to buy or sell currencies for future delivery.

The foreign exchange market is not a physical place; rather, it is an electronically linked network of banks, foreign exchange brokers, and dealers whose function is to bring together buyers and sellers of foreign exchange. It is not confined to any one country but is dispersed throughout the leading financial centers of the world: London, New York City, Paris, Zurich, Amsterdam, Tokyo, Toronto, Milan, Frankfurt, and other cities.

Trading is generally done by telephone or telex machine. Foreign exchange traders in each bank usually operate out of a separate foreign exchange trading room. Each trader has several telephones and is surrounded by display monitors and telex machines feeding up-to-the-minute information. It is a hectic existence, and many traders burn out by age 35. Most transactions are based on oral communications; written confirmation occurs later. Hence, an informal code of moral conduct has evolved over time in which the foreign exchange dealers' word is their bond.

The Participants

The major participants in the foreign exchange market are the large commercial banks; foreign exchange brokers in the interbank market; commercial customers, primarily multinational corporations; and central banks, which intervene in the market from time to time to smooth exchange rate fluctuations or to maintain target exchange rates. Central bank intervention involving buying or selling in the market is often indistinguishable from the foreign exchange dealings of commercial banks or of other private participants.

Only the head offices or regional offices of the major commercial banks are actually marketmakers—that is, actively deal in foreign exchange for their own accounts. These banks stand ready to buy or sell any of the major currencies on a more or less continuous basis. A large fraction of the interbank transactions in the United States is conducted through *foreign exchange brokers,* specialists in matching net supplier and demander banks. These brokers, of whom there are about a half dozen at present (located in New York City), receive a small commission on all trades. Some brokers tend to specialize in certain currencies, but they all handle major currencies such as the pound sterling, Canadian dollar, Deutsche mark, and Swiss franc.

Commercial and central bank customers buy and sell foreign exchange through their banks. However, most small banks and local offices of major banks do not deal directly in the interbank market. Rather, they typically will have a credit line with a large bank or with their home office. Thus, transactions with local banks will involve an extra step. The customer deals with a local bank that in turn deals with its head office or a major bank. The various linkages between banks and their customers are depicted in Exhibit 2.1. Note that

■ **EXHIBIT 2.1**   Structure of Foreign Exchange Markets

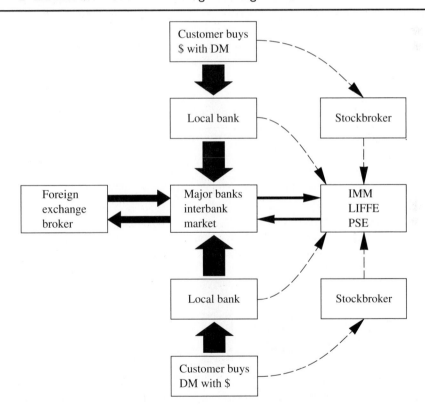

NOTE: The International Money Market (IMM) Chicago trades foreign exchange futures and DM futures options. The London International Financial Futures Exchange (LIFFE) trades foreign exchange futures. The Philadelphia Stock Exchange (PSE) trades foreign currency options.

SOURCE: *Review,* Federal Reserve Bank of St. Louis, March 1984, p. 9.

the diagram includes linkages with currency futures and options markets, which we will examine in the next chapter.

Size

The foreign exchange market is by far the largest financial market in the world. A recent estimate placed the average foreign exchange trading volume in 1990 at over $650 billion daily, or $160 trillion a year.[1] This figure compares with an average daily trading volume of about $6 billion on the New York Stock Exchange. Indeed, the New York Stock Exchange's biggest day, Black Monday (October 19, 1987), was only $21 billion, or 4% of the daily foreign exchange volume. As another benchmark, the U.S. gross national product was approximately $5.5 trillion in 1990.

According to recent data from the world's central banks, London is the world's largest currency trading market, with daily turnover in 1989 estimated at $187 billion.[2] The United States is second, at about $129 billion, followed by Japan, at $115 billion. However, Japan's share of world foreign exchange trading is growing, while London's is falling. The U.S. share has remained fairly stable in recent years. Exhibit 2.2 shows that the world foreign exchange market has more than doubled in volume between 1986 and 1989, far outpacing the growth of international trade and the world's output of goods and services. This explosive

■ **EXHIBIT 2.2**   Average Daily Foreign Exchange Trading

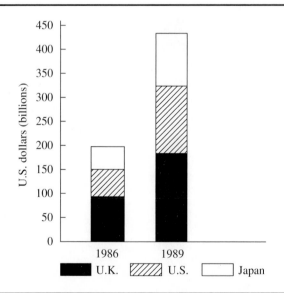

[1]This estimate appeared in *The Wall Street Journal,* March 1, 1990, p. C1.

[2]The results of this survey were reported in *The Wall Street Journal,* September 14, 1989, pp. C1, C11.

growth has been attributed to the growing integration of the world's economies and financial markets, as well as a growing desire on the part of companies and financial institutions to more actively manage their currency risk exposure.

Among smaller foreign exchange markets, the central banks reported average daily volume in the Swiss market at $57 billion, Hong Kong at $49 billion, France at $26 billion, Holland at $16 billion, and Canada at $15 billion. Germany's Bundesbank didn't participate in the survey. However, Germany's foreign exchange volume would certainly place it among the top four in the world.

■ 2.2 ■
THE SPOT MARKET

This section examines the spot market in foreign exchange. It covers spot quotations, transaction costs, and the mechanics of spot trading.

Spot Quotations

Almost all major newspapers print a daily list of exchange rates. For major currencies, up to four different quotes (prices) are displayed. One is the *spot price*. The others might include the 30-day, 90-day, and 180-day *forward prices*. These quotes are for trades among dealers in the interbank market. When interbank trades involve dollars (about 60% of such trades do), these rates will be expressed in either *American terms* (numbers of U.S. dollars per unit of foreign currency) or *European terms* (number of foreign-currency units per U.S. dollar). In *The Wall Street Journal,* quotes in both American and European terms are listed side by side (see Exhibit 2.3). For example, on February 6, 1990, the American quote for the Swiss franc was SFr 1 = $0.6766, and the European quote was $1 = SFr 1.4780. Nowadays, in trades involving dollars, all except U.K. and Irish exchange rates are expressed in European terms.

In their dealings with nonbank customers, banks in most countries use a system of *direct quotation*. A direct exchange rate quote gives the home currency price of a certain quantity of the foreign currency quoted (usually 100 units, but only one unit in the case of the U.S. dollar or the pound sterling). For example, the price of foreign currency is expressed in French francs (FF) in France and in Deutsche marks (DM) in Germany. Thus, in France, the Deutsche mark might be quoted at FF 4 while, in Germany, the franc would be quoted at DM 0.25.

There are exceptions to this rule, though. Banks in Great Britain quote the value of the pound sterling (£) in terms of the foreign currency—for example, £1 = $1.7625. This method of *indirect quotation* is also used in the United States for domestic purposes and for the Canadian dollar. In their foreign exchange activities abroad, however, U.S. banks adhere to the European method of direct quotation.

Banks do not normally charge a commission on their currency transactions, but profit from the spread between the buying and selling rates. Quotes are always given in pairs because a dealer usually does not know whether a prospective customer is in the market to buy or to sell a foreign currency. The first rate is the buy, or bid, price; the second is the sell,

■ **EXHIBIT 2.3** Foreign Exchange Rate Quotations

EXCHANGE RATES

Tuesday, February 6, 1990

The New York foreign exchange selling rates below apply to trading among banks in amounts of $1 million and more, as quoted at 3 p.m. Eastern time by Bankers Trust Co. Retail transactions provide fewer units of foreign currency per dollar.

Country	U.S. $ equiv. Tues.	U.S. $ equiv. Mon.	Currency per U.S. $ Tues.	Currency per U.S. $ Mon.
Argentina (Austral) ...	.0005128	.0005128	1950.00	1950.00
Australia (Dollar)	.7653	.7670	1.3067	1.3038
Austria (Schilling)	.08548	.08558	11.70	11.69
Bahrain (Dinar)	2.6522	2.6522	.3771	.3771
Belgium (Franc)				
Commercial rate	.02876	.02885	34.77	34.66
Financial rate	.02876	.02885	34.77	34.66
Brazil (Cruzado)	.05408	.05249	18.49	19.05
Britain (Pound)	1.7015	1.7000	.5877	.5882
30-Day Forward ...	1.6928	1.6914	.5907	.5912
90-Day Forward ...	1.6745	1.6731	.5972	.5977
180-Day Forward ...	1.6493	1.6483	.6063	.6067
Canada (Dollar)	.8405	.8421	1.1897	1.1875
30-Day Forward ...	.8398	.8393	1.1908	1.1915
90-Day Forward ...	.8335	.8335	1.1997	1.1997
180-Day Forward ...	.8271	.8268	1.2091	1.2095
Chile (Official rate) ...	.003482	.003482	287.22	287.22
China (Yuan)	.211811	.211811	4.7212	4.7212
Colombia (Peso)	.002250	.002250	444.50	444.50
Denmark (Krone)	.1558	.1563	6.4165	6.3995
Ecuador (Sucre)				
Floating rate	.001447	.001447	691.00	691.00
Finland (Markka)	.25465	.25265	3.9270	3.9580
France (Franc)	.17709	.17718	5.6470	5.6440
30-Day Forward ...	.17678	.17684	5.6568	5.6547
90-Day Forward ...	.17606	.17606	5.6800	5.6800
180-Day Forward ...	.17492	.17490	5.7170	5.7175
Greece (Drachma)	.006562	.006423	152.40	155.70
Hong Kong (Dollar) ..	.12806	.12804	7.8090	7.8100
India (Rupee)	.05921	.05921	16.89	16.89
Indonesia (Rupiah)	.0005565	.0005565	1797.01	1797.01
Ireland (Punt)	1.5980	1.5870	.6258	.6301
Israel (Shekel)	.5367	.5367	1.8632	1.8632
Italy (Lira)	.0008082	.0008117	1237.26	1232.01
Japan (Yen)	.006879	.006906	145.37	144.80
30-Day Forward ...	.006888	.006915	145.18	144.62

Country	U.S. $ equiv. Tues.	U.S. $ equiv. Mon.	Currency per U.S. $ Tues.	Currency per U.S. $ Mon.
90-Day Forward	.006902	.006928	144.89	144.35
180-Day Forward	.006906	.006948	144.80	143.93
Jordan (Dinar)	1.5188	1.5188	.6584	.6584
Kuwait (Dinar)	3.4640	3.4640	.2887	.2887
Lebanon (Pound)	.001826	.001826	547.50	547.50
Malaysia (Ringgit)	.3704	.3705	2.7000	2.6990
Malta (Lira)	3.0534	3.0534	.3275	.3275
Mexico (Peso)				
Floating rate	.0003679	.0003679	2718.06	2718.06
Netherland (Guilder) .	.5335	.5345	1.8745	1.8710
New Zealand (Dollar)	.6010	.6020	1.6639	1.6611
Norway (Krone)	.1558	.1553	6.4200	6.4400
Pakistan (Rupee)	.0471	.0471	21.25	21.25
Peru (Inti)	.00008389	.00008389	11920.37	11920.37
Philippines (Peso)	.04572	.04572	21.87	21.87
Portugal (Escudo)	.006781	.006781	147.48	147.48
Saudi Arabia (Riyal) ..	.26681	.26681	3.7480	3.7480
Singapore (Dollar)	.5388	.5362	1.8560	1.8650
South Africa (Rand)				
Commercial rate	.3954	.3932	2.5291	2.5432
Financial rate	.3134	.3105	3.1908	3.2206
South Korea (Won) ..	.0014584	.0014584	685.70	685.70
Spain (Peseta)	.009285	.009328	107.70	107.20
Sweden (Krona)	.1637	.1637	6.1100	6.1100
Switzerland (Franc) ..	.6766	.6784	1.4780	1.4740
30-Day Forward ...	.6759	.6778	1.4796	1.4754
90-Day Forward ...	.6743	.6765	1.4830	1.4783
180-Day Forward ...	.6724	.6748	1.4873	1.4820
Taiwan (Dollar)	.038654	.038715	25.87	25.83
Thailand (Baht)	.03909	.03909	25.58	25.58
Turkey (Lira)	.0004290	.0004290	2331.00	2331.00
United Arab (Dirham)	.2723	.2723	3.6725	3.6725
Uruguay (New Peso)				
Financial	.001248	.001248	801.50	801.50
Venezuela (Bolivar)				
Floating rate	.02299	.02299	43.50	43.50
W. Germany (Mark) ..	.6028	.6020	1.6590	1.6610
30-Day Forward ...	.6028	.6022	1.6588	1.6607
90-Day Forward ...	.6028	.6022	1.6588	1.6606
180-Day Forward ...	.6025	.6020	1.6598	1.6611
SDR	1.33580	1.32516	.74862	.75463
ECU	1.23171	1.21625	....	....

Special Drawing Rights (SDR) are based on exchange rates for the U.S., West German, British, French and Japanese curren-cies. Source: International Monetary Fund.

European Currency Unit (ECU) is based on a basket of community currencies. Source: European Community Commission.

SOURCE: *The Wall Street Journal,* February 6, 1990, p. C13. Reprinted with permission of *The Wall Street Journal,* © Dow Jones & Company, Inc. 1990. All rights reserved worldwide.

or ask, or offer, rate. Suppose the pound sterling is quoted at $1.7019–36. This quote means that banks are willing to buy pounds at $1.7019 and sell them at $1.7036. In practice, dealers do not quote the full rate to each other; instead, they quote only the last two digits of the decimal. Thus, sterling would be quoted at 19–36 in the above example. Any dealer who isn't sufficiently up-to-date to know the preceding numbers will not remain in business for long.

Transaction Costs. The *bid-ask spread*—that is, the spread between bid and ask rates for a currency—is based on the breadth and depth of the market for that currency as well as on the currency's volatility. This spread is usually stated as a percentage cost of transacting in the foreign exchange market, which is computed as follows:

$$\text{Percent spread} = \frac{\text{Ask price} - \text{Bid price}}{\text{Ask price}} \times 100$$

For example, with pound sterling quoted at $1.7019–36, the percentage spread equals 0.1%:

$$\text{Percent spread} = \frac{1.7036 - 1.7019}{1.7036} = 0.1\%$$

For widely traded currencies, such as the pound, DM, and yen, the spread might be on the order of 0.1–0.5%.[3] Less heavily traded currencies have higher spreads. These spreads have widened appreciably for most currencies since the general switch to floating rates in early 1973.

The quotes found in the financial press are not those that individuals or firms would get at a local bank. Unless otherwise specified, these quotes are for transactions in the interbank market exceeding $1 million. (The standard transaction amount in the interbank market is now $3 million.) But competition ensures that individual customers receive rates that reflect, even if they do not necessarily equal, interbank quotations. For example, a trader may believe that he or she can trade a little more favorably than the market rates indicate—that is, buy from a customer at a slightly lower rate or sell at a somewhat higher rate than the market rate. Thus, if the current spot rate for the Swiss franc is $0.6967–72, the bank may quote a customer a rate of $0.6964–75. On the other hand, a bank that is temporarily short in a currency may be willing to pay a slightly more favorable rate; or if the bank has overbought, it may be willing to sell at a lower rate.

For these reasons, many corporations will shop around at several banks for quotes before committing themselves to a transaction. On large transactions customers also may get a rate break inasmuch as it ordinarily does not take much more effort to process a large order than a small order.

The market for traveler's checks and smaller currency exchanges, such as might be made by a traveler going abroad, is quite separate from the interbank market. The spread on these smaller exchanges is much wider than that in the interbank market, reflecting the higher average costs banks incur on such transactions. As a result, individuals and firms involved in smaller retail transactions generally pay a higher price when buying and receive a lower price when selling foreign exchange than those quoted in newspapers.

Cross-Rates.   Because most currencies are quoted against the dollar, it may be necessary to work out the cross-rates for currencies other than the dollar. For example, if the Deutsche mark is selling for $0.60 and the buying rate for the French franc is $0.15, then the DM/FF cross-rate is DM 1 = FF 4. Exhibit 2.4 contains cross-rates for major currencies on February 6, 1990.

■ ───

ILLUSTRATION

Calculating the Direct Quote for the Pound in Frankfurt.   Suppose that sterling is quoted at $1.7019–36, while the Deutsche mark is quoted at $0.6250–67. What is the direct quote for the pound in Frankfurt?

---

[3]See, for example, Jacob A. Frenkel and Richard M. Levich, "Transaction Costs and Interest Arbitrage: Tranquil versus Turbulent Periods," *Journal of Political Economy,* November–December 1977, pp. 1209–1228.

■ **EXHIBIT 2.4**   Key Currency Cross-Rates

Key Currency Cross Rates Late New York Trading Feb. 6, 1990

	Dollar	Pound	SFranc	Guilder	Yen	Lira	D-Mark	FFranc	CdnDlr
Canada.........	1.1874	2.0227	.80447	.63514	.00817	.00096	.71664	.21048	......
France.........	5.6415	9.610	3.8222	3.0177	.03884	.00457	3.4049	....	4.7511
Germany.......	1.6569	2.8225	1.1226	.88628	.01141	.00134	....	.29370	1.3954
Italy...........	1234.3	2102.5	836.21	660.20	8.497	....	744.92	218.78	1039.5
Japan.........	145.25	247.43	98.408	77.695	....	.11768	87.664	25.747	122.33
Netherlands....	1.8695	3.1847	1.2666	....	.01287	.00151	1.1283	.33138	1.5744
Switzerland....	1.4760	2.5144	....	.78952	.01016	.00120	.89082	.26163	1.2431
U.K............	.58703	....	.39771	.31400	.00404	.00048	.35429	.10406	.49438
U.S............	....	1.7035	.67751	.53490	.00688	.00081	.60354	.17726	.84218

Source: Telerate

SOURCE: *The Wall Street Journal,* February 6, 1990, p. C13. Reprinted with permission of *The Wall Street Journal,* © Dow Jones & Company, Inc. 1990. All rights reserved worldwide.

Solution.   The bid rate for the pound in Frankfurt can be found by realizing that selling pounds for DM is equivalent to combining two transactions: (1) selling pounds for dollars at the rate of $1.7019 and (2) converting those dollars into DM 1.7019/0.6267 = DM 2.7157 per pound at the ask rate of $0.6267. Similarly, the DM cost of buying one pound (the ask rate) can be found by first buying $1.7036 (the ask rate for £1) with DM and then using those dollars to buy one pound. Because buying dollars for DM is equivalent to selling DM for dollars (at the bid rate of $0.6250), it will take DM 1.7036/0.6250 = DM 2.7258 to acquire the $1.7036 necessary to buy one pound. Thus, the direct quotes for the pound in Frankfurt are DM 2.7157–7258.   ■

Currency Arbitrage.   Until recently, the pervasive practice among bank dealers was to quote all currencies against the U.S. dollar when trading among themselves. Now, however, about 40% of all currency trades don't involve the dollar, and that percentage is growing.[4] For example, Swiss banks may quote the Deutsche mark against the Swiss franc, and German banks may quote pounds sterling in terms of Deutsche marks. Exchange traders are continually alert to the possibility of taking advantage, through *currency arbitrage* transactions, of exchange rate inconsistencies in different money centers. These transactions involve buying a currency in one market and selling it in another. Such activities tend to keep exchange rates uniform in the various markets.

For example, suppose that the pound sterling is bid at $1.9809 in New York, and the Deutsche mark at $0.6251 in Frankfurt. At the same time, London banks are offering pounds sterling at DM 3.1650. The astute trader would sell dollars for Deutsche marks in Frankfurt, use the Deutsche marks to acquire pounds sterling in London, and sell the pounds in New York.

---

[4]This estimate appeared in *The Wall Street Journal,* March 1, 1990, p. C1.

Specifically, the trader could acquire DM 1,599,744.04 for $1,000,000 in Frankfurt, sell these Deutsche marks for £505,448.35 in London, and resell the pounds in New York for $1,001,242.64. Thus, a few minutes' work would yield a profit of $1,242.64. In effect, the trader would, by arbitraging through the DM, be able to acquire sterling at $1.9784 in London ($0.6251 × 3.1650) and sell it at $1.9809 in New York. This sequence of transactions, known as *triangular currency arbitrage,* is depicted as follows:

1. Sell $1,000,000 in Frankfurt at DM 1 = $0.6251 for DM 1,599,744.04.
2. Sell these Deutsche marks in London at £1 = DM 3.1650 for £505,448.35.
3. Resell the pounds sterling in New York at £1 = $1.9809 for $1,001,242.64.
4. Net profit equals $1,242.64.

In the preceding example, the arbitrage transactions would tend to cause the Deutsche mark to appreciate vis-à-vis the dollar in Frankfurt and to depreciate against the pound sterling in London; at the same time, sterling would tend to fall in New York. Opportunities for such profitable currency arbitrage have been greatly reduced in recent years, given the extensive network of people—aided by high-speed, computerized information systems— who are continually collecting, comparing, and acting on currency quotes in all financial markets. The practice of quoting rates against the dollar makes currency arbitrage even simpler. The result of this activity is that rates for a specific currency tend to be the same everywhere, with only minimal deviations due to transaction costs.

■ ───

ILLUSTRATION

Calculating the Direct Quote for the Deutsche Mark in New York. If the direct quote for the dollar is DM 2.5 in Frankfurt, and transaction costs are 0.4%, what are the minimum and maximum possible direct quotes for the DM in New York?

Solution.   An arbitrageur who converted $1 into DM in Frankfurt would receive DM 2.5 × 0.996, after paying transaction costs of 0.4%. Converting these DM into dollars in New York at a direct quote of e, the arbitrageur would keep 2.5 × 0.996 × e × 0.996. Because in equilibrium this quantity must be less than or equal to $1 (otherwise there would be a money machine), $e < 1/[2.5(0.996)^2] = \$0.4032$. Alternatively, if the arbitrageur converted $1 into DM in New York at a rate of e, took those DM to Frankfurt, and exchanged them for dollars, the arbitrageur would wind up—after paying transaction costs in both New York and Frankfurt—with $(1/e) \times 0.996 \times 1/2.5 \times 0.996$. Because this quantity must be less than or equal to $1, the result is $(0.996)^2 \times (1/2.5e) < 1$ or $e > \$0.3968$. Combining these two inequalities yields $\$0.3968 < e < \$0.4032$.

─── ■

Settlement Date.   The *value date* for spot transactions, the date on which the monies must be paid to the parties involved, is set as the second working day after the date on which the transaction is concluded. Thus, a spot deal entered into on Thursday in Paris will not be settled until the following Monday (French banks are closed on Saturdays and Sundays). It is possible, although unusual, to get one-day or even same-day value, but the rates will be adjusted to reflect interest differentials on the currencies involved.

Exchange Risk.   Bankers also act as marketmakers, as well as agents, by taking positions in foreign currencies, thereby exposing themselves to *exchange risk*. The immediate adjustment of quotes as traders receive and interpret new political and economic information is the source of both exchange losses and gains by banks active in the foreign exchange market. For instance, suppose that a trader quotes a rate of £1:$1.3012 for £500,000, and it is accepted. The bank will receive $650,600 in return for the £500,000. If the bank doesn't have an offsetting transaction, it may decide within a few minutes to cover its exposed position in the interbank market. If during this brief delay, news of a lower-than-expected British trade deficit reaches the market, the trader may be unable to purchase pounds at a rate lower than $1.3101. Since it will cost the bank $655,050 to acquire £500,000 at this new rate, the result is a $4,450 ($655,050 – $650,600) exchange loss on a relatively small transaction within just a few minutes. Equally possible, of course, is a gain if the dollar strengthens against the pound.

Clearly, as a trader becomes more and more uncertain about the rate at which she can offset a given currency contract with other dealers or customers, she will demand a greater profit to bear this added risk. This expectation translates into a wider bid-ask spread. For example, during a period of volatility in the exchange rate between the French franc and U.S. dollar, a trader will probably quote a customer a bid for francs that is distinctly lower than the last observed bid in the interbank market; the trader will attempt to reduce the risk of buying francs at a price higher than that at which she can eventually resell them. Similarly, the trader may quote a price for the sale of francs that is above the current asking price.

The Mechanics of Spot Transactions

The simplest way to explain the process of actually settling transactions in the spot market is to work through an example. Suppose a U.S. importer requires FF 1 million to pay his French supplier. After receiving and accepting a verbal quote from the trader of a U.S. bank, the importer will be asked to specify two accounts: (1) the account in a U.S. bank that he wants debited for the equivalent dollar amount at the agreed exchange rate and (2) the French supplier's account that is to be credited by FF 1 million.

Upon completion of the verbal agreement, the trader will forward a dealing slip containing the relevant information to the settlement section of her bank. That same day, a *contract note*—that includes the amount of the foreign currency, the dollar equivalent at the agreed rate, and confirmation of the payment instructions—will be sent to the importer. The settlement section will then cable the bank's correspondent (or branch) in Paris, requesting transfer of FF 1 million from its *nostro account*—that is, working balances maintained with the correspondent to facilitate delivery and receipt of currencies—to the account specified by the importer. On the value date, the U.S. bank will debit the importer's account, and the exporter will have his account credited by the French correspondent.

At the time of the initial agreement, the trader provides a clerk with the pertinent details of the transaction. The clerk, in turn, constantly updates a *position sheet* that shows the bank's position by currency (as well as by maturities of forward contracts). A number of the major international banks have fully computerized this process to ensure accurate and instantaneous information on individual transactions and on the bank's cumulative currency exposure at any time. The head trader will monitor this information for evidence of possible fraud or excessive exposure in a given currency.

Because spot transactions are normally settled two working days later, a bank is never certain until one or two days after the deal is concluded whether the payment due the bank has actually been made. To keep this credit risk in bounds, most banks will transact large amounts only with prime names (other banks or corporate customers).

■ 2.3 ■
THE FORWARD MARKET

Forward exchange operations carry the same credit risk as spot transactions, but for longer periods of time; however, there are significant exchange risks involved.

A *forward contract* between a bank and a customer (which could be another bank) calls for delivery, at a fixed future date, of a specified amount of one currency against dollar payment; the exchange rate is fixed at the time the contract is entered into. Although the Deutsche mark is the most widely traded currency at present, active forward markets exist for the pound sterling, the Canadian dollar, the Japanese yen, and the major Continental currencies—particularly the Swiss franc, French franc, Belgian franc, Italian lira, and Dutch guilder. In general, forward markets for the currencies of less-developed countries (LDCs) are either limited or nonexistent.

In a typical forward transaction, for example, a U.S. company buys textiles from England with payment of £1 million due in 90 days. The importer, thus, is *short* pounds—that is, it owes pounds for future delivery. Suppose the present price of the pound is $1.71. Over the next 90 days, however, the pound might rise against the dollar, raising the dollar cost of the textiles. The importer can guard against this exchange risk by immediately negotiating a 90-day forward contract with a bank at a price of, say, £1 = $1.72. According to the forward contract, in 90 days the bank will give the importer £1 million (which it will use to pay for its textile order), and the importer will give the bank $1.72 million, which is the dollar equivalent of £1 million at the forward rate of $1.72.

In technical terms, the importer is offsetting a short position in pounds by going *long* in the forward market—that is, by buying pounds for future delivery. Exhibit 2.5 plots the importer's dollar cost of the textile shipment with and without the use of a forward contract. It also shows the gain or loss on the forward contract as a function of the contracted forward price and the spot price of the pound when the contract matures.

The gains and losses from long and short forward positions are related to the difference between the contracted forward price and the spot price of the underlying currency at the time the contract matures. In the case of the textile order, the importer is committed to buy pounds at $1.72 apiece. If the spot rate in 90 days is less than $1.72, the importer will suffer an implicit loss on the forward contract because it is buying pounds for more than its prevailing value. But if the spot rate in 90 days exceeds $1.72, the importer will enjoy an implicit profit because the contract obliges the bank to sell the pounds at a price less than its current value.

Three points are worth noting. First, the gain or loss on the forward contract is unrelated to the current spot rate of $1.71. Second, the forward contract gain or loss exactly offsets

■ **EXHIBIT 2.5**   Hedging a Future Payment with a Forward Contract

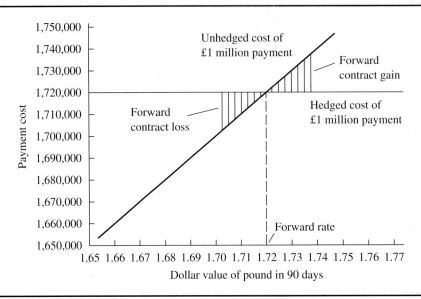

the change in the dollar cost of the textile order that is associated with movements in the pound's value. For example, if the spot price of the pound in 90 days is $1.75, the importer's cost of delivery is $1.75 million. However, the forward contract has a gain of $30,000, or 1,000,000 × (1.75 − 1.72). The net cost of the textile order when covering with a forward contract is $1.72 million, no matter what happens to the spot exchange rate in 90 days. (Chapter 9 elaborates on the use of forward contracts to manage exchange risk.) Third, the forward contract is not an option contract. Both parties must perform the agreed-upon behavior, unlike the situation with an option where the buyer can choose whether to exercise the contract or allow it to expire. The bank must deliver the pounds, and the importer must buy them at the prearranged price. Options are discussed in Chapter 3.

Forward Market Participants

The major participants in the forward market can be categorized as arbitrageurs, traders, hedgers, and speculators.

Arbitrageurs seek to earn risk-free profits by taking advantage of differences in interest rates among countries. They use forward contracts to eliminate the exchange risk involved in transferring their funds from one nation to another.

Traders use forward contracts to eliminate or cover the risk of loss on export or import orders that are denominated in foreign currencies. More generally, a forward-covering transaction relates to a specific payment or receipt expected at a specified point in time.

Hedgers, mostly multinational firms, engage in forward contracts to protect the home currency value of various foreign-currency-denominated assets and liabilities on their balance sheets that are not to be realized over the life of the contracts.

Arbitrageurs, traders, and hedgers seek to reduce (or eliminate, if possible) their exchange risks by "locking in" the exchange rate on future trade or financial operations.

In contrast to these three types of forward market participants, *speculators* actively expose themselves to currency risk by buying or selling currencies forward in order to profit from exchange rate fluctuations. Their degree of participation does not depend on their business transactions in other currencies; instead, it is based on prevailing forward rates and their expectations for spot exchange rates in the future.

Forward Quotations

Forward rates can be expressed in two ways. Commercial customers are usually quoted the actual price, otherwise known as the *outright rate.* In the interbank market, however, dealers quote the forward rate only as a discount from, or a premium on, the spot rate. This forward differential is known as the *swap rate.* A foreign currency is at a *forward discount* if the forward rate expressed in dollars is below the spot rate, whereas a *forward premium* exists if the forward rate is above the spot rate. As we shall see in Section 2.5, the forward premium or discount is closely related to the difference in interest rates on the two currencies.

According to Exhibit 2.3, spot Japanese yen on February 6, 1990, sold at $0.006879 while 90-day forward yen were priced at $0.006902. Based on these rates, the swap rate for the 90-day forward yen was quoted as a 23-point premium (0.006902 – 0.006879). Similarly, because the 90-day British pound was quoted at $1.6745 while the spot pound was $1.7015, the 90-day forward British pound sold at a 270-point discount. Alternatively, the discount or premium may be expressed as an annualized percentage deviation from the spot rate using the following formula:

$$\text{Forward premium or discount} = \frac{\text{Forward rate} - \text{Spot rate}}{\text{Spot rate}} \times \frac{12}{\text{Forward contract length in months}}$$

Thus, on February 6, 1990, the three-month forward Japanese yen was selling at a 1.34% annualized premium:

$$\text{Forward premium annualized} = \frac{0.006902 - 0.006879}{0.006879} \times \frac{12}{3} = 0.0134$$

The three-month British pound was selling at a 6.35% annualized discount:

$$\text{Forward discount annualized} = \frac{1.6745 - 1.7015}{1.7015} \times \frac{12}{3} = -0.0635$$

A swap rate can be converted into an outright rate by adding the premium (in points) to, or subtracting the discount (in points) from, the spot rate. Although the swap rates do not carry plus or minus signs, you can determine whether the forward rate is at a discount or premium using the following rule: When the forward bid in points is smaller than the offer rate in points, the forward rate is at a premium and the points should be added to the spot price to compute the outright quote. Conversely, if the bid in points exceeds the offer in points, the forward rate is at a discount and the points must be subtracted from the spot price to get the outright quotes.[5]

Suppose, for example, that the following quotes are received for spot, one-month, three-month, and six-month Swiss francs (SFr) and pounds sterling:

£:$2.0015–30   19–17   26–22   42–35
SFr:$0.6963–68   4–6   9–14   25–38

The outright rates are

Maturity	£			SFr		
	Bid	Ask	Spread (%)	Bid	Ask	Spread (%)
Spot	$2.0015	$2.0030	0.075	$0.6963	$0.6969	0.086
One-month	1.9996	2.0013	0.085	0.6967	0.6974	0.100
Three-month	1.9989	2.0008	0.095	0.6972	0.6982	0.143
Six-month	1.9973	1.9995	0.110	0.6988	0.7006	0.257

Thus, the Swiss franc is selling at a premium against the dollar and the pound is selling at a discount. Note the slightly wider percentage spread between outright bid and offer on the Swiss franc compared with the spread on the pound. This difference is due to the broader market in pounds. Note too the widening of spreads over time for both currencies. This widening is caused by the greater uncertainty surrounding future exchange rates.

Exchange Risk.   Spreads in the forward market are a function of both the breadth of the market (volume of transactions) in a given currency and the risks associated with forward contracts. The risks, in turn, are based on the variability of future spot rates. Even if the spot market is stable, there is no guarantee that future rates will remain invariant. This uncertainty will be reflected in the forward market. Furthermore, because beliefs about distant exchange rates are typically less secure than those about nearer-term rates, uncertainty will increase with lengthening maturities of forward contracts. Dealers will quote wider spreads on longer-term forward contracts to compensate themselves for the risk of being unable to profitably reverse their positions. Moreover, the greater unpredictability of future spot rates may reduce the number of market participants. This increased thinness will further widen

---

[5]This rule is based on two factors: (1) The buying rate, be it for spot or forward delivery, is always less than the selling price, and (2) the forward bid-ask spread always exceeds the spot bid-ask spread.

the bid-ask spread because it magnifies the dealer's risk in taking even a temporary position in the forward market.

Cross-Rates. Forward cross-rates are figured in much the same way as spot cross-rates. For instance, suppose a customer wants to sell one-month forward lire (Lit) against Dutch guilder (Dfl) delivery. The market rates (expressed in European terms of foreign currency units per dollar) are

$:Lit spot	1,890.00–1,892.00
One-month forward	1,894.25–1,897.50
$:Dfl spot	3.4582–3.4600
One-month forward	3.4530–3.4553

Based on these rates, the forward cross-rate for selling lire against guilders is found as follows: Forward lire are sold for dollars—that is, dollars are bought at the lira forward selling price of Lit 1,897.50 = $1—and are simultaneously sold for one-month forward guilders at a rate of Dfl 3.4530. Thus, Lit 1,897.50 = Dfl 3.4530 or the forward selling price for lire against guilders is Lit 1,897.50/3.4530 = Lit 549.52. Similarly, the forward buying rate for lire against guilders is Lit 1,894.25/3.4553 = Lit 548.22. The spot selling rate is Lit 1,892.0/3.4582 = Lit 547.11. Hence, the forward discount on selling lire against Dfl delivery equals (549.52 − 547.11)/547.11 = 0.0044 or 5.29% per annum (0.0044 × 12 = 0.0529).

Forward Contract Maturities

Forward contracts are normally available for one-month, two-month, three-month, six-month, or 12-month delivery. Banks will also tailor forward contracts for odd maturities (e.g., 77 days) to meet their customers' needs. Longer-term forward contracts can usually be arranged for widely traded currencies, such as the pound sterling, Deutsche mark, or Japanese yen; however, the bid-ask spread tends to widen for longer maturities. As with spot rates, these spreads have widened for almost all currencies since the early 1970s, probably because of the greater turbulence in foreign exchange markets. For widely traded currencies, the three-month bid-ask spread can vary from 0.1% to 1%.

Bank Policy on Speculation

Clearly, there is greater risk for a bank in its forward transactions than in spot contracts because of the more remote payment date and greater chance of unfavorable currency fluctuations. There are two types of risk here: (1) the risk of price fluctuations and (2) the risk that the contracts will not be carried out. The first risk will affect the bank only if it carries an open position in the forward contract. Typically, however, the bank will lay this risk off by engaging in an offsetting transaction. The bank carries the second risk, even if it has a net position of zero, because it stands in the middle. Banks are, therefore, concerned over the creditworthiness of their customers.

If a bank believes currency speculation is involved, it might require a customer to put up a margin of 10% of the forward contract to protect itself in case of default. Generally, however, banks prefer to discourage speculative transactions.

■ 2.4 ■
THE RELATIONSHIP BETWEEN THE FORWARD RATE AND THE FUTURE SPOT RATE

Our current understanding of the workings of the foreign exchange market suggests that, in the absence of government intervention in the market, both the spot rate and the forward rate are influenced heavily by current expectations of future events; and both rates move in tandem, with the link between them based on interest differentials. New information, such as a change in interest rate differentials, is reflected almost immediately in both spot and forward rates.

Suppose a depreciation of pounds sterling is anticipated. Recipients of sterling will begin selling sterling forward, while sterling-area dollar earners will slow their sales of dollars in the forward market. These actions will tend to depress the price of forward sterling. At the same time, banks will probably try to even out their long (net purchaser) positions in forward sterling by selling sterling spot. In addition, sterling-area recipients of dollars will tend to delay converting dollars into sterling, and earners of sterling will speed up their collection and conversion of sterling. In this way, pressure from the forward market is transmitted to the spot market, and vice versa.

Equilibrium is achieved only when the forward differential equals the expected change in the exchange rate. At this point, there is no longer any incentive to buy or sell the currency forward. This condition is illustrated in Exhibit 2.6. The vertical axis measures the expected change in the home currency (HC) value of the foreign currency, and the horizontal axis shows the forward discount or premium on the foreign currency. Parity prevails at point A, for example, where the expected foreign currency depreciation of 2% is just matched by the 2% forward discount on the foreign currency. Point B, however, is a position of disequilibrium because the expected 4% depreciation of the foreign currency exceeds the 3% forward discount on the foreign currency. We would, therefore, expect to see speculators selling the foreign currency forward for home currency, taking a 3% discount in the expectation of covering their commitment with 4% fewer units of HC.

A formal statement of the unbiased nature of the forward rate (UFR) is that the forward rate should reflect the expected future spot rate on the date of settlement of the forward contract:

$$f_1 = \bar{e}_1 \tag{2.1}$$

where $\bar{e}_1$ is the expected future exchange rate at time 1 (units of home currency per unit of foreign currency) and f_1 is the forward rate for settlement at time 1.

■ **EXHIBIT 2.6** Relationship Between the Forward Rate and the Future Spot Rate

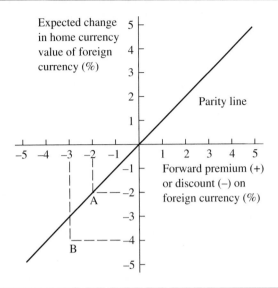

ILLUSTRATION

Using UFR to Forecast the Future \$/DM Spot Rate. If the 90-day forward rate is DM 1 = \$0.5987, what is the expected value of the DM in 90 days?

Solution. Arbitrage should ensure that the market expects the spot value of the DM in 90 days to be about \$0.5987. ■

Equation 2.1 can be transformed into the one reflected in the parity line appearing in Exhibit 2.6, which is that the forward differential equals the expected change in the exchange rate, by subtracting 1 (e_0/e_0), from both sides, where e_0 is the current spot rate (HC per unit of foreign currency):

$$\frac{f_1 - e_0}{e_0} = \frac{\bar{e}_1 - e_0}{e_0} \tag{2.2}$$

It should be noted that market efficiency requires that people process information and form reasonable expectations; it does not require that $f_1 = e_1$. Market efficiency allows for the possibility that risk-averse investors will demand a risk premium on forward contracts, much the same as they demand compensation for bearing the risk of investing in stocks. In this case, the forward rate will not reflect exclusively the expectation of the future spot rate.

The principal argument against the existence of a risk premium is that currency risk is largely diversifiable. If foreign exchange risk can be diversified away, no risk premium need be paid for holding a forward contract; the forward rate and expected future spot rate will be approximately equal. Ultimately, therefore, the unbiased nature of forward rates is an empirical, and not a theoretical, issue.

Empirical Evidence

A number of studies have examined the relation between forward rates and future spot rates.[6] Of course, it would be unrealistic to expect a perfect correlation between forward and future spot rates since the future spot rate will be influenced by events, such as an oil crisis, that can be forecast only imperfectly, if at all.

Nonetheless, the general conclusion from early studies was that forward rates are unbiased predictors of future spot rates. But more recent studies, using more powerful econometric techniques, argue that the forward rate is a biased predictor, probably because of a risk premium.[7] However, the premium appears to change signs—being positive at some times and negative at other times—and averages near zero. In the absence of a detailed econometric model, therefore, it would not be stretching things to treat the forward rate as an unbiased forecast of the future spot rate.

■ 2.5 ■
INTEREST RATE PARITY THEORY

As noted in the previous section, the movement of funds between two currencies to take advantage of interest rate differentials is also a major determinant of the spread between forward and spot rates. In fact, the forward discount or premium is closely related to the interest differential between the two currencies.

According to interest rate parity theory, the currency of the country with a lower interest rate should be at a forward premium in terms of the currency of the country with the higher rate. More specifically, in an efficient market with no transaction costs, the interest differential should be (approximately) equal to the forward differential. When this condition is met, the forward rate is said to be at *interest parity,* and equilibrium prevails in the money markets.

Interest parity ensures that the return on a hedged (or "covered") foreign investment will just equal the domestic interest rate on investments of identical risk, thereby eliminating the possibility of having a money machine. When this condition holds, the *covered interest differential*—the difference between the domestic interest rate and the hedged foreign rate—is zero. If the covered interest differential between two money markets is nonzero, there is an arbitrage incentive to move money from one market to the other.

[6]See, for example, Ian Giddy and Gunter Dufey, "The Random Behavior of Flexible Exchange Rates," *Journal of International Business Studies,* Spring 1975, pp. 1–32; and Bradford Cornell, "Spot Rates, Forward Rates, and Market Efficiency," *Journal of Financial Economics,* January 1977, pp. 55–65.

[7]See, for example, L.P. Hansen and R.J. Hodrick, "Forward Rates as Optimal Predictions of Future Spot Rates," *Journal of Political Economy,* October 1980, pp. 829–853.

For example, suppose the interest rate on pounds sterling is 12% in London, and the interest rate on a comparable dollar investment in New York is 7%. The pound spot rate is $1.75 and the one-year forward rate is $1.68. These rates imply a forward discount on sterling of 4% [(1.68 − 1.75)/1.75] and a covered yield on sterling approximately equal to 8% (12% − 4%). Since there is a covered interest differential in favor of London, funds will flow from New York to London. This movement of money to take advantage of a covered interest differential is known as *covered interest arbitrage*.

To illustrate the profits associated with covered interest arbitrage, we will assume that the borrowing and lending rates are identical and the bid-ask spread in the spot and forward markets is zero. Here are the steps the arbitrageur can take to profit from the discrepancy in rates based on a $1 million transaction. Specifically, the arbitrageur will

1. Borrow $1,000,000 in New York at an interest rate of 7%. This means that at the end of one year, the arbitrageur must repay principal plus interest of $1,070,000.
2. Immediately convert the $1,000,000 to pounds at the spot rate of £1 = $1.75. This yields £571,428.57 available for investment.
3. Invest the principal of £571,428.57 in London at 12% for one year. At the end of the year, the arbitrageur will have £640,000.
4. Simultaneously with the other transactions, sell the £640,000 in principal plus interest forward at a rate of £1 = $1.68 for delivery in one year. This transaction will yield $1,075,200 next year.
5. At the end of the year, collect the £640,000, deliver it to the bank's foreign exchange department in return for $1,075,200, and use $1,070,000 to repay the loan. The arbitrageur will earn $5,200 on this set of transactions.

The transactions associated with covered interest arbitrage will affect prices in both the money and foreign exchange markets. As pounds are bought spot and sold forward, boosting the spot rate and lowering the forward rate, the forward discount will tend to widen. Simultaneously, as money flows from New York, interest rates there will tend to increase; at the same time, the inflow of funds to London will depress interest rates there. The process of covered interest arbitrage will continue until interest parity is achieved, unless there is government interference.

If this process is interfered with, covered interest differentials between national money markets will not be arbitraged away. Interference often occurs since many governments regulate and restrict flows of capital across their borders. Moreover, just the risk of controls will be sufficient to yield prolonged deviations from interest rate parity.

The relationship between the spot and forward rates and interest rates in a free market can be shown graphically, as in Exhibit 2.7. Plotted on the vertical axis is the interest differential in favor of the home country. The horizontal axis plots the percentage forward discount (negative) or premium (positive) on the foreign currency relative to the home currency. The interest parity line joins those points for which the forward exchange rate is in equilibrium with the interest differential. For example, if the interest differential in favor of the foreign country is 2%, then the currency of that country must be selling at a 2% forward discount for equilibrium to exist.

■ **EXHIBIT 2.7**   Interest Rate Parity Theory

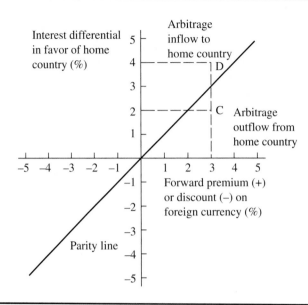

Point C indicates a situation of disequilibrium. Here, the interest differential is 2%, whereas the forward premium on the foreign currency is 3%. The transfer of funds abroad with exchange risks covered will yield an additional 1% annually. At point D, the forward premium remains at 3%, but the interest differential increases to 4%. Now it becomes profitable to reverse the flow of funds. The 4% higher interest rate more than makes up for the 3% loss on the forward exchange transaction, leading to a 1% increase in the interest yield.

In reality, the interest parity line is a band because transaction costs, arising from the spread on spot and forward contracts and brokerage fees on security purchases and sales, cause effective yields to be lower than nominal yields. For example, if transaction costs are 0.75%, then a covered yield of only 0.5% will not be sufficient to induce a flow of funds. That is, for interest arbitrage to occur, the covered yield must be at least equal to the transaction costs involved.

The covered interest arbitrage relationship can be stated formally. Let e_0 be the current spot rate (dollar value of one unit of foreign currency), and f_1 the end-of-period forward rate. If r_h and r_f are the prevailing interest rates in New York and, say, London, respectively, then one dollar invested in New York will yield $1 + r_h$ at the end of the period; the same dollar invested in London will be worth $(1 + r_f)f_1/e_0$ dollars at maturity. This latter result can be seen as follows: One dollar will convert into $1/e_0$ pounds that, when invested at r_f, will yield $(1 + r_f)/e_0$ pounds at the end of the period. By selling the proceeds forward today, this amount will be worth $(1 + r_f)f_1/e_0$ dollars when the investment matures.

It can be seen that funds will flow from New York to London if and only if

$$1 + r_h < \frac{(1 + r_f)f_1}{e_0}$$

Conversely, funds will flow from London to New York if and only if

$$1 + r_h > \frac{(1 + r_f)f_1}{e_0}$$

Interest rate parity holds when there are no covered interest arbitrage opportunities. Based on the previous discussion, this no-arbitrage condition can be stated as follows:

$$\frac{1 + r_h}{1 + r_f} = \frac{f_1}{e_0} \tag{2.3}$$

■ ─────────────────────────

ILLUSTRATION

Using IRP to Calculate the \$/¥ Forward Rate. The interest rate in the United States is 10%; in Japan, the comparable rate is 7%. The spot rate for the yen is \$0.003800. If interest rate parity holds, what is the 90-day forward rate?

Solution. According to interest rate parity, the 90-day forward differential on the yen f_{90} should be

$$f_{90} = \$0.003800 \, [(1 + 0.10/4)(1 + 0.07/4)]$$
$$= \$0.003828$$

In other words, the 90-day forward Japanese yen should be selling at an annualized premium of about 2.95% ($4 \times 0.000028/0.0038$). ■

Interest rate parity is often approximated by Equation 2.4:[8]

$$r_h - r_f = \frac{f_1 - e_0}{e_0} \tag{2.4}$$

In effect, interest rate parity says that *high interest rates on a currency are offset by forward discounts and that low interest rates are offset by forward premiums.*

Empirical Evidence

Interest rate parity is one of the best-documented relationships in international finance. In fact, in the Eurocurrency markets (to be studied in Chapter 22), the forward rate is calculated from the interest differential between the two currencies using the no-arbitrage condition. Deviations from interest parity do occur between national capital markets,

---

[8]Subtracting 1 from both sides of Equation 2.3 yields $(f_1 - e_0)/e_0 = (r_h - r_f)/(1 + r_f)$. Equation 2.4 follows if r_f is relatively small.

however, owing to capital controls (or the threat of them), the imposition of taxes on interest payments to foreigners, and transaction costs.

■ 2.6 ■
SUMMARY AND CONCLUSIONS

In this chapter, we saw that the primary function of the foreign exchange market is to transfer purchasing power denominated in one currency to another and, thereby, facilitate international trade and investment. The foreign exchange market consists of two tiers: the interbank market, in which major banks trade with each other, and the retail market, in which banks deal with their commercial customers.

In the spot market, currencies are traded for settlement within two business days after the transaction has been concluded. In the forward market, contracts are made to buy or sell currencies for future delivery. Spot and forward quotations are given in either American terms—the dollar price of a foreign currency—or in European terms—the foreign-currency price of a dollar. Quotations can also be expressed on a direct basis—the home-currency price of another currency—or an indirect basis—the foreign-currency price of the home currency.

The major participants in the forward market were categorized as arbitrageurs, traders, hedgers, and speculators. Forward rates can be stated on an outright basis, or as a discount from, or a premium on, the spot rate. This forward differential is known as the swap rate. Because all currencies are quoted against the dollar, the exchange rate between two nondollar currencies—known as a cross-rate—must be calculated on the basis of their direct quotes against the dollar.

Finally, we examined the links between the spot and forward markets. In particular, the theory of the unbiased forward rate says that the forward rate should equal the expected future spot rate. Both spot and forward exchange rates move in tandem, with the link between them based on interest differentials. We also saw that the movement of funds between two currencies to take advantage of interest rate differentials is also a major determinant of the spread between forward and spot rates. According to interest rate parity, the forward discount or premium is approximately equal to the interest differential between currencies. In technical terms, these two conditions can be expressed as follows:

■ The forward rate as an unbiased predictor of the future spot rate

$$f_1 = \bar{e}_1$$

where $\bar{e}_1$ = the expected home currency value of the foreign currency at time 1
         f_1 = the forward rate for delivery of one unit of foreign currency at time 1

■ Interest rate parity

$$\frac{1 + r_h}{1 + r_f} = \frac{f_1}{e_0}$$

where r_h = the home currency interest rate
        r_f = the foreign currency interest rate
        e_0 = the home currency value of the foreign currency at time 0

■ QUESTIONS ■

1. Answer the following questions based on data in Exhibit 2.3.

   a. How many Swiss francs can you get for one dollar?

   b. How many dollars can you get for one Swiss franc?

   c. What is the three-month forward rate for the Swiss franc?

   d. Is the Swiss franc selling at a forward premium or discount?

   e. What is the 90-day forward discount or premium on the Swiss franc?

2. What risks confront dealers in the foreign exchange market? How can they cope with those risks?

3. Suppose a currency increases in volatility. What is likely to happen to its bid-ask spread? Why?

4. Who are the principal users of the forward market? What are their motives?

5. How does a company pay for the foreign exchange services of a commercial bank?

6. The spot rate on the Deutsche mark is $0.63, and the 180-day forward rate is $0.64. What are possible reasons for the difference between the two rates?

7. What factors might lead to persistent covered interest arbitrage opportunities among countries?

■ PROBLEMS ■

1. The $:DM exchange rate is DM 1 = $0.35, and the DM:FF exchange rate is FF 1 = DM 0.31. What is the FF:$ exchange rate?

2. Suppose the direct quote for sterling in New York is 1.1110–5. What is the direct quote for dollars in London?

3. Suppose the spot quote on the Deutsche mark is $0.3302–10, and the spot quote on the French franc is $0.1180–90.

   a. What is the direct spot quote for the franc in Frankfurt?

   b. Compute the percentage bid-ask spreads on the DM and franc.

4. The spot and 90-day forward rates for the pound are $1.1376 and $1.1350, respectively. What is the forward premium or discount on the pound?

5. Suppose you observe the following direct spot quotations in New York and Toronto, respectively: 0.8000–50 and 1.2500–60. What are the arbitrage profits per $1 million?

6. Suppose the DM is quoted at 0.2074–80 in London, and the pound sterling is quoted at 4.7010–32 in Frankfurt.

   a. Is there a profitable arbitrage situation? Describe it.

   b. Compute the percentage bid-ask spreads on the pound and DM.

7. Assuming no transaction costs, suppose £1 = $2.4110 in New York, $1 = FF 3.997 in Paris, and FF 1 = £0.1088 in London. How could you take profitable advantage of these rates?

8. Using the data in Exhibit 2.3, calculate the 30-day, 90-day, and 180-day forward discounts for the British pound.

9. An investor wishes to buy French francs spot (at $0.1080) and sell French francs forward for 180 days (at $0.1086).

   a. What is the swap rate on French francs?

   b. What is the premium on 180-day French francs?

10. Assume the pound sterling is worth FF 9.80 in Paris and SFr 5.40 in Zurich.

    a. Show how British arbitrageurs can make profits given that the Swiss franc is worth two French francs. What would be the profit per pound transacted?

    b. What would be the eventual outcome on exchange rates in Paris and Zurich given these arbitrage activities?

    c. Rework part a, assuming that transaction costs amount to 0.6% of the amount transacted. What would be the profit per pound transacted?

    d. Suppose the Swiss franc is quoted at FF 2 in Zurich. Given a transaction cost of 0.6% of the amount transacted, what are the minimum/maximum French franc prices for the Swiss franc that you would expect to see quoted in Paris?

11. A foreign exchange trader in London could not understand why the 180-day forward rate on the yen was $1 = ¥135 when she believed that the dollar would be worth ¥125 in six months. What is the trader's expected profit on a 180-day forward sale of $1 million for yen delivery?

12. Assume the interest rate is 16% on pounds sterling and 7% on Deutsche marks. If the Deutsche mark is selling at a one-year forward premium of 10% against the pound, is there an arbitrage opportunity? Explain.

13. Suppose the Eurosterling rate is 15%, and the Eurodollar rate is 11.5%. What is the forward premium on the dollar? Explain.

14. If the Swiss franc is $0.68 on the spot market and the 180-day forward rate is $0.70, what is the annualized interest rate in the United States over the next six months? The annualized interest rate in Switzerland is 2%.

15. The interest rate in the United States is 8%; in Japan the comparable rate is 2%. The spot rate for the yen is $0.007692. If interest rate parity holds, what is the 90-day forward rate on the Japanese yen?

16. Suppose today's spot exchange rate is $0.51:DM 1. The six-month interest rates on dollars and DM are 13% and 6%, respectively. The six-month forward rate is $0.5170:DM 1. A foreign exchange advisory service has predicted that the DM will appreciate to $0.54:DM 1 within six months.

    a. How would you use forward contracts to profit in the above situation?

    b. How would you use borrowing and lending transactions to profit?

17. Suppose the spot rates for the Deutsche mark, pound sterling, and Swiss franc are $0.32, $1.13, and $0.38, respectively. The associated 90-day interest rates (annualized) are 8%, 16%, and 4%; the U.S. 90-day rate (annualized) is 12%. What is the 90-day forward rate on an ACU (ACU 1 = DM 1 + £1 + SFr 1) if interest parity holds?

18. Here are some prices in the international money markets:

Spot rate	= $0.75/DM
Forward rate (one year)	= $0.77/DM
Interest rate (DM)	= 7% per year
Interest rate ($)	= 9% per year

    a. Assuming no transaction costs or taxes exist, do covered arbitrage profits exist in the above situation? Describe the flows.

    b. Suppose now that transaction costs in the foreign exchange market equal 0.25% per transaction. Do unexploited covered arbitrage profit opportunities still exist?

   c. Suppose no transaction costs exist. Let the capital gains tax on currency profits equal 25%, and the ordinary income tax on interest income equal 50%. In this situation, do covered arbitrage profits exist? How large are they? Describe the transactions required to exploit these profits.

■ BIBLIOGRAPHY ■

Chrystal, K. Alec. "A Guide to Foreign Exchange Markets." *Federal Reserve Bank of St. Louis Review,* March 1984, pp. 5–18.

Kubarych, Roger M. *Foreign Exchange Markets in the United States.* New York: Federal Reserve Bank of New York, 1983.

3

Currency Futures and
Options Markets

I dipt into the future far as human eye could see, Saw the vision of the world and all the wonder that would be.

—Tennyson—

■ Foreign currency futures and options contracts are a new breed of financial instrument. This chapter describes the nature of these contracts and shows how they can be used to manage foreign exchange risk or take speculative positions on currency movements. It also shows how to read the prices of these contracts as they appear in the financial press.

■ 3.1 ■
FUTURES CONTRACTS

In 1972, the *Chicago Mercantile Exchange* opened its *International Monetary Market* (IMM) division. The IMM provides an outlet for currency speculators and for those looking to reduce their currency risks. Trade takes place in *currency futures,* which are contracts for specific quantities of given currencies; the exchange rate is fixed at the time the contract is entered into, and the delivery date is set by the board of directors of the IMM. These contracts, which represented the first step in the development of financial futures, are patterned after those for grain and commodity futures contracts, which have been traded on Chicago's exchanges for over 100 years.

Currency futures contracts are currently available for the British pound, Canadian dollar, Deutsche mark, Swiss franc, French franc, Japanese yen, Australian dollar, and European Currency Unit. Contracts in the Dutch guilder and Mexican peso have been dropped. Private individuals are encouraged, rather than discouraged, to participate in the market. Contract sizes are standardized according to amount of foreign currency—for example, £62,500; C$100,000; SFr 125,000. Exhibit 3.1 shows contract specifications.

■ **EXHIBIT 3.1** Contract Specifications for Foreign Currency Futures

	Australian Dollar	British Pound	Canadian Dollar	Deutsche Mark	French Franc	Japanese Yen	Swiss Franc
Contract size	A$100,000	£62,500	C$100,000	DM 125,000	FF 250,000	¥12,500,000	SFr 125,000
Symbol	AD	BP	CD	DM	FR	JY	SF
Margin requirements							
Initial	$1,200	$2,000	$700	$1,400	$700	$1,700	$1,700
Maintenance	900	1,500	500	1,000	500	1,300	1,300
Miminum price change	0.0001 (1 pt.)	0.0002 (2 pts.)	0.0001 (1 pt.)	0.0001 (1 pt.)	0.00005 (5 pts.)	0.000001 (1 pt.)	0.0001 (1 pt.)
Value of 1 point	$10.00	$6.25	$10.00	$12.50	$2.50	$12.50	$12.50

Months traded _____ January, March, April, June, July, September, _____
October, December and spot month
Trading hours _____ 7:20 A.M.–2:00 P.M. (Central time) _____
Last day of trading _____ Third Wednesday of the delivery month _____

SOURCE: *Contract Specifications and Minimum Margin Requirements,* Chicago Mercantile Exchange, April 11, 1989.

Leverage is high; margin requirements average less than 4% of the value of the futures contract. The leverage assures that investors' fortunes will be decided by tiny swings in exchange rates.

Instead of using the bid-ask spreads found in the interbank market, traders charge commissions. Though commissions will vary, a *round trip*—that is, one buy and one sell—costs as little as $15. This cost works out to less than 0.05% of the value of a sterling contract. The low cost, along with the high degree of leverage, has provided a major inducement for speculators to participate in the market. Other market participants include importers and exporters, companies with foreign-currency assets and liabilities, and bankers.

Although volume in the futures market is still small compared to the forward market, it is growing rapidly. Exhibit 3.2 shows just how rapid this growth is. The IMM can be viewed as an expanding part of a growing foreign exchange market. As we will see shortly, the different segments of this market are linked by arbitrage.

A notable feature of the IMM and other futures markets is that deals are struck by brokers face to face on a trading floor, rather than over the telephone. There are a number of other, more important distinctions between the futures and forward markets.

Forward Contract Versus Futures Contract

One way to understand futures contracts is to compare them to forward contracts. *Futures contracts* are standardized contracts that trade on organized futures markets. Because contract sizes and maturities are standardized, all participants in the market are familiar with the types of contracts available, and trading is facilitated. Forward contracts,

■ **EXHIBIT 3.2**   IMM Currency Futures Trading Volume, 1975–1991

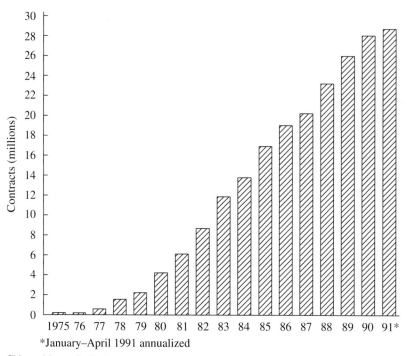

*January–April 1991 annualized

SOURCE: Chicago Mercantile Exchange.

on the other hand, are private deals between two individuals who can sign any type of contract they agree on. For example, two individuals may sign a forward contract for DM 70,000 in 20 months to be paid in Belgian francs. However, IMM contracts trade only in round lots of DM 125,000 priced in U.S. dollars and with a limited range of maturities available. With only a few standardized contracts traded, the trading volume in available contracts is higher, leading to superior liquidity, smaller price fluctuations, and lower transaction costs in the futures market.

The organization of futures trading with a clearing house reduces the default risks of trading. The exchange members, in effect, guarantee both sides of a contract. In contrast, a forward contract is a private deal between two parties and is subject to the risk that either side may default on the terms of the agreement.

Profits and losses of futures contracts are paid over every day at the end of trading, a practice called *marking to market*. This daily-settlement feature can best be illustrated with an example. On Tuesday morning, an investor takes a long position in a Swiss-franc futures contract that matures on Thursday afternoon. The agreed-upon price is $0.75 for SFr125,000. At the close of trading on Tuesday, the futures price has risen to $0.755. Due to daily settlement, three things occur. First, the investor receives her cash profit of $625

(125,000 × 0.005). Second, the existing futures contract with a price of $0.75 is canceled. Third, the investor receives a new futures contract with the prevailing price of $0.755. Thus, the value of the futures contracts is set to zero at the end of each trading day.

At Wednesday close, the price has declined to $0.752. The investor must pay the $375 loss (125,000 × 0.003) to the other side of the contract and trade in her old contract for a new one with a price of $0.752. At Thursday close, the price drops to $0.74, and the contract matures. The investor pays her $1,500 loss to the other side and takes delivery of the Swiss francs, paying the prevailing price of $0.74. Exhibit 3.3 details the daily settlement process.

Daily settlement reduces the default risk of futures contracts relative to forward contracts. Every day, futures investors must pay over any losses or receive any gains from the day's price movements. An insolvent investor with an unprofitable position would be forced into default after only one day's trading, rather than being allowed to build up huge losses that lead to one large default at the time the contract matures (as could occur with a forward contract).

Futures contracts also can be closed out easily with an *offsetting trade*. For example, if a company's long position in DM futures has proved to be profitable, it need not literally take delivery of the DM at the time the contract matures. Rather, the company can sell futures contracts on a like amount of DM just prior to the maturity of the long position. The two positions cancel on the books of the futures exchange and the company receives its profit in cash. These and other differences between forward and futures contracts are summarized in Exhibit 3.4.

Advantages and Disadvantages of Futures Contracts.   The smaller size of a futures contract and the freedom to liquidate the contract at any time before its maturity in a well-organized futures market differentiate the futures contract from the forward contract. These features of the futures contract attract many users. On the other hand, the limited

■ **EXHIBIT 3.3**   An Example of Daily Settlement with a Futures Contract

Time	Action	Cash Flow
Tuesday morning	Investor buys SFr futures contract that matures in two days. Price is $0.75.	None
Tuesday close	Futures price rises to $0.755. Position is marked to market.	Investor receives $125,000 \times (0.755 - 0.75) = \$625$.
Wednesday close	Futures price drops to $0.752. Position is marked to market.	Investor pays $125,000 \times (0.755 - 0.752) = \$375$.
Thursday close	Futures price drops to $0.74. (1) Contract is marked to market. (2) Investor takes delivery of SFr 125,000.	(1) Investor pays $125,000 \times (0.752 - 0.74) = \$1,500$. (2) Investor pays $125,000 \times 0.74 = \$92,500$.

■ **EXHIBIT 3.4**   Basic Differences Between Forward and Futures Contracts

1. **Trading:**
   Forward contracts are traded by telephone or telex.
   Futures contracts are traded in a competitive arena.
2. **Regulation:**
   The forward market is self-regulating.
   The IMM is regulated by the Commodity Futures Trading Commission.
3. **Frequency of Delivery:**
   More than 90% of all forward contracts are settled by actual delivery.
   By contrast, less than 1% of the IMM futures contracts are settled by delivery.
4. **Size of Contract:**
   Forward contracts are individually tailored and tend to be much larger than the standardized contracts on the futures market.
   Futures contracts are standardized in terms of currency amount.
5. **Delivery date:**
   Banks offer forward contracts for delivery on any date.
   IMM futures contracts are available for delivery on only a few specified dates a year.
6. **Settlement:**
   Forward contract settlement occurs on the date agreed upon between the bank and its customer.
   Futures contract settlements are made daily via the Exchange's Clearing House; gains on position values may be withdrawn and losses are collected daily. This practice is known as marking to market.
7. **Quotes:**
   Forward prices generally are quoted in European terms (units of local currency per U.S. dollar).
   Futures contracts are quoted in American terms (dollars per one foreign-currency unit).
8. **Transaction Costs:**
   Costs of forward contracts based on bid-ask spread.
   Futures contracts entail brokerage fees for buy and sell orders.
9. **Margins:**
   Margins are not required in the forward market.
   Margins are required of all participants in the futures market.
10. **Credit Risk:**
    The credit risk is borne by each party to a forward contract. Credit limits must therefore be set for each customer.
    The Exchange's Clearing House becomes the opposite side to each futures contract, thereby reducing credit risk substantially.

---

number of currencies traded, the limited delivery dates, and the rigid contractual amounts of currencies to be delivered are disadvantages of the futures contract to many commercial users. Only by chance will contracts conform exactly to corporate requirements. The contracts are of value mainly to those commercial customers who have a fairly stable and continuous stream of payments or receipts in the traded foreign currencies.

Arbitrage Between the Futures and Forward Markets. Arbitrageurs play an important role on the IMM. They translate IMM futures rates into interbank forward rates and, by realizing profit opportunities, keep IMM futures rates in line with bank forward rates.

■ ───

ILLUSTRATION

Forward-Futures Arbitrage. Suppose that the interbank forward bid for June 18 on pounds sterling is $1.2927 at the same time that the price of IMM sterling futures for delivery on June 18 is $1.2915. How could the dealer use arbitrage to profit from this situation?

Solution. The dealer would simultaneously buy the June sterling futures contract for $80,718.75 (62,500 × $1.2915) and sell an equivalent amount of sterling forward, worth $80,793.75 (62,500 × $1.2927), for June delivery. Upon settlement, the dealer would earn a profit of $75. Alternatively, if the markets come back together before June 18, the dealer could unwind his position (by simultaneously buying £62,500 forward and selling a futures contract, both for delivery on June 18) and earn the same $75 profit. Although the amount of profit on this transaction is tiny, it becomes $7,500 if 100 futures contracts are traded. ■

Such arbitrage transactions will bid up the futures price and bid down the forward price until approximate equality is restored. The word approximate is used because there is a difference between the two contracts. Unlike the forward contract, where gains or losses are not realized until maturity, marking to market means that day-to-day futures contract gains (or losses) will have to be invested (or borrowed) at uncertain future interest rates. However, a study of actual rates for the British pound, Canadian dollar, Deutsche mark, Swiss franc, and Japanese yen found that forward and futures prices do not differ significantly from each other.[1]

■ 3.2 ■
CURRENCY OPTIONS

Whatever advantages the forward or the futures contract might hold for their purchaser, they have a common disadvantage: While they protect the holder against the risk of adverse movements in exchange rates, they eliminate the possibility of gaining a windfall profit from favorable movements. This was apparently one of the considerations that led some commercial banks to offer *currency options* to their customers. Exchange-traded currency options were first offered in 1983 by the *Philadelphia Stock Exchange* (PHLX).

In principle, an *option* is a financial instrument that gives the holder the right—but not the obligation—to sell (put) or buy (call) another financial instrument at a set price and expiration date. The seller of the put option or call option must fulfill the contract if the buyer so desires it. Because the option not to buy or sell has value, the buyer must pay the seller of the option some premium for this privilege. As applied to foreign currencies, *call options* give the customer the right to purchase, and *put options* give the right to sell, the contracted currencies at the expiration date. An *American option* can be exercised at any time up to the expiration date; a *European option* can only be exercised at maturity.

---

[1]Bradford Cornell and Marc Reinganum, "Forward and Futures Prices: Evidence from the Foreign Exchange Markets," *Journal of Finance,* December 1981, pp. 1035–1045.

An option that would be profitable to exercise at the current exchange rate is said to be *in-the-money*. Conversely, an *out-of-the-money* option is one that would not be profitable to exercise at the current exchange rate. The price at which the option is exercised is called the *exercise price* or *strike price*. An option whose exercise price is the same as the spot exchange rate is termed *at-the-money*.

Using Currency Options

To see how currency options might be used, consider a U.S. importer that has a DM 62,500 payment to make to a German exporter in 60 days. The importer could purchase a European call option to have the Deutsche marks delivered to it at a specified exchange rate (the strike price) on the due date. Suppose the option premium is $0.02 per DM, and the exercise price is $0.64. The importer has paid $1,250 for the right to buy DM 62,500 at a price of $0.64 per mark at the end of 60 days. If at the time the importer's payment falls due, the value of the Deutsche mark has risen to, say, $0.70, the option would be in-the-money. In this case, the importer exercises its call option, and purchases Deutsche marks for $0.64. The importer would earn a profit of $3,750 (62,500 × 0.06), which would more than cover the $1,250 cost of the option. If the rate has declined below the contracted rate to, say, $0.60, the option would be out-of-the-money. Consequently, the importer would let the option expire and purchase the Deutsche marks in the spot market. Despite losing the $1,250 option premium, the importer would still be $1,250 better off than if it had locked in a rate of $0.64 with a forward or futures contract.

Exhibit 3.5 illustrates the importer's gains or losses on the call option. At a spot rate on expiration of $0.64 or lower, the option will not be exercised, resulting in a loss of the $1,250 option premium. Between $0.64 and $0.66, the option will be exercised, but the gain is insufficient to cover the premium. The *break-even price*—where the gain on the option just equals the option premium—is $0.66. Above $0.66 per DM, the option is sufficiently deep in-the-money to cover the option premium and yield a—potentially unlimited—net profit. Since this is a zero-sum game, the profit from selling a call is the mirror image of the profit from buying the call.

In contrast, a put option at the same terms (exercise price of $0.64 and put premium of $0.02 per DM) would be in-the-money at a spot price of $0.60 and out-of-the-money at $0.70. Exhibit 3.6 illustrates the profits available on this DM put option. If the spot price falls to, say, $0.58, the holder of a put option will deliver DM 62,500 worth $36,250 (0.58 × 62,500) and receive $40,000 (0.64 × 62,500). The option holder's profit, net of the $1,250 option premium, is $2,500. As the spot price falls further, the value of the put option rises. At the extreme, if the spot rate falls to 0, the buyer's profit on the contract will reach $38,750 (0.64 × 62,500 − 1,250). Below a spot rate of $0.62, the gain on the put option will more than cover the $1,250 option premium. Between $0.62—the break-even price for the put option—and $0.64, the holder would exercise the option, but the gain will be less than the option premium. At spot prices above $0.64, the holder would not exercise the option and so would lose the $1,250 premium. Both the put and the call options will be at-the-money if the spot rate in 60 days is $0.64, and the call or put option buyer will lose the $1,250 option premium.

Typical users of currency options might be financial firms holding large investments overseas where sizable unrealized gains had occurred because of exchange rate changes and

■ **EXHIBIT 3.5**   Profit from Buying a Call Option for Various Spot Prices at Expiration

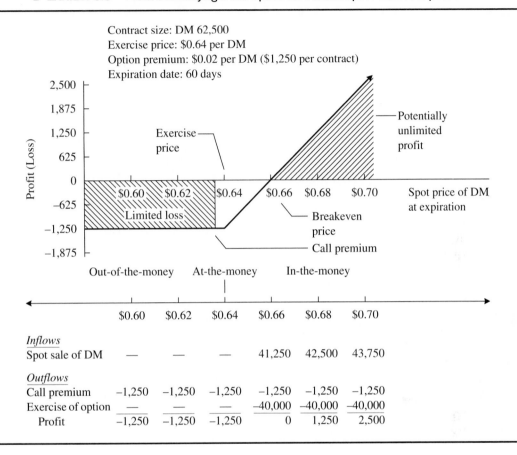

Contract size: DM 62,500
Exercise price: $0.64 per DM
Option premium: $0.02 per DM ($1,250 per contract)
Expiration date: 60 days

	$0.60	$0.62	$0.64	$0.66	$0.68	$0.70
Inflows						
Spot sale of DM	—	—	—	41,250	42,500	43,750
Outflows						
Call premium	−1,250	−1,250	−1,250	−1,250	−1,250	−1,250
Exercise of option	—	—	—	−40,000	−40,000	−40,000
Profit	−1,250	−1,250	−1,250	0	1,250	2,500

where these gains were thought likely to be partially or fully reversed. Limited use of currency options has also been made by firms that have a foreign currency inflow or outflow that is possibly forthcoming, but not definitely. In such cases, where future foreign-currency cash flows are contingent on an event such as acceptance of a bid, long call or put positions can be safer hedges than either futures or forwards.

For example, assume that a U.S. investor makes a firm bid in pounds sterling to buy a piece of real estate in London. If the firm wishes to hedge the dollar cost of the bid, it could buy pounds forward so that if the pound sterling appreciates, the gain on the forward contract would offset the increased dollar cost of the prospective investment. But, if the bid is eventually rejected, and if the pound has fallen in the interim, losses from the forward position would have no offset. If no forward cover is taken and the pound appreciates, the real estate will cost more than expected.

Currency call options can provide a better hedge in such a case. Purchased-pound call options would provide protection against a rising pound; and yet, if the bid were rejected and the pound had fallen, the uncovered hedge loss would be limited to the premium paid

■ **EXHIBIT 3.6**   Profit from Buying a Put Option for Various Spot Prices at Expiration

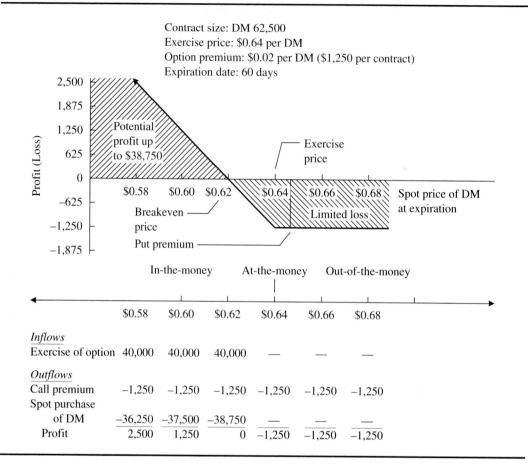

Contract size: DM 62,500
Exercise price: $0.64 per DM
Option premium: $0.02 per DM ($1,250 per contract)
Expiration date: 60 days

	$0.58	$0.60	$0.62	$0.64	$0.66	$0.68
Inflows						
Exercise of option	40,000	40,000	40,000	—	—	—
Outflows						
Call premium	−1,250	−1,250	−1,250	−1,250	−1,250	−1,250
Spot purchase of DM	−36,250	−37,500	−38,750	—	—	—
Profit	2,500	1,250	0	−1,250	−1,250	−1,250

for the calls. Note that a U.S. company in the opposite position, such as one bidding on a British project, whose receipt of future pound cash inflows is contingent on acceptance of its bid, would use a long pound put position to provide the safest hedge.

Currency options can also be used by pure speculators, those without an underlying foreign-currency transaction to protect against. The presence of speculators in the options markets adds to the breadth and depth of these markets, thereby making them more liquid and lowering transactions costs and risk.

Option Pricing and Valuation

From a theoretical standpoint, the value of an option is comprised of two components: intrinsic value and time value. The *intrinsic value* of the option is the amount by which the option is in-the-money, or $S - E$, where S is the current spot price and E the exercise price. In other words, the intrinsic value equals the immediate exercise value of the option. Thus,

the further into-the-money an option is, the more valuable it is. An out-of-the-money option
has no intrinsic value. For example, the intrinsic value of a call option on Swiss francs with
an exercise price of $0.74 and a spot rate of $0.77 would be $0.03 per franc. The intrinsic
value of the option for spot rates less than the exercise price is zero. Any excess of the option
value over its intrinsic value is called the *time value* of the contract. An option will generally
sell for at least its intrinsic value. The more out-of-the-money an option is, the lower the
option price. These features are shown in Exhibit 3.7.

During the time remaining before an option expires, the exchange rate can move so as
to make exercising the option profitable or more profitable. That is, an out-of-the-money
option can move into the money, or one already in-the-money can become more so. The
chance that an option will become profitable or more profitable is always greater than zero.
Consequently, the time value of an option is always positive for an out-of-the-money option
and is usually positive for an in-the-money option. Moreover, the more time that remains
until an option expires, the higher the time value tends to be. For example, an option with
six months remaining until expiration will tend to have a higher price than an option with
the same strike price but with only three months until expiration. As the option approaches
its maturity, the time value declines to zero.

The value of an American option always exceeds its intrinsic value because the time
value is always positive up to the expiration date. For example, if $S > E$, then $C(E) > S - E$,
where $C(E)$ is the dollar price of an American call option on one unit of foreign currency.
However, the case is more ambiguous for European options because increasing the time to
maturity may not increase its value, given that it can only be exercised on the maturity date.[2]

■ **EXHIBIT 3.7**   The Value of a Call Option Prior to Maturity

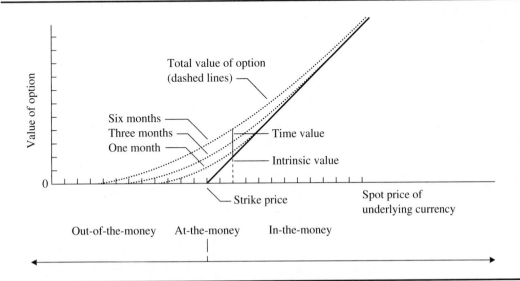

[2]For a technical discussion of foreign currency option pricing, see Mark B. Garman and Steven W. Kohlhagen,
"Foreign Currency Option Values," *Journal of International Money and Finance,* December 1983, pp. 231–238.

That is, a European currency option may be in-the-money before expiration, yet it may be out-of-the-money by the maturity date.

Before expiration, an out-of-the-money option has only time value, but an in-the-money option has both time value and intrinsic value. At expiration, an option can have only intrinsic value. The time value of a currency option reflects the probability that its intrinsic value will increase before expiration; this probability depends, among other things, on the volatility of the exchange rate. An increase in currency volatility increases the chance of an extremely high or low exchange rate at the time the option expires. The chance of a very high exchange rate benefits the call owner. The chance of a very low exchange rate, however, is irrelevant; the option will be worthless for any exchange rate less than the striking price, whether the exchange rate is "low" or "very low." Inasmuch as the effect of increased volatility is beneficial, the value of the call option is higher. Put options similarly benefit from increased volatility in the exchange rate.

Another aspect of time value involves interest rates. In general, options have a present intrinsic value, determined by the exercise price and price of the underlying asset. Since the option is a claim on a specified amount of an asset over a period of time into the future, that claim must have a return in line with market interest rates on comparable instruments. Therefore, a rise in the interest rate will cause call values to rise and put values to fall.

Pricing foreign-currency options is more complex because it requires consideration of both domestic and foreign interest rates. A foreign currency is normally at a forward premium or discount vis-à-vis the domestic currency. As we will see in Chapter 7, this premium or discount is determined by relative interest rates. Consequently, for foreign-currency options, call values rise and put values fall when the domestic interest rate increases or the foreign interest rate decreases.

The flip side of a more valuable put or call option is a higher option premium. Hence, options become more expensive when exchange rate volatility rises. Similarly, when the domestic-foreign interest differential increases, call options become more expensive and put options less expensive.

Using Forward or Futures Contracts
Versus Options Contracts

Suppose that on July 1, an American company makes a sale for which it will receive DM 125,000 on September 1. The firm will want to convert those DM into dollars, so it is exposed to the risk that the mark will fall below its current spot rate of $0.6922 in the meantime. The firm can protect itself against a declining Deutsche mark by selling its expected DM receipts forward (using a futures contract) or by buying a DM put option.

Exhibit 3.8 shows possible results for each choice, using options with strike prices just above and just below the spot exchange of July 1 ($0.68 and $0.70). The example assumes a DM decline to $0.6542 and the consequent price adjustments of associated futures and options contracts. The put quotes are the option premiums per DM. Thus, the dollar premium associated with a particular quote equals the quote multiplied by the number of DM covered by the put options. For example, the quote of $0.0059 for a September put option with a strike price of 68 (in cents) represents a premium for covering the exporter's DM 125,000 transaction equal to $0.0059 \times 125,000 = \$737.50$.

■ **EXHIBIT 3.8**   Declining Exchange Rate Scenario

	July 1	September 1
Spot	$0.6922	$0.6542
September futures	0.6956	0.6558
September 68 put	0.0059	0.0250
September 70 put	0.0144	0.0447

In the above example, a decision to remain unhedged would yield a loss of 125,000 × (0.6922 – 0.6542) or $4750. The outcomes of the various hedge possibilities are shown in Exhibit 3.9.

Exhibit 3.9 demonstrates the following differences between the futures and options hedging strategies:

1. The futures hedge offers the closest offset to the loss due to the decline of the Deutsche mark.
2. The purchase of the in-the-money put option (the 70 strike price) offers greater protection (but at a higher premium) than the out-of-the-money put (the 68 strike price).

Note that the September futures price is unequal to the spot rate on September 1 because settlement is not until later in the month. As the DM declines in value, the company would suffer a larger loss on its DM receivables, to be offset by a further increase in the value of the put and futures contracts.

While the company wants to protect against the possibility of a DM depreciation, what would happen if the DM appreciates? To answer this question—so as to fully assess the options and futures hedge strategies—assume the hypothetical conditions in Exhibit 3.10.

In this scenario, the rise in the DM would increase the value of the unhedged position by 125,000 × (0.7338 – 0.6922), or $5200. This gain would be offset by losses on the futures or options contracts, as shown in Exhibit 3.11.

We can see that the futures hedge again provides the closest offset. However, because these hedges generate losses, the company would be better served under this scenario by the smallest offset. With rapidly rising exchange rates, the company would benefit most from hedging with a long put position as opposed to a futures contract; conversely, with rapidly

■ **EXHIBIT 3.9**   Hedging Alternatives: Offsetting a $4,750 Loss Due to a Declining DM

Result of Selling Futures
  (0.6956 – 0.6558) × 125,000 = $4,975 profit

Results of Buying Put Options
  68 put: (0.0250 – 0.0059) × 125,000 = $2,387.50 profit
  70 put: (0.0447 – 0.0144) × 125,000 = $3,787.50 profit

■ **EXHIBIT 3.10**   Rising Exchange Rate Scenario

	July 1	September 1
Spot	$0.6922	$0.7338
September futures	0.6956	0.4374
September 68 put	0.0059	0.0001
September 70 put	0.0144	0.0001

falling exchange rates, the company would benefit most from hedging with a futures contract.

Market Structure

Options are purchased and traded either on an organized exchange (such as the PHLX) or in the *over-the-counter* (OTC) market. *Exchange-traded options* or *listed options* are standardized contracts with predetermined exercise prices, standard maturities (one, three, six, nine, and 12 months), and fixed maturities (March, June, September, and December). Options on the PHLX are available in the ECU and seven currencies—Deutsche mark, pound sterling, French franc, Swiss franc, Japanese yen, Canadian dollar, and Australian dollar—and are traded in standard contracts half the size of the IMM futures contracts. Contract specifications are shown in Exhibit 3.12. The PHLX trades both American-style and European-style currency options. Other organized options exchanges are located in Amsterdam (European Options Exchange), Chicago (Chicago Mercantile Exchange), and Montreal (Montreal Stock Exchange).

Trading volume in exchange-traded currency options has grown dramatically since their introduction in 1983, with more than ten million contracts representing approximately $500 billion in underlying value traded in 1990. Exhibit 3.13 shows the growth in contract volume on the PHLX since 1983.

OTC options are contracts whose specifications are generally negotiated as to the amount, exercise price and rights, underlying instrument, and expiration. *OTC currency options* are traded by commercial and investment banks in virtually all financial centers. OTC activity is concentrated in London and New York and it centers on the major currencies, most often involving U.S. dollars against pounds sterling, Deutsche marks, Swiss francs, Japanese yen, and Canadian dollars. Branches of foreign banks in the major financial centers

■ **EXHIBIT 3.11**   Hedging Alternatives: Offsetting a $5,200 Gain Due to a Rising DM

Result of Selling Futures
$(0.7374 - 0.6956) \times 125,000 = \$5,225$ loss

Results of Buying Put Options
68 put: $(0.0059 - 0.0001) \times 125,000 = \$725$ loss
70 put: $(0.0144 - 0.0001) \times 125,000 = \$1,787.50$ profit

■ **EXHIBIT 3.12**   Philadelphia Stock Exchange Currency Options Specifications

	Australian Dollar	British Pound	Canadian Dollar	Deutsche Mark	European Currency Unit	Swiss Franc	French Franc	Japanese Yen
Symbol								
American style	XAD	XBP	XCD	XDM	ECU	XSF	XFF	XJY
European style	CAD	CBP	CCD	CDM	n.a.	CSF	CFF	CJY
Contract size	A$50,000	£31,250	C$50,000	DM 62,500	ECU 62,500	SFr 62,500	FF 250,000	¥6,250,000
Exercise Price Intervals	1¢	2.5¢	0.5¢	1¢**	2¢	1¢**	0.25¢	0.01¢**
Premium Quotations	Cents per unit	Cents per unit	Cents per unit	Cents per unit	Cents per unit	Cents per unit	Tenths of a cent per unit	Hundredths of a cent per unit
Minimum Price Change	$0.(00)01	$0.(00)01	$0.(00)01	$0.(00)01	$0.(00)01	$0.(00)01	$0.(000)02	$0.(0000)01
Minimum Contract Price Change	$5.00	$3.125	$5.00	$6.25	$6.25	$6.25	$5.00	$6.25

Expiration Months & Cycle _____ March, June, September, and December _____
+ 2 additional near-term months/1, 2, 3, 6, 9, and 12 months

Exercise Notice _____ No automatic exercise of in-the-money options _____

Expiration Date ____ Saturday before third Wednesday of the month (Preceding Friday is the last trading day) _____

Expiration Settlement Date _____ Third Wednesday of month _____

Daily Price Limits _____ None _____

Issuer & Guarantor _____ Options Clearing Corporation (OCC) _____

Margin for Uncovered Writer ___ Option premium plus 4% of the underlying contract value less _____
out-of-the-money amount, if any, to a minimum of the option
premium plus 3/4% of the underlying contract value. Contract
value equal spots price times unit of currency per contract.

Position & Exercise Limits _____ 100,000 contracts _____

Trading Hours _____ 4:30 A.M.–2:30 P.M. EST/EDT—6:00 P.M.–10:00 P.M. EST/7:00–11:00 P.M. EDT* _____

*For the Australian dollar, British pound, Deutsche mark, Japanese yen, and Swiss franc (Sunday through Thursday).

**Half-point strike prices for DM (0.5¢), SFr (0.5¢), and ¥ (0.005¢) in the two near-term months only.

SOURCE: Philadelphia Stock Exchange, 1991.

are generally willing to write options against the currency of their home country. For example, Australian banks in London write options on the Australian dollar. OTC options are generally traded in round lots, commonly $5–10 million in New York and $2–3 million in London. The average maturity of OTC options ranges from two to six months, and very few options are written for more than one year. American options are most common, but European options are popular in Switzerland and Germany because of familiarity.

■ EXHIBIT 3.13   PHLX Currency Options Trading Volume, 1983–1991

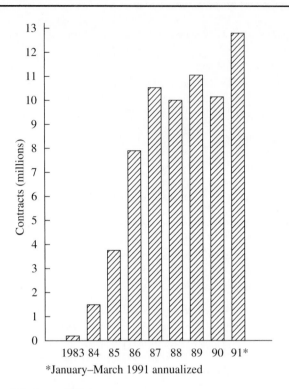

*January–March 1991 annualized

SOURCE: Philadelphia Stock Exchange, 1991.

The OTC options market consists of two sectors: (1) a *retail market* composed of nonbank customers who purchase from banks what amounts to customized insurance against adverse exchange rate movements and (2) a *wholesale market* among commercial banks, investment banks, and specialized trading firms; this market may include interbank OTC trading or trading on the organized exchanges. The interbank market in currency options is analogous to the interbank markets in spot and forward exchange. Banks use the wholesale market to hedge or "reinsure" the risks undertaken in trading with customers and to take speculative positions in options.

Most retail customers for OTC options are either corporations active in international trade or financial institutions with multicurrency asset portfolios. These customers could purchase foreign exchange puts or calls on organized exchanges, but they generally turn to the banks for options in order to find precisely the terms that match their needs. Contracts are generally tailored with regard to amount, strike price, expiration date, and currency.

OTC currency options predate exchange-traded options by many years, but trading in OTC options grew rapidly at the same time that PHLX trading began. For example, OTC trading volume in foreign currency options was estimated at $10 billion daily in 1988, double the volume in 1986.[3] The acceleration in the growth of options trading in both markets appears to spring from the desire by companies to manage foreign-currency risks more effectively and, in particular, from an increased willingness to pay a fee in order to transfer such risks to another party. Most commentators suggest that corporate demand has increased because the greater volatility of exchange rates has increasingly exposed firms to risks from developments that are difficult to predict and beyond their control.

The growth of listed options, especially for "wholesale" purposes, is apparently putting pressure on the OTC markets for greater standardization in interbank trading. In some instances, OTC foreign currency options are traded for expiration on the third Wednesday of March, June, September, and December, to coincide with expiration dates on the U.S. exchanges.

Although the buyer of an option can lose only the premium paid for the option, the seller's risk of loss is potentially unlimited. Because of this asymmetry between income and risk, few customers are willing to write options. For this reason, the market structure is distinctly asymmetrical when compared with the ordinary market for spot and forward foreign exchange—where there is a balance between customers purchasing or selling currency and where the interbank market likewise has a reasonable balance.

Futures Options

In January 1984, the IMM introduced a market in options on Deutsche-mark futures contracts. Since then the *futures option* market has grown to include options on futures in British pounds, Japanese yen, Swiss francs, and Canadian dollars as well. Trading involves purchases and sales of puts and calls on a contract calling for delivery of a standard IMM futures contract in the currency rather than the currency itself. When exercised, the holder receives a short or long position in the currency futures contract that expires one week after the expiration of the option contract. Once the option contract is exercised and the futures contract delivered, the holder may sell the contract on the IMM at a price that provides the holder with exactly the same profit as the holder would have realized with a straight currency option. The introduction of the futures option has been hailed by many observers as an important step toward providing traders and investors with a greater variety of instruments to reduce the risks associated with international business and investment.

■ 3.3 ■
READING FUTURES AND OPTIONS PRICES

Futures and exchange-listed options prices appear daily in the financial press. Exhibit 3.14 shows prices for February 6, 1990, as displayed in *The Wall Street Journal* on the following day. Futures prices on the IMM are listed for six currencies, with one to four contracts quoted for each currency: March and June 1990 for all but the Australian dollar,

---

[3]These estimates appear in *The Economist,* May 28, 1988, p. 82.

■ **EXHIBIT 3.14**   Foreign Currency Futures and Options Quotations

FUTURES

	Open	High	Low	Settle	Change	Lifetime High	Lifetime Low	Open Interest
JAPANESE YEN (IMM) 12.5 million yen; $ per yen (.00)								
Mar	.6939	.6939	.6885	.6891	− .0027	.8357	.6780	58,856
June	.6956	.6957	.6906	.6910	− .0028	.7530	.6850	3,475
Est vol 25,952; vol Mon 17,365; open int 62,385, +1,404.								
W. GERMAN MARK (IMM) − 125,000 marks; $ per mark								
Mar	.6043	.6044	.6015	.6028	+ .0004	.6044	.5000	72,528
June	.6043	.6044	.6014	.6025	+ .0002	.6044	.5057	4,458
Sept	.6021	.6021	.6015	.6023	+ .0001	.6021	.5410	238
Mr91	....	....	....	.6020	− .0004	.5975	.5915	375
Est vol 41,236; vol Mon 54,579; open int 77,621, +10,728.								
CANADIAN DOLLAR (IMM) − 100,000 dlrs.; $ per Can $								
Mar	.8371	.8386	.8368	.8375	− .0002	.8595	.7890	24,854
June	.8296	.8310	.8302	.8302	− .0001	.8522	.8107	3,456
Sept	.8250	.8250	.8250	.8240	− .0001	.8468	.8100	234
Dec	.8210	.8210	.8210	.8193	− .0005	.8420	.8120	176
Est vol 1,539; vol Mon 1,883; open int 28,779, −64.								
BRITISH POUND (IMM) − 62,500 pds.; $ per pound								
Mar	1.6914	1.6928	1.6858	1.6896	+ .0026	1.6928	1.4600	26,214
June	1.6668	1.6674	1.6610	1.6638	+ .0024	1.6950	1.4400	2,417
Sept	1.6430	1.6440	1.6380	1.6402	+ .0026	1.6440	1.5290	121
Est vol 8,313; vol Mon 9,215; open int 28,752, +1,234.								
SWISS FRANC (IMM) − 125,000 francs-$ per franc								
Mar	.6775	.6780	.6744	.6756	− .0021	.6780	.5740	40,927
June	.6760	.6760	.6725	.6736	− .0022	.6760	.5850	1,429
Mr91	....	....	....	.6731	− .0022	.6725	.6540	799
Est vol 19,135; vol Mon 22,444; open int 43,155, +2,480.								
AUSTRALIAN DOLLAR (IMM) − 100,000 dlrs.; $ per A.$								
Mar	.7604	.7610	.7584	.7588	− .0001	.7854	.7055	3,275
Est vol 256; vol Mon 203; open int 3,350, −12.								

FUTURES OPTIONS

JAPANESE YEN (IMM) 12,500,000 yen; cents per 100 yen

Strike Price	Calls−Settle Feb-c	Mar-c	Jun-c	Puts−Settle Feb-p	Mar-p	Jun-p
67	1.92	2.01	....	0.01	0.13	0.55
68	0.96	1.21	1.92	0.05	0.31	0.85
69	0.21	0.61	1.37	0.30	0.70	1.27
70	0.04	0.27	0.95	1.13	1.35	1.82
71	0.01	0.13	0.63	2.10	2.20	2.47
72	0.00	0.06	0.41	....	3.15	3.23

Est. vol. 8,312, Mon vol. 6,381 calls, 2,553 puts
Open interest Mon; 92,630 calls, 45,527 puts

W. GERMAN MARK (IMM) 125,000 marks; cents per mark

Strike Price	Calls−Settle Feb-c	Mar-c	Jun-c	Puts−Settle Feb-p	Mar-p	Jun-p
58	2.29	2.43	2.94	0.01	0.16	0.74
59	1.32	1.62	2.27	0.04	0.34	1.06
60	0.48	0.96	1.74	0.20	0.68	1.48
61	0.11	0.52	1.30	0.83	1.23	2.03
62	0.03	0.27	0.94	....	1.98	2.66
63	0.01	0.13	0.67	....	....	....

Est. vol. 32,070, Mon vol. 18,489 calls, 5,671 puts
Open interest Mon; 63,558 calls, 93,310 puts

CANADIAN DOLLAR (IMM) 100,000 Can.$, cents per Can.$

Strike Price	Calls−Settle Feb-c	Mar-c	Jun-c	Puts−Settle Feb-p	Mar-p	Jun-o
830	0.75	0.91	0.93	0.00	0.16	0.93
835	0.30	0.58	0.72	0.05	0.33	1.20
840	0.05	0.33	0.53	0.30	0.58	1.51
845	0.00	0.17	0.39	0.75	0.91	1.85
850	0.00	0.07	0.28	1.25	1.32	2.22
855	0.00	0.03	0.19	1.75	1.77	2.62

Est. vol. 406, Mon vol. 196 calls, 949 puts
Open interest Mon; 9,208 calls, 13,385 puts

BRITISH POUND (IMM) 62,500 pounds; cents per pound

Strike Price	Calls−Settle Feb-c	Mar-c	Jun-c	Puts−Settle Feb-p	Mar-p	Jun-p
1650	3.98	4.68	4.98	0.04	0.72	3.60
1675	1.64	2.96	3.80	0.22	1.50	4.88
1700	0.32	1.66	2.86	1.36	2.70	6.36
1725	0.04	0.88	2.10	....	4.40	....
1750	....	0.42	1.52	....	....	....
1775	....	....	....	....	....	....

Est. vol. 1,650, Mon vol. 843 calls, 1,172 puts
Open interest Mon; 10,383 calls, 13,603 puts

SWISS FRANC (IMM) 125,000 francs; cents per franc

Strike Price	Calls−Settle Feb-c	Mar-c	Jun-c	Puts−Settle Feb-p	Mar-p	Jun-p
66	1.59	1.93	2.58	0.03	0.37	1.26
67	0.73	1.26	2.03	0.17	0.70	1.67
68	0.19	0.74	1.57	0.63	1.18	....
69	0.04	0.42	1.19	1.48	1.85	....
70	0.01	0.23	0.89	....	....	....
71	....	0.13	0.66	....	....	....

Est. vol. 3,630, Mon vol. 2,344 calls, 3,669 puts
Open interest Mon; 33,210 calls, 40,361 puts

−OTHER CURRENCY FUTURES OPTIONS−

Final or settlement prices of selected contracts. Volume and open interest are totals in all contract months.

Australian Dollar (IMM) $100,000; $ per $

Strike	Feb-c	Mar-c	Jun-c	Feb-p	Mar-p	Jun-p
76	0.30	0.90	....	....	1.00	....

Est. vol. 1, Mon vol. 30, Op. int. 976.

Sterling (LIFFE) £250,000, ots. of 100%

Strike	Feb-c	Mar-c	Apr-c	Feb-p	Mar-p	Apr-p
155	15.20	15.20	15.20	0.00	0.05	0.24

Act. vol. Tues. vol. 0. Op. Int. 86.

FINEX−Financial Instrument Exchange, a division of the New York Cotton Exchange. IMM-International Monetary Market at Chicago Mercantile Exchange. LIFFE-London International Financing Futures Exchange.

(b)

OPTIONS

PHILADELPHIA EXCHANGE

Option & Underlying	Strike Price	Calls−Last Feb	Mar	Jun	Puts−Last Feb	Mar	Jun
50,000 Australian Dollars-cents per unit.							
ADollr	...73	r	r	r	r	r	1.30
76.53	...75	r	r	r	0.15	0.79	r
76.53	...76	r	r	r	0.41	1.28	r
76.53	...77	0.38	0.73	r	r	r	r
76.53	...78	r	0.41	r	r	r	r
76.53	...79	r	0.23	r	r	3.15	r
31,250 British Pounds-cents per unit.							
BPound	155	r	r	r	r	r	0.82
170.11	157½	r	r	r	r	r	1.35
170.11	162½	r	r	r	r	0.50	r
170.11	.165	5.20	5.32	r	r	0.90	r
170.11	167½	r	3.60	4.35	0.43	1.76	4.95
170.11	.170	1.30	2.18	r	1.65	3.00	r
170.11	172½	0.45	r	r	r	4.60	r
50,000 Canadian Dollars-cents per unit.							
CDollr	...83	r	r	r	r	r	0.19
84.19	...84	r	r	0.66	0.25	0.65	r
84.19	84½	r	r	r	r	0.98	r
84.19	...85	r	r	r	r	1.31	r
84.19	...86	r	r	r	r	2.16	r
62,500 West German Marks-cents per unit.							
DMark	. 54	r	r	r	r	r	0.14
60.27	...55	r	5.30	r	r	0.03	r
60.27	...56	r	r	r	r	0.05	r
60.27	...57	3.19	r	r	0.01	0.11	0.53
60.27	57½	r	r	s	r	0.14	s
60.27	...58	2.39	2.54	3.01	r	0.22	0.80
60.27	58½	r	r	s	0.08	0.32	s
60.27	...59	1.44	1.62	r	0.12	0.44	1.10
60.27	59½	1.06	1.33	s	0.22	0.55	s
60.27	...60	0.62	1.01	r	0.40	0.72	r
60.27	60½	0.40	0.84	s	0.56	r	s
60.27	...61	0.20	0.64	1.38	r	r	r
60.27	61½	0.13	0.56	s	r	r	s
60.27	...62	0.09	0.34	r	r	r	r
60.27	...63	r	0.18	0.75	r	r	r
62,500 West German Marks-European Style.							
60.27	58½	r	r	s	0.05	r	s
60.27	...59	r	r	r	r	0.37	r
60.27	59½	r	r	s	0.18	0.51	s
60.27	60½	0.39	r	s	r	r	s
60.27	...61	0.20	r	r	r	r	r
6,250,000 Japanese Yen-100ths of a cent per unit.							
JYen	...65	r	r	r	r	r	0.03
68.77	...67	r	r	r	r	r	0.13
68.77	...68	r	r	r	r	0.07	0.33
68.77	68½	0.55	r	r	r	r	s
68.77	...69	0.28	0.67	1.52	r	r	1.12
68.77	69½	0.14	r	s	r	r	s
68.77	...70	r	0.34	r	r	r	r
68.77	70½	r	0.31	s	r	r	s
68.77	...71	r	0.16	0.67	r	r	r
68.77	71½	r	0.12	s	r	r	s
68.77	...72	r	0.07	0.51	r	r	r
68.77	...73	r	0.04	r	r	r	r
62,500 Swiss Francs-cents per unit.							
SFranc	.63	4.70	r	r	r	r	0.46
67.62	...64	3.70	r	r	r	r	r
67.62	...65	r	r	3.34	0.05	0.21	r
67.62	...66	1.84	r	2.75	r	0.41	1.28
67.62	...67	1.01	1.42	r	0.32	0.75	r
67.62	...68	r	0.92	1.71	r	r	r
67.62	68½	r	0.52	r	r	r	s
67.62	...69	0.14	0.52	r	r	r	r
67.62	...71	r	0.16	r	r	r	r
62,500 Swiss Francs-European Style.							
67.62	...66	r	r	2.70	r	r	r
62,500 European Currency Units-cents per unit.							
ECU	...116	6.70	r	r	r	r	r
122.79	...122	r	1.89	r	r	r	3.16

Total call vol. 59,537   Call open int. 397,772
Total put vol. 36,591   Put open int. 402,264
r−Not traded. s−No option offered.
Last is premium (purchase price).

(c)

and September and December 1990 and March 1991 for some currencies. Included are the opening and last settlement (settle) prices, the change from the previous trading day, the range for the day, and the number of contracts outstanding (open interest). For example, the June Deutsche mark futures contract opened at $0.6043 per DM and closed at $0.6025 per DM. Futures prices are shown in Exhibit 3.14a.

Exhibit 3.14b shows the Chicago Mercantile Exchange (IMM) options on this same futures contract. To interpret the numbers in this column, consider the call options. These are rights to buy the June DM futures contract at specified prices—the strike prices. For example, the call option with a strike price of 60 means that you can purchase an option to buy a June DM futures contract, up to the June settlement date, for $0.6000 per mark. This option will cost $0.0174 per Deutsche mark, or $2175, plus brokerage commission for a DM 125,000 contract. The price is high because the option is in-the-money. In contrast, the June futures option with a strike price of 63, which is well out-of-the-money, costs only $0.0067 per mark, or $837.50 for one contract. These option prices indicate that the market expects the dollar price of the Deutsche mark to exceed $0.6000 but not to rise much above $0.6300 by June.

A futures call option allows you to buy the relevant futures contract, which is settled at maturity. On the other hand, the Philadelphia call options contract is an option to buy foreign exchange spot, which is settled when the call option is exercised; the buyer receives foreign currency immediately.

Price quotes usually reflect this difference. For example, PHLX call options for the June DM (shown in Exhibit 3.14c), with strike price $0.6300 are $0.0075 per mark (versus $0.0067 for the June futures call option), or $468.75, plus brokerage fees for one contract of DM 62,500. Brokerage fees here would be about the same as on the IMM: about $16 per transaction round trip, per contract.

Exhibit 3.15 summarizes how to read price quotations for futures and options on futures using a DM illustration.

■ 3.4 ■
PUT-CALL OPTION INTEREST RATE PARITY

As we saw in Chapter 2, interest rate parity relates the forward (and futures) rate differential to the interest differential. Another parity condition relates options prices to the interest differential and, by extension, to the forward differential. We are now going to derive the relation between put and call option prices, the forward rate, and domestic and foreign interest rates. To do this, we must first define the following parameters:

C = call option premium on a one-period contract
P = put option premium on a one-period contract
E = exercise price on the put and call options (dollars per unit of foreign currency)
e_0 = current spot rate (dollars per unit of foreign currency)
e_1 = end-of-period spot rate (dollars per unit of foreign currency)
f_1 = one-period forward rate (dollars per unit of foreign currency)
r_h = U.S. interest rate for one period
r_f = foreign interest rate for one period

For illustrative purposes, Germany is taken to be the representative foreign country in the following derivation.

In order to price a call option on the DM with a strike price of E in terms of a put option and forward contract, create the following portfolio:

Futures

Prices represent the
open, high, low,
and settlement (or
closing) price for
the previous day.

One day's change
in the settlement
price

The extreme prices
recorded for the
contract over its
trading life

GERMAN MARK (IMM)—125,000 marks; $ per mark

The number of
contracts still in
effect at the end
the previous day
trading session.
Each unit represe
a buyer *and* a sel
who still have a
contract position

	Open	High	Low	Settle	Chg	Lifetime high	Low	Open interest
Mar.	.5415	.5452	.5401	.5436	−.0011	.5520	.4370	56,576
June	.5435	.5472	.5422	.5459	−.0011	.5538	.4850	1,839
Sept.	.5460	.5494	.5460	.5483	−.0010	.5525	.4868	270

Est. vol. 26,426; vol. Thur. 35,278; open int. 58,706, — 1,399.

Contract delivery
months that are
currently traded

Number of trades
transacted in the
previous two
trading sessions

The total of the
right column, and
the change from the
prior trading day

Options on Futures

Closing prices for call options*

Closing prices
for put options*

GERMAN MARK (CME)—125,000 marks; cents per mark

Most active
strike prices

Expiration
month

Strike price	Calls–Settle Feb-C	Mar-C	Apr-C	Puts-Settle Feb-P	Mar-P	Apr-P
52	2.46	2.63	. . . .	0.11	0.29	. . . .
53	1.63	1.87	2.21	0.28	0.52	0.65
54	0.96	1.27	1.60	0.60	0.91	. . . .
55	0.50	0.80	. . . .	1.14	1.44	. . . .
56	0.25	0.50	. . . .	. . . .	2.13	. . . .
57	. . . .	0.30	. . . .	. . . .	. . . .	. . . .

Est. vol. 8,145, Thur. vol. 9,077 calls, 9,024 puts
Open interest Thur.; 47,855 calls, 46,767 puts

Volume of options
transacted in the previous
two trading sessions.
Each unit represents both
the buyer *and* the seller.

The number of options
that were still open
positions at the end of
the previous day's
trading session.

* The dollar price represented by a premium quotation equals the quote multiplied by the number
of currency units covered in the underlying futures. For example, a quote of 0.50¢ for a 55 call
represents a dollar premium of 0.50¢ × DM 125,000 = $625.

SOURCE: *Opportunities in Currency Trading,* Chicago Mercantile Exchange, 1986, p. 25

1. Lend $1/(1 + r_f)$ Deutsche marks in Germany. In one period, this investment will be worth DM 1, which is equivalent to e_1 dollars.
2. Buy a DM put option for DM 1 with an exercise price of E.
3. Borrow $E/(1 + r_h)$ dollars. This loan will cost E dollars to repay at the end of the period.

The payoffs on the portfolio and the call option at expiration depend on the relation between the spot rate at expiration and the exercise price. These payoffs, which are shown pictorially in Exhibit 3.16, are as follows:

Security	Dollar Value on Expiration Date If	
	$e_1 > E$	$e_1 < E$
I. Portfolio		
1. Lend DM $1/(1 + r_f)$	e_1	e_1
2. Buy a DM put option	0	$E - e_1$
3. Borrow $E/(1 + r_h)$ dollars	$-E$	$-E$
Total	$e_1 - E$	0
II. Buy a DM call option	$e_1 - E$	0

Since the payoffs on the portfolio and the call option are identical, both securities must sell for identical prices in the marketplace. Otherwise, a risk-free arbitrage opportunity will exist. Therefore, the dollar price of the call option (which is the call premium, C) must equal the dollar value of the DM loan plus the price of the put option (the put premium, P) less the amount of dollars borrowed. Algebraically, this can be expressed as

$$C = \frac{e_0}{1 + r_f} - \frac{E}{1 + r_h} + P \tag{3.1}$$

According to interest rate parity,

$$\frac{e_0}{1 + r_f} = \frac{f_1}{1 + r_h} \tag{3.2}$$

Substituting Equation 3.2 into Equation 3.1 yields a new equation:

$$C = \frac{f_1 - E}{1 + r_h} + P \tag{3.3}$$

or

$$C - P = \frac{f_1 - E}{1 + r_h} \tag{3.4}$$

These parity relations say that a long call is equivalent to a long put plus a forward (or futures) contract. The term $f_1 - E$ is discounted because the put and call premia are paid upfront whereas the forward rate and exercise price apply to the expiration date.

■ **EXHIBIT 3.16**   Illustration of Put-Call Option Interest Rate Parity

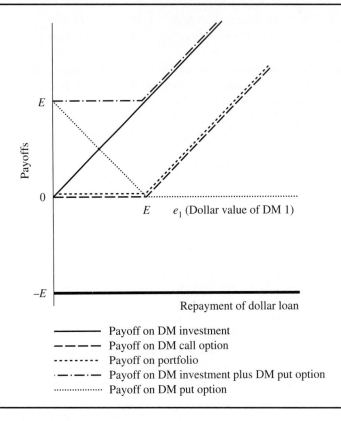

Payoff on DM investment
Payoff on DM call option
Payoff on portfolio
Payoff on DM investment plus DM put option
Payoff on DM put option

ILLUSTRATION

Pricing a December Deutsche Mark Call Option. Suppose that the premium on September 15 on a December 15 DM put option is 0.23 cents per DM at a strike price of $0.73. The December 15 forward rate is DM 1 = $0.74 and the quarterly U.S. interest rate is 2.5%. Then, according to Equation 3.3, the December 15 call option should equal

$$C = 0.0023 + (0.74 - 0.73)/1.025 = 0.0121$$

or 1.21 cents per DM.

■ 3.5 ■
SUMMARY AND CONCLUSIONS

   In this chapter, we have examined the currency futures and options markets and looked at some of the institutional characteristics and mechanics of these markets. We saw that currency futures and options offer alternative hedging (and speculative) mechanisms for companies and individuals. Like forward contracts, futures contracts must be settled at maturity. By contrast, currency options give the owner the right but not the obligation to buy (call option) or sell (put option) the contracted currency. An *American option* can be exercised at any time up to the expiration date; a *European option* can only be exercised at maturity.

Futures contracts are standardized contracts that trade on organized exchanges. Forward contracts, on the other hand, are custom-tailored contracts, typically entered into between a bank and its customers. Options contracts are sold on both organized exchanges and in the over-the-counter market. Like forward contracts, OTC options are contracts whose specifications are generally negotiated as to the terms and conditions between a bank and its customers.

We also derived a put-call parity condition that relates option prices to interest rates and the forward rate. As with interest rate parity, this condition relies on arbitrage for its existence.

■ QUESTIONS ■

1. On April 1, the spot price of the British pound was $1.86 and the price of the June futures contract was $1.85. During April the pound appreciated, so that by May 1 it was selling for $1.91. What do you think happened to the price of the June pound futures contract during April? Explain.

2. Suppose that Texas Instruments must pay a French supplier FF 10 million in 90 days.

   a. Explain how TI can use currency futures to hedge its exchange risk. How many futures contracts will TI need to fully protect itself?

   b. Explain how TI can use currency options to hedge its exchange risk. How many options contracts will TI need to fully protect itself?

   c. Discuss the advantages and disadvantages of using currency futures versus currency options to hedge TI's exchange risk.

3. Since a forward market already existed, why was it necessary to establish currency futures and currency options contracts?

4. What are the basic differences between forward and futures contracts? Between futures and options contracts?

5. Which contract is likely to be more valuable, an American or a European call option? Explain.

6. In Exhibit 3.7, the value of the call option is shown as approaching its intrinsic value as the option goes deeper and deeper in-the-money or further and further out-of-the-money. Explain why this is so.

7. Suppose that Bechtel Group wants to hedge a bid on a Japanese construction project. But since the yen exposure is contingent on acceptance of its bid, Bechtel decides to buy a put option for the ¥15 billion bid amount rather than sell it forward. In order to reduce its hedging cost, however, Bechtel simultaneously sells a call option for ¥15 billion with the same strike price. Bechtel reasons that it wants to protect its downside risk on the contract and is willing to sacrifice the upside potential in order to collect the call premium. Comment on Bechtel's hedging strategy.

■ PROBLEMS ■

1. On Monday morning, an investor takes a long position in a pound futures contract that matures on Wednesday afternoon. The agreed-upon price is $1.78 for £62,500. At the close of trading on Monday,

the futures price has risen to $1.79. At Tuesday close, the price rises further to $1.80. At Wednesday close, the price falls to $1.785, and the contract matures. The investor takes delivery of the pounds at the prevailing price of $1.796. Detail the daily settlement process (see Exhibit 3.3). What will be the investor's profit (loss)?

2. On Monday morning, an investor takes a short position in a DM futures contract that matures on Wednesday afternoon. The agreed-upon price is $0.6370 for DM 125,000. At the close of trading on Monday, the futures price has fallen to $0.6315. At Tuesday close, the price falls further to $0.6291. At Wednesday close, the price rises to $0.6420, and the contract matures. The investor delivers the Deutsche marks at the prevailing price of $0.63. Detail the daily settlement process (see Exhibit 3.3). What will be the investor's profit (loss)?

3. Suppose that the forward ask price for March 20 on DM is $0.7127 at the same time that the price of IMM mark futures for delivery on March 20 is $0.7145. How could an arbitrageur profit from this situation? What will be the arbitrageur's profit per futures contract (size is DM 125,000)?

4. Suppose that DEC buys a Swiss franc futures contract (contract size is SFr 125,000) at a price of $0.83. If the spot rate for the Swiss franc at the date of settlement is SFr 1 = $0.8250, what is DEC's gain or loss on this contract?

5. Citicorp sells a call option on Deutsche marks (contract size is DM 500,000) at a premium of $0.04 per DM. If the exercise price is $0.71 and the spot price of the mark at date of expiration is $0.73, what is Citicorp's profit (loss) on the call option?

6. Ford buys a French franc put option (contract size is FF 250,000) at a premium of $0.01 per franc. If the exercise price is $0.21 and the spot price of the franc at date of expiration is $0.216, what is Ford's profit (loss) on the put option?

7. Apex Corporation must pay its Japanese supplier ¥125 million in three months. It is thinking of buying 20 yen call options (contract size is ¥6.25 million) at a strike price of $0.00800 in order to protect against the risk of a rising yen. The premium is 0.015 cents per yen. Alternatively, Apex could buy 10 three-month yen futures contracts (contract size is ¥12.5 million) at a price of $0.007940/¥. The current spot rate is ¥1 = $0.007823. Apex's treasurer believes that the most likely value for the yen in 90 days is $0.007900, but the yen could go as high as $0.008400 or as low as $0.007500.

   a. Diagram Apex's gains and losses on the call option position and the futures position within its range of expected prices (see Exhibit 3.5). Ignore transaction costs and margins.

   b. Calculate what Apex would gain or lose on the option and futures positions if the yen settled at its most likely value.

   c. What is Apex's break-even future spot price on the option contract? On the futures contract?

   d. Calculate and diagram the corresponding profit and loss and break-even positions on the futures and options contracts for the sellers of these contracts.

8. Biogen expects to receive royalty payments totaling £1.25 million next month. It is interested in protecting these receipts against a drop in the value of the pound. It can sell 30-day pound futures at a price of $1.6513/£ or it can buy pound put options with a strike price of $1.6612 at a premium of 2.0 cents per pound. The spot price of the pound is currently $1.6560, and the pound is expected to trade in the range of $1.6250 to $1.70100. Biogen's treasurer believes that the most likely price of the pound in 30 days will be $1.6400.

   a. How many futures contracts will Biogen need to protect its receipts? How many options contracts?

   b. Diagram Biogen's profit and loss on the put option position and the futures position within its range of expected exchange rates (see Exhibit 3.6). Ignore transaction costs and margins.

    c. Calculate what Biogen would gain or lose on the option and futures positions within the range of expected future exchange rates and if the pound settled at its most likely value.

    d. What is Biogen's break-even future spot price on the option contract? On the futures contract?

    e. Calculate and diagram the corresponding profit and loss and break-even positions on the futures and options contracts for those who took the other side of these contracts.

9. Suppose that the premium on March 20 on a June 20 yen put option is 0.0514 cents per yen at a strike price of $0.0077. The forward rate for June 20 is ¥1 = $0.00787 and the quarterly U.S. interest rate is 2%. If put-call parity holds, what is the current price of a June 20 yen call option with an exercise price of $0.0077?

10. On June 25, the call premium on a December 25 contract is 6.65 cents per pound at a strike price of $1.81. The 180-day interest rate is 7.5% in London and 4.75% in New York. If the current spot rate is £1 = $1.8470 and put-call parity holds, what is the put premium on a December 25 pound contract with an exercise price of $1.81?

■ BIBLIOGRAPHY ■

Using Currency Futures and Options. Chicago: Chicago Mercantile Exchange, 1987.

Garman, Mark B., and Steven W. Kohlhagen. "Foreign Currency Option Values." *Journal of International Money and Finance,* December 1983, pp. 231–238.

4

The Determination of
Exchange Rates

*Experience shows that neither a state nor a bank ever have had the unrestricted
power of issuing paper money without abusing that power.*

—David Ricardo (1817)—

■ Chapters 2 and 3 described the workings of the foreign exchange market and its
offshoots—the forward, futures, and options markets. However, although they discussed
quotes on foreign currencies, they did not explain the nature of exchange rates and how they
are set. Such an understanding is critical to dealing with currency risk. The purpose of this
chapter is to provide that understanding.

The chapter first describes what an exchange rate is and how it is determined in a *freely
floating exchange rate* regime—that is, in the absence of government intervention. The chapter
next discusses the role of expectations in exchange rate determination. It also examines the
different forms and consequences of central bank intervention in the foreign exchange market.
Chapter 5 describes the political aspects of currency determination under alternative exchange rate
systems and presents a brief history of the international monetary system.

Before proceeding further, here are definitions of several terms commonly used to
describe currency changes. Technically, a *devaluation* refers to a decrease in the stated par
value of a *pegged currency,* one whose value is set by the government; an increase in par
value is known as a *revaluation*. By contrast, a *floating currency*—one whose value is set
primarily by market forces—is said to *depreciate* if it loses value and to *appreciate* if it gains
value. However, discussions in this book will use the terms devaluation and depreciation
and revaluation and appreciation interchangeably.

■ 4.1 ■
SETTING THE EQUILIBRIUM SPOT EXCHANGE RATE

On the most fundamental level, *exchange rates* are market-clearing prices that equilibrate supplies and demands in foreign exchange markets. The determinants of currency

supplies and demands are first discussed with the aid of the following two-country model featuring the United States and Germany. Later, the various currency influences will be studied more closely.

The demand for the Deutsche mark (DM), Germany's currency, in the foreign exchange market (which in this two-country world is equivalent to the supply of dollars) derives from the American demand for German goods and services and DM-denominated financial assets. An increase in the DM's dollar value is equivalent to an increase in the dollar price of German products. This higher dollar price will normally reduce the U.S. demand for German goods, services, and assets. Conversely, as the dollar value of the DM falls, Americans will demand more DM to buy the less-expensive German products, resulting in a downward sloping demand curve for Deutsche marks.

Similarly, the supply of Deutsche marks (which is equivalent to the demand for dollars) is based on German demand for U.S. goods and services and dollar-denominated financial assets. As the dollar value of the Deutsche mark increases, which lowers the DM cost of U.S. goods, the increased German demand for U.S. goods will cause an increase in the German demand for dollars and, hence, an increase in the amount of Deutsche marks supplied.[1]

In Exhibit 4.1, e is the spot exchange rate (dollar value of one DM), and Q is the quantity of Deutsche marks supplied and demanded. The DM supply *(S)* and demand *(D)* curves intersect at e_0, the equilibrium exchange rate. The quantity of DM exchanged at this price is Q_0.

Suppose that the supply of dollars increases relative to its demand. This excess growth in the money supply will cause inflation in the United States, which means that U.S. prices

■ **EXHIBIT 4.1**   Equilibrium Exchange Rates

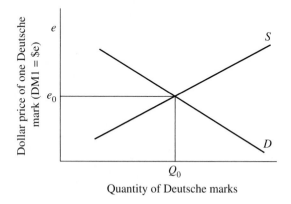

Quantity of Deutsche marks

---

[1]This statement holds provided the price elasticity of German demand, E, is greater than 1. In general, $E = -(\Delta Q/Q)/(\Delta P/P)$, where Q is the quantity of goods demanded, P is the price, and ΔQ is the change in quantity demanded for a change in price, ΔP. If $E > 1$, then total spending goes up when price declines.

begin to rise relative to prices of German goods and services. German consumers are likely to buy fewer U.S. products and begin switching to German substitutes, leading to a decrease in the amount of Deutsche marks supplied at every exchange rate. The result is a leftward shift in the DM supply curve to S' in Exhibit 4.2. Similarly, higher prices in the United States will lead American consumers to substitute German imports for U.S. products, resulting in an increase in the demand for Deutsche marks as depicted by D'. In effect, both Germans and Americans are searching for the best deals worldwide and will switch their purchases accordingly. Hence, a higher rate of inflation in the United States than in Germany will simultaneously increase German exports to the United States and reduce U.S. exports to Germany.

A new equilibrium rate $e_1 > e_0$ results. In other words, a higher rate of inflation in the United States than in Germany will lead to a depreciation of the dollar relative to the Deutsche mark or, equivalently, to an appreciation of the mark relative to the dollar.

In general, a nation running a relatively high rate of inflation will find its currency declining in value relative to the currencies of countries with lower inflation rates. This relationship will be formalized in Chapter 7 as purchasing power parity (PPP).

Depending on the current value of the Deutsche mark relative to the dollar, the amount of DM appreciation or depreciation is computed as the fractional increase or decrease in the dollar value of the DM:

$$\text{Amount of DM appreciation (depreciation)} = \frac{\text{New dollar value of DM} - \text{Old dollar value of DM}}{\text{Old dollar value of DM}}$$

$$= \frac{e_1 - e_0}{e_0} \tag{4.1}$$

Alternatively, the dollar is said to have depreciated (appreciated) by the fractional decrease (increase) in the DM value of the dollar:

■ **EXHIBIT 4.2**   Impact of U.S. Inflation on the Equilibrium Exchange Rate

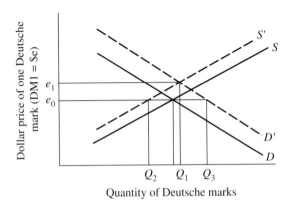

Quantity of Deutsche marks

Amount of dollar depreciation (appreciation) $= \dfrac{\text{New DM value of dollar} - \text{Old DM value of dollar}}{\text{Old DM value of dollar}}$

$$= \frac{1/e_1 - 1/e_0}{1/e_0} = \frac{e_0 - e_1}{e_1} \tag{4.2}$$

For example, an increase in the exchange rate from \$0.64 to \$0.68 is equivalent to a DM appreciation of 6.25% [(0.68 – 0.64)/0.64 = 0.0625] or a dollar depreciation of 5.88% [(0.64 – 0.68)/0.68 = –0.0588]. (Why don't the two exchange rate changes equal each other?[2])

■ ──

ILLUSTRATION

Calculating Dollar Appreciation Against the Italian Lira. On July 19, 1985, the Italian lira devalued by 17% against the U.S. dollar. By how much has the dollar appreciated against the lira?

Solution. If e_0 is the initial dollar value of the lira and e_1 is the post-devaluation exchange rate, then we know from Equation 4.1 that $(e_1 - e_0)/e_0 = -17\%$. Solving for e_1 in terms of e_0 yields $e_1 = 0.83e_0$. From Equation 4.2, we know that the dollar's appreciation against the lira equals $(e_0 - e_1)/e_1$ or $(e_0 - 0.83e_0)/0.83e_0 = 0.17/0.83 = 20.48\%$.   ■
──

Interest rate differentials will also affect the equilibrium exchange rate. A rise in U.S. interest rates relative to German rates, all else being equal, will cause investors in both nations to switch from DM- to dollar-denominated securities to take advantage of the higher dollar rates. The net result will be depreciation of the DM in the absence of government intervention. Similarly, because a stronger economy attracts capital, economic growth should lead to a stronger currency. Empirical evidence supports this hypothesis.

Other factors that can influence exchange rates include political and economic risks. Investors prefer to hold lesser amounts of riskier assets; thus, low-risk currencies—those associated with more politically and economically stable nations—are more highly valued than high-risk currencies.

■ ──

ILLUSTRATION

East-West Politics Affect the Deutsche Mark. Following the reform movement that swept Eastern Europe in late 1989, West Germany's stock market soared. The rise in the West German stock market reflected the general belief among investors that West German industry stood to benefit significantly from the opening of Eastern Europe. For example, economists estimated that the modernization of East Germany's economy alone would cost up to \$300 billion over the coming decade, with much of the reconstruction to be performed by West German industry.

---

[2]The reason the DM appreciation is unequal to the amount of dollar depreciation depends on the fact that the value of one currency is the inverse of the value of the other one. Hence, the percentage change in currency values differs because the base off which the change is measured differs.

■ **EXHIBIT 4.3**   How Political Factors Affect Exchange Rates

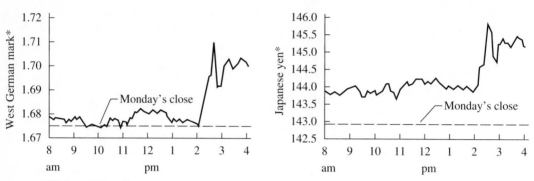

*Value of West German marks and Japanese yen at five-minute intervals

As foreign capital flowed into West Germany, attracted by its strong growth prospects in Eastern Europe, the demand for Deutsche marks in the foreign exchange market led to a steady increase in the DM's value. On January 30, 1990, however, the DM fell about 3% as panicked traders and investors dumped Deutsche marks and other foreign currencies and bought dollars following an unconfirmed report on Cable News Network that Mikhail Gorbachev, the architect of the Soviet Union's reform policies, might resign as head of the Soviet Communist Party. The dollar has traditionally been considered a safe haven for investors during periods of international turmoil.

The foreign exchange consequences of the CNN report, which was televised just after 2 p.m. EST and raised the specter of an unraveling of the reform movement in the Soviet Union and Eastern Europe, are vividly illustrated in Exhibit 4.3. By later in the day, the dollar retreated after the White House said that it had no information to support the CNN report. Over the next two days, the DM rose another 1.4% when Mr. Gorbachev denied the report. These currency fluctuations illustrate the importance of political factors in the foreign exchange market.   ■

■ 4.2 ■
EXPECTATIONS AND THE ASSET MARKET
MODEL OF EXCHANGE RATES

Although currency values are affected by current events and current supply and demand flows in the foreign exchange market, they also depend on expectations about future exchange rate movements. And exchange rate expectations are influenced by every conceivable economic, political, and social factor.

The role of expectations in determining exchange rates depends on the fact that currencies are financial assets and that an exchange rate is simply the relative price of two financial assets—one country's currency in terms of another's. Thus, currency prices are determined in the same manner that the prices of assets such as stocks, bonds, gold, or real estate are determined. Unlike the prices of services or products with short storage lives, asset prices are influenced comparatively little by current events. Rather, they are determined by people's willingness to hold the existing quantities of assets, which in turn depends on their expectations of the future worth of these assets. Thus, for example, frost in Florida can bump up the price of oranges, but it should have little impact on the price of the citrus groves producing the oranges; instead, longer-term expectations of the demand and supply of oranges governs the values of these groves.

Similarly, the value today of a given currency, say, the dollar, depends on whether or not—and how strongly—people still want the amount of dollars and dollar-denominated assets they held yesterday. According to this view—known as the *asset market model* of exchange rate determination—the exchange rate between two currencies represents the price that just balances the relative supplies of, and demands for, assets denominated in those currencies. Consequently, shifts in preferences can lead to massive shifts in currency values.

A brief examination of the dollar's ups and downs, using some stylized facts, provides further insight into the relation of exchange rate movements to the asset-like character of money. In the early 1960s, the United States was clearly the dominant nation in the world. The U.S. political system was stable and its economic health was good: U.S. inflation averaged about 1% annually; economic growth averaged almost 5% annually. Not surprisingly, the world was willing to hold a large fraction of its wealth in the form of dollars and dollar-denominated assets.

In the late 1960s and 1970s, problems appeared. The Vietnam War was sharply divisive, and the U.S. political system was shaken. One president was driven from office, another was forced to resign, and two others lost the confidence of the American people. Monetary growth accelerated, leading to double-digit inflation and sharply higher effective tax rates as inflation forced everyone into higher tax brackets. Economic growth slowed to about 3% annually, compared to about 4% in other developed nations. These factors, combined with increased government regulation, lowered the attractiveness of holding dollars and U.S. assets relative to foreign assets; the world decided to hold a much smaller fraction of its wealth in the form of dollars and dollar-denominated assets. This massive portfolio shift caused a sharp decline in the value of the dollar.

Then, in the early 1980s, Americans elected a new president who was committed to cutting inflation, taxes, and government regulation. The authority of the presidency was restored, taxes and inflation were sharply reduced, and after a brief recession, economic growth accelerated and reached 6.5% in 1984, compared to average growth of 0.9% in other developed countries. Capital was attracted to the United States by the strength of its economy, the high after-tax real (inflation-adjusted) rate of return, and the favorable political climate—conditions superior to those attainable elsewhere. Foreigners once again found the United States to be a safer and more rewarding place in which to invest, so they added substantially more U.S. assets to their portfolios. The dollar rose sharply.

As U.S. growth slowed down in 1985 and foreign growth accelerated, foreign assets became attractive again. At the same time, foreigners fled U.S. assets when they perceived that the U.S. government itself wanted the dollar to decline. The world's decreased willingness to hold U.S. assets led to another massive portfolio rebalancing; this time, investors substituted foreign assets for U.S. assets. The dollar declined once again.

Since the desire to hold a currency today depends critically on expectations of the factors that can affect the currency's future value, what matters is not only what is happening today but what markets expect will happen in the future. Thus, currency values are forward looking; they are set by investor expectations of their issuing countries' future economic prospects rather than by contemporaneous events alone.

The Nature of Money and Currency Values

To understand the factors that affect currency values, it helps to examine the special character of money. To begin, money has value because people are willing to accept it in exchange for goods and services. The value of money, therefore, depends on its purchasing power. Money also provides *liquidity*—that is, you can readily exchange it for goods or other assets, thereby facilitating economic transactions. Thus, money represents both a *store of value* and a *store of liquidity*. The demand for money, therefore, depends on money's ability to maintain its value and on the level of economic activity. Hence, the lower the expected inflation rate, the more money people will demand. Similarly, higher economic growth means more transactions and a greater demand for money to pay bills.

The demand for money is also affected by the demand for assets denominated in that currency. The higher the expected real return and the lower the riskiness of a country's assets, the greater is the demand for its currency to buy those assets. In addition, as people who prefer assets denominated in that currency (usually residents of the country) accumulate wealth, the value of the currency rises.

Because the exchange rate reflects the relative demands for two moneys, factors that increase the demand for the home currency should also increase the price of home currency on the foreign exchange market. In summary, the economic factors that affect a currency's value include its usefulness as a store of value, determined by its expected rate of inflation; the demand for liquidity, determined by the volume of transactions in that currency; and the demand for assets denominated in that currency, determined by the risk-return pattern on investment in that nation's economy and by the wealth of its residents. The first factor depends primarily on the country's future monetary policy, while the latter two factors depend largely on expected economic growth and political and economic stability. All three factors ultimately depend on the soundness of the nation's economic policies. The sounder these policies, the more valuable the nation's currency will be; conversely, the more uncertain a nation's future economic and political course, the riskier its assets will be, and the more depressed and volatile its currency's value.

■ ───

ILLUSTRATION

An Earthquake Hits the Mexican Peso. After the devastating Mexico City earthquake in September 1985, the Mexican government expropriated private property in what was called "a bold gesture to speed the rebuilding of the capital." But the abrupt, carelessly executed expropriation shredded private-sector confidence in the government. People rushed to sell Mexican assets and the peso plunged 30%.

The asset market view that sound economic policies strengthen a currency is challenged by critics who point to the links between the huge U.S. budget deficits, high real interest rates, and the strong dollar in the early 1980s. But others find this argument unconvincing, especially now that the dollar has fallen while the deficit has risen further. If the big deficits were responsible for high real U.S. interest rates, there would be more evidence that private borrowing was being crowded out in interest-sensitive areas, such as fixed business investment and residential construction. Yet the rise in real interest rates coincided with rapid growth in capital spending.

An alternative explanation for high real interest rates is that a vigorous U.S. economy, combined with a major cut in business taxes in 1981, raised the after-tax profitability of business investments. The result was a capital spending boom and a strong dollar.

Indeed, if large government deficits and excessive government borrowing cause currencies to strengthen, then the Argentine austral and Brazilian cruzeiro should be among the strongest currencies in the world. Instead, they are among the weakest currencies since their flawed economic policies scare off potential investors.

Central Bank Reputations and Currency Values

Another critical determinant of currency values is central bank behavior. A *central bank* is the nation's official monetary authority; its job is to use the instruments of monetary policy, including the sole power to create money, so as to achieve one or more of the following objectives: price stability, low interest rates, or a target currency value. As such, the central bank affects the risk associated with holding money. This risk is inextricably linked to the nature of a *fiat money.* Until 1971, every major currency was linked to a commodity. Today no major currency is linked to a commodity. With a commodity base, usually gold, there was a stable, long-term anchor to the price level. Prices varied a great deal in the short term, but they eventually returned to where they had been.

With a fiat money, there is no anchor to the price level—that is, there is no standard of value that investors can use to find out what the currency's future value might be. Instead, a currency's value is largely determined by the central bank through its control of the money supply. If the central bank creates too much money, inflation will occur and the value of money will fall. *Expectations* of central bank behavior will also affect exchange rates today; a currency will decline if people *think* the central bank will expand the money supply in the future.

Viewed this way, money becomes a brand name product whose value is backed by the reputation of the central bank that issues it. And just as reputations among automobiles vary—from Mercedes Benz to Yugo—so currencies come backed by a range of quality reputations—from the Deutsche mark, Swiss franc, and Japanese yen on the high side to the Mexican peso, Brazilian cruzeiro, and Argentine austral on the low side. Underlying these reputations is trust in the willingness of the central bank to maintain price stability.

The high-quality currencies are those expected to maintain their purchasing power because they are issued by reputable central banks. In contrast, the low-quality currencies are those that bear little assurance their purchasing power will be maintained. And as in the car market, high-quality currencies sell at a premium, and low-quality currencies sell at a discount (relative to their values based on economic fundamentals alone). That is, investors demand a risk premium to hold a riskier currency, whereas safer currencies will be worth more than their economic fundamentals would indicate.

Because good reputations are slow to build and quick to disappear, many economists recommend that central banks adopt rules for price stability that are verifiable, unambiguous, and enforceable.[3] Absent such rules, the natural accountability of central banks to government becomes an avenue for political influence. The greater scope for political influence will, in turn, add to the perception of inflation risk.

The importance of expectations and central bank reputations in determining currency values was dramatically illustrated on June 2, 1987, when the financial markets learned that Paul Volcker was resigning as chairman of the Federal Reserve Board. Within seconds after this news appeared on the ubiquitous video screens used by traders to watch the world, both the price of the dollar on foreign exchange markets and the prices of bonds began a steep decline. By day's end, the dollar had fallen 2.6% against the Japanese yen, and the price of Treasury bonds declined 2.3%—one of the largest one-day declines ever. The price of corporate bonds fell by a similar amount. All told, the value of U.S. bonds fell by more than $100 billion.

The response by the financial markets reveals the real forces that are setting the value of the dollar and interest rates under our current monetary system. On that day, there was no other economic news of note. There was no news about American competitiveness. There was no change in Federal Reserve (Fed) policy or inflation statistics; nor was there any change in the size of the budget deficit, the trade deficit, or the growth rate of the U.S. economy.

What actually happened on that announcement day? Foreign exchange traders and investors simply became less certain of the path U.S. monetary policy would take in the days and years ahead. Volcker was a known inflation fighter. Alan Greenspan, the incoming Fed chairman, was an unknown quantity. The possibility that he would emphasize growth over price stability raised the specter of a more expansive monetary policy. Because the natural response to risk is to hold less of the asset whose risk has risen, investors tried to reduce their holdings of dollars and dollar-denominated bonds, driving down their prices in the process.

The import of what happened on June 2, 1987, is that prices of the dollar and those billions of dollars in bonds were changed by nothing more or less than investors changing their collective assessment of what actions the Fed would or wouldn't take. A critical lesson for business people and policymakers alike surfaces: A shift in the trust that people have for a currency can change its value now by changing its expected value in the future. The level of interest rates is also affected by trust in the future value of money. All else being equal,

---

[3]See, for example, W. Lee Hoskins, "A European System of Central Banks: Observations from Abroad," *Economic Commentary,* Federal Reserve Bank of Cleveland, November 15, 1990.

the greater the trust in the promise that money will maintain its purchasing power, the lower interest rates will be. This theory will be formalized in Chapter 7 as the Fisher effect.

■ 4.3 ■
THE FUNDAMENTALS OF CENTRAL BANK INTERVENTION

The exchange rate is one of the most important prices in a country because it links the domestic economy and the rest-of-world economy. As such, it affects relative national competitiveness.

We have already seen the link between exchange rate changes and relative inflation rates. The important point for now is that an appreciation of the exchange rate beyond that necessary to offset the inflation differential between two countries raises the price of domestic goods relative to the price of foreign goods. This rise in the *real* or *inflation-adjusted exchange rate*—measured as the nominal exchange rate adjusted for changes in relative price levels—proves to be a mixed blessing. For example, the rise in the value of the U.S. dollar from 1980 to 1985 translated directly into a reduction in the dollar prices of imported goods and raw materials. As a result, prices of imports and of products that compete with imports began to ease. This development contributed significantly to the slowing of U.S. inflation in the early 1980s.

Yet the rising dollar had some distinctly negative consequences for the U.S. economy as well. Declining dollar prices of imports had their counterpart in the increasing foreign currency prices of U.S. products sold abroad. As a result, American exports became less competitive in world markets, and American-made import substitutes became less competitive in the United States. Sales of domestic traded goods declined, generating unemployment in the traded-goods sector and inducing a shift in resources from the traded-to the nontraded-goods sector of the economy.

Alternatively, home currency depreciation results in a more competitive traded-goods sector, stimulating domestic employment and inducing a shift in resources from the non-traded- to the traded-goods sector. The bad part is that currency weakness also results in higher prices for imported goods and services, eroding living standards and worsening domestic inflation.

From its peak in mid-1985, the U.S. dollar fell by more than 50% over the next few years, enabling Americans to experience the joys and sorrows of both a strong and a weak currency in less than a decade. The weak dollar made U.S. companies more competitive worldwide; at the same time, it lowered the living standards of Americans who enjoyed consuming foreign goods and services. Exhibit 4.4 charts the real value of the U.S. dollar from 1976 to 1990.

Depending on their economic goals, some governments will prefer an overvalued domestic currency, whereas others will prefer an undervalued currency. Still others just want a correctly valued currency, but economic policymakers may feel that the rate set by the market is irrational; that is, they feel they can better judge the correct exchange rate than the marketplace can.

■ **EXHIBIT 4.4**   Real Value of the U.S. Dollar, 1976–1990

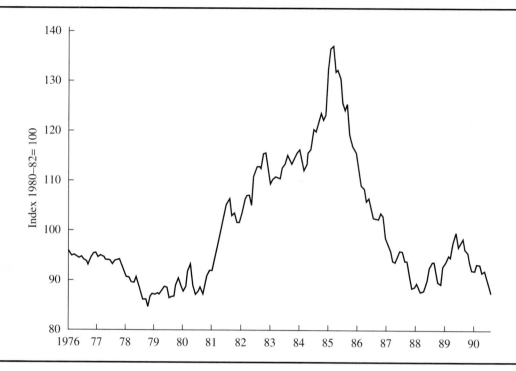

No matter what category they fall in, most governments will be tempted to intervene in the foreign exchange market to move the exchange rate to the level consistent with their goals or beliefs. *Foreign exchange market intervention* refers to official purchases and sales of foreign exchange that nations undertake through their central banks to influence their currencies.

For example, looking back at Section 4.1, suppose the U.S. and German governments decide to maintain the old exchange rate e_0 in the face of the new equilibrium rate e_1. According to Exhibit 4.2, the result will be an excess demand for Deutsche marks equal to $Q_3 - Q_2$; this DM shortage is the same as an excess supply of $(Q_3 - Q_2)e_0$ dollars. Either the Federal Reserve (the American central bank), or the Bundesbank (the German central bank), or both will then have to intervene in the market to supply this additional quantity of Deutsche marks (to buy up the excess supply of dollars). Absent some change, the United States will face a perpetual balance-of-payments deficit equal to $(Q_3 - Q_2)e_0$ dollars, which is the dollar value of the German balance-of-payments surplus of $(Q_3 - Q_2)$ Deutsche marks.

Foreign Exchange Market Intervention

Although the mechanics of central bank intervention vary, the general purpose of each variant is basically the same: to increase the market demand for one currency by increasing the market supply of another. To see how this purpose can be accomplished, suppose in the previous example that the Bundesbank wants to reduce the value of the DM from e_1 to its previous equilibrium value of e_0. To do so, the Bundesbank must sell an additional $(Q_3 - Q_2)$ DM in the foreign exchange market, thereby eliminating the shortage of DM that would otherwise exist at e_0. This sale of DM (which involves the purchase of an equivalent amount of dollars) will also eliminate the excess supply of $(Q_3 - Q_2)e_0$ dollars that now exists at e_0. The simultaneous sale of DM and purchase of dollars will balance the supply and demand for DM (and dollars) at e_0.

If the Fed also wants to raise the value of the dollar, it will buy dollars with Deutsche marks. Regardless of whether the Fed or the Bundesbank initiates this foreign exchange operation, the net result is the same: The U.S. money supply will fall, and Germany's money supply will rise.

Sterilized Versus Unsterilized Intervention

The two examples just discussed are instances of *unsterilized* intervention; that is, the monetary authorities have not insulated their domestic money supplies from the foreign exchange transactions. In both cases, the U.S. money supply will fall, and the German money supply will rise. As noted earlier, an increase (decrease) in the supply of money, all other things held constant, will result in more (less) inflation. Thus, the foreign exchange market intervention will not only change the exchange rate, it will also increase German inflation, while reducing U.S. inflation. Recall it was the jump in the U.S. money supply that caused this inflation. These money supply changes will also affect interest rates in both countries.

To neutralize these effects, the Fed and/or the Bundesbank can *sterilize* the impact of their foreign exchange market intervention on the domestic money supply through an *open-market operation,* which is just the sale or purchase of U.S. Treasury securities. For example, the purchase of U.S. Treasury bills by the Fed supplies reserves to the banking system and increases the U.S. money supply. Following the open-market operation, therefore, the public will hold more cash and bank deposits and fewer Treasury securities; if the Fed buys enough T-bills, the U.S. money supply will return to its preintervention level. Similarly, the Bundesbank could neutralize the impact of intervention on the German money supply by subtracting reserves from its banking system through sales of German Treasury securities.

The Effects of Foreign Exchange Market Intervention

The basic problem with intervention is that it is likely to be either ineffectual or irresponsible. Because sterilized intervention entails a substitution of DM-denominated securities for dollar-denominated ones, the exchange rate will be permanently affected only if investors view domestic and foreign securities as being imperfect substitutes. If this is the case, then the exchange rate and relative interest rates must change to induce investors to hold the new portfolio of securities.

But if investors consider these securities to be perfect substitutes, then no change in the exchange rate or interest rates will be necessary to convince investors to hold this portfolio. In this case, sterilized intervention is ineffectual. This conclusion is consistent with the experiences of the United States and other industrial nations in their intervention policies. Between March 1973 and April 1983, industrial nations bought and sold a staggering $772 billion of foreign currencies to influence exchange rates. More recently, the U.S. government bought over $36 billion of foreign currencies between July 1988 and July 1990 to stem the rise in the value of the dollar. Despite these large interventions, exchange rates appear to have been moved largely by basic market forces.

On the other hand, unsterilized intervention can have a lasting effect on exchange rates, but insidiously—by creating inflation in some nations and deflation in others. In the example presented above, Germany would wind up with a permanent (and inflationary) increase in its money supply, and the United States would end up with a deflationary decrease in its money supply. If the resulting increase in German inflation and decrease in U.S. inflation were sufficiently large, the exchange rate would remain at e_0 without the need for further government intervention. But it is the money supply changes, and not the intervention by itself, that affect the exchange rate. Moreover, moving the *nominal* (or actual) exchange rate from e_1 to e_0 should not affect the real exchange rate because the change in inflation rates offsets the nominal exchange rate change.

If forcing a currency below its equilibrium level causes inflation, it follows that devaluation cannot be much use as a means of restoring competitiveness. A devaluation improves competitiveness only to the extent that it does not cause higher inflation. If the devaluation causes domestic wages and prices to rise, any gain in competitiveness is quickly eroded.

■ ───

ILLUSTRATION

Britain Pegs the Pound to the Mark. In early 1987, Nigel Lawson, Britain's Chancellor of the Exchequer, began pegging the pound sterling against the Deutsche mark. Unfortunately, his exchange rate target greatly undervalued the pound. In order to prevent sterling from rising against the DM he had to massively intervene in the foreign exchange market. The resulting explosion in the British money supply reignited the inflation that Prime Minister Margaret Thatcher had spent so long subduing. With high inflation, the pound fell against the mark and British interest rates surged. The combination of high inflation and high interest rates led first to Mr. Lawson's resignation in October 1989 and then to Mrs. Thatcher's resignation a year later, in November 1990.   ■

Of course, when the world's central banks execute a coordinated surprise attack, the impact on the market can be dramatic—for a short period. Early in the morning on February 27, 1985, for example, Western European central bankers began telephoning banks and investment firms in London, Frankfurt, Milan, and other financial centers to order the sale of hundreds of millions of dollars; the action—joined a few hours later by the Federal Reserve in New York—panicked the markets and drove the dollar down by 5% that day.

But keeping the market off balance requires credible repetitions. Shortly after the February 27 blitzkrieg, the dollar was back on the rise. The Fed intervened again, but it wasn't until clear signs of a U.S. economic slowdown emerged that the dollar turned down in March.

Open-Market Operations

To summarize, exchange market intervention will have a lasting influence on exchange rates only if the intervention leads to permanent changes in relative money supplies. Thus, if the DM appreciation is viewed as resulting from a shortage of DM, an alternative to foreign exchange market intervention is for the Bundesbank to expand the supply of DM by buying Treasury bills from the public. Some of these added DM will be spent on foreign goods, services, and assets. More DM will be sold in the foreign exchange market to buy dollars to carry out these planned purchases. If the Bundesbank expands the money supply sufficiently through its open-market operations, the increased supply of DM in the foreign exchange market will cause the equilibrium exchange rate to return to e_0.

Conversely, if the depreciating dollar is traced to an excess of dollars, the Fed could reduce the U.S. money supply by selling Treasury bills to the public. As the U.S. money supply declines, fewer dollars will be sold in the foreign exchange market. If the drop in the U.S. money supply is large enough, the demand for DM will drop sufficiently to return the equilibrium exchange rate to e_0.

Open-market operations affect the equilibrium exchange rate in a manner analogous to unsterilized intervention—primarily through their impact on inflation rates. In the case of Bundesbank open-market operations, the increased supply of DM will raise the German inflation rate. If enough DM are created, German inflation will rise to the level of U.S. inflation, and the old equilibrium exchange rate e_0 will be restored. Alternatively, if the U.S. money supply is reduced sufficiently, the initial inflation that shifted the equilibrium exchange rate will end, and e_0 will again be the equilibrium rate. In either event, the real exchange rate and relative competitiveness should remain unchanged because the shift in inflation rates offsets the nominal currency change.

To summarize the empirical evidence, *real* exchange rates are primarily determined by real economic variables, such as relative national incomes and interest rates between countries; real exchange rates, in turn, determine the magnitudes and the direction of flows of goods, services, and capital among countries. A change in the supply-demand relationship in the foreign exchange market that was brought about by intervention may temporarily influence the movement of the real exchange rate. However, unless the underlying economic variables that typically give rise to broadly based, market-generated supply-and-demand forces change, these forces will eventually swamp the impact of the intervention. Thus, nations intent on fixing their exchange rate in defiance of market forces must ultimately bow to those forces or else resort to currency controls.

■ 4.4 ■

THE EQUILIBRIUM APPROACH TO EXCHANGE RATES

We have seen that changes in the nominal exchange rate are largely affected by variations or expected variations in relative money supplies. These nominal exchange rate changes are also highly correlated with changes in the real exchange rate. Indeed, many commentators believe that nominal exchange rate changes *cause* real exchange rate changes. As defined earlier, the *real* exchange rate is the relative price of foreign goods in terms of domestic goods. Thus, changes in the nominal exchange rate, through their impact on the real exchange rate, are said to help or hurt companies and economies.

One explanation for the correlation between nominal and real exchange rate changes is supplied by the disequilibrium theory of exchange rates.[4] According to this view, various frictions in the economy cause goods prices to adjust slowly over time, whereas nominal exchange rates adjust quickly in response to new information or changes in expectations. As a direct result of the differential speeds of adjustment in the goods and currency markets, changes in nominal exchange rates caused by purely monetary disturbances are naturally translated into changes in real exchange rates and can lead to exchange rate "overshooting," whereby the short-term change in the exchange rate exceeds, or overshoots, the long-term change in the equilibrium exchange rate (see Exhibit 4.5). This view underlies most popular accounts of exchange rate changes and policy discussions that appear in the media. It implies that currencies may become "overvalued" or "undervalued" relative to equilibrium, and that these disequilibria affect international competitiveness in ways that are not justified by changes in comparative advantage.

■ **EXHIBIT 4.5**   Exchange Rate Overshooting According to the Disequilibrium Theory of Exchange Rates

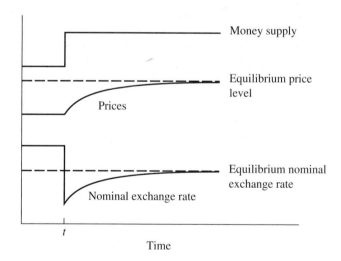

[4]The most elegant presentation of a disequilibrium theory is in Rudiger Dornbusch, "Expectations and Exchange Rate Dynamics," *Journal of Political Economy,* December 1976, pp. 1161–1176.

However, the disequilibrium theory has been criticized by some economists in recent years. In its place, they have suggested an equilibrium approach to exchange rate changes.[5] The basis for the equilibrium approach is that markets clear—supply and demand are equated—through price adjustments. Real disturbances to supply or demand in the goods market cause changes in relative prices, including the real exchange rate. These changes in the real exchange rate are often accomplished, in part, through changes in the nominal exchange rate. Repeated shocks in supply or demand thereby create a correlation between changes in nominal and real exchange rates.

The equilibrium approach has three important implications for exchange rates. First, exchange rates do not "cause" changes in relative prices but are part of the process through which the changes occur in equilibrium; that is, changes in relative prices and in real exchange rates occur simultaneously, and both are related to more fundamental economic factors.

Second, attempts by government to affect the real exchange rate via foreign exchange market intervention will fail. The direction of causation runs from the real exchange rate change to the nominal exchange rate change, and not vice versa; changing the nominal exchange rate by altering money supplies will affect relative inflation rates in such a way as to leave the real exchange rate unchanged.

Finally, there is no simple relation between changes in the exchange rate and changes in international competitiveness, employment, or the trade balance. With regard to the latter, trade deficits do not "cause" currency depreciation, nor does currency depreciation by itself help reduce a trade deficit.

Some of the implications of the equilibrium approach may appear surprising. They conflict with many of the claims that are commonly made in the financial press and by politicians; they also seem to conflict with experience. But according to the equilibrium view of exchange rates, many of the assumptions and statements commonly made in the media are simply wrong, and experiences may be very selective.

Econometric testing of these models is in its infancy, but there is some evidence that supports the equilibrium models, although it is far from conclusive. According to the disequilibrium approach, a change in the real exchange rate occurs in response to changes in the nominal exchange rate because of sticky prices. But as prices eventually adjust toward their new equilibrium levels, the real exchange rate should return to its equilibrium value. Monetary disturbances, then, should create temporary movements in real exchange rates. Initial increases in the real exchange rate should be followed by later decreases as nominal prices adjust to equilibrium.

But statistical evidence indicates that changes in real exchange rates tend, on average, to be nearly permanent or to persist for very long periods of time. The evidence also indicates that changes in nominal exchange rates—even very short-term day-to-day changes—are largely permanent. This persistence is inconsistent with the view that monetary shocks, or even temporary real shocks, cause most of the major changes in real exchange rates. On the other hand, it is consistent with the view that most changes in real exchange rates are due to real shocks with a large permanent component. Changes in real and nominal exchange rates

---

[5]See, for example, Alan C. Stockman, "The Equilibrium Approach to Exchange Rates," *Economic Review,* Federal Reserve Bank of Richmond, March/April 1987, pp. 12–30. This section is based on his article.

are also very highly correlated and have similar variances, supporting the view that most changes in nominal exchange rates are due to largely permanent, real disturbances.

An alternative explanation is that we are seeing the effects of a sequence of monetary shocks, so that even if any given exchange rate change is temporary, the continuing shocks keep driving the exchange rate from its long-run equilibrium value. Thus, the sequence of these temporary changes is a permanent change. Moreover, if the equilibrium exchange rate is itself constantly subject to real shocks, we would not expect to see reversion in real exchange rates. The data do not allow us to distinguish between these hypotheses.

Another feature of the data is that the exchange rate varies much more than the ratio of price levels. The equilibrium view attributes this "excess variability" to shifts in demand and/or supply between domestic and foreign goods; the shifts affect the exchange rate but not relative inflation rates. Supply-and-demand changes also operate indirectly to alter relative prices of foreign and domestic goods by affecting the international distribution of wealth.

Although the equilibrium theory of exchange rates is consistent with selected empirical evidence, it may stretch its point too far. Implicit in the equilibrium theory is the view that money is just a unit of account—a measuring rod for value—with no intrinsic value. However, because money is an asset it is possible that monetary and other policy changes, by altering the perceived usefulness and importance of money as a store of value or liquidity, could alter real exchange rates. The evidence presented earlier that changes in anticipated monetary policy can alter real exchange rates supports this view. Moreover, the equilibrium theory fails to explain a critical fact: The variability of real exchange rates has been much greater when currencies are floating than when they are fixed. This fact is easily explained, if we view money as an asset, by the greater instability in relative monetary policies in a floating rate system. The real issue then is not whether monetary policy—including its degree of stability—has any impact at all on real exchange rates but whether that impact is of first- or second-order importance.

Despite important qualifications, the equilibrium theory of exchange rates provides a useful addition to our understanding of exchange rate behavior. Its main contribution is to suggest an explanation for exchange rate behavior that is consistent with the notion that markets work reasonably well if they are permitted to.

■ 4.5 ■
SUMMARY AND CONCLUSIONS

This chapter studied the process of determining exchange rates under a floating exchange rate system. We saw that in the absence of government intervention, exchange rates respond to the forces of supply and demand, that in turn are dependent on relative inflation rates, interest rates, and GNP growth rates. Monetary policy is crucial here. If the central bank expands the money supply at a faster rate than the growth in money demand, the purchasing power of money declines both at home (inflation) and abroad (currency depreciation). In addition, the healthier the economy is, the stronger the currency is likely to be. Exchange rates are also crucially affected by expectations of future exchange rate changes, which depend on forecasts of future economic and political conditions.

In order to achieve certain economic or political objectives, governments often intervene in the currency markets to affect the exchange rate. Although the mechanics of such intervention vary, the general purpose of each variant is basically the same: to increase the market demand for one currency by increasing the market supply of another. Alternatively, the government can control the exchange rate directly by setting a price for its currency and then restricting access to the foreign exchange market.

A critical factor that helps explain the volatility of exchange rates is that with a fiat money there is no anchor to a currency's value, nothing around which beliefs can coalesce. In this situation, where people are unsure of what to expect, any new piece of information can dramatically alter their beliefs. Thus, if the underlying domestic economic policies are unstable, exchange rates will be volatile as traders react to new information.

■ QUESTIONS ■

1. Suppose prices start rising in the United States relative to prices in Japan. What would we expect to see happen to the dollar:yen exchange rate? Explain.

2. If a foreigner purchases a U.S. government security, what happens to the supply of, and demand for, dollars?

3. Describe how these three typical transactions should affect present and future exchange rates.

   a. Seagram imports a year's supply of French champagne. Payment in French francs is due immediately.

   b. American Motors sells a new stock issue to Renault, the French car manufacturer. Payment in dollars is due immediately.

   c. Korean Airlines buys five Boeing 747s. As part of the deal, Boeing arranges a loan to KAL for the purchase amount from the U.S. Export-Import Bank. The loan is to be paid back over the next seven years with a two-year grace period.

4. In 1987, the British government cut taxes significantly, raising the after-tax return on investments in Great Britain. What would be the likely consequence of this tax cut on the equilibrium value of the British pound?

5. Some economists have argued that a lower government deficit could cause the dollar to drop by reducing high real interest rates in the United States. What does the asset view of exchange rates predict will happen if the United States lowers its budget deficit? What is the evidence from countries such as Mexico and Brazil?

6. The maintenance of money's value is said to depend on the monetary authorities. What might the monetary authorities do to a currency that would cause its value to drop?

7. For each of the following six scenarios, say whether the value of the dollar will appreciate, depreciate, or remain the same relative to the Japanese yen. Explain each answer. Assume that exchange rates are free to vary and that other factors are held constant.

   a. The growth rate of national income is higher in the United States than in Japan.

   b. Inflation is higher in the United States than in Japan.

   c. Prices in Japan and the United States are rising at the same rate.

   d. Real interest rates are higher in the United States than in Japan.

e. The United States imposes new restrictions on the ability of foreigners to buy American companies and real estate.

f. U.S. wages rise relative to Japanese wages, while American productivity falls behind Japanese productivity.

8. The Fed adopts an easier monetary policy. How is this likely to affect the value of the dollar and U.S. interest rates?

9. What is there about a fiat money that makes its exchange rate especially volatile?

10. Comment on the following headline (*The Wall Street Journal,* January 17, 1985): "Sterling Drops Sharply Despite Good Health of British Economy: Oil Price Slump Is Blamed."

11. Suppose the Soviet Union makes threatening moves against Western Europe. How is this threat likely to affect the dollar's value? Why?

12. Comment on the following statement: "One of the puzzling aspects of central bank intervention is how those who manage our economic affairs think they know what is the 'right' price for a dollar in terms of francs, pounds, yen, or Deutsche marks. And if they do know, why do they keep changing their minds?"

13. In a widely anticipated move, on August 30, 1990, the Bank of Japan raised the discount rate (the rate it charges on loans to financial institutions) to 6% from 5.25% in a move to reduce inflationary pressures in Japan. Many currency traders had expected the Japanese central bank to raise its rate by more than 0.75%. What was the likely consequence of this interest rate rise on the yen:dollar exchange rate?

14. On November 28, 1990, Federal Reserve Chairman Alan Greenspan told the House Banking Committee that despite possible benefits to the U.S. trade balance, "a weaker dollar also is a cause for concern." This statement departed from what appeared to be an attitude of benign neglect by U.S. monetary officials toward the dollar's depreciation. He also rejected the notion that the Fed should aggressively ease monetary policy, as some Treasury officials had been urging. At the same time, Mr. Greenspan didn't mention foreign exchange market intervention to support the dollar's value.

a. What was the likely reaction of the foreign exchange market to Mr. Greenspan's statements. Explain.

b. Can Mr. Greenspan support the value of the U.S. dollar without intervening in the foreign exchange market? If so, how?

15. In the late 1980s, the Bank of Japan bought billions of dollars in the foreign exchange market to prop up the dollar's value against the yen. What were the likely consequences of this foreign exchange market intervention for the Japanese economy?

16. Countries with high inflation need to keep devaluing their currencies to maintain competitiveness. But countries that try to maintain their competitiveness by devaluing their currencies only end up with even higher inflation. Discuss.

■ PROBLEMS ■

1. Suppose the Mexican peso devalues by 75% against the dollar. What is the percentage appreciation of the dollar against the peso?

2. Suppose the dollar appreciates by 500% against the Brazilian cruzeiro. How much has the cruzeiro devalued against the dollar?

3. Between 1988 and 1991, the price of a room at the Milan Hilton rose from Lit 346,400 to Lit 475,000. At the same time, the exchange rate went from Lit 1,302 = $1 in 1988 to Lit 1,075 = $1 in 1991.

   a. By how much has the dollar cost of a room at the Milan Hilton changed over this three-year period?

   b. What has happened to the lira's dollar value during this period?

■ BIBLIOGRAPHY ■

Batten, Dallas S., and Mack Ott. "What Can Central Banks Do About the Value of the Dollar?" *Federal . Reserve Bank of St. Louis Review,* May 1984, pp. 16–26.

Dornbusch, Rudiger. "Expectations and Exchange Rate Dynamics." *Journal of Political Economy,* December 1976, pp. 1161–1176.

Frenkel, Jacob A., and Harry G. Johnson, eds. *The Economics of Exchange Rates.* Reading, Mass.: Addison-Wesley, 1978.

Levich, Richard M. "Empirical Studies of Exchange Rates: Price Behavior, Rate Determination and Market Efficiency." In *Handbook of International Economics,* vol. II. Ronald W. Jones and Peter B. Kenen, eds. Netherlands: Elsevier B.V., 1985, pp. 980–1040.

Marrinan, Jane. "Exchange Rate Determination: Sorting Out Theory and Evidence." *New England Economic Review,* November/December 1989, pp. 39–51.

Stockman, Alan C. "The Equilibrium Approach to Exchange Rates." *Economic Review,* Federal Reserve Bank of Richmond, March/April 1987, pp. 12–30.

◖ 5 ◗

The International Monetary System

The monetary and economic disorders of the past fifteen years . . . are a reaction to a world monetary system that has no historical precedent. We have been sailing on uncharted waters and it has been taking time to learn the safest routes.

—Milton Friedman —
Winner of Nobel Prize in Economics

■ The currency problems faced by firms today have been exacerbated by the breakdown of the postwar international monetary system established at the Bretton Woods Conference in 1944. The main features of the *Bretton Woods system* were the relatively fixed exchange rates of individual currencies in terms of the U.S. dollar and the convertibility of the dollar into gold for foreign official institutions. These fixed exchange rates were supposed to reduce the riskiness of international transactions, thus promoting growth in world trade.

Yet in 1971, the Bretton Woods system fell victim to the international monetary turmoil it was designed to avoid. It was replaced by the present regime of rapidly fluctuating exchange rates, resulting in major problems and opportunities for multinational corporations. The purpose of this chapter is to help managers, both financial and nonfinancial, understand what the international monetary system is and how the choice of system affects currency values. It also provides a historical background of the international monetary system to enable managers to gain perspective when trying to interpret the likely consequences of new policy moves in the area of international finance. After all, although the types of government foreign exchange policies may at times appear to be limitless, they are all variations on a common theme.

■ 5.1 ■
ALTERNATIVE EXCHANGE RATE SYSTEMS

The *international monetary system* refers primarily to the set of policies, institutions, practices, regulations, and mechanisms that determine the rate at which one currency is exchanged for another. This section considers five different market mechanisms for establishing exchange rates: free float, managed float, target-zone arrangement, fixed-rate system, and the current hybrid system.

Free Float

We have already seen that free market exchange rates are determined by the interaction of currency supplies and demands. The supply-and-demand schedules, in turn, are influenced by price level changes, interest differentials, and economic growth. In a *free float,* as these economic parameters change—for example, due to new government policies or acts of nature—market participants will adjust their current and expected future currency needs. In the two-country example of Germany and the United States, the shifts in the Deutsche mark supply-and-demand schedules will, in turn, lead to new equilibrium positions. Over time, the exchange rate will fluctuate randomly as market participants assess and react to new information, much as security and commodity prices in other financial markets respond to news. These shifts and oscillations are illustrated in Exhibits 5.1 and 5.2; D_t and S_t are the hypothetical DM demand-and-supply curves, respectively, for period t. Such a system of freely floating exchange rates is usually referred to as a *clean float.*

■ **EXHIBIT 5.1**   Supply-and-Demand Curve Shifts

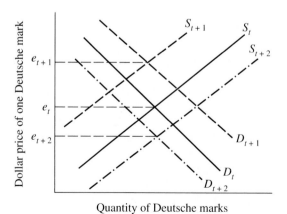

Quantity of Deutsche marks

■ **EXHIBIT 5.2**   Fluctuating Exchange Rate

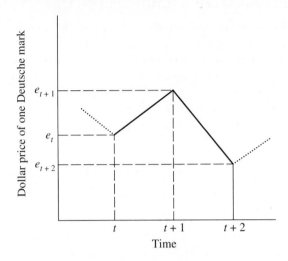

Managed Float

Not surprisingly, few countries have been able to resist for long the temptation to actively intervene in the foreign exchange market in order to reduce the economic uncertainty associated with a clean float. Too abrupt a change in the value of its currency, it is feared, could imperil a nation's export industries (if the currency appreciates) or lead to a higher rate of inflation (if the currency depreciates). Moreover, the experience with floating rates in the 1980s has not been encouraging. Instead of reducing economic volatility, as they were supposed to do, floating exchange rates appear to have increased it. Exchange rate uncertainty also reduces economic efficiency by acting as a tax on trade and foreign investment. Therefore, most countries with floating currencies have attempted, via central bank intervention, to smooth out exchange rate fluctuations. Such a system of managed exchange rates, called a *managed float,* is also known as a *dirty float.*

Managed floats fall into three distinct categories of central bank intervention. The approaches, which vary in their reliance on market forces, are as follows.

1. *Smoothing out daily fluctuations*: Governments following this route attempt only to preserve an orderly pattern of exchange rate changes. They occasionally enter the market on the buy or sell side to ease the transition from one rate to another, rather than resist fundamental market forces, tending to bring about longer-term currency appreciation or depreciation.

2. *"Leaning against the wind"*: This approach is an intermediate policy designed to moderate or prevent abrupt short- and medium-term fluctuations brought about by random events whose effects are expected to be only temporary. The rationale for this policy—which is primarily aimed at delaying, rather than resisting, fundamental exchange rate adjustments—is that government intervention can reduce for exporters and importers the uncertainty caused by disruptive exchange rate changes. It is questionable, though, whether governments are more capable than private forecasters in distinguishing between fundamental and temporary (irrational) values.

3. *Unofficial pegging*: This strategy evokes memories of a fixed-rate system. It involves resisting fundamental upward or downward exchange rate movements for reasons clearly unrelated to exchange market forces. Thus, Japan has historically resisted revaluation of the yen for fear of its consequences for Japanese exports. With unofficial pegging, however, there is no publicly announced government commitment to a given exchange rate level.

Target-Zone Arrangement

Many economists and policy makers have argued that the industrialized countries could minimize exchange rate volatility and enhance economic stability if the United States, Germany, and Japan linked their currencies in a target-zone system. Under a *target-zone arrangement,* countries adjust their national economic policies to maintain their exchange rates within a specific margin around agreed-upon, fixed central exchange rates. Such a system already exists for the major European currencies participating in the European Monetary System.

The *European Monetary System* (EMS) began operating in March 1979. Its purpose is to foster monetary stability in the European Community (EC, or the Common Market). As part of this system, the members have established the European Currency Unit, which plays a central role in the functioning of the EMS. The *European Currency Unit* or ECU is a composite currency that consists of fixed amounts of ten European currencies. The quantity of each country's currency in the ECU reflects that country's relative economic strength in the European Community. The ECU functions as a unit of account, as a means of settlement, and as a reserve asset for the members of the EMS.

At the heart of the system is an exchange-rate mechanism (ERM), which provides for each member to determine a mutually agreed upon central exchange rate for its currency; each rate is denominated in currency units per ECU. These central rates attempt to establish equilibrium exchange values, but members can seek adjustments to the central rates. With the last realignment on January 12, 1987, the ECU central rates were the following: 42.4582 Belgian francs, 7.85212 Danish kroner, 2.05853 Deutsche marks, 6.90403 French francs, 2.31943 Dutch guilders, 0.798411 Irish pounds, and 1483.58 Italian lire.

Central rates establish a grid of bilateral cross-exchange rates between the currencies. For example, 2.05853 Deutsche marks per ECU, divided by 7.85212 Danish kroner per ECU, equals 0.26216 DM per krone, which also implies 3.81443 kroner per DM (see Exhibit 5.3). Nations (except Spain and Britain) participating in the ERM pledged to keep their currencies within a 2.25% margin on either side of these central cross-exchange rates. (Spain and Britain have 6% margins.) Thus, if the Danish krone should strengthen against the Deutsche mark and reach the upper intervention limit, the Bundesbank will sell kroner to commercial banks at 3.73 kroner per DM, and Denmark's National Bank will buy DM at 0.26810 kroner per DM.

■ **EXHIBIT 5.3** European Monetary System Parity Grid

	Germany	Denmark	Ireland	France
Deutsche Mark				
+ 2.25		3.9016	.38182	3.4305
Central rate	1	3.81443	.37328	3.35386
− 2.25		3.7300	.36496	3.2792
Danish Krone				
+ 2.25	.26810	1	.10008	.89225
Central rate	.26216		.09786	.87925
− 2.25	.25630		.09568	.85970
Irish Pound				
+ 2.25	2.740	10.451		9.1890
Central rate	2.678	10.2186	1	8.9848
− 2.25	2.619	9.9913		8.7850
French Franc				
+ 2.25	.30495	1.1632	.11383	
Central rate	.298164	1.13732	.111299	1
− 2.25	.29150	1.1120	.108825	

NOTE: All exchange rates are expressed in terms of national currencies rather than in terms of ECUs.

SOURCE: Nicholas V. Karamouzis, "Lessons from the European Monetary System," *Economic Commentary,* Federal Reserve Bank of Cleveland, August 15, 1987, p. 2.

Fixed-Rate System

Under a *fixed-rate system,* such as Bretton Woods, governments are committed to maintaining target exchange rates. Each central bank actively buys or sells its currency in the foreign exchange market whenever its exchange rate threatens to deviate from its stated par value by more than an agreed-upon percentage. The resulting coordination of monetary policy ensures that each member nation has the same inflation rate. Put another way, in order for a fixed-rate system to work, each member must accept the group's joint inflation rate as its own.

Under the Bretton Woods system, whenever the commitment to the official rate became untenable, it was abruptly changed and a new rate was announced publicly. Currency devaluation or revaluation, however, was usually the last in a string of temporizing alternatives for solving a persistent balance-of-payments deficit or surplus.

Policy Alternatives. We will now examine the efficacy of four alternatives to devaluation. In general, these policies and their effects would be reversed in the case of revaluation.

1. *Foreign borrowing*: As we saw in Chapter 4, an overvalued currency will lead to a balance-of-payments deficit. Governments typically try to finance these payments deficits by borrowing abroad. However, foreign borrowing is only a temporary solution to a persistent payments deficit. Foreign money can be withdrawn as easily as it was brought in. If capital controls are imposed to counter this possibility, few additional funds will be forthcoming. Even the threat of controls is likely to lead to large capital outflows and further worsen a country's deficit.

Government access to foreign capital markets can be maintained only as long as investors have a reasonable expectation of being repaid. For example, Mexico financed large payments deficits during the late 1970s with increasingly heavy foreign borrowing. However, by early 1982, investors began withholding additional funds from Mexico when they perceived a decrease in the country's ability to pay its debts. The peso was devalued shortly thereafter.

2. *Austerity*: Austerity brought about by a combination of reduced government expenditures and increased taxes can be a permanent substitute for devaluation. If austerity works as intended, national income will be reduced, bringing about a decline in imports; the greater the decline in imports, the more effective austerity will be at reducing a trade deficit. But if a fall in imports were the only consequence of the decline in national income, austerity would not boost the value of the currency. As we saw previously, a decline in national income is likely to lower, not raise, a currency's value.

Thus, to work properly, the primary effect of austerity must be to bring about a lower rate of domestic inflation (disinflation). Disinflation will strengthen the currency's value, lessening the need for a devaluation. However, disinflation often leads to a short-run increase in unemployment, a cost of austerity that politicians today generally consider to be unacceptable.

3. *Wage and price controls*: An alternative to austerity is the imposition of wage and price controls. Although varying in its popularity, this alternative is perhaps more politically palatable. However, the historical evidence on these controls emphasizes the futility of attacking symptoms rather than the problem itself. Moreover, the policy is likely to increase pressure on the currency because it clearly indicates that the government doesn't possess the political will to deal with fundamental causes.

4. *Exchange controls*: In addition to other measures, many governments attempt to achieve a balance-of-payments equilibrium by imposing exchange controls. Exchange controls have become a way of life in most developing countries. Nations with overvalued currencies ration foreign exchange, while countries facing revaluation, such as South Korea and Switzerland, may restrict capital inflows.

In effect, government controls supersede the allocative function of the foreign exchange market. The most drastic situation is when all foreign exchange earnings must be surrendered to the central bank which, in turn, apportions these funds to users on the basis of government priorities. The buying and selling rates need not be equal, nor need they be uniform across all transaction categories. Exhibit 5.4 lists the most frequently used currency control measures. These controls are a major source of market imperfection, providing opportunities as well as risks for multinational corporations.

■ **EXHIBIT 5.4**   Typical Currency Control Measures

- Restriction or prohibition of certain remittance categories such as dividends or royalties.
- Ceilings on direct foreign investment outflows (e.g., the elaborate U.S. Office of Foreign Direct Investment controls in effect 1968–1975)
- Controls on overseas portfolio investments
- Import restrictions
- Required surrender of hard-currency export receipts to central bank
- Limitations on prepayments for imports
- Requirements to deposit in interest-free accounts with central bank, for a specified time, some percentage of the value of imports and/or remittances
- Foreign borrowings restricted to a minimum or maximum maturity
- Ceilings on granting of credit to foreign firms
- Imposition of taxes and limitations on foreign-owned bank deposits
- Multiple exchange rates for buying and selling foreign currencies, depending on category of goods or services each transaction falls into

Some countries, such as Italy and France, have established (and abandoned) *two-tier* foreign exchange markets. This arrangement involves an official market (at the official rate) for current account transactions and a free market for capital account transactions. The incentive for arbitrage between these two markets increases as the rate spread widens; arbitrage, however, is illegal.

The Current System of Exchange Rate Determination

The current international monetary system is a hybrid, with major currencies floating on a managed basis, some currencies freely floating, and other currencies moving in and out of various types of pegged exchange rate relationships. Exhibit 5.5 presents a currency map that describes the various zones and blocs linking the world's currencies as of January 31, 1991.

■ 5.2 ■
A BRIEF HISTORY OF THE INTERNATIONAL MONETARY SYSTEM

Almost from the dawn of history, gold has been used as a medium of exchange because of its desirable properties. It is durable, storable, portable, easily recognized, divisible, and easily standardized. Another valuable attribute of gold is that short-run changes in its stock are limited by high production costs, making it costly for governments to manipulate. Most importantly, because gold is a commodity money, it ensures a long-run tendency toward price stability. The reason is that the purchasing power of an ounce of gold, or what it will buy in terms of all other goods and services, will tend toward equality with its long-run cost of production.

For these reasons, most major currencies, until recently, were on a gold standard, which defined their relative values or exchange rates. The *gold standard* essentially involved a

■ EXHIBIT 5.5 Exchange Rate Arrangements, January 31, 1990

Currency Pegged to				Flexibility Limited	More Flexible	
U.S. Dollar	**French Franc**	**Other Currency**	**Other Composite**[1]	**Single Currency**[2]	**Managed Floating**	**Independently Floating**

U.S. Dollar
Afghanistan
Angola
Antigua & Barbuda
Bahamas, The
Barbados
Belize
Djibouti
Dominica
Dominican Rep.
Ethiopia
Grenada
Guyana
Haiti
Iraq
Liberia
Oman
Panama
St. Kitts & Nevis
St. Lucia
St. Vincent & the Grenadines
Sudan
Suriname
Syrian Arab Rep.
Trinidad & Tobago
Yemen, Republic of

French Franc
Benin
Burkina Faso
Cameroon
C. African Rep.
Chad
Comoros
Congo
Côte d'Ivoire
Equatorial Guinea
Gabon
Mali
Niger
Senegal
Togo

Other Currency
Bhutan (Indian Rs.)
Kiribati (A$)
Lesotho (So. African R)
Swaziland (So. African R)
Tonga (A$)
Yugoslavia (DM)

SDR
Burundi
Iran, I. R. of
Libya
Myanmar
Rwanda
Seychelles

Other Composite[1]
Algeria
Austria
Bangladesh
Botswana
Bulgaria
Cape Verde
Cyprus
Czechoslovakia
Fiji
Finland
Hungary
Iceland
Israel
Jordan
Kenya
Kuwait
Malawi
Malaysia
Malta
Mauritius
Morocco
Nepal
Norway
Papua New Guinea
Poland
Romania
Sao Tome & Principe
Solomon Islands
Sweden
Tanzania
Thailand
Uganda
Vanuatu
Western Samoa
Zimbabwe

Single Currency[2]
Bahrain
Qatar
Saudi Arabia
United Arab Emirates

Cooperative Arrangements[3]
Belgium
Denmark
France
Germany
Ireland
Italy
Luxembourg
Netherlands
Spain
United Kingdom

Managed Floating
China, P.R.
Costa Rica
Ecuador
Egypt
Greece
Guinea
Guinea-Bissau
Honduras
India
Indonesia
Korea
Lao P.D. Rep.
Mauritania
Mexico
Nicaragua
Pakistan
Portugal
Singapore
Somalia
Sri Lanka
Tunisia
Turkey
Vietnam

Independently Floating
Argentina
Australia
Bolivia
Brazil
Canada
El Salvador
Gambia, The
Ghana
Guatemala
Jamaica
Japan
Lebanon
Maldives
Nambia
New Zealand
Nigeria
Paraguay
Peru
Philippines
Sierra Leone
South Africa
United States
Uruguay
Venezuela
Zaïre

Adjusted[4]
Chile
Colombia
Madagascar
Mozambique
Zambia

Classification Status, End of Period	1984	1985	1986	1987	1988			1989				1990			
					QII	QIII	QIV	QI	QII	QIII	QIV	QI	QII	QIII	QIV
Currency pegged to															
U.S. dollar	34	31	32	38	38	38	36	31	32	32	32	30	28	25	25
French franc	14	14	14	14	14	14	14	14	14	14	14	14	14	14	14
Other currency	5	5	5	5	5	5	5	5	5	5	5	5	5	5	6
of which: pound sterling	(1)	(1)	(—)	(—)	(—)	(—)	(—)	(—)	(—)	(—)	(—)	(—)	(—)	(—)	(—)
SDR	11	12	10	8	7	7	8	8	7	7	7	7	7	7	6
Other currency composite	31	32	30	27	31	31	31	31	31	34	34	34	35	37	35
Flexibility limited vis-à-vis a single currency	7	5	5	4	4	4	4	4	4	4	4	4	4	4	4
Cooperative arrangements	8	8	8	8	8	8	8	8	9	9	9	9	9	9	10
Adjusted according to a set of indicators	6	5	6	5	5	5	5	5	5	5	5	4	4	3	5
Managed floating	20	21	21	20	20	22	22	25	24	25	21	23	21	23	23
Independently floating	12	15	19	18	18	17	17	19	18	18	20	21	23	26	25
Total[5]	148	149	151	151	151	151	151	151	151	152	152	152	151	154	154

NOTE: Table excludes the currency of Democratic Kampuchea, for which no current information is available. For members with dual or multiple exchange markets, the arrangement shown is that in the major market.

[1]Comprises currencies which are pegged to various "baskets" of currencies of the members' own choice, as distinct from the SDR basket.

[2]Exchange rates of all currencies have shown limited flexibility in terms of the U.S. dollar.

[3]Refers to the cooperative arrangment maintained under the European Monetary System.

[4]Includes exchange arrangements under which the exchange rate is adjusted at relatively frequent intervals, on the basis of indicators determined by the respective member countries.

[5]Includes the currency of Democratic Kampuchea. Effective May 22, 1990, the Yemen Arab Republic and the People's Democratic Republic of Yemen merged as the Republic of Yemen.

SOURCE: *International Financial Statistics,* International Monetary Fund, February 1990, p. 22.

commitment by the participating countries to fix the prices of their domestic currencies in terms of a specified amount of gold. The countries maintained these prices by being willing to buy or sell gold to anyone at that price. For example, from 1821 to 1914, Great Britain maintained a fixed price of gold at £3, 17s, 10½d per ounce; the United States, over the 1834–1933 period, maintained the price of gold at $20.67 per ounce (with the exception of the Greenback period from 1861 to 1878). Thus, over the period 1834–1914 (with the exception of 1861–1878), the dollar/pound sterling exchange rate was perfectly determined. The fixed exchange rate of $4.867 per pound was referred to as the *par exchange rate*.

Since the value of gold relative to other goods and services does not change much over long periods of time, the monetary discipline imposed by a gold standard should ensure long-run price stability for both individual countries and groups of countries. Indeed, there was remarkable long-run price stability in the period before World War I when most countries were on a gold standard. As Exhibit 5.6 shows, price levels at the start of World War I were roughly the same as they had been in the late 1700s before the Napoleonic Wars began.

This record is all the more remarkable when contrasted with the post–World War II inflationary experience of the industrialized nations of Europe and North America. As shown in Exhibit 5.7, 1985 price levels in all these nations were several times as high as they were in 1950. Even in Germany the value of the currency in 1985 was less than one-third of its 1950 level, while the comparable magnitude was less than one-tenth for France, Italy, and the United Kingdom. Although there were no episodes of extremely rapid inflation, price levels rose steadily and substantially.

How the Gold Standard Worked in Theory

A gold standard is often considered an anachronism in our modern, high-tech world because of its needless expense; on the most basic level, it means digging up gold in one corner of the globe for burial in another corner. John Maynard Keynes, the famous British economist, labeled gold a "barbarous metal." Nikolai Lenin predicted that socialism would eventually reduce the value of gold to where it would be used to "coat the walls and floors of public lavatories." The data in Exhibit 5.6 indicate that even under the gold standard,

■ **EXHIBIT 5.6**   Wholesale Price Indices, Pre–World War I

Year	Belgium	Britain	France	Germany	United States
1776	na	101	na	na	84
1793	na	120	na	98	100
1800	na	186	155	135	127
1825	na	139	126	76	101
1850	83	91	96	71	82
1875	100	121	111	100	80
1900	87	86	85	90	80
1913	100	100	100	100	100

SOURCE: Data from B. R. Mitchell, *European Historical Statistics;* Bureau of the Census, *Historical Statistics of the United States.*

■ **EXHIBIT 5.7**   Consumer Price Indices, Post–World War II

Nation	CPI, 1950	CPI, 1985	Loss of Purchasing Power During Period (%)
Belgium	100	466.8	76.8
France	100	1012.2	90.1
Germany	100	308.7	67.6
Italy	100	1369.1	92.7
Netherlands	100	513.4	80.5
United Kingdom	100	1056.0	90.5
United States	100	446.9	77.6

SOURCE: *International Financial Statistics,* International Monetary Fund, various issues.

there were substantial fluctuations in the price level. The long-run stability of the price level includes alternating periods of inflation and deflation. Nonetheless, discontent with the current monetary system, which has produced over two decades of worldwide inflation and widely fluctuating exchange rates, has prompted interest in a return to some form of a gold standard.

To put it bluntly, calls for a new gold standard reflect a fundamental distrust of government's willingness to maintain the integrity of fiat money. *Fiat money* is nonconvertible paper money backed only by faith in the monetary authorities that they will not cheat (by issuing more money). This faith has been tempered by hard experience; the 100% profit margin on issuing new fiat money has proved to be an irresistible temptation for most governments.

By contrast, the net profit margin on issuing more money under a gold standard is zero. The government must acquire more gold before it can issue more money, and the government's cost of acquiring the extra gold equals the value of the money it issues. Thus, expansion of the money supply is constrained by the available supply of gold. This fact is crucial in understanding how a gold standard works.

Under the classical gold standard, disturbances in the price level in one country would be wholly or partly offset by an automatic balance-of-payments adjustment mechanism called the *price-specie-flow mechanism.* (Specie refers to gold coins.) To see how this adjustment mechanism worked to equalize prices across countries and automatically bring international payments back in balance, consider the following example.

Suppose that a technological advance increases productivity in the nongold-producing sector of the U.S. economy. This productivity will lower the price of other goods and services relative to the price of gold, and the U.S. price level will decline. The fall in U.S. prices will result in lower prices of U.S. exports; export prices will decline relative to import prices (determined largely by supply and demand in the rest of the world). Consequently, foreigners will demand more U.S. exports, and Americans will buy fewer imports.

Starting from a position of equilibrium in its international payments, the United States will now run a balance-of-payments surplus. The difference will be made up by a flow of gold into the United States. The gold inflow will increase the U.S. money supply (under a gold standard, more gold means more money in circulation), reversing the initial decline in prices. At the same time, the other countries will experience gold outflows, reducing their money supplies (less gold, less money in circulation) and, thus, their price levels. In final equilibrium, price levels in all countries will be slightly lower than they were before, due to the increase in the worldwide supply of other goods and services relative to the supply of gold. Exchange rates will remain fixed.

Thus, the operation of the price-specie-flow mechanism tended to keep prices in line for those countries that were on the gold standard. As long as the world was on a gold standard, all adjustments were automatic, and although there were many undesirable things that might have happened under a gold standard, enduring inflation was not one of them.

How the Classical Gold Standard Worked in Practice: 1821–1914

In 1821, following the Napoleonic Wars and their associated inflation, England returned to the gold standard. From 1821 to 1880, more and more countries joined the gold standard. By 1880, the majority of the nations of the world were on some form of gold standard. There was some discretionary management, to be sure, because of the costs of maintaining a pure gold standard. For example, strict adherence to a gold standard entailed periodic bouts of inflation and deflation—felt by most nations to impose too high a price. Moreover, gold was expensive to locate, mine, and mint. Hence, most nations evolved substitutes for pure commodity money and attempted to shield domestic economic activity from external disturbances.

Substitutes for gold included both government-issued paper money and privately produced fiduciary money (bank notes and bank deposits). As long as governments backed their notes with a fixed amount of gold, and commercial banks maintained a fixed ratio of gold to their liabilities, a gold standard could be sustained.

Many nations frequently followed policies of sterilizing gold flows—attempting to neutralize the effects of gold flows on the domestic money supply by open-market purchases or sales of domestic securities. Moreover, much of the balance-of-payments adjustment mechanism in the pre–World War I period did not require actual gold flows. Instead, the adjustment consisted primarily of transfers of sterling and other currency balances in the London, Paris, and New York money markets. The result was a managed gold standard, not the pure gold standard discussed earlier.

Nonetheless, the period from 1880 to 1914, during which the classical gold standard prevailed in its most pristine form, was a remarkable period in world economic history. The period was characterized by a rapid expansion of virtually free international trade, stable exchange rates and prices, a free flow of labor and capital across political borders, rapid economic growth, and, in general, world peace. Advocates of the gold standard harken back to this period.

Opponents of a rigid gold standard, in contrast, point to some less-than-idyllic economic conditions during this period: a major depression during the 1890s, a severe economic contraction in 1907, and repeated recessions. Whether these sharp ups and downs could have been prevented under a fiat money standard cannot be known.

The Gold Exchange Standard: 1925–1931

The gold standard broke down during World War I and was briefly reinstated from 1925–1931 as the Gold Exchange Standard. Under this standard, the United States and England could hold only gold reserves, but other nations could hold both gold and dollars or pounds as reserves. In 1931, England departed from gold in the face of massive gold and capital flows, owing to an unrealistic exchange rate, and the Gold Exchange Standard was finished.

Following the devaluation of sterling, 25 other nations devalued their currencies to maintain trade competitiveness. The result was a "beggar-thy-neighbor" trade war in which nations cheapened their currencies in order to increase their exports at others' expense and reduce imports. Many economists and policymakers believed that the protectionist exchange rate and trade policy fueled the global depression. In order to avoid such destructive economic policies in the future, the Allied nations agreed to a new postwar monetary system at a conference held in Bretton Woods, New Hampshire, in 1944. The conference also created two new institutions—the International Monetary Fund (IMF) and the International Bank for Reconstruction and Development (World Bank)—to implement the new system.

The Bretton Woods System: 1946–1971

Under the *Bretton Woods Agreement,* implemented in 1946, each government pledged to maintain a fixed, or pegged, exchange rate for its currency vis-à-vis the dollar or gold. Since one ounce of gold was set equal to $35, fixing a currency's gold price was equivalent to setting its exchange rate relative to the dollar. For example, the Deutsche mark was set equal to 1/140 of an ounce of gold, meaning it was worth $0.25 ($35/140). The exchange rate was allowed to fluctuate only within 1% of its stated par value (usually less in practice).

The fixed exchange rates were maintained by official intervention in the foreign exchange markets. The intervention took the form of purchases and sales of dollars by foreign central banks against their own currencies whenever the supply and demand conditions in the market caused rates to deviate from the agreed-upon par values. The IMF stood ready to provide the necessary foreign exchange to member nations defending their currencies against pressure resulting from temporary factors. Any dollars acquired by the monetary authorities in the process of such intervention could then be exchanged for gold at the U.S. Treasury, at a fixed price of $35 per ounce.

These technical aspects of the system had important practical implications for all trading nations participating in it. In principle, the stability of exchange rates removed a great deal of uncertainty from international trade and investment transactions, thus promoting their growth for the benefit of all the participants. Also, the functioning of the system imposed a degree of discipline on the participating nations' economic policies.

For example, a country that followed policies leading to a higher rate of inflation than that experienced by its trading partners would experience a balance-of-payments deficit as its goods became more expensive, reducing its exports and increasing its imports. The necessary consequences of the deficit would be an increase in the supply of the deficit country's currency on the foreign exchange markets. The excess supply would depress the exchange value of that country's currency, forcing its authorities to intervene. The country would be obligated to "buy" with its reserves the excess supply of its own currency, effectively reducing the domestic money supply. Moreover, as the country's reserves were gradually depleted through intervention, the authorities would be forced, sooner or later, to change economic policies in order to eliminate the source of the reserve-draining deficit. The reduction in the money supply and the adoption of restrictive policies would reduce the country's inflation, thus bringing it in line with the rest of the world.

Changes in these fixed rates were permitted only in the case of fundamental disequilibrium. In over 25 years of operation, however, fundamental disequilibrium was never adequately defined. This ambiguity proved useful to governments because they perceived large political costs to any exchange rate changes. Most governments were also unwilling to coordinate their monetary policies, even though this coordination was necessary to maintain existing currency values.

The reluctance of governments to adjust currency values or to make the necessary economic adjustments to ratify the current values of their currencies led to periodic foreign exchange crises. Dramatic battles between the central banks and the foreign exchange markets ensued. Those battles were invariably won by the markets. However, because devaluation or revaluation was used only as a last resort, exchange rate changes were infrequent and large.

In fact, Bretton Woods was a fixed exchange rate system in name only. Of 21 major industrial countries, only the United States and Japan had no change in par value during the period 1946–1971. Of the 21 countries, 12 devalued their currencies more than 30% against the dollar, four had revaluations, and four were floating their currencies by mid-1971 when the system collapsed.

The maintenance of price stability under the Bretton Woods system was largely the responsibility of the United States. As long as the system remained intact, all currencies were subject to the same rate of inflation as the U.S. dollar. If the United States kept the price of gold at $35 an ounce, it would stabilize prices around the world.

Unfortunately, the Federal Reserve did not arrange monetary policy to keep gold at $35. The U.S. government avoided this discipline by using every means of keeping gold at $35 except the one that counted—restricting the issuance of dollars. The United States issued nonmarketable Treasury bonds as a substitute for redemption of foreign gold holdings; prohibited U.S. citizens from holding gold abroad as well as at home; abolished the gold cover for U.S. dollars; eliminated private redemption of gold; restricted capital outflows by MNCs; and pressured other governments not to convert dollars for gold. The deathblow for the system came on August 15, 1971, when President Nixon, convinced that the "run" on the dollar was reaching alarming proportions, abruptly ordered U.S. authorities to terminate convertibility even for central banks. At the same time, he devalued the dollar to deal with America's emerging trade deficit.

The fixed exchange rate system collapsed along with the dissolution of the gold standard. There are two related reasons for the collapse of the Bretton Woods system. First, inflation reared its ugly head in the United States. In the mid-1960s, the Johnson administration financed the escalating war in Vietnam and its equally expensive Great Society programs by, in effect, printing money instead of raising taxes. As a result, it was difficult for the United States to maintain the price of gold at $35 an ounce without resorting to the various dilatory tactics referred to above.

Second, the fixed exchange rate system collapsed because some countries—primarily West Germany, Japan, and Switzerland—refused to accept the inflation that a fixed exchange rate with the dollar would have imposed on them. Thus, the dollar depreciated sharply relative to the currencies of these three countries.

The Post–Bretton Woods System: 1971 to the Present

In December 1971, under the Smithsonian Agreement, the dollar was devalued to 1/38 of an ounce of gold, and other currencies were revalued by agreed-on amounts vis-à-vis the dollar. After months of such last-ditch efforts to set new fixed rates, the world officially turned to floating exchange rates in 1973.

OPEC and the Oil Crisis of 1973–1974.   October 1973 marked the beginning of successful efforts by OPEC to raise the price of oil. By 1974, oil prices had quadrupled. Nations responded in various ways to the vast shift of resources to the oil-exporting countries. Some nations, such as the United States, tried to offset the effect of higher energy bills by boosting spending, pursuing expansionary monetary policies, and controlling the price of oil. The result was high inflation, economic dislocation, and a misallocation of resources, without bringing about the real economic growth that was desired. Other nations, such as Japan, allowed the price of oil to rise to its market level and followed more prudent monetary policies.

The first group of nations experienced balance-of-payments deficits (because their governments kept intervening in the foreign exchange market to maintain overvalued currencies); the second group of nations, along with the OPEC nations, wound up with balance-of-payments surpluses. These surpluses were recycled to debtor nations, setting the stage for the international debt crisis of the 1980s.

U.S. Dollar Crisis of 1977–1978.   During 1977–1978, the value of the dollar plummeted, and U.S. balance-of-payments difficulties were exacerbated as the Carter administration pursued an expansionary monetary policy that was significantly out of line with other strong currencies. A run on the dollar was provoked, in part, by Treasury Secretary Michael Blumenthal's 1977 announcement that the dollar was overvalued. The turnaround in the dollar's fortunes can be dated to October 6, 1979, when the Fed announced a major change in its conduct of monetary policy. From here on, in order to curb inflation and inflationary expectations, it would focus its efforts on stabilizing the money supply, even if that meant more volatile interest rates. Prior to this date, the Fed had attempted to stabilize interest rates, indirectly causing the money supply to be highly variable.

The Rising Dollar: 1980–1985.   This shift had its desired effect on both the inflation rate and the value of the U.S. dollar. During President Reagan's first term in office (1981–1984), inflation plummeted and the dollar rebounded extraordinarily. This rebound has been attributed to vigorous economic expansion in the United States and to high real interest rates (due largely to strong economic growth) that combined to attract capital from around the world.

The Sinking Dollar: 1985–1987.   The dollar peaked in March 1985 and then began a long downhill slide. The slide is largely attributable to changes in government policy and relative national economic performances. Most important was the slowdown in U.S. economic growth relative to growth in the rest of the world. However, this factor was compounded by the effects of foreign exchange market intervention and confusing signals concerning U.S. monetary and fiscal policies.

By September 1985, the dollar had fallen about 15% from its March high. But this decline was considered inadequate to dent the growing U.S. trade deficit. In late September of 1985, the Group of Five, or *G–5 nations* (the United States, France, Japan, Great Britain, and West Germany), met at the Plaza Hotel in New York City at the initiative of U.S. Treasury Secretary James Baker. His purpose was to defuse mounting protectionist pressures associated with the U.S. trade deficit. The outcome was the *Plaza Agreement,* a coordinated program designed to force down the dollar against other major currencies and thereby improve American competitiveness.

The policy to bring down the value of the dollar worked too well. The dollar slid so fast during 1986 that the central banks of Japan, Germany, and Britain reversed their policies and began buying dollars to stem the dollar's decline.

By early 1987, Baker and his counterparts abroad had had enough. Meeting in Paris in February, the United States, Japan, West Germany, France, Britain, Canada, and Italy—also known as the Group of Seven or *G–7 nations*—agreed to an ambitious plan to slow the dollar's fall. The *Louvre Accord,* named for the Paris landmark where it was negotiated, called for the G–7 nations to support the falling dollar by pegging exchange rates within a narrow, undisclosed range, while they also moved to bring their economic policies into line.

The United States promised to cut its bulging budget deficit; the Germans and Japanese agreed to stimulate their economies to offset slowing growth in the United States. However, as always, it proved much easier to talk about coordinating policy than to change it. The United States failed to cut its deficit. At the same time, inflation-sensitive governments in Bonn and Tokyo resisted U.S. pressure for major tax cuts, increases in money growth rates, or spending increases to stimulate their economies. They chose instead to limit their actions to token measures. The hoped-for economic cooperation faded, and the dollar continued to fall (see Exhibit 5.8).

During the week of October 12, 1987, tensions reached a peak as Baker criticized West Germany for tightening credit and thus running counter to the Louvre provisions that called on Bonn to stimulate growth. Markets, already nervous, headed downward after a White House news briefing on October 15 suggested the United States might allow a further fall in the dollar unless German monetary policy eased. The decline became a free fall on Black Monday (October 19) after Baker seemed to reaffirm that position on Sunday (October 18).

Simply put, the U.S. threat to drive the dollar further down terrified the markets. Many felt that the Louvre Accord was dead and that the United States had abruptly changed to a policy of letting the dollar fall. What the markets almost surely feared was the possibility

■ **EXHIBIT 5.8**   Effects of Government Actions and Statements on the Value of 1987 Dollar

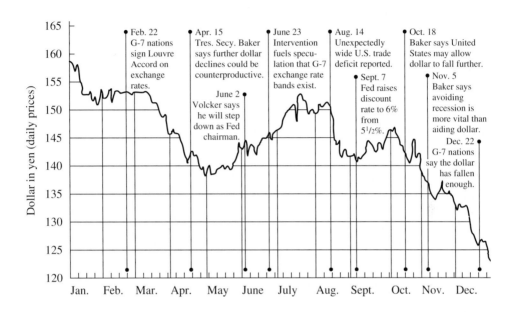

that foreign investors would flee dollar assets, causing a collapse of the dollar and, inevitably, a burst of inflation.

The already fractured Louvre Accord broke fast after the stock market crashed. Alan Greenspan, the chairman of the Federal Reserve, reacted as a central banker must in a financial panic: He flooded the markets with money. This move helped quell the panic, but it also put extreme pressure on the dollar. Less than two weeks later, Karl Otto Poehl, the president of the Bundesbank, pronounced rate pegging dead. Although Baker said the United States remained committed to the Louvre Accord, it appeared that hardly anyone else was; when the world's central banks let the dollar go in November, it sank fast.

The failure of the Louvre Accord provides further proof that currency manipulation is fruitless in a world of sovereign states. Intervening in currency markets—even strong statements of an intention to intervene—can have a powerful effect on exchange rates for a while. The dollar, for instance, dropped 5% the day after the Plaza Agreement was announced. But intervention has a lasting effect only if it is accompanied by equally lasting changes in monetary and fiscal policies. Short-term intervention is costly and merely delays the inevitable triumph of the market's judgment.

Recent History: 1988–1991.   Beginning in early 1988, the U.S. dollar rallied somewhat and then maintained its strength against most currencies through 1989. It fell sharply again in 1990 but recovered in early 1991, continuing its roller coaster ride of the past decade. Its future course is unpredictable given the absence of an anchor for its value.

■ ───

ILLUSTRATION

Iraq Invades Kuwait. Following the Iraqi invasion of Kuwait in August 1990, investors initially sought refuge in the dollar and it surged in value. Then they had second thoughts, switched out of dollars, and the dollar slumped. The reversal reflected investor nervousness about the possibility that the United States would repeat its past mistakes. In particular, the reaction of many Americans to the rise in the price of oil following the invasion evoked memories of the 1970s. Large oil companies—attacked unmercifully by politicians and the media throughout the 1970s—were once again in the spotlight, accused of profiteering on the Persian Gulf crisis and threatened with new price controls. At the same time, U.S. Treasury policymakers began pushing again for a falling dollar to improve American trade competitiveness. In other words, the dollar's fall reflected lack of confidence in the ability of the U.S. political system to deal with economic crises and its willingness to protect the integrity of the dollar. The subsequent war in the Persian Gulf and its successful conclusion, brought a reminder of American strength and renewed prospects for the U.S. economy—and a stronger dollar. The dollar's strength was reinforced by doubts about how well German economic integration was working.

─── ■

Assessment of the Floating-Rate System

At the time floating rates were adopted in 1973, proponents said that the new system would reduce economic volatility and facilitate free trade. In particular, floating exchange rates would offset international differences in inflation rates so that trade, wages, employment, and output would not have to adjust. High-inflation countries would see their currencies depreciate, allowing their firms to stay competitive without having to cut wages or employment. At the same time, currency appreciation would not place firms in low-inflation countries at a competitive disadvantage. Real exchange rates would stabilize, even if permitted to float in principle, since the underlying conditions affecting trade and the relative productivity of capital would change only gradually. And if countries would coordinate their monetary policies to achieve a convergence of inflation rates, then nominal exchange rates would also stabilize.

The experience to date, however, is disappointing. The dollar's ups and downs have had little to do with actual inflation, and everything to do with expectations of future government policies and economic conditions. Put another way, real exchange rate volatility has increased, not decreased, since floating began. Partly, this instability reflects shocks to the world economy, but these shocks were not greater during the 1980s than they were in earlier periods. Instead, uncertainty over future government policies has increased.

Given this evidence, a number of economists and others have called for a return to fixed exchange rates. To the extent that fixed exchange rates more tightly constrain the types of monetary and other policies governments can pursue, this should make expectations less volatile and hence reduce fluctuations in the real exchange rate.

Although history offers no convincing model for a system that will lead to long-term exchange rate stability, it does point to two basic requirements. First, the system must be credible. If the market expects an exchange rate to be changed, the battle to keep it fixed is already lost. Second, the system must have price stability built into its very core. Without price stability the system will not be credible. Recall that under a fixed-rate system, each member must accept the group's inflation rate as its own. Only a zero rate of inflation will be mutually acceptable. If the inflation rate is much above zero, prudent governments will defect from the system.

■ 5.3 ■
THE EUROPEAN MONETARY SYSTEM

A review of the European Monetary System provides valuable insights into the operation of a target-zone system and illustrates the problems that such mechanisms are likely to encounter. Perhaps the most important lesson that the EMS illustrates is that the exchange rate stability afforded by any target-zone arrangement requires a coordination of economic policy objectives and practices. Nations should achieve convergence of those economic variables that directly affect exchange rates—variables such as fiscal deficits, monetary growth rates, and real economic growth differentials.

Although the system has helped keep its member currencies in a remarkably narrow zone of stability during the past few years, it has had a history of ups and downs. In its early years, the exchange-rate mechanism offered little anti-inflationary discipline, with Italy and France undergoing regular devaluations to offset higher inflation than in West Germany. By January 1987, the values of the EMS currencies had been realigned 12 times despite heavy central bank intervention. Relative to their positions in March 1979, the Deutsche mark and the Dutch guilder soared, while the French franc and the Italian lira nose-dived. For example, between 1979 and 1988, the franc devalued relative to the DM by over 50%.

The reason for the past failure of the European Monetary System to provide the currency stability it promised is straightforward: Germany's economic policymakers, responding to an electorate hypersensitive to inflation, have put a premium on price stability; in contrast, the French have generally pursued a more expansive monetary policy in response to high domestic unemployment. Moreover, neither country has been willing to permit exchange rate considerations to override political priorities.

Consider, for example, the situation in early 1983. Both Germany and France were facing a general election in early March, and each government was reluctant to undertake economic measures that could adversely affect the outcome. The German government was reluctant to revalue the Deutsche mark for fear that a change would reduce the country's ability to export and thus increase domestic unemployment. In France, the Socialist government of Francois Mitterrand was reluctant to devalue the franc for fear that such a step (the third since it took office in May 1981) would deal a blow to the national "prestige," and would amount to an admission of failure of its domestic economic policies. Consequently, even though the pressures in the foreign exchange markets mounted, each government stood by its increasingly misaligned currency exchange rates.

The politically motivated intransigence proved costly to the French treasury. In early March, while the political debates raged on, the exchange markets were turned into "sure bet" gambling casinos. The French government is reported to have spent over $5 billion in two weeks to defend its overvalued currency, mostly to the benefit of the speculators. Finally, by mid-March and with the elections behind them, the two governments turned their attention to the exchange rates. The outcome was a 2.5% devaluation of the French franc and a 5.5% revaluation of the Deutsche mark.

The experience of the EMS also demonstrates once again that foreign exchange market intervention not supported by a change in a nation's monetary policy has only a limited influence on exchange rates. The heavy intervention preceding the January 12, 1987, EMS realignment was generally not accompanied by changes in national monetary policies. Germany, in particular, made only small adjustments to monetary policy in response to the exchange rate pressures. Consequently, the intervention failed to contain speculation, and a realignment became unavoidable.

The bottom line is that the maintenance of target zones narrow enough to eliminate the uncertainty associated with exchange rate volatility requires a close degree of macroeconomic coordination. Ironically, if nations maintain a mutually consistent and stable set of monetary, fiscal, and trade policies, a system of rigid target zones becomes unnecessary. Coordination and cooperation by themselves could maintain exchange rate stability. The principal argument, therefore, for a target-zone arrangement is that it could provide the mechanism to induce such coordination and cooperation.

Unfortunately, the experience to date is mixed. Bretton Woods, for example, broke down when politics overrode economics; instead of changing policies to stay with the system, the major countries of the world simply dropped the system. Similarly, the Louvre Accord has produced more bickering than cooperation.

On the other hand, the EMS has achieved significant success lately. By improving monetary policy coordination among its member states in recent years, the EMS has succeeded in narrowing inflation differentials in Europe. In 1980 the gap between the highest inflation rate (Italy's 21.2%) and the lowest (West Germany's 5.5%) was 16 percentage points. By 1990 the gap had narrowed to less than four percentage points. The narrowing of inflation rates, in turn, has reduced exchange rate volatility. Indeed, since January 1987 currencies have remained fixed. Moreover, the importance of Germany to the European economy and the Bundesbank's unwillingness to compromise its monetary policy mean that other members of the EMS have been forced to adjust their monetary policies to more closely mimic Germany's low-inflation policy. As a result, inflation rates have tended to converge toward Germany's lower rate. For example, in 1990 the Netherlands, France, Belgium, Denmark, and Ireland all had inflation rates within one percentage point of Germany's (see Exhibit 5.9). In effect, the EMS has moved to a Deutsche-mark standard. Conversely, the gap between British and German inflation widened over time. In recognition of the benefits to be derived from a strong and stable monetary system, Prime Minister Thatcher finally relented on "monetary sovereignty" in late 1990 and entered Britain in the EMS.

Monetary Union

The current debate in the European Community is whether to move towards *monetary union*. Under this scenario, the EC nations would establish a single central bank with the sole power to issue a single European currency. Business would clearly benefit from lower cross-border currency conversion costs. For example, Philips, the giant Dutch electronics

■ **EXHIBIT 5.9**   The European Monetary System Forces Convergence Toward Germany's Inflation Rate

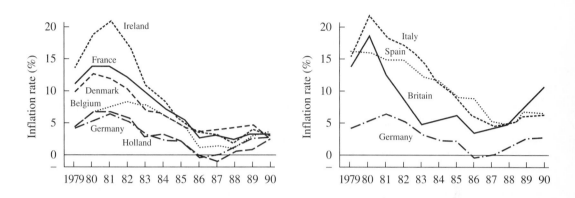

company, estimates that a single European currency would save it $300 million a year in currency transaction costs.

More importantly, monetary union—such as exists among the 50 states of the United States, where the exchange rate between states is immutably set at 1—would provide the ultimate in coordination of monetary policy. Inflation rates under monetary union would converge, but not in the same way as in the current system. The common inflation rate would be decided by the monetary policy of the European central bank. It would tend to reflect the average preferences of the people running the bank, rather than giving automatic weight to the most anti-inflationary nation as in the current system. Thus, in order for the European Monetary Union (EMU) to be an improvement over the current state of affairs, the new European central bank must be as averse to inflation as is the central bank Europe in effect already has—the Bundesbank.

To ensure the EMU's inflation-fighting success, the new central bankers would have to be granted independence along with a statutory duty to devote monetary policy to keeping the price level stable. One way to protect the central bank's independence is to appoint the governing body, as in the United States and Germany, on long-term contracts that cut across national electoral cycles. Only then would a European central bank be able to do what William McChesney Martin, a former Fed chairman, said a sound central bank must always do: "take away the punch-bowl just when the party gets going."

■ ──

ILLUSTRATION

German Monetary Union. As a first step toward economic reunification, East and West Germany formed a monetary union. On July 2, 1990, the East German mark or Ostmark was replaced by the Deutsche mark as the single German currency. It was agreed that East Germans would trade their Ostmarks to the West German Bundesbank for Deutsche marks at an exchange rate fixed in advance. In addition, the East German central bank had to cede its power to issue currency or create bank balances; otherwise, the Bundesbank would lose control over the money supply. At the same time, restrictions on movements of capital across the border were eliminated, making it possible for East Germans to hold bank accounts in West Germany and for West Germans to invest freely in East Germany. All transactions would be denominated in DM.

Most economists believed that a key to smooth transition toward German monetary union—and ultimately economic integration—was to get the exchange rate between Deutsche marks and Ostmarks right. Valuing the DM too high would destroy the worth of East German savings. But overvaluing the Ostmark would keep East German wages and goods from being competitive. Businesses in East Germany would suffer, leading to a further exodus of workers to West Germany.

Most economists felt that the best approach would be to err on the side of undervaluation, making East German industry more competitive and attracting investors from West Germany and other countries. Ultimately though Chancellor Helmut Kohl decided on political grounds to convert East German savings, debts, wages, and prices from Ostmarks into DM at vastly overvalued rates ranging between one and two Ostmarks to one Deutsche mark. The result will be an inflationary expansion in the DM money supply, unless the German government engages in open market operations to sop up many of the new DM. ∎

Optimum Currency Area

Most discussion of European monetary union has highlighted its benefits, such as eliminating currency uncertainty and lowering the costs of doing business. The potential costs of currency integration have been overlooked. In particular, it may sometimes pay to be able to change the value of one currency relative to another. Suppose, for example, that the worldwide demand for French goods falls sharply. To cope with such a drop in demand, France must make its goods less expensive and attract new industries to replace its shrinking old ones. The quickest way to do this is to reduce French wages, thereby making its workers more competitive. But this reduction is unlikely to be accomplished quickly. Over time, of course, high unemployment might persuade French workers to accept lower pay. But in the interim, the social and economic costs of reducing wages by, say, 10% will be high. In contrast, a 10% depreciation of the franc would achieve the same thing quickly and relatively painlessly.

Conversely, a worldwide surge in demand for French goods could give rise to French inflation—unless France allowed the franc to appreciate. In other words, currency changes can substitute for periodic bouts of inflation and deflation caused by various economic shocks. Once France has entered the monetary union, it no longer has the option of changing its exchange rate to cope with these shocks.

Taking this logic to its extreme would imply that not only should each nation have its own currency, but so should each region within a nation. Why not a Southern California dollar, or indeed a Los Angeles dollar? The answer is that having separate currencies brings costs as well as benefits.

The more currencies there are, the higher the costs of doing business and the more currency risk there is. Both factors impair the functions of money as a medium of exchange and a store of value. So maintaining more currencies acts as a barrier to international trade and investment, even as it reduces vulnerability to economic shocks.

According to the theory of the *optimum currency area,* this trade-off becomes less and less favorable as the size of the economic unit shrinks. So how large is the optimum currency area? No one knows. But some economists argue that Europe might be better off with four or five regional currencies than with only one.[1] Similarly, some have argued that the United States too might do better with several regional currencies to cushion shocks such as afflicted the Midwest and the Southwest during the 1980s, and the Northeast in the 1990s. Nonetheless, the experience with floating exchange rates since the early 1970s will likely give pause to anyone seriously thinking of pushing that idea further. That experience suggests that exchange rate changes can add to economic volatility, as well as absorb it.

■ 5.4 ■
SUMMARY AND CONCLUSIONS

This chapter studied the process of exchange rate determination under four different market mechanisms—free float, managed float, target-zone system, and fixed-rate system—as well as the current hybrid system. In the latter three systems, governments intervene in the currency markets in various ways to affect the exchange rate.

Regardless of the form of intervention, however, fixed rates do not remain fixed for long. Neither do floating rates. The basic reason that exchange rates don't stay fixed for long in either a fixed- or floating-rate system is that governments subordinate exchange rate considerations to domestic political considerations.

We saw that the gold standard is a specific type of fixed exchange rate system, one that required participating countries to maintain the value of their currencies in terms of gold. Calls for a new gold standard remind us of the fundamental lack of trust in fiat money due to the historical unwillingness of the monetary authorities to desist from tampering with the money supply.

Finally, we conclude that intervention to maintain a disequilibrium rate is generally ineffective or injurious when pursued over lengthy periods of time. Seldom have policymakers been able to outsmart for any extended period the collective judgment of buyers and sellers. The current volatile market environment, a consequence of unstable U.S. and world financial conditions, cannot be arbitrarily directed by government officials for long.

Examining U.S. experience since the abandonment of fixed rates, we find that free-market forces did correctly reflect economic realities thereafter. The dollar's value dropped sharply between 1973 and 1980 when the United States experienced high inflation and weakened economic conditions. Beginning in 1981, the dollar's value rose when American policies dramatically changed under the leadership of the Federal Reserve and a new president, but fell when foreign economies strengthened relative to the U.S. economy. Nonetheless, the resulting shifts in U.S. cost competitiveness have led many to question the current international monetary system.

The principal alternative to the current system of floating currencies with its economic volatility is a fixed exchange rate system. History offers no entirely convincing model for

---

[1]See, for example, Geoffrey M.B. Tootell, "Central Bank Flexibility and the Drawbacks to Currency Unification," *New England Economic Review,* May/June 1990, pp. 3–18; and Paul Krugman, "A Europe-Wide Currency Makes No Economic Sense," *Los Angeles Times,* August 5, 1990, p. D2.

how such a system should be constructed, but it does point to two requirements. To succeed in reducing economic volatility, a system of fixed exchange rates must be credible, and it must have price stability built into its very fabric. Otherwise, the market's expectations of exchange rate changes combined with an unsatisfactory rate of inflation will lead to periodic battles among central banks and between central banks and the financial markets.

■ QUESTIONS ■

1. Have exchange rate movements under the current system of managed floating been excessive? Explain.

2. Why has speculation failed to smooth exchange rate movements?

3. Is a floating-rate system more inflationary than a fixed-rate system? Explain.

4. Find a recent example of a nation's foreign exchange market intervention and note what the government's justification was. Does this justification make economic sense?

5. Gold has been called "the ultimate burglar alarm." Explain what this expression means.

6. Comment on the following statement: "A system of floating exchange rate fails when governments ignore the verdict of the exchange markets on their policies and resort to direct controls over trade and capital flows."

7. Suppose nations attempt to pursue independent monetary and fiscal policies. How will exchange rates behave?

8. Will coordination of economic policies make exchange rates more or less stable? Explain.

9. The experiences of fixed exchange rate systems and target-zone arrangements have not been entirely satisfactory.

   a. What lessons can economists draw from the breakdown of the Bretton Woods system?

   b. What lessons can economists draw from the exchange rate experiences of the European Monetary System?

10. Despite official parity between the Deutsche mark and the Ostmark, the black market rate in early 1990 was about ten Ostmarks for one Deutsche mark. What problems might setting the exchange rate at one Ostmark for each DM create for Germany?

11. Historically, Spain has had high inflation and has seen its peseta continuously depreciate. In 1989, though, Spain joined the EMS and pegged the peseta to the DM. According to a Spanish banker, EMS membership means that "the government has less capability to manage the currency but, on the other hand, the people are more trusting of the currency for that reason."

   a. What underlies the peseta's historical weakness?

   b. Comment on the banker's statement.

   c. What are the likely consequences of EMS membership on the Spanish public's willingness to save and invest?

12. When Britain announced its entry into the exchange-rate mechanism of the EMS on October 5, 1990, the price of British gilts (long-term government bonds) soared and sterling rose in value.

   a. What might account for these price jumps?

   b. Sterling entered the ERM at a central rate against the DM of DM 2.95, and it is allowed to move within a band of plus and minus 6% of this rate. What are sterling's upper and lower rates against the DM?

13. In discussing European Monetary Union, a recent government report stressed a need to make the central bank accountable to the "democratic process." What are the likely consequences for price stability and exchange rate stability in the EMS if the "Eurofed" becomes accountable to the "democratic process?"

■ BIBLIOGRAPHY ■

Bordo, Michael David. "The Classical Gold Standard: Some Lessons for Today." *Federal Reserve Bank of St. Louis Review,* May 1981, pp. 2–17.

Coombs, Charles A. *The Arena of International Finance.* New York: John Wiley & Sons, 1976.

Friedman, Milton, and Robert V. Roosa. "Free Versus Fixed Exchange Rates: A Debate." *Journal of Portfolio Management,* Spring 1977, pp. 68–73.

Mundell, Robert A. "A Theory of Optimum Currency Areas." *American Economic Review,* September 1961, pp. 657–665.

6

The Balance of Payments and International Economic Linkages

I had a trade deficit in 1986 because I took a vacation in France. I didn't worry about it; I enjoyed it.

—Herbert Stein—
Chairman of the Council
of Economic Advisors under
Presidents Nixon and Ford

We have almost a crisis in trade and this is the year Congress will try to turn it around with trade legislation.

—Lloyd Bentsen—
U.S. Senator from Texas

Despite all the cries for protectionism to cure the trade deficit, protectionism will not lower the trade deficit.

—Phil Gramm—
U.S. Senator from Texas

■ A key theme of this book is that companies today operate within a global marketplace, and they can ignore this fact only at their peril. In line with this theme, the purpose of this chapter is to present the financial and real linkages between the domestic and world economies and examine how these linkages affect business viability. The chapter identifies the basic forces underlying the flows of goods, services, and capital between countries and relates these flows to key political, economic, and cultural factors.

Politicians and the business press realize the importance of these trade and capital flows. They pay attention to the balance of payments, on which these flows are recorded, and to the massive and continuing U.S. trade deficits. As we saw in Chapter 5, government foreign exchange policies are often geared toward dealing with balance-of-payments problems. But as the three quotes above indicate, many people disagree on the nature of the trade deficit problem and its solution. In the process of studying the balance of payments, this chapter will sort out some of these issues.

■ 6.1 ■
BALANCE-OF-PAYMENTS CATEGORIES

The *balance of payments* is an accounting statement that summarizes all the economic transactions between residents of the home country and residents of all other countries. Balance-of-payments statistics are published quarterly in the United States by the Commerce Department and include such transactions as trade in goods and services, transfer payments, loans, and short- and long-term investments. The statistics are followed closely by bankers and business people, economists, and foreign exchange traders; the publication affects the value of the home currency if these figures are more, or less, favorable than anticipated.

Currency inflows are recorded as *credits,* and outflows are recorded as *debits.* Credits show up with a plus sign, and debits have a minus sign. There are three major balance-of-payments categories:

- *Current account,* which records flows of goods, services, and transfers
- *Capital account,* which shows public and private investment and lending activities
- *Official reserves account,* which measures changes in holdings of gold and foreign currencies—*reserve assets*—by official monetary institutions

Exports of goods and services are credits; imports of goods and services are debits. Interest and dividends are treated as services because they represent payment for the use of capital. Capital inflows appear as credits since the nation is selling (exporting) to foreigners valuable assets—buildings, land, stock, bonds, and other financial claims—and receiving cash in return. Capital outflows show up as debits because they represent purchases (imports) of valuable foreign assets. The increase in a nation's official reserves also shows up as a debit item because the purchase of gold and other reserve assets is equivalent to importing these assets.

The balance-of-payments statement is based on double-entry bookkeeping; every economic transaction recorded as a credit brings about an equal and offsetting debit entry, and vice versa. For example, if a foreigner sells a painting to a U.S. resident, a debit is recorded to indicate an increase in purchases made by the United States (the painting); a credit is recorded to reflect an increase in liabilities to the foreigner (payment for the painting).

Because double-entry bookkeeping ensures that debits equal credits, the sum of all transactions is zero. That is, the sum of the balance on the current account, capital account, and official reserves account must equal zero.

These features of balance-of-payments accounting are illustrated in Exhibit 6.1, which shows the U.S. balance of payments for 1990, and in Exhibit 6.2, which gives examples of entries in the U.S. balance-of-payments accounts.

Current Account

The balance on current account reflects the net flow of goods, services, and unilateral transfers (gifts). It includes exports and imports of merchandise (trade balance), military transactions, and service transactions (invisibles). The service account includes investment income (interest and dividends), tourism, financial charges (banking and insurance), and transportation expenses (shipping and air travel). *Unilateral transfers* include pensions, remittances, and other transfers for which no specific services are rendered. In 1990, for example, the U.S. balance of trade registered a deficit of $111.3 billion, while the overall current-account deficit was $92.9 billion, a difference of $18.4 billion.

■ **EXHIBIT 6.1**   The U.S. Balance of Payments for 1990 (U.S. $ Billions)

Credits		**Debits**	
a: Exports of civilian goods	$385.6	*b:* Imports of civilian goods	$491.1
c: Military sales abroad	9.7	*d:* Military purchases abroad	15.1
Trade balance	$= a + c - (b + d)$		
	$=$ Deficit of 111.3		
e: Exports of services (investment income and fees earned, foreign tourism in United States, etc.)	246.5	*f:* Imports of services (investment income paid out, U.S. tourism abroad, etc.)	212.3
		g: Net unilateral transfers (gifts)	15.8
Current-account balance	$= a + c + e - (b + d + f + g)$		
	$=$ Deficit of 92.9		
h: Foreign private investment in United States	45.3	*i:* U.S. private investment overseas	29.8
j: Foreign official lending in United States	14.6	*k:* U.S. government lending overseas	2.5
Capital-account balance	$= h + j - (i + k)$		
	$=$ Surplus of 27.6		
		l: Net increase in U.S. official reserves	1.5
Official reserves balance	$=$ Deficit of 1.5		
m: Statistical discrepancy	66.8		

SOURCE: Data from *Survey of Current Business*, U.S. Department of Commerce, December 1990.

■ **EXHIBIT 6.2**   Examples of Entries in the U.S. Balance-of-Payments Accounts

Credits	Debits
Current Account	
a: Sales of wheat to Great Britain; sales of computers to West Germany	*b:* Purchases of oil from Saudi Arabia; purchases of Japanese automobiles
c: Sales of Phantom jets to Canada	*d:* Payments to Filipino workers at U.S. bases in the Philippines
e: Interest earnings on loans to Argentina; profits on U.S.-owned auto plants abroad; licensing fees earned by Lotus 1-2-3; spending by Japanese tourists at Disneyland	*f:* Profits on sales by Nestle's U.S. affiliate; hotel bills of U.S. tourists in Paris
	g: Remittances by Mexican-Americans to relatives in Mexico; Social Security payments to Americans living in Italy; economic aid to Pakistan
Capital Account	
h: Purchases by the Japanese of U.S. real estate; increases in Arab bank deposits in New York banks; purchases by the French of IBM stock; investment in plant expansion in Ohio by Honda	*i:* New investment in a German chemical plant by Du Pont; increases in U.S. bank loans to Mexico; deposits in Swiss banks by Americans; purchases of Japanese stocks and bonds by Americans
j: Purchases of U.S. Treasury bonds by Bank of Japan; increases in holdings of New York bank deposits by Saudi Arabian government	*k:* Deposits of funds by the U.S. Treasury in British banks; purchases of Swiss-franc bonds by the Federal Reserve
Official Reserve Account	
	l: Purchases of gold by the U.S. Treasury; increases in holdings of Japanese yen by the Federal Reserve

The U.S. current-account deficit at $92.9 billion in 1990 is the world's largest, but as a percent of GNP the deficit has fallen to 1.8% in 1990—half its peak in 1987. As seen in Exhibit 6.3, nine industrial countries had larger deficits than the United States as a percent of GNP in 1990.

Capital Account

Capital-account transactions affect a nation's wealth and net creditor position. These transactions are classified as either portfolio, direct, or short-term investments. *Portfolio investments* are purchases of financial assets with a maturity greater than one year, while *short-term investments* involve securities with a maturity of less than one year. *Direct investments* are those where management control is exerted. Government borrowing and lending is included in the balance on capital account. As shown in Exhibit 6.1, the U.S. balance on capital account in 1990 was a surplus of $27.6 billion.

■ **EXHIBIT 6.3**   Current-Account Balances as Percent of GNP/GDP

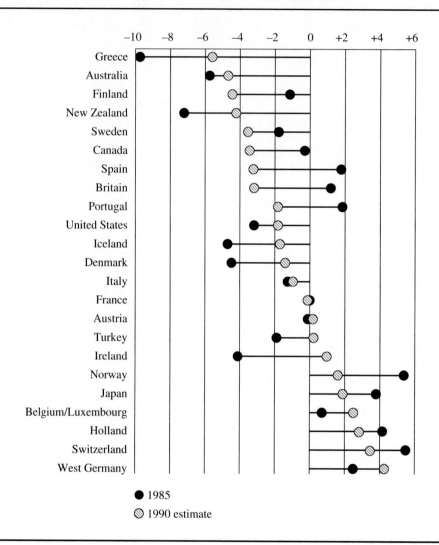

Official Reserves Account

The change in official reserves measures a nation's surplus or deficit on its current- and capital-account transactions by netting reserve liabilities from reserve assets. For example, a surplus will lead to an increase in official holdings of foreign currencies and/or gold; a deficit will normally cause a reduction in these assets. However, U.S. balance-of-payments deficits have not been matched exactly by net changes in reserve assets because foreigners have been willing to hold many billions of dollars (over $100 billion it is estimated) for liquidity and other purposes. Instead of being converted into foreign currencies, many dollars have been placed on deposit in the Eurodollar market. For most countries, though, there is a close correlation between balance-of-payments deficits and reserve declines. A drop in reserves will occur, for instance, when a nation sells gold to acquire foreign currencies that it can then use to meet a deficit in its balance of payments.

Balance-of-Payments Measures

There are a number of balance-of-payments definitions available. The *basic balance* focuses on transactions that are considered to be fundamental to the economic health of a currency. Thus, it includes the balance on current account and long-term capital, but it excludes such ephemeral items as short-term capital flows—mainly bank deposits—that are heavily influenced by temporary factors—short-run monetary policy, changes in interest differentials, and anticipations of currency fluctuations.

The *net liquidity balance* measures the change in private domestic borrowing or lending that is required to keep payments in balance without adjusting official reserves. Nonliquid, private, short-term capital flows and errors and omissions are included in the balance, while liquid assets and liabilities are excluded.

The *official reserve transactions balance* measures the adjustment required in official reserves to achieve balance-of-payments equilibrium. The assumption here is that official transactions are different from private transactions.

Each of these measures has shortcomings, primarily because of the increasing complexity of international financial transactions. For example, changes in the official reserve balance may now reflect investment flows as well as central bank intervention. Similarly, critics of the basic balance argue that the distinction between short-and long-term capital flows has become blurred. Direct investment is still determined by longer-term factors, but investment in stocks and bonds can be just as speculative as bank deposits and sold just as quickly. The astute international financial manager, therefore, must analyze the payments figures rather than rely on a single summarizing number.

The Missing Numbers

In going over the numbers in Exhibit 6.1, you will note an item referred to as *statistical discrepancy*. This number reflects errors and omissions in collecting data on international transactions. In 1982, that item reached a then record $41.4 billion on the plus side. (A plus figure reflects a mysterious inflow of funds; a minus amount an outflow.) The statistical discrepancy in 1990 was even higher, a huge $66.8 billion.

This discrepancy coincides with such worrisome foreign events as the Iraqi invasion of Kuwait, the turmoil in China, the unrest in Central and Latin America, and the upheaval in the Soviet Union. Many experts believe that the statistical discrepancy is primarily the result of foreigners surreptitiously moving money into what they deem to be a safe political haven—the United States.

■ 6.2 ■
THE INTERNATIONAL FLOW OF GOODS, SERVICES, AND CAPITAL

This section provides an analytical framework that links the international flows of goods and capital to domestic economic behavior. The framework consists of a set of basic *macroeconomic accounting identities* that links domestic spending and production to savings, consumption, and investment behavior, and thence to the capital-account and current-account balances. By manipulating these equations, we will identify the nature of the links between the U.S. and world economies and assess the effects on the domestic economy of international economic policies, and vice versa. As we shall see in the next section, ignoring these links leads to political solutions to international economic problems—such as the trade deficit—that create greater problems. At the same time, authors of domestic policy changes are often unaware of the effect these changes can have on the country's international economic affairs.

Domestic Savings and Investment and the Capital Account

The national income and product accounts provide an accounting framework for recording our national product and showing how its components are affected by international transactions. This framework begins with the observation that *national income,* which is the same as *national product,* is either spent on consumption or saved:

$$\text{National product} = \text{Consumption} + \text{Savings} \tag{6.1}$$

Similarly, *national expenditure,* the total amount that the nation spends on goods and services, can be divided into spending on consumption and spending on domestic real investment. *Real investment* refers to plant and equipment, R&D, and other expenditures designed to increase the nation's productive capacity. This equation provides the second national accounting identity:

$$\text{National spending} = \text{Consumption} + \text{Investment} \tag{6.2}$$

Subtracting Equation 6.2 from Equation 6.1 yields a new identity:

$$\frac{\text{National}}{\text{income}} - \frac{\text{National}}{\text{spending}} = \text{Savings} - \text{Investment} \tag{6.3}$$

This identity says if a nation's income exceeds its spending, then savings will exceed domestic investment, yielding surplus capital. The surplus capital must be invested overseas (if it were invested domestically there wouldn't be a capital surplus). In other words, savings equals domestic investment plus net foreign investment. Net foreign investment equals the nation's net public and private capital outflows plus the increase in official reserves. The net private and public capital outflows equal the capital-account deficit if the outflow is positive (a capital-account surplus if negative), while the net increase in official reserves equals the balance on official reserves account. In a freely floating exchange rate system—that is, no government intervention and no official reserve transactions—excess savings will equal the capital-account deficit. Alternatively, a national savings deficit will equal the capital-account surplus (net borrowing from abroad); this borrowing finances the excess of national spending over national income.

Here is the bottom line: A nation that produces more than it spends will save more than it invests domestically and will have a net capital outflow. This capital outflow will appear as some combination of a capital-account deficit and an increase in official reserves. Conversely, a nation that spends more than it produces will invest domestically more than it saves and have a net capital inflow. This capital inflow will appear as some combination of a capital-account surplus and a reduction in official reserves.

The Link Between the Current and Capital Accounts

Beginning again with national product, we can subtract from it spending on domestic goods and services. The remaining goods and services must equal exports. Similarly, if we subtract spending on domestic goods and services from total expenditures, the remaining spending must be on imports. Combining these two identities leads to another national income identity:

$$\frac{\text{National}}{\text{income}} - \frac{\text{National}}{\text{spending}} = \text{Exports} - \text{Imports} \tag{6.4}$$

Equation 6.4 says that a current-account surplus arises when national output exceeds domestic expenditures; similarly, a current-account deficit is due to domestic expenditures exceeding domestic output. Exhibit 6.4 illustrates this latter point for the United States. Moreover, when Equation 6.4 is combined with Equation 6.3, we have a new identity:

$$\text{Savings} - \text{Investment} = \text{Exports} - \text{Imports} \tag{6.5}$$

According to Equation 6.5, if a nation's savings exceed its investment, then that nation will run a current-account surplus. This equation explains the Japanese current-account surplus: The Japanese have an extremely high savings rate, both in absolute terms and relative to their investment rate. Conversely, a nation such as the United States that saves less than it invests must run a current-account deficit. Noting that savings minus investment equals net foreign investment, we have the following identity:

$$\frac{\text{Net foreign}}{\text{investment}} = \text{Exports} - \text{Imports} \tag{6.6}$$

Equation 6.6 says that the balance on the current account must equal the net capital outflow; that is, any foreign exchange earned by selling abroad must either be spent on imports or exchanged for claims against foreigners. The net amount of these IOUs equals

■ **EXHIBIT 6.4**   The Trade Balance Falls as Spending Rises Relative to GNP

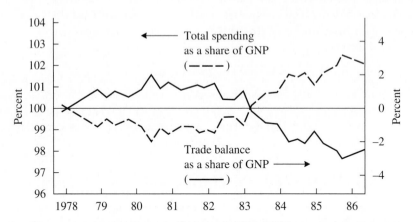

NOTE: Total spending is "Gross Domestic Purchases"; trade balance
is "Net Exports of Goods and Services."

the nation's capital outflow. If the current account is in surplus, then the country must be a
net exporter of capital; a current-account deficit indicates that the nation is a net capital
importer. This equation explains why Japan, with its large current-account surpluses, is a
major capital exporter, while the United States, with its large current-account deficits, is a
major capital importer. Bearing in mind that trade is goods plus services, to say that the
United States has a *trade deficit* with Japan is simply to say that the United States is buying
more goods and services from Japan than Japan is buying from the United States, and that
Japan is investing more in the United States than the United States is investing in Japan.
Between the United States and Japan, any deficit in the current account is exactly equal to
the surplus in the capital account. Otherwise, there would be an imbalance in the foreign
exchange market, and the exchange rate would change.

Another interpretation of Equation 6.6 is that the excess of goods and services bought
over goods and services produced domestically must be acquired through foreign trade and
must be financed by an equal amount of borrowing from abroad (the capital-account surplus
and/or official reserves deficit). Thus, in a freely floating exchange rate system, the
current-account balance and the capital-account balance must exactly offset each other. With
government intervention in the foreign exchange market, the sum of the current-account
balance plus the capital-account balance plus the balance on official reserves account must
be zero. These relations are shown in Exhibit 6.5.

These identities are useful because they allow us to assess the efficacy of proposed
"solutions" for improving the current-account balance. It is clear that a nation cannot reduce
its current-account deficit nor increase its current-account surplus unless it meets two

■ **EXHIBIT 6.5**   Linking National Economic Activity with Balance-of-Payments Accounts: Basic Identities

---

	Our national product (Y) – Our total spending (E)
minus	Our spending for consumption minus Our spending for consumption

= Our national savings (S) – Our investment in new real assets (I_d)

= Net foreign investment, or the net increase in claims on foreigners and official reserve assets, e.g., gold (I_f)

	Our national product (Y) – Our total spending (E)
minus	Our spending on our own goods minus Our spending on our own goods and and services services

= Our exports of goods and services (X) – Our imports of goods and services (M)
= Balance on current account
= – (Balance on capital and official reserves accounts)

$$Y - E = S - I_d = X - M = I_f$$

Conclusions: A nation that produces more than it spends will save more than it invests, export more than it imports, and wind up with a capital outflow. A nation that spends more than it produces will invest more than it saves, import more than it exports, and wind up with a capital inflow.

---

conditions: (1) Raise national product relative to national spending, and (2) increase savings relative to domestic investment. A proposal to improve the current-account balance by reducing imports (say, via higher tariffs) that doesn't affect national output/spending and national savings/investment leaves the trade deficit the same; and the proposal cannot achieve its objective without violating fundamental accounting identities.

Government Budget Deficits and Current-Account Deficits

Up to now, government spending and taxation have been included in aggregate domestic spending and income figures. By differentiating between the government and private sectors, we can see the effect of a government deficit on the current-account deficit.

National spending can be divided into household spending plus private investment plus government spending. Household spending, in turn, equals national income less the sum of private savings and taxes. Combining these terms yields the following identity:

$$\frac{\text{National}}{\text{spending}} = \frac{\text{Household}}{\text{spending}} + \frac{\text{Private}}{\text{investment}} + \frac{\text{Government}}{\text{spending}}$$

$$= \frac{\text{National}}{\text{income}} - \frac{\text{Private}}{\text{savings}} - \text{Taxes} + \frac{\text{Private}}{\text{investment}} + \frac{\text{Government}}{\text{spending}} \qquad (6.7)$$

Rearranging Equation 6.7 yields a new expression for excess spending:

$$\frac{\text{National}}{\text{spending}} - \frac{\text{National}}{\text{income}} = \frac{\text{Private}}{\text{investment}} - \frac{\text{Private}}{\text{savings}} + \frac{\text{Government}}{\text{budget deficit}} \qquad (6.8)$$

■ **EXHIBIT 6.6**   U.S. National Income Accounts and the Current-Account Deficit, 1973–
1990 (Percent of GNP)

Year	Gross Private Savings	Gross Private Investment	Savings Less Investment	Total Government Deficit	Current-Account Balance*
1973–79 (average)	18.0	16.8	1.2	–0.9	0.1
1980	17.5	16.0	1.5	–1.3	0.5
1981	18.0	16.9	2.9	–1.0	0.3
1982	18.3	14.7	3.6	–3.6	0.0
1983	17.4	14.7	2.7	–3.8	–1.0
1984	17.9	17.6	0.3	–2.7	–2.4
1985	17.2	16.5	0.7	–3.4	–2.9
1986	16.2	16.3	–0.1	–3.4	–3.4
1987	14.7	15.7	–0.8	–2.3	–3.5
1988	15.1	15.4	–0.3	–2.0	–2.5
1989	15.0	14.8	0.2	–1.7	–1.9
1990**	14.3	13.6	0.7	–2.3	–1.7

*The sum of the savings-investment balance and the government budget deficit should equal the current-account balance. Any discrepancy between these figures is due to rounding or minor data adjustments.
**Preliminary data.
SOURCE: *Economic Report of the President,* February 1991, Table B–28.

where the *government budget deficit* equals government spending minus taxes. Equation 6.8 says that excess national spending is composed of two parts: the excess of private domestic investment over private savings and the total government (federal, state, and local) deficit. Since national spending minus national product equals the net capital inflow, Equation 6.8 also says that the nation's excess spending equals its net borrowing from abroad.

Rearranging and combining Equations 6.4 and 6.8 provides a new accounting identity:

$$\text{Current account balance} = \text{Savings surplus} - \text{Government budget deficit} \qquad (6.9)$$

Equation 6.9 reveals that a nation's current-account balance is identically equal to its private savings-investment balance less the government budget deficit. According to this expression, a nation running a current-account deficit is not saving enough to finance its private investment and government budget deficit. Conversely, a nation running a current-account surplus is saving more than is needed to finance its private investment and government deficit.

In 1986, for example, private savings in the United States totaled $681 billion; private investment equaled $686 billion; and the government budget deficit amounted to $143 billion. Excess domestic spending thus equaled $148 billion, and the United States experienced a $143 billion current-account deficit. The $5 billion discrepancy reflects errors and omissions in the measurements of international transactions plus other small adjustments.

Exhibit 6.6 presents similar data for the United States since 1980, along with the averages for the period 1973 to 1979. To facilitate comparisons over time, the data are expressed as percentages of gross national product (GNP). The table shows that the increase in the U.S. current-account deficit since 1980 has been associated with an increase in the total government budget deficit and, since 1982, with a narrowing in private savings relative to private investment. The growth in the total government budget deficit reflects the huge federal budget deficit, since state and local governments typically run surpluses. In general, a current-account deficit represents a decision to consume, both publicly and privately, and to invest more than the nation currently is producing.

The purpose of Exhibit 6.6 is not to specify a channel of causation, but simply to show a tautological relationship among private savings, private investment, the government budget deficit, and the current-account balance. Nevertheless, the important implication is that steps taken to correct the current-account deficit can only be effective if they also change private savings, private investment, and/or the government deficit. Policies or events that fail to affect both sides of the relationship shown in Equation 6.9 will not alter the current-account deficit.

■ 6.3 ■
COPING WITH THE CURRENT-ACCOUNT DEFICIT

Conventional wisdom suggests some oft-repeated solutions to a current-account deficit. The principal suggestions are currency devaluation and protectionism. Yet, there are important, though subtle, reasons why neither is likely to work.

Currency Depreciation

An overvalued currency acts as a tax on exports and a subsidy to imports, reducing the former and increasing the latter. The result, as we saw in Chapter 4, is that a nation maintaining an overvalued currency will run a trade deficit. Permitting the currency to return to its equilibrium level will help reduce the trade deficit.

Many academics, politicians, and business people also believe that devaluation can reduce a trade deficit in a floating-rate system. Key to the effectiveness of devaluation is sluggish adjustment of nominal prices, which translates changes in nominal exchange rates into changes in real (inflation-adjusted) exchange rates. This view of exchange rate changes implies a systematic relation between the exchange rate and the current-account balance. For example, it implies that the current U.S. trade deficit will be reduced eventually by a fall in the value of the dollar.

By contrast, we saw in Chapter 4 that all exchange rates do is to equate currency supplies and demands; they do not determine the distribution of these currency flows between trade flows (the current-account balance) and capital flows (the capital-account balance). This view of exchange rates predicts that there is no simple relation between the exchange rate and the current-account balance. Trade deficits do not "cause" currency depreciation, nor does currency depreciation by itself help reduce a trade deficit: That is, both exchange rate changes and trade balances are determined by more fundamental economic factors.

These diametrically opposed theories can be evaluated by studying evidence on trade deficits and exchange rate changes. A good place to start is with recent U.S. experience.

From 1976 to 1980, the value of the dollar declined as the current-account deficit for the United States first worsened and then improved; but from 1980 to 1985, the dollar strengthened even as the current account steadily deteriorated. Many analysts attributed the rise in the U.S. trade deficit in the early 1980s to the sharp rise in the value of the U.S. dollar over that period. As the dollar rose in value against the currencies of America's trading partners, it took fewer dollars to buy a given amount of foreign goods and more foreign currencies to buy a fixed amount of U.S. goods. Responding to these price changes, Americans bought more foreign goods; and foreign consumers reduced their purchases of U.S.-made goods. U.S. imports increased and exports declined.

After reaching its peak in early March 1985, the value of the dollar began to decline. This decline was actively encouraged by the United States and by several foreign governments in hope of reducing the U.S. trade deficit. Conventional wisdom suggested that the very same basic economic forces affecting the trade account during the dollar's run-up would now be working in the opposite direction, reducing the U.S. trade deficit. As Exhibit 6.7 documents, however, the theory didn't work. The U.S. trade deficit kept rising, reaching new record levels month after month. By 1987, it had risen to $150 billion and remained at that level in 1988. What went wrong?

J-Curve Theory.   One explanation is based on the J-curve theory, illustrated in Exhibit 6.8. The letter J describes a curve that, viewed from left to right, goes down sharply for a short time, flattens out, then rises steeply for an extended period. That's how J-curve proponents have been expecting the U.S. trade deficit to behave. According to the *J-curve theory,* a country's trade deficit worsens just after its currency depreciates because price

■ **EXHIBIT 6.7**   The Dollar and the Deficit

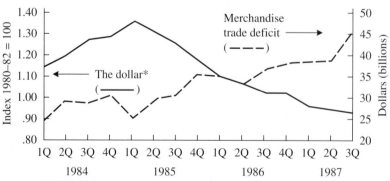

*The dollar's value against 15 industrial-country currencies weighted by trade

■ **EXHIBIT 6.8**   The Theoretical J-Curve

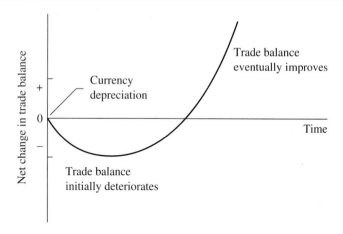

effects will dominate the effect on volume of imports in the short run: That is, the higher cost of imports will more than offset the reduced volume of imports. Thus, the J-curve says that a decline in the value of the dollar should be followed by a temporary worsening in the trade deficit before its longer term improvement.

The initial worsening of the trade deficit occurred as predicted in 1985 but it wasn't until over four years later, in 1989, that the trade deficit started coming down. Moreover, what little improvement occurred in 1989 may owe more to the jump in Social Security taxes, which reduced the federal budget deficit, than to depreciation of the dollar. In other words, the upturn of the J-curve has proved elusive.

U.S. Deficits and the Demand for U.S. Assets.   Another possible reason for the failure of dollar devaluation to cure the persistent U.S. trade deficit is that the earlier analysis mixed up cause and effect. The argument that the strong dollar was the main culprit of the massive U.S. trade deficit rested on the obvious fact that the dollar's high price made it cheaper to import than to export. But that was not the complete picture. The dollar's price was not a cause nor even a symptom of the problem. It is axiomatic that price is a reflection of a fundamental value in the market. To argue that the high dollar hurt the U.S. economy does not explain how or why the price got there.

Here is a plausible explanation. For a variety of reasons, including an increasingly attractive investment climate in the United States and added political and economic turmoil elsewhere in the world, foreign investors in the early 1980s wanted to expand their holdings of U.S. assets. They bid up the value of the dollar to a level at which Americans were willing to exchange their assets for foreign goods and services. The result was a capital-account surplus balanced by a current-account deficit. In effect, the capital-account surplus drove the current-account deficit. The net result was excess American spending financed by borrowing from abroad.

Adding fuel to the current-account deficit, particularly after 1982, was the growth of the federal government's budget deficit. The U.S. budget deficit could only be funded in one of three ways: restricting investment, increasing savings, or exporting debt. The United States rejected the first alternative, was unable to accomplish the second, and thus relied heavily on the third. Accordingly, the trade deficit was the equilibrating factor that enabled the United States to satisfy its extralarge debt appetite. The price of the dollar determined the terms on which the rest of the world was willing to finance that deficit. When foreigners wanted to hold U.S. assets, the terms were quite attractive (they were willing to pay a high price for dollars); when foreigners no longer found U.S. assets so desirable, the financing terms became more onerous (they reduced the price they were willing to pay for dollars). However, since private savings were insufficient to finance private investment plus the government deficit, the U.S. current-account deficit persisted even as the lower dollar led Americans to consume fewer foreign goods and services. How could this be? It occurred because devaluation without a change in savings and spending behavior meant that the lower volume of imports cost more dollars: That is, Americans were buying less abroad, but paying more.

In general, unless the drop in imports exceeds the devaluation-induced increase in import prices, the total import bill in dollars will actually increase. For example, if a foreign currency appreciation of 20% causes an increase of 15% in the dollar price of imports, the volume of imports must drop by at least 15% for the dollar amount of imports to drop. At the same time, the dollar volume of exports should rise following dollar depreciation. The net effect of devaluation on the current account, therefore, depends on the price elasticities of export and import demand.

Unless the federal budget deficit shrinks, the current-account deficit will disappear only if the U.S. private savings rate rises significantly or the rate of investment falls. Hence, currency devaluation will work only if some mechanism is in place that leads to a rise in private savings, a cut in private investment, or a reduction in the government budget deficit. Otherwise, any rise in exports is offset by the adverse effects of higher-priced imports.

Although a policy of forcing down the dollar may not improve the current-account balance, it does have two clear-cut effects. It makes Americans poorer, since it takes a greater volume of domestic output to acquire a unit of imports. Dollar depreciation also reduces the incentives U.S. industry has to improve international competitiveness by cutting costs and increasing productivity.

Protectionism

Another response to a current-account deficit is *protectionism*—that is, the imposition of tariffs, quotas, or other forms of restraint against foreign imports. A *tariff* is essentially a tax that is imposed on a foreign product sold in a country. Its purpose is to increase the price of the product, thereby discouraging purchase of that product and encouraging the purchase of a substitute, domestically produced product. A *quota* specifies the quantity of particular products that can be imported to a country, typically an amount that is considerably less than the amount currently being imported. By restricting the supply relative to the demand, the quota causes the price of foreign products to rise. In both cases, the results are ultimately a rise in the price of products consumers buy, an erosion of purchasing power, and a collective decline in the standard of living.

These results present a powerful argument against selective trade restrictions as a means of correcting a nation's trade imbalance. An even more powerful argument is that such restrictions don't work. Either other imports rise or exports fall. This conclusion follows from the basic national income accounting identity: Savings – Investment = Exports – Imports. Unless saving or investment behavior changes, this identity says that a $1 reduction in imports will lead to a $1 decrease in exports.

The mechanism that brings about this result depends upon the basic market forces that shape the supply and demand for currencies in the foreign exchange market. For example, when the U.S. government imposes restrictions on steel imports, the reduction in purchases of foreign steel effectively reduces the U.S. demand for foreign exchange. Fewer dollars tendered for foreign exchange means a higher value for the dollar. The higher-valued dollar raises the price of U.S. goods sold overseas and causes proportionately lower sales of U.S. exports. A higher-valued dollar also lowers the cost in the United States of foreign goods, thereby encouraging the purchase of those imported goods on which there is no tariff. Thus, any reduction in imports from tariffs or quotas will be offset by the reduction in exports and increase in other imports.

Restrictions on importing steel will also raise the price of steel, reducing the competitiveness of U.S. users of steel, such as automakers and capital goods manufacturers. Their ability to compete will be constrained both at home and abroad. Ironically, it is the most efficient and most internationally competitive producers—those who are exporting or are able to compete against imports—who are being punished, while the inefficient producers are being sheltered.

Ending Foreign Ownership of Domestic Assets

One approach that would eliminate a current-account deficit is to forbid foreigners from owning domestic assets. If foreigners cannot hold claims on the nation, they will export an amount equal in value to what they are willing to import, ending net capital inflows. The microeconomic adjustment mechanism that will balance imports and exports under this policy is as follows.

The cessation of foreign capital inflows, by reducing the available supply of capital, will raise real domestic interest rates. Higher interest rates will stimulate more savings because the opportunity cost of consumption rises with the real interest rate; higher rates will cause domestic investment to fall because fewer projects will have positive net present values. The outcome will be a balance between savings/investment and elimination of excess domestic spending that caused the current-account deficit in the first place. Although such an approach would work, most observers would consider the resulting slower economic growth too high a price to pay to eliminate a current-account deficit.

Although many observers are troubled by the role of foreign investors in U.S. financial markets, as long as Americans continue to spend more than they produce, there will be a continuing need for foreign capital. This foreign capital is helping to improve America's industrial base, while at the same time providing capital gains to those Americans who are selling their assets to foreigners. Foreign investors often introduce improved management, better production, or new technology that increases the quality and variety of goods available to U.S. consumers, who benefit from lower prices as well. Foreign investment also raises labor productivity which, in turn, leads to higher wages. Restrictions on foreign investment may also provoke reciprocal restrictions by foreign governments.

■ ——

ILLUSTRATION

Japan's Transplanted Auto Parts Suppliers Raise Quality. Japanese auto plants located in the United States buy about 60% of their parts from American sources. This figure includes purchases from Japanese component makers that have followed their customers to the United States. Japan's transplanted parts makers allow the Japanese carmakers to be very choosy customers. Many American parts suppliers have been rejected as not producing to the requisite quality. The good news is that the tough, new competition has forced many U.S. companies to raise their standards and cut their costs.

Japanese buyers put would-be suppliers through exhausting qualification trials, which often require suppliers to make fundamental improvements in their manufacturing. Since auto suppliers form a pyramid, those feeding car manufacturers at the top can meet stringent requirements only with better performance from their own suppliers. And so on, down the chain. In this way, demands from quality-conscious Japanese customers ripple down to the base of the industrial supplier infrastructure. For example, when Honda demanded a smoother steel coating, Inland Steel had to insist on better zinc. Moreover, suppliers to the Japanese-owned auto plants are also supplying Detroit's Big Three. As the supplier base improves, so do the components that make up a Ford, Chevy, or Chrysler. ■

Boosting the Savings Rate

As we have seen, a low savings rate tends to lead to a current-account deficit. Thus, another way to reduce the current-account deficit would be to stimulate savings behavior. Yet, the data indicate that the rate of U.S. private savings has declined over time. In particular, personal savings, which averaged about 8% of disposable income in the 1970s, slid to 4.3% in 1986, and to 3.2% in the second quarter of 1987. Future U.S. wealth will be impaired if the low U.S. personal savings rate persists.

One possible explanation for the decline in personal savings is that Social Security benefits expanded greatly during the 1970s. By attenuating the link between savings behavior and retirement income, Social Security may have reduced the incentive for Americans to save for retirement. By contrast, Japan—which has only a rudimentary social security system and no welfare to speak of—has an extraordinarily high personal savings rate. Presumably, the inability of the Japanese to throw themselves on the mercy of the state has affected their willingness to save for a rainy day.

Similarly, changes in tax regulations and tax rates may greatly affect savings and investment behavior and, therefore, the nation's trade and capital flows. Thus, purely domestic policies may have dramatic—and unanticipated—consequences for a nation's international economic transactions. The lesson is clear: In an integrated world economy, everything connects to everything else; politicians can't tinker with one parameter without affecting the entire system.

Current-Account Deficits and Unemployment

One rationale for attempting to eliminate a current-account deficit is that such a deficit leads to unemployment. Underlying this rationale is the notion that imported goods and services are substituting for domestic goods and services and costing domestic jobs. It is argued that reducing imports would raise domestic production and employment. However, the view that reducing a current-account deficit promotes jobs is based on single-entry bookkeeping.

If a country buys fewer foreign goods and services, it will demand less foreign exchange. As discussed above, this result will raise the value of the domestic currency, thereby reducing exports and encouraging the purchase of other imports. Jobs are saved in some industries, but other jobs are lost by the decline in exports and rise in other imports. According to this line of reasoning, the net impact of a trade deficit or surplus on jobs should be nil.

Judging by the claims of some politicians, however, it would appear that the economic performance of the United States has been dismal because of its huge current-account deficits. But if the alternative story is correct—that a current-account deficit reflects excess spending and has little to do with the health of an economy—then there should be no necessary relation between economic performance and the current-account balance.

The appropriate way to settle this dispute is to examine the evidence. Here are some facts:

1. Although its current-account deficit nearly quadrupled between 1982 and 1987, the United States created over 13 million new jobs during this period, more than Europe and Japan combined in the past decade.
2. Between 1983 and 1987, U.S. unemployment declined by 28%; the unemployment rate in Japan rose by 17%; and the unemployment rate in the Common Market countries rose by more than 20%.
3. Between 1982 and 1986 as the trade deficit increased, the United States gained 406,000 jobs in manufacturing.
4. Not only did the number of jobs in manufacturing increase in the United States, but real wages in manufacturing, which declined by 7% from 1977 to 1981 (when the United States was generally running a current-account surplus), increased by 6% from 1982 to 1986.

In short, from 1982 to 1986, the trade deficit soared, but the United States created jobs 3 times as fast as Japan and 20 times as fast as West Germany. Also, in the same time period, America's GNP grew 43% faster than that of Japan or West Germany, even though both nations had huge trade surpluses with the United States.

In general, no systematic relationship between net exports and economic growth should be expected. Exhibit 6.9 shows the annual growth rate of U.S. real GNP from 1970 to 1986, together with the real value of the current account. Strong output growth has been associated with both an improving current account, as in 1978, and a worsening current account, as in 1984. The evidence shows that current-account surpluses—in and of themselves—are neither good nor bad. They are not correlated with growth, decline, competitiveness, or weakness. What matters is why they occur.

■ **EXHIBIT 6.9**   No Systematic Relationship Between Current Account and Economic Growth

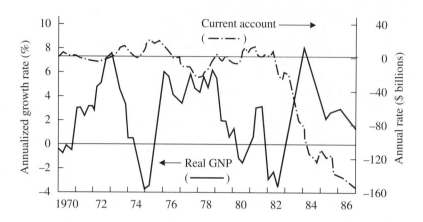

The Bottom Line on Current-Account Deficits and Surpluses

To summarize the previous discussion of current-account deficits and surpluses, consider the following stylized facts. Suppose that the United States is a country whose citizens, for one reason or another, have a low propensity to save. And suppose also that for a variety of reasons, the United States is an attractive place to invest. Finally, suppose that in the rest of the world, people have high propensities to save, but their opportunities for investment are less attractive. In these circumstances, there will be a flow of capital from the rest of the world and a corresponding net inflow of goods and services to the United States. The United States would have a current-account deficit.

In the above situation, the current-account deficit would not be viewed as a problem. Rather, it would be viewed as an efficient adaptation to different savings propensities and investment opportunities in the United States and the rest of the world. From this perspective, a current-account deficit becomes a solution, not a problem.

The real problem, if there is one, is either too much consumption and thus too little savings or too much investment. Regardless of what one's opinions are, the situation confronting the United States and the rest of the world is an expression of national preferences, to which trade flows have adjusted in a timely manner. An economist has no further wisdom to shed on this matter.

What are the long-term consequences for the United States or for any other nation that runs a current-account deficit? Here, an economist can speak with some authority. If the current-account deficit and resulting capital-account surplus finances productive domestic investment, then the nation is better off; the returns from these added investments will service the foreign debts with income left over to increase living standards. Conversely, a capital-account surplus that finances consumption will increase the nation's well-being today at the expense of its future well-being. That trade-off, however, has little to do with the balance of payments per se.

■ 6.4 ■
SUMMARY AND CONCLUSIONS

The balance of payments is an accounting statement of the international transactions of one nation over a specific period. The statement shows the sum of economic transactions of individuals, businesses, and government agencies located in one nation with those located in the rest of the world during the period. Thus, the U.S. balance of payments for a given year is an accounting of all transactions between U.S. residents and residents of all other countries during that year.

The statement is based on double-entry bookkeeping; every economic transaction recorded as a credit brings about an equal and offsetting debit entry, and vice versa. A debit entry shows a purchase of foreign goods, services, or assets, or a decline in liabilities to foreigners. A credit entry shows a sale of domestic goods, services, or assets, or an increase in liabilities to foreigners. For example, if a foreign company sells a car to a U.S. resident, a debit is recorded to indicate an increase in purchases made by the United States (the car); a credit is recorded to reflect an increase in liabilities to the foreigner (payment for the car).

The balance of payments is often divided into several different components. Each shows a particular kind of transaction, such as merchandise exports or foreign purchases of U.S. government securities. Transactions that represent purchases and sales of goods and services in the current period are called the current account; those that represent capital transactions are called the capital account. Changes in official reserves appear on the official reserves account.

Because double-entry bookkeeping ensures that debits equal credits, the sum of all transactions is zero. In the absence of official reserve transactions, a capital-account surplus must offset the current-account deficit; and a capital-account deficit must offset a current-account surplus.

The United States is presently running a large current-account deficit. Much public discussion about why the United States imports more than it exports has focused on claims of unfair trading practices or the high value of the dollar (the latter claim seems less realistic today). However, economic theory indicates that the total size of the current-account deficit is a macroeconomic phenomenon; there is a basic accounting identity that a nation's current-account deficit reflects excess domestic spending. Equivalently, a current-account deficit equals the excess of domestic investment over domestic savings. Explicitly taking government into account yields a new relation: The domestic spending balance equals the private savings-investment balance minus the government budget deficit. Since private savings and investment are approximately in balance for the United States, the trade deficit can be traced to the federal budget deficit.

We saw that failure to consider the elementary economic accounting identities can mislead policymakers into relying on dollar depreciation, trade restrictions, or trade subsidies in order to reduce U.S. trade deficits without doing anything about excess domestic spending. To reduce the current-account deficit, domestic savings must rise; private investment must decline; or the government deficit must be reduced. Absent any of these changes, the current-account deficit will not diminish, regardless of the trade barriers imposed or the amount of dollar depreciation.

■ QUESTIONS ■

1. In a freely floating exchange rate system, if the current account is running a deficit, what are the consequences for the nation's balance on capital account and its overall balance of payments?

2. As the inflation-adjusted value of the U.S. dollar rises, what is likely to happen to the U.S. balance on current account?

3. Currently, social security is minimal in Japan. Suppose Japan institutes a comprehensive social security system. How is this policy switch likely to affect Japan's trade surplus?

4. Suppose Lufthansa buys $400 million worth of Boeing jets in 1992 and is financed by the U.S. Eximbank with a five-year loan that has no principal or interest payments due until 1993. What is the net impact of this sale on the U.S. current account, capital account, and overall balance of payments for 1992?

5. How does a trade deficit affect the current-account balance?

6. On which balance-of-payments account does tourism show up?

7. Suppose the United States expropriates all foreign holdings of American assets. What will happen to the U.S. current-account deficit? What will likely happen to U.S. savings and investment? Why?

8. What happens to Mexico's ability to repay its foreign loans if the United States restricts imports of Mexican agricultural produce?

9. In order for Brazil to service its foreign debts without borrowing more money, what must be true of its trade balance?

10. Suppose the United States imposes import restrictions on Japanese steel. What is likely to happen to the U.S. current-account deficit? What else is likely to happen?

11. Suppose that Brazil starts welcoming foreign investment with open arms. How is this likely to affect the value of the cruzeiro? The Brazilian current-account balance?

12. In 1990, Germany's current-account surplus was over $50 billion. However, it is estimated that the process of reunification will require that Germany invest several hundred billion dollars in its eastern states over the coming decade.

    a. What implications does this huge investment have for Germany's current-account balance in the future? Explain.

    b. How should the Deutsche mark's value change to facilitate the necessary shift in Germany's economy?

13. Suppose that the trade imbalances of the 1980s largely disappear during the 1990s. What is likely to happen to the huge global capital flows of the 1980s? What is the link between the trade imbalances and the global movement of capital?

14. In 1965, about 34% of all adult workers were under the age of 34, compared with almost 47% by 1980. Meanwhile, the share of the workforce between 35 years and 59 years shrank from about 60% to 49%. What impact might this dramatic shift in the age distribution of the U.S. workforce have had on the U.S. current-account balance over this 15-year period? (*Hint:* Consider the difference in savings behavior between younger and older workers.)

■ PROBLEMS ■

1. The following transactions (expressed in U.S.$ billions) take place during a year. Calculate the U.S. merchandise-trade, current-account, capital-account, and official reserves balances.

   a. The United States exports $300 of goods and receives payment in the form of foreign demand deposits abroad.

   b. The United States imports $225 of goods and pays for them by drawing down its foreign demand deposits.

   c. The United States pays $15 to foreigners in dividends drawn on U.S. demand deposits here.

   d. American tourists spend $30 overseas using traveler's checks drawn on U.S. banks here.

   e. Americans buy foreign stocks with $60, using foreign demand deposits held abroad.

   f. The U.S. government sells $45 in gold for foreign demand deposits abroad.

   g. In a currency support operation, the U.S. government uses its foreign demand deposits to purchase $8 from private foreigners in the United States.

2. Ruritania is calculating its balance of payments for the year. As usual, its data are perfectly accurate. All of the transactions for the year are listed below (in Rur$ millions). Fill in the correct number for each balance-of-payments account a through j.

   a. Ruritania received weapons worth $200 from the United States under its military aid program; no payment is necessary.

   b. A Ruritanian firm exported $400 of cloth and received an IOU from the foreign importer.

   c. A Ruritanian resident paid $10 in interest on a loan from a foreigner; the check was drawn on a domestic Ruritanian bank.

   d. Foreign tourists visited Ruritania and spent $100 in traveler's checks drawn on foreign banks.

   e. The Ruritanian central bank sold $60 in gold to a foreign government and received U.S. Treasury bills in return.

   f. A foreign central bank deposited $120 in a private domestic Ruritanian bank and paid with a check drawn on a private bank in the United States.

       1. Exports
         a. goods
         b. services
       Imports
         c. goods
         d. services
         e. unilateral transfers
       2. Ruritanian assets abroad
         f. privately owned
         g. officially owned
       3. Foreign assets in Ruritania
         h. privately owned
         i. officially owned
         j. current account

3.* Select a country and undertake an analysis of that country's balance of payments for 8 to 12 years, subject to availability of data. The analysis must include examinations (presentation of statistical data with discussion) of the trade balance, current-account balance, capital-account balance, basic balance, and overall balance. Your report should also address the following issues:

a. What accounts for swings in these various balances over time?

b. What is the relationship between shifts in the current-account balance and changes in savings and investment? Include an examination of government budget deficits and surpluses, explaining how they relate to the savings-investment and current-account balances.

*Project suggested by Donald T. Buck.

■ 7 ■

Parity Conditions in International Finance and Currency Forecasting

It is not for its own sake that men desire money, but for the sake of what they can purchase with it.

—Adam Smith (1776)—

■ On the basis of the flows of goods and capital discussed in Chapter 4, this chapter presents a simple, yet elegant, set of equilibrium relationships that should apply to product prices, interest rates, and spot and forward exchange rates if markets are not impeded. These relationships, or *parity conditions,* provide the foundation for much of the remainder of this text; they should be clearly understood before you proceed further. The final section of this chapter examines the usefulness of a number of models and methodologies in profitably forecasting currency changes under both fixed-rate and floating-rate systems.

■ 7.1 ■
ARBITRAGE AND THE LAW OF ONE PRICE

In competitive markets, characterized by numerous buyers and sellers having low-cost access to information, exchange-adjusted prices of identical tradable goods and financial assets must be within transactions costs of equality worldwide. This idea, referred to as the *law of one price,* is enforced by international arbitrageurs who follow the profit-guaranteeing dictum of "buy low, sell high" and prevent all but trivial deviations from equality. Similarly, in the absence of market imperfections, risk-adjusted expected returns on financial assets in different markets should be equal.

Five key theoretical economic relationships, which are depicted in Exhibit 7.1, result from these arbitrage activities. Two of these conditions, interest rate parity and unbiased forward rates, were already discussed in Chapter 2.

■ Purchasing power parity (PPP)
■ Fisher effect (FE)
■ International Fisher effect (IFE)
■ Interest rate parity (IRP)
■ Forward rates as unbiased predictors of future spot rates (UFR)

The framework of Exhibit 7.1 emphasizes the links among prices, spot exchange rates, interest rates, and forward exchange rates. According to the diagram, if inflation in, say, France is expected to exceed inflation in the United States by 3% for the coming year, then the French franc should decline in value by about 3% relative to the dollar. By the same token, the one-year forward French franc should sell at a 3% discount relative to the U.S. dollar. Similarly, one-year interest rates in France should be about 3% higher than one-year interest rates on securities of comparable risk in the United States.

The common denominator of these parity conditions is the adjustment of the various rates and prices to inflation. According to modern monetary theory, inflation is the logical outcome of an expansion of the money supply in excess of real output growth. Although this view of the origin of inflation is not universally subscribed to, it has a solid microeconomic

■ **EXHIBIT 7.1**   Five Key Theoretical Relationships Among Spot Rates, Forward Rates, Inflation Rates, and Interest Rates

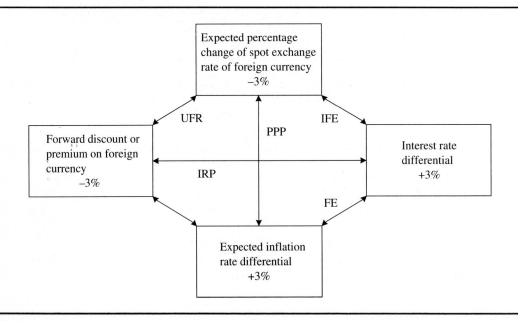

foundation. In particular, it is a basic precept of price theory that as the supply of one commodity increases relative to supplies of all other commodities, the price of the first commodity must decline relative to the prices of other commodities. Thus, for example, a bumper crop of corn should cause corn's value in exchange—its exchange rate—to decline. Similarly, as the supply of money increases relative to the supply of goods and services, the purchasing power of money—the exchange rate between money and goods—must decline.

The mechanism that brings this adjustment about is simple and direct. Suppose, for example, that the supply of U.S. dollars exceeds the amount that individuals desire to hold. In order to reduce their excess holdings of money, individuals increase their spending on goods, services, and securities, causing U.S. prices to rise.

■ _____

ILLUSTRATION

Bolivia Ends Its Hyperinflation.   In the Spring of 1985, Bolivia's inflation rate was running at 25,000% a year, one of the highest rates in history. At the time, Bolivian government revenues covered less than 15% of its spending, with most of the rest being paid for by printing new pesos. Inflation threatened the very fabric of society. Prices changed by the minute, and people literally carried money around in suitcases. Currency, which was printed abroad, was the third-largest import in 1984. The two-inch stack of money needed to buy a chocolate bar far outweighed the candy. The government eventually solved the stacks-of-money problem by issuing 1-million-, 2-million-, and 10-million-peso notes. But its failure to solve the inflation problem led to its replacement by a new government that announced an anti-inflation program on August 29. The program had two basic thrusts: Cut spending and shut down the printing presses. To cut spending, the new government adopted the simple rule that it would not spend more than it received. Each day the finance minister signed checks only up to the value of the revenues the treasury had received that day. By October, the monthly inflation rate had fallen to zero, from more than 60% in August. Economists consider this performance to be an extraordinary verification of basic monetary theory. ■

A further link in the chain relating money supply growth, inflation, interest rates, and exchange rates is the notion that money is neutral. That is, money should have no impact on real variables. Thus, for example, a 10% increase in the supply of money relative to the demand for money should cause prices to rise by 10%. This view has important implications for international finance. Specifically, although a change in the quantity of money will affect prices and exchange rates, this change should not affect the rate at which domestic goods are exchanged for foreign goods or the rate at which goods today are exchanged for goods in the future. These ideas are formalized as purchasing power parity and the Fisher effect, respectively. We will examine them here briefly and then in greater detail in Sections 7.2 and 7.3, respectively.

The international analogue to inflation is home-currency depreciation relative to foreign currencies. The analogy derives from the observation that inflation involves a change in the exchange rate between the home currency and domestic goods, whereas home-currency depreciation—a decline in the foreign currency value of the home currency—results in a change in the exchange rate between the home currency and foreign goods.

That inflation and currency depreciation are related is no accident. Excess money-supply growth, through its impact on the rate of aggregate spending, affects the demand for goods produced abroad as well as goods produced domestically. In turn, the domestic demand for foreign currencies changes and, consequently, the foreign exchange value of the domestic currency changes. Thus, the rate of domestic inflation and changes in the exchange rate are jointly determined by the rate of domestic money growth relative to the growth of the amount that people—domestic and foreign—want to hold.

If international arbitrage enforces the law of one price, then the exchange rate between the home currency and domestic goods must equal the exchange rate between the home currency and foreign goods. In other words, a unit of home currency (HC) should have the same purchasing power worldwide. Thus, if a dollar buys a pound of bread in the United States, it should also buy a pound of bread in Great Britain. For this to happen, the foreign exchange rate must change by (approximately) the difference between the domestic and foreign rates of inflation. This relationship is called *purchasing power parity.*

Similarly, the *nominal interest rate,* the price quoted on lending and borrowing transactions, determines the exchange rate between current and future dollars (or any other currency). For example, an interest rate of 10% on a one-year loan means that one dollar today is being exchanged for 1.1 dollars a year from now. But what really matters according to the *Fisher effect* is the exchange rate between current and future purchasing power, as measured by the real interest rate. Simply put, the lender is concerned with how many more goods can be obtained in the future by forgoing consumption today, while the borrower wants to know how much future consumption must be sacrificed to obtain more goods today. This condition is the case regardless of whether the borrower and lender are located in the same or different countries. As a result, if the exchange rate between current and future goods—the *real interest rate*—varies from one country to the next, arbitrage between domestic and foreign capital markets, in the form of international capital flows, should occur. These flows will tend to equalize real interest rates across countries. By looking more closely at these and related parity conditions, we can see how they can be formalized and used for management purposes.

■ 7.2 ■
PURCHASING POWER PARITY

Purchasing power parity (PPP) was first stated in a rigorous manner by the Swedish economist Gustav Cassel in 1918; he used it as the basis for recommending a new set of official exchange rates at the end of World War I that would allow for the resumption of normal trade relations.[1] Since then, PPP has been widely used by central banks as a guide to establishing new par values for their currencies when the old ones were clearly in disequilibrium. From a management standpoint, purchasing power parity is often used to forecast future exchange rates, for purposes ranging from deciding on the currency denomination of long-term debt issues to determining in which countries to build plants.

---

[1] Gustav Cassel, "Abnormal Deviations in International Exchanges," *Economic Journal,* December 1918, pp. 413–415.

In its *absolute* version, purchasing power parity states that exchange-adjusted price levels should be identical worldwide. In other words, a unit of home currency (HC) should have the same purchasing power around the world. This theory is just an application of the law of one price to national price levels rather than to individual prices. (That is, it rests on the assumption that free trade will equalize the price of any good in all countries; otherwise, arbitrage opportunities would exist.) However, absolute PPP ignores the effects on free trade of transportation costs, tariffs, quotas and other restrictions, and product differentiation.

The *relative* version of purchasing power parity, which is used more commonly now, states that the exchange rate between the home currency and any foreign currency will adjust to reflect changes in the price levels of the two countries. For example, if inflation is 5% in the United States and 1% in Japan, then in order to equalize the dollar price of goods in the two countries, the dollar value of the Japanese yen must rise by about 4%.

Formally, if i_h and i_f are the periodic price level increases (rates of inflation) for the home country and the foreign country, respectively; e_0 is the dollar (HC) value of one unit of foreign currency at the beginning of the period; and e_t is the spot exchange rate in period t, then

$$\frac{e_t}{e_0} = \frac{(1 + i_h)^t}{(1 + i_f)^t} \tag{7.1}$$

For example, if the United States and Germany are running annual inflation rates of 5% and 3%, respectively, and the initial exchange rate was DM 1 = $0.75, then according to Equation 7.1 the value of the DM in three years should be

$$e_3 = 0.75(1.05/1.03)^3$$
$$= \$0.7945$$

The one-period version of Equation 7.1 is commonly used. It is

$$\frac{e_1}{e_0} = \frac{1 + i_h}{1 + i_f} \tag{7.2}$$

■ ──

ILLUSTRATION

Calculating the PPP Rate for the DM. Suppose the current U.S. price level is at 112 while the German price level is at 107, relative to base price levels of 100. If the initial value of the Deutsche mark was $0.48, then according to PPP, the dollar value of the DM should have risen to approximately $0.5024 (0.48 × 112/107), an appreciation of 4.67%. On the other hand, if the German price level now equals 119, then the Deutsche mark should have depreciated by about 5.88%, to $0.4518 (0.48 × 112/119). ──────────── ■

Purchasing power parity is often represented by the following approximation of Equation 7.2:[2]

───

[2]Subtracting 1 from both sides of Equation 7.2 yields $(e_1 - e_0)/e_0 = (i_h - i_f)/(1 + i_f)$. Equation 7.3 follows if i_f is relatively small.

$$\frac{e_1 - e_0}{e_0} = i_h - i_f \tag{7.3}$$

That is, the exchange rate change during a period should equal the inflation differential for that same time period. In effect, PPP says that *currencies with high rates of inflation should devalue relative to currencies with lower rates of inflation.*

Equation 7.3 is illustrated in Exhibit 7.2. The vertical axis measures the percentage currency change, and the horizontal axis shows the inflation differential. Equilibrium is reached on the parity line, which contains all those points at which these two differentials are equal. At point A, for example, the 3% inflation differential is just offset by the 3% appreciation of the foreign currency relative to the home currency. Point B, on the other hand, depicts a situation of disequilibrium, where the inflation differential of 3% is greater than the appreciation of 1% in the HC value of the foreign currency.

The Lesson of Purchasing Power Parity

Purchasing power parity bears an important message: Just as the price of goods in one year cannot be meaningfully compared to the price of goods in another year without adjusting for interim inflation, so exchange rate changes may indicate nothing more than the reality that countries have different inflation rates. In fact, according to PPP, exchange rate movements should just cancel out changes in the foreign price level relative to the domestic price level. These offsetting movements should have no effects on the relative competitive positions of domestic firms and their foreign competitors. Thus, changes in the

■ **EXHIBIT 7.2**   Purchasing Power Parity

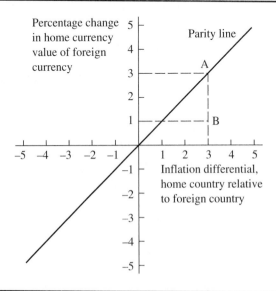

nominal exchange rate—that is, the actual exchange rate—may be of little significance in determining the true effects of currency changes on a firm and a nation. In terms of currency changes affecting relative competitiveness, therefore, the focus must be not on nominal exchange rate changes but instead on changes in the real purchasing power of one currency relative to another. Here we consider the concept of the real exchange rate.

The Real Exchange Rate. As we will see in the next section, although purchasing power parity is a fairly accurate description of long-run behavior, deviations from PPP do occur. These deviations give rise to changes in the real exchange rate. As defined in Chapter 4, the *real exchange rate* is the nominal exchange rate adjusted for changes in the relative purchasing power of each currency since some base period. Specifically, the real exchange rate at time t, e_t', is designated as

$$e_t' = e_t \frac{(1 + i_f)^t}{(1 + i_h)^t} \tag{7.4}$$

where the various parameters are the same as those defined previously.

If purchasing power parity holds exactly, that is,

$$e_t = e_0 \frac{(1 + i_h)^t}{(1 + i_f)^t}$$

then e_t' equals e_0. In other words, if changes in the nominal exchange rate are fully offset by changes in the relative price levels between the two countries, then the real exchange rate remains unchanged. Alternatively, a change in the real exchange rate is equivalent to a deviation from PPP.

ILLUSTRATION

Calculating Real Exchange Rates for the Pound and DM. Between June 1979 and June 1980, the U.S. rate of inflation was 13.6%, and the German rate of inflation was 7.7%. In line with the relatively higher rate of inflation in the United States, the West German Deutsche mark revalued from $0.54 in June 1979 to $0.57 in June 1980. Based on the above definition, the real rate of exchange in June 1980 equaled $0.57(1.077)/1.136 = $0.54. In other words, the real (inflation-adjusted) dollar/Deutsche mark exchange rate held constant at $0.54. During this same time period, England experienced a 17.6% rate of inflation, and the pound sterling revalued from $2.09 to $2.17. Thus, the real value of the pound in June 1980 (relative to June 1979) was 2.17(1.176)/1.136 = $2.25. Hence, the real exchange rate increased between June 1979 and June 1980 from $2.09 to $2.25, a real appreciation of 7.6% in the value of the pound.

The distinction between the nominal exchange rate and the real exchange rate has important implications for foreign exchange risk measurement and management. As we will see in Chapter 10, if the real exchange rate remains constant (i.e., if purchasing power parity holds), currency gains or losses from nominal exchange rate changes will generally be offset over time by the effects of differences in relative rates of inflation, thereby reducing the net impact of nominal devaluations and revaluations. Deviations from purchasing power parity, however, will lead to real exchange gains and losses.

For example, the U.K.'s Wedgwood Ltd. was significantly hurt by the real appreciation of the British pound described above. The strong pound made Wedgwood's china exports more expensive, costing it foreign sales and putting downward pressure on its prices, while its costs—primarily labor and raw materials from local sources—rose apace with British inflation. The result was a decline in sales and greatly reduced profit margins. Wedgwood's competitive position improved with pound devaluation in the early 1980s.

Expected Inflation and Exchange Rate Changes

Changes in expected, as well as actual, inflation will cause exchange rate changes. An increase in a currency's expected rate of inflation, all other things equal, makes that currency more expensive to hold over time (because its value is being eroded at a faster rate) and less in demand at the same price. Consequently, the value of higher-inflation currencies will tend to be depressed relative to the value of lower-inflation currencies, other things being equal.

Empirical Evidence

The strictest version of purchasing power parity—that all goods and financial assets obey the law of one price—is demonstrably false. The risks and costs of shipping goods internationally, as well as government-erected barriers to trade and capital flows, are at times high enough to cause exchange-adjusted prices to systematically differ between countries. On the other hand, there is clearly a relationship between relative inflation rates and changes in exchange rates. This relationship is shown in Exhibit 7.3, which compares the relative change in the purchasing power of 47 currencies (as measured by their relative inflation rates) with the relative change in the exchange rates for those currencies for the period 1982 through 1988. As expected, those currencies with the largest relative decline (gain) in purchasing power saw the sharpest erosion (appreciation) in their foreign exchange values.

The general conclusion from empirical studies of PPP is that the theory holds up well in the long run, but not as well over shorter time periods.[3] A common explanation for the failure of PPP to hold is that goods prices are sticky, leading to short-term violations of the law of one price. Adjustment to PPP eventually occurs, but it does so with a lag. An alternative explanation for the failure of most tests to support PPP in the short run is that these tests ignore the problems caused by the combination of differently constructed price indices, relative price changes, and nontraded goods and services.

One problem arises because the price indices used to measure inflation vary substantially between countries as to the goods and services included in the "market basket" and the weighting formula used. Thus, changes in the relative prices of various goods and services will cause differently constructed indices to deviate from each other, falsely signaling deviations from PPP. Careful empirical work by Kravis and others demonstrates

---

[3]Perhaps the best known of these studies is Henry J. Gailliot, "Purchasing Power Parity as an Explanation of Long-Term Changes in Exchange Rates," *Journal of Money, Credit, and Banking,* August 1971, pp. 348–357.

■ **EXHIBIT 7.3** Purchasing Power Parity: Empirical Data, 1982–1988

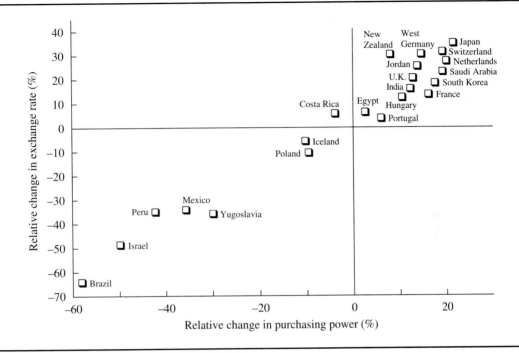

that measured deviations from PPP are far smaller when using the same weights than when using different weights in calculating the U.S. and foreign price indices.[4]

In addition, relative price changes could lead to changes in the equilibrium exchange rate, even in the absence of changes in the general level of prices. For example, an increase in the relative price of oil will lead to an increase in the exchange rates of oil-exporting countries, even if other prices adjust so as to keep all price levels constant. In general, a relative price change that increases a nation's wealth will also increase the value of its currency. Similarly, an increase in the real interest rate in one nation relative to real interest rates elsewhere will induce flows of foreign capital to the first nation. The result will be an increase in the real value of that nation's currency.

Finally, price indices heavily weighted with nontraded goods and services will provide misleading information about a nation's international competitiveness. Over the longer term, increases in the price of medical care or the cost of education will affect the cost of producing traded goods. But, in the short run, such price changes will have little effect on the exchange rate.

Exhibit 7.4 shows the often substantial gaps that can arise between nontraded goods and services between countries. You can't easily substitute a Hong Kong Big Mac costing

---

[4]Irving Kravis, et al., *A System of International Comparisons of Gross Product and Purchasing Power* (Baltimore: Johns Hopkins University Press, 1975).

■ **EXHIBIT 7.4**   Comparison of Prices of Nontraded Goods and Services

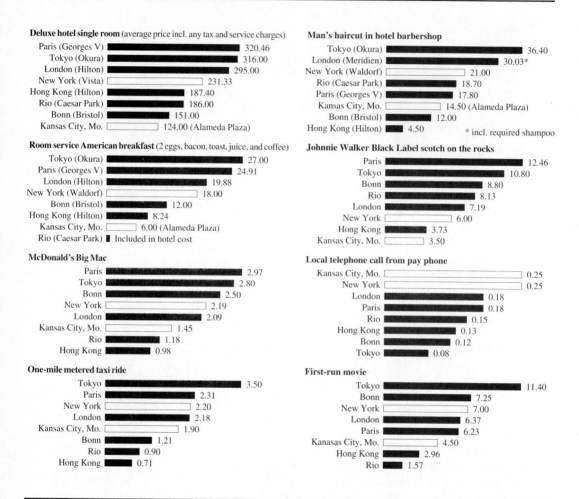

Deluxe hotel single room (average price incl. any tax and service charges)

Paris (Georges V)	320.46
Tokyo (Okura)	316.00
London (Hilton)	295.00
New York (Vista)	231.33
Hong Kong (Hilton)	187.40
Rio (Caesar Park)	186.00
Bonn (Bristol)	151.00
Kansas City, Mo.	124.00 (Alameda Plaza)

Room service American breakfast (2 eggs, bacon, toast, juice, and coffee)

Tokyo (Okura)	27.00
Paris (Georges V)	24.91
London (Hilton)	19.88
New York (Waldorf)	18.00
Bonn (Bristol)	12.00
Hong Kong (Hilton)	8.24
Kansas City, Mo.	6.00 (Alameda Plaza)
Rio (Caesar Park)	Included in hotel cost

McDonald's Big Mac

Paris	2.97
Tokyo	2.80
Bonn	2.50
New York	2.19
London	2.09
Kansas City, Mo.	1.45
Rio	1.18
Hong Kong	0.98

One-mile metered taxi ride

Tokyo	3.50
Paris	2.31
New York	2.20
London	2.18
Kansas City, Mo.	1.90
Bonn	1.21
Rio	0.90
Hong Kong	0.71

Man's haircut in hotel barbershop

Tokyo (Okura)	36.40
London (Meridien)	30.03*
New York (Waldorf)	21.00
Rio (Caesar Park)	18.70
Paris (Georges V)	17.80
Kansas City, Mo.	14.50 (Alameda Plaza)
Bonn (Bristol)	12.00
Hong Kong (Hilton)	4.50

* incl. required shampoo

Johnnie Walker Black Label scotch on the rocks

Paris	12.46
Tokyo	10.80
Bonn	8.80
Rio	8.13
London	7.19
New York	6.00
Hong Kong	3.73
Kansas City, Mo.	3.50

Local telephone call from pay phone

Kansas City, Mo.	0.25
New York	0.25
London	0.18
Paris	0.18
Rio	0.15
Hong Kong	0.13
Bonn	0.12
Tokyo	0.08

First-run movie

Tokyo	11.40
Bonn	7.25
New York	7.00
London	6.37
Paris	6.23
Kanasas City, Mo.	4.50
Hong Kong	2.96
Rio	1.57

$0.98 for a Paris Big Mac at $2.97. Similarly, if you're in Tokyo and you don't like the $316 price of a room at the Hotel Okura, you can't easily substitute a $124 room at the Alameda Plaza hotel in Kansas City. Because PPP is driven by arbitrage, including such prices in estimating PPP will not help to determine whether exchange rates are in equilibrium.

Despite the problems caused by relative price changes, most tests of relative PPP as a long-term theory of exchange rate determination seem to support its validity. The reason is that over long periods of time with a moderate inflation differential, the general trend in the price level ratio will tend to dominate the effects of relative price changes. This factor also explains why standard tests of PPP support it even in the short run during periods of hyperinflation: With high inflation, changes in the general level of prices quickly swamp the effects of relative price changes.

Deviations from PPP and Exchange Rate Equilibrium

Despite the fact that currencies deviate from their PPP values, these deviations do not indicate that the currencies are mispriced. For example, although commentators have claimed at various times that the U.S. dollar was overvalued or undervalued, it is not clear how a freely floating currency can be overvalued or undervalued, especially in a market in which as much as a trillion dollars changes hands daily. Presumably, these individuals are arguing that the dollar is mispriced with respect to PPP. But there are dangers in attributing too much importance to a deviation from PPP because PPP is not a complete theory of exchange-rate determination.

Deviations from PPP have prevailed throughout the history of the world. Either these deviations signal slow adjustment to equilibrium, or we must acknowledge that PPP is a poor proxy for the true equilibrium exchange rate. For example, if the dollar was overvalued from 1981 to September 1985 when official intervention against the dollar was initiated, then we must assume that a four-year period is insufficient time for market forces to restore equilibrium. If this is the case, then equilibrium becomes a meaningless concept.

The alternative view is that the dollar was in equilibrium during this period, and the true equilibrium rate was changing over time as new information reached the market about relative economic and political factors. This latter view is consistent with the evidence (presented in Chapter 4) that there are many economic and political factors aside from relative rates of inflation that affect currency values. For example, we saw that relative price changes, economic growth, and political risk affect spot exchange rates.

To summarize, despite often lengthy departures from PPP, there is a clear correspondence between relative inflation rates and changes in the nominal exchange rate. But, for reasons that have nothing to do with market disequilibrium, the correspondence is not perfect.

■ 7.3 ■
THE FISHER EFFECT

The interest rates that are quoted in the financial press are nominal rates. That is, they are expressed as the rate of exchange between current and future dollars. For example, a nominal interest rate of 8% on a one-year loan means that $1.08 must be repaid in one year for $1.00 loaned today. But what really matters to both parties to a loan agreement is the *real* interest rate, the rate at which current goods are being converted into future goods.

Looked at one way, the real rate of interest is the net increase in wealth that people expect to achieve when they save and invest their current income. Alternatively, it can be viewed as the added future consumption promised by a corporate borrower to a lender in return for the latter's deferring current consumption. From the company's standpoint, this exchange is worthwhile as long as it can find suitably productive investments.

However, because virtually all financial contracts are stated in nominal terms, the real interest rate must be adjusted to reflect expected inflation. The *Fisher effect* states that the nominal interest rate r is made up of two components: (1) a real required rate of return a and (2) an inflation premium equal to the expected amount of inflation i. Formally, the Fisher effect is

1 + Nominal rate = (1 + Real rate)(1 + Expected inflation rate)
$1 + r = (1 + a)(1 + i)$

or

$$r = a + i + ai \tag{7.5}$$

Equation 7.5 is often approximated by the equation $r = a + i$.

The Fisher equation says, for example, that if the required real return is 3% and expected inflation is 10%, then the nominal interest rate will be about 13% (13.3%, to be exact). The logic behind this result is that $1 next year will have the purchasing power of $0.90 in terms of today's dollars. Thus, the borrower must pay the lender $0.103 to compensate for the erosion in the purchasing power of the $1.03 in principal and interest payments, in addition to the $0.03 necessary to provide a 3% real return.

■ ———————————————————————————————————————

ILLUSTRATION

Brazilians Shun Negative Interest Rates on Savings. In 1981, the Brazilian government spent $10 million on an advertising campaign to help boost national savings, which dropped sharply in 1980. According to *The Wall Street Journal* (January 12, 1981, p. 23), the decline in savings occurred, "because the pre-fixed rates on savings deposits and treasury bills for 1980 were far below the rate of inflation, currently 110%." Clearly, the Brazilians were not interested in investing money at interest rates less than the inflation rate.

—— ■

The generalized version of the Fisher effect asserts that real returns are equalized across countries through arbitrage—that is, $a_h = a_f$, where the subscripts h and f refer to home and foreign. If expected real returns were higher in one currency than another, capital would flow from the second to the first currency. This process of arbitrage would continue, in the absence of government intervention, until expected real returns were equalized.

In equilibrium, then, with no government interference, it should follow that the nominal interest rate differential will approximately equal the anticipated inflation rate differential, or

$$\frac{1 + r_h}{1 + r_f} = \frac{1 + i_h}{1 + i_f} \tag{7.6}$$

where r_h and r_f are the nominal home- and foreign-currency interest rates, respectively.

If r_f and i_f are relatively small, then this exact relationship can be approximated by Equation 7.7:[5]

$$r_h - r_f = i_h - i_f \tag{7.7}$$

———————————————————————————————————————

[5]Equation 7.6 can be converted into Equation 7.7 by subtracting 1 from both sides and assuming that r_f and i_f are relatively small.

In effect, the generalized version of the Fisher effect says that *currencies with high rates of inflation should bear higher interest rates than currencies with lower rates of inflation.*

For example, if inflation rates in the United States and the United Kingdom are 4% and 7%, respectively, the Fisher effect says that nominal interest rates should be about about 3% higher in the United Kingdom than in the United States. A graph of Equation 7.7 is shown in Exhibit 7.5. The horizontal axis shows the expected difference in inflation rates between the home country and the foreign country, and the vertical axis shows the interest differential between the two countries for the same time period. The parity line shows all points for which $r_h - r_f = i_h - i_f$.

Point C, for example, is a position of equilibrium since the 2% higher rate of inflation in the foreign country ($i_h - i_f = -2\%$) is just offset by the 2% lower HC interest rate ($r_h - r_f = -2\%$). At point D, however, where the real rate of return in the home country is 1% higher than in the foreign country (an inflation differential of 3% versus an interest differential of only 2%), funds should flow from the foreign country to the home country to take advantage of the real differential. This flow will continue until expected real returns are again equal.

Empirical Evidence

Exhibit 7.6 illustrates the relationship between interest rates and subsequent inflation rates for 43 countries during the period 1982 through 1988. It is evident from the graph that nations with higher inflation rates generally have higher interest rates. Thus, the empirical evidence is consistent with the hypothesis that most of the variation in nominal interest rates across countries can be attributed to differences in inflationary expectations.

■ **EXHIBIT 7.5**   The Fisher Effect

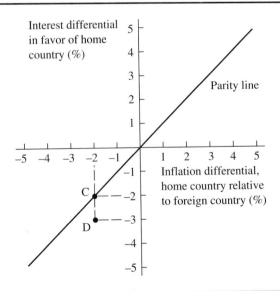

■ **EXHIBIT 7.6**   Fisher Effect: Empirical Data, 1982–1988

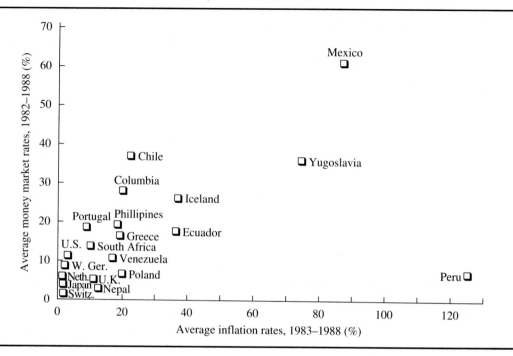

The proposition that expected real returns are equal between countries cannot be tested directly. However, many observers believe it unlikely that significant real interest differentials could long survive in the increasingly internationalized capital markets. Most market participants agree that arbitrage, via the huge pool of liquid capital that operates in international markets these days, is forcing pretax real interest rates to converge across all the major nations.

To the extent that arbitrage is permitted to operate unhindered, capital markets are integrated worldwide. *Capital market integration* means that real interest rates are determined by the global supply and global demand for funds. This is in contrast to *capital market segmentation,* where real interest rates are determined by local credit conditions. The difference between capital market segmentation and capital market integration is depicted in Exhibit 7.7. With a segmented capital market, the real interest rate in the United States, a_{us}, is based on the national demand D_{us} and national supply S_{us} of credit. Conversely, the real rate in the rest of the world, a_{rw}, is based on the rest-of-world supply S_{rw} and demand D_{rw}. In this example, the U.S. real rate is higher than the real rate outside the United States or $a_{us} > a_{rw}$.

Once the U.S. market opens up, the U.S. real interest rate falls (and the rest-of-world rate rises) to the new world rate a_w, which is determined by the world supply S_w ($S_{us} + S_{rw}$) and world demand D_w ($D_{us} + D_{rw}$) for credit. The mechanism whereby equilibrium is brought

■ **EXHIBIT 7.7**   The Distinction Between Capital Market Integration and Capital Market
Segmentation

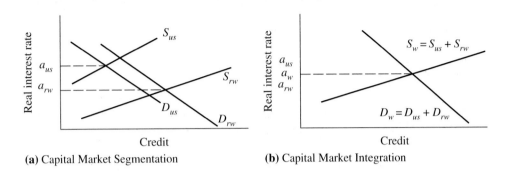

(a) Capital Market Segmentation   **(b)** Capital Market Integration

about is a capital inflow to the United States. It is this same capital flow that drives up the real interest rate outside the United States.

As shown by Exhibit 7.7, in an integrated capital market, the domestic real interest rate depends on what is happening outside as well as inside the United States. For example, a rise in the demand for capital by German companies to finance investments in Eastern Europe will raise the real interest rate in the United States as well as in Germany. Similarly, a rise in the U.S. savings rate, other things being equal, will lower the real cost of capital both in the United States and in the rest of the world. Conversely, a fall in U.S. inflation will lower the nominal U.S. interest rate (the Fisher effect), while leaving unchanged real interest rates worldwide.

Capital market integration has homogenized markets around the world, eroding much— although apparently not all—of the real interest rate differentials between comparable domestic and offshore securities, and strengthening the link between assets that are denominated in different currencies but carry similar credit risks.[6] To the extent that real interest differentials do exist, they must be due to either currency risk or some form of political risk.

A real interest rate differential could exist without being arbitraged away if investors strongly prefer to hold domestic assets in order to avoid currency risk, even if the expected real return on foreign assets was higher. Despite this theoretical possibility, the data indicate a convergence in real interest rates internationally, even if they don't appear to be equal.[7] Moreover, some evidence suggests that currency risk is not systematic and thus, according to the capital asset pricing model, should not command a risk premium. Indeed, for

---

[6]An offshore security is one denominated in the home currency but issued abroad. They are generally referred to as Eurosecurities.

[7]See, for example, Frederick S. Mishkin, "Are Real Interest Rates Equal Across Countries? An International Investigation of Parity Conditions," *Journal of Finance,* December 1984, pp. 1345–1357. He finds that although capital markets may be integrated, real interest rates appear to differ across countries because of currency risk.

consumers who prefer foreign goods and services, investing overseas could reduce their exchange risk by generating foreign currency revenues to offset their foreign currency expenses.

Absent currency risk, the only way to reintroduce real interest rate differentials in this closely integrated world economy is for countries to pursue sharply differing tax policies, impose regulatory barriers to the free flow of capital, or consciously present varying risks for would-be investors. None of these options is attractive to policymakers of the major industrial countries.

In many developing countries, however, currency controls and other government policies impose political risk on foreign investors. In effect, political risk can drive a wedge between the returns available to domestic investors and those available to foreign investors. For example, if political risk in Argentina causes foreign investors to demand a 7% higher interest rate than they demand elsewhere, then foreign investors would consider a 10% expected real return in Argentina to be equivalent to a 3% expected real return in the United States. Hence, real interest rates in developing countries can exceed those in developed countries without presenting attractive arbitrage opportunities to foreign investors. The combination of a relative shortage of capital and high political risk in most developing countries is likely to cause real interest rates in these countries to exceed real interest rates in the developed countries.

Before moving to the next parity condition, a caveat is in order. We must keep in mind that there are numerous interest differentials just as there are many different interest rates in a market. The rate on bank deposits, for instance, will not be identical to that on Treasury bills. When computing an interest differential, therefore, the securities on which this differential is based must be of identical risk characteristics save for currency risk. Otherwise, there is the danger of comparing apples with oranges (or at least temple oranges with navel oranges).

Adding Up Capital Markets Internationally.   Central to understanding how we can add yen and DM and dollar capital markets together is to recognize that money is only a veil: All financial transactions, no matter how complex, ultimately involve exchanges of goods today for goods in the future. As we saw in Chapter 6, you supply credit (capital) when you consume less than you produce; you demand credit when you consume more than you produce. Thus, the supply of credit can be thought of as the excess supply of goods and the demand for credit as the excess demand for goods. So when we add up the capital markets around the world we are adding up the excess demands for goods and the excess supplies of goods. A car is still a car, whether it is valued in yen or dollars.

■ 7.4 ■
THE INTERNATIONAL FISHER EFFECT

The key to understanding the impact of relative changes in nominal interest rates among countries on the foreign exchange value of a nation's currency is to recall the implications of PPP and the generalized Fisher effect. PPP implies that exchange rates will move to offset changes in inflation rate differentials. Thus, a rise in the U.S. inflation rate relative to those of other countries will be associated with a fall in the dollar's value. It will also be associated with a rise in the U.S. interest rate relative to foreign interest rates. Combine these two conditions and the result is the *international Fisher effect*:

$$\frac{(1 + r_h)^t}{(1 + r_f)^t} = \frac{\overline{e}_t}{e_0} \tag{7.8}$$

where $\overline{e}_t$ is the expected exchange rate in period t. The single period analogue to Equation 7.8 is

$$\frac{1 + r_h}{1 + r_f} = \frac{\overline{e}_1}{e_0} \tag{7.9}$$

Note the relation here to interest rate parity. If the forward rate is an unbiased predictor of the future spot rate—that is, $f_1 = \overline{e}_1$—then Equation 7.9 becomes the interest rate parity condition:

$$\frac{1 + r_h}{1 + r_f} = \frac{f_1}{e_0} \tag{7.10}$$

According to both Equations 7.9 and 7.10, the expected return from investing at home, $1 + r_h$, should equal the expected HC return from investing abroad, $(1 + r_f)\overline{e}_1/e_0$ or $(1 + r_f)f_1/e_0$. As discussed in the previous section, however, despite the intuitive appeal of equal expected returns, domestic and foreign expected returns might not equilibrate if the element of currency risk restrained the process of international arbitrage.

■ ───

ILLUSTRATION

Using the IFE to Forecast U.S.\$ and SFr Rates. In July, the one-year interest rate is 4% on Swiss francs and 13% on U.S. dollars.
a. If the current exchange rate is SFr 1 = \$0.63, what is the expected future exchange rate in one year?
    Solution.   According to the international Fisher effect, the spot exchange rate expected in one year equals $0.63 \times 1.13/1.04 = \$0.6845$.
b. If a change in expectations regarding future U.S. inflation causes the expected future spot rate to rise to \$0.70, what should happen to the U.S. interest rate?
    Solution.   If r_{us} is the unknown U.S. interest rate, and the Swiss interest rate stayed at 4% (because there has been no change in expectations of Swiss inflation), then according to the international Fisher effect, $0.70/0.63 = (1+r_{us})/1.04$, or $r_{us} = 15.56\%$.   ■

If r_f is relatively small, Equation 7.11 provides a reasonable approximation to the international Fisher effect (IFE):[8]

───

[8]Subtracting 1 from both sides of Equation 7.9 yields $(\overline{e}_1 - e_0)/e_0 = (r_h - r_f)/(1 + r_f)$. Equation 7.11 follows if i_f is relatively small.

$$r_h - r_f = \frac{\bar{e}_1 - e_0}{e_0} \qquad\qquad (7.11)$$

In effect, the IFE says that *currencies with low interest rates are expected to appreciate relative to currencies with high interest rates.*

A graph of Equation 7.10 is shown in Exhibit 7.8. The vertical axis shows the expected change in the home-currency value of the foreign currency, and the horizontal axis shows the interest differential between the two countries for the same time period. The parity line shows all points for which $r_h - r_f = (e_1 - e_0)/e_0$.

Point E is a position of equilibrium because it lies on the parity line, with the 4% interest differential in favor of the home country just offset by the anticipated 4% appreciation in the HC value of the foreign currency. Point F, however, illustrates a situation of disequilibrium. If the foreign currency is expected to appreciate by 3% in terms of the HC, but the interest differential in favor of the home country is only 2%, then funds would flow from the home to the foreign country to take advantage of the higher exchange-adjusted returns there. This capital flow will continue until exchange-adjusted returns are equal in both nations.

Essentially what the IFE says is that arbitrage between financial markets—in the form of international capital flows—should ensure that the interest differential between any two countries is an *unbiased predictor* of the future change in the spot rate of exchange. This condition does not mean, however, that the interest differential is an especially accurate predictor; it just means that prediction errors tend to cancel out over time.

■ **EXHIBIT 7.8**   International Fisher Effect

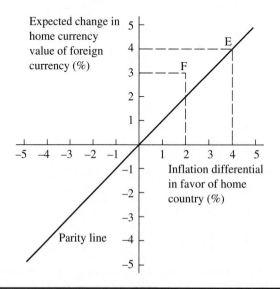

Empirical Evidence

As predicted, there is a clear tendency for currencies with high interest rates (for example, Mexico and Brazil) to depreciate and those with low interest rates (for example, Japan and Switzerland) to appreciate. This is shown in Exhibit 7.9, which graphs the nominal interest differential (relative to the U.S. interest rate) against exchange rate changes (relative to the U.S. dollar) for 45 currencies over the period 1982 to 1988. The ability of interest differentials to anticipate currency changes is also supported by several empirical studies that indicate the long-run tendency for these differentials to offset exchange rate changes.[9] Thus, at any given time, currencies bearing higher nominal interest rates can reasonably be expected to depreciate relative to currencies bearing lower interest rates.

However, the effect on exchange rates of a change in the nominal interest differential is not so easily determined. According to the Fisher effect, changes in the nominal interest

■ **EXHIBIT 7.9**   International Fisher Effect: Empirical Data, 1982–1988

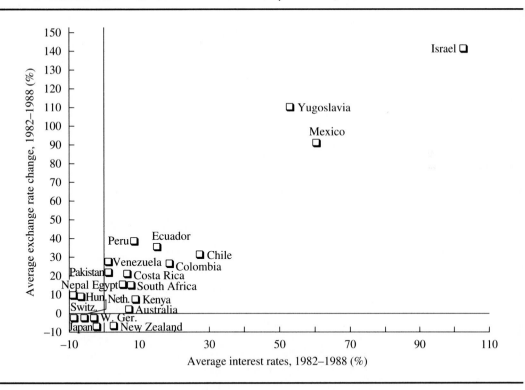

[9]See, for example, Ian H. Giddy and Gunter Dufey, "The Random Behavior of Flexible Exchange Rates," *Journal of International Business Studies,* Spring 1975, pp. 1–32; and Robert A. Aliber and Clyde P. Stickney, "Accounting Measures of Foreign Exchange Exposure: The Long and Short of It," *The Accounting Review,* January 1975, pp. 44–57.

differential can be due to changes in either the real interest differential or relative inflationary expectations. These two possibilities have opposite effects on currency values. For example, suppose that the nominal interest differential widens in favor of the United States. If this spread is due to a rise in the real interest rate in the United States relative to that of other countries, the value of the dollar will rise. Alternatively, if the change in the nominal interest differential is caused by an increase in inflationary expectations for the United States, the dollar's value will drop.

The key to understanding short-run changes in the value of the dollar or other currency, then, is to distinguish changes in nominal interest rate differentials that are caused by changes in real interest rate differentials from those caused by changes in relative inflation expectations. Historically, changes in the nominal interest differential have been dominated, at times, by changes in the real interest differential; at other times, they have been dominated by changes in relative inflation expectations. Consequently, there is no stable, predictable relationship between changes in the nominal interest differential and exchange rate changes.

■ 7.5 ■
INFLATION RISK AND ITS IMPACT ON FINANCIAL MARKETS

We have seen from the Fisher effect that both borrowers and lenders factor expected inflation into the nominal interest rate. The problem, of course, is that actual inflation could turn out to be higher or lower than expected. This possibility introduces the element of inflation risk, by which is meant the divergence between actual and expected inflation.

It is easy to see why inflation risk can have such a devastating impact on bond prices. Bonds promise investors fixed cash payments until maturity. Even if those payments are guaranteed, as in the case of default-free U.S. Treasury bonds, investors face the risk of random changes in the dollar's purchasing power. If actual inflation could vary between 5% and 15% annually, then the real interest rate associated with a 13% nominal rate could vary between 8% (13 – 5) and –2% (13 – 15). Since what matters to people is the real value—not the quantity—of the money they will receive, a high and variable rate of inflation will result in lenders demanding a premium to bear inflation risk.

Borrowers also face inflation risk. Assume a firm issues a 20-year bond priced to yield 15%. If this nominal rate is based on a 12% expected rate of inflation, then the firm's expected real cost of debt will be about 3%. But suppose the rate of inflation averages 2% over the next 20 years. Instead of a 3% real cost of debt, the firm must pay a real interest rate of 13%. Thus, borrowers will also demand to be compensated for bearing inflation risk. Of course, if inflation turns out to be higher than expected, the borrower will gain by having a lower real cost of funds than anticipated. Since inflation is a zero-sum game, the lender will lose exactly what the borrower gains. When inflation is lower than expected, however, the lender will profit at the borrower's expense. Thus, the presence of uncertain inflation introduces an element of risk into financial contracts even when, as with government debt, default risk is absent. Under conditions of high and variable inflation, therefore, we would expect to find an inflation risk premium, p, added to the basic Fisher equation. The modified Fisher equation would then be

$$r = a + i + ai + p \tag{7.12}$$

Yet a basic problem remains. Although inflation risk on a financial contract stated in nominal terms affects both borrower and lender, both cannot be compensated simultaneously for bearing this risk. Therefore, lender and borrower will decide under some circumstances to shun fixed-rate debt contracts altogether.

Inflation and Bond Price Fluctuations

The effect of inflation on bond prices is comparable to that of interest rate changes because both affect the real value of cash flows to be received in the future. For example, the real or inflation-adjusted value of a dollar to be received in one year when inflation is 5% per annum equals 1/1.05 or $0.9524. That same dollar to be received two years hence has a real value of $1/(1.05)^2 = \$0.9070$. An increase in the inflation rate to 8% per annum will change the real values of the dollars received in the first and second years to $0.9259 and $0.8573, respectively. The 3% increase in the rate of inflation reduces the real value of the dollar received in year 1 by $0.0265, while the real value of the dollar received in year 2 drops by $0.0497.

This example illustrates a more general phenomenon: The longer the maturity of a bond, the greater the impact on the present value of that bond associated with a given change in the rate of inflation. In effect, a change in the inflation rate is equivalent to a change in the rate at which future cash flows are discounted back to the present. Thus, inflation risk is most devastating on long-term, fixed-rate bonds.

Responses to Inflation Risk

Since the problem of inflation risk increases with the maturity of a bond, the presence of volatile inflation will make corporate borrowers less willing to issue, and investors less willing to buy, long-term, fixed-rate debt. The result will be a decline in the use of long-term, fixed-rate financing and an increased reliance on debt with shorter maturities, floating-rate bonds, and indexed bonds.

Shorter Maturities.   With shorter maturities, investors and borrowers lock themselves in for shorter periods of time. They reduce their exposure to inflation risk because the divergence between actual and expected inflation decreases as the period of time over which inflation is measured decreases. When the security matures, the loan can be "rolled over" or borrowed again at a new rate that reflects revised expectations of inflation.

Floating-Rate Bonds.   The problem with short maturities for the corporate borrower, however, is that there is no guarantee that additional funds will be available at maturity. A floating-rate bond solves this problem. The funds are automatically rolled over every three to six months, or so, at an adjusted interest rate. The new rate is typically set at a fixed margin above a mutually agreed-upon interest rate "index" such as the London interbank offer rate (LIBOR) for Eurodollar deposits (see Chapter 20), the corresponding Treasury bill rate, or the prime rate. For example, if the floating rate is set at prime plus 2, then a prime rate of 8.5% will yield a loan rate of 10.5%.

Indexed Bonds.   The real interest rate on a floating-rate bond can still change if real interest rates in the market change. This problem can be alleviated by issuing indexed bonds that pay interest tied to the inflation rate. For example, the British government has sold several billion pounds of indexed bonds since 1981. The way indexation works is that the interest rate is set equal to, say, 3% plus an adjustment for the amount of inflation during the past year. If inflation was 17%, the interest rate will be 3 + 17 = 20%. In this way, although the nominal rate of interest will fluctuate with inflation, the real rate of interest will be fixed at 3%. Both borrower and lender are protected against inflation risk.

The international evidence clearly supports these conjectures. In highly inflationary countries—such as Argentina, Brazil, Israel, and Mexico—long-term fixed-rate financing is no longer available. Instead, long-term financing is done with floating-rate bonds or indexed debt. Similarly, in the United States during the late 1970s and early 1980s, when inflation risk was at its peak, 30-year conventional fixed-rate mortgages were largely replaced with so-called adjustable-rate mortgages. The interest rate on this type of mortgage is adjusted every month or so in line with the changing short-term cost of funds. To the extent that short-term interest rates track actual inflation rates closely—a reasonable assumption according to the available evidence—an adjustable-rate mortgage protects both borrower and lender from inflation risk.

■ 7.6 ■
CURRENCY FORECASTING

Forecasting exchange rates has become an occupational hazard for financial executives of multinational corporations. The potential for periodic—and unpredictable—government intervention makes currency forecasting all the more difficult. But this has not dampened the enthusiasm for currency forecasts, nor the willingness of economists and others to supply them. Unfortunately, though, enthusiasm and willingness are not sufficient conditions for success.

Requirements for Successful Currency Forecasting

Currency forecasting can lead to consistent profits only if the forecaster meets at least one of the following four criteria:[10] He or she

- Has exclusive use of a superior forecasting model
- Has consistent access to information before other investors
- Exploits small, temporary deviations from equilibrium
- Can predict the nature of government intervention in the foreign exchange market

---

[10]These criteria were suggested by Giddy and Dufey, "Random Behavior of Flexible Exchange Rates."

The first two conditions are self-correcting. Successful forecasting breeds imitators, while the second situation is unlikely to last long in the highly informed world of international finance. The third situation describes how foreign exchange traders actually earn their living and also why deviations from equilibrium are not likely to last long. The fourth situation is the one worth searching out. Countries that insist on managing their exchange rates, and are willing to take losses to achieve their target rates, present speculators with potentially profitable opportunities. Simply put, consistently profitable predictions are possible in the long run only if it is not necessary to outguess the market to win.

As a general rule, when forecasting in a fixed-rate system, the focus must be on the governmental decision-making structure because the decision to devalue or revalue at a given time is clearly political. During the Bretton Woods system, for example, many speculators did quite well by "stepping into the shoes of the key decisionmakers" to forecast their likely behavior. The basic forecasting methodology in a fixed-rate system, therefore, involves first ascertaining the pressure on a currency to devalue or revalue and then determining how long the nation's political leaders can, and will, persist with this particular level of disequilibrium. Exhibit 7.10 depicts a five-step procedure for performing this analysis. In the case of a floating-rate system, where government intervention is sporadic or nonexistent, currency prognosticators have the choice of using either market- or model-based forecasts, neither of which guarantees success.

Market-Based Forecasts

So far, we have identified several equilibrium relationships that should exist between exchange rates and interest rates. The empirical evidence on these relationships implies that, in general, the financial markets of developed countries efficiently incorporate expected currency changes in the cost of money and forward exchange. This means that currency forecasts can be obtained by extracting the predictions already embodied in interest and forward rates.

Forward Rates. Market-based forecasts of exchange rate changes can be derived most simply from current forward rates. Specifically, f_1—the forward rate for one period from now—will usually suffice for an unbiased estimate of the spot rate as of that date. In other words, f_1 should equal $\bar{e}_1$, where $\bar{e}_1$ is the expected future spot rate.

Interest Rates. Although forward rates provide simple and easy to use currency forecasts, their forecasting horizon is limited to about one year because of the general absence of longer-term forward contracts. Interest rate differentials can be used to supply exchange rate predictions beyond one year. For example, suppose five-year interest rates on dollars and Deutsche marks are 12% and 8%, respectively. If the current spot rate for the DM is $0.40 and the (unknown) value of the DM in five years is e_5, then $1.00 invested today in Deutsche marks will be worth $(1.08)^5 e_5/0.4$ dollars at the end of five years; if invested in the dollar security, it will be worth $(1.12)^5$ in five years. The market's forecast of e_5 can be found by assuming that investors demand equal returns on dollar and DM securities, or

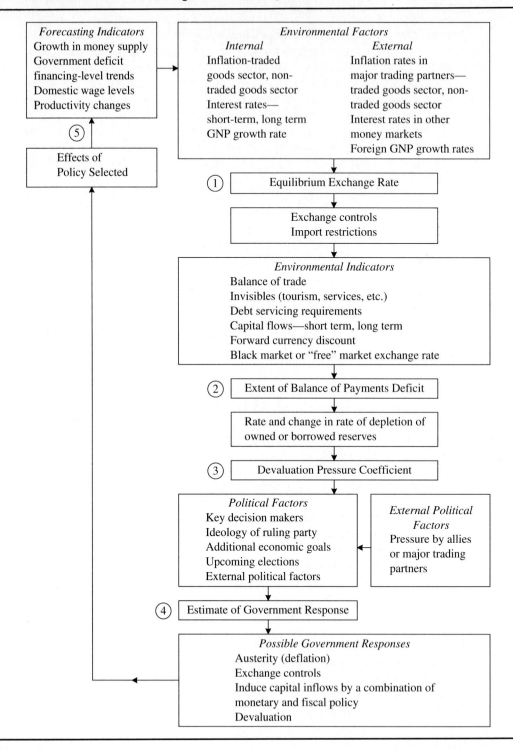

$$(1.08)^5 e_5/0.4 = (1.12)^5$$

Thus, the five-year DM spot rate implied by the relative interest rates is $e_5 = \$0.4798$ (0.40 $\times 1.12^5/1.08^5$).

Model-Based Forecasts

The two principal model-based approaches to currency prediction are known as fundamental analysis and technical analysis. Each approach has its advocates and detractors.

Fundamental Analysis. *Fundamental analysis* is the most common approach to forecasting future exchange rates. It relies on painstaking examination of the macroeconomic variables and policies that are likely to influence a currency's prospects. The variables examined include relative inflation and interest rates, national income growth, and changes in money supplies. The interpretation of these variables and their implications for future exchange rates depend on the analyst's model of exchange rate determination.

The simplest form of fundamental analysis involves the use of PPP. We have previously seen the value of PPP in explaining exchange rate changes. Its application in currency forecasting is straightforward.

■ ───────────────────────────────

ILLUSTRATION

Using PPP to Forecast the Peseta's Future Spot Rate. The U.S. inflation rate is expected to average about 4% annually, while the Spanish rate of inflation is expected to average about 9% annually. If the current spot rate for the peseta is $0.008, what is the expected spot rate in two years?

Solution. According to PPP (Equation 7.1), the expected spot rate for the peseta in two years is $\$0.008 \times (1.04/1.09)^2 = \$0.00728$. ───────── ■

Most analysts use more complicated forecasting models whose analysis usually centers on how the different macroeconomic variables are likely to affect the demand and supply for a given foreign currency. The currency's future value is then determined by estimating the exchange rate at which supply just equals demand—when any current-account imbalance is just matched by a net capital flow.

Technical Analysis. *Technical analysis* is the antithesis of fundamental analysis in that it focuses exclusively on past price and volume movements—while totally ignoring economic and political factors—to forecast currency winners and losers. Success depends on whether technical analysts can discover price patterns that repeat themselves and are, therefore, useful for forecasting.

There are two primary methods of technical analysis: *charting* and *trend analysis.* Chartists examine bar charts or use more sophisticated computer-based extrapolation techniques to find recurring price patterns. They then issue buy or sell recommendations if prices diverge from their past pattern. Trend-following systems seek to identify price trends via various mathematical computations.

Model Evaluation

The possibility that either fundamental or technical analysis can be used to profitably forecast exchange rates is inconsistent with the efficient market hypothesis, which says that current exchange rates reflect all publicly available information. Because markets are forward looking, exchange rates will fluctuate randomly as market participants assess and then react to new information, much as security and commodity prices in other asset markets respond to news. Thus, exchange rate movements are unpredictable; otherwise, it would be possible to earn arbitrage profits. Such profits could not persist in a market—like the foreign exchange market—that is characterized by free entry and exit and an almost unlimited amount of money, time, and energy that participants are willing to commit in pursuit of profit opportunities.

Despite the theoretical skepticism over successful currency forecasting, a study of 14 forecast advisory services by Richard Levich indicates that the profits associated with using several of these forecasts seem too good to be explained by chance.[11] Of course, if the forward rate contains a risk premium, these returns would have to be adjusted for the risks borne by speculators. It is also questionable whether currency forecasters would continue selling their information rather than acting on it themselves if they truly believed it could yield excess risk-adjusted returns.

Forecasting Controlled Exchange Rates

A major problem in currency forecasting is that the widespread existence of exchange controls, as well as restrictions on imports and capital flows, often masks the true pressures on a currency to devalue. In such situations, forward markets and capital markets are invariably nonexistent or subject to such stringent controls that interest and forward differentials are of little practical use in providing market-based forecasts of exchange rate changes. An alternative forecasting approach in such a controlled environment is to use *black-market exchange rates* as useful indicators of devaluation pressure on the nation's currency.

Black-market exchange rates for a number of countries are regularly reported in *Pick's Currency Yearbook and Reports*. These black markets for foreign exchange are likely to appear whenever exchange controls cause a divergence between the equilibrium exchange rate and the official, or controlled, exchange rate. Those potential buyers of foreign exchange without access to the central banks will have an incentive to find another market in which to buy foreign currency. Similarly, sellers of foreign exchange will prefer to sell their holdings at the higher black-market rate.

The black-market rate depends on the difference between the official and equilibrium exchange rates, as well as on the expected penalties for illegal transactions. The existence of these penalties and the fact that some transactions do go through at the official rate mean that the black-market rate is not influenced by exactly the same set of supply-and-

---

[11]Richard M. Levich, "The Use and Analysis of Foreign Exchange Forecasts: Current Issues and Evidence," paper presented at the Euromoney Treasury Consultancy Program, New York, September 4–5, 1980.

demand forces that influences the free-market rate. Therefore, the black-market rate in itself cannot be regarded as indicative of the true equilibrium rate that would prevail in the absence of controls. Economists normally assume that for an overvalued currency, the hypothetical equilibrium rate lies somewhere between the official rate and the black-market rate.

The usefulness of the black-market rate is that it is a good indicator of where the official rate is likely to go if the monetary authorities give in to market pressure. However, although the official rate can be expected to move toward the black-market rate, we should not expect to see it coincide with that rate due to the bias induced by government sanctions. The black-market rate seems to be most accurate in forecasting the official rate one month ahead and is progressively less accurate as a forecaster of the future official rate for longer time periods.[12]

Exhibit 7.11(a) graphs monthly movements in the official and black-market rates for the Brazilian cruzeiro from December 1968 to March 1977. Exhibit 7.11(b) graphs monthly movements in the two rates from 1981 to 1983. The data clearly show that the black-market cruzeiro rate is invariably above the official rate and is a useful indicator of future devaluations.

■ 7.7 ■
SUMMARY AND CONCLUSIONS

In this chapter, we examined three relationships, or parity conditions, that should apply to spot rates, inflation rates, and interest rates in different currencies: purchasing power parity, the Fisher effect, and the international Fisher effect. These parity conditions follow from the law of one price, the notion that in the absence of market imperfections, arbitrage ensures that exchange-adjusted prices of identical traded goods and financial assets are within transaction costs worldwide.

The technical description of these three equilibrium relationships is summarized as follows:

■ Purchasing power parity

$$\frac{e_t}{e_0} = \frac{(1 + i_h)^t}{(1 + i_f)^t}$$

where e_t = the home currency value of the foreign currency at time t
   e_0 = the home currency value of the foreign currency at time 0
   i_h = the periodic domestic inflation rate
   i_f = the periodic foreign inflation rate

---

[12]See, for example, Ian H. Giddy, "Black Market Exchange Rates as a Forecasting Tool," working paper, Columbia University, May 1978.

■ **EXHIBIT 7.11**   Black Market Versus Official Exchange Rates: Brazilian Cruzeiro

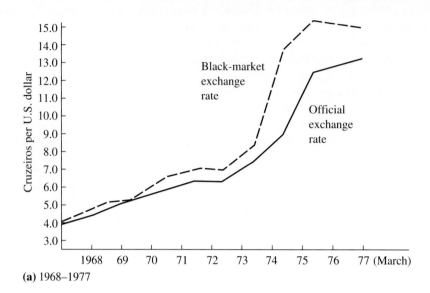

(a) 1968–1977

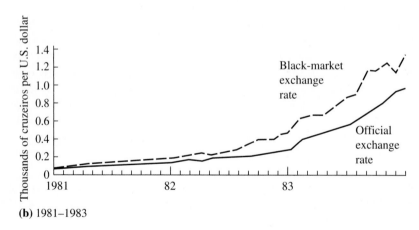

(b) 1981–1983

■ Fisher effect

$$1 + r = (1 + a)(1 + i)$$

where r = the nominal rate of interest
        a = the real rate of interest
        i = the rate of expected inflation

■ Generalized version of Fisher effect:

$$\frac{(1 + r_h)_t}{(1 + r_f)^t} = \frac{(1 + i_h)^t}{(1 + i_f)^t}$$

where r_h = the periodic home currency interest rate
   r_f = the periodic foreign currency interest rate

■ International Fisher effect

$$\frac{(1 + r_h)^t}{(1 + r_f)^t} = \frac{\overline{e}_t}{e_0}$$

where $\overline{e}_t$ = the expected home currency value of the foreign currency at time t

Despite the mathematical precision with which these parity conditions are expressed, they are only approximations to reality. A variety of factors can lead to significant and prolonged deviations from parity. For example, both currency risk and inflation risk may cause real interest rates to differ across countries.

The chapter also defined the real exchange rate, e_t', as the nominal, or actual, exchange rate adjusted for changes in the relative purchasing power of each currency since some base period. Specifically,

$$e_t' = e_t \times \frac{(1 + i_f)^t}{(1 + i_h)^t}$$

Finally, we analyzed a series of forecasting models that purport to outperform the market's own forecasts of future exchange rates as embodied in interest and forward differentials. We concluded that the foreign exchange market is no different from any other financial market in its susceptibility to profitable predictions.

Those who have inside information about events that will affect the value of a currency or a security should benefit handsomely. Those who do not have this access will have to trust either to luck or to the existence of a market imperfection, such as government intervention, to assure themselves of above average, risk-adjusted profits. In fact, given the widespread availability of information and the many knowledgeable participants in the foreign exchange market, only the latter situation—government manipulation of exchange rates—holds the promise of superior returns from currency forecasting. When governments spend money to control exchange rates, this money flows into the hands of private participants who bet against the government. The trick is to predict government actions.

■ QUESTIONS ■

1. What are some reasons for deviations from purchasing power parity?

2. Under what circumstances can purchasing power parity be applied?

3. One proposal to stabilize the international monetary system involves setting exchange rates at their purchasing power parity rates. Once exchange rates are correctly aligned (according to PPP), each

nation would adjust its monetary policy so as to maintain them. What problems might arise from using the PPP rate as a guide to the equilibrium exchange rate?

4. If the average rate of inflation in the world rises from 5% to 7%, what will be the effect on the U.S. dollar's forward premium or discount relative to foreign currencies?

5. Comment on the following statement. "It makes sense to borrow during times of high inflation because you can repay the loan in cheaper dollars."

6. Which is likely to be higher, a 150% cruzeiro return in Brazil or a 15% dollar return in the United States?

7. The interest rate in England is 12%, while in Switzerland it is 5%. What are possible reasons for this interest rate differential? What is the most likely reason?

8. In Exhibit 7.6, Peru and Chile stand out as countries whose interest rates are not consistent with their inflation experience.

   a. How would you characterize the real interest rates of Peru and Chile (e.g., close to zero, highly positive, highly negative)?

   b. What might account for Peru's low interest rate relative to its high inflation rate? What are the likely consequences of this low interest rate?

   c. What might account for Chile's high interest rate relative to its inflation rate? What are the likely consequences of this high interest rate?

   d. In Exhibit 7.9, Peru is shown as having a small interest differential and yet a large average exchange rate change. How would you reconcile this experience with the international Fisher effect and with your answer to part b?

9. A number of countries (e.g., Pakistan, Hungary, Venezuela) are shown in Exhibit 7.9 as having a small or negative interest rate differential and a large average annual depreciation against the dollar. How would you explain these data? Can you reconcile these data with the international Fisher effect?

10. The empirical evidence shows that there is no consistent relationship between the spot exchange rate and the nominal interest rate differential. Why might this be?

11. During 1988, the U.S. prime rate—the rate of interest banks charge on loans to their best customers—stood at 9.5%. Japan's prime rate, meanwhile, was about 3.5%. Pointing to that discrepancy, a number of commentators argued that the cost of capital must come down for U.S. business to remain competitive with Japanese companies. What additional information would you need to properly assess this claim? Why might interest rates be lower in Japan than in the United States?

12. In the late 1960s, Firestone Tire decided that Swiss francs at 2% were cheaper than U.S. dollars at 8% and borrowed about SFr 500 million. Comment on this choice.

13. Comment on the following quote from a story in *The Wall Street Journal* (August 27, 1984, p. 6) that discusses the improving outlook for Britain's economy: "Recovery here will probably last longer than in the U.S. because there isn't a huge budget deficit to pressure interest rates higher."

14. In early 1989, Japanese interest rates were about 4 percentage points below U.S. rates. The wide difference between Japanese and U.S. interest rates prompted some U.S. real estate developers to borrow in yen to finance their projects. Comment on this strategy.

15. In early 1990, Japanese and German interest rates rose while U.S. rates fell. At the same time, the yen and DM fell against the U.S. dollar. What might explain the divergent trends in interest rates?

16. In late December 1990, one-year German Treasury bills yielded 9.1%, whereas one-year U.S. Treasury bills yielded 6.9%. At the same time, the inflation rate during 1990 was 6.3% in the United States, double the German rate of 3.1%.

    a. Are these inflation and interest rates consistent with the Fisher effect?

    b. What might explain this difference in interest rates between the United States and Germany?

17. Comment on the following headline that appeared in *The Wall Street Journal* (December 19, 1990, p. C10): "Dollar Falls Across the Board as Fed Cuts Discount Rate to 6.5% From 7%." The discount rate is the interest rate the Fed charges member banks for loans.

18. In late 1990, the U.S. government announced that it might try to reduce the budget deficit by imposing a 0.5% transfer tax on all sales and purchases of securities in the United States, with the exception of Treasury securities. It projected the tax would raise $10 billion in federal revenues—an amount arrived at by multiplying 0.5% by the value of the $2 trillion trading on the New York Stock Exchange each year.

    a. What are the likely consequences of this tax? Consider its effects on trading volume in the United States and stock and bond prices.

    b. Why does the U.S. government plan to exclude its securities from this tax?

    c. Critically assess the government's estimates of the revenue it will raise from this tax.

■ PROBLEMS ■

1. From base price levels of 100 in 1987, West German and U.S. price levels in 1988 stood at 102 and 106, respectively. If the 1987 $:DM exchange rate was $0.54, what should the exchange rate be in 1988? In fact, the exchange rate in 1988 was DM 1 = $0.56. What might account for the discrepancy? (Price levels were measured using the consumer price index.)

2. Two countries, the United States and England, produce only one good, wheat. Suppose the price of wheat in the United States is $3.25 and in England it is £1.35.

    a. According to the law of one price, what should the $:£ spot exchange rate be?

    b. Suppose the price of wheat over the next year is expected to rise to $3.50 in the United States and to £1.60 in England. What should the one-year $:£ forward rate be?

    c. If the U.S. government imposes a tariff of $0.50 per bushel on wheat imported from England, what is the maximum possible change in the spot exchange rate that could occur?

3. In July, the one-year interest rate is 12% on British pounds and 9% on U.S. dollars.

    a. If the current exchange rate is $1.63:£1, what is the expected future exchange rate in one year?

    b. Suppose a change in expectations regarding future U.S. inflation causes the expected future spot rate to decline to $1.52:£1. What should happen to the U.S. interest rate?

4. If expected inflation is 100% and the real required return is 5%, what will the nominal interest rate be according to the Fisher effect?

5. Suppose that in Japan the interest rate is 8% and inflation is expected to be 3%. Meanwhile, the expected inflation rate in France is 12%, and the English interest rate is 14%. To the nearest whole number, what is the best estimate of the one-year forward exchange premium (discount) at which the pound will be selling relative to the French franc?

6. Chase Econometrics has just published projected inflation rates for the United States and Germany for the next five years. U.S. inflation is expected to be 10% per year, while German inflation is expected to be 4% per year. If the current exchange rate is DM 1 = $0.50, what should the exchange rates for the next five years be?

7. If the $:¥ spot rate is $1 =¥218 and interest rates in Tokyo and New York are 6% and 12%, respectively, what is the expected $:¥ exchange rate one year hence?

8. The inflation rate in Great Britain is expected to be 4% per year, and the inflation rate in France is expected to be 6% per year. If the current spot rate is £1 = FF 12.50, what is the expected spot rate in two years?

9. Suppose three-year deposit rates on Eurodollars and Eurofrancs (Swiss) are 12% and 7%, respectively. If the current spot rate for the Swiss franc is $0.3985, what is the spot rate implied by these interest rates for the franc three years from now?

10. Suppose the dollar appreciates by 10% relative to the Deutsche mark during a year in which U.S. inflation was 7% and German inflation was 4%. What has happened to the real value of the Deutsche mark relative to the dollar?

11. Suppose the U.S. dollar:yen exchange rate moves from ¥270 = $1 at the beginning of the year to ¥245 = $1 by the end of the year. At the same time, the U.S. price index rises from 130 to 145, and the Japanese index moves from 110 to 115. What is the real appreciation of the yen during this year?

12. Suppose that on January 1, the cost of borrowing French francs for the year is 18%. During the year, U.S. inflation is 5%, and French inflation is 9%. At the same time, the exchange rate changes from FF 1 = $0.15 on January 1 to FF 1 = $0.10 on December 31. What was the real U.S. dollar cost of borrowing francs for the year?

13. In late 1990, following Britain's entry into the exchange-rate mechanism of the European Monetary System, 10-year British Treasury bonds yielded 11.5%, whereas the German equivalent offered a yield of just 9%. Under terms of its entry, Britain established a central rate against the DM of DM 2.95 and pledged to maintain this rate within a band of plus and minus 6%.

   a. By how much would sterling have to fall against the DM over a 10-year period for the German bond to offer a higher overall return than the British one? Assume the Treasuries are zero-coupon bonds with no interest paid until maturity.

   b. How does the exchange rate established in part a compare to the lower limit that the British government is pledged to maintain for sterling against the DM?

   c. What accounts for the difference between the two rates? Does this difference violate the international Fisher effect?

■ BIBLIOGRAPHY ■

Cornell, Bradford. "Relative Price Changes and Deviations from Purchasing Power Parity." *Journal of Banking and Finance,* 3 (1979), pp. 263–279.

Dufey, Gunter, and Ian H. Giddy. *The International Money Market.* Englewood Cliffs, N.J.: Prentice-Hall, 1978.

———. "Forecasting Exchange Rates in a Floating World." *Euromoney,* November 1975, pp. 28–35.

Gailliot, Henry J. "Purchasing Power Parity as an Explanation of Long-Term Changes in Exchange Rates." *Journal of Money, Credit, and Banking,* August 1970, pp. 348–357.

Giddy, Ian H. "An Integrated Theory of Exchange Rate Equilibrium." *Journal of Financial and Quantitative Analysis,* December 1976, pp. 883–892.

————, and Gunter Dufey. "The Random Behavior of Flexible Exchange Rates." *Journal of International Business Studies,* Spring 1975, pp. 1–32.

Levich, Richard M. "Analyzing the Accuracy of Foreign Exchange Advisory Services: Theory and Evidence." In *Exchange Risk and Exposure.* Richard Levich and Clas Wihlborg, eds. Lexington, Mass: D.C. Heath, 1980.

Officer, Lawrence H. "The Purchasing-Power-Parity Theory of Exchange Rates: A Review Article." *IMF Staff Papers,* March 1976, pp. 1–60.

Roll, Richard. "Violations of the Law of One Price and Their Implications for Differentially-Denominated Assets." In *International Finance and Trade,* vol. I. Marshall Sarnat and George Szego, eds. Cambridge, Mass.: Ballinger, 1979.

Shapiro, Alan C. "What Does Purchasing Power Parity Mean?" *Journal of International Money and Finance,* December 1983, pp. 295–318.

Strongin, Steve. "International Credit Market Connections." *Economic Perspectives,* July/August 1990, pp. 2–10.

Treuherz, Rolf M. "Forecasting Foreign Exchange Rates in Inflationary Economies." *Financial Executive,* February 1969, pp. 57–60.

■ PART I ■
■ Case Studies ■

■ Case I.1
Oil Levies: The Economic Implications

BACKGROUND

The combination of weakening oil prices and the failure of Congress to deal with the budget deficit by cutting spending has led some to see the possibility of achieving two objectives at once: (1) protecting U.S. oil producers from "cheap" foreign competition and (2) reducing the budget deficit. The solution is an oil-import fee or tariff. A tax on imported crude and refined products that matches a world oil-price decline, for example, would leave oil and refined-product prices in the United States unchanged. Thus, it is argued, such a tax will have little effect on U.S. economic activity. It merely represents a transfer of funds from foreign oil producers to the U.S. Treasury. Moreover, it would provide some price relief to struggling U.S. refineries and encourage the production of U.S. oil. Finally, at the current level of imports, a $5/barrel tariff on foreign crude oil and a separate tariff of $10/barrel-equivalent on refined products would raise more than $11.5 billion a year.

QUESTIONS

1. Suppose the tariff were levied solely on imported crude. In an integrated world economy, who will bear the burden of the import tariff? Who will benefit? Why? What will be the longer-term consequences?

2. If a $10/barrel tariff were levied on imported refined products (but no tariff were levied on crude oil), who would bear the burden of such a tariff? Who would benefit? Why? What will be the longer-term consequences?

3. What would be the economic consequences of the combined $5/barrel tariff on imported crude and a $10/barrel tariff on refined oil products? How would these tariffs affect domestic consumers, oil producers, refiners, companies competing against imports, and exporters?

4. How would these proposed import levies affect foreign suppliers to the United States of crude oil and refined products?

5. During the 1970s, price controls on crude oil—but not on refined products—were in effect in the United States. Based on your previous analysis, what differences would you expect to see between heating oil and gasoline prices in New York and in Rotterdam (the major refining center in northwestern Europe)?

■ Case I.2
President Carter Lectures the Foreign Exchange Markets

At a press conference in March 1978, President Jimmy Carter—responding to a falling dollar—lectured the international financial markets as follows:

I've spent a lot of time studying about the American dollar, its value in international monetary markets, the causes of its recent deterioration as it relates to other major currencies. I can say with complete assurance that the basic principles of monetary values are not being adequately addressed on the current international monetary market.*

President Carter then offered three reasons why the dollar should improve: (1) the "rapidly increasing" attractiveness of investment in the U.S. economy due to high nominal interest rates, (2) an end to growth in oil imports, and (3) a decline in the real growth of the U.S. economy relative to the rest of the world's economic growth.

QUESTIONS

1. How were financial markets likely to respond to President Carter's lecture? Explain.

2. At the time President Carter made his remarks, the inflation rate was running at about 10% annually and accelerating as the Federal Reserve continued to pump up the money supply to finance the growing government budget deficit. Meanwhile, the interest rate on long-term Treasury bonds had risen to about 8.5%. Was President Carter correct in his assessment of the positive effects on the dollar of the higher interest rates? Explain. Note that during 1977, the movement of private capital had switched to an outflow of $6.6 billion in the second half of the year, from an inflow of $2.9 billion in the first half.

3. Comment on the consequences of a reduction in U.S. oil imports for the value of the U.S. dollar. Next, consider that President Carter's energy policy involved heavily taxing U.S. oil production, imposing price controls on domestically produced crude oil and gasoline, and providing rebates to users of heating oil. How was this energy policy likely to affect the value of the dollar? Explain.

4. What were the likely consequences of the slowdown in U.S. economic growth for the value of the U.S. dollar? For the U.S. trade balance?

5. If President Carter had listened to the financial markets instead of trying to lecture them, what might he have heard? That is, what were the markets trying to tell him about his policies?

---

*"President Canute," *The Wall Street Journal,* March 8, 1978, p. 16. Used with permission.

PART II

Foreign Exchange Risk Management

◼ 8 ◼

Measuring Accounting Exposure

The stream of time sweeps away errors, and leaves the truth for the inheritance of humanity.

—George Brandes—

◼ The general concept of *exposure* refers to the degree to which a company is affected by exchange rate changes. *Accounting exposure* arises from the need, for purposes of reporting and consolidation, to convert the financial statements of foreign operations from the local currencies (LC) involved to the home currency (HC). If exchange rates have changed since the previous reporting period, this *translation,* or restatement, of those assets, liabilities, revenues, expenses, gains, and losses that are denominated in foreign currencies will result in foreign exchange gains or losses. The possible extent of these gains or losses is measured by the translation exposure figures. The rules that govern translation are devised by an accounting association such as the *Financial Accounting Standards Board* (FASB) in the United States, the parent firm's government, or the firm itself.

This chapter presents alternative accounting methods for determining translation exposure, focusing on *Statements of Financial Accounting Standards No. 8* and *No. 52*—the past (No. 8) and present (No. 52) currency translation methods prescribed by the FASB. The chapter also discusses the differences between accounting requirements and economic reality, making recommendations to accountants and financial executives on how to adjust reporting standards in order to reconcile those differences. The next chapter discusses how companies can manage their accounting exposure.

◼ 8.1 ◼
ALTERNATIVE CURRENCY TRANSLATION METHODS

Companies with international operations will have foreign-currency-denominated assets and liabilities, revenues, and expenses. However, because home-country investors and the entire financial community are interested in home-currency values, the foreign currency balance-sheet accounts and income statement must be assigned HC values. In particular, the financial statements of an MNC's overseas subsidiaries must be translated from local currency to home currency prior to consolidation with the parent's financial statements.

If currency values change, foreign exchange translation gains or losses may result. Assets and liabilities that are translated at the current (postchange) exchange rate are considered to be exposed; those translated at a historical (prechange) exchange rate will maintain their historic HC values and, hence, are regarded as not exposed. *Translation exposure* is simply the difference between exposed assets and exposed liabilities. The controversies among accountants center on which assets and liabilities are exposed and on when accounting-derived foreign exchange gains and losses should be recognized (reported on the income statement). A crucial point to realize in putting these controversies in perspective is that such gains or losses are of an accounting nature—that is, no cash flows are necessarily involved.

Four principal translation methods are available: the current/noncurrent method, the monetary/nonmonetary method, the temporal method, and the current rate method. In practice, there are also variations of each method.

Current/Noncurrent Method

At one time, the *current/noncurrent method,* whose underlying theoretical basis is maturity, was used by almost all U.S. multinationals. With this method, all the foreign subsidiary's current assets and liabilities are translated into home currency at the *current exchange rate.* Each noncurrent asset or liability is translated at its *historical exchange rate;* that is, at the rate in effect at the time the asset was acquired or the liability incurred. Hence, a foreign subsidiary with positive local-currency working capital will give rise to a translation loss (gain) from a devaluation (revaluation) with the current/noncurrent method, and vice versa if working capital is negative.

The income statement is translated at the average exchange rate of the period, except for those revenues and expense items associated with noncurrent assets or liabilities. The latter items, such as depreciation expense, are translated at the same rates as the corresponding balance-sheet items. Thus, it is possible to see different revenue and expense items with similar maturities being translated at different rates.

Monetary/Nonmonetary Method

The *monetary/nonmonetary method* differentiates between *monetary* assets and liabilities—that is, those items that represent a claim to receive, or an obligation to pay, a fixed amount of foreign currency units—and *nonmonetary,* or physical, assets and liabilities. Monetary items (for example, cash, accounts payable and receivable, and long-term debt) are translated at the current rate; nonmonetary items (for example, inventory, fixed assets, and long-term investments) are translated at historical rates.

Income statement items are translated at the average exchange rate during the period, except for revenue and expense items related to nonmonetary assets and liabilities. The latter items, primarily depreciation expense and cost of goods sold, are translated at the same rate as the corresponding balance-sheet items. As a result, the cost of goods sold may be translated at a rate different from that used to translate sales.

Temporal Method

This method appears to be a modified version of the monetary/nonmonetary method. The only difference is that under the monetary/nonmonetary method, inventory is always translated at the historical rate. Under the *temporal method,* inventory is normally translated at the historical rate, but it can be translated at the current rate if the inventory is shown on the balance sheet at market values. Despite the similarities, however, the theoretical basis of each method is different. The choice of exchange rate for translation is based on the type of asset or liability in the monetary/nonmonetary method; in the temporal method, it is based on the underlying approach to evaluating cost (historical versus market). Under a historical cost accounting system, as the United States now has, most accounting theoreticians would probably argue that the temporal method is the appropriate method for translation.

Income statement items are normally translated at an average rate for the reporting period. However, cost of goods sold and depreciation and amortization charges related to balance-sheet items carried at past prices are translated at historical rates.

Current Rate Method

The *current rate method* is the simplest; all balance-sheet and income items are translated at the current rate. As the method recommended by the Institute of Chartered Accountants of England and Wales and the Institute of Chartered Accountants of Scotland, it is widely employed by British companies. Under this method, if a firm's foreign-currency-denominated assets exceed its foreign-currency-denominated liabilities, a devaluation must result in a loss and a revaluation, in a gain. One variation is to translate all assets and liabilities except net fixed assets at the current rate.

Exhibit 8.1 applies the four different methods to a hypothetical balance sheet that is affected by both a 25% devaluation and a revaluation of 37.5%. Depending on the method chosen, the translation results for the devaluation can range from a loss of $205,000 to a gain of $215,000; revaluation results can vary from a gain of $615,000 to a loss of $645,000.

■ 8.2 ■
STATEMENT OF FINANCIAL ACCOUNTING STANDARDS NO. 8

Such a wide variation in results as those of Exhibit 8.1 led the FASB to issue a new ruling: *Statement of Financial Accounting Standards No. 8* (FASB–8). FASB–8 established uniform standards for the translation into dollars of foreign-currency-denominated financial statements and transactions of U.S.-based multinational companies.

FASB–8, which was based on the temporal method, became effective on January 1, 1976. Its principal virtue was its consistency with generally accepted accounting practice

■ **EXHIBIT 8.1** Financial Statement Impact of Translation Alternatives (U.S.$ Thousands)

	Local Currency	U.S. Dollars Prior to Exchange Rate Change (LC 4 = $1)	After Devaluation of Local Currency (LC 5 = $1)				After Revaluation of Local Currency (LC 2.5 = $1)			
			Monetary/ Non-monetary	Temporal	Current/ Non-current	Current Rates for All Assets and Liabilities	Monetary/ Non-Monetary	Temporal	Current/ Non-current	Current Rates for All Assets and Liabilities
Assets										
Current assets										
Cash, marketable securities, and receivables	2,600	$ 650	$ 520	$ 520	$ 520	$ 520	$1,040	$1,040	$1,040	$1,040
Inventory (at market)	3,600	900	900	720	720	720	900	1,440	1,440	1,440
Prepaid expenses	200	50	50	50	40	40	50	50	80	80
Total current assets	6,400	1,600	1,470	1,290	1,280	1,280	1,990	2,530	2,560	2,560
Fixed assets less accumulated depreciation	3,600	900	900	900	900	720	900	900	900	1,440
Goodwill	1,000	250	250	250	250	200	250	250	250	400
Total assets	LC 11,000	$2,750	$2,620	$2,440	$2,430	$2,200	$3,140	$3,680	$3,710	$4,400
Liabilities										
Current liabilities	3,400	850	680	680	680	680	1,360	1,360	1,360	1,360
Long-term debt	3,000	750	600	600	750	600	1,200	1,200	750	1,200
Deferred income taxes	500	125	100	100	125	100	200	200	125	200
Total liabilities	6,900	1,725	1,380	1,380	1,555	1,380	2,760	2,760	2,235	2,760
Capital stock	1,500	375	375	375	375	375	375	375	375	375
Retained earnings	2,600	650	865	685	500	445	5	545	1,100	1,265
Total equity	4,100	1,025	1,240	1,060	875	820	380	920	1,475	1,640
Total liabilities plus equity	LC 11,000	$2,750	$2,620	$2,440	$2,430	$2,200	$3,140	$3,680	$3,710	$4,400
Translation Gain (Loss)	—	—	$ 215	$ 35	$ (150)	$ (205)	$ (645)	$ (105)	$ 450	$ 615

that requires balance-sheet items to be valued (translated) according to their underlying measurement basis (that is, current or historical).

Almost immediately upon its adoption, controversy ensued over FASB–8. A major source of corporate dissatisfaction with FASB–8 was the ruling that all reserves for currency losses be disallowed. Before FASB–8, many companies established a reserve and were able to defer unrealized translation gains and losses by adding them to, or charging them against, the reserve. In that way corporations generally were able to cushion the impact of sharp changes in currency values on reported earnings. With FASB–8, however, fluctuating values of pesos, pounds, marks, Canadian dollars, Australian dollars, and other foreign currencies often had far more impact on profit-and-loss statements than did the sales and profit margins of multinational manufacturers' product lines.

The experience of Sony, the Japanese electronics producer, which follows U.S. accounting rules because its shares are traded on the New York Stock Exchange, illustrates the impact of FASB–8. In 1979, Sony's consolidated second-quarter earnings were reduced by a foreign exchange loss of $49.3 million, whereas in 1978, the second-quarter net was restated to include a $19.3 million gain on currency conversion—a $68.6 million swing in pretax net income that might never be realized. The result was a 49% slump in Sony's second-quarter consolidated earnings, despite a near tripling in operating earnings from a year earlier. For the first half of 1979, Sony reported that net earnings had declined by 36% from the year before, despite a 98% increase in operating earnings. Sony's plight was caused almost entirely by an $84.8 million earnings movement resulting from a 1979 first-half foreign exchange loss of $59.4 million, compared to a gain of $26.4 million a year earlier.

■ 8.3 ■
STATEMENT OF FINANCIAL ACCOUNTING STANDARDS NO. 52

In 1981, widespread dissatisfaction by corporate executives over FASB–8 led to a new translation standard: *Statement of Financial Accounting Standards No. 52* (FASB–52). According to FASB–52, firms must use the current rate method to translate foreign-currency-denominated assets and liabilities into dollars. All foreign currency revenue and expense items on the income statement must be translated at either the exchange rate in effect on the date these items are recognized or at an appropriately weighted average exchange rate for the period. The most important aspect of the new standard is that unlike the case with FASB–8, most FASB–52 translation gains and losses bypass the income statement and are accumulated in a separate equity account on the parent's balance sheet. This account is usually called something like "cumulative translation adjustment."

FASB–52 differentiates for the first time between the functional currency and the reporting currency. An affiliate's *functional currency* is the currency of the primary economic environment in which the affiliate generates and expends cash. If the enterprise's operations are relatively self-contained and integrated within a particular country, the functional currency would generally be the currency of that country. An example of this case would be an English affiliate that both manufactures and sells most of its output in England. Alternatively, if the foreign affiliate's operations are a direct and integral component or extension of the parent company's operations, the functional currency would be the U.S. dollar. An example would be a Hong Kong assembly plant for radios that sources the components in the United States and sells the assembled radios in the United States. It is also possible that the functional currency is neither the local currency nor the dollar but, rather, is a third currency. However, in the remainder of this chapter, we will assume that if the functional currency is not the local currency, then it is the U.S. dollar.

Guidelines for selecting the appropriate functional currency are presented in Exhibit 8.2. There is sufficient ambiguity, however, to give companies some leeway in selecting the functional currency. However, in the case of a *hyperinflationary country*—defined as one that has cumulative inflation of approximately 100% or more over a three-year period—the functional currency must be the dollar.

Companies will usually explain in the notes to their annual report how they accounted for foreign currency translation. A typical statement is that found in Dow Chemical's 1989 Annual Report:

> The U.S. dollar has been used as the functional currency throughout the world except for operations in Germany and Japan, for which local currencies have been used. Effective December 31, 1988, the functional currency of the subsidiary companies in six European countries was changed to the local currency. These countries are Belgium, France, Italy, the Netherlands, Spain, and U.K. The impact on the balance sheet is noted in the Consolidated Statement of Stockholders' Equity. This change did not impact income in 1988.
>
>   Where the U.S. dollar is used as the functional currency, foreign currency gains and losses are reflected in income currently. Translation gains and losses of those operations that use local currencies as the functional currency, and the effects of exchange rate changes on transactions designated as hedges of net foreign investments are included as a separate component of stockholders' equity.

The *reporting currency* is the currency in which the parent firm prepares its own financial statements; that is, U.S. dollars for a U.S. firm. FASB–52 requires that the financial statements of a foreign unit first be stated in the functional currency, using generally accepted accounting principles of the United States. At each balance-sheet date, any assets and liabilities denominated in a currency other than the functional currency of the recording entity must be adjusted to reflect the current exchange rate on that date. Transaction gains and losses that result from adjusting assets and liabilities denominated in a currency other than the functional currency, or from settling such items, generally must appear on the foreign unit's income statement. The only exceptions to the general requirement to include transaction gains and losses in income as they arise are listed as follows:

1. Gains and losses attributable to a foreign-currency transaction that is designated as an economic hedge of a net investment in a foreign entity must be included in the separate component of shareholders' equity in which adjustments arising from translating foreign-currency financial statements are accumulated. An example of such a transaction would be a Deutsche mark borrowing by a U.S. parent. The transaction would be designated as a hedge of the parent's net investment in its German subsidiary. See, for example, the statement in Dow's 1989 Annual Report.

■ **EXHIBIT 8.2**   Factors Indicating the Appropriate Functional Currency

Foreign Unit's	Local Currency Indicators	Dollar Indicators
Cash flows	Primarily in the local currency; do not directly affect parent company cash flows	Direct impact on parent company; cash flow available for remittance
Sales prices	Not responsive to exchange rate changes in the short run; determined more by local conditions	Determined more by world wide competition; affected in the short run by exchange rate changes
Sales market	Active local market for entity's products	Products sold primarily in the United States; sales contracts denominated in dollars
Expenses	Labor, materials, and other costs denominated primarily in local currency	Inputs primarily from sources in the United States or otherwise denominated in dollars
Financing	Primarily in local currency; operations generate sufficient funds to service these debts	Primarily from the parent company or otherwise denominated in dollars; operations don't generate sufficient dollars to service its dollar debts
Intercompany transactions	Few intracorporate transactions; little connection between local and parent operations	High volume of intracorporate transactions; extensive interrelationship between local and parent operations

2. Gains and losses attributable to intercompany foreign-currency transactions that are of a long-term investment nature must be included in the separate component of shareholders' equity. The parties to the transaction in this case are accounted for by the equity method in the reporting entity's financial statements.

3. Gains and losses attributable to foreign-currency transactions that hedge identifiable foreign-currency commitments are to be deferred and included in the measurement on the basis of the related foreign transactions.

The requirements regarding translation of transactions apply both to transactions entered into by a U.S. company and denominated in a currency other than the U.S. dollar and to transactions entered into by a foreign affiliate of a U.S. company and denominated in a currency other than its functional currency. Thus, for example, if a German subsidiary of a U.S. company owed $180,000 and the DM declined from $0.60 to $0.50, the Deutsche mark amount of the liability would increase from DM 300,000 (180,000/0.60) to DM 360,000 (180,000/0.50), for a loss of DM 60,000. If the subsidiary's functional currency is the Deutsche mark, the DM 60,000 loss must be translated into dollars at the average exchange rate for the period (say $0.55), and the resulting amount ($33,000) must be included as a transaction loss in the U.S. company's consolidated statement of income. This loss results even though the liability is denominated in the parent company's reporting currency because the subsidiary's functional currency is the Deutsche mark, and its financial statements must be measured in terms of that currency. Under FASB–8, there was no gain or loss included in consolidated net income on debt denominated in the parent company's reporting currency. Similarly, under FASB–52, if the subsidiary's functional currency is the U.S. dollar, no gain or loss would arise on the $180,000 liability.

After all financial statements have been converted into the functional currency, the functional currency statements are then translated into dollars, with translation gains and losses flowing directly into the parent's foreign exchange equity account.

If the functional currency is the dollar, the unit's local currency financial statements must be remeasured in dollars. The objective of the remeasurement process is to produce the same results that would have been reported if the accounting records had been kept in dollars rather than the local currency. Translation of the local currency accounts into dollars takes place according to the temporal method previously required by FASB–8; thus, the resulting translation gains and losses *must* be included in the income statement.

A large majority of firms have opted for the local currency as the functional currency for most of their subsidiaries. The major exceptions are those subsidiaries operating in Latin American and other highly inflationary countries that must use the dollar as their functional currency.

Application of FASB No. 52

Sterling Ltd.—the British subsidiary of a U.S. company—started business and acquired fixed assets at the beginning of a year when the exchange rate for the pound sterling was £1 = $1.50. The average exchange rate for the period was $1.40, the rate at the end of the period was $1.30, and the historical rate for inventory was $1.45. Refer to Exhibits 8.3 and 8.4 for the discussion that follows.

During the year, Sterling Ltd. has income after tax of £20 million, which goes into retained earnings—that is, no dividends are paid. Thus, retained earnings rise from £0 to £20 million. Exhibit 8.3 shows how the income statement would be translated into dollars under two alternatives: (1) The functional currency is the pound sterling, and (2) the functional currency is the U.S. dollar. The second alternative yields results similar to those under FASB–8.

If the functional currency is the pound sterling, Sterling Ltd. will have a translation loss of $22 million, which bypasses the income statement (because the functional currency is identical to the local currency) and appears on the balance sheet as a separate item called *cumulative translation adjustment* under the shareholder's equity account. The translation loss is calculated as the number that reconciles the equity account with the remaining translated accounts to balance assets with liabilities and equity. Exhibit 8.4 shows the balance-sheet translations for Sterling Ltd. under the two alternative functional currencies.

Similarly, if the dollar is the functional currency, the foreign exchange translation gain of $108 million, which appears on Sterling Ltd.'s income statement (because the functional currency differs from the local currency), is calculated as the difference between translated income before currency gains ($23 million) and the retained earnings figure ($131 million). This amount just balances Sterling Ltd.'s books.

Two comments are appropriate here.

■ **EXHIBIT 8.3**   Translation of Sterling Ltd.'s Income Statement Under FASB–52 (Millions)

| | | Functional Currency | | | |
| | | Pound Sterling | | U.S. Dollar | |
	Pounds Sterling	**Rates Used**	**U.S. Dollars**	**Rates Used**	**U.S. Dollars**
Revenue	£120	1.40	$168	1.40	$168
Cost of goods sold	(50)	1.40	(70)	1.45	(73)
Depreciation	(20)	1.40	(28)	1.50	(30)
Other expenses, net	(10)	1.40	(14)	1.40	(14)
Foreign exchange gain					108
Income before taxes	40		56		159
Income taxes	(20)	1.40	(28)		(28)
Net income	£ 20		$ 28		$131
Ratios					
Net income to revenue	0.17		0.17		0.78
Gross profit to revenue	0.58		0.58		0.57
Debt to equity	7.33		7.33		4.07

■ **EXHIBIT 8.4**   Translation of Sterling Ltd.'s Balance Sheet Under FASB–52 (Millions)

| | | Functional Currency | | | |
| | | Pound Sterling | | U.S. Dollar | |
	Pounds Sterling	**Rates Used**	**U.S. Dollars**	**Rates Used**	**U.S. Dollars**
Assets					
Cash	£ 120	1.30	$ 130	1.30	$ 130
Receivables	200	1.30	260	1.30	260
Inventory	300	1.30	390	1.45	435
Fixed assets, net	400	1.30	520	1.50	600
Total assets	£1,000		$1,300		$1,425
Liabilities					
Current liabilities	180	1.30	234	1.30	234
Long-term debt	700	1.30	910	1.30	910
Stockholders' equity					
Common stock	100	1.50	150	1.50	150
Retained earnings	20		28		131
Cumulative translation adjustment			(22)		
Total liabilities plus equity	£1,000		$1,300		$1,425

1. Fluctuations in reported earnings in the example above are reduced significantly under FASB–52 when the local currency is the functional currency, as compared to the case when the U.S. dollar is the functional currency. Using the U.S. dollar as the functional currency is similar to the situation that prevailed when FASB–8 was in effect.

2. Key financial ratios and relationships—such as net income-to-revenue, gross profit, and debt-to-equity—are the same when translated into dollars under FASB–52, using the local currency as the functional currency, as they are in the local-currency financial statements. These ratios and relationships were significantly different under FASB–8, represented here by using the dollar as the functional currency. The ratios appear at the bottom of Exhibit 8.3.

■ 8.4 ■
TRANSACTION EXPOSURE

Companies often include transaction exposure as part of their accounting exposure. *Transaction exposure* stems from the possibility of incurring future exchange gains or losses on transactions already entered into and denominated in a foreign currency. For example, when IBM sells a mainframe computer to Royal Dutch Shell in England, it typically will not be paid until a later date. If that sale is priced in pounds, IBM has a pound transaction exposure.

A company's transaction exposure is measured currency by currency and equals the difference between contractually fixed future cash inflows and outflows in each currency. Some of these unsettled transactions, including foreign-currency-denominated debt and accounts receivable, are already listed on the firm's balance sheet. But other obligations, such as contracts for future sales or purchases, are not.

■ 8.5 ■
ACCOUNTING PRACTICE AND ECONOMIC REALITY

Many multinationals have responded to increased currency volatility by devoting more resources to the management of *foreign exchange risk.* In order to develop an effective strategy for managing currency risk, management must first determine what is at risk. This determination requires an appropriate definition of foreign exchange risk. However, there is a major discrepancy between accounting practice and economic reality in terms of measuring exposure.

Accounting measures of exposure focus on the effect of currency changes on previous decisions of the firm, as reflected in the book values of assets acquired and liabilities incurred in the past. However, book values—which represent historical cost—and market values—which reflect future cash flows—of assets and liabilities typically differ. Therefore, *retrospective* accounting techniques, no matter how refined, cannot truly account for the economic (that is, cash flow) effects of a devaluation or revaluation on the value of a firm because these effects are primarily *prospective* in nature.

Since the change in accounting net worth produced by a movement in exchange rates often bears little relationship to the change in the market value of the firm, information derived from a historical-cost accounting system can provide a misleading picture of a firm's true economic exposure. Here, *economic exposure* is defined as the extent to which the value of the firm—as measured by the present value of its expected cash flows—will change when exchange rates change. Although all items on a firm's balance sheet represent future cash flows, not all future flows appear there. Moreover, these items are not adjusted to reflect the distorting effects of inflation and relative price changes on their associated future cash flows.

The definition of exposure based on market value assumes that management's goal is to maximize the value of the firm. Whether management actually behaves in this fashion has been vigorously debated. Some managers will undoubtedly prefer to pursue other objectives. Nevertheless, the assumption that management seeks to maximize (risk-adjusted) cash flow remains standard in much of the finance literature. Moreover, the principle of maximizing stockholder wealth provides a rational guide to financial decision making.

Our evolving understanding of what exchange risk is, however, is often at odds with current management practice. Many top managers seem to be preoccupied with potential accounting-based currency gains or losses; perhaps these managers believe that the stock market evaluates a firm on the basis of its reported earnings or changes in accounting net worth, regardless of the underlying cash flows. Or perhaps their compensation is tied to earnings instead of market value. For whatever reason, failure to distinguish between the accounting description of foreign exchange risk and the business reality of the effects of currency movements can cause corporate executives to make serious errors of judgment.

Recommendations for International Financial Executives

Most chief executives want to generate the smooth pattern of year-to-year earnings gains so cherished by security analysts. That is probably why empirical research by academicians, as well as statements by practitioners, show such a strong relationship between accounting translation methods and corporate financial policies that are designed to manage currency risk. But since the real effect of currency changes is on a firm's future cash flows, it is obvious that information based on retrospective accounting techniques may bear no relationship to a firm's actual operating results. Furthermore, basing management decisions on these flawed accounting data can lead to financial policies that will adversely affect the real economic growth of foreign operations.

The myopia of acting on the basis of *balance-sheet exposure* rather than economic impact has been scathingly portrayed by Gunter Dufey.[1] In Dufey's example, the French subsidiary of an American multinational corporation was instructed to reduce its working-capital balances in light of a forecasted French-franc devaluation. To do so would have forced it to curtail its operations; however, the French subsidiary was selling all of its output to other subsidiaries located in Germany and Belgium. Because the dollar value of its output would remain constant while franc costs expressed in dollars would decline, a 10% franc devaluation was expected to increase the French subsidiary's dollar profitability by over 25%. The French manager, therefore, argued (correctly) that the plant should begin expand-

---

[1]Gunter Dufey, "Corporate Finance and Exchange Rate Variations," *Financial Management,* Summer 1978, pp. 51–57.

ing its operations, rather than contracting them, to take advantage of the anticipated devaluation.

To be sure, the distortions associated with accounting measures of exposure do not mean that accounting statements are irrelevant; clearly the statements serve a useful purpose and are necessary for consolidating the results of a worldwide network of operating units. The danger is that the results will be misinterpreted—not by financial executives, but by stockholders, bankers, security analysts, and the board of directors. In fact, financial managers generally are aware of the misleading nature of many of these results. Despite that knowledge, however, most financial executives undertake cosmetic exchange risk management actions because they worry that others will not understand the real, as opposed to the accounting, effects of currency changes. Clearly, if the capital markets did not rationally price corporate securities, managers would be hard pressed to design a foreign exchange strategy that could be expected to maximize the firm's value.

Is there a solution to this dichotomy between accounting and economic reality? Fortunately, the problem may be more apparent than real. A large body of research on financial markets suggests that investors are relatively sophisticated in responding to publicly available information; they appear able to understand detailed financial statements and properly interpret various accounting conventions behind corporate balance sheets and income statements.

Although the view of efficient capital markets in which stock prices correctly reflect all available information is not universally held, there is a good deal of empirical evidence that investors can effectively discriminate between accounting gimmickry and economic reality. In particular, when accounting numbers diverge significantly from cash flows, changes in security prices generally reflect changes in cash flows rather than reported earnings. Consider, as an example, changes in accounting practices for reporting (but not tax) purposes, such as switching depreciation and/or inventory valuation methods, that affect reported earnings but not cash flows. The changes do not appear to have any discernible, statistically significant effect on security prices.[2]

The implication of these results for multinational firms is that as long as there is complete disclosure, it probably doesn't matter which translation method is used. In an efficient market, translation gains or losses will be placed in a proper perspective by investors and, therefore, should not affect an MNC's stock price. To help the market correctly interpret the translation outcomes, though, companies should clearly and openly disclose which translation methods they use. Furthermore, nothing prevents management from including a note in the financial statement explaining its view of the economic consequences of exchange rate changes.

Despite its inconclusive nature, the debate over the adoption by the Financial Accounting Standards Board of new currency translation methods has helped increase Wall Street's insight into the effects of currency changes on foreign operations. The debate has focused attention on the all-important distinction between the accounting and the cash-flow approaches to measuring exposure.

---

[2]See, for example, Robert S. Kaplan and Richard Roll, "Investor Evaluation of Accounting Information: Some Empirical Evidence," *Journal of Business,* April 1972, pp. 225–257.

Against that background, a number of multinational firms are now taking a longer-term look at their degree of exchange risk. This look involves an examination of the risk due to the potential impact of uncertain exchange rate changes on future cash flows. Chapter 10 looks more closely at what constitutes this real exposure.

■ 8.6 ■
SUMMARY AND CONCLUSIONS

In this chapter, we have examined the concept of exposure to exchange rate changes from the perspective of the accountant. The accountant's concern is the appropriate way to translate foreign-currency-denominated items on financial statements to their home-currency values. If currency values change, translation gains or losses may result. We have surveyed the four principal translation methods available: the current/noncurrent method, the monetary/nonmonetary method, the temporal method, and the current rate method. In addition, we analyzed the past and present translation methods mandated by the Financial Accounting Standards Board, FASB–8 and FASB–52, respectively.

Regardless of the translation method selected, measuring accounting exposure is conceptually the same. It involves determining which foreign-currency-denominated assets and liabilities will be translated at the current (postchange) exchange rate and which will be translated at the historical (prechange) exchange rate. The former items are considered to be exposed, while the latter items are regarded as not exposed. Translation exposure is simply the difference between exposed assets and exposed liabilities.

By far the most important feature of the accounting definition of exposure is the exclusive focus on the balance-sheet effects of currency changes. We saw that this focus is misplaced since it has led the accounting profession to ignore the more important effect that these changes may have on future cash flows.

■ QUESTIONS ■

1. What is translation exposure? Transaction exposure?

2. What are the basic translation methods? How do they differ?

3. Why was FASB–8 so widely criticized? How did the Financial Accounting Standards Board respond to this criticism?

■ PROBLEMS ■

1. Suppose that on January 1, American Golf's French subsidiary, Golf du France, had a balance sheet that showed current assets of FF 1 million; current liabilities of FF 300,000; total assets of FF 2.5 million; and total liabilities of FF 900,000. On December 31, Golf du France's balance sheet in francs was unchanged from the figures given above, but the franc had declined in value from $0.1270 at the start of the year to $0.1180 at the end of the year. Under FASB–52, what is the translation amount to be shown on American Golf's equity account for the year if the franc is the functional currency? How would your answer change if the dollar were the functional currency?

2. Suppose that at the start and at the end of the year, Bell U.K. had current assets of £1 million, fixed assets of £2 million, and current liabilities of £1 million. Bell has no long-term liabilities. If the pound depreciated during that year from $1.50 to $1.30, what is the FASB–52 translation gain (loss) to be included in the equity account of Bell's U.S. parent?

3. Zapata Auto Parts, the Mexican affiliate of American Diversified, Inc., had the following balance sheet on January 1, 1992:

Assets (Ps millions)		Liabilities (Ps millions)	
Cash, marketable securities	Ps 1,000	Current liabilities	Ps 47,000
Accounts receivable	50,000	Long-term debt	12,000
Inventory	32,000	Equity	135,000
Net fixed assets	111,000		
	Ps 194,000		Ps 194,000

The exchange rate on January 1, 1992 was Ps 8,000 = $1.

a. What is Zapata's FASB–52 peso translation exposure on January 1, 1992?

b. Suppose the exchange rate on December 31, 1992 is Ps 12,000. What will be Zapata's translation loss for the year?

c. Zapata can borrow an additional Ps 15,000. What will this do to its translation exposure if it uses the funds to pay a dividend to its parent? If it uses the funds to increase its cash position?

■ BIBLIOGRAPHY ■

Accounting for the Translation of Foreign Currency Transactions and Foreign Currency Financial Statements, Statement of Financial Accounting Standards No. 8. Stamford, Conn.: Financial Accounting Standards Board, October 1975.

Dukes, Roland. *An Empirical Investigation of the Effects of Statement of Financial Accounting Standards No. 8 on Security Return Behavior.* Stamford, Conn.: Financial Accounting Standards Board, 1978.

Evans, Thomas G., William R. Folks, Jr., and Michael Jilling. *The Impact of Statement of Financial Accounting Standards No. 8 on the Foreign Exchange Risk Management Practices of American Multinationals.* Stamford, Conn.: Financial Accounting Standards Board, November 1978.

Statement of Financial Accounting Standards No. 52. Stamford, Conn.: Financial Accounting Standards Board, December 1981.

Giddy, Ian H. "What Is FAS No. 8's Effect on the Market's Valuation of Corporate Stock Prices?" *Business International Money Report,* May 26, 1978, p. 165.

9

Managing Accounting Exposure

Unfortunately the values of today's currencies oscillate wildly—to the despair of international companies that want to plan ahead.

—The Economist, May 28, 1988, p. 81—

■ The pressure to monitor and manage foreign currency risks has led many companies to develop sophisticated computer-based systems to keep track of their foreign exchange exposure and aid in managing that exposure. This chapter deals with the management of accounting exposure, including both translation and transaction exposure. Management of accounting exposure centers around the concept of hedging. *Hedging* a particular currency exposure means establishing an offsetting currency position such that whatever is lost or gained on the original currency exposure is exactly offset by a corresponding foreign exchange gain or loss on the currency hedge. Regardless of what happens to the future exchange rate, therefore, hedging locks in a dollar (home currency) value for the currency exposure. In this way, hedging can protect a firm from unforeseen currency movements.

A variety of hedging techniques are available, but before a firm uses them it must decide on which exposures to manage. Once the firm has determined the exposure position it intends to manage, how should it manage that position? How much of that position should it hedge, and which exposure-reducing technique(s) should it employ? In addition, how should exchange rate considerations be incorporated into operating decisions that will affect the firm's exchange risk posture? This chapter deals with these and other issues.

■ 9.1 ■
MANAGING TRANSACTION EXPOSURE

A transaction exposure arises whenever a company is committed to a foreign currency-denominated transaction. Since the transaction will result in a future foreign currency cash inflow or outflow, any change in the exchange rate between the time the transaction is entered into and the time it is settled in cash will lead to a change in the dollar (HC) amount of the cash inflow or outflow. Protective measures to guard against transaction exposure involve entering into foreign currency transactions whose cash flows exactly offset the cash flows of the transaction exposure.

These protective measures include using forward contracts, price adjustment clauses, currency options, and borrowing or lending in the foreign currency. Alternatively, the company could try to invoice all transactions in dollars and to avoid transaction exposure entirely. However, eliminating transaction exposure doesn't eliminate all foreign exchange risk. The firm is still subject to exchange risk on its future revenues and costs—its operating cash flows.

We will now look at the various techniques for managing transaction exposure by examining the case of General Electric's Deutsche mark exposure. Suppose that on January 1, GE is awarded a contract to supply turbine blades to Lufthansa, the German airline. On December 31, GE will receive payment of DM 25 million for these blades. The most direct way for GE to hedge this receivable is to sell a DM 25 million forward contract for delivery in one year. Alternatively, it can use a money market hedge, which would involve borrowing DM 25 million for one year, converting it into dollars, and investing the proceeds in a security that matures on December 31. As we will see, if interest rate parity holds, both methods will yield the same results. GE can also manage its transaction exposure through risk shifting, risk sharing, exposure netting, and currency options.

Forward Market Hedge

In a *forward market hedge,* a company that is long a foreign currency will sell the foreign currency forward, whereas a company that is short a foreign currency will buy the currency forward. In this way, the company can fix the dollar value of future foreign currency cash flow. For example, by selling forward the proceeds from its sale of turbine blades, GE can effectively transform the currency denomination of its DM 25 million receivable from Deutsche marks to dollars, thereby eliminating all currency risk on the sale. For example, suppose the current spot price for the Deutsche mark is DM 1 = $0.40, and the one-year forward rate is DM 1 = $0.3828. Then, a forward sale of DM 25 million for delivery in one year will yield GE $9.57 million on December 31. Exhibit 9.1 shows the cash-flow

■ **EXHIBIT 9.1**   Possible Outcomes of Forward Market Hedge as of December 31

Spot Exchange Rate	Value of Original Receivable (1)	+	Gain (Loss) on Forward Contract (2)	=	Total Cash Flow (3)
DM 1 = $0.40	$10,000,000		($430,000)		$9,570,000
DM 1 = $0.3828	9,570,000		0		9,570,000
DM 1 = $0.36	9,000,000		570,000		9,570,000

consequences of combining the forward sale with the Deutsche mark receivable, given three possible exchange rate scenarios.

Regardless of what happens to the future spot rate, Exhibit 9.1 demonstrates that GE still gets to collect $9.57 million on its turbine sale. Any exchange gain or loss on the forward contract will be offset by a corresponding exchange loss or gain on the receivable. The effects of this transaction can also be seen with the following simple T-account describing GE's position as of December 31:

December 31: GE T-Account (Millions)

| Account receivable | DM 25 | Forward contract payment | DM 25 |
| Forward contract receipt | $9.57 | | |

Without hedging, GE will have a DM 25 million asset whose value will fluctuate with the exchange rate. The forward contract creates an equal DM liability, offset by an asset worth $9.57 million dollars. The DM asset and liability cancel each other out, and GE is left with a $9.57 million asset.

The True Cost of Hedging.   Exhibit 9.1 also shows that the true cost of hedging can't be calculated in advance because it depends on the future spot rate, which is unknown at the time the forward contract is entered into. In the example above, the actual cost of hedging can vary from +$430,000 to –$570,000; a plus (+) represents a cost, and a minus (–) represents a negative cost or a gain. In percentage terms, the cost varies from –5.7% to +4.3%.

This example points out the distinction between the traditional method of calculating the cost of a forward contract and the correct method, which measures its opportunity cost. Specifically, the cost of a forward contract is usually measured as its forward discount or premium:

$$\frac{e_0 - f_1}{e_0}$$

where e_0 is the current spot rate (dollar price) of the foreign currency and f_1 is the forward rate. In GE's case, this cost would equal 4.3%.

However, this approach is wrong because the relevant comparison must be between the dollars per unit of foreign currency received with hedging, f_1, and the dollars received in the absence of hedging, e_1, where e_1 is the future (unknown) spot rate on the date of settlement. That is, the real cost of hedging is an *opportunity cost*. In particular, if the forward contract had not been entered into, the future value of each unit of foreign currency would have been e_1 dollars. Thus, the true dollar cost of the forward contract per dollar's worth of foreign currency sold forward equals

$$\frac{e_1 - f_1}{e_0}$$

In fact, in an efficient market, the expected cost (value) of a forward contract must be zero. Otherwise, there would be an arbitrage opportunity. Suppose, for example, that management at General Electric believes that despite a one-year forward rate of $0.3828, the Deutsche mark will actually be worth about $0.3910 on December 31. Then GE could profit by buying (rather than selling) Deutsche marks forward for one year at $0.3828 and, on December 31, completing the contract by selling Deutsche marks in the spot market at $0.3910. If GE is correct, it will earn $0.0082 (0.3910 − 0.3828) per Deutsche mark sold forward. On a DM 25 million forward contract, this would amount to $205,000—a substantial reward for a few minutes of work.

As we saw in Chapter 2, the prospect of such rewards would not go unrecognized for long, which is why the forward rate is likely to be an unbiased estimate of the future spot rate. Therefore, unless GE or any other company has some special information about the future spot rate that it has good reason to believe is not adequately reflected in the forward rate, it should accept the forward rate's predictive validity as a working hypothesis and avoid speculative activities. After the fact, of course, the actual cost of a forward contract will turn out to be positive or negative (unless the future spot rate equals the forward rate), but the sign can't be predicted in advance.

Money Market Hedge

An alternative to a forward market hedge is to use a money market hedge. A *money market hedge* involves simultaneous borrowing and lending activities in two different currencies to lock in the dollar value of a future foreign currency cash flow. For example, suppose Deutsche mark and U.S. dollar interest rates are 15% and 10%, respectively. Using a money market hedge, General Electric will borrow DM 25/1.15 million = DM 21.74 million for one year, convert it into $8.7 million in the spot market, and invest the $8.7 million for one year. On December 31, GE will receive $1.10 \times \$8.7$ million = $9.57 million from its dollar investment. GE will use these dollars to pay back the $1.15 \times$ DM 21.74 million = DM 25 million it owes in principal and interest. As Exhibit 9.2 shows, the exchange gain or loss on the borrowing and lending transactions exactly offsets the dollar loss or gain on GE's DM receivable.

The gain or loss on the money market hedge can be calculated simply by subtracting the cost of repaying the DM debt from the dollar value of the investment. For example, in the case of an end-of-year spot rate of $0.40, the DM 25 million in principal and interest

■ **EXHIBIT 9.2**   Possible Outcomes of Money Market Hedge on December 31

Spot Exchange Rate	Value of Original Receivable (1)	+	Gain (Loss) on Money Market Hedge (2)	=	Total Cash Flow (3)
DM 1 = $0.40	$10,000,000		($430,000)		$9,570,000
DM 1 = $0.3828	9,570,000		0		9,570,000
DM 1 = $0.36	9,000,000		570,000		9,570,000

will cost $10 million to repay. The return on the dollar investment is only $9.57 million, leaving a loss of $430,000.

We can also view the effects of this transaction with the simple T-account used earlier:

December 31: GE T-Account (Millions)

Account receivable	DM 25	Loan repayment (including	DM 25
Investment return (including		interest)	
interest)	$9.57		

As before, the DM asset and liability (the loan repayment) cancel each other out, and GE is left with a $9.57 million asset (its investment).

The equality of the net cash flows from the forward market and money market hedges is not coincidental. The interest rates and forward and spot rates were selected so that interest rate parity holds. In effect, the simultaneous borrowing and lending transactions associated with a money market hedge enable GE to create a "homemade" forward contract. The effective rate on this forward contract will equal the actual forward rate if interest rate parity holds. Otherwise, a covered interest arbitrage opportunity would exist.

Risk Shifting

General Electric could have avoided its transaction exposure altogether if Lufthansa had allowed it to price the sale of turbine blades in dollars. Dollar invoicing, however, does not eliminate currency risk; it simply shifts that risk from GE to Lufthansa (which now has dollar exposure). Lufthansa may or may not be better able, or more willing, to bear it. Despite the fact that this form of *risk shifting* is a zero-sum game, it is common in international business. Firms typically attempt to invoice exports in strong currencies and imports in weak currencies.

Is it possible to gain from risk shifting? Not if one is dealing with informed customers or suppliers. To see why, consider the GE-Lufthansa deal. If Lufthansa is willing to be invoiced in dollars for the turbine blades, that must be because Lufthansa calculates that its Deutsche mark equivalent cost will be no higher than the DM 25 million price it was originally prepared to pay. Since Lufthansa does not have to pay for the turbine blades until December 31, its cost will be based on the spot price of the dollars as of that date. By buying dollars forward at the one-year forward rate of DM 1 = $0.3828, Lufthansa can convert a dollar price of P into a DM cost of $P/0.3828$. Thus, the maximum dollar price P_M that Lufthansa should be willing to pay for the turbine blades is the solution to

$$P_M/0.3828 = DM\ 25\ million$$

or

$$P_M = \$9.57\ million$$

Considering that GE can guarantee itself $9.57 million by pricing in Deutsche marks and selling the resulting DM 25 million forward, it will certainly not accept a lower dollar price. The bottom line is that both Lufthansa and General Electric will be indifferent between a U.S. dollar price and a Deutsche mark price only if the two prices are equal at the forward exchange rate. Therefore, because the Deutsche mark price arrived at through arm's-length negotiations is DM 25 million, the dollar price that is equally acceptable to Lufthansa and GE can only be $9.57 million. Otherwise, one or both of the parties involved in the negotiations has ignored the possibility of currency changes. Such naiveté is unlikely to exist for long in the highly competitive world of international business.

Pricing Decisions

Notwithstanding the view expressed above, top management has sometimes failed to take anticipated exchange rate changes into account when making operating decisions, leaving financial management with the essentially impossible task, through purely financial operations, of recovering a loss already incurred at the time of the initial transaction. To illustrate this type of error, suppose that GE has priced Lufthansa's order of turbine blades at $10 million and then, because Lufthansa demands to be quoted a price in Deutsche marks, converts the dollar price to a Deutsche mark quote of DM 25 million, using the spot rate of DM 1 = $0.40.

In reality, the quote is worth only $9.57 million—even though it is booked at $10 million—because that is the risk-free price that GE can guarantee for itself by using the forward market. If GE management wanted to sell the blades for $10 million, it should have set a Deutsche mark price equal to DM 10,000,000/0.3828 = DM 26.12 million. Thus, GE lost $430,000 the moment it signed the contract (assuming that Lufthansa would have agreed to the higher price rather than turn to another supplier). This loss is not an exchange loss; it is a loss due to management inattentiveness.

The general rule on credit sales overseas is to convert between the foreign currency price and the dollar price by using the forward rate, not the spot rate. If the dollar price is high enough, the exporter should follow through with the sale. Similarly, if the dollar price on a foreign-currency-denominated import is low enough, the importer should follow through on the purchase. All this rule does is to recognize that a Deutsche mark (or any other foreign currency) tomorrow is not the same as a Deutsche mark today. This rule is the international analogue to the insight that a dollar tomorrow is not the same as a dollar today.

In the case of a sequence of payments to be received at several points in time, the foreign currency price should be a weighted average of the forward rates for delivery on those dates.

■ ——

ILLUSTRATION

Weyerhaeuser Quotes a French Franc Price for Its Lumber. Weyerhaeuser is asked to quote a price in French francs for lumber sales to a French company. The lumber will be shipped and paid for in four equal, quarterly installments. Weyerhaeuser requires a minimum price of $1 million to accept this contract. If P_F is the French franc price contracted for, then Weyerhaeuser will receive $0.25P_F$ every three months, beginning 90 days from now. Suppose the spot and forward rates for the French franc are as follows:

Spot	90-Day	180-Day	270-Day	360-Day
$0.1772	$0.1767	$0.1761	$0.1758	$0.1751

Based on these forward rates, the certainty-equivalent dollar value of this franc revenue is $0.25P_F(0.1767 + 0.1761 + 0.1758 + 0.1751)$ or $0.25P_F(0.7037) = \$0.1759P_F$. In order for Weyerhaeuser to realize $1 million from this sale, the minimum French franc price must be the solution to

$$\$0.1759P_F = \$1,000,000$$

or

$$P_F = \text{FF } 5,685,048$$

At any lower franc price, Weyerhaeuser cannot be assured of receiving the $1 million it demands for this sale. Note that the spot rate did not enter into any of these calculations. ∎

Exposure Netting

Exposure netting involves offsetting exposures in one currency with exposures in the same or another currency, where exchange rates are expected to move in such a way that losses (gains) on the first exposed position should be offset by gains (losses) on the second currency exposure. This portfolio approach to hedging recognizes that the total variability or risk of a currency exposure portfolio should be less than the sum of the individual variabilities of each currency exposure considered in isolation. The assumption underlying exposure netting is that the net gain or loss on the entire currency exposure portfolio is what matters, rather than the gain or loss on any individual monetary unit.

It is easy to see, for example, that a DM 1 million receivable and DM 1 million payable cancel each other out, with no net (before-tax) exposure. It may be less obvious that such exposure netting can also be accomplished by using positions in different currencies. But companies practice multicurrency exposure netting all the time. According to Frederick Dietz of B.F. Goodrich, the U.S.-based tire manufacturer: "We might be willing to tolerate a short position in Swiss francs if we had a long position in Deutsche marks. They're fellow travelers. We look at our exposures as a portfolio."[1]

In practice, exposure netting involves one of three possibilities:

1. A firm can offset a long position in a currency with a short position in that same currency.
2. If the exchange rate movements of two currencies are positively correlated (for example, the Swiss franc and Deutsche mark), then the firm can offset a long position in one currency with a short position in the other.
3. If the currency movements are negatively correlated, then short (or long) positions can be used to offset each other.

[1]"How Corporations Are Playing the Currency Game," *Institutional Investor,* May 1976, p. 31.

Currency Risk Sharing

In addition to, or instead of, a traditional hedge, General Electric and Lufthansa can agree to share the currency risks associated with their turbine blade contract. *Currency risk sharing* can be implemented by developing a customized hedge contract imbedded in the underlying trade transaction. This hedge contract typically takes the form of a *price adjustment clause,* whereby a base price is adjusted to reflect certain exchange rate changes. For example, the base price could be set at DM 25 million, but the parties would share the currency risk beyond a neutral zone. The *neutral zone* represents the currency range in which risk is not shared.

Suppose the neutral zone is specified as a band of exchange rates: $0.39–0.41:DM 1, with a base rate of DM 1 = $0.40. This means that the exchange rate can fall as far as $0.39:DM 1 or rise as high as $0.41:DM 1 without reopening the contract. Within the neutral zone, Lufthansa must pay GE the dollar equivalent of DM 25 million at the base rate of $0.40, or $10 million. Thus, Lufthansa's cost can vary from DM 24.39 million to DM 25.64 million (10,000,000/0.41 to 10,000,000/0.39). But if the DM depreciates from $0.40 to, say, $0.35, the actual rate will have moved $0.04 beyond the lower boundary of the neutral zone ($0.39:DM 1). This amount is shared equally. Thus, the exchange rate actually used in settling the transaction is $0.38:DM 1 ($0.40 − 0.04/2). The new price of the turbine blades becomes DM 25,000,000 × 0.38 or $9.5 million. Lufthansa's cost rises to DM 27.14 million (9,500,000/0.35). In the absence of a risk-sharing agreement, the contract value to GE would have been $8.75 million. Of course, if the Deutsche mark appreciates beyond the upper bound to, say, $0.45, GE does not get the full benefit of the DM's rise in value. Instead, the new contract exchange rate becomes $0.42 (0.40 + 0.04/2). GE collects DM 25,000,000 × 0.42, or $10.5 million; and Lufthansa pays a price of DM 23.33 million (10,500,000/0.45).

Exhibit 9.3 compares the currency risk protection features of the currency risk-sharing arrangement with that of a traditional forward contract (at a forward rate of $0.3828) and a no-hedge alternative. Within the neutral zone, the dollar value of GE's contract under the risk-sharing agreement stays at $10 million. This situation is equivalent to Lufthansa selling GE a forward contract at the current spot rate of $0.40. Beyond the neutral zone, the contract's dollar value rises or falls only half as much under the risk-sharing agreement as under the no-hedge alternative. The value of the hedged contract remains the same, regardless of the exchange rate.

Foreign Currency Options

Thus far, we have examined how firms can hedge known foreign currency transaction exposures. Yet, in many circumstances, the firm is uncertain whether the hedged foreign currency cash inflow or outflow will materialize. For example, the previous assumption was that GE learned on January 1 that it had won a contract to supply turbine blades to Lufthansa. But suppose that although GE's bid on the contract was submitted on January 1, the announcement of the winning bid would not be until April 1. During the three-month period from January 1 to April 1, GE does not know whether it will receive a payment of DM 25 million on December 31 or not. This uncertainty has important consequences for the appropriate hedging strategy.

- **EXHIBIT 9.3**　Currency Risk Sharing: GE and Lufthansa

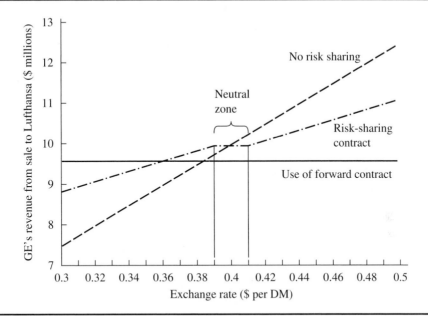

GE would like to guarantee that the exchange rate doesn't move against it between the time it bids and the time it gets paid, should it win the contract. The danger of not hedging is that its bid will be selected and the Deutsche mark will decline in value, possibly wiping out GE's anticipated profit margin. For example, if the forward rate on April 1 for delivery December 31 falls to DM 1 = $0.36, the value of the contract will drop from $9.57 million to $9 million, for a loss in value of $570,000.

The apparent solution is for GE to sell the anticipated DM 25 million receivable forward on January 1. However, if GE does that and loses the bid on the contract, it still has to sell the currency— which it will have to get by buying on the open market, perhaps at a big loss. For example, suppose the forward rate on April 1 for December 31 delivery has risen to $0.4008. To eliminate all currency risk on its original forward contract, GE would have to buy DM 25 million forward at a price of $0.4008. The result would be a loss of $450,000 [(0.3828 – 0.4008) × 25,000,000] on the forward contract entered into on January 1 at a rate of $0.3828.

Until recently, GE or any company that bid on a foreign contract in a foreign currency and was not assured of success would be unable to resolve its foreign exchange risk dilemma. The advent of *currency options* has changed all that. Specifically, the solution to managing its currency risk in this case is for GE, at the time of its bid, to purchase an option to sell DM 25 million on December 31. For example, suppose that on January 1, GE can buy for $100,000 the right to sell Citibank DM 25 million on December 31 at a price of $0.3828 per Deutsche mark. If it enters into this option contract with Citibank, GE will guarantee itself a minimum price ($9.57 million) should its bid be selected, while simultaneously ensuring that if it lost the bid, its loss would be limited to the price paid for the option contract (the premium of $100,000). Should the spot price of the Deutsche mark on December 31 exceed $0.3828, GE would let its option contract expire unexercised and convert the DM 25 million at the prevailing spot rate.

As we saw in Chapter 3, two types of options are available to manage exchange risk. A *put option,* such as the one appropriate to GE's situation, gives the buyer the right, but not the obligation, to sell a specified number of foreign currency units to the option seller at a fixed dollar price, up to the option's expiration date. Alternatively, a *call option* is the right, but not the obligation, to buy the foreign currency at a specified dollar price, up to the expiration date.

A call option is valuable, for example, when a firm has offered to buy a foreign asset, such as another firm, at a fixed foreign currency price, but is uncertain whether its bid will be accepted. By buying a call option on the foreign currency, the firm can lock in a maximum dollar price for its tender offer, while limiting its downside risk to the call premium in the event its bid is rejected.

Currency options are a valuable risk-management tool in other situations as well. Conventional transaction exposure management says you wait until your sales are booked or your orders placed before hedging them. But if a company does that, it faces potential losses from exchange rate movements because the foreign currency price doesn't necessarily adjust right away to changes in the value of the dollar. As a matter of policy, to avoid confusing customers and salespeople, most companies don't change their price list every time the exchange rate changes. Unless and until the foreign currency price changes, the unhedged company may suffer a decrease in its profit margin. Because of the uncertainty of anticipated sales or purchases, however, forward contracts are an imperfect tool to hedge the exposure.

For example, a company that commits to a foreign currency price list for, say, three months has a foreign currency exposure that depends on the unknown volume of sales at those prices during this period. Thus, the company does not know what volume of forward contracts to enter into to protect its profit margin on these sales. For the price of the premium, currency put options allow the company to insure its profit margin against adverse movements in the foreign currency while guaranteeing fixed prices to foreign customers. Without options, the firm might be forced to raise its foreign currency prices sooner than the competitive situation warranted.

■ ——

ILLUSTRATION

Hewlett-Packard Uses Currency Options to Protect Its Profit Margins. Hewlett-Packard, the California-based computer firm, uses currency options to protect its dollar profit margins on products built in the United States but sold in Europe. The firm needs to be able to lower local currency (LC) prices if the dollar weakens and hold LC prices steady for about three months (the price adjustment period) if the dollar strengthens.

Suppose H-P sells anticipated DM sales forward at DM 2.5:$1 to lock in a dollar value for those sales. If one month later the dollar weakens to DM 2:$1, H-P faces tremendous competitive pressure to lower its Deutsche mark prices. H-P would now be locked into a loss on the forward contracts that would not be offset by a gain on its sales (because it had to cut DM prices). With DM put options, H-P would just let them expire, and it would lose only the put premium. Conversely, options help H-P delay LC price increases when the dollar strengthens until it can raise them without suffering a competitive disadvantage. The reduced profit margin on local sales is offset by the gain on the put option.

Currency options can also be used to hedge exposure to shifts in a competitor's currency. Companies competing with firms from other nations may find their products at a price disadvantage if a major competitor's currency weakens, allowing the competitor to reduce its prices. Thus, the company will be exposed to fluctuations in the competitor's currency even if it has no sales in that currency. For example, a Swiss engine manufacturer selling in Germany will be placed at a competitive disadvantage if dollar depreciation allows its principal competitor, located in the United States, to sell at a lower price in Germany. Purchasing out-of-the-money put options on the dollar and selling them for a profit if they move into the money (which will happen if the dollar depreciates enough) will allow the Swiss firm to partly compensate for its lost competitiveness. Since the exposure is not contractually set, forward contracts are again not as useful as options in this situation.

The ideal use of forward contracts is when the exposure has a straight risk-reward profile: Forward contract gains or losses are exactly offset by losses or gains on the underlying transaction. But if the transaction exposure is uncertain, because the volume and/or the foreign currency prices of the items being bought or sold are unknown, a forward contract won't match it. By contrast, currency options are a good hedging tool in situations in which the quantity of foreign exchange to be received or paid out is uncertain.

ILLUSTRATION

How Cadbury Schweppes Uses Currency Options. Cadbury Schweppes, the British candy manufacturer, uses currency options to hedge uncertain payables. The price of its key product input, cocoa, is quoted in sterling but is really a dollar-based product. That is, as the value of the dollar changes, the sterling price of cocoa changes as well. The objective of the company's foreign exchange strategy is to eliminate the currency element in the decision to purchase the commodity, thus leaving the company's buyers able to concentrate on fundamentals. However, this task is complicated by the fact that the company's projections of its future purchases is highly uncertain.

As a result, Cadbury Schweppes has turned to currency options. After netting its total exposure, the company covers with forward contracts a base number of exposed, known payables. It covers the remaining—uncertain—portion with options. The options act as an insurance policy.

The general rules to follow when choosing between currency options and forward contracts for hedging purposes are summarized as follows:

1. When the quantity of a foreign currency cash outflow is known, buy the currency forward; when the quantity is unknown, buy a call option on the currency.
2. When the quantity of a foreign currency cash inflow is known, sell the currency forward; when the quantity is unknown, buy a put option on the currency.

3. When the quantity of a foreign currency cash flow is partially known and partially uncertain, use a forward contract to hedge the known portion and an option to hedge the maximum value of the uncertain remainder.[2]

These rules presume that the financial manager's objective is to reduce risk and not to speculate on the direction or volatility of future currency movements. They also presume that both forward and options contracts are fairly priced. In an efficient market, the expected value or cost of either of these contracts should be zero. Any other result would introduce the possibility of arbitrage profits. The presence of such profits would attract arbitrageurs as surely as bees are attracted to honey. Their subsequent attempts to profit from inappropriate prices will return these prices to their equilibrium values.

■ 9.2 ■
MANAGING TRANSLATION EXPOSURE

Firms have three available methods for managing their translation exposure: (1) adjusting fund flows, (2) entering into forward contracts, and (3) exposure netting. The basic hedging strategy for reducing translation exposure shown in Exhibit 9.4 uses these methods. Essentially, the strategy involves increasing *hard-currency* (likely to appreciate) assets and decreasing *soft-currency* (likely to depreciate) assets, while simultaneously decreasing hard-currency liabilities and increasing soft-currency liabilities. For example, if a devaluation appears likely, the basic hedging strategy would be executed as follows: Reduce the level of cash, tighten credit terms to decrease accounts receivable, increase LC borrowing, delay accounts payable, and sell the weak currency forward.

Despite their prevalence among firms, however, these hedging activities are not automatically valuable. If the market already recognizes the likelihood of currency appreciation or depreciation, this recognition will be reflected in the costs of the various hedging techniques. Only if the firm's anticipations differ from the market's and are also superior to the market's can hedging lead to reduced costs. Otherwise, the principal value of hedging would be to protect a firm from unforeseen currency fluctuations.

■ **EXHIBIT 9.4**   Basic Strategy for Hedging Translation Exposure

	Assets	Liabilities
Hard currencies (Likely to appreciate)	Increase	Decrease
Soft currencies (Likely to depreciate)	Decrease	Increase

[2]For elaboration, see Ian H. Giddy, "The Foreign Exchange Options as a Hedging Tool," *Midland Corporate Finance Journal,* Fall 1983, pp. 32–42.

Funds Adjustment

Most techniques for hedging an impending local currency (LC) devaluation reduce LC assets or increase LC liabilities, thereby generating LC cash. If accounting exposure is to be reduced, these funds must be converted into hard-currency assets. For example, a company will reduce its translation loss if, before an LC devaluation, it converts some of its LC cash holdings to the home currency. This conversion can be accomplished, either directly or indirectly, by means of various funds adjustment techniques.

Funds adjustment involves altering either the amounts or the currencies (or both) of the planned cash flows of the parent and/or its subsidiaries to reduce the firm's local currency accounting exposure. If an LC devaluation is anticipated, direct funds-adjustment methods include pricing exports in hard currencies and imports in the local currency, investing in hard-currency securities, and replacing hard-currency borrowings with local currency loans. The indirect methods, which will be elaborated in Chapter 15, include adjusting transfer prices on the sale of goods between affiliates; speeding up the payment of dividends, fees, and royalties; and adjusting the leads and lags of intersubsidiary accounts. The latter method, which is the one most frequently used by multinationals, involves speeding up the payment of intersubsidiary accounts payable and delaying the collection of intersubsidiary accounts receivable. These hedging procedures for devaluations would be reversed for revaluations (see Exhibit 9.5).

Some of these techniques or tools may require considerable lead time and—as is the case with a transfer price—once they are introduced, they cannot be easily changed. In

■ **EXHIBIT 9.5**   Basic Hedging Techniques

Depreciation	Appreciation
■ Sell local currency forward	■ Buy local currency forward
■ Reduce levels of local-currency cash and marketable securities	■ Increase levels of local-currency cash and marketable securities
■ Tighten credit (reduce local-currency receivables)	■ Relax local-currency credit terms
■ Delay collection of hard-currency receivables	■ Speed up collection of soft-currency receivables
■ Increase imports of hard-currency goods	■ Reduce imports of soft-currency goods
■ Borrow locally	■ Reduce local borrowing
■ Delay payment of accounts payable	■ Speed up payment of accounts payable
■ Speed up dividend and fee remittances to parent and other subsidiaries	■ Delay dividend and fee remittances to parent and other subsidiaries
■ Speed up payment of intersubsidiary accounts payable	■ Delay payment of intersubsidiary accounts payable
■ Delay collection of intersubsidiary accounts receivable	■ Speed up collection of intersubsidiary accounts receivable
■ Invoice exports in foreign currency and imports in local currency	■ Invoice exports in local currency and imports in foreign currency

addition, techniques such as transfer price, fee and royalty, and dividend flow adjustments fall into the realm of corporate policy and are not usually under the treasurer's control (although this situation may be changing). It is, therefore, incumbent on the treasurer to educate other decisionmakers about the impact of these tools on the costs and management of corporate exposure.

Although entering forward contracts is the most popular coverage technique, leading and lagging of payables and receivables is almost as important. For those countries in which a formal market in LC forward contracts doesn't exist, leading and lagging and LC borrowing are the most important techniques. The bulk of international business, however, is conducted in those few currencies for which forward markets do exist.

Forward contracts can reduce a firm's translation exposure by creating an offsetting asset or liability in the foreign currency. For example, suppose that IBM U.K. has translation exposure of £40 million (that is, sterling assets exceed sterling liabilities by that amount). IBM U.K. can eliminate its entire translation exposure by selling £40 million forward. Any loss (gain) on its translation exposure will then be offset by a corresponding gain (loss) on its forward contract. Note, however, that the gain (or loss) on the forward contract is of a cash-flow nature and is netted against an unrealized translation loss (or gain).

Selecting convenient (less-risky) currencies for invoicing exports and imports and adjusting transfer prices are two techniques that are less frequently used, perhaps because of constraints on the use of those techniques. It is often difficult, for instance, to make a customer or supplier accept billing in a particular currency.

Exposure netting is an additional exchange management technique that is available to multinational firms with positions in more than one foreign currency or with offsetting positions in the same currency. As defined earlier, this technique involves offsetting exposures in one currency with exposures in the same or another currency such that gains and losses on the two currency positions will offset each other.

Evaluating Alternative Hedging Mechanisms

Ordinarily, the selection of a funds-adjustment strategy cannot proceed by evaluating each possible technique separately without risking suboptimization; for example, whether or not a firm chooses to borrow locally is not independent of its decision to use or not use those funds to import additional hard-currency inventory. However, where the level of forward contracts that the financial manager can enter into is unrestricted, the following two-stage methodology allows the optimal level of forward transactions to be determined apart from the selection of what funds-adjustment techniques to use.[3] Moreover, this methodology is valid regardless of the manager's (or firm's) attitude toward risk.

Stage 1: Compute the profit associated with each funds-adjustment technique on a covered after-tax basis. Transactions that are profitable on a covered basis ought to be undertaken regardless of whether they increase or decrease the firm's accounting exposure.

---

[3]This methodology is presented in William R. Folks, Jr., "Decision Analysis for Exchange Risk Management," *Financial Management,* Winter 1972, pp. 101–112.

However, such activities should not be termed *hedging;* rather, they involve the use of *arbitrage* to exploit market distortions.

Stage 2: Any unwanted exposure resulting from the first stage can be corrected in the forward market. Stage two is the selection of an optimal level of forward transactions based on the firm's initial exposure, adjusted for the impact on exposure of decisions made in Stage 1. Where the forward market is nonexistent, or where access to it is limited, the firm must determine both what techniques to use and what their appropriate levels are. In the latter case, a comparison of the net cost of a funds-adjustment technique with the anticipated currency depreciation will indicate whether or not the hedging transaction is profitable on an expected-value basis.

■ 9.3 ■
DESIGNING A HEDGING STRATEGY

Management's objectives will largely determine its decision about the specific hedging tactics and strategy to pursue. These objectives, in turn, should reflect management's view of the world, particularly its beliefs about how markets work. The quality, or value to the shareholders, of a particular hedging strategy is, therefore, related to the congruence between those perceptions and the realities of the business environment.

The view taken here is that the basic purpose of hedging is to reduce exchange risk, where exchange risk is defined as that element of cash-flow variability that is due to currency fluctuations. Underlying the selection of a definition of exchange risk based on market value is the assumption that management's primary objective is to maximize the value of the firm. Hence, the focus is on the cash-flow effects of currency changes.

In operational terms, hedging to reduce the variance of cash flows translates into the following exposure management goal: to arrange a firm's financial affairs in such a way that however the exchange rate may move in the future, the effects on dollar returns are minimized. This objective is not universally subscribed to, however. Instead, many firms follow a selective hedging policy designed to protect against anticipated currency movements. But, if financial markets are efficient, firms cannot hedge against *expected* exchange rate changes. Interest rates, forward rates, and sales-contract prices should already reflect currency changes that are anticipated, thereby offsetting the loss-reducing benefits of hedging with higher costs. In the case of Mexico, for instance, the one-year forward discount in the futures market was close to 100% just before the peso was floated in 1982. The unavoidable conclusion is that a firm can protect itself only against *unexpected* currency changes.

Other standard techniques for responding to anticipated currency changes were summarized in Exhibit 9.5. Such techniques, however, are vastly overrated. If a devaluation is unlikely, they are costly and inefficient ways of doing business. If a devaluation is expected, the cost of using the techniques (like the cost of local borrowing) rises to reflect the anticipated devaluation. Just prior to the August 1982 peso devaluation, for example, every company in Mexico was trying to delay peso payments. Of course, this technique cannot produce a net gain because one company's payable is another company's receivable. As another example, if one company wants peso trade credit, another must offer it. Assuming that both the borrower and the lender are rational, a deal will not be struck until the interest cost rises to reflect the expected decline in the peso.

Even shifting funds from one country to another is not a costless means of hedging. The net effect of speeding up remittances while delaying receipt of intercompany receivables is to force a subsidiary in a devaluation-prone country to increase its local currency borrowings to finance the additional working capital requirements. The net cost of shifting funds, therefore, is the cost of the LC loan minus the profit generated from the use of the funds—for example, prepaying a hard-currency loan—with both adjusted for expected exchange rate changes. As mentioned previously, loans in local currencies subject to devaluation fears carry higher interest rates that are likely to offset any gains from LC devaluation.

Reducing the level of cash holdings to lower exposure can adversely affect a subsidiary's operations, while selling LC-denominated marketable securities can entail an opportunity cost (the lower interest rate on hard-currency securities). A firm with excess cash or marketable securities should reduce its holdings regardless of whether a devaluation is anticipated. Once cash balances are at the minimum level, however, any further reductions will involve real costs that must be weighed against the expected benefits.

Risk shifting by invoicing exports in the foreign currency and imports in the local currency may cause the loss of valuable sales or may reduce a firm's ability to extract concessions on import prices. Similarly, tightening credit may reduce profits more than costs.

To summarize, hedging exchange risk costs money and should be scrutinized like any other purchase of insurance. The costs of these hedging techniques are summarized in Exhibit 9.6.

■ **EXHIBIT 9.6**   Cost of the Basic Hedging Techniques

Depreciation	Costs
■ Sell local currency forward	■ Transaction costs; difference between forward and future spot rates
■ Reduce levels of local-currency cash and marketable securities	■ Operational problems; opportunity cost (loss of higher interest rates on LC securities)
■ Tighten credit (reduce local receivables)	■ Lost sales and profits
■ Delay collection of hard-currency receivables	■ Cost of financing additional receivables
■ Increase imports of hard-currency goods	■ Financing and holding costs
■ Borrow locally	■ Higher interest rates
■ Delay payment of accounts payable	■ Harm to credit reputation
■ Speed up dividend and fee remittances to parent and other subsidiaries	■ Borrowing cost if funds not available or loss of higher interest rates if LC securities must be sold
■ Speed up payment of intersubsidiary accounts payable	■ Opportunity cost of money
■ Delay collection of intersubsidiary accounts receivable	■ Opportunity cost of money
■ Invoice exports in foreign currency and imports in local currency	■ Lost export sales or lower price; premium price for imports

A company can benefit from the preceding techniques only to the extent that it can estimate the probability and timing of a devaluation more accurately than the general market can. Attempting to profit from foreign exchange forecasting, however, is speculating rather than hedging. The hedger is well advised to assume that the market knows as much as he or she does. Those who feel that they have superior information may choose to speculate, but this activity should not be confused with hedging.

Under some circumstances, it is possible for a company to benefit at the expense of the local government without speculating. Such a circumstance would involve the judicious use of market imperfections and/or existing tax asymmetries. In the case of an overvalued currency, such as the Mexican peso in 1982, if exchange controls are not imposed to prevent capital outflows and if hard currency can be acquired at the official exchange rate, then money can be moved out of the country via intercompany payments. For instance, a subsidiary can speed payments of intercompany accounts payable, make immediate purchases from other subsidiaries, or speed remittances to the parent. Unfortunately, governments are not unaware of these tactics. During a currency crisis, when hard currency is scarce, the local government can be expected to block such transfers or at least make them more expensive.

Another often-cited reason for market imperfection is that individual investors may not have equal access to capital markets. For example, since forward exchange markets exist only for the major currencies, hedging often requires local borrowing in heavily regulated capital markets. As a legal citizen of many nations, the MNC normally has greater access to these markets.

Similarly, if forward contract losses are treated as a cost of doing business, whereas gains are taxed at a lower capital gains rate, the firm can engage in tax arbitrage. In the absence of financial market imperfections or tax asymmetries, however, the net expected value of hedging over time should be zero. But, despite the questionable value to shareholders of hedging balance-sheet exposure or even transaction exposure, managers often try to reduce these exposures because they are evaluated, at least in part, on translation or transaction gains or losses.

Centralization Versus Decentralization

In the area of foreign exchange risk management, there are good arguments both for and against centralization. Favoring centralization is the reasonable assumption that local treasurers want to optimize their own financial and exposure positions, regardless of the overall corporate situation. An example is a multibillion-dollar U.S. consumer goods firm that gives its affiliates a free hand in deciding on their hedging policies. The firm's local treasurers ignored the possibilities available to the corporation to trade off positive and negative currency exposure positions by consolidating exposure worldwide. If subsidiary A sells to subsidiary B in sterling, then from the corporate perspective, these sterling exposures net out on a consolidated translation basis (but only before tax). If A and/or B hedge their sterling positions, however, unnecessary hedging takes place or a zero sterling exposure turns into a positive or negative position. Furthermore, in their dealings with external customers, some affiliates may wind up with a positive exposure and others with a negative exposure in the same currency. Through lack of knowledge or incentive, individual subsidiaries may undertake hedging actions that increase rather than decrease overall corporate exposure in a given currency.

A further benefit of centralized exposure management is the ability to take advantage, through exposure netting, of the portfolio effect discussed previously. Thus, centralization of exchange risk management should reduce the amount of hedging required to achieve a given level of safety.

Once the company has decided on the maximum currency exposure it is willing to tolerate, it can then select the cheapest option(s) worldwide to hedge its remaining exposure. Tax effects can be crucial at this stage, both in computing the amounts to hedge and the costs involved, but only headquarters will have the required global perspective. Centralized management is also needed to take advantage of the before-tax hedging cost variations that are likely to exist among subsidiaries because of market imperfections.

All these arguments for centralization of currency risk management are powerful. Against the benefits must be weighed the loss of local knowledge and the lack of incentive for local managers to take advantage of particular situations that only they may be familiar with. Companies that decentralize the hedging decision may allow local units to manage their own exposures by engaging in forward contracts with a central unit at negotiated rates. The central unit, in turn, may or may not lay off these contracts in the marketplace.

■ 9.4 ■
ILLUSTRATION: MANAGING TRANSACTION EXPOSURE FOR THE TORONTO BLUE JAYS

During the first half of the 1985 baseball season, the Toronto Blue Jays, an American League expansion team, had the best won-lost record in the major leagues. Yet their profits at the gate did not match their performance at the plate. Attendance was up, and so were ticket prices, but the Blue Jays budgeted for a loss of more than C$2 million in 1985. The reason: The Blue Jays get most of their revenue in the form of Canadian dollars (C$) but pay most of their bills in U.S. dollars.

Projected 1985 expenses included about $19 million in U.S. dollars and the equivalent of only about $4.5 million in Canadian currency. Projected revenues of roughly $21 million were almost all in Canadian dollars except for income from a U.S. television package and 20% of gate receipts from the Jays' games in U.S. ballparks. As a result of this imbalance of currency inflows and outflows, it was estimated that each $0.01 drop of the Canadian dollar against its U.S. counterpart cost the Jays about C$135,000 in 1985.

Although major-league teams usually lose money, it was believed that the Jays' ecstatic fans would have made the team profitable in 1985 if it weren't for the currency problem. The magnitude of this problem is indicated by the changed fortune of the Canadian dollar. When the Toronto franchise was created in 1976, the Canadian currency was worth $1.04; at midseason 1985, it was trading at about $0.73.

The biggest expense in 1985 was U.S. $10 million for players' salaries. (All major-league ballplayers are paid in U.S. dollars; none of the Jays' players are Canadians anyway.) By 1989, that figure had reached about U.S. $18 million. At an exchange rate of $0.80, a 1¢ drop in the Canadian dollar added C$285,000 to annual salary costs.

Like other businesses with foreign exchange problems, the Blue Jays and their fellow sufferers, the Montreal Expos, make forward purchases of U.S. dollars to protect against swings in exchange rates. Late in 1984, for example, the Jays contracted to buy about 60% of the team's projected 1985 U.S. currency needs at about 75 cents per Canadian dollar. The profit on this position enabled the team to offset most of the losses on its U.S. dollar outflows.

■ 9.5 ■
SUMMARY AND CONCLUSIONS

Firms normally cope with anticipated currency changes by engaging in forward contracts, borrowing locally, and adjusting their pricing and credit policies. However, there is reason to question the value of much of this activity. In fact, we have seen that, in normal circumstances, hedging cannot provide protection against expected exchange rate changes.

A number of empirical studies indicate that forward rates provide an unbiased estimate of future spot rates. Furthermore, according to the international Fisher effect, in the absence of government controls, interest rate differentials among countries should equal anticipated currency devaluations or revaluations. Empirical research substantiates that over time, gains or losses on debt in hard currencies tend to be offset by low interest rates; in soft currencies, they will be offset by higher interest rates unless, of course, there are various barriers that preclude equalization of real interest rates.

In fact, no other results would be consistent with the existence of a well-informed market with numerous participants—as is represented by the international financial community. Persistent differences between forward and future spot rates, for instance, would provide profitable opportunities for speculators. However, the very act of buying or selling forward to take advantage of these differences would tend to bring about equality between hedging costs and expected currency changes.

The other hedging methods, which involve factoring anticipated exchange rate changes into pricing and credit decisions, can be profitable only at the expense of others. Thus, to consistently gain by these trade-term adjustments, it is necessary to deal continuously with less-knowledgeable people. Certainly, though, a policy predicated on the continued existence of naive firms is unlikely to be viable for very long in the highly competitive and well-informed world of international business. The real value to a firm of factoring currency change expectations into its pricing and credit decisions is to prevent others from profiting at its expense.

The basic value of hedging, therefore, is to protect a company against unexpected exchange rate changes; however, by definition, these changes are unpredictable and, consequently, impossible to profit from. Of course, to the extent that a government does not permit interest and/or forward rates to fully adjust to market expectations, a firm with access to these financial instruments can expect, on average, to gain from currency changes. Nevertheless, the very nature of these imperfections severely restricts a company's ability to engage in such profitable financial operations.

■ QUESTIONS ■

1. A U.S. firm has fully hedged its sterling receivables and has bought credit insurance to cover the risk of default. Has this firm eliminated all risk on these receivables? Explain.

2. What is the basic translation hedging strategy? How does it work?

3. What alternative hedging transactions are available to a company seeking to hedge the translation exposure of its German subsidiary?

4. Referring to Question 3, how would the appropriate hedge change if the German affiliate's functional currency is the U.S. dollar?

5. Multinational firms can always reduce the foreign exchange risk faced by their foreign affiliates by borrowing in the local currency. True or false? Why?

6. Can hedging provide protection against expected exchange rate changes? Explain.

7. What is the domestic counterpart to exchange risk? Explain.

8. If a currency that a company is long in threatens to weaken, many companies will sell that currency forward. Comment on this policy.

■ PROBLEMS ■

1. In September 1984, Multinational Industries, Inc. assessed the March 1985 spot rate for sterling at the following rates:

    $1.30/£ with probability 0.15
    $1.35/£ with probability 0.20
    $1.40/£ with probability 0.25
    $1.45/£ with probability 0.20
    $1.50/£ with probability 0.20

   a. What is the expected spot rate for March 1985?

   b. If the six-month forward rate is $1.40, should the firm sell forward its pound receivables due in March 1985?

   c. What factors are likely to affect the firm's hedging decision?

2. An importer has a payment of £8 million due in 90 days.

   a. If the 90-day pound forward rate is $1.4201, what is the hedged cost of making that payment?

   b. If the spot rate expected in 90 days is $1.4050, what is the expected cost of payment?

   c. What factors will influence the hedging decision?

3. A foreign exchange trader assesses the French franc exchange rate three months hence as follows:

    $0.11 with probability 0.25
    $0.13 with probability 0.50
    $0.15 with probability 0.25

   The 90-day forward rate is $0.12.

   a. Will the trader buy or sell French francs forward against the dollar if she is concerned solely with expected values? In what volume?

   b. In reality, what is likely to limit the trader's speculative activities?

c. Suppose the trader revises her probability assessment as follows:

$0.09 with probability 0.33
$0.13 with probability 0.33
$0.17 with probability 0.33

Assuming the forward rate remains at $0.12, do you think this new assessment will affect the trader's decision?

4. International Worldwide would like to execute a money market hedge to cover a ¥250,000,000 shipment from Japan of sound systems it will receive in six months. The current exchange rate for yen is ¥124 = $1.

a. How would International structure the hedge? What would it do to hedge the Japanese yen it must pay in six months? The annual yen interest rate is 4%.

b. The yen may rise to as much as ¥140 = $1 or fall to ¥115 = $1. What will the total dollar cash flow be in six months in either case?

5. In January 1988, Arco bought a 24.3% stake in the British oil firm Britoil PLC. It intended to buy a further $1 billion worth of Britoil stock if Britoil was agreeable. However, Arco was uncertain whether Britoil, which had expressed a strong desire to remain independent, would accept its bid. To guard against the possibility of a pound appreciation in the interim, Arco decided to convert $1 billion into pounds and place them on deposit in London, pending the outcome of its discussions with Britoil's management. What exchange risk does Arco face and has it chosen the best way to protect itself from that risk?

6. Sumitomo Chemical of Japan has one week in which to negotiate a contract to supply products to a U.S. company at a dollar price that will remain fixed for one year. What advice would you give Sumitomo?

7. Kemp & Beatley, Inc., is a New York importer of table linens and accessories. It hedges all its import orders using forward contracts. Does Kemp & Beatley face any exchange risk? Explain.

8. U.S. Farm-Raised Fish Trading Co., a catfish concern in Jackson, Mississippi, tells its Japanese customers that it wants to be paid in dollars. According to its director of export marketing, this simple strategy eliminates all its currency risk. Is he right? Why?

9. The Montreal Expos are a major-league baseball team located in Montreal, Canada. What currency risk is faced by the Expos, and how can this exchange risk be managed?

10. Westinghouse recently had to put together a $50 million bid, denominated in Swiss francs, to upgrade a Swiss power plant. If it won, Westinghouse expected to pay subcontractors and suppliers in five currencies. The payment schedule for the contract stretched over a five-year period.

a. How should Westinghouse establish the Swiss franc price of its $50 million bid?

b. What exposure does Westinghouse face on this bid? How can it hedge that exposure?

11.* Metalgesselschaft, a leading German metal processor, has scheduled a supply of 20,000 metric tons of copper for October 1. On April 1, copper is quoted on the London Metals Exchange at £562 per metric ton for immediate delivery and £605 per metric ton for delivery on October 1. Monthly storage costs are £10 for a metric ton in London and DM 30 in Hamburg, payable on the first day of storage.

Exchange rate quotations are as follows: The pound is worth DM 3.61 on April 1 and is selling at a 6.3% annual discount. The opportunity cost of capital for Metalgesselschaft is estimated at 8%

* Problem contributed by Laurent Jacque.

annually, and the pound sterling is expected to depreciate at a yearly rate of 6.3% throughout the next 12 months.

Compute the Deutsche mark cost for Metalgesselschaft on April 1 of the following options:

a. Buy 20,000 metric tons of copper on April 1 and store it in London until October 1.

b. Buy a forward contract of 20,000 metric tons on April 1, for delivery in six months. Cover sterling debt by purchasing forward pounds sterling on April 1.

c. Buy 20,000 metric tons of copper on October 1. Can you identify other options available to Metalgesselschaft? Which one would you recommend?

■ BIBLIOGRAPHY ■

Cornell, Bradford, and Alan C. Shapiro. "Managing Foreign Exchange Risks." *Midland Corporate Finance Journal,* Fall 1983, pp. 16–31.

Dufey, Gunter, and S.L. Srinivasulu. "The Case for Corporate Management of Foreign Exchange Risk." *Financial Management,* Summer 1984, pp. 54–62.

Giddy, Ian H. "The Foreign Exchange Option as a Hedging Tool." *Midland Corporate Finance Journal,* Fall 1983, pp. 32–42.

Goeltz, Richard K. "Managing Liquid Funds on an International Scope," unpublished paper. New York: Joseph E. Seagram and Sons, 1971.

Shapiro, Alan C., and David P. Rutenberg. "Managing Exchange Risks in a Floating World." *Financial Management,* Summer 1976, pp. 48–58.

Srinivasulu, Sam, and Edward Massura. "Sharing Currency Risks in Long-Term Contracts." *Business International Money Reports,* February 23, 1987, pp. 57–59.

▪10▪

Measuring Economic Exposure

Let's face it. If you've got 75% of your assets in the U.S. and 50% of your sales outside it, and the dollar's strong, you've got problems.

—Donald V. Fites—
Executive Vice President
Caterpillar Tractor

▪ Chapter 8 focused on the accounting effects of currency changes. As we saw in that chapter, the adoption of FASB–52 has helped to moderate the wild swings in the translated earnings of overseas subsidiaries. Nevertheless, the problem of coping with volatile currencies remains essentially unchanged. Fluctuations in exchange rates will continue to have "real" effects on the cash profitability of foreign subsidiaries—complicating overseas selling, pricing, buying, and plant-location decisions.

This chapter develops an appropriate definition of foreign exchange risk. It discusses the nature and origins of exchange risk and presents a theory of the *economic*, as distinguished from the accounting, consequences of currency changes on a firm's value. The chapter also illustrates how economic exposure can be measured and provides an operational measure of exchange risk.

▪ 10.1 ▪
FOREIGN EXCHANGE RISK AND ECONOMIC EXPOSURE

The most important aspect of foreign exchange risk management is to incorporate currency change expectations into *all* basic corporate decisions. In performing this task, the firm must know what is at risk. However, there is a major discrepancy between accounting practice and economic reality in terms of measuring *exposure*, which is the degree to which a company is affected by exchange rate changes.

As we saw in Chapter 8, those who use an accounting definition of exposure—whether FASB–8, FASB–52, or some other method—divide the balance sheet's assets and liabilities into those accounts that will be affected by exchange rate changes and those that will not. In contrast, economic theory focuses on the impact of an exchange rate change on future cash flows; that is, *economic exposure* is based on the extent to which the value of the firm—as measured by the present value of its expected future cash flows—will change when exchange rates change.

Specifically, if *PV* is the present value of a firm, then that firm is exposed to currency risk if $\Delta PV/\Delta e$ is not equal to zero, where ΔPV is the change in the firm's present value associated with an exchange rate change, Δe. *Exchange risk,* in turn, is defined as the variability in the firm's value that is caused by uncertain exchange rate changes. Thus, exchange risk is viewed as the possibility that currency fluctuations can alter the expected amounts or variability of the firm's future cash flows.

Economic exposure can be separated into two components: transaction exposure and operating exposure. We saw that *transaction exposure* stems from exchange gains or losses on foreign-currency-denominated contractual obligations. Although transaction exposure is often included under accounting exposure, as it was in Chapter 8, it is more properly a cash-flow exposure and, hence, part of economic exposure. However, even if the company prices all contracts in dollars or otherwise hedges its transaction exposure, the residual exposure—longer-term operating exposure—still remains.

Operating exposure arises because currency fluctuations can alter a company's future revenues and costs—that is, its operating cash flows. Consequently, measuring a firm's operating exposure requires a longer-term perspective, viewing the firm as an ongoing concern with operations whose cost and price competitiveness could be affected by exchange rate changes.

Thus, the firm faces operating exposure the moment it invests in servicing a market subject to foreign competition or in sourcing goods or inputs abroad. This investment includes new-product development, a distribution network, foreign supply contracts, or production facilities. Transaction exposure arises later on, and only if the company's commitments lead it to engage in foreign-currency-denominated sales or purchases. Exhibit 10.1 shows the time pattern of economic exposure.

The measurement of economic exposure is made especially difficult because it is impossible to assess the effects of an exchange rate change without simultaneously considering the impact on cash flows of the underlying relative rates of inflation associated with each currency. Reconsidering the concept of the real exchange rate will help clarify the discussion of exposure. As presented in Chapter 7, the *real exchange rate* is defined as the nominal exchange rate (for example, the number of dollars per franc) adjusted for changes in the relative purchasing power of each currency since some base period. Specifically,

$$e'_t = e_t \times \frac{(1 + i_{f,t})}{(1 + i_{h,t})}$$

where e'_t = the real exchange rate (home currency per one unit of foreign currency) at time t

e_t = the nominal exchange rate (home currency per one unit of foreign currency) at time t

$i_{f,t}$ = the amount of foreign inflation between times 0 and t

$i_{h,t}$ = the amount of domestic inflation between times 0 and t

■ **EXHIBIT 10.1** The Time Pattern of Economic Exposure

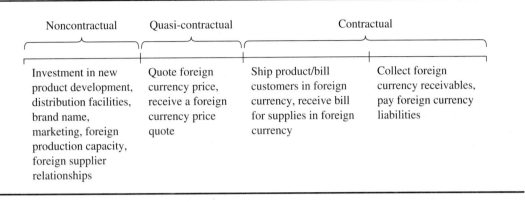

Importance of the Real Exchange Rate

The distinction between the nominal exchange rate and the real exchange rate is important because of their vastly different implications for exchange risk. A dramatic change in the nominal exchange rate accompanied by an equal change in the price level should have no effects on the relative competitive positions of domestic firms and their foreign competitors and, therefore, will not alter real cash flows. Alternatively, if the real exchange rate changes, it will cause relative price changes—changes in the ratio of domestic goods' prices to prices of foreign goods. In terms of currency changes affecting relative competitiveness, therefore, the focus must be not on nominal exchange rate changes, but instead on changes in the purchasing power of one currency relative to another.

Inflation and Exchange Risk

Let us begin by holding relative prices constant and looking only at the effects of general inflation. This condition means that if the inflation rate is 10%, the price of every good in the economy rises by 10%. In addition, we will initially assume that all goods are traded in a competitive world market without transaction costs, tariffs, or taxes of any kind. Given these conditions, economic theory tells us that the law of one price must prevail. That is, the price of any good, measured in a common currency, must be equal in all countries.

If the law of one price holds and if there is no variation in the relative prices of goods or services, then the rate of change in the exchange rate must equal the difference between the inflation rates in the two countries. The implications of a constant real exchange rate—that is, PPP holds—are worth exploring further. To begin, purchasing power parity does not imply that exchange rate changes will necessarily be small or easy to forecast. If a country has high and unpredictable inflation (for example, Argentina), then the country's exchange rate will also fluctuate randomly.

Nonetheless, without relative price changes, a multinational company faces no real operating exchange risk. As long as the firm avoids contracts fixed in foreign-currency terms, its foreign cash flows will vary with the foreign rate of inflation. Because the exchange rate also depends on the difference between the foreign and the domestic rates of inflation, the movement of the exchange rate exactly cancels the change in the foreign price level, leaving real dollar cash flows unaffected.

■ ───

ILLUSTRATION

Calculating the Effect of Exchange Rate Changes and Inflation on Apex Spain. Apex Spain, the Spanish subsidiary of Apex Company, produces and sells medical imaging devices in Spain. At the current peseta exchange rate of Ptas. 1 = $0.01, the devices cost Ptas. 40,000 ($400) to produce and sell for Ptas. 100,000 ($1000). The profit margin of Ptas. 60,000 provides a dollar margin of $600. Suppose that Spanish inflation during the year is 20%, while the U.S. inflation rate is zero. All prices and costs are assumed to move in line with inflation. Assuming that purchasing power parity holds, the peseta will devalue to $0.0083 (0.01 × 1/1.2). Since the real value of the peseta stays at $0.01 (0.0083 × 1.2/1.0), Apex Spain's dollar profit margin will remain at $600. These effects are shown in Exhibit 10.2. ■

Of course, the above conclusion does not hold if the firm enters into contracts fixed in terms of the foreign currency. Examples of such contracts are debt with fixed interest rates, long-term leases, labor contracts, and rent. However, if the real exchange rate remains constant, the risk introduced by entering into fixed contracts is not exchange risk; it is inflation risk. For instance, a Mexican firm with fixed-rate debt in pesos faces the same risk as the subsidiary of an American firm with peso debt. If the rate of inflation declines, the

■ **EXHIBIT 10.2** The Effects of Nominal Exchange Rate Changes and Inflation on Apex Spain

Price Level	Spain	United States			
Beginning of year	100	100			
End of year	120	100			

Exchange Rate	Beginning of Year		End of Year		
Nominal Rate	Ptas. 1 = $0.01		Ptas. 1 = $0.0083		
Real Rate	Ptas. 1 = $0.01		Ptas. 1 = $0.0083 × 1.2/1 = $0.01		

	Beginning of Year		End of Year	
Profit Impact	**Pesetas**	**U.S. Dollars**	**Pesetas**	**U.S. Dollars**
Price*	Ptas. 100,000	$1,000	Ptas. 120,000	$1,000
Cost of production*	40,000	400	48,000	400
Profit margin	Ptas. 60,000	$ 600	Ptas. 72,000	$ 600

*Peseta prices and costs are assumed to increase at the 20% rate of Spanish inflation.

real interest cost of the debt rises, and the real cash flow of both companies falls. The solution to the problem of inflation risk is to avoid writing contracts fixed in nominal terms in countries with unpredictable inflation. If the contracts are indexed and if the real exchange rate remains constant, exchange risk is eliminated.

Real Exchange Rate Changes and Exchange Risk

In general, a decline in the real value of a nation's currency makes its exports and import-competing goods more competitive. Conversely, an appreciating currency hurts the nation's exporters and those producers competing with imports.

During the late 1970s, for example, worldwide demand for Swiss franc-denominated assets caused the Swiss franc to appreciate in real terms. As a result, Swiss watchmakers were squeezed. Because of competition from Japanese companies, Swiss firms could not significantly raise the dollar price of watches sold in the United States. Yet, at the same time, the *dollar* cost of Swiss labor was rising because the franc was appreciating against the dollar.

American companies faced similar problems when the real value of the dollar began rising against other currencies during the early 1980s. U.S. exporters found themselves with the Hobson's choice of either keeping dollar prices constant and losing sales volume (because foreign currency prices rose in line with the appreciating dollar) or setting prices in the foreign currency to maintain market share, with a corresponding erosion in dollar revenues and profit margins. At the same time, the dollar cost of American labor remained the same or rose in line with U.S. inflation. The combination of lower dollar revenues and unchanged or higher dollar costs resulted in severe hardship for those U.S. companies selling abroad. Similarly, U.S. manufacturers competing domestically with imports whose dollar prices were declining saw both their profit margins and sales volumes reduced. But now the shoe is on the other foot, as Japanese firms attempt to cope with a yen that appreciated by more than 100% in real terms between 1985 and 1989.

■ ───

ILLUSTRATION

Yen Appreciation Harms Japanese TV Producers. For most of 1985, the yen traded at about ¥240 = $1. By 1988, the yen's value had risen to about ¥130 = $1. This rise had a highly negative impact on Japanese TV manufacturers. If it cost, say, ¥100,000 to build a color TV in Japan, ship it to the United States, and earn a normal profit, that TV could be sold in 1985 for about $417 (100,000/240). However, in 1988, the price would have had to be about $769 (100,000/130) for Japanese firms to break even. As the Japanese firms raise their dollar price to compensate for yen appreciation, Americans buy fewer Japanese color TVs, and the yen revenues fall. If the Japanese TV producers decide to keep their price constant at $417 to preserve market share in the United States, they will have to cut their yen price to about ¥54,210 (417 × 130). Whether they hold the line on yen prices or cut them, yen appreciation is bad news for Japanese TV manufacturers. ─────────────── ■

Alternatively, Industrias Penoles, the Mexican firm that is the world's largest refiner of newly mined silver, increased its dollar profits by over 200% following the real devaluation of the Mexican peso relative to the dollar in 1982. The reason for the firm's success is that its costs, which are in pesos, declined in dollar terms, while the dollar value of its revenues, which are derived from exports, held steady.

To summarize, the economic impact of a currency change on a firm depends on whether the exchange rate change is fully offset by the difference in inflation rates or whether (because of price controls, a shift in monetary policy, or some other reason) the real exchange rate and, hence, relative prices change. It is these relative price changes that ultimately determine a firm's long-run exposure.

A less obvious point is that a firm may face more exchange risk if nominal exchange rates do *not* change. Consider, for example, a Brazilian shoe manufacturer producing for export to the United States and Europe. If the Brazilian cruzeiro's exchange rate remains fixed in the face of Brazil's typically high rate of inflation, then both the cruzeiro's real exchange rate and the manufacturer's dollar costs of production will rise. Therefore, unless the cruzeiro devalues, the Brazilian exporter will be placed at a competitive disadvantage vis-à-vis producers located in countries with less rapidly rising costs, such as Taiwan and South Korea.

Suppose, for example, that the Brazilian firm sells its shoes in the U.S. market for $10. Its profit margin is $6, or Cr$300, because the shoes cost $4 to produce at the current cruzeiro exchange rate of Cr$1 = $0.02. If Brazilian inflation is 100% but the cruzeiro exchange rate remains constant, it will cost the manufacturer $8 to produce these same shoes by the end of the year. Assuming no U.S. inflation, the firm's profit margin will drop to $2. The basic problem is the 100% real appreciation of the cruzeiro (0.02 × 2/1). This situation is shown in Exhibit 10.3 as Scenario 1.

In order to preserve its dollar profit margin (but not its inflation-adjusted cruzeiro margin), the firm will have to raise its price to $14 (why?).[1] But if it does that, it will be placed at a competitive disadvantage. By contrast, Scenario 2 shows that if the cruzeiro devalues by 50%, to $0.01, the real exchange rate will remain constant at $0.02 ($.01 × 2/1), the Brazilian firm's competitive situation will be unchanged, and its profit margin will stay at $6. Its real cruzeiro profit margin also remains the same. Note that with 100% inflation, today's Cr$300 profit margin must rise to Cr$600 by year's end (which it does) to stay constant in real cruzeiro terms.

■ ──

ILLUSTRATION

Chile Mismanages Its Exchange Rate. A particularly dramatic illustration of the unfortunate effects of a fixed nominal exchange rate combined with high domestic inflation is provided by Chile. As part of its plan to bring down the rate of Chilean inflation, the government fixed the exchange rate in the middle of 1979 at 39 pesos to the U.S. dollar. Over the next two and one-half years, the Chilean price level rose 60%, while U.S. prices rose by only about 30%. Thus, by early 1982, the Chilean peso had appreciated in real terms by approximately 23% (1.6/1.3 − 1) against the U.S. dollar. These data are summarized in Exhibit 10.4.

───

[1]If the price is raised to $14, the profit margin is $6 ($14 − $8). However, at an exchange rate of Cr$1 = $0.02, the cruzeiro margin is still Cr$300. With 100% inflation, the inflation-adjusted value of this margin is equivalent to only half of today's margin of Cr$300 (Cr$2 at year's end has the purchasing power of Cr$1 today).

■ **EXHIBIT 10.3**   The Effects of Real Exchange Rate Changes on the Brazilian Shoe
Manufacturer

Price Level	Brazil	United States
Beginning of year	100	100
End of year	200	100

Scenario 1	Beginning of Year	End of Year
Nominal Exchange Rate	Cr$1 = $0.02	Cr$1 = $0.02
Real Exchange Rate	Cr$1 = $0.02	Cr$1 = $0.02 × 2/1 = $0.04

	Beginning of Year		End of Year	
Profit Impact	Cruzeiros	U.S. Dollars	Cruzeiros	U.S. Dollars
Price	500	10.00	500	10.00
Cost of production	200	4.00	400	8.00
Profit margin	300	6.00	100	2.00

Scenario 2	Beginning of Year	End of Year
Nominal Exchange Rate	Cr$1 = $0.02	Cr$1 = $0.01
Real Exchange Rate	Cr$1 = $0.02	Cr$1 = $0.01 × 2/1 = $0.02

	Beginning of Year		End of Year	
Profit Impact	Cruzeiros	U.S. Dollars	Cruzeiros	U.S. Dollars
Price	500	10.00	1,000	10.00
Cost of production	200	4.00	400	4.00
Profit margin	300	6.00	600	6.00

An 18% "corrective" devaluation was enacted in June 1982. But it was too late. The artificially high peso had already done its double damage to the Chilean economy: It made Chile's manufactured products more expensive abroad, pricing many of them out of international trade; and it made imports cheaper, undercutting Chilean domestic industries. The effects of the overvalued peso were devastating. Banks became insolvent, factories and copper smelters were thrown into bankruptcy, copper mines were closed, construction projects were shut down, and farms were put on the auction block. Unemployment approached 25%, and some areas of Chile resembled industrial graveyards. ■

The Chilean example illustrates a critical point: *An increase in the real value of a currency acts as a tax on exports and a subsidy on imports.* Hence, firms that export or that compete with imports are hurt by an appreciating home currency. Conversely, such firms

■ **EXHIBIT 10.4**   Nominal and Real Exchange Rates for Chile, 1979–1982

Price Level	Chile	United States	
1979	100	100	
1982	160	130	

Nominal Exchange Rate	1979	Ps. 1 = $0.02564	
	1982	Ps. 1 = $0.02564	
Real Exchange Rate	1979	Ps. 1 = $0.02564	
	1982	Ps. 1 = $0.02564 × $\dfrac{1.60}{1.30}$	
		= $0.03156	

Increase in Real Value of the Chilean Peso $\dfrac{0.03156 - 0.02564}{0.02564} = 23.1\%$

Result: Economic Devastation
—Loss of export markets
—Loss of domestic markets to imports
—Massive unemployment
—Numerous bankruptcies
—Numerous bank failures

benefit from home-currency depreciation. These general principles identify a company's economic exposure.

■ 10.2 ■
THE ECONOMIC CONSEQUENCES OF EXCHANGE RATE CHANGES

We now examine more closely the specifics of a firm's economic exposure. Solely for the purpose of exposition, the discussion of exposure is divided into its component parts: transaction exposure and real operating exposure.

Transaction Exposure

Transaction exposure arises out of the various types of transactions that require settlement in a foreign currency. Examples are cross-border trade, borrowing and lending in foreign currencies, and the local purchasing and sales activities of foreign subsidiaries. Strictly speaking, of course, the items already on a firm's balance sheet, such as loans and receivables, capture some of these transactions. However, a detailed transaction exposure report must also contain a number of off-balance-sheet items as well, including future sales and purchases, lease payments, forward contracts, loan repayments, and other contractual or anticipated foreign-currency receipts and disbursements.

In terms of measuring economic exposure, though, a transaction exposure report, no matter how detailed, has a fundamental flaw: the assumption that local-currency cost and revenue streams remain constant following an exchange rate change.

That assumption does not permit an evaluation of the typical adjustments that consumers and firms can be expected to undertake under conditions of currency change. Hence, attempting to measure the likely exchange gain or loss by simply multiplying the projected predevaluation (prerevaluation) local-currency cash flows by the forecast devaluation (revaluation) percentage will lead to misleading results. Given the close relationship between nominal exchange rate changes and inflation as expressed in purchasing power parity, measuring exposure to a currency change without reference to the accompanying inflation is also a misguided task.

We will now examine more closely the typical demand and cost effects that result from a real exchange rate change and how these effects combine to determine a firm's true operating exposure. In general, an appreciating real exchange rate can be expected to have the opposite effects. The dollar is assumed to be the home currency.

Operating Exposure

A real exchange rate change affects a number of aspects of the firm's operations. With respect to dollar (HC) appreciation, the key issue for a domestic firm is its degree of *pricing flexibility*—that is, can the firm maintain its dollar margins both at home and abroad? Can the company maintain its dollar price on domestic sales in the face of lower-priced foreign imports? In the case of foreign sales, can the firm raise its foreign currency selling price sufficiently to preserve its dollar profit margin?

The answers to these questions depend largely on the *price elasticity of demand.* The less price elastic the demand, the more price flexibility a company will have to respond to exchange rate changes. Price elasticity, in turn, depends on the degree of competition and the location of key competitors. The more *differentiated* (distinct) a company's products are, the less competition it will face and the greater its ability will be to maintain its domestic currency prices both at home and abroad. Examples here are IBM and Daimler-Benz (producer of Mercedes Benz cars). Similarly, if most competitors are based in the home country, then all will face the same change in their cost structure from home currency appreciation, and all can raise their foreign currency prices without putting any of them at a competitive disadvantage relative to their domestic competitors. Examples of this situation are in the precision instrumentation and high-end telecommunications industries, in which virtually all the important players are U.S.-based companies.

Conversely, the less differentiated a company's products are and the more internationally diversified its competitors (for example, the low-priced end of the auto industry) are, the greater the price elasticity of demand for its products will be and the less pricing flexibility it will have. These companies face the greatest amount of exchange risk.

■ ─────────────────────────────────

ILLUSTRATION

Product Differentiation and Susceptibility to Exchange Risk of the U.S. Apparel and Textile Industries. The U.S. textile and apparel industries are highly competitive, with each composed of many small manufacturers. In addition, nearly every country has a textile industry, and apparel industries are also common to most countries.

Despite these similarities, the textile industry exists in a more-competitive environment than the apparel industry because textile products are more standardized than apparel products. Buyers of textiles can easily switch from a firm that sells a standard good at a higher price to one that sells virtually the same good at a lower price. Because they are more differentiated, the products of competing apparel firms are viewed as more distinct and are less sensitive than textile goods to changes in prices. Thus, even though both textile and apparel firms operate in highly competitive industries, apparel firms—with their greater degree of pricing flexibility—are less subject to exchange risk than textile firms. ∎

Another important determinant of a company's susceptibility to exchange risk is its ability to shift production and the sourcing of inputs among countries. The greater a company's flexibility to substitute between home-country and foreign-country inputs or production, the less exchange risk the company will face. Other things being equal, firms with worldwide production systems can cope with currency changes by increasing production in a nation whose currency has undergone a real devaluation and decreasing production in a nation whose currency has revalued in real terms.

With respect to a multinational corporation's foreign operations, the determinants of its economic exposure will be similar to those just mentioned. A foreign subsidiary selling goods or services in its local market will generally be unable to raise its local-currency selling price to the full extent of an LC devaluation, causing it to register a decline in its postdevaluation dollar revenues. However, because an LC devaluation will also reduce import competition, the more import competition the subsidiary was facing prior to the devaluation, the smaller its dollar revenue decline will be.

The harmful effects of LC devaluation will be mitigated somewhat since the devaluation should lower the subsidiary's dollar production costs, particularly those attributable to local inputs. However, the higher the import content of local inputs, the less dollar production costs will decline. Inputs used in the export or import-competing sectors will decline less in dollar price than other domestic inputs.

An MNC using its foreign subsidiary as an export platform will be benefited by an LC devaluation since its export revenues should stay about the same, whereas its dollar costs will decline. The net result will be a jump in dollar profits for the exporter.

Local-currency movements can also affect the dollar value of the depreciation tax shield. The cash flow associated with the tax write-off of depreciable assets can have a substantial present value, particularly for a capital-intensive corporation. Unless indexation of fixed assets is permitted (as in Argentina, Brazil, and Israel), the dollar value of the local-currency-denominated tax shield will unambiguously decline by the percentage of nominal devaluation.

The major conclusion is that the sector of the economy in which a firm operates (export, import-competing, or purely domestic), the sources of the firm's inputs (imports, domestic traded or nontraded goods), and fluctuations in the real exchange rate are far more important in delineating the firm's true economic exposure than is any accounting definition. The economic effects are summarized in Exhibit 10.5.

■ **EXHIBIT 10.5**   Characteristic Economic Effects of Exchange Rate Changes on MNCs

Cash-Flow Categories	Relevant Economic Factors	Devaluation Impact	Revaluation Impact
Revenue		**Parent-Currency Revenue Impact**	**Parent-Currency Revenue Impact**
Export sales	Price-sensitive demand	Increase (+ +)	Decrease (– –)
	Price-insensitive demand	Slight increase (+)	Slight decrease (–)
Local sales	Weak prior import competition	Sharp decline (– –)	Increase (+ +)
	Strong prior import competition	Decrease (–) (less than devaluation %)	Slight increase (+)
Costs		**Parent-Currency Cost Impact**	**Parent-Currency Cost Impact**
Domestic inputs	Low import content	Decrease (– –)	Increase (+ +)
	High import content/inputs used in export or import-competing sectors	Slight decrease (–)	Slight increase (+)
Imported inputs	Small local market	Remain the same (0)	Remain the same (0)
	Large local market	Slight decrease (–)	Slight increase (+)
Depreciation		**Cash-Flow Impact**	**Cash-Flow Impact**
Fixed assets	No asset valuation adjustment	Decrease by devaluation % (– –)	Increase by revaluation % (+ +)
	Asset valuation adjustment	Decrease (–)	Increase (+)

NOTE: To interpret the above chart, and taking the impact of a devaluation on local demand as an example, it is assumed that if import competition is weak, local prices will climb slightly, if at all; in such a case, there would be a sharp contraction in parent-company revenue. If imports generate strong competition, local-currency prices are expected to increase, although not to the full extent of the devaluation; in this instance, only a moderate decline in parent-company revenue would be registered.

SOURCE: Alan C. Shapiro, "Developing a Profitable Exposure Management System." Reprinted from p. 188 of the June 17, 1977, issue of *Business International Money Report,* with the permission of Business International Corporation (New York).

A surprising implication of this analysis is that domestic facilities that supply foreign markets normally entail much greater exchange risk than do foreign facilities supplying local markets. The explanation is that material and labor used in a domestic plant are paid for in the home currency while the products are sold in a foreign currency. For example, take a Japanese company such as Nissan Motors that builds a plant to produce cars for export, primarily to the United States. The company will incur an exchange risk from the point at which it invests in facilities to supply a foreign market (the United States) because its yen expenses will be matched with dollar revenues rather than yen revenues. The point seems obvious; however, all too frequently, firms neglect those effects when analyzing a proposed foreign investment.

Similarly, a firm (or its affiliate) producing solely for the domestic market and using only domestic sources of inputs can be strongly affected by currency changes, even though its accounting exposure is zero. Consider, for example, American Motors (now a Chrysler subsidiary), which produces and sells cars only in the United States and uses only U.S. labor and materials. Because it buys and sells only in dollars, by U.S. accounting standards it has no balance-sheet exposure. However, its principal emphasis has been on the compact, economy-minded end of the auto market—the segment most subject to competition from less-expensive Korean, Japanese, Italian, and German imports. Dollar devaluations have certainly enhanced American Motors' competitive position or, at least, have slowed down its erosion, enabling the company to enjoy higher dollar profits than it would have in the absence of these currency changes. Appreciation of the dollar has had opposite effects.

■ 10.3 ■
IDENTIFYING ECONOMIC EXPOSURE

At this point it makes sense to illustrate some of the concepts just discussed by examining several firms to see in what ways they may be susceptible to exchange risk. The companies are Aspen Skiing Company, Petróleos Mexicanos, and Toyota Motor Company.

Aspen Skiing Company

Aspen owns and operates ski resorts in the Colorado Rockies, catering primarily to Americans. It buys all its supplies in dollars and uses only American labor and materials. All guests pay in dollars. Because it buys and sells only in dollars, by U.S. standards it has no accounting exposure. Yet, Aspen Skiing Company does face economic exposure because changes in the value of the dollar affect its competitive position. For example, the strong dollar in the early 1980s adversely affected the company because it led to bargains abroad that offered stiff competition for domestic resorts, including the Rocky Mountain ski areas.

Despite record snowfalls in the Rockies during the early 1980s, many Americans decided to ski in the European Alps instead. Although air fare to the Alps cost much more than a flight to Colorado, the difference between expenses on the ground made a European ski holiday less expensive. For example, in January 1984, American Express offered a basic one-week ski package in Aspen for $439 per person, including double-occupancy lodging, lift ticket, and free rental car or bus transfer from Denver.[2] Throw in round-trip air fare between New York and Denver of $300 and the trip's cost totaled $739.

At the same time, skiers could spend a week in Chamonix in the French Alps for $234, including lodging, lift ticket, breakfast, and a bus transfer from Geneva, Switzerland. Adding in round-trip air fare from New York of $579 brought the trip's cost to $813. The Alpine vacation became less expensive than the one in the Rockies when the cost of meals was included: an estimated $50 a day in Aspen versus $30 a day in Chamonix.

In effect, Aspen Skiing Company is operating in a global market for skiing or, more broadly, vacation services. As the dollar appreciates in real terms, both foreigners and Americans find less-expensive skiing and vacation alternatives outside the United States. In addition, even if California and other West Coast skiers find that high transportation costs continue to make it more expensive to ski in Europe than in the Rockies, they are not restricted to the American Rockies. They have the choice of skiing in the Canadian Rockies, where the skiing is fine and their dollars go further.

Conversely, a depreciating dollar makes Aspen Skiing Company more competitive and

---

[2]Reported in *The Wall Street Journal,* January 17, 1984, p.1.

should increase its revenues and profits. In either event, the use of American products and labor means that its costs will not be significantly affected by exchange rate fluctuations.

Petróleos Mexicanos

Petróleos Mexicanos, or Pemex, is the Mexican national oil company. It is the largest company in Mexico and ranked number 36 in the 1987 Fortune directory of the biggest non-U.S. industrial companies. Most of its sales are overseas. Suppose Pemex borrows U.S. dollars. If the peso devalues, is Pemex a better or worse credit risk?

The instinctive response of most people is that peso devaluation makes Pemex a poorer credit risk. This response is wrong. Consider Pemex's revenues. Assume that it exports all its oil. Because oil is priced in dollars, Pemex's dollar revenues will remain the same following peso devaluation. Its dollar costs, however, will change. Most of its operating costs are denominated in pesos. These costs include labor, local supplies, services, and materials. Although the peso amount of these costs may go up somewhat, they will not rise to the extent of the devaluation of the peso. Hence, the dollar amount of peso costs will decline. Pemex also uses a variety of sophisticated equipment and services to aid in oil exploration, drilling, and production. Because these inputs are generally from foreign sources, their dollar costs are likely to be unaffected by peso devaluation. Inasmuch as some costs will fall in dollar terms and other costs will stay the same, the overall effect of peso devaluation is a decline in Pemex's dollar costs.

Since its dollar revenue will stay the same while the dollar amount of its costs will fall, the net effect on Pemex of a peso devaluation is to increase its dollar cash flow. Hence, it becomes a better credit risk in terms of its ability to service dollar debt.

Might this conclusion be reversed if it turns out that Pemex sells much of its oil domestically? Surprisingly, the answer is no if we add the further condition that the Mexican government doesn't impose oil price controls. Suppose the price of oil is $20 a barrel. If the initial peso exchange rate is Ps 1 = $0.04, that means that the price of oil in Mexico must be Ps 500 a barrel. Otherwise, there would be an arbitrage opportunity because oil transportation costs are a small fraction of the price of oil. If the peso now devalues to $0.02, the price of oil must rise to Ps 1,000. Consider what would happen if the price stayed at Ps 500. The dollar equivalent price would now be $10. But why would Pemex sell oil in Mexico for $10 a barrel when it could sell the same oil outside Mexico for $20 a barrel? It wouldn't do so unless there were price controls in Mexico and the government allocated a certain amount of oil to the Mexican market at this price. Hence, in the absence of government intervention, the peso price of oil must rise to Ps 1,000 and Pemex's dollars profits will rise whether it exports all or part of its oil.

This situation points out the important distinction between the currency of denomination and the currency of determination. The *currency of denomination* is the currency in which contracts are stated. For example, oil prices in Mexico are stated in pesos. However, although the currency of denomination for oil sales in Mexico is the peso, the peso price itself is determined by the dollar price of oil; that is, as the peso:dollar exchange rate changes, the peso price of oil changes to equate the dollar-equivalent price of oil in Mexico with the dollar price of oil in the world market. Thus, the *currency of determination* for Pemex's domestic oil sales is the U.S. dollar.

Toyota Motor Company

Toyota is the largest Japanese auto company and the fourth largest non-U.S. industrial firm in the world. Over half of its sales are overseas, primarily in the United States. If the yen appreciates, Toyota has the choice of keeping its yen price constant or its dollar price constant. If Toyota holds its yen price constant, the dollar price of its auto exports will rise and sales volume will decline. On the other hand, if Toyota decides to maintain its U.S. market share, it must hold its dollar price constant. In either case, its yen revenues will fall.

Even if Toyota decides to focus on the Japanese market, it will face the *flow-back effect,* as previously exported products flow back into the home market. Flow-back occurs because other Japanese firms find that a high yen makes it difficult to export their cars and so they emphasize Japanese sales as well. The result is increased domestic competition and lower profit margins on domestic sales.

Toyota's yen production costs will also be affected by yen appreciation. Steel, copper, aluminum, oil (from which plastics are made), and other materials that go into making a car are all imported. As the yen appreciates, the yen cost of these imported materials will decline. Yen costs of labor and domestic services, products, and equipment will likely stay the same. The net effect of lower yen costs for some inputs and constant yen costs for other inputs is a reduction in overall yen costs of production.

The net effect on profits of lower yen revenues and lower yen costs is an empirical question. This question can be answered by examining the profit consequences of yen appreciation. Here, the answer is unambiguous: Yen appreciation hurts Toyota; the reduction in its revenues more than offsets the reduction in its costs.

These three examples illustrate a progression of ideas. Aspen Skiing Company's revenues were affected by exchange rate changes, but its costs were largely unaffected. By contrast, Pemex's costs were affected by exchange rate changes, but not its revenues. Toyota had both its costs and its revenues affected by exchange rate changes. The process of examining these companies includes a systematic approach to identifying a company's exposure to exchange risk. Exhibit 10.6 summarizes this approach by presenting a series of questions that underlie the analysis of economic exposure.

■ 10.4 ■
CALCULATING ECONOMIC EXPOSURE

We will now work through a hypothetical, though comprehensive, example illustrating all the various aspects of exposure that have been discussed so far. This example emphasizes the quantitative, rather than qualitative, determination of economic exposure. It shows how critical the underlying assumptions are.

Spectrum Manufacturing AB is the wholly owned Swedish affiliate of a U.S. multinational industrial plastics firm. It manufactures patented sheet plastic in Sweden, with 60% of its output currently being sold in Sweden and the remaining 40% exported to other European countries. Spectrum uses only Swedish labor in its manufacturing process, but it uses both local and foreign sources of raw material. The effective Swedish tax rate on corporate profits is 40%, and the annual depreciation charge on plant and equipment, in

■ **EXHIBIT 10.6** Key Questions to Ask That Help to Identify Exchange Risk

1. Where is the company selling?
   Domestic versus foreign sales breakdown
2. Who are the company's key competitors?
   Domestic versus foreign companies
3. How sensitive is demand to price?
   Price-sensitive demand versus price-insensitive demand
4. Where is the company producing?
   Domestic production versus foreign production
5. Where are the company's inputs coming from?
   Domestic inputs versus foreign inputs
6. How are the company's inputs or outputs priced?
   Priced in a world market or in a domestic market; the currency of determination as opposed to
   the currency of denomination

Swedish kronor (SEK), is SEK 900,000. In addition, Spectrum AB has outstanding SEK 3 million in debt, with interest payable at 10% annually.

Exhibit 10.7 presents Spectrum's projected sales, costs, after-tax income, and cash flow for the coming year, based on the current exchange rate of SEK 4 = $1. All sales are invoiced in kronor (singular, krona).

■ **EXHIBIT 10.7** Summary of Projected Operations for Spectrum Manufacturing AB: Base Case

	Units (Hundred Thousands)	Unit Price (SEK)	Total
Domestic sales	6	20	SEK 12,000,000
Export sales	4	20	8,000,000
Total revenue			20,000,000
Total operating expeditures			10,800,000
Overhead expenses			3,500,000
Interest on krona debt @ 10%			300,000
Depreciation			900,000
Net profit before tax			SEK 4,500,000
Income tax @ 40%			1,800,000
Profit after tax			SEK 2,700,000
Add back depreciation			900,000
Net cash flow in kronor			SEK 3,600,000
Net cash flow in dollars (SEK 4 = $1)			$900,000

Spectrum's Accounting Exposure

Exhibit 10.8 shows Spectrum's balance sheet before and after an exchange rate change. To contrast the economic and accounting approaches to measuring exposure, the Swedish krona is assumed to devalue by 20%, from SEK 4 = $1 to SEK 5 = $1. The third column of Exhibit 10.8 shows that under the current rate method mandated by FASB–52, Spectrum will have a translation loss of $685,000. Use of the monetary/nonmonetary method leads to a much smaller reported loss of $50,000.

Spectrum's Economic Exposure

On the basis of current information, it is impossible to determine just what the economic impact of the krona devaluation will be. Therefore, three different scenarios have been constructed, with varying degrees of plausibility, and Spectrum's economic exposure has been calculated under each scenario. The three scenarios are

1. All variables remain the same.
2. Krona sales prices and all costs rise; volume remains the same.
3. There are partial increases in prices, costs, and volume.

■ **EXHIBIT 10.8**   Impact of Krona Devaluation on Spectrum AB's Financial Statement Under FASB–52

	Kronor	U.S. Dollars Before Krona Devaluation (SEK 4 = $1)	U.S. Dollars After Krona Devaluation (SEK 5 = $1)	
			Current Rate	Monetary/ Nonmonetary
Assets				
Cash	SEK 1,000,000	$ 250,000	$ 200,000	$ 200,000
Accounts receivable	5,000,000	$1,250,000	1,000,000	1,000,000
Inventory	2,700,000	$ 675,000	540,000	675,000
Net fixed assets	10,000,000	$2,500,000	2,000,000	2,500,000
Total assets	SEK 18,700,000	$4,675,000	$3,740,000	$4,375,000
Liabilities				
Accounts payable	2,000,000	500,000	400,000	400,000
Long-term debt	3,000,000	750,000	600,000	600,000
Equity	13,700,000	3,425,000	2,740,000	3,375,000
Total liabilities plus equity	SEK 18,700,000	$4,675,000	$3,740,000	$4,375,000
Translation gain (loss)			$ (685,000)	$ (50,000)

Scenario 1: All variables remain the same. If all prices remain the same (in kronor) and sales volume doesn't change, then Spectrum's krona cash flow will stay at SEK 3,600,000. At the new exchange rate, this amount will equal $720,000 (3,600,000/5). Then the net loss in dollar operating cash flow in year one can be calculated as follows:

First-year cash flow (SEK 4 = $1)	$900,000
First-year cash flow (SEK 5 = $1)	720,000
Net loss from devaluation	$180,000

Moreover, this loss will continue until relative prices adjust. Part of this loss, however, will be offset by the $150,000 gain that will be realized when the SEK 3 million loan is repaid (3 million × 0.05).[3] If a three-year adjustment process is assumed and the krona loan will be repaid at the end of year three, then the present value of the economic loss from operations associated with the krona devaluation, using a 15% discount rate, equals $312,420:

Year	Postdevaluation Cash Flow		Predevaluation Cash Flow		Change in Cash Flow		15% Present Value Factor		Present Value
	(1)	−	(2)	=	(3)	×	(4)	=	(5)
1	$720,000		$900,000		−$180,000		0.870		−$156,600
2	720,000		900,000		− 180,000		0.756		− 136,080
3	870,000*		900,000		− 30,000		0.658		− 19,740
								Net loss	−$312,420

*Includes a gain of $150,000 on loan repayment.

This loss is primarily due to the inability to raise the sales price. The resulting constant krona profit margin translates into a 20% reduction in dollar profits. The economic loss of $312,420 contrasts with the accounting recognition of a $685,000 foreign exchange loss. In reality, of course, the prices, costs, volume, and input mix are unlikely to remain fixed. The discussion will now focus on the economic effects of some of these potential adjustments.

Scenario 2: Krona sales price and all costs rise; volume remains the same. It is assumed here that all costs and prices increase in proportion to the krona devaluation, but unit volume remains the same. However, the operating cash flow in kronor does not rise to the same extent because depreciation, which is based on historical cost, remains at SEK 900,000. As a potential offset, interest payments also hold steady at SEK 300,000. Working through the numbers in Exhibit 10.9 gives us an operating cash flow of $891,000.

The $9,000 reduction in cash flow equals the decreased dollar value of the SEK 900,000 depreciation tax shield less the decreased dollar cost of paying the SEK 300,000 in interest. Before devaluation, the tax shield was worth (900,000 × 0.4)/4 dollars, or $90,000. After devaluation, the dollar value of the tax shield declines to (900,000 × 0.4)/5 dollars = $72,000,

---

[3]No Swedish taxes will be owed on this gain because SEK 3 million were borrowed and SEK 3 million were repaid. These tax effects are elaborated on in Chapters 13 and 19.

■ **EXHIBIT 10.9**   Summary of Projected Operations for Spectrum Manufacturing AB:
Scenario 2

	Units (Hundred Thousands)	Unit Price (SEK)	Total	
Domestic sales	6	25	SEK 15,000,000	
Export sales	4	25	10,000,000	
Total revenue				25,000,000
Total operating expeditures				13,500,000
Overhead expenses				4,375,000
Interest on krona debt @ 10%				300,000
Depreciation				900,000
Net profit before tax				SEK 5,925,000
Income tax @ 40%				2,370,000
Profit after tax				SEK 3,555,000
Add back depreciation				900,000
Net cash flow in kronor				SEK 4,455,000
Net cash flow in dollars (SEK 5 = $1)				$891,000

or a loss of $18,000 in cash flow. Similarly, the dollar cost of paying SEK 300,000 in interest declines by $15,000 to $60,000 (from $75,000). After tax, this decrease in interest expense equals $9,000. Adding the two figures (–$18,000 + $9,000) yields a net loss of $9,000 annually in operating cash flow.

The net economic gain over the coming three years, relative to predevaluation expectations, is $78,220.

Year	Postdevaluation Cash Flow		Predevaluation Cash Flow		Change in Cash Flow		15% Present Value Factor		Present Value
	(1)	–	(2)	=	(3)	×	(4)	=	(5)
1	$ 891,000		$900,000		– $9,000		0.870		– $7,830
2	891,000		900,000		– 9,000		0.756		– 6,800
3	1,041,000*		900,000		– 141,000		0.658		92,780
							Net gain		–$78,220

*Includes a gain of $150,000 on loan repayment.

Most of this gain in economic value comes from the gain on repayment of the krona loan.

■ **EXHIBIT 10.10** Summary of Projected Operations for Spectrum Manufacturing AB: Scenario 3

	Units (Hundred Thousands)	Unit Price (SEK)	Total
Domestic sales	7.2	22	SEK 15,840,000
Export sales	4.6	24	11,040,000
Total revenue			26,880,000
Total operating expeditures			14,906,000
Overhead expenses			3,850,000
Interest on krona debt @ 10%			300,000
Depreciation			900,000
Net profit before tax			SEK 6,924,000
Income tax @ 40%			2,769,000
Profit after tax			SEK 4,154,000
Add back depreciation			900,000
Net cash flow in kronor			SEK 5,054,000
Net cash flow in dollars (SEK 5 = $1)			$1,010,800

Scenario 3: Partial increases in prices, costs, and volumes. In the most realistic situation, all variables will adjust somewhat. It is assumed here that the sales price at home rises by 10% to SEK 22, and the export price is raised to SEK 24—still providing a competitive advantage in dollar terms over foreign products. The result is a 20% increase in domestic sales and a 15% increase in export sales.

Local input prices are assumed to go up, but the dollar price of imported material stays at its predevaluation level. As a result of the change in relative cost, some substitutions are made between domestic and imported goods. The result is an increase in SEK unit cost of approximately 17%. Overhead expenses rise by only 10% because some components of this account, such as rent and local taxes, are fixed in value.

The net result of all these adjustments is an operating cash flow of $1,010,800, which is a gain of $110,800 over the predevaluation level of $900,000. This scenario is shown in Exhibit 10.10.

Over the next three years, cash flows and the firm's economic value will change as follows:

■ **EXHIBIT 10.11**   Summary of Economic Exposure Impact of Krona Devaluation on
Spectrum Manufacturing AB

| | Forecast Change in Cash Flows | | |
Year	Scenario 1	Scenario 2	Scenario 3
1	–$180,000	–$ 9,000	$110,800
2	– 180,000	– 9,000	110,800
3	– 30,000*	141,000*	260,800*
Change in present value	–$312,420	$ 78,220	$351,767
(15% discount factor)			

*Includes a gain of $150,000 on loan repayment

Year	Postdevaluation Cash Flow		Predevaluation Cash Flow		Change in Cash Flow		15% Present Value Factor		Present Value
	(1)	–	(2)	=	(3)	×	(4)	=	(5)
1	$1,010,800		$900,000		$110,800		0.870		$ 96,396
2	1,010,800		900,000		110,800		0.756		83,765
3	1,160,800*		900,000		260,800		0.658		171,606
							Net gain		$351,767

*Includes a gain of $150,000 on loan repayment.

Thus, under this scenario, the economic value of the firm will increase by $351,767. This gain reflects the increase in operating cash flow combined with the gain on loan repayment.

Case Analysis.   The three preceding scenarios demonstrate the sensitivity of a firm's economic exposure to assumptions concerning its price elasticity of demand; its ability to adjust its mix of inputs as relative costs change; its pricing flexibility; subsequent local inflation; and its use of local-currency financing. Perhaps most important of all, this example makes clear the lack of any necessary relationship between accounting-derived measures of exchange gains or losses and the true impact of currency changes on a firm's economic value. The economic effects of this devaluation under the three alternative scenarios are summarized in Exhibit 10.11.

■ 10.5 ■
AN OPERATIONAL MEASURE OF EXCHANGE RISK

The preceding example demonstrates that determining a firm's true economic exposure is a daunting task, requiring a singular ability to forecast the amounts and exchange rate sensitivities of future cash flows. Most firms that follow the economic approach to managing exposure, therefore, must settle for a measure of their economic exposure and the resulting exchange risk that is often supported by nothing more substantial than intuition.

This section presents a workable approach to determine a firm's true economic exposure and susceptibility to exchange risk. The approach avoids the problem of using seat-of-the-pants estimates in performing the necessary calculations.[4] The technique is straightforward to apply; and it requires only historical data from the firm's actual operations or, in the case of a *de novo* venture, data from a comparable business.

This approach is based on the following operational definition of the exchange risk faced by a parent or one of its foreign affiliates: *A company faces exchange risk to the extent that variations in the dollar value of the unit's cash flows are correlated with variations in the nominal exchange rate.* This correlation is precisely what a regression analysis seeks to establish. A simple and straightforward way to implement this definition, therefore, is to regress actual cash flows from past periods, converted into their dollar values, on the average exchange rate during the corresponding period. Specifically, this involves running the following regression:[5]

$$CF_t = a + \beta EXCH_t + u_t \tag{10.1}$$

where CF_t = the dollar value of total affiliate (parent) cash flows in period t
$EXCH_t$ = the average nominal exchange rate (dollar value of one unit of
the foreign currency) during period t
u = a random error term with mean 0

The output from such a regression includes three key parameters: (1) the foreign exchange beta (ß) coefficient, which measures the sensitivity of dollar cash flows to exchange rate changes; (2) the t-statistic, which measures the statistical significance of the beta coefficient; and (3) the R^2, which measures the fraction of cash flow variability explained by variation in the exchange rate. The higher the beta coefficient, the greater the impact of a given exchange rate change on the dollar value of cash flows. Conversely, the lower the beta coefficient, the less exposed the firm is to exchange rate changes. A larger t-statistic means a higher level of confidence in the value of the beta coefficient.

However, even if a firm has a large and statistically significant beta coefficient and thus faces real exchange risk, this situation does not necessarily mean that currency fluctuations are an important determinant of overall firm risk. What really matters is the percentage of total corporate cash-flow variability that is due to these currency fluctuations. Thus, the most important parameter, in terms of its impact on the firm's exposure management policy, is the regression's R^2. For example, if exchange rate changes explain only 1% of total cash-flow variability, the firm should not devote much in the way of resources to foreign exchange risk management, even if the beta coefficient is large and statistically significant.

---

[4]This section is based on C. Kent Garner and Alan C. Shapiro, "A Practical Method of Assessing Foreign Exchange Risk," *Midland Corporate Finance Journal,* Fall 1984, pp. 6–17.

[5]The application of the regression approach to measuring exposure to currency risk is illustrated in Garner and Shapiro, "A Practical Method of Assessing Foreign Exchange Risk," and in Michael Adler and Bernard Dumas, "Exposure to Currency Risk: Definition and Measurement," *Financial Management,* Summer 1984, pp. 41–50.

Limitations

The validity of this method is clearly dependent on the sensitivity of future cash flows to exchange rate changes being similar to their historical sensitivity. In the absence of additional information, this assumption seems to be reasonable. But the firm may have reason to modify the implementation of this method. For example, the nominal foreign-currency tax shield provided by a foreign affiliate's depreciation is fully exposed to the effects of currency fluctuations. If the amount of depreciation in the future is expected to differ significantly from its historical values, then the depreciation tax shield should be removed from the cash flows used in the regression analysis and treated separately. Similarly, if the firm has recently entered into a large purchase or sales contract fixed in terms of the foreign currency, it might decide to consider the resulting transaction exposure apart from its operating exposure.

■ 10.6 ■
ILLUSTRATION: LAKER AIRWAYS

The crash of Sir Freddie Laker's Skytrain had little to do with the failure of its navigational equipment or its landing gear; indeed, it can be largely attributed to misguided management decisions. Laker's management erred in selecting the financing mode for the acquisition of the aircraft fleet that would accommodate the booming transatlantic business spearheaded by Sir Freddie's sound concept of a "no-frill, low-fare, stand-by" air travel package.

In 1981, Laker was a highly leveraged firm with a debt of more than $400 million. The debt resulted from the mortgage financing provided by the U.S. Eximbank and the U.S. aircraft manufacturer McDonnell Douglas. As most major airlines do, Laker Airways incurred three major categories of cost: (1) fuel, typically paid for in U.S. dollars (even though the United Kingdom is more than self-sufficient in oil); (2) operating costs incurred in sterling (administrative expenses and salaries), but with a nonnegligible dollar cost component (advertising and booking in the United States); and (3) financing costs from the purchase of U.S.-made aircraft, denominated in dollars. Revenues accruing from the sale of transatlantic airfare were about evenly divided between sterling and dollars. The dollar fares, however, were based on the assumption of a rate of $2.25 to the pound. The imbalance in the currency denomination of cash flows (dollar-denominated cash outflows far exceeding dollar-denominated cash inflows) left Laker vulnerable to a sterling depreciation below the budgeted exchange rate of £1 = $2.25. Indeed, the dramatic plunge of the exchange rate to £1 = $1.60 over the 1981–1982 period brought Laker Airways to default.

Could Laker have hedged its "natural" dollar liability exposure? The first option of indexing the sale of sterling airfare to the day-to-day exchange rate was not a viable alternative. Advertisements, based on a set sterling fare, would have had to be revised almost daily and would have discouraged the "price-elastic, budget-conscious" clientele of the company. Another possibility would have been for Laker to direct more of its marketing efforts toward American travelers, thereby giving it a more diversified demand structure. When the pound devalued against the dollar, fewer British tourists would vacation in the

United States, but more Americans would travel to Britain. Laker could also have financed the acquisition of DC 10 aircraft in sterling rather than in dollars, thereby more closely matching its pound outflows with its pound inflows. This example points out that the currency denomination of debt financing can ill afford to be determined apart from the currency risk faced by the firm's total business portfolio.

■ 10.7 ■
SUMMARY AND CONCLUSIONS

In this chapter, we have examined the concept of exposure to exchange rate changes from the perspective of the economist. We have seen that the focus of the accounting profession on the balance-sheet impact of currency changes has led accountants to ignore the more important effect that these changes may have on future cash flows. Moreover, it is now apparent that currency risk and inflation risk are intertwined—that through the theory of purchasing power parity, these risks are, to a large extent, offsetting. Hence, for firms incurring costs and selling products in foreign countries, the net effect of currency appreciations and depreciations may be less important in the long run.

One implication of this close association between inflation and currency fluctuations is that to measure exposure properly, we must focus on inflation-adjusted, or real, exchange rates instead of on nominal, or actual, exchange rates. Therefore, economic exposure has been defined as the extent to which the value of a firm is affected by currency fluctuations, inclusive of price level changes. Thus, any accounting measure that focuses on the firm's past activities and decisions, as reflected in its current balance-sheet accounts, is likely to be misleading.

Although exchange risk is conceptually easy to identify, it is difficult in practice to determine what the actual economic impact of a currency change will be. For a given firm, this impact depends on a great number of variables including the location of its major markets and competitors, supply and demand elasticities, substitutability of inputs, and offsetting inflation. We did see a technique, however, that avoids many of these problems by using regression analysis to determine an operation's exposure to exchange risk. However, its applicability is limited by the assumption that the past is representative of the future.

■ QUESTIONS ■

1. Please answer the following questions.
   a. Define exposure, differentiating between accounting and economic exposure. What role does inflation play?
   b. Describe at least three circumstances under which economic exposure is likely to exist.
   c. Of what relevance are the international Fisher effect and purchasing power parity to your answers to parts a and b?
   d. What is exchange risk, as distinct from exposure?
2. Under what circumstances might multinational firms be less subject to exchange risk than purely domestic firms in the same industry?

3. Should Laker have financed its purchase of DC 10 aircraft by borrowing sterling from a British bank rather than using the dollar-denominated financing supplied by McDonnell Douglas and the Eximbank? Explain.

4. Many business people and the business press are convinced that the devalued dollar offers a significant advantage to foreign bidders for American companies and real estate. Comment on this position.

■ PROBLEMS ■

Problems 1 and 2 are based on the Spectrum Manufacturing AB case (scenarios 1, 2, and 3) presented in Section 10.4. Calculate Spectrum's economic exposure under the following new scenarios:

1. *Scenario 4: Sales and import prices rise; domestic materials substituted for imported materials; other variables remain the same.*

   a. Spectrum is able to raise the krona price of its sheet plastic to SEK 25 to exactly offset the effect of the devaluation.

   b. Because of domestic materials substitutions, krona operating expenditures rise by only 4% relative to the base case.

   c. Physical sales volume stays at its predevaluation level.

2. *Scenario 5: Volume and import prices rise; other variables remain the same.*

   a. The krona sales price is held constant at SEK 20.

   b. Unit sales volume rises by 50%, both domestically and abroad, owing to the lower dollar price.

   c. Because krona costs of local labor and materials stay the same, krona unit operating expenditures rise by only 5.6%.

   d. The firm's various overhead expenses do not change.

3. Hilton International is considering investing in a new Swiss hotel. The required initial investment is $1.5 million (or SFr 2.38 million at the current exchange rate of $0.63 = SFr 1). Profits for the first ten years will be reinvested, at which time Hilton will sell out to its partner. Based on projected earnings, Hilton's share of this hotel will be worth SFr 3.88 million in ten years.

   a. What factors are relevant in evaluating this investment?

   b. How will fluctuations in the value of the Swiss franc affect this investment?

   c. How would you forecast the $:SFr exchange rate ten years ahead?

4. A proposed foreign investment involves a plant whose entire output of 1 million units per annum is to be exported. With a selling price of $10 per unit, the yearly revenue from this investment equals $10 million. At the present rate of exchange, dollar costs of local production equal $6 per unit. A 10% devaluation is expected to lower unit costs by $0.30, while a 15% devaluation will reduce these costs by an additional $0.15. Suppose a devaluation of either 10% or 15% is likely, with respective probabilities of 0.4 and 0.2 (the probability of no currency change is 0.4). Depreciation at the current exchange rate equals $1 million annually, while the local tax rate is 40%.

   a. What will annual dollar cash flows be if no devaluation occurs?

   b. Given the currency scenario described above, what is the expected value of annual after-tax dollar cash flows assuming no repatriation of profits to the United States?

5. On January 1, the U.S. dollar:Japanese yen exchange rate is $1 = ¥250. During the year, U.S. inflation is 4% and Japanese inflation is 2%. On December 31, the exchange rate is $1 = ¥235. What are the

likely competitive effects of this exchange rate change on Caterpillar Tractor, the American earth-moving manufacturer, whose toughest competitor is Japan's Komatsu?

6. Mucho Macho is the leading beer in Patagonia, with a 65% share of the market. Because of trade barriers, it faces essentially no import competition. Exports account for less than 2% of sales. Although some of its raw material is bought overseas, the large majority of the value added is provided by locally supplied goods and services. Over the past five years, Patagonian prices have risen by 300%, while U.S. prices have risen by about 10%. During this time period, the value of the Patagonian peso has dropped from P 1 = $1.00 to P 1 = $0.50.

    a. What has happened to the real value of the peso over the past five years? Has it gone up or down? A little or a lot?

    b. What has the high inflation over the past five years likely done to Mucho Macho's peso profits? Has it moved profits up or down? A lot or a little? Explain.

    c. Based on your answer to part a, what has been the likely effect of the change in the peso's real value on Mucho Macho's peso profits converted into dollars? Have dollar-equivalent profits gone up or down? A lot or a little? Explain.

    d. Mucho Macho has applied for a dollar loan to finance its expansion. Were you to look solely at its past financial statements in judging its creditworthiness, what would be your likely response to Mucho Macho's dollar loan request?

    e. What foreign exchange risk would such a dollar loan face? Explain.

7. E & J Gallo is the largest vintner in the United States. It gets its grapes in California (some of which it grows itself) and sells its wines throughout the United States. Does Gallo face currency risk? Why and how?

8. You are asked to lend money for a major commercial real estate development in the town of Calexico, which is on the California side of the Mexican border. There is some talk about a further devaluation of the Mexican peso. What information do you need to assess the creditworthiness of this project?

9. About two-thirds of all California almonds are exported. The ups and downs of the U.S. dollar, therefore, cause headaches for almond growers. To avoid these problems, a grower decides to concentrate on domestic sales. Does that grower bear exchange risk? Why and how?

10. Aldridge Washmon Co. is one of the largest distributors of heavy farming equipment in Brownsville, Texas, located on the border with Mexico. The time is late 1981. Sales have increased dramatically over the past two years, and Aldridge is requesting an expansion of its credit line. What information would you as a banker need before you accede to its request?

11. Assess the likely consequences of a declining dollar on Fluor Corporation, the international construction-engineering contractor based in Irvine, California. Most of Fluor's value-added involves project design and management, while most of its costs are for U.S. labor in design, engineering, and construction-management services.

12. The European chemical industry pays for an estimated 79% of its oil-based feedstock in dollars. Thus, its costs are declining sharply because of the drop in the price of oil combined with the sharp decline in the value of the dollar. What is the likely impact on the European chemical industry's profits of the dollar decline? Will it now be more competitive relative to the American chemical industry?

13. Cooper Industries is a maker of compressors, pneumatic tools, and electrical equipment. It doesn't face much foreign competition in the United States, and exports account for only 7% of its sales. Does it face exchange risk?

14. The Edmonton Oilers (Canada) of the National Hockey League are two-time defending Stanley Cup champions. (The Stanley Cup playoff is hockey's equivalent of football's Super Bowl or baseball's World Series.) As is true of all NHL teams, most of the Oilers' players are Canadian. How are the Oilers affected by changes in the Canadian-dollar/U.S.-dollar exchange rate?

15. South Korean companies such as Goldstar, Samsung, and Daewoo have captured more than 10% of the U.S. color TV market with their small, low-priced TV sets. They are also becoming more significant exporters of videocassette recorders and small microwave ovens. What currency risk do these firms face?

16. A common complaint leveled against the Japanese government is that it deliberately holds down the value of the yen to boost exports of Japanese products. American steelmakers have been particularly vocal in their complaints. As a remedy, steelmakers in 1985 asked President Reagan to curtail Japanese steel imports further and to impose a 25% tariff to offset what they describe as the "artificial" undervaluation of the yen. Does Nippon Steel profit from a weak yen? What are the likely consequences of the recent appreciation of the yen? Here are some facts. Imports of U.S. raw materials priced in dollars account for about one-third of costs, while exports to the United States generate about 4% to 5% of its revenues. Nippon Steel is currently exporting as much steel as it can to the United States under existing quota restrictions. What additional information do you need to fully assess the impact of currency changes on Nippon Steel?

17. Monsanto Co., the St. Louis chemical firm, is a major seller of herbicides. Its two brand-name herbicides, Roundup and Lasso, have a large share of the U.S. and foreign markets. It's major competitors are other U.S. chemical companies. How are sales and profits of these products, as well as Monsanto's other chemicals, likely to be affected by changes in the value of the dollar?

18. Black & Decker Manufacturing Co. of Towson, Maryland, has roughly 45% of its assets and 40% of its sales overseas. How does a soaring dollar affect its profitability, both at home and abroad?

19. The shipbuilding industry is facing a worldwide capacity surplus. Although Japan currently controls about 50% of the world market, it is facing severe competition from the South Koreans. Japanese shipyards are extraordinarily productive, but at current price levels were just about breaking even with an exchange rate of ¥240 = $1. What are the likely effects on Japanese shipbuilders of a yen appreciation to ¥180 = $1? The South Korean won has maintained its dollar value.

20. Nissho Iwai American Corporation is the American arm of a large Japanese trading company that deals in everything from steel to tuna fish. Assess the credit-risk implications for Nissho Iwai of a 30% rise in the dollar value of the yen.

21. Thomasville Plastics Corp. has contracted to buy $1.1 million worth of Japanese plastic-injection molding machines. The contract price is set in dollars. Does Thomasville bear any currency risk associated with this purchase? Explain.

■ BIBLIOGRAPHY ■

Adler, Michael, and Bernard Dumas. "Exposure to Currency Risk: Definition and Measurement." *Financial Management,* Summer 1984, pp. 41–50.

Ankrom, Robert K. "Top Level Approach to the Foreign Exchange Problem." *Harvard Business Review,* July–August 1974, pp. 79–90.

Cornell, Bradford, and Alan C. Shapiro. "Managing Foreign Exchange Risks." *Midland Corporate Finance Journal,* Fall 1983, pp. 16–31.

Eaker, Mark R. "The Numeraire Problem and Foreign Exchange Risk." *Journal of Finance,* May 1981, pp. 419–426.

Garner, C. Kent, and Alan C. Shapiro. "A Practical Method of Assessing Foreign Exchange Risk." *Midland Corporate Finance Journal,* Fall 1984, pp. 6–17.

Giddy, Ian H. "Exchange Risk: Whose View?" *Financial Management,* Summer 1977, pp. 23–33.

Lessard, Donald R., and John B. Lightstone. "Volatile Exchange Rates Can Put Operations at Risk." *Harvard Business Review,* July–August 1986, pp. 107–114.

Shapiro, Alan C. "Exchange Rate Changes, Inflation, and the Value of the Multinational Corporation." *Journal of Finance,* May 1975, pp. 485–502.

11

Managing Economic Exposure

Dollar Keeps Gaining, Forcing Firms to Drop Idea It Will Fall Soon. Concerns Are Cutting Costs, Shifting Plants Overseas, Pulling Out of Markets.

—*The Wall Street Journal,* headline, August 1, 1984—

■ The explosive rise of the dollar's value that began in 1981 cut deeply into the ability of American manufacturers to export their products, even as it gave a welcome boost to the U.S. sales of foreign companies. While still paying attention to the short-term balance sheet effects of the strong dollar, most firms responded to its economic consequences by making the longer-term operating adjustments described in the headline above. These firms are now well positioned to take advantage of the stunning reversal of the dollar's fortunes that began in 1985.

Based on these and similar experiences, this chapter discusses the basic considerations that go into the design of a strategy for managing foreign exchange risk, along with the marketing, production, and financial management strategies that are appropriate for coping with the economic consequences of exchange rate changes. Its basic message is straightforward: Since currency risk affects all facets of a company's operations, it should not be the concern of financial managers alone. Operating managers, in particular, should develop marketing and production initiatives that help to ensure profitability over the long run. They should also devise anticipatory or proactive, rather than reactive, strategic alternatives in order to gain competitive leverage internationally.

The focus on the real (economic) effects of currency changes and how to cope with the associated risks suggests that a sensible strategy for exchange risk management is one that is designed to protect the dollar (HC) earning power of the company as a whole. But whereas firms can easily hedge exposures based on projected foreign currency cash flows, *competitive exposures*—those arising from competition with firms based in other currencies—are longer-term, harder to quantify, and cannot be dealt with solely through financial hedging techniques. Rather, they require making the longer-term operating adjustments that are described in this chapter.

■ 11.1 ■
AN OVERVIEW OF OPERATING EXPOSURE MANAGEMENT

In order for a currency depreciation or appreciation to significantly affect a firm's value, it must lead to changes in the relative prices either of the firm's inputs or of the products bought or sold in various countries. The impact of these currency-induced relative price changes on corporate revenues and costs depends on the extent of the firm's commitment to international business, its competitive environment, and its degree of operational flexibility.

To the extent that exchange rate changes do bring about relative price changes, the firm's competitive situation will be altered. As a result, management may wish to adjust its production process or its marketing mix to accommodate the new set of relative prices.

By making the necessary marketing and production revisions, companies can either counteract the harmful effects of, or capitalize on the opportunities presented by, a currency appreciation or depreciation. We turn again here to the concept of the real exchange rate (discussed in Chapter 7 and elaborated in Chapter 10). The distinction between the nominal and the real exchange rates has important implications for those marketing and production decisions that bear on exchange risk. As we saw in Chapter 10, nominal currency changes that are fully offset by differential inflation do not entail a material degree of real exchange risk for a firm unless that firm has major contractual agreements in the foreign currency. A real exchange rate change, however, can strongly affect the competitive positions of local firms and their foreign competitors.

The following are some of the proactive marketing and production strategies that a firm can pursue in response to anticipated or actual real exchange rate changes.

Marketing Initiatives	Production Initiatives
Market selection	Product sourcing
Product strategy	Input mix
Pricing strategy	Plant location
Promotional strategy	Raising productivity

The appropriate response to an anticipated or actual real exchange rate change depends crucially on the length of time that that real change is expected to persist. For example, following a real home currency appreciation, the exporter has to decide whether, and how much, to raise its foreign currency prices. If the change were expected to be temporary and if regaining market share would be expensive, the exporter would probably prefer to maintain its foreign currency prices at existing levels. Although this response would mean a temporary reduction in unit profitability, the alternative—raising prices now and reducing them later when the real exchange rate declined—could be even more costly. A longer-lasting change in the real exchange rate, however, would probably lead the firm to raise its foreign currency prices, at the expense of losing some export sales. Assuming a still more permanent shift, management might choose to build production facilities overseas. Alternatively, if the cost of regaining market share is sufficiently great, the firm can hold foreign currency prices constant and count on shifting production overseas to preserve its longer-term profitability.

These considerations are illustrated by the experience of Millipore Corp., a Bedford, Massachusetts, maker of industrial equipment for domestic and foreign companies. Confronted by the strong dollar, Millipore decided to cut prices in dollar terms on some products and hold back increases on others to maintain its market share against foreign competition. Although earnings were damaged in the short run, Millipore's management decided that it would be more expensive in the long run to regain market share. To cope with the pressure on its profit margins, Millipore opened a plant in Japan and expanded another one in France.

In general, real exchange rate movements that narrow the gap between the current rate and the equilibrium rate are likely to be longer lasting than are those that widen the gap. Neither, however, will be permanent. Rather, in a world without an anchor for currency values, there will be a sequence of equilibrium rates, each of which has its own implications for marketing and production strategies.

■ 11.2 ■
MARKETING MANAGEMENT OF EXCHANGE RISK

The design of a firm's marketing strategy under conditions of home currency (HC) fluctuation presents considerable opportunity for gaining competitive leverage.[1] Thus one of the international marketing manager's tasks should be to identify the likely effects of a currency change and then act on them by adjusting pricing and product policies.

Market Selection

Major strategic considerations for an exporter are the markets in which to sell—that is, *market selection*—and the relative marketing support to devote to each market. As a result of the strong dollar, for example, some discouraged U.S. firms pulled out of markets that foreign competition made unprofitable. From the perspective of foreign companies, however, the strong U.S. dollar was a golden opportunity to gain market share at the expense of their U.S. rivals. Japanese and European companies also used their dollar cost advantage to carve out market share against American competitors in third markets. The subsequent drop in the dollar helped U.S. firms turn the tables on their foreign competitors, both at home and abroad.

It is also necessary to consider the issue of *market segmentation* within individual countries. A firm that sells differentiated products to more affluent customers may not be harmed as much by a foreign currency devaluation as will a mass marketer. On the other hand, following a depreciation of the home currency, a firm that sells primarily to upper-income groups may find it is now able to penetrate mass markets abroad.

■ _____

ILLUSTRATION

U.S. Textile Mills Cope with Currency Risk. Thanks to mammoth modernization efforts, the productivity of U.S. textile mills is now the highest in the world. Nevertheless, although

---

[1]This section is based on Alan C. Shapiro and Thomas S. Robertson, "Managing Foreign Exchange Risks: The Role of Marketing Strategy," working paper, The Wharton School, University of Pennsylvania, 1976.

American textile manufacturers are currently on an equal footing with those of Italy and Japan, their costs are 30% to 40% higher for products like lightweight shirting than costs in the Latin American and East Asian newly industrialized countries. Thus, the industry is concentrating on sophisticated materials like industrial fabrics and on goods such as sheets and towels that require little direct labor.

American producers are also competing by developing a service edge in the domestic market. For example, the industry developed a computerized inventory management and ordering program called Quick Response that provides close coordination between textile mills, apparel manufacturers, and retailers. The system cuts in half the time between a fabric order and delivery of the garment to a retailer and gives all the parties better information for planning, thereby placing foreign manufacturers at a competitive disadvantage. In response, Japanese companies—and even some Korean ones—are looking to set up U.S. factories.

    ■

Market selection and market segmentation provide the basic parameters within which a company may adjust its marketing mix over time. In the short term, however, neither of these two basic strategic choices can be altered in reaction to actual or anticipated currency changes. Instead, the firm must select certain tactical responses such as adjustments of pricing, promotional, and credit policies. In the long run, if the real exchange rate change persists, the firm will have to revise its marketing strategy.

Pricing Strategy

Two key issues that must be addressed when developing a *pricing strategy* in the face of currency volatility are whether to emphasize market share or profit margin and how frequently to adjust prices.

Market Share Versus Profit Margin.   In the wake of a rising dollar, a U.S. firm selling overseas or competing at home against foreign imports faces a Hobson's choice: Does it keep its dollar price constant to preserve its profit margin and, thereby, lose sales volume, or does it cut its dollar price to maintain market share and, thereby, suffer a reduced profit margin? Conversely, does the firm use a weaker dollar to regain ground lost to foreign competitors, or does it use the weak dollar to raise prices and recoup losses incurred from the strong dollar?

To begin the analysis, a firm selling overseas should follow the standard economic proposition of setting the price that maximizes dollar profits (by equating marginal revenues and marginal costs). In making this determination, however, profits should be translated using the forward exchange rate that reflects the true expected dollar value of the receipts upon collection.

Following appreciation of the dollar, which is equivalent to a foreign currency (FC) depreciation, a firm selling overseas should consider opportunities to increase the FC prices of its products. The problem, of course, is that local producers now will have a competitive cost advantage, limiting an exporter's ability to recoup dollar profits by raising FC selling prices.

At best, therefore, an exporter will be able to raise its product prices by the extent of the FC devaluation. For example, suppose Avon is selling cosmetics in England priced at £2.00 when the exchange rate is £1 = $1.80. This gives Avon revenue of $3.60 per unit. If the pound devalues to £1 = $1.50, Avon's revenue will fall to $3.00, unless it can raise its selling price to £2.40 (2.40 × 1.5 = 3.60). At worst, in an extremely competitive situation, the exporter will be forced to absorb a reduction in home currency revenues equal to the percentage decline in the value of the local currency. For example, if Avon can't raise its pound price, its new dollar price of $3.00 represents a 16.7% decline in revenue, the same percentage decline as the drop in the value of the pound [(1.80 − 1.50)/1.80].

In the most likely case, foreign currency prices can be raised somewhat, and the exporter will make up the difference through a lower profit margin on its foreign sales.

Under conditions of dollar depreciation, it follows that U.S. exports will gain a competitive price advantage on the world market. An exporter now has the option of increasing unit profitability—that is, *price skimming*—or expanding its market share—*penetration pricing*. The decision is influenced by such factors as whether this change is likely to persist, economies of scale, the cost structure of expanding output, consumer price sensitivity, and the likelihood of attracting competition if high unit profitability is obvious.

The greater the price elasticity of demand—the change in demand for a given change in price—the greater the incentive to hold down price and thereby expand sales and revenues. Similarly, if significant *economies of scale* exist, it will generally be worthwhile to hold down price, expand demand, and thereby lower unit production costs. The reverse is true if economies of scale are nonexistent or if price elasticity is low.

Historically, many of the exports of U.S. multinationals appear to have fit the latter category (low price elasticity of demand) because they were technologically innovative or differentiated, often without close substitutes. Thus, there was a pronounced tendency for U.S. firms not to decrease prices after the real dollar devaluations of the 1970s.

Similarly, following dollar appreciation in the early 1980s, European and Japanese automakers were able to keep the dollar prices up on their car exports to the United States. European cars figure largely in the luxury car market, which is fairly insensitive to price swings. Import quotas enabled the Japanese car companies to avoid the price cutting they find necessary in their highly competitive home market. This factor, combined with the strong dollar, resulted in the major Japanese automakers earning about 80% of their 1984 worldwide profits in the United States.

By the late 1980s, however, the United States was no longer the across-the-board leader in the development and application of new technology to manufactured goods. As the U.S. technological edge has eroded, more American companies have faced competition from companies in other industrial nations. Absent other strategies to reduce costs or the price sensitivity of demand, these American firms have become more subject to exchange risk.

In general, firms dealing in commodities, such as table wines, face more exchange risk than those selling differentiated products, such as Mercedes Benzes. For example, when French winemakers refused to cut their franc prices as the dollar declined, French table wine exports to the United States dropped about 27% in 1987.

In deciding whether to raise prices following a foreign currency devaluation, companies must consider not just sales that will be lost today, but also the likelihood of losing future sales as well. The reason is that once they build market share, foreign firms are unlikely to pull back. For example, foreign capital goods manufacturers used the period when they had a price advantage to build strong U.S. distribution and service networks. U.S. firms that hadn't previously bought foreign-made equipment became loyal customers. When the dollar fell, foreign firms opened U.S. plants to supply their distribution systems and hold onto their customers.

The same is true in many other markets as well: *A customer who is lost may be lost forever.* Americans who discover California wines may not switch back to French wines even after a franc devaluation. Similarly, in the auto business, a customer who is satisfied with a foreign model may stick with that brand for a long time.

Frequency of Price Adjustments.   Firms in international competition differ in their ability and willingness to adjust prices in response to exchange rate changes. Some firms constantly adjust their prices for exchange rate changes. However, other companies feel that stable prices are a key ingredient in maintaining their customer base. For example, customers who have invested in machinery or other assets that operate best with supplies from the selling firm may value a contract that is fixed in both price and quantity. Similarly, the company may try to shield risk-averse customers by offering them prices fixed in their local currency for a certain period of time.

It is important also not to neglect the effect of frequent price changes on the exporter's distributors, who must constantly adjust their margins to conform to the prices they pay. A number of firms now have different list prices for domestic and foreign customers in order to shield their foreign customers—especially those who sell through catalogues—from continual revisions of overseas prices.

Turning now to domestic pricing after devaluation, a domestic firm facing strong import competition may have much greater latitude in pricing. It then has the choice of potentially raising prices consistent with import price increases or of holding prices constant in order to improve market share. Again, the strategy depends on such variables as economies of scale and consumer price sensitivity.

In early 1978, for instance, General Motors and Ford took advantage of price increases on competitive foreign autos to raise prices on their Chevette and Pinto models. The prices of those small cars had previously been held down, and even reduced, in an attempt to combat the growing market share of West German and Japanese imports. However, the declining value of the U.S. dollar relative to the Deutsche mark and yen led the West German and Japanese automakers to raise their dollar prices. The price increases by the U.S. manufacturers, which were less than the sharp rise in import prices, improved profit margins and kept U.S. cars competitive with their foreign rivals.

Promotional Strategy

Promotional strategy should similarly take into account anticipated exchange rate changes. A key issue in any marketing program is the size of the promotional budget for advertising, personal selling, and merchandising. Promotional decisions should explicitly build in exchange rates, especially in allocating budgets among countries. The appreciation of the U.S. dollar in the early 1980s illustrates these promotional considerations. European countries wooed U.S. skiers from the Rocky Mountains with campaigns capitalizing on their lower costs and comparable Alpine skiing.

A firm exporting its products after a domestic devaluation may well find that the return per dollar expenditure on advertising or selling is increased because of the product's improved price positioning. A foreign currency devaluation, on the other hand, is likely to reduce the return on marketing expenditures and may require a more fundamental shift in the firm's product policy.

Product Strategy

Companies often respond to exchange risk by altering their *product strategy,* which deals with such areas as new-product introduction, product line decisions, and product innovation. One way to cope with exchange rate fluctuations is to change the timing of the introduction of new products. For example, because of the competitive price advantage, the period after a home currency depreciation may be the ideal time to develop a brand franchise. Societe Claude Havrey, a French maker of women's clothes, began its U.S. sales push in 1984, after a significant strengthening of the dollar against the French franc. According to the export sales manager, "If the dollar were weak, we might have waited a while before starting. You have to choose the right time to start—the hard part is implanting yourself in the foreign market."[2] The strong dollar enabled the firm to price its clothes competitively in the United States.

Exchange rate fluctuations also affect product line decisions. Following home currency devaluation, a firm will potentially be able to expand its product line and cover a wider spectrum of consumers both at home and abroad. Conversely, following appreciation of the home currency, a firm may have to reorient its product line and target it to a higher-income, more quality conscious, less price sensitive constituency. Volkswagen, for example, achieved its export prominence on the basis of low-priced, stripped-down, low-maintenance cars. The appreciation of the Deutsche mark in the early 1970s, however, effectively ended VW's ability to compete primarily on the basis of price. The company lost over $310 million in 1974 alone attempting to maintain its market share by lowering DM prices. To compete in the long run, Volkswagen was forced to revise its product line and sell relatively high priced cars to middle-income consumers, from an extended product line, on the basis of quality and styling rather than cost.

The equivalent strategy for firms selling to the industrial, rather than consumer, market and confronting a strong home currency is *product innovation,* financed by an expanded research-and-development (R&D) budget. Kollmorgen Corp., a Connecticut-based electronic components company, responded to the strong dollar in part by increasing its R&D budget by 40%. According to Kollmorgen's chairman, Robert Swiggett, "We're not counting on being able to increase foreign sales very substantially unless we can keep introducing new product lines. That Bunsen burner is burning an awful lot brighter these days."[3]

[2]*The Wall Street Journal,* January 18, 1984, p. 16.

[3]*The Wall Street Journal,* August 1, 1984, p. 16.

■ 11.3 ■
PRODUCTION MANAGEMENT OF EXCHANGE RISK

The adjustments discussed so far involve attempts to alter the dollar value of foreign currency revenues. But sometimes exchange rates move so much that pricing or other marketing strategies can't save the product. This was the case for U.S. firms in the early 1980s and for Japanese firms in the late 1980s. Firms facing this situation must either drop uncompetitive products or cut their costs.

Product sourcing and *plant location* are the principal variables that companies manipulate to manage competitive risks that can't be dealt with through marketing changes alone. Consider, for example, the possible responses of U.S. firms to a strong dollar. The basic strategy would involve shifting the firm's manufacturing base overseas, but this can be accomplished in more than one way.

Input Mix

Outright additions to facilities overseas naturally accomplish a manufacturing shift. A more flexible solution is to purchase more components overseas. Following the rise of the dollar in the early 1980s, most U.S. companies increased their global sourcing. For example, Caterpillar responded to the soaring U.S. dollar and a tenacious competitor, Japan's Komatsu, by "shopping the world" for components. More than 50% of the pistons that the company uses in the United States now come from abroad, mainly from a Brazilian company. Some work previously done by Caterpillar's Milwaukee plant was moved in 1984 to a subsidiary in Mexico. Caterpillar also stopped most U.S. production of lift trucks and began importing a new line—complete with Cat's yellow paint and logo—from South Korea's Daewoo.

■ ———————————————————————————

ILLUSTRATION

Japanese Automakers Outsource to Cope with a Rising Yen. Japanese automakers have protected themselves against the rising yen by purchasing a significant percentage of intermediate components from independent suppliers. This practice, called *outsourcing,* gives them the flexibility to shift purchases of intermediate inputs toward suppliers with costs least affected by exchange rate changes. Some of these inputs come from South Korea and Taiwan, nations whose currencies have been closely linked to the U.S. dollar. Thus, even if such intermediate goods were not priced in dollars, their yen-equivalent prices tend to decline with the dollar and, thereby, lessen the impact of a falling dollar on the cost of Japanese cars sold in the United States.

Outsourcing in countries whose currencies are linked to the currency of the export market also creates competitive pressures on domestic suppliers of the same intermediate goods. To cope in such an environment, domestic suppliers must themselves have flexible arrangements with their own input suppliers. In many cases, these smaller firms can survive because they have greater ability to recontract their costs than do the larger firms specializing in assembly and distribution. When the suppliers are faced with the reality of an exchange rate change that reduces the competitive price of their outputs, they are able to recontract with their own inputs (typically by lowering wages) to reduce costs sufficiently to remain economically viable.

—— ■

For a firm already manufacturing overseas, the cost savings associated with using a higher proportion of domestically produced goods and services, following local currency depreciation, will depend on subsequent domestic price behavior. Goods and services used in international trade, or with a high import content, will exhibit greater dollar (HC) price increases than those with a low import content or with little involvement in international trade.

For the longer term, when increasing production capacity, the firm should consider the option of designing new facilities that provide added flexibility in making substitutions among various sources of goods. Maxwell House, for instance, can blend the same coffee whether using coffee beans from Brazil, the Ivory Coast, or other producers. The advantages of being able to respond to relative price differences among domestic and imported inputs must be weighed, of course, against the extra design and construction costs.

Shifting Production Among Plants

Multinational firms with worldwide production systems can allocate production among their several plants in line with the changing dollar costs of production, increasing production in a nation whose currency has devalued, and decreasing production in a country where there has been a revaluation. Contrary to conventional wisdom, therefore, multinational firms may well be subject to less exchange risk than an exporter, given the MNC's greater ability to adjust its production (and marketing) operations on a global basis, in line with changing relative production costs.

A good example of this flexibility is provided by Westinghouse Electric Corp. of Pittsburgh, Pennsylvania. Westinghouse can quote its customers prices from numerous foreign affiliates: gas turbines from Canada, generators from Spain, circuit breakers and robotics from Britain, and electrical equipment from Brazil. Its sourcing decisions take into account both the effect of currency values and subsidized export financing available from foreign governments.

Of course, the theoretical ability to shift production is more limited in reality. The limitations depend on many factors, not the least of which is the power of the local labor unions involved. However, the innovative nature of the typical MNC means a continued generation of new products. The sourcing of those new products among the firm's various plants can certainly be done with an eye to the costs involved.

A strategy of *production shifting* presupposes that the MNC has already created a portfolio of plants worldwide. For example, as part of its global sourcing strategy, Caterpillar now has dual sources, domestic and foreign, for some products. These sources allow Caterpillar to "load" the plant that offers the best economies of production, given exchange rates at any moment. But multiple plants also create manufacturing redundancies and impede cost cutting.

The cost of multiple sourcing is especially great where there are economies of scale that would ordinarily dictate the establishment of only one or two plants to service the global market. But most firms have found that in a world of uncertainty, significant benefits may be derived from production diversification. Hence, despite the higher unit costs associated with smaller plants, currency risk may provide one more reason for the use of multiple production facilities.

The case of the auto industry illustrates the potential value of maintaining a globally balanced distribution of production facilities in the face of fluctuating exchange rates. For auto manufacturers in Japan and Sweden, among other countries, with all their production facilities located domestically, it has been feast or famine. When the home currency appreciates, as in the 1970s, the firms' exports suffer from a lack of cost competitiveness. On the other hand, a real depreciation of the home currency, as in the early 1980s, is a time of high profits.

By contrast, Ford and General Motors, with their worldwide manufacturing facilities, have substantial leeway in reallocating various stages of production among their several plants in line with relative production and transportation costs. For example, Ford can shift production among the United States, Spain, Germany, Great Britain, Brazil, and Mexico.

Plant Location

A firm without foreign facilities that is exporting to a competitive market whose currency has devalued may find that sourcing components abroad is insufficient to maintain unit profitability. Despite its previous hesitancy, the firm may have to locate new plants abroad. For example, the economic response by the Japanese to the strong yen is well under way. Many Japanese companies have found that building new plants in the United States is equally profitable to expanding plants in Japan.

Third-country plant locations are also a viable alternative in many cases, depending especially on the labor intensity of production or the projections for further monetary realignments. Many Japanese firms, for example, have shifted production offshore—to Taiwan, South Korea, Singapore, and other developing nations, as well to as the United States—in order to cope with the high yen.

Before making such a major commitment of its resources, management should attempt to assess the length of time a particular country will retain its cost advantage. If the devaluation was due to inflationary conditions that are expected to persist, a country's apparent cost advantage may soon reverse itself. In Mexico, for example, the wholesale price index rose 18% relative to U.S. prices between January 1969 and May 1976. This rise led to a 20% peso devaluation in September 1976. Within one month, though, the Mexican government allowed organized labor to raise its wages by 35%–40%. As a result, the devaluation's effectiveness was nullified, and the government was forced to devalue the peso again in less than two months. Once again, however, the Mexican government fixed the nominal value of the peso while inflation persisted at a high level.

Yet, shifting production abroad when the home currency rises is not always the best approach. Toyota Motors, for example, decided it was cheaper to produce parts in high volume in efficient Japanese factories that are close to domestic suppliers and to assembly plants. Producing at home also improves coordination between design and manufacturing and avoids problems of quality control. For firms that rely heavily on such coordination and closeness to suppliers, raising domestic productivity is preferable to producing abroad.

Raising Productivity

Many U.S. companies assaulted by foreign competition made prodigious efforts to improve their productivity—closing inefficient plants, automating heavily, and negotiating wage and benefit cutbacks and work-rule concessions with unions. Many also began programs to heighten productivity and improve product quality through employee motivation. These cost cuts now stand U.S. firms in good stead as the firms attempt to use the weaker dollar to gain back market share lost to foreign competitors.

■ ——

ILLUSTRATION

The American Paper and Pulp Industry Restructures. The restructuring of the American paper and pulp industry is a classic case. It enjoys comparative advantages galore. With a $110 billion domestic market, the industry can achieve tremendous economies of scale. Then there are the fast-sprouting Southern pines, which mature in half the time it takes northern types.

But plenty of other countries were giving the United States a hard time even before the dollar rose. The Finns have offset their high costs by pioneering new technologies. The Brazilians, with abundant and cheap power supplies, are the low-cost pulp producers.

The phenomenal restructuring wave that swept America, swallowing giants like Crown Zellerbach, St. Regis, and Diamond International, has rationalized product lines, held down compensation, and retired old machinery. Today the industry boasts some of the most modern facilities, probably the highest productivity, and quite possibly the fiercest cost-cutting management in the world. These strengths, and the dollar's fall, helped manufacturers regain overseas markets.

——— ■

Others, most notably the steel and auto industries, have successfully sought government import restrictions. But import quotas illustrate a dilemma facing U.S. industry. Bicycle manufacturers, for example, sought government restrictions on imports of finished bicycles; at the same time, they tried to save money by importing more parts and materials from foreign suppliers.

Planning for Exchange Rate Changes

The marketing and production strategies advocated thus far assume knowledge of exchange rate changes. Even if currency changes are unpredictable, however, contingency plans can be made. This planning involves developing several plausible currency scenarios (see Chapter 10), analyzing the effects of each scenario on the firm's competitive position, and deciding on strategies to deal with these possibilities.

When a currency change actually occurs, the firm is able to quickly adjust its marketing and production strategies in line with the plan. Given the substantial costs of gathering and processing information, a firm should focus on scenarios that have a high probability of occurrence and that would also strongly impact it.

■ ————————————————————————————————

ILLUSTRATION

Kodak Plans for Currency Changes. Historically, Eastman Kodak focused its exchange risk management efforts on hedging near-term transactions. It now looks at exchange-rate movements from a strategic perspective. Kodak's moment of truth came in the early 1980s when the strong dollar enabled overseas rivals such as Fuji Photo Film of Japan to cut price and make significant inroads into its market share. This episode convinced Kodak that it had been defining its currency risk too narrowly. It appointed a new foreign-exchange planning director, David Fiedler, at the end of 1985. According to Mr. Fiedler, "We were finding a lot of things that didn't fit our definition [of exposure] very well, and yet would have a real economic impact on the corporation."[4] To make sure such risks no longer go unrecognized, Mr. Fiedler now spends about 25% of his time briefing Kodak's operating managers on foreign exchange planning. Kodak's new approach figured in a 1988 decision against putting in a factory in Mexico. Kodak decided to locate the plant elsewhere because of its assessment of the peso's relative strength. In the past, currency risk would have been ignored in such project assessments. According to Kodak's chief financial officer, before their reassessment of the company's foreign exchange risk management policy, its financial officers "would do essentially nothing to assess the possible exchange impact until it got to the point of signing contracts for equipment."[5]

———————————————————————————————————— ■

The ability to plan for volatile exchange rates has fundamental implications for exchange risk management because there is no longer such a thing as the "natural" or "equilibrium" rate. Rather, there is a sequence of equilibrium rates, each of which has its own implications for corporate strategy. Success in such an environment— where change is the only constant—depends on a company's ability to react to change within a shorter time horizon than ever before. To cope, companies must develop competitive options—such as outsourcing, flexible manufacturing systems, a global network of production facilities, and shorter product cycles.

In a volatile world, these investments in flexibility are likely to yield high returns. For example, flexible manufacturing systems permit faster production response times to shifting market demand. Similarly, foreign facilities, even if they are uneconomical at the moment, can pay off by enabling companies to shift production in response to changing exchange rates or other relative cost shocks.

[4]Quoted in Cristopher J. Chipello, "The Market Watcher," *The Wall Street Journal,* September 23, 1988, p. 14.

[5]Quoted in Chipello, "The Market Watcher."

The greatest boost to competitiveness comes from compressing the time it takes to bring new and improved products to market. The edge a company gets from shorter *product cycles* is dramatic: Not only can it charge a premium price for its exclusive products, but it can also incorporate more up-to-date technology in its goods and respond faster to emerging market niches and changes in taste. Often held up as the ideal is the speedy way that retailers such as The Limited operate (see Chapter 1, Exhibit 1.2): If they see an item catching on with the public, they can have it manufactured in quantity and on their shelves within perhaps three weeks.

This speedy delivery is harder for a company that produces, say, automobiles or heavy machinery. Apparently, however, radical improvements in new-product delivery time are within reach even in these industries. In response to *endaka*—the soaring yen—which made their old products less competitive, Japanese automakers are making a frantic effort to reduce—from four years to less than two years—the time between the initial design and the actual production of a new car. With better planning and more competitive options, corporations can now change their strategies substantially before the impact of any currency change can make itself felt.

As a result, the adjustment period following a large exchange rate change has been compressed dramatically. The 100% appreciation of the Japanese yen against the dollar from 1985 to 1988, for example, sparked some changes in corporate strategy that are likely to be long-lasting: increased direct investment in the United States and East Asia by Japanese companies to cope with the high yen and to protect their markets from any trade backlash; upscaling by Japanese manufacturers to reduce the price sensitivity of their products and broaden their markets; massive cost-reduction programs by Japanese plants, with a long-term impact on production technology; and an increase in joint ventures between competitors.

■ ———————————————————————————————————————

ILLUSTRATION

Toshiba Copes with a Rising Yen by Cutting Costs. By 1988, Toshiba's cost cutting reduced its cost-to-sales ratio to where it was before the yen began rising. The company shifted production of low-tech products to developing nations and moved domestic production to high-value-added products. At a VCR plant outside of Tokyo, it halved the number of assembly-line workers by minimizing inventories and simplifying operations. Other cost-reducing international activities included production of color picture tubes with Westinghouse in the United States, photocopier production in a joint venture with Rhone-Poulenc in France, assembly of video cassette recorders in Tennessee, production of similar VCRs in West Germany, and establishment of a new plant in California for assembling and testing telephones and medical electronics equipment. Overall, Toshiba is estimated to have saved ¥115 billion—¥53 billion by redesigning products, ¥47 billion in parts cutbacks and lower raw material costs, and ¥15 billion in greater operating efficiency. Similarly, by 1989, with the dollar around ¥125, Fujitsu Fanuc, a robot maker had streamlined itself so thoroughly and differentiated its products so effectively that it estimated it could break even with only a fifth of its plant in use and a dollar down to ¥70.

—— ■

■ 11.4 ■
FINANCIAL MANAGEMENT OF EXCHANGE RISK

The one attribute that all the strategic marketing and production adjustments have in common is that they take time to accomplish in a cost-effective manner. The role of financial management in this process is to structure the firm's liabilities in such a way that during the time the strategic operational adjustments are underway, the reduction in asset earnings is matched by a corresponding decrease in the cost of servicing these liabilities.

One possibility is to finance the portion of a firm's assets used to create export profits so that any shortfall in operating cash flows due to an exchange rate change is offset by a reduction in debt servicing expenses. For example, a firm that has developed a sizable export market should hold a portion of its liabilities in that country's currency. The portion to be held in the foreign currency depends on the size of the loss in profitability associated with a given currency change. No more definite recommendations are possible because the currency effects will vary from one company to another.

Volkswagen is a case in point. To hedge its operating exposure, VW should have used dollar financing in proportion to its net dollar cash flow from U.S. sales. This strategy would have cushioned the impact of the DM revaluation that almost brought VW to its knees. For the longer term, though, VW could only manage its competitive exposure by developing new products with lower price elasticities of demand and by establishing production facilities in lower-cost nations.

The implementation of a hedging policy is likely to be quite difficult in practice, if only because the specific cash-flow effects of a given currency change are hard to predict. Trained personnel are required to implement and monitor an active hedging program. Consequently, hedging should be undertaken only when the effects of anticipated exchange rate changes are expected to be significant.

A highly simplified example can illustrate the application of the financing rule developed previously; namely, that the liability structure of the combined MNC—parent and subsidiaries—should be set up in such a way that any change in the inflow on assets due to a currency change should be matched by a corresponding change in the outflow on the liabilities used to fund those assets. Consider the effect of a local currency change on the subsidiary depicted in Exhibit 11.1. In the absence of any exchange rate changes, the subsidiary is forecast to have an operating profit of $800,000. If a predicted 20% devaluation of the local currency from LC 1 = $0.25 to LC 1 = $0.20 occurs, the subsidiary's LC profitability is expected to rise to LC 3.85 million from LC 3.2 million because of price increases. However, that LC profit rise still entails a loss of $30,000, despite a reduction in the dollar cost of production.

Suppose the subsidiary requires assets equaling LC 20 million, or $5 million at the current exchange rate. It can finance these assets by borrowing dollars at 8% and converting them into their local currency equivalent, or it can use LC funds at 10%. How can the parent structure its subsidiary's financing in such a way that a 20% devaluation will reduce the cost of servicing the subsidiary's liabilities by $30,000 and thus balance operating losses with a decrease in cash outflows?

Actually, a simple procedure is readily available. If S is the dollar outflow on local debt service, then it is necessary that $0.2S$, the dollar gain on devaluation, equal $30,000, the

■ **EXHIBIT 11.1**   Statement of Projected Cash Flow

	Units (hundred thousands)	Unit Price (LC)	Total	
LC 1 = $0.25				
Domestic sales	4	20	8,000,000	
Export sales	4	20	8,000,000	
Total revenue				16,000,000
Local labor (hours)	8	10	8,000,000	
Local material	8	3	2,400,000	
Imported material	6	4	2,400,000	
Total expeditures				12,800,000
Net Cash Flow from Operations				LC 3,200,000
Net Cash Flow from Operations				$800,000
LC 1 = $0.20				
Domestic sales	3	24	7,200,000	
Export sales	5	24	12,000,000	
Total revenue				19,200,000
Local labor (hours)	8	12	9,600,000	
Local material	10	3.5	3,500,000	
Imported material	4.5	5	2,250,000	
Total expeditures				15,350,000
Net Cash Flow from Operations				LC 3,850,000
Net Cash Flow from Operations				$770,000

■ **EXHIBIT 11.2**   Effect of Financial Structure on Net Cash Flow

	LC 1 = $0.25		LC 1 = $0.20	
	Local Currency	Dollars	Local Currency	Dollars
Operating cash flows	LC 3,200,000	$800,000	LC 3,850,000	$770,000
Debt service requirements:				
Local currency debt	600,000	150,000	600,000	120,000
Dollar debt	1,120,000	280,000	1,400,000	280,000
Total debt service outflow	1,720,000	430,000	2,000,000	400,000
Net cash flow	LC 1,480,000	$370,000	LC 1,850,000	$370,000

operating loss on devaluation. Hence, $S = \$150,000$, or LC 600,000 at the current exchange rate. At a local currency interest rate of 10%, that debt service amount corresponds to local currency debt of LC 6 million. The remaining LC 14 million can be provided by borrowing $3.5 million. Exhibit 11.2 illustrates the offsetting cash effects associated with such a financial structure.

This example would certainly become more complex if the effects of taxes, depreciation, and working capital were included. Although the execution becomes more difficult, a rough equivalence between operating losses (gains) and debt service gains (losses) can still be achieved as long as all cash flows are accounted for. The inclusion of other foreign operations just requires the aggregation of the cash-flow effects over all affiliates because the corporation's total exchange risk is based on the sum of the changes of the profit contributions of each individual subsidiary.

As mentioned earlier, this approach concentrates exclusively on risk reduction rather than on cost reduction. Where financial market imperfections are significant, a firm might consider exposing itself to more exchange risk in order to lower its expected financing costs.

■ 11.5 ■
SUMMARY AND CONCLUSIONS

We have seen in this chapter that currency risk affects all facets of a company's operations; therefore, it should not be the concern of financial managers alone. Operating managers, in particular, should develop marketing and production initiatives that help to ensure profitability over the long run. They should also devise anticipatory or proactive, rather than reactive, strategic alternatives in order to gain competitive leverage internationally.

The key to effective exposure management is to integrate currency considerations into the general management process. One approach used by a number of MNCs to develop the necessary coordination among executives responsible for different aspects of exchange risk management is to establish a committee for managing foreign currency exposure. Besides financial executives, such committees should—and often do—include the senior officers of the company such as the vice president-international, top marketing and production executives, the director of corporate planning, and the chief executive officer. This arrangement is desirable because top executives are exposed to the problems of exchange risk management, so they can incorporate currency expectations into their own decisions.

In this kind of integrated exchange risk program, the role of the financial executive is fourfold: (1) to provide local operating management with forecasts of inflation and exchange rates, (2) to identify and highlight the risks of competitive exposure, (3) to structure evaluation criteria such that operating managers are not rewarded or penalized for the effects of unanticipated currency changes, and (4) to estimate and hedge whatever operating exposure remains after the appropriate marketing and production strategies have been put in place.

■ QUESTIONS ■

1. Why should managers focus on marketing and production strategies to cope with foreign exchange risk?

2. What marketing and production techniques can firms initiate to cope with exchange risk?

3. What is the role of finance in protecting against exchange risk?

4. Comment on the following statement: "The sharp appreciation of the U.S. dollar during the early 1980s might have been the best thing that ever happened to American industry."

5. In what sense is the boost in profits of American companies due to a falling dollar artificial?

6. How does a shorter product-cycle time help companies reduce the exchange risk they face?

7. Why do exchange rate changes bring feast or famine for Volvo, but neither feast nor famine for Ford? Consider the distribution and concentration of their production facilities worldwide.

■ PROBLEMS ■

1.* Nissan produces a car that sells in Japan for ¥1.8 million. On September 1, the beginning of the model year, the exchange rate is ¥150:$1. Consequently, Nissan sets the U.S. sticker price at $12,000. By October 1, the exchange rate has dropped to ¥125:$1. Nissan is upset because it now receives only $12,000 × 125 = ¥1.5 million per sale.

   a. What scenarios are consistent with the U.S. dollar's depreciation?

   b. What alternatives are open to Nissan to improve its situation?

   c. How should Nissan respond in this situation?

   d. Suppose that on November 1, the U.S. Federal Reserve intervenes to rescue the dollar, and the exchange rate adjusts to ¥220:$1 by the following July. What problems and/or opportunities does this situation present for Nissan and for General Motors?

2.* Middle American Corporation (MAC) produces a line of corn silk cosmetics. All of the inputs are purchased domestically and processed at the factory in Des Moines, Iowa. Sales are only in the United States, primarily west of the Mississippi.

   a. Is there any sense in which MAC is exposed to the risk of foreign exchange rate changes that effect large multinational firms? If yes, how could MAC protect itself from these risks?

   b. If MAC opens a sales office in Paris, will this move increase its exposure to exchange rate risks? Explain.

3.* Gizmo, U.S.A. is investigating medium-term financing of $10 million in order to build an addition to its factory in Toledo, Ohio. Gizmo's bank has suggested the following alternatives:

Type of loan	Rate (%)
Three-year U.S. dollar loan	14
Three-year Deutsche mark loan	8
Three-year Swiss franc loan	4

   a. What information does Gizmo require to decide among the three alternatives?

*Problems 1-3 contributed by Richard M. Levich.

    b. Suppose the factory will be built in Geneva, Switzerland, rather than Toledo. How does this affect your answer in part a?*

4. Chemex, a U.S. maker of specialty chemicals, exports 40% of its $600 million in annual sales: 5% goes to Canada and 7% each to Japan, Britain, Germany, France, and Italy. It incurs all its costs in U.S. dollars, while most of its export sales are priced in the local currency.

    a. How is Chemex affected by exchange rate changes?

    b. Distinguish between Chemex's transaction exposure and its operating exposure.

    c. How can Chemex protect itself against transaction exposure?

    d. What financial, marketing, and production techniques can Chemex use to protect itself against operating exposure?

    e. Can Chemex eliminate its operating exposure by hedging its position every time it makes a foreign sale or by pricing all foreign sales in dollars? Why or why not?

5. Boeing Commercial Airplane Co. manufactures all its planes in the United States and prices them in dollars, even the 50% of its sales destined for overseas markets. Assess Boeing's currency risk. How can it cope with this risk?

6. Fire King International, an Indiana manufacturer of fire-resistant filing cabinets and disk storage units, has sought to protect itself from currency risk by pricing its export sales in dollars and holding firm on price. What currency risk does Fire King face from a rising dollar? How can Fire King manage that risk?

7. Cost Plus Imports is a West Coast chain specializing in low-cost imported goods, principally from Japan. It has to put out its semiannual catalogue with prices that are good for six months. Advise Cost Plus Imports on how it can protect itself against currency risk.

8. Matsushita exports about half of its TV set production to the United States under its Panasonic, Quasar, and Technics brand names. It prices its products in yen. Suppose the yen moves from ¥130 = $1 to ¥110 = $1. What currency risk is Matsushita facing? How can it cope with this currency risk?

9. Lyle Shipping, a British company, has chartered out ships at fixed-U.S.-dollar freight rates. How can Lyle use financing to hedge against its exposure? How will your recommendation affect Lyle's translation exposure? Lyle uses the current rate method to translate foreign currency assets and liabilities. However, the charters are off-balance-sheet items.

10. Di Giorgio International, a subsidiary of California-based Di Giorgio Corp., processes fruit juices and packages condiments in Turnhout, Belgium. It buys Brazilian orange concentrate in dollars, German apples in marks, Italian peaches in lire, and cartons in Dutch guilders. At the same time, its exports 85% of its production. Assess Di Giorgio International's currency risk and determine how it can structure its financing to reduce this risk.

11. In order to cut costs when the dollar was at its peak, Caterpillar shifted production of small construction equipment overseas. By contrast, Caterpillar's main competitors in that area, Deere & Co. and J.I. Case, make most of their small construction equipment in the United States. What are the most likely competitive consequences of this restructuring?

12. Walt Disney Company is in the process of building a new Euro Disneyland theme park in a sugar beet field 20 miles east of Paris. Euro Disneyland is expected to draw visitors from all over Western Europe, with the lion's share of tourists coming from France and Germany. The project is estimated to cost $1 billion, and the French government is offering to provide $400 million of that amount in franc financing at very favorable terms.

    a. What exchange risk is this project subject to from the standpoint of Disney?

   b. How can financing be used to mitigate this exchange risk?

   c. Suppose it turns out that having $400 million in franc financing actually adds to Disney's economic exposure. How should this affect Disney's willingness to accept the full amount of financing offered by the French government?

13. Texas Instruments (TI) manufactures integrated circuits and memory chips that it sells around the world. It has major markets in Europe. TI's primary competitors are Japanese companies.

   a. What factors will influence TI's exposure to movements in the dollar value of European currencies?

   b. Does TI's European business have yen exposure? Explain.

   c. How can TI use financing to reduce its yen exposure, to the extent this exposure exists?

■ BIBLIOGRAPHY ■

Dufey, Gunter. "Corporate Financial Policies and Floating Exchange Rates." Address presented at the meeting of the International Fiscal Association in Rome, October 14, 1974.

Lessard, Donald R., and John B. Lightstone. "Volatile Exchange Rates Can Put Operations at Risk." *Harvard Business Review,* July–August 1986, pp. 107–114.

Shapiro, Alan C.; and Thomas S. Robertson. "Managing Foreign Exchange Risks: The Role of Marketing Strategy." Working paper, The Wharton School, University of Pennsylvania, 1976.

■ PART II ■
■ Case Studies ■

■ Case II.1
British Materials Corporation

In January 1981, Vulkan Inc., a U.S. firm relatively new to international business, acquired British Materials Corp., or BMC, an English firm. BMC operated two detinning plants in England, one in Manchester and the other in Birmingham, and a scrap collection depot just outside of London.

Detinning involves the separation and recovery of tin and detinned steel from tinplate scrap. The principal sources of tinplate scrap are the waste cuttings and stampings from the manufacture of articles made from tinplate by can manufacturers, food packers, bottlecap manufacturers, and others. Other sources are tinplate trimmings and rejects from steel companies which manufacture tinplate. Both the steel and the tin recovered in this process are high-quality, high-purity premium metals.

BMC was the only detinning company operating in the United Kingdom and had established clear domination of the industrial tinplate scrap market. At the time of its acquisition, approximately 80% of BMC's scrap supply was provided by 39 tinplate fabricators, the largest of which provided nearly half of BMC's scrap. BMC did not buy the scrap supplied to it by these firms. Rather, it had signed contracts with them to process their scrap for a fee. These contracts all had similar provisions. They were cost-plus, and they prescribed a profit to BMC equal to 15% of the prices BMC received for the detinned steel and the recovered tin.

Costs covered by the contracts included all variable costs as well as an agreed-upon amount for fixed costs excluding depreciation and financing charges. The management of Vulkan felt that the fixed-cost recovery provisions were adequate to cover projected out-of-pocket fixed costs. The remaining 20% of BMC's tinplate scrap requirement was met through open market purchases.

Detinned steel recovered by BMC was sold primarily to British Steel, with the remainder exported to companies in Western Europe. During 1974–1976, only 2% of BMC's detinned steel sales revenue arose from foreign sales, whereas 33% of its 1980 sales revenue came from export sales. Most of the tin recovered is sold to various firms in the market areas surrounding the detinning plants. These firms convert the tin into inorganic tin chemicals consumed by the glass, plating, and chemical industries.

The acquisition of BMC was effected through Vulkan's newly formed United Kingdom subsidiary, Vulkan U.K. or VUK, which purchased all of the outstanding common and preference shares of BMC. Subsequently, BMC and its primary subsidiaries were liquidated into VUK. As it considered the alternatives for funding this acquisition, a paramount concern of Vulkan was the possible foreign exchange exposure associated with the sterling revenues and costs generated by VUK. Based upon 1980s proportions of pound sterling- and U.S. dollar-denominated sales, and assuming that sterling prices were invariant to exchange rate changes, Vulkan tested the sensitivity of VUK's income and debt service capacity to likely changes in the dollar-sterling exchange rate. These analyses tended to indicate that dollar-denominated earnings and cash flows were sensitive to exchange rate fluctuations. Additionally, Thomas Alan, Vulkan's financial vice president, consulted with several investment and commercial bankers. A typical opinion is the one from Diane Ronningen, the partner in charge of international finance at the investment banking firm of Ronningen and Simnowitz (see Exhibit II 1.1).

■ **EXHIBIT II 1.1**   Opinion on BMC's Exchange Risk

January 5, 1981

Mr. Thomas Alan
Vice President–Finance
Vulkan, Inc.
30 Golden Triangle
Pittsburgh, Pennsylvania 15217

Dear Tom:

Following our recent conversations, I am writing to give you our thoughts on the appropriate currency Vulkan should use for financing the acquisition of British Materials Corp. (BMC). You have asked specifically that we review alternatives in pounds sterling, U.S. dollars, Deutsche marks, and Swiss francs.

We believe that financing the acquisition of BMC with sterling or a sterling equivalent makes the most financial and business sense. It is sterling revenues and income which BMC generates in its daily operations and sterling which Vulkan would then have available to service any debt used for the acquisition. If BMC were a substantial exporter or competed in the United Kingdom against firms which set their prices on a dollar base (e.g., the U.K. computer industry, North Sea oil, etc.) the appropriate currency might be dollars. Since this is not the case, a financing in dollars places an unnecessary foreign exchange exposure burden on Vulkan. Vulkan's primary business is not currency speculation. Since neither you nor we know the future movements of the sterling exchange rate over the next few years and since sterling has been one of the most volatile and least predictable currencies in the world recently, incurring such an exchange risk would, in our opinion, be ill-advised.

Borrowing on the Deutsche mark or Swiss franc markets on an unhedged basis to fund the acquisition makes even less sense for Vulkan since you have no natural exposure in either of these currencies. On a hedged basis, the cost would theoretically be similar to those for the dollar borrowing alternative.

I hope this letter clarifies our recommendation. Please don't hesitate to call if you have questions. Best regards.

Sincerely,

Diane M. Ronningen
Senior Partner
Ronningen & Simnowitz

To minimize the economic gains and losses on its investment in BMC resulting from fluctuations in the rate of exchange between the U.S. dollar and the pound sterling, Vulkan concluded that the acquisition should be funded entirely in pounds sterling. This decision was based on the following factors:

- All BMC's assets would be denominated in pounds sterling
- The high probability that most, if not all, of BMC's future revenues and costs would be denominated in pounds sterling or would be determined on a pound sterling-equivalent basis.
- Vulkan's projected income and debt service sensitivity analyses
- U.K. and U.S. tax laws and U.K. corporate law
- The advice of Vulkan's investment and commercial banks

Accordingly, in January 1981, Vulkan and VUK borrowed £2,355,000 and £1,137,000, respectively, for 10 years on a floating-rate basis (LIBOR plus a margin) to fund part of the purchase of all the outstanding common and preference shares of BMC. The balance of the purchase price was funded by VUK's borrowing under a sterling overdraft facility and its issuance of short-term sterling notes. VUK's obligations were not guaranteed by Vulkan. On the date of these borrowings, the exchange rate was $2.4060:£1.00.

It should be emphasized that Vulkan decided to finance its acquisition of BMC with sterling debt to hedge against the effects of unanticipated exchange rate changes, not to profit from the possibility that sterling would devalue by more than the amount already reflected in the sterling-dollar interest rate differential. Pursuing the latter objective would have constituted currency speculation, not hedging. And it was an article of faith among Vulkan's management that its comparative advantage lay in production and marketing, not in currency speculation.

During April 1983, the average U.S. dollar-pound sterling exchange rate was $1.5362. Based on quarterly exchange rates between 1981:1 and 1983:1, the nominal or actual, sterling depreciation against the dollar was 33.6%. In real or inflation-adjusted terms, using the implicit price indexes in both countries to measure inflation, sterling depreciated 31.0% This significant and rapid depreciation of the pound sterling in both nominal and real terms raised the question: Had the sterling borrowing to finance the acquisition of BMC provided an effective hedge of the economic foreign exchange exposure believed to be inherent in its operations? Vulkan's management accordingly decided to reexamine its original conclusion that the acquisition of BMC created a "long" pound sterling exposure.

Although Ms. Ronningen's reasoning still seemed persuasive, Mr. Alan has decided to call in an independent consultant, Robert Daniels, for a second opinion on the advisability of funding VUK with pound debt. Mr. Daniels, who is noted for his expertise in the area of currency risk management, requested all available data on BMC's past operations.

Thomas Alan managed to assemble operating data for BMC from the first quarter of 1974 through the first quarter of 1983. Due to unusual transactions which occurred during the second quarter of 1981, he decided to exclude this data. In addition, Mr. Alan included the average exchange rate (dollars/pound), as well as some price data on detinned steel, for each quarter. These data are contained in Exhibit II 1.2.

Now it was up to Mr. Daniels to interpret these data and come to some conclusion concerning the extent to which VUK was subject to exchange risk. His opinion would have a major impact on whether Vulkan would maintain its pound sterling debt or refund this debt and replace it with dollar financing.

■ **EXHIBIT II 1.2**   Operating Data for BMC, 1972–1983

Year: Quarter	Exchange Rate[1]	£Cash Flow (BIT)[2]	£Cash Flow (BDIT)[3]	Home Price[4]	Export Price[5]	Average Price[6]
72:1	2.599	—	—	—	—	—
72:2	2.599	—	—	—	—	—
72:3	2.445	—	—	—	—	—
72:4	2.364	—	—	—	—	—
73:1	2.420	—	—	—	—	—
73:2	2.530	—	—	—	—	—
73:3	2.480	—	—	—	—	—

continues

■ **EXHIBIT II 1.2**   Continued

Year: Quarter	Exchange Rate[1]	£Cash Flow (BIT)[2]	£Cash Flow (BDIT)[3]	Home Price[4]	Export Price[5]	Average Price6
73:4	2.379	—	—	—	—	—
74:1	2.279	127.000	51.000	21.190	25.860	21.930
74:2	2.397	186.000	142.000	28.020	36.280	28.920
74:3	2.350	−11.000	−57.000	34.040	—	34.040
74:4	2.330	220.000	171.000	39.120	51.500	39.570
75:1	2.391	325.000	280.000	40.740	—	40.740
75:2	2.325	392.000	345.000	36.720	38.400	36.750
75:3	2.129	235.000	175.000	35.160	29.990	35.030
75:4	2.043	354.000	305.000	33.610	30.140	33.430
76:1	2.000	32.000	−10.000	39.010	—	39.010
76:2	1.807	693.000	648.000	48.010	—	48.010
76:3	1.767	416.000	363.000	40.490	—	40.490
76:4	1.651	207.000	154.000	39.300	—	39.300
77:1	1.714	65.000	40.000	36.290	—	36.290
77:2	1.719	−54.000	−146.000	35.050	28.180	33.350
77:3	1.735	417.000	365.000	32.250	26.410	30.410
77:4	1.815	688.000	638.000	29.600	22.460	27.040
78:1	1.927	53.000	2.000	29.240	21.900	28.020
78:2	1.835	597.000	539.000	33.360	30.610	32.830
78:3	1.932	401.000	342.000	38.830	35.760	38.250
78:4	1.984	800.000	728.000	45.230	42.210	44.690
79:1	2.016	−35.000	−94.000	57.800	65.380	58.350
79:2	2.080	616.000	553.000	59.580	53.420	58.530
79:3	2.232	760.000	693.000	60.310	47.400	58.420
79:4	2.159	829.000	760.000	51.890	47.390	50.450
80:1	2.254	186.000	109.000	53.750	51.410	52.770
80:2	2.285	379.000	299.000	46.870	46.360	46.640
80:3	2.381	120.000	27.000	35.290	36.190	35.870
80:4	2.386	−141.000	−246.000	30.910	31.280	31.120
81:1	2.310	838.000	803.000	34.620	33.310	34.180
81:2	2.081	—	—	35.130	39.270	35.990
81:3	1.837	332.000	274.000	35.920	38.930	36.600
81:4	1.884	545.000	477.000	39.720	35.530	39.210
82:1	1.847	552.000	496.000	47.880	40.320	46.150
82:2	1.780	177.000	116.000	42.260	45.620	42.920
82:3	1.725	5.000	−60.000	41.740	44.720	42.360
82:4	1.650	370.000	297.000	35.310	38.880	36.180
83:1	1.534	−57.000	−171.000	36.140	37.920	36.500

[1]Average spot exchange rate during the quarter (U.S. dollars/British pounds)   [2]Cash flow equals income before interest and taxes plus depreciation plus or minus changes in working capital.   [3]Same as in note 2 but without depreciation   [4]Average sales price in U.K. in £/ton   [5]Average export sales price in £/ton   [6]Volume weighted, average total sales price in £/ton

QUESTIONS

1. Is VUK subject to exchange risk? How, if at all, do your analysis and conclusions differ from those of Ms. Ronningen?

2. Should Vulkan refund the pound debt it used for the acquisition of BMC and replace it with dollar financing? Why or why not? What criteria are you using to reach your decision?

3. Suppose it is concluded that VUK is not subject to exchange risk. Should Vulkan repay its pound debts? Should VUK repay its pound loans and replace them with dollar financing? Consider the tax consequences of replacing the pound debt with dollar financing in both the United Kingdom and the United States.

4. Does Vulkan's foreign exchange risk management objective make sense? From what perspective?

■ Case II.2
Euclides Engineering Ltd.

The submission of a bid to the Mexican government's agency in charge of the rural electrification project had been most disappointing. In November 1984, Sam Finkel, Manager-Finance of the Power Systems Management Division at Euclides Engineering, was notified that Euclides had been underbid to the tune of $13 million by the Swiss–West German consortium Brown-Boveri & Siemens.

Euclides had entered the bidding contest for the installation of five high-voltage transmission units near Monterey, Mexico's second largest industrial center. The bid submitted in March 1984 was in the amount of $67 million to be paid in three equal installments on July 1, 1986; December 31, 1986; and July 1, 1987, with installation to be completed in the last six months of 1985. Attached with the reply from the Mexican government was a photocopy of the two bids, which were virtually identical from the standpoint of technical specifications but which varied in terms of payment.

- Brown-Boveri & Siemens: equivalent of $54 million (denominated in Deutsche marks at the rate of DM 3.14:$1). Same payment schedule as Euclides, but in three equal installments of Deutsche marks.
- Euclides Engineering: $67 million

A second round of bidding was to be held on December 10, with the winner to be announced on December 20. Sam Finkel was concerned that a strong dollar has just about closed his export market, where Euclides used to be price competitive even when lavish export credits were offered by its foreign competitors. Sam felt that in spite of his new financial responsibilities, his background and the last 15 years of his career as a civil engineer with Euclides did not quite equip him with the creative financing skills that could close the seemingly unbridgeable gap between the two bids. Fortunately, Sam felt he could depend on his newly hired assistant, Gerardo Wehmann, a Mexican national with graduate education in electrical engineering from Stanford and an MBA in international business from the Wharton School.

Gerardo, who had gone over the files, felt that the exchange rate consideration had much to do with Euclides's problem. He decided to study the situation further. To begin, he examined the Deutsche mark exchange rate forecasts put out by Wharton Econometric Forecasting Associates (WEFA). He

SOURCE: Copyright © 1985 by Laurent L. Jacque. Revised by Alan C. Shapiro.

274   Part II   Foreign Exchange Risk Management

also studied the forward rates and the rates on several options contracts as of December 3. These data are contained in Exhibits II 2.1 and II 2.2, respectively.

QUESTIONS

1. In view of the relative values of the U.S. dollar and the Deutsch mark, how can you explain the discrepancy between the U.S. and the Swiss-West German bids?

2. Can Euclides match the Swiss-West German bid without changing its dollar price? How?

3. If you were to advise the Mexican government on how to compare bids denominated in different currencies, what would your advice be?

■ **EXHIBIT II 2.1**   WEFA Exchange Rate Forecasts (DM per U.S. $, End of Period)

Year	Jan.	Feb.	Mar.	Apr.	May	June
1985	3.18	3.16	3.14	3.11	3.09	3.07
1986	2.87	2.83	2.80	2.77	2.74	2.71
1987	2.55	2.54	2.53	2.51	2.49	2.47
Year	July	Aug.	Sept.	Oct.	Nov.	Dec.
1985	3.05	3.02	2.99	2.96	2.93	2.90
1986	2.68	2.66	2.64	2.61	2.59	2.57
1987	2.46	2.44	2.43	2.41	2.39	2.38

■ **EXHIBIT II 2.2**   Exchange Rate Quotations (DM per U.S. Dollar)

WEFA Forecast for the Deutsche Mark, December 3, 1984

	1 Month	3 Months	6 Months	12 Months
Forecast	3.1563	3.1611	3.0899	2.9285
Forward	3.1045	3.0863	3.0550	2.9875

Foreign Currency Options (Philadelphia Exchange), 1985

	Premium on Call Contract		Premium on Put Contract	
Strike Price	March	June	March	June
0.31	1.20	2.25	0.33	0.55
0.32	1.10	1.65	0.67	0.92
0.33	0.62	1.19	1.19	
0.34	0.33	0.79		
0.35	0.20	0.52		

NOTE: Strike prices are expressed in U.S. dollars per DM and premiums in cents per DM.

■ Case II.3
Polygon Appliances, Inc.

Larry Osborn, the newly appointed vice president-purchasing of Polygon Appliances, Inc. (PAI) is reviewing the terms of the procurement contract signed October 1, 1983, with two Italian manufacturers, Necci and Aspera. PAI's foreign sourcing strategy for compressors had been initiated in 1980 as a response to strong import competition from Italian and Japanese household appliance manufacturers. The procurement contract first signed in October 1980 had been renewed three times with the same firms and had reached the amount of $50 million by October 1983, thus accounting for over 70% of the total supplies of compressors used by PAI in its U.S. line of refrigerators.

Generally, PAI remained a largely domestic firm selling the totality of its line of household appliances in the United States. Turning to foreign manufacturers for sourcing subassemblies marked a key departure from past company practices and explained perhaps the directives issued by the Board of Directors that under no condition was PAI to incur exposure to foreign exchange risk.

Of primary concern to Larry Osborn was the issue of foreign exchange. Risk was to be apportioned between PAI (the importer) and Necci and Aspera (the exporters). Although the sourcing contract was not to be signed for another four months, Larry wished to initiate the renegotiation well ahead of schedule so as to maintain maximum flexibility.

The current contractual scheme, which had been progressively refined over the course of the last three years, called for a fixed price set in Italian lire, adjusted monthly by the Italian rate of inflation (as measured by the consumer price index). Furthermore, PAI had obtained the guarantee that exchange risk outside a band of $\pm$ Lit 50 around the exchange rate prevailing at the signing of the contract would be split evenly between the two parties. Within the $\pm$ Lit 50 band, PAI was to assume the full impact of exchange risk. As Larry Osborn reviewed the outcome of sourcing contracts over the first six months of the 1983–1984 year, he listed some of the issues that had to be discussed in his forthcoming negotiations with Necci and Aspera.

- The currency in which the price of imported compressors had to be denominated
- Whether or not a real price increase had to be provided to the Italian companies as part of the agreement
- The exchange rate to be used for apportioning exchange risk between the two parties
- The width of the band of fluctuations within which PAI was to assume fully the exchange risk

QUESTIONS

1. Evaluate the current contracting scheme in view of the actual price/exchange rate for the last 18 months (See Exhibit II 3.1 for selected statistics on the Italian economy).

2. Develop an alternative contracting scheme that would better serve the interests of PAI.

3. Assuming that the invoice would continue to be denominated in lire, should PAI be prepared to hedge its exposure through forward contracts? Should the cost of such forward contracts be incorporated in the lira price of compressors? Prepare general guidelines within which the forthcoming lira exposure should be managed. As of today (April 2, 1984), the 30-day, 90-day, 180-day, and 360-day forward rates are, respectively, Lit 1621.0, Lit 1653.0, Lit 1680.0, and Lit 1734.0.

SOURCE: Copyright © 1985 by Laurent L. Jacque.

■ **EXHIBIT II 3.1**   Selected Statistics on the Italian Economy

Year: Quarter	Italy		United States		Exchange Rate (Lira:Dollar)
	CPI	WPI	CPI	WPI	
78:1	146.8	151.5	116.9	115.4	861.85
78:2	151.4	155.1	120.0	118.9	862.39
78:3	155.0	157.8	122.8	120.8	837.95
78:4	159.7	161.4	125.2	123.5	832.47
79:1	165.8	168.4	128.4	128.0	839.11
79:2	172.0	176.2	132.8	132.5	847.00
79:3	177.9	183.8	137.2	136.7	816.68
79:4	187.9	194.1	141.2	141.5	820.65
80:1	200.0	207.0	146.7	148.0	824.82
80:2	207.9	214.4	152.0	151.1	851.46
80:3	216.6	219.1	154.8	156.0	843.45
80:4	228.9	227.3	158.9	159.3	906.07
81:1	236.7	237.0	163.1	163.9	1001.36
81:2	247.2	249.1	166.9	167.9	1134.09
81:3	254.6	257.9	171.7	169.2	1215.43
81:4	266.3	268.1	171.4	169.1	1196.18
82:1	277.0	276.8	175.6	170.5	1261.84
82:2	285.4	282.5	178.2	170.7	1319.33
82:3	297.1	291.5	181.6	171.6	1393.6
82:4	310.4	301.3	182.0	171.7	1435.2
83:1	321.7	306.1	181.9	171.8	1399.4
83:2	331.1	311.1	184.2	172.4	1477.5
83:3	338.6	327.1	186.3	174.1	1573.7
83:4	350.3	328.9	188.0	174.9	1624.8
84:1	360.5	339.3	190.0	176.9	1662.4

NOTE: CPI = Consumer Price Index; WPI = Wholesale Price Index. Italian and U.S. price indexes are expressed as 1975 = 100. All data are period averages.

SOURCE: *International Financial Statistics, 1978–1984*, International Monetary Fund.

■ **Case II.4**
Rolls-Royce Limited

Rolls-Royce Limited, the British aeroengine manufacturer, suffered a loss of £58 million in 1979 on worldwide sales of £848. The company's annual report for 1979 (p. 4) blamed the loss on the dramatic revaluation of the pound sterling against the dollar, from £1 = $1.71 in early 1977 to £1 = $2.12 by the end of 1979.

SOURCE: Written in collaboration with Laurent L. Jacque.

The most important was the effect of the continued weakness of the U.S. dollar against sterling. The large civil engines which Rolls-Royce produces are supplied to American air frames. Because of U.S. dominance in civil aviation, both as producer and customer, these engines are usually priced in U.S. dollars and escalated accordingly to U.S. indices. . . .

A closer look at Rolls-Royce's competitive position in the global market for jet engines reveals the sources of its dollar exposure. For the previous several years Rolls-Royce export sales had accounted for a stable 40% of total sales and had been directed at the U.S. market. This market is dominated by two U.S. competitors, Pratt and Whitney Aircraft Group (United Technologies) and General Electric's aerospace division. As the clients of its mainstay engine, the RB 211, were U.S. aircraft manufacturers (Boeing's 747SP and 747,200 and Lockheed's L1011), Rolls-Royce had little choice in the currency denomination of its export sales but to use the dollar.

Indeed, Rolls-Royce won some huge engine contracts in 1978 and 1979 that were fixed in dollar terms. Rolls-Royce's operating costs, on the other hand, were almost exclusively incurred in sterling (wages, components, and debt servicing). These contracts were mostly pegged to an exchange rate of about $1.80 for the pound, and Rolls-Royce officials, in fact, expected the pound to fall further to $1.65. Hence, they didn't cover their dollar exposures. If the officials were correct, and the dollar strengthened, Rolls-Royce would enjoy windfall profits. When the dollar weakened instead, the combined effect of fixed dollar revenues and sterling costs resulted in foreign exchange losses in 1979 on its U.S. engine contracts that were estimated by *The Wall Street Journal* (March 11, 1980, p. 6) to be equivalent to as much as $200 million.

Moreover, according to that same *Wall Street Journal* article, "the more engines produced and sold under the previously negotiated contracts, the greater Rolls-Royce's losses will be."

QUESTIONS

1. Describe the factors you would need to know to assess the economic impact on Rolls-Royce of the change in the dollar:sterling exchange rate. Does inflation affect Rolls-Royce's exposure?

2. Given these factors, how would you calculate Rolls-Royce's economic exposure?

3. Suppose Rolls-Royce had hedged its dollar contracts. Would it now be facing any economic exposure? How about inflation risk?

4. What alternative financial management strategies might Rolls-Royce have followed that would have reduced or eliminated its economic exposure on the U.S. engine contracts?

5. What nonfinancial tactics might Rolls-Royce now initiate to reduce its exposure on the remaining engines to be supplied under the contracts? On future business (e.g., diversification of export sales)?

6. What additional information would you require to ascertain the validity of the statement that "the more engines produced and sold under the previously negotiated contracts, the greater Rolls-Royce's losses will be"?

■ Case II.5
The Mexican Peso

The basic purpose of this case is to have you conduct an in-depth analysis of the impact of government macroeconomic policies on firms and banks doing business with that country. The vehicle being used is the Mexican peso. See Exhibit II 5.1 for statistics related to exchange rates and price indexes in the United States and Mexico for the period 1975–1987. Using these data, please address the following questions.

QUESTIONS

1. What are the causes of the continuing devaluation of the peso since August 1976? Analyze both the immediate causes (e.g., balance-of-payments deficits) and longer-term, more fundamental causes (e.g., inflation, the political and economic environment). Concentrate especially on the 1982 and subsequent devaluations of the peso.

2. What role did oil price changes play in Mexico's difficulties?

3. What indicators of peso devaluation prior to 1982 were there?

4. What were the likely effects of the peso devaluation between 1976 and January 1982 on

    a. Mexican companies?

    b. Foreign firms operating in Mexico?

    c. U.S. companies in border towns catering to Mexicans?

5. Redo question 4, focusing on the effects of peso devaluation subsequent to February 1982.

6. In August 1982, the Mexican government devalued the peso, froze all dollar accounts in Mexican banks, and imposed currency controls. What were the government's objectives? How did these actions affect the black market value of the peso? Why?

7. How did the Mexican government's expropriation of Mexico City real estate, following the September 1985 earthquake, affect the value of the peso and why?

8. Consider the trust factor with respect to Mexican policies. What have been the probable effects of trust or its lack on investment in Mexico, Mexican citizens' investment choices, and the peso's value?

9. Are dollar loans to the Mexican government and Mexican companies exposed to exchange risk? Explain.

10. How did Mexico's economic policies contribute to its debt crisis?

■ **EXHIBIT II 5.1**   Exchange Rates

| Year:Quarter | Nominal Exchange Rates (Period Average) | | CPI Mexico | CPI United States |
	Peso/Dollar	Dollar/Peso		
75:1	12.50	0.08000	100.0	100.0
75:2	12.50	0.08000	103.2	101.9
75:3	12.50	0.08000	107.0	104.1
75:4	12.50	0.08000	110.4	105.8
76:1	12.50	0.08000	115.2	106.8
76:2	12.50	0.08000	118.2	108.2
76:3	19.85	0.05038	122.0	109.8
76:4	19.95	0.05013	137.3	111.0
77:1	22.69	0.04407	149.1	113.0

continues

■ **EXHIBIT II 5.1**   Continued

Year:Quarter	Nominal Exchange Rates (Period Average)		CPI Mexico	CPI United States
	Peso/Dollar	**Dollar/Peso**	**CPI Mexico**	**CPI United States**
77:2	23.00	0.04348	155.7	115.5
77:3	22.69	0.04407	162.4	117.1
77:4	22.73	0.04399	168.6	118.5
78:1	22.74	0.04398	177.7	120.4
78:2	22.81	0.04384	183.9	123.6
78:3	22.73	0.04399	191.4	126.5
78:4	22.72	0.04401	197.6	129.0
79:1	22.83	0.04380	209.5	132.3
79:2	22.84	0.04378	217.0	136.8
79:3	22.78	0.04390	225.2	141.3
79:4	22.80	0.04386	235.6	145.4
80:1	22.85	0.04376	256.8	151.1
80:2	22.93	0.04361	271.5	156.6
80:3	23.06	0.04337	289.3	159.4
80:4	23.25	0.04301	303.9	163.7
81:1	23.76	0.04209	328.5	168.0
81:2	24.37	0.04103	348.4	171.9
81:3	25.20	0.03968	365.9	176.9
81:4	26.29	0.03804	389.4	179.3
82:1	45.50	0.02198	435.0	180.9
82:2	48.04	0.02082	501.5	183.5
82:3	50.00	0.02000	606.1	187.0
82:4	96.48	0.01036	730.8	187.5
83:1	102.02	0.00980	926.2	187.3
83:2	120.01	0.00833	1076.9	189.7
83:3	131.97	0.00758	1217.2	191.9
83:4	143.93	0.00695	1369.6	193.6
84:1	155.76	0.00642	1601.9	195.7
84:2	167.59	0.00597	1807.3	197.9
84:3	179.55	0.00557	1987.7	200.1
84:4	192.56	0.00519	2196.5	201.5
85:1	208.90	0.00479	2552.7	202.8
85:2	228.01	0.00439	2800.9	205.3
85:3	305.10	0.00328	3097.0	206.7
85:4	371.70	0.00269	3527.5	212.6
86:1	473.60	0.00211	4254.7	213.1
86:2	575.40	0.00174	4957.8	212.6
86:3	752.00	0.00133	5930.4	214.3
86:4	923.50	0.00108	7164.7	215.4
87:1	1126.00	0.00089	8909.4	217.8
87:2	1353.70	0.00074	11120.8	220.7
87:3	1570.80	0.00064	13889.6	223.1
87:4	2209.70	0.00045	17795.7	225.0

PART III

Multinational Working Capital Management

▪ 12 ▪

Short-Term Financing

Money is a wonderful thing, but it is possible to pay too high a price for it.

—Anonymous—

▪ Financing the working capital requirements of a multinational corporation's foreign affiliates poses a complex decision problem. This complexity stems from the large number of financing options available to the subsidiary of an MNC. Subsidiaries have access to funds from sister affiliates and the parent, as well as from external sources. This chapter focuses on developing policies for borrowing from either within or without the corporation when the risk of exchange rate changes is present and different tax rates and regulations are in effect.

This chapter is concerned with the following five aspects of developing a short-term overseas financing strategy: (1) identifying the key factors, (2) formulating and evaluating objectives, (3) describing available short-term borrowing options, (4) developing a methodology for calculating and comparing the effective after-tax dollar costs of these alternatives, and (5) integrating the borrowing strategy with exposure management considerations.

▪ 12.1 ▪
KEY FACTORS IN SHORT-TERM FINANCING STRATEGY

Expected costs and risk, the basic determinants of any funding strategy, are strongly influenced in an international context by six key factors.

1. If forward contracts are unavailable, the crucial issue is whether differences in nominal interest rates among currencies are matched by anticipated exchange rate changes. For example, is the difference between an 8% dollar interest rate and a 3% Swiss franc interest rate due solely to expectations that the dollar will devalue by 5% relative to the franc? The key issue here, in other words, is whether there are deviations from the international Fisher effect. If deviations do exist, then expected dollar borrowing costs will vary by currency, leading to a decision problem. Trade-offs must then be made between the expected borrowing costs and the exchange risks associated with each financing option.

2. The element of exchange risk is the second key factor. Many firms borrow locally to provide an offsetting liability for their exposed local currency assets. On the other hand, borrowing a foreign currency in which the firm has no exposure will increase its exchange risk. What matters is the covariance between the operating and financing cash flows. That is, the risks associated with borrowing in a specific currency are related to the firm's degree of exposure in that currency.

3. The third essential element is the firm's degree of risk aversion. The more risk averse the firm (or its management) is, the higher the price it should be willing to pay to reduce its currency exposure. Risk aversion affects the company's risk-cost trade-off and consequently, in the absence of forward contracts, influences the selection of currencies it will use to finance its foreign operations.

4. If forward contracts are available, however, currency risk should not be a factor in the firm's borrowing strategy. Instead, relative borrowing costs, calculated on a covered basis, become the sole determinant of which currencies to borrow in. The key issue here is whether the nominal interest differential equals the forward differential—that is, whether interest rate parity holds. If it does hold, then in the absence of tax considerations, the currency denomination of the firm's debt is irrelevant. Covered after-tax costs can differ among currencies because of government capital controls or the threat of such controls. Due to this added element of risk, the annualized forward discount or premium may not offset the difference between the interest rate on the LC loan versus the dollar loan—that is, interest rate parity will not hold.

5. Even if interest rate parity does hold before tax, the currency denomination of corporate borrowings does matter where tax asymmetries are present. These tax asymmetries are based on the differential treatment of foreign exchange gains and losses on either forward contracts or loan repayments. For example, English firms or affiliates have a disincentive to borrow in strong currencies because Inland Revenue, the British tax agency, taxes exchange gains on foreign currency borrowings, but disallows the deductibility of exchange losses on the same loans. An opposite incentive (to borrow in stronger currencies) is created in countries such as Australia that may permit exchange gains on forward contracts to be taxed at a lower rate than the rate at which forward contract losses are deductible. In such a case, even if interest parity holds before tax, after-tax forward contract gains may be greater than after-tax interest costs. Such tax asymmetries lead to possibilities of borrowing arbitrage, even if interest rate parity holds before tax. The essential point is that, in comparing relative borrowing costs, these costs must be computed on an after-tax covered basis.

6. A final factor that may enter into the borrowing decision is *political risk.* Even if local financing is not the minimum cost option, multinationals will often still try to maximize their local borrowings if they believe that expropriation or exchange controls are serious possibilities. If either event occurs, an MNC has fewer assets at risk if it has used local, rather than external, financing.

■ 12.2 ■

SHORT-TERM FINANCING OBJECTIVES

This section considers four possible objectives that can guide a firm in deciding where and in which currencies to borrow.

1. *Minimize expected cost.* By ignoring risk, this objective reduces information requirements, allows borrowing options to be evaluated on an individual basis without considering the correlation between loan cash flows and operating cash flows, and lends itself readily to break-even analysis (see Section 12.4). One problem with this approach is that if risk affects the company's operating cash flows (see Chapter 1), the validity of using expected cost alone is questionable. If forward contracts are available, however, there is a theoretically justifiable reason for ignoring risk; namely, loan costs should be evaluated on a covered (riskless) basis. In that case, minimizing expected cost is the same as minimizing actual cost.

2. *Minimize risk without regard to cost.* A firm that followed this advice to its logical conclusion would dispose of all its assets and invest the proceeds in government securities. In other words, this objective is impractical and contrary to shareholder interests.

3. *Trade off expected cost and systematic risk.* The advantage of this objective is that, like the first objective, it allows a company to evaluate different loans without considering the relationship between loan cash flows and operating cash flows from operations. Moreover, it is consistent with shareholder preferences as described by the capital asset pricing model. In practical terms, however, there is probably little difference between expected borrowing costs adjusted for systematic risk and expected borrowing costs without that adjustment. This lack of difference is because the correlation between currency fluctuations and a well-diversified portfolio of risky assets is likely to be quite small.

4. *Trade off expected cost and total risk.* The theoretical rationale for this approach was described in Chapter 1. Basically, it relies on the existence of potentially substantial costs of financial distress. On a more practical level, management generally prefers greater stability of cash flows (regardless of investor preferences). Management will typically self-insure against most losses, but might decide to use the financial markets to hedge against the risk of large losses. To implement this approach, it is necessary to take into account the covariances between operating and financing cash flows. This approach (trading off expected cost and total risk) is valid only where forward contracts are unavailable. Otherwise, selecting the lowest-cost borrowing option, calculated on a covered after-tax basis, is the only justifiable objective.[1]

■ 12.3 ■

SHORT-TERM FINANCING OPTIONS

Firms typically prefer to finance the temporary component of current assets with short-term funds. This section briefly describes three short-term financing options that may

---

[1]These possible objectives are suggested by Donald R. Lessard, "Currency and Tax Considerations in International Financing," Teaching Note No. 3, Massachusetts Institute of Technology, Spring 1979.

be available to an MNC: (1) the intercompany loan, (2) the local currency loan, and (3) Euronotes and Euro-commercial paper.

Intercompany Financing

A frequent means of affiliate financing is to have either the parent company or sister affiliate provide an *intercompany loan*. At times, however, these loans may be limited in amount or duration by official exchange controls, such as the restrictions between 1968 and 1974 imposed by the U.S. government's Office of Foreign Direct Investment. In addition, interest rates on intercompany loans are frequently required to fall within set limits. Normally, the lender's government will want the interest rate on an intercompany loan to be set as high as possible for both tax and balance-of-payments purposes, while the borrower's government will demand a low interest rate for similar reasons. The relevant parameters in establishing the cost of such a loan include the lender's opportunity cost of funds, the interest rate set, tax rates and regulations, the currency of denomination of the loan, and expected exchange rate movements over the term of the loan.

Local Currency Financing

Like most domestic firms, affiliates of multinational corporations generally attempt to finance their working capital requirements locally, for both convenience and exposure management purposes. Since all industrial nations and most LDCs have well-developed commercial banking systems, firms desiring local financing generally turn there first. The major forms of bank financing include overdrafts, discounting, and term loans. Nonbank sources of funds include commercial paper and factoring.

Bank Loans. Loans from commercial banks are the dominant form of short-term interest-bearing financing used around the world. These loans are described as *self-liquidating* because they are usually used to finance temporary increases in accounts receivable and inventory. These increases in working capital are soon converted into cash, which is used to repay the loan.

Short-term bank credits are typically unsecured. The borrower signs a note evidencing its obligation to repay the loan when it is due, along with accrued interest. Most notes are payable in 90 days; the loans must, therefore, be repaid or renewed every 90 days. The need to periodically roll over bank loans gives a bank substantial control over the use of its funds, reducing the need to impose severe restrictions on the firm. To further ensure that short-term credits are not being used for permanent financing, a bank will usually insert a *cleanup clause* requiring the company to be completely out of debt to the bank for a period of at least 30 days during the year.

Forms of Bank Credit. Bank credit provides a highly flexible form of financing because it is readily expandable and, therefore, serves as a financial reserve. Whenever the firm needs extra short-term funds that can't be met by trade credit, it is likely to turn first to bank credit. Unsecured bank loans may be extended under a line of credit, under a revolving-credit arrangement, or on a transaction basis. Bank loans can be originated either in the domestic or Eurodollar market.

1. *Term loans.* Term loans are straight loans, often unsecured, that are made for a fixed period of time, usually 90 days. They are attractive because they give corporate treasurers complete control over the timing of repayments. A term loan is typically made for a specific purpose with specific conditions and is repaid in a single lump sum. The loan provisions are contained in the promissory note that is signed by the customer. This type of loan is used most often by borrowers who have an infrequent need for bank credit.

2. *Line of credit.* Arranging separate loans for frequent borrowers is a relatively expensive means of doing business. One way to reduce these transaction costs is to use a line of credit. This informal agreement permits the company to borrow up to a stated maximum amount from the bank. The firm can draw down its line of credit when it requires funds and pay back the loan balance when it has excess cash. Although the bank is not legally obligated to honor the line-of-credit agreement, it almost always does unless it or the firm encounters financial difficulties. A line of credit is usually good for one year, with renewals renegotiated every year.

3. *Overdrafts.* In countries other than the United States, banks tend to lend through overdrafts. An overdraft is simply a line of credit against which drafts (checks) can be drawn (written) up to a specified maximum amount. These overdraft lines are often extended and expanded year after year, thus providing, in effect, a form of medium-term financing. The borrower pays interest on the debit balance only.

4. *Revolving credit agreement.* A revolving credit agreement is similar to a line of credit except that now the bank (or syndicate of banks) is *legally committed* to extend credit up to the stated maximum. The firm pays interest on its outstanding borrowings plus a commitment fee, ranging between 0.125% and 0.5% per annum, on the *unused* portion of the credit line. Revolving credit agreements are usually renegotiated every two or three years.

The danger that short-term credits are being used to fund long-term requirements is particularly acute with a revolving credit line that is continuously renewed. Inserting an out-of-debt period under a cleanup clause validates the temporary need for funds.

5. *Discounting.* The discounting of trade bills is the preferred short-term financing technique in many European countries—especially in France, Italy, Belgium, and, to a lesser extent, Germany. It is also widespread in Latin America, particularly in Argentina, Brazil, and Mexico. These bills often can be rediscounted with the central bank.

Discounting usually results from the following set of transactions. A manufacturer selling goods to a retailer on credit draws a bill on the buyer, payable in, say, 30 days. The buyer endorses (accepts) the bill or gets his or her bank to accept it, at which point it becomes a *banker's acceptance*. The manufacturer then takes the bill to his or her bank, and the bank accepts it for a fee if the buyer's bank has not already accepted it. The bill is then sold at a discount to the manufacturer's bank or to a money market dealer. The rate of interest varies with the term of the bill and the general level of local money market interest rates.

The popularity of discounting in European countries stems from the fact that according to European commercial law, which is based on the Code Napoleon, the claim of the bill holder is independent of the claim represented by the underlying transaction. (For example, the bill holder must be paid even if the buyer objects to the quality of the merchandise.) This right makes the bill easily negotiable and enhances its liquidity (or tradability), thereby lowering the cost of discounting relative to other forms of credit.

Interest Rates on Bank Loans. The interest rate on bank loans is based on personal negotiation between the banker and the borrower. The loan rate charged to a specific customer reflects that customer's creditworthiness, previous relationship with the bank, the maturity of the loan, and other factors. Ultimately, of course, bank interest rates are based on the same factors as the interest rates on the financial securities issued by a borrower: the risk-free return, which reflects the time value of money, plus a risk premium based on the borrower's credit risk. However, there are certain bank loan pricing conventions that you should be familiar with.

Interest on a loan can be paid at maturity or in advance. Each payment method gives a different effective interest rate, even if the quoted rate is the same. The *effective interest rate* is defined as follows:

$$\text{Effective interest rate} = \frac{\text{Annual interest paid}}{\text{Funds received}}$$

Suppose you borrow $10,000 for one year at 11% interest. If the interest is paid at maturity, you owe the lender $11,100 at the end of the year. This payment method yields an effective interest rate of 11%, the same as the stated interest rate:

$$\frac{\text{Effective interest rate when}}{\text{interest is paid at maturity}} = \frac{\$1,100}{\$10,000} = 11\%$$

If the loan is quoted on a *discount* basis, the bank deducts the interest in advance. On the $10,000 loan, you will receive only $8,900 and must repay $10,000 in one year. The effective rate of interest exceeds 11% because you are paying interest on $10,000, but only have the use of $8,900:

$$\frac{\text{Effective interest rate}}{\text{on discounted loan}} = \frac{\$1,100}{\$8,900} = 12.36\%$$

An extreme illustration of the difference in the effective interest rate between paying interest at maturity and paying interest in advance is provided by the Mexican banking system. In 1985, the nominal interest rate on a peso bank loan was 70%, about 15 percentage points higher than the inflation rate. But high as it was, the nominal figure didn't tell the whole story. By collecting interest in advance, Mexican banks boosted the effective rate dramatically. Consider, for example, the cost of a Ps 10,000 loan. By collecting interest of 70%, or Ps 7,000, in advance, the bank actually loaned out only Ps 3,000 and received Ps 10,000 at maturity. The effective interest rate on the loan is 233%:

$$\frac{\text{Effective interest rate}}{\text{on Mexican loan}} = \frac{\text{Ps } 7,000}{\text{Ps } 3,000} = 233\%$$

Compensating Balances.   Many banks require borrowers to hold from 10% to 20% of their outstanding loan balance on deposit in a noninterest-bearing account. These compensating balance requirements raise the effective cost of a bank credit since not all of the loan is available to the firm:

$$\text{Effective interest rate with compensating balance requirement} = \frac{\text{Annual interest paid}}{\text{Usable funds}}$$

Usable funds equal the net amount of the loan less the compensating balance requirement.

Returning to the previous example, suppose you borrow $10,000 at 11% interest paid at maturity, and the compensating balance requirement is 15%, or $1,500. Thus, the $10,000 loan provides only $8,500 in usable funds for an effective interest rate of 12.9%:

$$\text{Effective interest rate when interest is paid at maturity} = \frac{\$1,100}{\$8,500} = 12.9\%$$

If the interest is prepaid, the amount of usable funds declines by a further $1,100—that is, to $7,400—and the effective interest rate rises to 14.9%:

$$\text{Effective interest rate on discounted loan} = \frac{\$1,100}{\$7,400} = 14.9\%$$

In both instances, the compensating balance requirement raises the effective interest rate above the stated interest rate. This higher rate is the case even if the bank pays interest on the compensating balance deposit because the loan rate invariably exceeds the deposit rate.

Commercial Paper.   One alternative to borrowing short term from a bank is to issue commercial paper. *Commercial paper* (CP) is a short-term unsecured promissory note that is generally sold by large corporations on a discount basis to institutional investors and to other corporations. Because commercial paper is unsecured and bears only the name of the issuer, the market has generally been dominated by the largest and most creditworthy companies.

Commercial paper is one of the most-favored short-term nonbank financing methods for MNCs. But CP markets are not all alike. Perhaps the most telling difference is the depth and popularity of CP markets, as best measured by the amount outstanding. The United States dwarfs all other national markets. In September 1987, U.S. commercial paper outstanding was $350 billion. By contrast, CP outstanding in the Netherlands was only about $300 million.

Available maturities are fairly standard across the spectrum, but average maturities—reflecting the terms companies actually use—vary from 20–25 days in the United States to over three months in the Netherlands. The minimum denomination of paper also varies widely: In Australia, Canada, Sweden, and the United States, firms can issue CP in much smaller amounts than in other markets. In most countries, the instrument is issued at a discount, with the full face value of the note redeemed upon maturity. In other markets, however, interest-bearing instruments are also offered.

By going directly to the market rather than relying on a financial intermediary such as a bank, large, well-known corporations can save substantial interest costs, often on the order of 1% or more. In addition, because commercial paper is sold directly to large institutions, U.S. CP is exempt from SEC registration requirements. This exemption reduces the time and expense of readying an issue of commercial paper for sales.

There are three major noninterest costs associated with using commercial paper as a source of short-term funds: (1) back-up lines of credit, (2) fees to commercial banks, and (3) rating service fees. In most cases, issuers back their paper 100% with lines of credit from commercial banks. Because its average maturity is very short, commercial paper poses the risk that an issuer might not be able to pay off or roll over maturing paper. Consequently, issuers use back-up lines as insurance against periods of financial stress or tight money, when lenders ration money directly rather than raise interest rates. For example, the market for Texaco paper, which provided the bulk of its short-term financing, disappeared following the $11.1 billion judgment against it. Texaco replaced these funds by drawing on its bank lines of credit.

Back-up lines are usually paid for through compensating balances, typically about 10% of the unused portion of the credit line plus 20% of the amount of credit actually used. As an alternative to compensating balances, issuers sometimes pay straight fees ranging from 0.375% to 0.75% of the line of credit; this explicit pricing procedure has been used increasingly in recent years.

Another cost associated with issuing commercial paper is fees paid to the large commercial banks that act as issuing and paying agents for the paper issuers and handle all the associated paper work. Finally, rating services charge fees ranging from $5,000 to $25,000 per year for ratings, depending on the rating service. Credit ratings are not legally required by any nation, but they are often essential for placing paper.

Euronotes and Euro-Commercial Paper

A recent innovation in nonbank short-term credits that bears a strong resemblance to commercial paper is the so-called Euronote. *Euronotes* are short-term notes usually denominated in dollars and issued by corporations and governments. The prefix "Euro" indicates that the notes are issued outside the country in whose currency they are denominated. The interest rates are adjusted each time the notes are rolled over. Euronotes are often called *Euro-commercial paper* (Euro-CP, for short). Typically, though, the name Euro-CP is reserved for those Euronotes that are not underwritten.

There are some differences between the U.S. commercial paper and the Euro-CP markets. For one thing, the average maturity of Euro-CP is about twice as long as the average maturity of U.S. CP. Also, Euro-CP is actively traded in a secondary market, but most U.S. CP is held to maturity by the original investors. Central banks, commercial banks, and corporations are important parts of the investor base for particular segments of the Euro-CP market; the most important holders of U.S. CP are money market funds, which are not very important in the Euro-CP market. In addition, the distribution of U.S. issuers in the Euro-CP market is of significantly lower quality than the distribution of U.S. issuers in the U.S.-CP market. An explanation of this finding may lie in the importance of banks as buyers of less-than-prime paper in the Euro-CP market.

Another important difference in practice between the two markets is in the area of ratings. Only about 45% of active Euro-CP issuers at year-end 1986 were rated. Credit ratings in the United States, on the other hand, are ubiquitous. This difference may prove transitory, however, as investors become accustomed to the concept and the rating agencies facilitate the use of their services. For example, Standard and Poor's Corporation charges an entity with a U.S. rating only $5,000 on top of the $25,000 annual U.S. fee for a Euro-CP rating. Moody's has gone a step further by making its CP ratings global paper ratings that are applicable in any market or currency.

■ 12.4 ■
CALCULATING THE DOLLAR COSTS OF ALTERNATIVE FINANCING OPTIONS

This section presents explicit formulas to compute the effective dollar costs of a local currency loan and a dollar loan for both the no-tax and tax cases.[2] These cost formulas can be used to calculate the least expensive financing source for each future exchange rate. A computer can easily perform this analysis—called *break-even analysis*—and determine the range of future exchange rates within which each particular financing option is cheapest.

With this break-even analysis, the treasurer can readily see the amount of currency appreciation or depreciation necessary to make one type of borrowing less expensive than another. The treasurer will then compare the firm's actual forecast of currency change, determined objectively or subjectively, with this benchmark.

The logic of this break-even analysis can be extended to financing alternatives other than the two that are presented in this section. In all situations, the cost of each source of funds must be calculated in terms of the relevant parameters (for example, nominal interest rate, tax rate, and future exchange rate) and the expense compared with that of all other possibilities. These calculations and comparisons will differ little from those that are performed here.

Suppose that Du Pont's Brazilian affiliate requires funds to finance its working capital needs for one year. It can borrow cruzeiros at 45% or dollars at 11%. To determine an appropriate borrowing strategy, this section will first develop explicit cost expressions for each of these loans using the numbers given above. These expressions will then be generalized to obtain analytical cost formulas that are usable under a variety of circumstances.

Case 1: No Taxes

In the absence of taxes and forward contracts, costing these loans is relatively straightforward.

---

[2]This section draws on material in Alan C. Shapiro, "Evaluating Financing Costs for Multinational Subsidiaries," *Journal of International Business Studies,* Fall 1975, pp. 25–32.

1. *Local currency loan.* Suppose the current exchange rate e_0 ($\$e_0$ = Cr\$1) is Cr\$1 = $\$0.0025 = 1/400$, or Cr\$400 = \$1. Then, the cruzeiro cost of repaying the principal plus interest (45%) at the end of one year on one dollar's worth of cruzeiros is $400(1.45) = $Cr\$580. The dollar cost is $400(1.45)e_1$, where e_1 is the (unknown) ending exchange rate. Subtracting the dollar principal yields an effective dollar cost of $400(1.45)e_1 - 1$. For example, if the ending exchange rate is \$0.002 (or Cr\$500 = \$1), then the cost per dollar borrowed equals

$$(400)(1.45)(0.002) - 1 = 0.16 \text{ or } 16\%$$

A simpler expression for the borrowing cost can be found by substituting $1/e_0$ for 400, yielding $1.45(e_1/e_0) - 1$. This expression equals $0.45(1 - d) - d$, where d is the (unknown) cruzeiro devaluation and is defined as $d = (e_0 - e_1)/e_0$. Thus, the effective dollar interest rate on borrowed cruzeiros equals $0.45(1 - d) - d$. In general, the dollar (HC) cost of borrowing local currency at an interest rate of r_L and a currency change of d is the sum of the dollar interest cost less the exchange gain (loss) on repaying the principal:

$$\frac{\text{Dollar cost}}{\text{of LC loan}} = \text{Interest cost} - \text{Exchange gain (loss)}$$
$$= r_L(1 - d) - d \tag{12.1}$$

The first term in Equation 12.1 is the dollar interest cost (paid at year end after an LC devaluation of d); the second term is the exchange gain or loss involved in repaying an LC loan valued at \$1 at the beginning of the year with local currency worth $(1 - d)$ dollars at year end. As before, $d = (e_0 - e_1)/e_0$, where e_0 and e_1 are the beginning and ending exchange rates (LC 1 = $\$e$).

2. *Dollar loan.* The Brazilian affiliate can borrow dollars at 11%. In general, the cost of a dollar (HC) loan to the affiliate is the interest rate on the dollar (HC) loan r_H.

Analysis.   The cruzeiro loan costs $0.45(1 - d) - d$, and the dollar loan costs 11%. To find the break-even rate of currency depreciation at which the dollar cost of cruzeiro borrowing is just equal to the cost of dollar financing, equate the two costs and solve for d:

$$0.45(1 - d) - d = 0.11$$

or

$$d = (0.45 - 0.11)/1.45 = 0.234$$

In other words, the Brazilian cruzeiro must devalue by 23.4%, to Cr\$522 = \$1, before it is less expensive to borrow cruzeiros at 45% than dollars at 11%. Ignoring the factor of exchange risk, the borrowing decision rule is as follows:

If $d < 23.4\%$, borrow dollars
If $d > 23.4\%$, borrow cruzeiros

Each of these cost formulas can be represented as a straight line with a positive intercept (equal to the effective interest rate when $d = 0$) and a negative (or zero) slope equal to the coefficient of the d term. The points at which these lines intersect (unless they are parallel) provide the break-even values of d. These straight-line equations are plotted in Exhibit 12.1. A cruzeiro devaluation of 31% will yield an effective interest rate of zero on the cruzeiro loan.

In the general case, the break-even rate of currency change is found by equating the dollar costs of dollar and local currency financing:

$$r_H = r_L(1 - d) - d \tag{12.2}$$

The solution to Equation 12.2 is

$$d* = \frac{r_L - r_H}{1 + r_L} \tag{12.3}$$

If the international Fisher effect holds, then we saw in Chapter 7 (Equation 7.6) that $d*$ also equals the expected LC devaluation (revaluation); that is, the expected cruzeiro devaluation should equal 23.4% unless there is reason to believe that some form of market imperfection is not permitting interest rates to adjust to reflect anticipated currency changes.

Case 2: Taxes

Taxes complicate the calculating of various loan costs. Suppose the effective tax rate on the earnings of Du Pont's Brazilian affiliate is 40%.

■ **EXHIBIT 12.1**   Loan Cost Comparisons: No Taxes

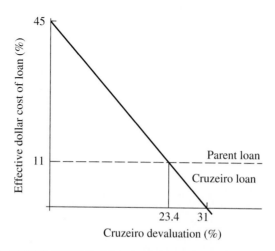

1. *Local currency loan.* The interest expense on one dollar's worth of cruzeiros is 0.45 $\times 400 = $ Cr\$180. After Brazilian tax, this cost is $180 \times (1 - 0.40) = $ Cr\$108. The total after-tax cruzeiro cost of repaying the loan plus interest equals Cr\$508 (the principal amount of Cr\$400 plus the after-tax interest expense of Cr\$108). The dollar cost equals $508e_1$. Subtracting the dollar principal produces the after-tax dollar cost of $508e_1 - 1$. This cost can be separated into two terms:

$$0.45 \times \frac{e_1}{e_0} \times 0.6 + \frac{e_1}{e_0} - 1$$

Substituting d for $(e_0 - e_1)/e_0$ yields

$$0.45(1 - d)0.6 - d = 0.27(1 - d) - d$$

The first term is the after-tax dollar interest cost of the cruzeiro interest expense, and the second term is the gain from the reduced dollar cost of repaying the cruzeiro principal.

In general, the after-tax dollar cost of borrowing in the local currency for a foreign affiliate equals the after-tax interest expense less the exchange gain (loss) on principal repayment, or

$$\frac{\text{After-tax dollar}}{\text{cost of LC loan}} = \text{Interest cost} - \text{Exchange gain (loss)}$$

$$= r_L(1 - d)(1 - t_a) - d \qquad\qquad\qquad \textbf{(12.4)}$$

where t_a is the affiliate's marginal tax rate. The first term in Equation 12.4 is the after-tax dollar interest cost paid at year end after an LC devaluation (revaluation) of d; the second is the exchange gain or loss in dollars of repaying a local currency loan valued at one dollar with local currency worth $(1 - d)$ dollars at the end of the year. The gain or loss has no tax effect for the affiliate because the same amount of local currency was borrowed and repaid.

2. *Dollar loan.* The after-tax cost of a dollar loan equals the Brazilian affiliate's after-tax interest expense, $0.11(1 - 0.4)$, minus the dollar value to the Brazilian affiliate of the tax write-off on the increased number of cruzeiros necessary to repay the dollar principal following a cruzeiro devaluation, $0.4d$. This latter term is calculated in the following way: The dollar loan is converted to $1/e_0$ cruzeiros, or Cr\$400. The number of cruzeiros needed to repay this principal equals $1/e_1$ or an increase of

$$\frac{1}{e_1} - 400 = \frac{1}{e_1} - \frac{1}{e_0}$$

This extra expense is tax-deductible. The cruzeiro value of this tax deduction is $0.40(1/e_1 - 1/e_0)$, with a dollar value equal to $0.4(1/e_1 - 1/e_0)e_1$, or $0.4d$. Adding these two components yields a cost of dollar financing equal to

$$0.11(1 - 0.4) - 0.4d = 0.066 - 0.4d$$

We can generalize this analysis as follows: The total cost of the dollar loan is the after-tax interest expense less the tax write-off associated with the dollar principal repayment, or

$$\frac{\text{After-tax cost}}{\text{of dollar loan}} = \frac{\text{Interest cost}}{\text{to subsidiary}} - \text{Tax gain (loss)}$$
$$= r_H(1 - t_a) - dt_a \qquad\qquad\qquad\qquad\qquad \textbf{(12.5)}$$

The only change from the no-tax case, other than using after-tax instead of before-tax interest rates, is the addition of the second term, dt_a. This term equals the dollar value of the tax write-off (cost) associated with the increased (decreased) amount of local currency required to repay the dollar principal following an LC depreciation (appreciation).

Similarly, an LC revaluation will lead to a foreign exchange gain that is taxable, resulting in an increase in taxes equaling dt_a dollars. Hence, due to the tax effects, an LC devaluation will decrease the total cost of the dollar (HC) loan, and an LC revaluation will increase it.

Analysis.   As in case 1, we will set the cost of dollar financing, $0.066 - 0.4d$, equal to the cost of local currency financing, $0.27(1 - d) - d$, in order to find the break-even rate of cruzeiro depreciation necessary to leave the firm indifferent between borrowing in dollars or cruzeiros.

The break-even value of d occurs when

$$0.066 - 0.4d = 0.27(1 - d) - d$$

or

$$d = 0.234$$

Thus, the cruzeiro must devalue by 23.4% to Cr\$522 = \$1 before it is cheaper to borrow cruzeiros at 45% than dollars at 11%. This is the same break-even exchange rate as in the before-tax case. Although taxes affect the after-tax costs of the dollar and LC loans, they don't affect the relative desirability of the two loans. That is, if one loan has a lower cost before tax, it will also be less costly on an after-tax basis.

As in the no-tax case, effective dollar interest rates can be graphically illustrated as a function of alternative rates of cruzeiro devaluation. The intersection of the lines in Exhibit 12.2 provides the break-even values of cruzeiro devaluation—that is, the devaluation percentages at which the firm would just be indifferent between one form of financing and another. Surprisingly, perhaps the most visible effect of taxes is the negative after-tax costs of the two loans at the break-even rate of currency depreciation.[3] In contrast, the interest rate of 11% at the break-even level of cruzeiro depreciation in the no-tax case is highly positive.

In general, the break-even rate of currency appreciation or depreciation can be found by equating the dollar costs of local currency and dollar financing and solving for d:

---

[3]The negative after-tax loan costs here are analogous to the negative real after-tax interest expenses often encountered during periods of high inflation.

■ **EXHIBIT 12.2**   Loan Cost Comparisons: Taxes

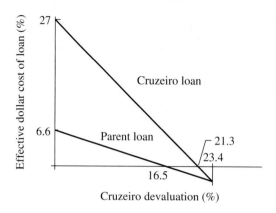

$$r_H(1 - t_a) - dt_a = r_L(1 - d)(1 - t_a) - d$$

or

$$d^* = \frac{r_L(1 - t_a) - r_H(1 - t_a)}{(1 + r_L)(1 - t_a)} = \frac{r_L - r_H}{1 + r_L} \qquad (12.6)$$

The tax rates cancel out and we are left with the same break-even value for d as in the before-tax case (see Equation 12.3). This result is the same as in the case of Du Pont's Brazilian affiliate and demonstrates that the earlier result was not a fluke.

■ 12.5 ■
BORROWING STRATEGY AND EXCHANGE RISK MANAGEMENT

This section provides a simple illustration of the interaction between financing choice and exchange risk management.[4] Assume that Du Pont's Brazilian affiliate is going to invest the funds it borrows in a project that pays a relatively certain return of 50% annually in cruzeiros.

Du Pont is concerned not only with its expected dollar profits from the investment but also with the effects of its loan choice on the project's exchange risk. It is assumed here that there are no taxes and that forward contracts are unavailable. If I is the local currency (cruzeiro) value of the investment, s is the percentage LC return on the investment, and σ refers to a standard deviation, then we can derive several important equations.

---

[4]This section is based on material in Lessard, "Currency and Tax Considerations in International Financing."

Operating Profit on Investment. The dollar profit, π, equals the difference between dollar revenue and dollar cost, or

$$\pi = I(1 + s)e_1 - Ie_0$$

with a standard deviation for these profits of

$$\sigma(\pi) = I(1 + s)\sigma(e_1)$$

Cost of Dollar Financing. Using the dollar loan as an example, we have already seen that the cost (C_H) of dollar financing is

$$C_H = Ie_0 r_H$$

with a standard deviation of

$$\sigma(C_H) = 0$$

Cost of Local Currency Financing. The dollar cost of local currency financing, C_L, is

$$C_L = Ie_1(1 + r_L) - Ie_0$$

with a standard deviation of

$$\sigma(C_L) = I(1 + r_L)\sigma(e_1)$$

Profits Net of Financing Costs. By subtracting financing costs from the operating profit, net home currency profits can be computed if financing is done in home currency (π_H) or local currency (π_L):

$$\pi_H = [I(1 + s)e_1 - Ie_0] - Ie_0 r_H = I[(1 + s)e_1 - (1 + r_H)e_0]$$

with a standard deviation of

$$\sigma(\pi_H) = I(1 + s)\sigma(e_1)$$

and

$$\pi_L = [I(1 + s)e_1 - Ie_0] - [I(1 + r_L)e_1 - Ie_0] = I(s - r_L)e_1$$

with a standard deviation of

$$\sigma(\pi_L) = I(s - r_L)\,\sigma(e_1)$$

We saw that if Du Pont is concerned solely with minimizing expected cost, it will borrow cruzeiros only if the cruzeiro is anticipated to devalue by more than 23.4%. If risk is an important consideration, however, then cruzeiro financing becomes relatively more attractive at any given exchange rate. The standard deviation of net profits with cruzeiro financing, $I(s - r_L)\sigma(e_1)$, is much smaller than the standard deviation with dollar (HC) financing, $I(1 + s)\sigma(e_1)$, because variation in dollar profits due to currency fluctuations is offset by equal variation in dollar financing costs. The difference in standard deviations of net profit between dollar and LC financing is

$$\sigma(\pi_H) - \sigma(\pi_L) = I(1 + r_L)\sigma(e_1) > 0$$

Assuming that $I = $ Cr\$400 million = \$1 million at the current exchange rate of $e_0 = \$0.0025$, with $\sigma(e_1) = 0.02275$ and $r_L = 0.45$, then

$$\sigma(\pi_H) = \$136,500$$

and

$$\sigma(\pi_L) = \$4,550$$

If the expected value of e_1 is 0.001915 (i.e., an expected devaluation of 23.4%, just large enough for the international Fisher effect to hold), then expected dollar profit in either case equals \$38,300. It seems obvious that, in this case at least, most firms would prefer to use cruzeiro financing even if they expected a cruzeiro devaluation of somewhat less than 23.4%. In fact, given the large downside risk with dollar financing and the relatively slender profit margin, it is unlikely that most firms would even consider this investment unless it could be financed with borrowed cruzeiros.

■ 12.6 ■
SUMMARY AND CONCLUSIONS

This chapter has examined the various short-term financing alternatives available to a firm, focusing on parent company loans, local currency bank loans, and commercial paper. We saw how factors such as relative interest rates, anticipated currency changes, tax rates, the existence of forward contracts, and economic exposure combine to affect a firm's short-term borrowing choices. Various objectives that a firm might use to arrive at its borrowing strategy were evaluated. It was concluded that if forward contracts exist, the only valid objective is to minimize covered after-tax interest costs. In the absence of forward contracts, firms can either attempt to minimize expected costs or establish some trade-off between reducing expected costs and reducing the degree of cash-flow exposure. The latter goal involves offsetting operating cash inflows in a currency with financing cash outflows in that same currency.

This chapter also developed formulas to compute effective dollar costs of loans denominated in dollars (home currency) or local currency in the presence and absence of taxes. These formulas were then used to calculate the break-even rates of currency appreciation or depreciation that would equalize the costs of borrowing in the local currency or in the home currency.

■ QUESTIONS ■

1. Comment on the following statement: "One should borrow in those currencies expected to depreciate and invest in those expected to appreciate."

2. How can taxes affect the choice of currency denomination for loans?

3. How can the choice of currency denomination of loans enable a firm to reduce its exchange risk?

4. What are the three basic types of bank loans? Describe their differences.

5. How does each of the following affect the relationship of stated and effective interest rates?

   a. The lending bank requires the borrower to repay principal and interest at the end of the borrowing period only.

   b. The lending bank requires the borrower to maintain a compensating balance.

   c. Interest is deducted from the amount borrowed before the borrower receives the proceeds.

   d. What is the likely ranking of the above from least to most expensive?

6. Explain the characteristics of commercial paper that tend to limit its use to financially sound firms.

■ PROBLEMS ■

1. Apex Supplies borrows FF 1 million at 12%, payable in one year. If Apex is required to maintain a compensating balance of 20%, what is the effective percentage cost of its loan (in FF)?

2. The Olivera Corp., a manufacturer of olive oil products, needs to acquire Lit 100 million in funds today to expand a pimento-stuffing facility. Banca di Roma has offered them a choice of an 11% loan payable at maturity or a 10% loan on a discount basis. Which loan should Olivera choose?

3. To finance production of its new F-16 bubble gum, Hong Kong-based Top Gum Co. has been offered a one-year loan of HK$1.25 million at 9% payable at maturity with a 10% compensating balance.

   a. What is the effective interest rate on this loan (in HK$)?

   b. If the compensating balance requirement is 20%, what will be the effective interest rate?

   c. If the compensating balance is 10%, but the loan is on a discount basis, what will be the effective interest rate?

   d. If the company requires HK$1.25 million, how much must it borrow in part c to receive this amount?

4. If Consolidated Corp. issues a Eurobond denominated in yen, the 7% interest rate on the $1-million, one-year borrowing will be 2% less than rates in the United States. However, ConCorp would have to pay back the principal and interest in Japanese yen. Currently, the exchange rate is ¥183 = $1. By how much could the yen rise against the dollar before the Euroyen bond would lose its advantage to ConCorp?

5. Although the one-year interest rate is 10% in the United States, one-year, yen-denominated corporate bonds in Japan yield only 5%.

   a. Does this present a riskless opportunity to raise capital at low yen interest rates?

   b. Suppose the current exchange rate is ¥140 = $1. What is the lowest future exchange rate at which borrowing yen would be no more expensive than borrowing U.S. dollars?

6. Ford can borrow dollars at 12% or pesos at 80% for one year. The peso:dollar exchange rate is expected to move from $1 = Ps 3300 currently to $1 = Ps 4500 by year's end.

   a. What is the expected after-tax dollar cost of borrowing dollars for one year if the Mexican corporate tax rate is 53%?

   b. What is Ford's expected after-tax dollar cost of borrowing pesos for one year?

   c. At what end-of-year exchange rate will the after-tax peso cost of borrowing dollars equal the after-tax peso cost of borrowing pesos?

7. The manager of an English subsidiary of a U.S. firm is trying to decide whether to borrow, for one year, dollars at 7.8% or pounds sterling at 12%. If the current value of the pound is $1.70, at what end-of-year exchange rate would the firm be indifferent now between borrowing dollars and pounds?

8. Suppose that a firm located in Belgium can borrow dollars at 8% or Belgian francs at 14%.

   a. If the Belgian franc is expected to depreciate from BF 58 = $1 at the beginning of the year to BF 61 = $1 at the end of the year, what is the expected before-tax dollar cost of the Belgian franc loan?

   b. If the Belgian corporate tax rate is 42%, what is the expected after-tax dollar cost of borrowing dollars, assuming the same currency change scenario?

   c. Given the expected exchange rate change, which currency yields the lower expected after-tax dollar cost?

BIBLIOGRAPHY

Financing Foreign Operations. New York: Business International Corporation, various issues.

Lessard, Donald R. "Currency and Tax Considerations in International Financing." Teaching Note No. 3, Massachusetts Institute of Technology, Spring 1979.

Shapiro, Alan C. "Evaluating Financing Costs for Multinational Subsidiaries." *Journal of International Business Studies,* Fall 1975, pp. 25–32.

———. Chapter 29 in *Modern Corporate Finance.* New York: Macmillan, 1990.

◣ 13 ◢

Financing Foreign Trade

The development of a new product is a three-step process: first, a U.S. firm announces an invention; second, the Russians claim they made the same discovery 20 years ago; third, the Japanese start exporting it.

—Anonymous—

■ Most multinational corporations are heavily involved in foreign trade in addition to their other international activities. The financing of trade-related working capital requires large amounts of money, as well as financial services such as letters of credit and acceptances. It is vital, therefore, that the multinational financial executive have knowledge of the institutions and documentary procedures that have evolved over the centuries to facilitate the international movement of goods. Much of the material in this chapter is descriptive in nature, but interspersed throughout will be discussions of the role of these special financial techniques and their associated advantages and disadvantages.

The main purpose of this chapter is to describe and analyze the various payment terms possible in international trade, along with the necessary documentation associated with each procedure. It also examines the different methods and sources of export financing and credit insurance that are available from the public sector. The final section discusses the rise of countertrade, a sophisticated word for barter.

■ 13.1 ■
PAYMENT TERMS IN INTERNATIONAL TRADE

Every shipment abroad requires some kind of financing while in transit. The exporter also needs financing to buy or manufacture its goods. Similarly, the importer has to carry these goods in inventory until the goods are sold. Then, it must finance its customers' receivables.

A financially strong exporter can finance the entire trade cycle out of its own funds by extending credit until the importer has converted these goods into cash. Alternatively, the importer can finance the entire cycle by paying cash in advance. Usually, however, some in-between approach is chosen, involving a combination of financing by the exporter, the importer, and one or more financial intermediaries.

The five principal means of payment in international trade, ranked in terms of increasing risk to the exporter, are

- Cash in advance
- Letter of credit
- Draft
- Consignment
- Open account

As a general rule, the greater the protection afforded the exporter, the less convenient are the payment terms for the buyer (importer). Some of these methods, however, are designed to protect both parties against commercial and/or political risks. It is up to the exporter when choosing among these payment methods to weigh the benefits in risk reduction against the cost of lost sales.

The five basic means of payment are discussed in the following paragraphs.

Cash in Advance

Cash in advance affords the exporter the greatest protection because payment is received either before shipment or upon arrival of the goods. This method also allows the exporter to avoid tying up its own funds. Although less common than in the past, cash payment upon presentation of documents is still widespread.

Cash terms are used where there is political instability in the importing country or where the buyer's credit is doubtful. Political crises or exchange controls in the purchaser's country may cause payment delays or even prevent fund transfers, leading to a demand for cash in advance. In addition, where goods are made to order, prepayment is usually demanded, both to finance production and to reduce marketing risks.

Letter of Credit

Importers will often balk at paying cash in advance, however, and will demand credit terms instead. When credit is extended, the *letter of credit* (L/C) offers the exporter the greatest degree of safety.

If the importer is not well known to the exporter or if exchange restrictions exist or are possible in the importer's country, the exporter selling on credit may wish to have the importer's promise of payment backed by a foreign or domestic bank. On the other hand, the importer may not wish to pay the exporter until it is reasonably certain that the merchandise has been shipped in good condition. A letter of credit satisfies both of these conditions.

In essence, the letter of credit is a letter addressed to the seller, written and signed by a bank acting on behalf of the buyer. In the letter, the bank promises it will honor drafts drawn on itself if the seller conforms to the specific conditions set forth in the L/C. (The draft, which is a written order to pay, is discussed in the next part of this section.) Through an L/C, the bank substitutes its own commitment to pay for that of its customer (the importer). The letter of credit, therefore, becomes a financial contract between the issuing bank and a designated beneficiary that is separate from the commercial transaction.

The advantages to the exporter are as follows:

1. Most important, an L/C eliminates credit risk if the bank that opens it is of undoubted standing. Therefore, the firm need check only on the credit reputation of the issuing bank.

2. An L/C also reduces the danger that payment will be delayed or withheld due to exchange controls or other political acts. Countries generally permit local banks to honor their letters of credit. Failure to honor them could severely damage the country's credit standing and credibility.

3. An L/C reduces uncertainty. The exporter knows all the requirements for payment because they are clearly stipulated on the L/C.

4. The L/C can also guard against preshipment risks. The exporter who manufactures under contract a specialized piece of equipment runs the risk of contract cancellation before shipment. Opening a letter of credit will provide protection during the manufacturing phase.

5. Last, and certainly not least, the L/C facilitates financing because it ensures the exporter a ready buyer for its product. It also becomes especially easy to create a banker's acceptance—a draft accepted by a bank.

Most advantages of an L/C are realized by the seller; nevertheless, there are some advantages to the buyer as well.

1. Because payment is only in compliance with the L/C's stipulated conditions, the importer is able to ascertain that the merchandise is actually shipped on, or before, a certain date by requiring an on-board bill of lading. The importer can also require an inspection certificate.

2. Any documents required are carefully inspected by clerks with years of experience. Moreover, the bank bears responsibility for any oversight.

3. Because an L/C is about as good as cash in advance, the importer can usually command better credit terms and/or prices.

4. Some exporters will sell only on a letter of credit. Willingness to provide one expands a firm's sources of supply.

5. L/C financing may be cheaper than the alternatives. There is no tie-up of cash if the L/C substitutes for cash in advance.

6. If prepayment is required, the importer is better off depositing its money with a bank than with the seller because it is then easier to recover the deposit if the seller is unable or unwilling to make a proper shipment.

The mechanics of letter-of-credit financing are quite simple. To illustrate its application, consider the case of U.S.A. Importers, Inc., of Los Angeles. The company is buying spare auto parts worth $38,000 from Japan Exporters, Inc., of Tokyo, Japan. U.S.A. Importers applies for, and receives, a letter of credit for $38,000 from its bank, Wells Fargo. The actual L/C is shown in Exhibit 13.1. Exhibit 13.2, in turn, shows the relationships between the three parties to the letter of credit.

After Japan Exporters has shipped the goods, it draws a draft against the issuing bank (Wells Fargo) and presents it, along with the required documents, to its own bank, the Bank of Tokyo. The Bank of Tokyo, in turn, forwards the bank draft and attached documents to Wells Fargo; Wells Fargo pays the draft upon receiving evidence that all conditions set forth in the L/C have been met. Exhibit 13.3 details the sequence of steps in the L/C transaction.

Most L/Cs issued in connection with commercial transactions are *documentary*—that is, the seller must submit, together with the draft, any necessary invoices and the like. The documents required from Japan Exporters are listed on the face of the letter of credit in Exhibit 13.1 following the words "accompanied by the following documents." A *nondocumentary,* or *clean,* L/C is normally used in other than commercial transactions.

The letter of credit can be revocable or irrevocable. A *revocable L/C* is a means of arranging payment, but it does not carry a guarantee. It can be revoked, without notice, at any time up to the time a draft is presented to the issuing bank. An *irrevocable L/C,* on the other hand, cannot be revoked without the specific permission of all parties concerned, including the exporter. Most credits between unrelated parties are irrevocable; otherwise, the advantage of commitment to pay is lost. In the case of Japan Exporters, the L/C is irrevocable.

Although the essential character of a letter of credit—the substitution of the bank's name for the merchant's—is absent with a revocable credit, this type of L/C is useful in some respects. Just the fact that a bank is willing to open a letter of credit for the importer gives an indication of the customer's creditworthiness. Thus, it is safer than sending goods on a collection basis, where payment is made by a draft only after the goods have been shipped. Of equal, if not greater, importance is the probability that imports covered by letters of credit will be given priority in the allocation of foreign exchange should currency controls be imposed.

A letter of credit can also be confirmed or unconfirmed. A *confirmed L/C* is an L/C issued by one bank and confirmed by another, obligating both banks to honor any drafts drawn in compliance. An *unconfirmed L/C* is the obligation of only the issuing bank.

An exporter will prefer an irrevocable letter of credit by the importer's bank with confirmation by a domestic bank. In this way, the exporter need look no further than a bank in its own country for compliance with terms of the letter of credit. For example, if the Bank of Tokyo had confirmed the letter of credit issued by Wells Fargo and Wells Fargo, for whatever reason, fails to honor its irrevocable L/C, Japan Exporters can collect $38,000 from the Bank of Tokyo, assuming that Japan Exporters has met all the necessary conditions. This arrangement serves two purposes. Most exporters are not in a position to evaluate or deal with a foreign bank directly should difficulties arise. Domestic confirmation avoids this problem. In addition, should the foreign bank be unable to fulfill its commitment to pay, whether because of foreign exchange controls or political directives, that is of no concern to the exporter. The domestic confirming bank must still honor all drafts in full.

Thus, the three main types of L/C, in order of safety for the exporter, are (1) the irrevocable, confirmed L/C; (2) the irrevocable, unconfirmed L/C; and (3) the revocable L/C. Selecting the type of L/C to use depends on an evaluation of the risks associated with

■ **EXHIBIT 13.1** Letter of Credit

IRREVOCABLE
COMMERCIAL
LETTER OF
CREDIT

Since 1852

WELLS FARGO BANK,N.A.

☐ 475 SANSOME STREET, SAN FRANCISCO, CALIFORNIA 94111

☐ 770 WILSHIRE BLVD., LOS ANGELES, CALIFORNIA 90017

INTERNATIONAL DIVISION **COMMERCIAL L/C DEPARTMENT** CABLE ADDRESS: **WELLS**

OUR LETTER OF CREDIT NO. XYZ9000 AMOUNT US$38,000 DATE MAY 6, 19XX
THIS NUMBER MUST BE MENTIONED
ON ALL DRAFTS AND CORRESPONDENCE

. JAPAN EXPORTERS INC.   . BANK OF TOKYO
. TOKYO, JAPAN   . TOKYO, JAPAN
.   .
.   .

GENTLEMEN:

BY ORDER OF U.S.A. IMPORTERS INC.

AND FOR ACCOUNT OF SAME

WE HEREBY AUTHORIZE YOU TO DRAW ON OURSELVES

UP TO AN AGGREGATE AMOUNT OF THIRTY EIGHT THOUSAND AND NO/100 U.S. DOLLARS

AVAILABLE BY YOUR DRAFTS AT ON OURSELVES, IN DUPLICATE, AT 90 DAYS SIGHT
ACCOMPANIED BY
SIGNED INVOICE IN TRIPLICATE
PACKING LIST IN DUPLICATE
FULL SET OF CLEAN OCEAN BILLS OF LADING, MADE OUT TO ORDER OF SHIPPER,
   BLANK ENDORSED, MARKED FREIGHT PREPAID AND NOTIFY: U.S.A. IMPORTERS,
   INC., LOS ANGELES, DATED ON BOARD NOT LATER THAN MAY 30, 19XX.
INSURANCE POLICY/CERTIFICATE IN DUPLICATE FOR 110% OF INVOICE VALUE,
   COVERING ALL RISKS.

COVERING: SHIPMENT OF AUTOMOBILE SPARE PARTS, AS PER BUYER'S ORDER NO.
   900 DATED MARCH 15, 19XX FROM ANY JAPANESE PORT C.I.F.
   LOS ANGELES, CALIFORNIA
PARTIAL SHIPMENTS ARE PERMITTED.
TRANSHIPMENT IS NOT PERMITTED.
DOCUMENTS MUST BE PRESENTED WITHIN 7 DAYS AFTER THE BOARD DATE OF
   THE BILLS OF LADING, BUT IN ANY EVENT NOT LATER THAN JUNE 6, 19XX.

SPECIMEN

DRAFTS MUST BE DRAWN AND NEGOTIATED NOT LATER THAN JUNE 6, 19XX
ALL DRAFTS DRAWN UNDER THIS CREDIT MUST BEAR ITS DATE AND NUMBER AND THE AMOUNTS
MUST BE ENDORSED ON THE REVERSE SIDE OF THIS LETTER OF CREDIT BY THE NEGOTIATING BANK.
WE HEREBY AGREE WITH THE DRAWERS, ENDORSERS, AND BONA FIDE HOLDERS OF ALL DRAFTS
DRAWN UNDER AND IN COMPLIANCE WITH THE TERMS OF THIS CREDIT, THAT SUCH DRAFTS WILL
BE DULY HONORED UPON PRESENTATION TO THE DRAWEE.
THIS CREDIT IS SUBJECT TO THE UNIFORM CUSTOMS AND PRACTICE FOR DOCUMENTARY CREDITS
(1974 REVISION). INTERNATIONAL CHAMBER OF COMMERCE PUBLICATION NO. 290.

SPECIMEN

AUTHORIZED SIGNATURE

Used with the permission of Wells Fargo Bank.

■ **EXHIBIT 13.2**   Relationships Between the Three Parties to a Letter of Credit

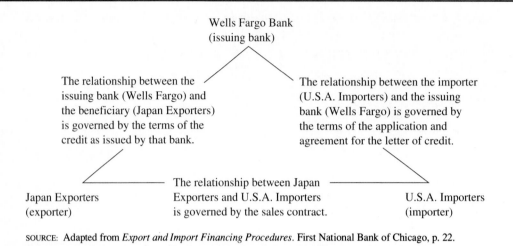

SOURCE: Adapted from *Export and Import Financing Procedures*. First National Bank of Chicago, p. 22.

the transaction and the relative costs involved. One of the costs is the possibility of lost sales if the importer can get better credit terms elsewhere.

An exporter who acts as an intermediary may have to provide some assurance to its supplier that the supplier will be paid. It can provide this assurance by transferring or assigning the proceeds of the letter of credit opened in its name to the manufacturer.

A *transferable L/C* is one under which the beneficiary has the right to instruct the paying bank to make the credit available to one or more secondary beneficiaries. No L/C is transferable unless specifically authorized in the credit; moreover, it can be transferred only once. The stipulated documents are transferred along with the L/C.

An *assignment,* in contrast to a transfer, assigns part or all of the proceeds to another party, but does not transfer to the party the required documents. This provision is not as safe to the assignee as a transfer because the assignee does not have control of the required merchandise and documentation.

The Draft

Commonly used in international trade, a *draft* is an unconditional order in writing— usually signed by the exporter (seller) and addressed to the importer (buyer) or the importer's agent—ordering the importer to pay on demand, or at a fixed or determinable future date, the amount specified on its face. Such an instrument, also known as a *bill of exchange,* serves three important functions:

- To provide written evidence, in clear and simple terms, of a financial obligation
- To enable both parties to potentially reduce their costs of financing
- To provide a negotiable and unconditional instrument (That is, payment must be made to any holder in due course despite any disputes over the underlying commercial transaction.)

Using a draft also enables an exporter to employ its bank as a collection agent. The bank forwards the draft or bill of exchange to the foreign buyer (either directly or through a branch or correspondent bank), collects on the draft, and then remits the proceeds to the exporter. The bank has all the necessary documents for control of the merchandise and turns them over to the importer only when the draft has been paid or accepted in accordance with the exporter's instructions.

The conditions for a draft to be negotiable under the U.S. Uniform Commercial Code are that it must be

- In writing
- Signed by the issuer (drawer)
- An unconditional order to pay
- A certain sum of money
- Payable on demand or at a definite future time
- Payable to order of bearer

There are usually three parties to a draft. The party who signs and sends the draft to the second party is called the *drawer;* payment is made to the third party, the *payee.* Normally,

■ **EXHIBIT 13.3**   Example of Letter of Credit Financing of U.S. Imports

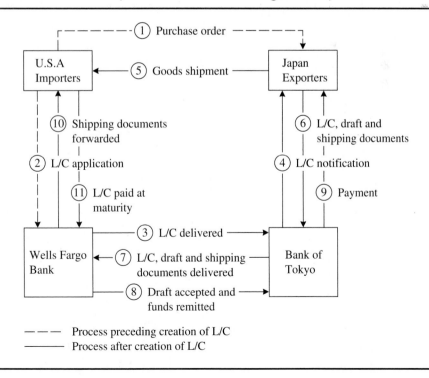

the drawer and payee are the same person. The party to whom the draft is addressed is the *drawee,* who may be either the buyer or if a letter of credit was used, the buyer's bank. In the case of a confirmed L/C, the drawee would be the confirming bank.

In the previous example, Japan Exporters is the drawer and the Bank of Tokyo is the payee. The drawee is Wells Fargo under the terms of the L/C. This information is included in the draft shown in Exhibit 13.4.

Drafts may be either sight or time drafts. *Sight drafts* must be paid on presentation or else dishonored. *Time drafts* are payable at some specified future date and as such become a useful financing device. The maturity of a time draft is known as its *usance* or *tenor.* As mentioned earlier, to qualify as a negotiable instrument, the date of payment must be determinable. For example, a time draft payable "upon delivery of goods" is not specific enough, given the vagaries of ocean freight, and, hence, will likely nullify its negotiability. As shown in Exhibit 13.4, the draft drawn under the letter of credit by Japan Exporters is a time draft with a tenor of 90 days, indicated by the words "at ninety days sight." Thus, the draft will mature on August 24, 90 days after it was drawn (May 26).

A time draft becomes an *acceptance* after being accepted by the drawee. Accepting a draft means writing *accepted* across its face, followed by an authorized person's signature and the date. The party accepting a draft incurs the obligation to pay it at maturity. A draft accepted by a bank becomes a *banker's acceptance;* one drawn on and accepted by a commercial enterprise is termed a *trade acceptance.* Exhibit 13.5 is the time draft in Exhibit 13.4 after being accepted by Wells Fargo.

The exporter can hold the acceptance or sell it at a discount from face value to its bank, to some other bank, or to an acceptance dealer. The discount normally is less than the prevailing prime rate for bank loans. These acceptances enjoy a wide market and are an important tool in the financing of international trade. They are discussed in more detail in

■ **EXHIBIT 13.4**   Time Draft

TOKYO, JAPAN	MAY 26	, 19 XX	**No.** 712

AT NINETY DAYS _____SIGHT OF THIS **ORIGINAL** OF EXCHANGE (DUPLICATE UNPAID)

PAY TO THE ORDER OF ___ BANK OF TOKYO _____ U.S. $ 38,000.00

THE SUM OF ___ THIRTY EIGHT THOUSAND AND NO/100 * U.S. Dollars

DRAWN UNDER LETTER OF CREDIT NO.	DATED	ISSUED BY
X Y Z 9000	MAY 6, 19XX	WELLS FARGO BANK

To ___ WELLS FARGO BANK

770 WILSHIRE BLVD.   *SPECIMEN*

LOS ANGELES, CALIFORNIA   JAPAN EXPORTERS INC.

16-178 (REV 10-71)

Used by permission of Wells Fargo Bank.

■ **EXHIBIT 13.5**   Banker's Acceptance

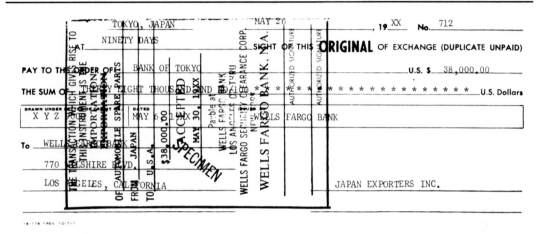

Used by permission of Wells Fargo Bank.

the next section. An acceptance can be transferred from one holder to another simply by endorsement.

Drafts can be clean or documentary. A *clean draft,* one unaccompanied by any other papers, is normally used only for nontrade remittances. Its primary purpose is to put pressure on a recalcitrant debtor that must pay or accept the draft or else face damage to its credit reputation.

Most drafts used in international trade are documentary. A *documentary draft,* which can be either sight or time, is accompanied by documents that are to be delivered to the drawee on payment or acceptance of the draft. Typically, these documents include the bill of lading in negotiable form, the commercial invoice, the consular invoice where required, and an insurance certificate. The bill of lading in negotiable form is the most important document because it gives its holder the right to control the goods covered. A documentary sight draft is also known as a D/P (documents against payment) draft; if documents are delivered on acceptance, it is a D/A draft.

There are two significant aspects to shipping goods under documentary time drafts for acceptance. First, the exporter is extending credit to the importer for the usance of the draft. Second, the exporter is relinquishing control of the goods in return for a signature on the acceptance to assure it of payment.

It is important to bear in mind that sight drafts are not always paid at presentation, nor are time drafts always paid at maturity. Firms can get bank statistics on the promptness of sight and time draft payments, by country, from bank publications such as Chase Manhattan's *Collection Experience* bulletin.

Unless a bank has accepted a draft, the exporter must ultimately look to the importer for payment. Thus, use of a sight or accepted time draft is warranted only when the exporter has faith in the importer's financial strength and integrity.

Consignment

Goods sent on *consignment* are only shipped to the importer, but they are not sold. The exporter (consignor) retains title to the goods until the importer (consignee) has sold them to a third party. This arrangement is normally made only with a related company because of the large risks involved. There is little evidence of the buyer's obligation to pay, and should the buyer default, it will prove difficult to collect.

The seller must carefully consider the credit risks involved and also the availability of foreign exchange in the importer's country. Imports covered by documentary drafts receive priority over imports shipped on consignment.

Open Account

Open account selling is shipping goods first and billing the importer later. The credit terms are arranged between the buyer and the seller, but the seller has little evidence of the importer's obligation to pay a certain amount at a certain date. Sales on open account, therefore, are made only to a foreign affiliate or to a customer with which the exporter has a long history of favorable business dealings. However, open account sales have greatly expanded due to the major increase in international trade, the improvement in credit information about importers, and the greater familiarity with exporting in general. The benefits include greater flexibility (no specific payment dates are set) and involve lower costs, including fewer bank charges than with other methods of payment. As with shipping on consignment, the possibility of currency controls is an important factor because of the low priority in allocating foreign exchange normally accorded this type of transaction.

Exhibit 13.6 summarizes some of the advantages and disadvantages associated with the various means of arranging payment in international trade.

Collecting Overdue Accounts

Typically, 1%-3% of a company's export sales go uncollected. Small businesses, however, take more risks than do large ones, often selling on terms other than a confirmed letter of credit. One reason is that they are eager to develop a new market opportunity; another reason is that they aren't as well versed in the mechanics of foreign sales. Thus, their percentage of uncollected export sales may be higher than is that of large companies.

Once an account becomes delinquent, sellers have three options: (1) They can try to collect the account themselves; (2) they can hire an attorney who is experienced in international law; or (3) they can engage the services of a collection agency.

The first step is for sellers to attempt to recover the money themselves. Turning the bill over to a collection agency or a lawyer too quickly will hurt the customer relationship. However, after several telephone calls, telexes, and/or personal visits, the firm must decide whether to write the account off or pursue it further.

The cost of hiring a high-priced U.S. lawyer, who then contacts an expensive foreign lawyer, is a deterrent to following the second option for receivables of less than $100,000. With such a relatively small amount, a collection agency would usually be more appropriate.

■ **EXHIBIT 13.6** International Methods of Payment: Advantages and Disadvantages (Ranked by Risk)

Method	Risk*	Chief Advantage	Chief Disadvantage
Cash in advance	L	No credit extension required	Can limit sales potential, disturb some potential customers
Sight draft	M/L	Retains control and title; ensures payment before goods are delivered	If customer does not or cannot accept goods, goods remain at port of entry and no payment is due.
Letters of credit Irrevocable Revocable	 M M/H	Banks accept responsibility to pay; payment upon presentation of papers; costs go to buyer	If revocable, terms can change during contract work.
Time draft	M/H	Lowers customer resistance by allowing extended payment after receipt of goods	Same as sight draft, plus goods are delivered before payment is due or received
Consignment sales	M/H	Facilitates delivery; lowers customer resistance	Capital tied up until sales; must establish distributor's creditworthiness; need political risk insurance in some countries; increased risk from currency controls
Open account	H	Simplified procedure; no customer resistance	High risk; seller must finance production; increased risk from currency controls

*L: low risk; M: medium risk; H: high risk

Whereas internationally experienced attorneys in large law firms generally charge from $100–$200 an hour for their services, regardless of the amount recovered, collection agencies work on a percentage basis. A typical fee is 20%–25% of the amount collected, but if the claim is over $25,000 or so, the agency will often negotiate a more favorable rate.

Even with professional help, there are no guarantees of collecting on foreign receivables. This reality puts a premium on checking a customer's credit prior to filling an order.

One good source of credit information is the U.S. Department of Commerce's International Trade Administration (ITA). Its *World Data Trade Reports* covers nearly 200,000 foreign establishments and can be obtained from district offices of ITA for $75. Other places to check on the creditworthiness of foreign companies and governments are export management companies and the international departments of commercial banks. Also, Dun & Bradstreet International publishes *Principal International Businesses,* a book with information on about 50,000 foreign enterprises in 133 countries.

Banks and Trade Financing

Historically, banks have been involved in only a single step in international trade transactions such as providing a loan or a letter of credit. But as financing has become an integral part of many trade transactions, U.S. banks—especially major money center banks—have evolved as well. They have gone from financing individual trade deals to providing comprehensive solutions to trade needs. This includes combining bank lending with subsidized funds from government export agencies, international leasing, and other nonbank financing sources, along with political and economic risk insurance.

■ 13.2 ■
DOCUMENTS IN INTERNATIONAL TRADE

The most important supporting document required in commercial bank financing of exports is the bill of lading. Of secondary importance are the commercial invoice, consular invoice, and insurance certificate.

Bill of Lading

Of the shipping documents, the *bill of lading* (B/L) is the most important. It serves three main and separate functions:

1. It is a contract between the carrier and shipper (exporter) in which the former agrees to carry the goods from port of shipment to port of destination.
2. It is the shipper's receipt for the goods.
3. The negotiable B/L, its most common form, is a document that establishes control over the goods.

A bill of lading can be either a straight or order B/L. A *straight B/L* consigns the goods to a specific party, normally the importer, and is not negotiable. Because title cannot be transferred to a third party merely by endorsement and delivery, a straight B/L is not good collateral and, therefore, is used only when no financing is involved.

Most trade transactions do involve financing, which requires transfer of title, so the vast majority of bills of lading are order B/Ls. Under an *order B/L,* the goods are consigned to the order of a named party, usually the exporter. In this way, the exporter retains title to the merchandise until it endorses the B/L on the reverse side. The exporter's representative may endorse to a specific party or endorse it in blank by simply signing his or her name. The shipper delivers the cargo in the port of destination to the bearer of the endorsed order B/L, who must surrender it.

Because an order B/L represents goods in transit that are probably readily marketable and fully insured, this document is generally considered to be good collateral by banks. It is required under L/C financing and for discounting of drafts.

Bills of lading can also be classified in several other ways. An *on-board* B/L certifies that the goods have actually been placed on board the vessel. By contrast, a *received-for-shipment* B/L merely acknowledges that the carrier has received the goods for shipment. It does not state that the ship is in port or that space is available. The cargo can, therefore, sit on the dock for weeks, or even months, before it is shipped. When goods are seasonal or perishable, therefore, the received-for-shipment B/L is never satisfactory to either the shipper or the importer. A received-for-shipment B/L can easily be converted into an on-board B/L by stamping it "on-board" and supplying the name of the vessel, the date, and the signature of the captain or the captain's representative.

A *clean B/L* indicates that the goods were received in apparently good condition. However, the carrier is not obligated to check beyond the external visual appearance of the boxes. If boxes are damaged or in poor condition, this observation is noted on the B/L, which then becomes a *foul B/L*. It is important that the exporter get a clean B/L—that is, one with no such notation—because foul B/Ls are generally not acceptable under a letter of credit.

Commercial Invoice

A *commercial invoice* contains an authoritative description of the merchandise shipped, including full details on quality, grades, price per unit, and total value. It also contains the names and addresses of the exporter and importer, the number of packages, any distinguishing external marks, the payment terms, other expenses such as transportation and insurance charges, any fees collectible from the importer, the name of the vessel, the ports of departure and destination, and any required export or import permit numbers.

Insurance

All cargoes going abroad are insured. Most of the insurance contracts used today are under an *open,* or *floating,* policy. This policy automatically covers all shipments made by the exporter, thereby eliminating the necessity of arranging individual insurance for each shipment. To evidence insurance for a shipment under an open policy, the exporter makes out an *insurance certificate* on forms supplied by the insurance company. This certificate contains information on the goods shipped. All entries must conform exactly with the information on the B/L, on the commercial invoice and, where required, on the consular invoice.

Consular Invoice

Exports to many countries require a special *consular invoice.* This invoice, which varies in its details and information requirements from nation to nation, is presented to the local consul in exchange for a visa. The form must be filled out very carefully, for even trivial inaccuracies can lead to substantial fines and delays in customs clearance. The consular invoice does not convey any title to the goods being shipped and is not negotiable.

■ 13.3 ■
FINANCING TECHNIQUES IN INTERNATIONAL TRADE

In addition to straight bank financing, there are several other techniques available for trade financing: bankers' acceptances, discounting, factoring, and forfaiting.

Bankers' Acceptances

Bankers' acceptances have played an important role in financing international trade for many centuries. As we saw in the previous section, a banker's acceptance is a time draft drawn on a bank. By "accepting" the draft, the bank makes an unconditional promise to pay the holder of the draft a stated amount on a specified day. Thus, the bank effectively substitutes its own credit for that of a borrower, and in the process, it creates a negotiable instrument that may be freely traded.

Creating an Acceptance. A typical acceptance transaction is shown in Exhibit 13.7. An importer of goods seeks credit to finance its purchase until the goods can be resold. The importer requests its bank to issue a letter of credit on its behalf, authorizing the foreign exporter to draw a time draft on the bank in payment for the goods. Based on this authorization, the exporter ships the goods on an order B/L made out to itself and presents a time draft and the endorsed shipping documents to its bank. The foreign bank then forwards the draft and the appropriate shipping documents to the importer's bank; the importer's bank accepts the draft and, thus, creates a banker's acceptance. The exporter discounts the draft with the accepting bank and receives payment for the shipment. The shipping documents are delivered to the importer, and the importer may now claim the shipment. The accepting bank may either buy (discount) the B/A and hold it in its own portfolio or sell (rediscount) the B/A in the money market; in Exhibit 13.7, the bank sells the acceptance in the money market.

Terms of Acceptance Financing. Typical maturities on bankers' acceptances are 30 days, 90 days, and 180 days, with the average being 90 days. Maturities can be tailored, though, to cover the entire period needed to ship and dispose of the goods financed.

For an investor, a banker's acceptance is a close substitute for other bank liabilities, such as certificates of deposit (CDs). Consequently, bankers' acceptances trade at rates very close to those on CDs. Market yields, however, do not give a complete picture of the costs of acceptance financing to the borrower because the accepting bank levies a fee, or commission, for accepting the draft. The fee varies depending on the maturity of the draft as well as the creditworthiness of the borrower, but it averages less than 1% per annum. The bank also receives a fee if a letter of credit is involved. In addition, the bank may hope to realize a profit on the difference between the price at which it purchases and the price at which it resells the acceptance.

On the maturity date of the acceptance, the accepting bank is required to pay the current holder the amount stated on the draft. The holder of a bank acceptance has recourse for the full amount of the draft from the last endorser in the event of the importer's unwillingness or inability to pay at maturity. The authenticity of an accepted draft is separated from the underlying commercial transaction and may not be dishonored for reason of a dispute between the exporter and importer. This factor, of course, significantly enhances its marketability and reduces its riskiness.

In recent years, the demand for acceptance financing has fallen off. One factor has been the increased availability of funding from nonbank investors in the U.S. commercial paper market. Prime commercial paper generally trades at rates near those on acceptance liabilities

■ **EXHIBIT 13.7** Example of Banker's Acceptance Financing of U.S. Imports: Created, Discounted, Sold, and Paid at Maturity

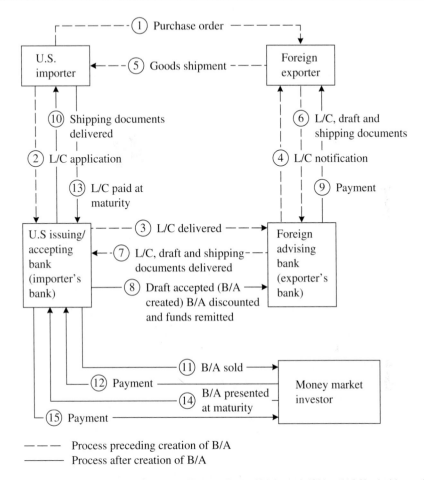

SOURCE: *Instruments of the Money Market.* Federal Reserve Bank of Richmond, 1981, p. 116. Used with permission.

---

of prime banks; for firms with access to this market, the overall cost—including placement fees charged by dealers and fees for back-up line of credit—is usually below the all-in cost of acceptance financing.

Discounting

Even if a trade draft is not accepted by a bank, the exporter can still convert the trade draft into cash by means of *discounting*. The exporter places the draft with a bank or other financial institution and, in turn, receives the face value of the draft less interest and commissions. By insuring the draft against both commercial and political risks, the exporter will often pay a lower interest rate. If losses covered by the insurer do occur, the insuring agency will reimburse the exporter or any institution to which the exporter transfers the draft.

The discount rate for trade paper is often lower than interest rates on overdrafts, bank loans, and other forms of local funding. This lower rate is usually a result of export promotion policies that lead to direct or indirect subsidies of rates on export paper.

Discounting may be done with or without *recourse*. With recourse, the bank can collect from the exporter if the importer fails to pay the bill when due. The bank bears the collection risk if the draft is sold without recourse.

Factoring

Firms with a substantial export business and companies too small to afford a foreign credit and collections department can turn to a *factor*. Factors buy a company's receivables at a discount, thereby accelerating their conversion into cash. Most factoring is done on a *nonrecourse* basis, which means that the factor assumes all the credit and political risks except for those involving disputes between the transacting parties. The exporter assumes these risks in factoring *with recourse*.

Factoring is becoming increasingly popular as a trade financing vehicle. In 1989, the value of world exports financed through factoring topped $10 billion, a 22% increase over 1988. By using a factor, a firm can ensure that its terms are in accord with local practice and are competitive. For instance, customers can be offered payment on open account rather than being asked for a letter of credit or stiffer credit requirements. If the margin on its factored sales is not sufficiently profitable, then the firm can bear the credit risks itself or forgo that business. Even if an exporter chooses not to discount its foreign receivables with a factor, it can still use the factor's extensive credit information files to ascertain the creditworthiness of prospective customers.

An exporter that has established an ongoing relationship with a factor will submit new orders directly to the factor. After evaluating the creditworthiness of the new claim, the factor will make a recourse/nonrecourse decision within two days to two weeks, depending on the availability of information.

Although the factors may consider their fees to be nominal considering the services provided, they are not cheap. Export factoring fees are determined on an individual company basis and are related to the annual turnover (usually a minimum of $500,000 to $1 million is necessary), the average invoice size (smaller invoices are more expensive because of the fixed information-gathering costs), the creditability of the claims, and the terms of sale. In general, these fees run from 1.75% to 2% of sales.

Despite these high costs, factoring can be quite worthwhile to many firms for one principal reason: The cost of bearing the credit risk associated with a given receivable can be substantially lower to a factor than to the selling firm. First, the factor's greater credit information makes it more knowledgeable of the actual, as opposed to the perceived, risks involved and, thereby, reduces its required risk premium. Second, by holding a well-diversified portfolio of receivables, the factor can eliminate some of the risks associated with individual receivables.

In general, factoring is most useful for (1) the occasional exporter and (2) the exporter having a geographically diverse portfolio of accounts receivable. In both cases, it would be organizationally difficult and expensive to internalize the accounts receivable collection process. Such companies would generally be small or else be involved on a limited scale in foreign markets.

Forfaiting

The specialized factoring technique known as forfaiting is sometimes used in the case of extreme credit risk. *Forfaiting* is the discounting—at a fixed rate without recourse—of medium-term export receivables denominated in fully convertible currencies (U.S. dollar, Swiss franc, Deutsche mark). This technique is usually used in the case of capital-goods exports with a five-year maturity and repayment in semiannual installments. The discount is set at a fixed rate: about 1.25% above the local cost of funds or above the *London interbank offer rate* (LIBOR).

Forfaiting is especially popular in Western Europe (primarily in Switzerland and Austria), and many forfaiting houses are subsidiaries of major international banks, such as Credit Suisse. These houses also provide help with administrative and collection problems.

■ 13.4 ■
GOVERNMENT SOURCES OF EXPORT FINANCING AND CREDIT INSURANCE

In the race for export orders, particularly for capital equipment and other "big-ticket" items requiring long repayment arrangements, most governments of developed countries have attempted to provide their domestic exporters with a competitive edge in the form of low-cost export financing and concessionary rates on political and economic risk insurance. Nearly every developed nation has its own export-import agency for development and trade financing.

Export Financing

Procedures for extending credit vary greatly among agencies. Many agencies offer funds in advance of the actual export contract, whereas private sources extend financing only after the sale has been made. Some programs extend credit only to the supplier—called *supplier credits*—to pass on to the importer; others grant credit directly to the buyer—called *buyer credits*—who then pays the supplier. The difference is that in the first arrangement, the supplier bears the credit risk, whereas in the latter case, the government is the risk bearer. Of course, the government often provides credit insurance in conjunction with supplier credits.

Export-Import Bank.   The *Export-Import Bank* (*Eximbank*) is the only U.S. government agency dedicated solely to financing and facilitating U.S. exports. Eximbank loans provide competitive, fixed-rate financing for U.S. export sales facing foreign competition backed with subsidized official financing. Evidence of foreign competition is not required for exports produced by small businesses where the loan amount is $2.5 million or less. Eximbank also provides guarantees of loans made by others. The loan and guarantee programs cover up to 85% of the U.S. export value and have repayment terms of one year or more.

Eximbank operations generally conform to five basic principles:

1. Loans are made for the specific purpose of financing U.S. exports of goods and services. If a U.S. export item contains foreign-made components, Eximbank will cover up to 100% of the U.S. content of exports provided that the total amount financed or guaranteed does not exceed 85% of the total contract price of the item and that the total U.S. content accounts for at least half of the contract price.
2. Eximbank will not provide financing unless private capital is unavailable in the amounts required. It supplements, rather than competes with private capital.
3. Loans must have reasonable assurance of repayment and must be for projects that have a favorable impact on the country's economic and social well-being. The host government must be aware of, and not object to, the project.
4. Fees and premiums charged for guarantees and insurance are based on the risks covered.
5. In authorizing loans and other financial assistance, Eximbank is obliged to take into account any adverse effects on the U.S. economy or balance of payments that might occur.

The interest rates on Eximbank's loans are based on an international arrangement among the 22 members of the Organization for Economic Cooperation and Development (OECD). The purpose of the arrangement, which sets minimum rates that an official export finance agency must charge on export credits, is to limit the interest subsidies used by many industrial countries to gain competitive advantage vis-à-vis other nations. The OECD minimum rates are based on the weighted average interest rate on government bond issues denominated in the U.S. dollar, German mark, British pound, French franc, and Japanese yen. In this way, rates on export credits are brought closer to market interest rates.

Eximbank extends direct loans to foreign buyers of U.S. exports and intermediary loans to financial institutions that extend loans to the foreign buyers. Both direct and intermediary loans are provided when U.S. exporters face officially subsidized foreign competition.

Eximbank's medium-term loans to intermediaries (where the loan amount is $10 million or less and the term is seven years or less) are structured as "standby" loan commitments. The intermediary may request disbursement by Eximbank at any time during the term of the underlying debt obligation.

Eximbank guarantees provide repayment protection for private sector loans to credit-worthy buyers of exported U.S. goods and services. The guarantees are available alone or may be combined with an intermediary loan. Most guarantees provide comprehensive coverage of both political and commercial risks. Eximbank will also guarantee payments on cross-border or international leases.

Exporters may also have access to an Eximbank program that guarantees export-related working-capital loans to creditworthy small and medium-sized businesses. Since all Eximbank guarantees carry the full faith and credit of the U.S. government, loans provided under these guarantee programs are made at close to the risk-free interest rate. In effect, low-cost guarantees are another form of government-subsidized export financing.

Repayment terms vary with the project and type of equipment purchased. For capital goods, long-term credits are normally provided for a period of five years to ten years. Loans for projects and large product acquisitions are eligible for longer terms, while lower-unit-value items receive shorter terms. Loan amortization is made in semiannual installments, beginning six months after delivery of the exported equipment.

Another program run by Eximbank provides a *preliminary commitment* that outlines the amount, terms, and conditions of financing it will extend to importers of U.S. goods and services. This commitment gives U.S. firms a competitive advantage in bidding on foreign projects because it enables the firms to offer financing along with their equipment proposals. Preliminary commitments are issued without cost (there is a $100 processing fee) or obligation to applicants.

Eximbank charges a front-end *exposure fee,* assessed on each disbursement of a loan by Eximbank or the guaranteed or intermediary lender. Exposure fees, which are adjusted periodically, vary according to the term of the loan, the classification of the borrower or guarantor, and the borrower's country. For exposure-fee purposes, Eximbank classifies countries in five country categories according to risk. Under each country category, there are three borrower/guarantor classifications:

- Class I: Sovereign borrowers or guarantors, or for political-risks-only cover
- Class II: Creditworthy nonsovereign public institutions or banks, or highly credit-worthy private buyers
- Class III: Other creditworthy private buyers

In recent years, Eximbank has become more aggressive in fighting perceived abuses by foreign export-credit agencies. One area that Eximbank has targeted is foreign *mixed-credit financing*—the practice of tying grants and low-interest loans to the acceptance of specific commercial contracts. For years, U.S. capital-equipment exporters, engineering firms, and high-tech producers have lost overseas bids to foreign firms backed by government mixed credits. Eximbank now offers its own mixed credits. It will even offer mixed-credit deals before the fact. Any deal that has a chance of attracting a foreign mixed-credit bid is considered. However, an Eximbank spokesperson noted, "This is not an export promotion. We are not out there to match every mixed credit. We're out to end mixed credits, and will only offer one if it helps us to make a specific negotiating point."[1]

Private Export Funding Corporation.   The *Private Export Funding Corporation* (PEFCO) was created in 1970 by the *Bankers' Association for Foreign Trade* to mobilize private capital for financing the export of big-ticket items by U.S. firms. It purchases the medium- to long-term debt obligations of importers of U.S. products at fixed interest rates.

[1] "How U.S. Firms Benefit from Eximbank's War on Foreign Mixed Credits," *Business International Money Report,* February 10, 1986, p. 41.

PEFCO finances its portfolio of foreign importer loans through the sale of its own securities. Eximbank fully guarantees repayment of all PEFCO foreign obligations.

PEFCO normally extends its credits jointly with one or more commercial banks and Eximbank. The maturity of the importers' notes purchased by PEFCO varies from 2.5 years to 12 years; the banks take the short-term maturity and Eximbank, the long-term portion of a PEFCO loan. Much of this money goes to finance purchases of U.S.-manufactured jet aircraft and related equipment such as jet engines.

Trends.   There are several trends in public-source export financing. These trends include:

1. *A shift from supplier to buyer credits*: Many capital goods exports that cannot be financed under the traditional medium-term supplier credits become feasible under buyer credits, where the payment period can be stretched up to 20 years.
2. *A growing emphasis on acting as catalysts to attract private capital*: This action includes participating with private sources, either as a member of a financial consortium or as a partner with an individual private investor, in supplying export credits.
3. *Public agencies as a source of refinancing*: Public agencies are becoming an important source for refinancing loans made by bankers and private financiers. Refinancing enables a private creditor to discount its export loans with the government.
4. *Attempts to limit competition among agencies*: The virtual export-credit war among governments has led to several attempts to agree upon and coordinate financing terms. These attempts, however, have been honored more in the breach than in the observance.

The Effect of Export-Credit Subsidies

The benefits of the Eximbank do not come free of charge. Through much of the 1980s, the Eximbank has absorbed losses of more than $250 million a year. In fiscal 1987, it posted a record loss of $387 million. The bank borrows through the U.S. Treasury, which means that the credit terms it receives are first rate. However, lending below the market to help U.S. companies export ensures a persistent deficit. The obligation that American taxpayers take on to support this activity translates into a credit break for foreign firms that buy U.S. airplanes and the like.

Although the Eximbank claims that cut-rate loans are necessary to allow U.S. firms to compete with foreign exporters, the truth is that the Eximbank loans subsidize less than 3% of American merchandise exports. Another argument used by Eximbank officials is that their activities are justified because foreign governments subsidize exports. But a nation that subsidizes exports simply gives away part of its wealth. Moreover, there is reason to question whether export subsidies really improve the balance of trade. Any increase in exports achieved by a subsidy would necessarily increase the demand for dollars by foreign purchasers of U.S. goods. The increase in demand would boost the dollar's value. Dollar appreciation would, of course, encourage further imports and discourage unsubsidized exports. Since savings and investment are unaffected by these subsidies, the trade deficit is unlikely to respond to export subsidies.

Export-Credit Insurance

Export financing covered by government credit insurance, also known as *export-credit insurance,* provides protection against losses from political and/or commercial risks. It serves as collateral for the credit and is often indispensable in making the sale. The insurance does not usually provide an ironclad guarantee against all risks, however. Having this insurance results in lowering the cost of borrowing from private institutions because the government agency is bearing those risks set forth in the insurance policy. The financing is nonrecourse to the extent that risks and losses are covered. Often, however, the insurer requires additional security in the form of a guarantee by a foreign local bank or a certificate from the foreign central bank that foreign exchange is available for repayment of the interest and principal.

The purpose of export-credit insurance is to encourage a nation's export sales by protecting domestic exporters against nonpayment by importers. The existence of medium- and long-term credit insurance policies makes banks more willing to provide nonrecourse financing of big-ticket items that require lengthy repayment maturities, provided the goods in question have been delivered and accepted.

Foreign Credit Insurance Association. In the United States, the export-credit insurance program is administered by the *Foreign Credit Insurance Association* (FCIA). The FCIA is a cooperative effort of Eximbank and a group of approximately 50 of the leading marine, casualty, and property insurance companies. FCIA insurance offers protection from political and commercial risks to U.S. exporters: The private insurers cover commercial risks, and the Eximbank covers political risks. The exporter (or the financial institution providing the loan) must self-insure that portion not covered by the FCIA.

Short-term insurance is available for export credits up to 180 days (360 days for bulk agricultural commodities and consumer durables) from the date of shipment. Coverage is of two types: comprehensive (90%–100% of political and 90%–95% of commercial risks) and political only (90%–100% coverage). Coinsurance is required presumably because of the element of moral hazard: the possibility that exporters might take unreasonable risks knowing that they would still be paid in full.

Rather than sell insurance on a case-by-case basis, the FCIA approves discretionary limits within which each exporter can approve its own credits. Insurance rates are based on the terms of sale, type of buyer, and the country of destination. The FCIA also offers preshipment insurance up to 180 days from the time of sale.

Medium-term insurance, guaranteed by Eximbank and covering big-ticket items sold on credit usually from 181 days to 5 years, is available on a case-by-case basis. As with short-term coverage, the exporter must reside in, and ship from, the United States. However, the FCIA will provide medium-term coverage for that portion only of the value-added that originated in the United States. As before, the rates depend on the terms of sale and the destination.

Under the FCIA lease insurance program, lessors of U.S. equipment and related services can cover both the stream of lease payments and the fair market value of products leased outside the United States. The FCIA charges a risk-based premium that is determined by country, lease term, and the type of lease.

■ 13.5 ■
COUNTERTRADE

In recent years, more and more multinationals have had to resort to *countertrade* to sell overseas: purchasing local products to offset the exports of their own products to that market. Countertrade transactions can often be complex and cumbersome. They may involve two-way or three-way transactions, especially where a company is forced to accept unrelated goods for resale by outsiders.

If swapping goods for goods sounds less efficient than using cash or credit, that's because it is less efficient; but it is preferable to having no sales in a given market. More firms are finding it increasingly difficult to conduct business without being prepared to countertrade. Although precise numbers are impossible to come by, this transaction is growing in importance. One recent estimate places countertrade volume at from 20% to 30% of all international trade.[2]

When a company exports to a nation requiring countertrade, it must take back goods that the country can't (or won't try to) sell in international markets. To unload these goods, the company usually has to cut the prices at which the goods are nominally valued in the barter arrangement. Recognizing this necessity, the firm will typically pad the price of the goods it sells to its countertrade customer. When a German machine-tool maker sells to Rumania, for instance, it might raise prices by 20%. Then, when it unloads the blouses it gets in return, the premium covers the reduction in price.

Usually, an exporting company wants to avoid the trouble of marketing those blouses, so it hands over the 10% premium to a countertrade specialist. This middleman splits the premium with a blouse buyer, keeping perhaps 2% and passing the remaining 8% along in price cuts. The result: Rumania pays above the market for imports, making international trade less attractive than it should be, and dumps its own goods through backdoor price shaving. In the long run, however, the practice is self-defeating. Having failed to set up continuing relationships with customers, Rumania never learns what the market really wants—what style blouses, for instance—or how it might improve its competitiveness.

Countertrade takes several specific forms.

1. *Barter*: a direct exchange of goods between two parties without the use of money. For example, Iran might swap oil for guns.
2. *Counterpurchase*: also known as parallel barter, the sale and purchase of goods that are unrelated to each other. For example, Pepsico sells soft drinks to the Soviet Union for vodka.
3. *Buyback*: repayment of the original purchase price through the sale of a related product. For example, Western European countries delivered various pipeline materials to the Soviet Union for construction of a gas pipeline from Siberian gas fields and in return will purchase 28 billion cubic meters of gas per year.

---

[2]Thomas R. Hofstedt, "An Overview of Countertrade," July 29, 1987, unpublished.

The unanswered question in countertrade is, Why go through such a convoluted sales process? Why not sell the goods directly at their market price (which is what ultimately happens anyway) using experts to handle the marketing? One argument is that counter-trade enables members of cartels such as OPEC to undercut an agreed-upon price without formally doing so. Another argument is that countertrade keeps bureaucrats busy in centrally planned economies. Countertrade may also reduce the risk faced by a country that contracts for a new manufacturing facility. If the contractor's payment is received in the form of goods supplied by the facility, the contractor has an added incentive to do quality work and to ensure that the plant's technology is suitable for the skill levels of the available workers.

Regardless of its reason for being, countertrading is replete with problems for the firms involved. First, the goods that can be taken in countertrade are usually undesirable. Those that could be readily converted into cash have already been converted. So, although a firm shipping computers to Brazil might prefer to take coffee beans in return, the only goods available might be Brazilian shoes. Second, the trading details are difficult to work out (how many tons of naphtha is a pile of shoddy Eastern European goods worth?). The inevitable result is a very high ratio of talk to action, with only a small percentage of deals that are talked about getting done. And lost deals cost money.

Until recently, most countertrade centered on the governmental foreign trade organiza-tions (FTOs) of Eastern European countries. In order to sell a machine or an entire plant to an FTO, a Western firm might be required to take at least some of its pay in goods (for example, tomatoes, linen, and machine parts). Sometimes these deals will stretch over a period of several years. Centered in Vienna, the countertrade experts in this business use their contacts with Eastern European officials and their knowledge of available products to earn their keep. However, the restructuring currently taking place in Eastern Europe has already reduced the scale and profitability of their business.

The loss of Eastern European business, however, has been more than offset by the explosive growth in countertrade with Third World countries. The basis for the new wave of countertrade is the cutting off of bank credit to developing nations. Third World countertrade involves more commodities and fewer hard-to-sell manufactured goods. A typical deal, arranged by Sears World Trade, involved bartering U.S. breeding swine for Dominican sugar. Another countertrader swapped BMWs for Ecuadoran tuna fish.

In an effort to make it easier for Third World countries to buy their products, big manufacturers—including General Motors, General Electric, and Caterpillar—have set up countertrading subsidiaries. Having sold auto and truck parts to Mexico, for example, GM's countertrade subsidiary, Motors Trading Corp., arranged tour groups to the country and imported Mexican slippers and gloves. Similarly, arms manufacturers selling to developing countries are often forced to accept local products in return—for example, Iraqi oil for French Exocet missiles or Peruvian anchovies for Spanish Piranha patrol boats.

Authorities in countertrading countries are concerned that goods taken in countertrade will cannibalize their existing cash markets. Proving that countertrade goods go to new markets is difficult enough in the area of manufactured goods; it's impossible for commod-ities, whose ultimate use cannot be identified with its source. For example, some Indonesian rubber taken in countertrade will invariably displace rubber that Indonesia sells for cash.

Interest in countertrade and its variations appears to be growing, even among developed countries, despite the obvious difficulties it presents to the firms and countries involved. For example, in order for McDonnell Douglas to sell F-15s to the Japanese air force, it had to offset the cost to Japan in currency and jobs by agreeing to teach Japanese manufacturers to make military aircraft.

The growth in countertrade is reflected in the scramble for experienced specialists. It has been said that a good countertrader combines the avarice and opportunism of a commodities trader, the inventiveness and political sensitivity of a crooked bureaucrat, and the technical knowledge of a machine-tool salesperson.

■ 13.6 ■
SUMMARY AND CONCLUSIONS

In this chapter, we have examined a number of different financing arrangements and documents involved in international trade. The most important documents encountered in bank-related financing are the draft, which is a written order to pay; the letter of credit, which is a bank guarantee of payment provided that certain stipulated conditions are met; and the bill of lading, the document covering actual shipment of the merchandise by a common carrier and title. Documents of lesser importance include commercial and consular invoices and the insurance certificate.

These instruments serve four primary functions:

- To reduce both buyer and seller risk
- To pinpoint who bears those risks that remain
- To facilitate the transfer of risk to a third party
- To facilitate financing

Each instrument evolved over time as a rational response to the additional risks in international trade posed by greater distances, the lack of familiarity between exporters and importers, the possibility of government imposition of exchange controls, and the greater costs involved in bringing suit against a party domiciled in another nation. Were it not for the latter two factors and publicly financed export promotion programs, we might expect that, with the passage of time, the financial arrangements in international trade would differ little from those encountered in purely domestic commercial transactions.

We also examined some of the government-sponsored export financing programs and credit insurance programs. The number of these institutions and their operating scope have grown steadily, in line with national export drives. From the standpoint of international financial managers, the most significant difference between public and private sources of financing is that public lending agencies offer their funds and credit insurance at less than normal commercial rates. The multinational firm can take advantage of these subsidized rates by structuring its marketing and production programs in accord with the different national financial programs.

■ QUESTIONS ■

1. The principal problem in analyzing different forms of export financing is the distribution of risks between the exporter and the importer. Analyze the following export financing instruments in this respect.

   a. Confirmed, revocable letter of credit

   b. Confirmed, irrevocable letter of credit

   c. Open account credit

   d. Time draft, D/A

   e. Cash with order

   f. Cash in advance

   g. Consignment

   h. Sight draft

2. In order to "meet the competition" from its counterparts overseas, Eximbank will mechanically match the terms of a loan provided by a rival export-financing agency—including the interest rate—when it finances U.S. exports.

   a. What problems might arise from this rule of matching nominal interest rates?

   b. As of January 15, 1988, the minimum interest rate on government-supplied export credits to rich countries was set at a flat rate of 10.4% for all nations providing such credits. What problems might arise with this rule? Comment on which governments would push for such a rule. Which would be against it?

   c. How should minimum interest rates on export credits be set so as to ensure comparability across countries?

   d. Suppose that instead of subsidizing interest rates, governments turn to export insurance subsidies. Is this move an improvement vis-à-vis export-credit subsidies? Explain.

   e. Why has the U.S. government fought against export-credit subsidies?

3. One of the purposes of Eximbank is to absorb credit risks on export sales that the private sector will not accept. Comment on this purpose.

4. Comment on the following statement: "Eximbank does not compete with private financial institutions. It offers assistance only in cases in which the export-credit transaction would not take place without its help. Eximbank does not offer direct-loan assistance to foreign buyers when private institutions will provide comparable financing on reasonable terms."

5. What is countertrade? Why is it termed a sophisticated form of barter?

6. What are some benefits and costs of countertrade for the parties involved?

■ BIBLIOGRAPHY ■

Financing Foreign Operations. New York: Business International Corporation, various issues.
Methods of Export Financing, 2d ed. New York: Chase World Information Corporation, 1976.
Schneider, Gerhard W. *Export-Import Financing.* New York: The Ronald Press, 1974.

◾ 14 ◾

Current Asset Management

A penny saved is a penny earned.

—Benjamin Franklin—

◾ The management of working capital in the multinational corporation is similar to its domestic counterpart. Both are concerned with selecting that combination of *current assets*—cash, marketable securities, accounts receivable, and inventory—that will maximize the value of the firm. The essential differences between domestic and international working-capital management include the impact of currency fluctuations, potential exchange controls, and multiple tax jurisdictions on these decisions, in addition to the wider range of short-term financing and investment options available.

Chapter 15 discusses the mechanisms by which the multinational firm can shift liquid assets among its various affiliates; it also examines the tax and other consequences of these maneuvers. This chapter deals with the management of working-capital items available to each affiliate. The focus includes discussions of international cash, accounts receivable, and inventory management.

◾ 14.1 ◾
INTERNATIONAL CASH MANAGEMENT

International money managers attempt to attain on a worldwide basis the traditional domestic objectives of cash management: (1) bringing the company's cash resources within control as quickly and efficiently as possible and (2) achieving the optimum conservation and utilization of these funds. Accomplishing the first goal requires establishing accurate, timely forecasting and reporting systems, improving cash collections and disbursements, and decreasing the cost of moving funds among affiliates. The second objective is achieved by minimizing the required level of cash balances, making money available when and where it is needed, and increasing the risk-adjusted return on those funds that can be invested.

The principles of domestic and international cash management are identical. The latter is a more complicated exercise, however, and not only because of its wider scope and the need to recognize the customs and practices of other countries. When considering the movement of funds across national borders, a number of external factors inhibit adjustment and constrain the money manager. The most obvious is a set of restrictions that impedes the free flow of money into or out of a country. Numerous examples exist: the former U.S. Office of Foreign Direct Investment (OFDI) restrictions, Germany's Bardepot, and the requirements of many countries that their exporters repatriate the proceeds of foreign sales within a specific period. These regulations impede the free flow of capital and, thereby, hinder an international cash management program.

There is really only one generalization that can be made about this type of regulation: Controls become more stringent during periods of crisis, precisely when financial managers want to act. Thus, a large premium is placed on foresight, planning, and anticipation. Government restrictions must be scrutinized on a country-by-country basis to determine realistic options and limits of action.

Other complicating factors in international money management include multiple tax jurisdictions and currencies and the relative absence of internationally integrated interchange facilities—such as are available domestically in the United States and in other Western nations—for moving cash swiftly from one location to another. Despite these difficulties, however, MNCs may have significant opportunities for improving their global cash management. For example, multinationals can often achieve higher returns overseas on short-term investments that are denied to purely domestic corporations, and the MNCs can frequently keep a higher proportion of these returns after tax by taking advantage of various tax laws and treaties. In addition, by considering all corporate funds as belonging to a central reservoir or "pool" and managing it as such (where permitted by the exchange control authorities), overall returns can be increased while simultaneously reducing the required level of cash and marketable securities worldwide.

This section is divided into seven key areas of international cash management: (1) organization, (2) collection and disbursement of funds, (3) netting of interaffiliate payments, (4) investment of excess funds, (5) establishment of an optimal level of worldwide corporate cash balances, (6) cash planning and budgeting, and (7) bank relations.

Organization

When compared to a system of autonomous operating units, a fully centralized international cash management program offers a number of advantages:

1. The corporation is able to operate with a smaller amount of cash; pools of excess liquidity are absorbed and eliminated; each operation will maintain transactions balances only and not hold speculative or precautionary ones.
2. By reducing total assets, profitability is enhanced and financing costs reduced.
3. The headquarters staff, with its purview of all corporate activity, can recognize problems and opportunities that an individual unit might not perceive.
4. All decisions can be made using the overall corporate benefit as the criterion.
5. By increasing the volume of foreign exchange and other transactions done through headquarters, banks provide better foreign exchange quotes and better service.

6. Greater expertise in cash and portfolio management exists if one group is responsible for these activities.
7. Less will be lost in the event of an expropriation or currency controls restricting the transfer of funds because the corporation's total assets at risk in a foreign country can be reduced.

The foregoing benefits have long been understood by many experienced multinational firms. Today the combination of volatile currency and interest rate fluctuations, questions of capital availability, increasingly complex organizations and operating arrangements, and a growing emphasis on profitability virtually mandates a highly centralized international cash management system. There is also a trend to place much greater responsibility in corporate headquarters.

Centralization does not necessarily imply control by corporate headquarters of all facets of cash management. Instead, a concentration of decision making at a sufficiently high level within the corporation is required so that all pertinent information is readily available and can be used to optimize the firm's position.

Collection and Disbursement of Funds

Accelerating collections both within a foreign country and across borders is a key element of international cash management. Material potential benefits exist because long delays are often encountered in collecting receivables, particularly on export sales, and in transferring funds among affiliates and corporate headquarters. Allowing for mail time and bank processing, delays of eight to ten business days are common from the moment an importer pays an invoice to the time when the exporter is credited with *good funds*—that is, when the funds are available for use. Given high interest rates, wide fluctuations in the foreign exchange markets, and the periodic imposition of credit restrictions that have characterized financial markets in recent years, cash in transit has become more expensive and more exposed to risk.

With increasing frequency, corporate management is participating in the establishment of an affiliate's credit policy and the monitoring of collection performance. The principal goals of this intervention are to minimize *float*—that is, the transit time of payments—to reduce the investment in accounts receivable, and to lower banking fees and other transaction costs. By converting receivables into cash as rapidly as possible, a company can increase its portfolio or reduce its borrowing and, thus, earn a higher investment return or save interest expense.

Considering either national or international collections, accelerating the receipt of funds usually involves the following: (1) defining and analyzing the different available payment channels, (2) selecting the most efficient method (which can vary by country and by customer), and (3) giving specific instructions regarding procedures to the firm's customers and banks.

In addressing the first two points, the full costs of using the various methods must be determined, and the inherent delay of each must be calculated. There are two main sources of delay in the collections process: the time between the dates of payment and of receipt and the time for the payment to clear through the banking system. Inasmuch as banks will be as "inefficient" as possible to increase their float, understanding the subtleties of domestic and international money transfers is requisite if a firm is to reduce the time that funds are held and extract the maximum value from its banking relationships. Exhibit 14.1 lists the different methods multinationals use to expedite their collection of receivables.

With respect to payment instructions to customers and banks, the use of *cable remittances* is a crucial means for companies to minimize delays in receipt of payments and in conversion of payments into cash, especially in Europe because European banks tend to defer the value of good funds when the payment is made by check or draft.

Turning to international cash movements, having all affiliates transfer funds by telex enables the corporation to better plan because the vagaries of mail time are eliminated. Third parties, too, will be asked to use wire transfers. For most amounts, the fees required for telex are less than the savings generated by putting the money to use more quickly.

One of the cash manager's biggest problems is that bank-to-bank wire transfers do not always operate with great efficiency or reliability. Delays, crediting the wrong account, availability of funds, and many other operational problems are common. One solution to these problems is to be found in the *SWIFT* network (Society for Worldwide Interbank Financial Telecommunications). SWIFT has standardized international message formats and employs a dedicated computer network to support funds transfer messages.

The SWIFT network connects over 900 banks in North America, Western Europe, and the Far East. Its mission is to quickly transmit standard forms to allow its member banks to automatically process data by computer. All types of customer and bank transfers are transmitted as well as foreign exchange deals, bank account statements, and administrative messages. To use SWIFT the corporate client must deal with domestic banks that are subscribers and with foreign banks that are highly automated. Appendix 14A discusses electronic methods of transferring funds internationally.

To cope with some of the transmittal delays associated with checks or drafts, customers are instructed to remit to "mobilization" points that are centrally located in regions with large sales volumes. These funds are managed centrally or are transmitted to the selling subsidiary. For example, European customers may be told to make all payments to Switzerland, where the corporation maintains a staff specializing in cash and portfolio management and collections.

Sometimes customers are asked to pay directly into a designated account at a branch of the bank that is mobilizing the MNC's funds internationally. This method is particularly useful when banks have large branch networks. Another technique used is to have customers

■ **EXHIBIT 14.1**   How Multinationals Expedite Their Collection of Receivables

Procedures for Expediting Receipt of Payments	Procedures for Expediting Conversion of Payments into Cash
Cable remittances	Cable remittances
Mobilization centers	Establishing accounts in customers' banks
Lock boxes	Negotiations with banks on value-dating
Electronic fund transfers	

remit funds to a designated *lock box,* which is a postal box in the company's name. One or more times daily, a local bank opens the mail received at the lock box and deposits any checks immediately.

Multinational banks now provide firms with rapid transfers of their funds among branches in different countries, generally giving their customers *same-day value*—that is, funds are credited that same day. Rapid transfers can also be accomplished through a bank's correspondent network, although it becomes somewhat more difficult to arrange same-day value for funds.

Chief financial officers are increasingly relying on computers and worldwide telecommunications networks to help manage the company cash portfolio. Many multinational firms will not deal with a bank that doesn't have a leading-edge electronic banking system.

At the heart of today's high-tech corporate treasuries are the *treasury workstation* software packages that many big banks sell as supplements to their cash management systems. Linking the company with its bank and branch offices, the workstations let treasury personnel compute a company's worldwide cash position on a "real-time" basis, meaning that the second a transaction is made in, say, Rio de Janeiro, it is electronically recorded in Tokyo as well. This simultaneous record keeping lets companies keep their funds active at all times. Treasury personnel can use their workstations to initiate fund transfers from units with surplus cash to those units that require funds, thereby reducing the level of bank borrowings.

■ ──

ILLUSTRATION

International Cash Management at National Semiconductor. After computerizing its cash management system, National Semiconductor was able to save significant interest expenses by quickly transfering money from locations with surplus cash to those needing money. In a typical transaction, the company shifted a surplus $500,000 from its Japanese account to its Phillipine operations—avoiding the need to borrow the half million dollars and saving several thousand dollars in interest expense. Before computerization, it would have taken five or six days to discover the surplus. ■

Management of disbursements is a delicate balancing act: holding onto funds versus staying on good terms with suppliers. It requires a detailed knowledge of individual country and supplier nuances, as well as the myriad of payment instruments and banking services available around the world. Exhibit 14.2 presents some questions that corporate treasurers should address in reviewing their disbursement policies.

Payments Netting in International Cash Management

Many multinational corporations are now in the process of rationalizing their production on a global basis. This process involves a highly coordinated international interchange of materials, parts, subassemblies, and finished products among the various units of the MNC, with many affiliates both buying from, and selling to, each other.

The importance of these physical flows to the international financial executive is that they are accompanied by a heavy volume of *interaffiliate fund flows*. Of particular impor-

■ **EXHIBIT 14.2**   Reviewing Disbursements: Auditing Payment Instruments

1. What payment instruments are you using to pay suppliers, employees, and government entities (e.g., checks, drafts, wire transfers, direct deposits)?
2. What are the total disbursements made through each of these instruments annually?
3. What is the mail and clearing float for these instruments in each country?
4. What techniques, such as remote disbursement, are being used to prolong the payment cycle?
5. How long does it take suppliers to process the various instruments and present them for payment?
6. What are the bank charges and internal processing costs for each instrument?
7. Are banking services such as controlled disbursement and zero-balance accounts used where available?

tance is the fact that there is a measurable cost associated with these cross-border fund transfers, including the cost of purchasing foreign exchange (the foreign exchange spread), the opportunity cost of float (time in transit), and other transaction costs, such as cable charges. These transaction costs are estimated to vary from 0.25% to 1.5% of the volume transferred. Thus, there is a clear incentive to minimize the total volume of intercompany fund flows. This can be achieved by payments netting.

Bilateral and Multilateral Netting.   The idea behind a *payments netting* system is very simple: Payments among affiliates go back and forth, whereas only a netted amount need be transferred. Suppose, for example, the German subsidiary of an MNC sells goods worth $1 million to its Italian affiliate that in turn sells goods worth $2 million to the German unit. The combined flows total $3 million. On a net basis, however, the German unit need remit only $1 million to the Italian unit. This type of *bilateral netting* is valuable, though, only if subsidiaries sell back and forth to each other.

Bilateral netting would be of little use where there is a more complex structure of internal sales, such as in the situation depicted in Exhibit 14.3 where no company both buys from, and sells to, any one affiliate. Note, however, that each affiliate's inflows equal its outflows. On a multilateral basis, therefore, total transfers would net out to zero.

Since a large percentage of multinational transactions are internal—leading to a relatively large volume of interaffiliate payments—the payoff from *multilateral netting* can be large, relative to the costs of such a system. Many companies find they can eliminate 50% or more of their intercompany transactions through multilateral netting, with annual savings in foreign exchange transactions costs and bank transfer charges that average about 1.5% per dollar netted. For example, SmithKline Beckman estimates that it saves $300,000 annually in foreign exchange transactions costs and bank transfer charges by using a multilateral netting system.[1] Similarly, Baxter International estimates it saves $200,000 per year by eliminating approximately 60% of its intercompany transactions through netting.[2]

[1]"How Centralized Systems Benefit Managerial Control: SmithKline Beckman," *Business International Money Report,* June 23, 1986, p. 198.

[2]*Solving International Financial and Currency Problems* (New York: Business International Corporation, 1976), p. 29.

■ **EXHIBIT 14.3**   Multilateral Netting

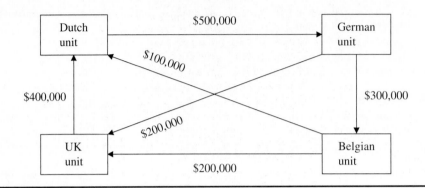

Information Requirements.   Essential to any netting scheme is a centralized control point that can collect and record detailed information on the intracorporate accounts of each participating affiliate at specified time intervals. The control point, called a *netting center,* is a subsidiary company set up in a location with minimal exchange controls for trade transactions.

The netting center will use a matrix of payables and receivables to determine the net payer or creditor position of each affiliate at the date of clearing. An example of such a matrix is provided in Exhibit 14.4. It is assumed that there is a U.S. parent corporation with subsidiaries in France, Belgium, and Sweden. Each of the amounts due to and from the

■ **EXHIBIT 14.4**   Intercompany Payments Matrix (U.S. $ Millions)

	Paying Affiliates				
Receiving Affiliates	**United States**	**France**	**Sweden**	**Belgium**	**Total**
United States	—	8	7	4	19
France	6	—	4	2	12
Sweden	2	0	—	3	5
Belgium	1	2	5	—	8
Total	9	10	16	9	44

	Receipt	**Payment**	**Net Receipt**	**Net Payment**
United States	19	9	10	—
France	12	10	2	—
Sweden	5	16	—	11
Belgium	8	9	—	1

affiliated companies is converted into a common currency (the U.S. dollar in this example) and entered onto the matrix. Note that in an intercompany system, the payables will always equal the receivables on both a gross basis and a net basis. Typically, to minimize the impact of currency changes on the amounts scheduled for transfer, the exchange rate at which these transactions occur is fixed during the week that netting takes place.

Without netting, the total payments in the system would equal $44 million. Multilateral netting will pare these transfers to $12 million, a net reduction of 73%. If all payments and disbursements are made through a central pool, the payers in the system—Sweden and Belgium in this example—will remit the local currency equivalent of their net obligations to the pool, where those currencies are sold in exchange for the receiving units' currencies. Alternatively, the payers can be asked to remit funds directly to specified recipients.

The choice of which affiliate(s) each payer pays depends on the relative costs of transferring funds between each pair of affiliates. The per unit costs of sending funds between two affiliates can vary significantly from month to month because one subsidiary may receive payment from a third party in a currency that is needed by the other subsidiary. By using this currency for payment, one or more foreign exchange conversions can be eliminated. This conclusion implies that the cost of sending funds from Germany to France, for example, can differ greatly from the cost of moving money from France to Germany.

For example, Volvo has a policy of transferring a currency, without conversion, to a unit needing that currency to pay a creditor.[3] To see how this policy works, suppose that Volvo Sweden buys automotive components from a German manufacturer and Volvo Belgium purchases automotive kits from Volvo Sweden. At the same time, a German dealer buys automobiles from Volvo Belgium and pays in Deutsche marks. Volvo Belgium will then use these DM to pay Volvo Sweden, which in turn will use them to pay its German creditor.

Foreign Exchange Controls. Before implementing a payments netting system, a company needs to know whether any restrictions on netting exist. Firms may sometimes be barred from netting or be required to obtain permission from the local monetary authorities.

Analysis. The higher the volume of intercompany transactions and the more back-and-forth selling that takes place, the more worthwhile netting is likely to be. A useful approach to evaluating a netting system would be to establish the direct cost savings of the netting system and then use this figure as a benchmark against which to measure the costs of implementation and operation. These set-up costs have been estimated at less than $20,000.[4]

An additional benefit from running a netting system is the tighter control that management can exert over corporate fund flows. The same information required to operate a netting system will also enable an MNC to shift funds in response to expectations of currency movements, changing interest differentials, and tax differentials.

---

[3]Op cit, p. 32.

[4]"The State of the Art," *New Techniques in International Exposure and Cash Management,* Vol. 1 (New York: Business International Corporation, 1977), p. 244.

■ ───

ILLUSTRATION

Cost/Benefit Analysis of an International Cash Management System. Although company A already operates a multilateral netting system, it commissioned a study to show where additional improvements in cash management could be made.[5] The firm proposed to establish a finance company (FINCO) in Europe. FINCO'S primary function would be to act as a collecting and paying agent for divisions of company A that export to third parties. All receivables would be gathered into the international branch network of bank X. Each branch would handle receivables denominated in the currency of its country of domicile. These branch accounts would be monitored by both FINCO and the exporting unit via the bank's electronic reporting facility.

Intercompany payments and third-party collection payments from FINCO to each exporter would be included in the existing multilateral netting system, which would be administered by FINCO. Payments for imports from third-party suppliers would also be included. Finally, the netting system would be expanded to include intercompany payments from operations in the United States, Canada, and one additional European country.

The feasibility study examined six basic savings components and two cost components. The realizable, annualized savings are summarized below:

Savings Component	Cost Savings
1. Optimized multilateral netting	$ 29,000
2. Reduced remittance-processing time by customer and remitting bank	26,000
3. Reduction in cross-border transfer float by collecting currencies in their home country	46,000
4. Reduction in cross-border transfer comissions and charges by collecting currencies in their home country	41,000
5. Use of incoming foreign currencies to source outgoing foreign payments in the same currencies	16,000
6. Use of interest-bearing accounts	8,000
Total Estimated Annual Savings	$166,000
Cost Component	**Cost**
1. Computer time-sharing charges for accessing Bank X's system	$ 17,000
2. Communications charges for additional cross-border funds transfers	13,000
Total Estimated Annual Costs	$ 30,000
Total Net Savings	$136,000 ■

Management of the Short-Term Investment Portfolio

A major task of international cash management is to determine the levels and currency denominations of the multinational group's investment in cash balances and money market instruments. Firms with seasonal or cyclical cash flows have special problems, such as

───────────────────────────────────

[5]This illustration appears in "Cost/Benefit Analysis of One Company's Cash Management System," *Business International Money Report,* April 14, 1986, pp. 119–120.

spacing investment maturities to coincide with projected needs. To manage this investment properly requires (1) a forecast of future cash needs based on the company's current budget and past experience and (2) an estimate of a minimum cash position for the coming period. These projections should take into account the effects of inflation and anticipated currency changes on future cash flows.

Successful management of an MNC's required cash balances and of any excess funds generated by the firm and its affiliates depends largely on the astute selection of appropriate short-term money market instruments. Rewarding opportunities exist in many countries, but the choice of an investment medium depends on government regulations, the structure of the market, and the tax laws, all of which vary widely. Available money instruments differ among the major markets, and at times, foreign firms are denied access to existing investment opportunities. Only a few markets, such as the broad and diversified U.S. market and the Eurocurrency markets, are truly free and international. Capsule summaries of key money market instruments are provided in Exhibit 14.5.

Once corporate headquarters has fully identified the present and future needs of its affiliates, it must then decide on a policy for managing its liquid assets worldwide. This policy must recognize that the value of shifting funds across national borders to earn the highest possible risk-adjusted return depends not only on the risk-adjusted yield differential, but also on the transaction costs involved. In fact, the basic reason for holding cash in several currencies simultaneously is the existence of currency conversion costs. If these costs are zero and government regulations permit, all cash balances should be held in the currency having the highest effective risk-adjusted return net of withdrawal costs.

Given that transaction costs do exist, the appropriate currency denomination mix of an MNC's investment in money and near-money assets is probably more a function of the currencies in which it has actual and projected inflows and outflows than of effective yield differentials or government regulations. The reason why is simple: Despite government controls, it would be highly unusual to see an annualized risk-adjusted interest differential of even 2%. Although seemingly large, a 2% annual differential yields only an additional 0.167% for a 30-day investment or 0.5% extra for a 90-day investment. Such small differentials can easily be offset by foreign exchange transaction costs. Thus, even large annualized risk-adjusted interest spreads may not justify shifting funds for short-term placements.

Portfolio Guidelines.   Common-sense guidelines for globally managing the marketable securities portfolio are as follows.

1. Diversify the instruments in the portfolio to maximize the yield for a given level of risk. Don't invest only in government securities. Eurodollar and other instruments may be nearly as safe.
2. Review the portfolio daily to decide which securities should be liquidated and what new investments should be made.
3. In revising the portfolio, make sure that the incremental interest earned more than compensates for such added costs as clerical work, the income lost between investments, fixed charges such as the foreign exchange spread, and commissions on the sale and purchase of securities.

■ **EXHIBIT 14.5**   Key Money Market Instruments

Instrument	Borrower	Maturities	Comments
Treasury bills (T-bills)	Central governments of many countries	Up to 1 year	Safest and most-liquid short-term investment
Federal funds (U.S.)	U.S. commercial banks temporarily short of legal reserve requirements	Overnight to 3 days	Suitable for very short-term investment of large amounts ($1 million or more)
Government agency notes (U.S.)	Issued by U.S. government agencies such as Federal National Mortgage Association	30 days to 270 days	Similar to local authority notes in the United Kingdom. Both offer slightly higher yields than T-bills.
Demand deposits	Commercial banks	On demand	Governments sometimes impose restrictions on interest rates banks can offer (as in the U.S.).
Time deposits	Commercial banks	Negotiable but advance notice usually required	Governments sometimes regulate interest rates and/or maturities.
Deposits with nonbank financial institutions	Nonbank financial institutions	Negotiable	Usually offer higher yields than banks do
Certificates of deposit (CDs)	Commercial banks	Negotiable but normally 30, 60, or 90 days	Negotiable papers representing a term bank deposit; more liquid than straight deposits since they can be sold
Bankers' acceptances	Bills of exchange guaranteed by a commercial bank	Up to 180 days	Highest-quality investment next to T-bills
Commercial paper (also known as trade paper or, in the United Kingdom, fine trade bills)	Large corporations with high credit ratings	30 days to 270 days	Negotiable, unsecured promissory notes; available in all major money markets
Temporary corporate loans	Corporations	Negotiable	Usually offer higher returns than those available from financial institutions but are not liquid since they must be held to maturity

4. If rapid conversion to cash is an important consideration, then carefully evaluate the security's marketability (liquidity). Ready markets exist for some securities, but not for others.

5. Tailor the maturity of the investment to the firm's projected cash needs. Or a secondary market with high liquidity should exist.

6. Carefully consider opportunities for covered or uncovered interest arbitrage.

Optimal Worldwide Cash Levels

Centralized cash management typically involves the transfer of an affiliate's cash in excess of minimal operating requirements into a centrally managed account, or *cash pool*. Some firms have established a special corporate entity that collects and disburses funds through a single bank account.

With cash pooling, each affiliate need hold locally only the minimum cash balance required for transactions purposes. All precautionary balances are held by the parent or in the pool. As long as the demands for cash by the various units are reasonably independent of each other, centralized cash management can provide an equivalent degree of protection with a lower level of cash reserves.

Another benefit from pooling is that either less borrowing need be done or more excess funds are available for investment where returns will be maximized. Consequently, interest expenses are reduced or investment income is increased. In addition, the larger the pool of funds, the more worthwhile it becomes for a firm to invest in cash management expertise. Furthermore, pooling permits exposure arising from holding foreign currency cash balances to be centrally managed.

Evaluation and Control.   Taking over control of an affiliate's cash reserves can create motivational problems for local managers unless some adjustments are made to the way in which these managers are evaluated. One possible approach is to relieve local managers of profit responsibility for their excess funds. The problem with this solution is that it provides no incentive for local managers to take advantage of specific opportunities that only they may be aware of.

An alternative approach is to present local managers with interest rates for borrowing or lending funds to the pool that reflect the opportunity cost of money to the parent corporation. In setting these *internal interest rates* (IIRs), the corporate treasurer, in effect, is acting as a bank, offering to borrow or lend currencies at given rates. By examining these IIRs, local treasurers will have a greater awareness of the opportunity cost of their idle cash balances, as well as an added incentive to act on this information. In many instances, they will prefer to transfer at least part of their cash balances (where permitted) to a central pool in order to earn a greater return. To make pooling work, managers must have access to the central pool whenever they require money.

■ ───

ILLUSTRATION

An Italian Cash Management System. An Italian firm has created a centralized cash management system for its 140 operating units within Italy. At the center is a holding company that manages banking relations, borrowings, and investments. In the words of the firm's treasurer, "We put ourselves in front of the companies as a real bank and say, 'If you have a surplus to place, I will pay you the best rates.' If the company finds something better than that, they are free to place the funds outside the group. But this doesn't happen very often."[6] In this way, the company avoids being overdrawn with one bank while investing with another.

                                                                                                       ∎

Cash Planning and Budgeting

The key to the successful global coordination of a firm's cash and marketable securities is a good reporting system. Cash receipts must be reported and forecast in a comprehensive, accurate, and timely manner. If the headquarters staff is to fully and economically use the company's worldwide cash resources, they must know the financial positions of affiliates, the forecast cash needs or surpluses, the anticipated cash inflows and outflows, local and international money market conditions, and likely currency movements.

As a result of rapid and pronounced changes in the international monetary arena, the need for more frequent reports has become acute. Firms that had been content to receive information quarterly now require monthly, weekly, or even daily data. Key figures are often transmitted by telex or fax machine instead of by mail.

Multinational Cash Mobilization.   A *multinational cash mobilization* system is designed to optimize the use of funds by tracking current and near-term cash positions. The information gathered can be used to aid a multilateral netting system, to increase the operational efficiency of a centralized cash pool, and to determine more effective short-term borrowing and investment policies.

The operation of a multinational cash mobilization system is illustrated here with a simple example centered around a firm's four European affiliates. Assume the European headquarters maintains a regional cash pool in London for its operating units located in England, France, Germany, and Italy. Each day, at the close of banking hours, every affiliate reports to London its current cash balances in *cleared funds*—that is, its cash accounts net of all receipts and disbursements that have cleared during the day. All balances are reported in a common currency, which is assumed here to be the U.S. dollar, with local currencies translated at rates designated by the manager of the central pool.

One report format is presented in Exhibit 14.6. It contains the end-of-day balance as well as a revised five-day forecast. According to the report for July 12, the Italian affiliate has a cash balance of $400,000. This balance means the affiliate could have disbursed an additional $400,000 that day without creating a cash deficit or having to use its overdraft facilities. The French affiliate, on the other hand, has a negative cash balance of $150,000, which it is presumably covering with an overdraft. Alternatively, it might have borrowed funds from the pool to cover this deficit. The British and German subsidiaries report cash surpluses of $100,000 and $350,000, respectively.

---

[6]"Central Cash Management Step by Step: The European Approach," *Business International Money Report,* October 19, 1984, p. 331.

■ **EXHIBIT 14.6**   Daily Cash Reports of European Central Cash Pool (U.S. $ Thousands)

Date: July 12, 199X
Affiliate: France
Cash Position: –150
Five-Day Forecast:

Day	Deposit	Disburse	Net
1	400	200	+200
2	125	225	–100
3	300	700	–400
4	275	275	0
5	250	100	+150
		Net for period	–150

Date: July 12, 199X
Affiliate: Germany
Cash Position: +350
Five-Day Forecast:

Day	Deposit	Disburse	Net
1	430	50	+380
2	360	760	–400
3	500	370	+130
4	750	230	+520
5	450	120	+330
		Net for period	+960

Date: July 12, 199X
Affiliate: Italy
Cash Position: +400
Five-Day Forecast:

Day	Deposit	Disburse	Net
1	240	340	–100
2	400	275	+125
3	480	205	+275
4	90	240	–150
5	300	245	+ 55
		Net for period	+205

Date: July 12, 199X
Affiliate: England
Cash Position: +100
Five-Day Forecast:

Day	Deposit	Disburse	Net
1	100	50	+ 50
2	260	110	+150
3	150	350	–200
4	300	50	+250
5	200	300	–100
		Net for period	+150

The manager of the central pool can then assemble these individual reports into a more usable form, such as that depicted in Exhibit 14.7. This report shows the cash balance for each affiliate, its required minimum operating cash balance, and the resultant cash surplus or deficit for each affiliate individually and for the region as a whole. According to the report, both the German and Italian affiliates ended the day with funds in excess of their operating needs, while the English unit wound up with $25,000 less than it normally requires in operating funds (even though it had $100,000 in cash). The French affiliate was short $250,000, including its operating deficit and minimum required balances. For the European region as a whole, however, there was excess cash of $75,000.

The information contained in these reports can be used to decide how to cover any deficits and where to invest temporary surplus funds. Netting can also be facilitated by breaking down each affiliate's aggregate inflows and outflows into their individual currency components. This breakdown will aid in deciding what netting operations to perform and in which currencies.

The cash forecasts contained in the daily reports can aid in determining when to transfer funds to or from the central pool and the maturities of any borrowings or investments. For

■ **EXHIBIT 14.7**   Aggregate Cash Position of European Central Cash Pool (U.S. $ Thousands)

	Daily Cash Position, July 12, 199X		
Affiliate	Closing Balance	Minimum Required	Cash Balance Surplus (Deficit)
France	−150	100	−250
Germany	+350	250	100
Italy	+400	150	250
England	+100	125	− 25
Regional surplus (deficit)			+ 75

example, although the Italian subsidiary currently has $250,000 in excess funds, it projects a deficit tomorrow of $100,000. One possible strategy is to have the Italian unit remit $250,000 to the pool today and, in turn, have the pool return $100,000 tomorrow to cover the projected deficit. However, unless interest differentials are large and/or transaction costs are minimal, it may be preferable to instruct the Italian unit to remit only $150,000 to the pool and invest the remaining $100,000 overnight in Italy.

Similarly, the five-day forecast shown in Exhibit 14.8, based on the data provided in Exhibit 14.7, indicates that the $75,000 European regional surplus generated today can be invested for at least two days before it is required (because of the cash deficit forecasted two days from today).

The cash mobilization system illustrated here has been greatly simplified in order to bring out some key details. In reality, such a system should include longer-term forecasts of

■ **EXHIBIT 14.8**   Five-Day Cash Forecast of European Central Cash Pool (U.S. $ Thousands)

	Days from July 12, 199X					
Affiliate	+1	+2	+3	+4	+5	Five-Day Total
France	+200	−100	−400	0	+150	−150
Germany	+380	−400	+130	+520	+330	+960
Italy	−100	+125	+275	−150	+ 55	+205
England	+ 50	+150	−200	+250	−100	+150
Forecast regional surplus (deficit) by day	+530	−225	−195	+620	+435	+1165

cash flows broken down by currency, forecasts of intercompany transactions (for netting purposes), and interest rates paid by the pool (for decentralized decision making).

Bank Relations

Good bank relations are central to a company's international cash management effort. Although some companies may be quite pleased with their banks' services, others may not even realize that they are being poorly served by their banks. Poor cash management services mean lost interest revenues, overpriced services, and inappropriate or redundant services. Many firms that have conducted a bank relations audit find that they are dealing with too many banks. Here are some considerations involved in auditing the company's banks.

Some common problems in bank relations are

1. *Too many relations*: Using too many banks can be expensive. It also invariably generates idle balances, higher compensating balances, more check-clearing float, suboptimal rates on foreign exchange and loans, a heavier administrative workload, and diminished control over every aspect of banking relations.

2. *High banking costs*: To keep a lid on bank expenses, treasury management must carefully track not only the direct costs of banking services—including rates, spreads, and commissions—but also the indirect costs rising from check float, *value-dating*—that is, when value is given for funds—and compensating balances. This monitoring is especially important in developing countries of Latin America and Asia; in these countries, compensating balance requirements may range as high as 30%–35%, and check-clearing times may drag on for days or even weeks. It also pays off in such European countries as Italy, where banks enjoy value-dating periods of as long as 20–25 days.

3. *Inadequate reporting*: Banks often don't provide immediate information on collections and account balances. This delay can cause excessive amounts of idle cash and prolonged float. To avoid such problems, firms should instruct their banks to provide daily balance information and to clearly distinguish between ledge and collected balances—that is, posted totals versus immediately available funds.

4. *Excessive clearing delays*: In many countries, bank float can rob firms of funds availability. In such nations as Mexico, Spain, Italy, and Indonesia, checks drawn on banks located in remote areas can take weeks to clear to headquarters accounts in the capital city. Fortunately, firms that negotiate for better float times often meet with success. Whatever method is used to reduce clearing time, it is crucial that companies constantly check up on their banks to ensure that funds are credited to accounts as expected.

Negotiating better service is easier if the company is a valued customer. Demonstrating that it is a valuable customer requires the firm to have ongoing discussions with its bankers to determine the precise value of each type of banking activity and the value of the business it generates for each bank. Armed with this information, the firm should make up a monthly report that details the value of its banking business. By compiling this report, the company knows precisely how much business it is giving to each bank it uses. With such information in hand, the firm can negotiate better terms and better service from its banks.

■ ───

ILLUSTRATION

How Morton Thiokol Manages Its Bank Relations. Morton Thiokol, a Chicago-based manufacturer with international sales of about $300 million, centralizes its banking policy for three main reasons: Cash management is already centralized; small local staffs may not have time to devote to bank relations; and overseas staffs often need the extra guidance of centralized bank relations. Morton Thiokol is committed to trimming its overseas banking relations to cut costs and streamline cash management. A key factor in maintaining relations with a bank is a bank's willingness to provide the firm with needed services at reasonable prices. Although Morton Thiokol usually tries to reduce the number of banks with which it maintains relations, it will sometimes add banks to increase competition and, thereby, improve its chances of getting quality services and reasonable prices. ─────────────── ■

■ 14.2 ■
ACCOUNTS RECEIVABLE MANAGEMENT

Firms grant trade credit to customers, both domestically and internationally, because they expect the investment in receivables to be profitable, either by expanding sales volume or by retaining sales that otherwise would be lost to competitors. Some companies also earn a profit on the financing charges they levy on credit sales.

The need to scrutinize *credit terms* is particularly important in countries experiencing rapid rates of inflation. The incentive for customers to defer payment, liquidating their debts with less valuable money in the future, is great. Furthermore, credit standards abroad are often more relaxed than in the home market, especially in countries lacking alternative sources of credit for small customers. To remain competitive, MNCs may feel compelled to loosen their own credit standards. Finally, the compensation system in many companies tends to reward higher sales more than it penalizes an increased investment in accounts receivable. Local managers frequently have an incentive to expand sales even if the MNC overall does not benefit.

The effort to better manage receivables overseas will not get far if finance and marketing don't coordinate their efforts. In many companies, finance and marketing work at cross purposes. Marketing thinks about selling, and finance thinks about speeding up cash flows. One way to ease the tensions between finance and marketing is to educate the sales force on how credit and collection affect company profits. Another way is to tie bonuses for salespeople to *collected* sales or to adjust sales bonuses for the interest cost of credit sales. Forcing managers to bear the opportunity cost of working capital ensures that their credit, inventory, and other working-capital decisions will be more economical.

■ ───

ILLUSTRATION

Nestle Charges for Working Capital. Nestle charges local subsidiary managers for the interest expense of net working capital using an internally devised standard rate. The inclusion of this finance charge encourages country managers to keep a tight rein on accounts receivable and inventory because the lower the net working capital, the lower the theoretical interest charge, and the higher their profits.

■

Credit Extension

Two key credit decisions to be made by a firm selling abroad are the amount of credit to extend and the currency in which credit sales are to be billed. Nothing need be added here to Chapter 9's discussion of the latter decision except to note that competitors will often resolve the currency-of-denomination issue.

The easier the credit terms are, the more sales are likely to be made. Generosity is not always the best policy. Balanced against higher revenues must be the risk of default, increased interest expense on the larger investment in receivables, and the deterioration (through currency devaluation) of the dollar value of accounts receivable denominated in the buyer's currency. These additional costs may be partly offset if liberalized credit terms enhance a firm's ability to raise its prices.

The bias of most personnel evaluation systems is in favor of higher revenues, but another factor often tends to increase accounts receivable in foreign countries. An uneconomic expansion of local sales may occur if managers are credited with dollar sales when accounts receivable are denominated in the local currency. Sales managers should be charged for the expected depreciation in the value of local currency accounts receivable. For instance, if the current exchange rate is LC 1 = $0.10, but the expected exchange rate 90 days hence (or the three-month forward rate) is $0.09, managers providing three-month credit terms should be credited with only $0.90 for each dollar in sales booked at the current spot rate.

Whether judging the implications of inflation, devaluation, or both, it must be remembered that when a unit of inventory is sold on credit, a real asset has been transformed into a monetary asset. The opportunity to raise the local currency selling price of the item to maintain its dollar value is lost. This point is obvious, but is frequently disregarded.

Assuming that both buyer and seller have access to credit at the same cost and reflect in their decisions anticipated currency changes and inflation, it should normally make no difference to a potential customer whether it receives additional credit or an equivalent cash discount. However, the MNC may benefit by revising its credit terms in three circumstances:

1. The buyer and seller hold different opinions concerning the future course of inflation or currency changes, leading one of the two to prefer term/price discount trade-offs (that is, a lower price if paid within a specified period).
2. The MNC has a lower risk-adjusted cost of credit than does its customer because of market imperfections. In other words, the buyer's higher financing cost must not be a result of its greater riskiness.
3. During periods of credit restraint in a country, the affiliate of an MNC may have access to funds (because of its parent) that local companies do not have and may, thereby, gain a marketing advantage over its competitors. Absolute availability of money, rather than its cost, may be critical.

The following five-step approach enables a firm to compare the expected benefits and costs associated with extending credit internationally:

1. Calculate the current cost of extending credit.
2. Calculate the cost of extending credit under the revised credit policy.
3. Using the information from steps 1 and 2, calculate incremental credit costs under the revised credit policy.
4. Ignoring credit costs, calculate incremental profits under the new credit policy.
5. If, and only if, incremental profits exceed incremental credit costs, select the new credit policy.

■ _____

ILLUSTRATION

Evaluating Credit Extension Overseas. Suppose a subsidiary in France currently has annual sales of $1 million with 90-day credit terms. It is believed that sales will increase by 6%, or $60,000, if terms are extended to 120 days. Of these additional sales, the cost of goods sold is $35,000. Monthly credit expenses are 1% in financing charges. In addition, the French franc is expected to depreciate an average of 0.5% every 30 days.

Ignoring currency changes for the moment, but considering financing costs, the value today of one dollar of receivables to be collected at the end of 90 days is approximately $0.97. Taking into account the 1.5% ($3 \times 0.5\%$) expected French franc depreciation over the 90-day period, this value declines to 0.97(1 − 0.015), or $0.955, implying a 4.5% cost of carrying French franc receivables for three months. Similarly, one dollar of receivables collected 120 days from now is worth $[1 − 4 \times 0.01][1 − 0.02]$ today, or $0.941. Then the incremental cost of carrying French franc receivables for the fourth month equals 0.955 − 0.941 dollars, or 1.4%.

Using the information mentioned previously, annual credit costs are currently $1,000,000 \times 0.045 = \$45,000$. Lengthening terms to 120 days will raise this cost to $1,000,000 \times 0.059 = \$59,000$. The cost cf carrying for 120 days the incremental sales of $60,000 is $60,000 \times 0.059 = \$3,540$. Thus, incremental credit costs under the new policy equal $59,000 + $3,540 − $45,000 = $17,540. Since this amount is less than the incremental profit of $25,000 (60,000 − 35,000), it is worthwhile providing a fourth month of credit.
_____ ■

In the general case, let ΔS and ΔC be the incremental sales and costs associated with an easing of credit terms. If the expected credit cost per unit of sales revenues, R, is expected to increase to $R + \Delta R$ because of a more lenient credit policy, then terms should be eased if, and only if, incremental profits are greater than incremental credit costs, or

$$\Delta S - \Delta C \geq S\Delta R + \Delta S(R + \Delta R)$$

It should be noted that R reflects forecasted changes in currency values as well as the cost of funds over the longer collection period. This analysis can also be used to ascertain whether it would be worthwhile to tighten credit, accepting lower sales but reducing credit costs at the same time.

This same methodology of comparing incremental benefits and costs can be used to solve some of the important problems firms face in trying to manage inventory abroad.

■ 14.3 ■
INVENTORY MANAGEMENT

Inventory in the form of raw materials, work in process, or finished goods is held (1) to facilitate the production process by both ensuring that supplies are at hand when needed and allowing a more even rate of production and (2) to make certain that goods are available for delivery at the time of sale.

Although, conceptually, the inventory management problems faced by multinational firms are not unique, they may be exaggerated in the case of foreign operations. For instance, MNCs typically find it more difficult to control their overseas inventory and realize inventory turnover objectives. There are a variety of reasons: long and variable transit times if ocean transportation is used, lengthy customs proceedings, dock strikes, import controls, higher duties, supply disruption, and anticipated changes in currency values.

Production Location and Inventory Control

Many U.S. companies have eschewed domestic manufacturing for offshore production to take advantage of both low-wage labor and a grab bag of tax holidays, low-interest loans, and other government largess. But a number of firms have found that low manufacturing cost isn't everything. Aside from the strategic advantages associated with U.S. production, such as maintaining close contact with domestic customers, onshore manufacturing allows for a more efficient use of capital. In particular, because of the delays in international shipment of goods and potential supply disruptions, firms producing abroad typically hold larger work-in-process and finished goods inventories. The result is higher inventory-carrying costs.

■ ——————————————————————————————————

ILLUSTRATION

Cypress Semiconductor Decides to Stay Onshore. The added inventory expenses that foreign manufacture would entail is an important reason that Cypress Semiconductor decided to manufacture integrated circuits in San Jose, California, instead of going abroad. Because Cypress makes relatively expensive circuits (they average around $8 apiece), time-consuming international shipments would have tied up the company's capital in a very expensive way. Even though offshore production would save about $0.032 per chip in labor costs, the company estimated that the labor saving would be more than offset by combined shipping and customs duties of $0.025, and an additional $0.16 in the capital cost of holding inventory.

According to Cypress chairman L.J. Sevin, "Some people just look at the labor rates, but it's inventory cost that matters. It's simply cheaper to sell a part in one week than in five or six. You have to figure out what you could have done with the inventory or the money you could have made simply by pulling the interest on the dollars you have tied up in the part."[7]

---

[7] Joel Kotkin, "The Case for Manufacturing in America," *Inc.,* March 1985, p. 54.

The estimate of 16 cents in carrying cost can be backed out as follows: As the preceding quotation indicates, parts manufactured abroad were expected to spend an extra five weeks or so in transit. This means that parts manufactured abroad would spend five more weeks in work-in-process inventory than would parts manufactured domestically. Assuming an opportunity cost of 20% (not an unreasonable number considering the volatility of the semiconductor market) and an average cost per chip of $8, the added inventory-related interest expense associated with overseas production equals:

$$\begin{aligned}\text{Added interest} \atop \text{expense} &= {\text{Opportunity cost} \atop \text{of funds}} \times {\text{Added time} \atop \text{in transit}} \times {\text{Cost per} \atop \text{part}} \\ &= 0.20 \times 5/52 \times \$8 = \$0.154\end{aligned}$$

■

Advance Inventory Purchases

In many developing countries, forward contracts for foreign currency are limited in availability or are nonexistent. In addition, restrictions often preclude free remittances, making it difficult, if not impossible, to convert excess funds into a hard currency. One means of hedging is to engage in anticipatory purchases of goods, especially imported items. The trade-off involves owning goods for which local currency prices may be increased, thereby maintaining the dollar value of the asset even if devaluation occurs, versus forgoing the return on local money market investments.

For example, suppose that Volkswagen do Brasil is trying to decide how many months' worth of components to carry in inventory. The present price of a component is DM 100, and this price is rising at the rate of 0.5% monthly. The Deutsche mark holding cost is estimated at 1% monthly, including insurance, warehousing, and spoilage, but excluding the opportunity cost of funds. Under these circumstances, where holding costs exceed antici-pated cost increases by 0.5% monthly, Volkswagen should maintain the minimum parts inventory necessary to achieve its targeted output in Brazil.

Assume now that Volkswagen has excess cruzeiro balances in Brazil on which it is earning a nominal monthly rate of 2%. However, under Brazil's system of minidevaluation, the cruzeiro is expected to devalue against the Deutsche mark by 3% in each of the next three months, 2% in the fourth month, and 1% thereafter. Since other investment opportu-nities are limited or nonexistent because of currency and financial market controls, VW's opportunity cost of funds in Deutsche marks (the 2% nominal rate it earns on cruzeiros less the expected devaluation) for the next six months, month by month, equals

Month	Opportunity Cost of Funds (%)
1	−1
2	−1
3	−1
4	0
5	1
6	1

Adding this opportunity cost of funds to the previously given monthly holding costs of 1% yields the total monthly individual and cumulative DM costs of carrying inventory for the next six months:

Beginning Month	Total Monthly Carrying Cost (%)	Cumulative Carrying Cost (5 mos.)	Cumulative Price Increase (%)
1	0	0	0.0
2	0	0	0.5
3	0	0	1.0
4	1	1	1.5
5	2	3	2.0
6	2	5	2.5

Based on the cumulative carrying costs and price increases, it is now apparent that the existence of anticipated cruzeiro devaluations, unmatched by correspondingly higher nominal interest rates—that is, the international Fisher effect is not expected to hold—should lead Volkswagen do Brasil to hedge a portion of its cash balances by purchasing four months' worth of inventory at today's prices (and at today's DM:cruzeiro exchange rate). In other words, it will pay Volkswagen to purchase this amount of inventory in advance in order to minimize losses in the real value of its cruzeiro cash balances. This conclusion is illustrated in Exhibit 14.9.

Inventory Stockpiling

Because of long delivery lead times, the often limited availability of transport for economically sized shipments, and currency restrictions, the problem of supply failure is of

■ **EXHIBIT 14.9**   The Value of Advance Purchases of Inventory

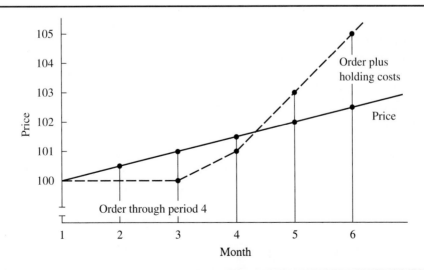

particular importance for any firm that is dependent on foreign sources These conditions may make the knowledge and execution of an optimal stocking policy, under a threat of a disruption to supply, more critical in the MNC than in the firm that purchases domestically.

The traditional response to such risks has been advance purchases. Holding large amounts of inventory can be quite expensive, though. In fact, the high cost of *inventory stockpiling*—including financing, insurance, storage, and obsolescence—has led many companies to identify low inventories with effective management. In contrast, production and sales managers typically desire a relatively large inventory, particularly when a cutoff in supply is anticipated.

Some firms do not charge their managers interest on the money tied up in inventory. A danger is that managers in these companies may take advantage of this situation by stockpiling sufficient quantities of material or goods before a potential cutoff in order to have close to a zero stock-out probability. Such a policy, established without regard to the trade-offs involved, can be very costly. For example, "In Singapore possible curtailment in shipments of air conditioners led to such heavy advance ordering that for the next two years the market was completely saturated because the warehouses were full of air conditioners."[8] Such an asymmetrical reward structure will distort the trade-offs involved. The profit performances of those managers who are receiving the benefits of additional inventory on hand should be adjusted to reflect the added costs of stockpiling.

It is obvious that as the probability of disruption increases or as holding costs go down, more inventory should be ordered. Similarly, if the cost of a stock-out rises or if future supplies are expected to be more expensive, it will pay to stockpile additional inventory. Conversely, if these parameters move in the opposite direction, less inventory should be stockpiled.

■ 14.4 ■
ILLUSTRATION: AMERICAN EXPRESS

In early 1980, American Express (Amex) completed an eight-month study of the cash cycles of its travel, credit card, and traveler's check businesses operating in seven European countries.[9] On the basis of that project, Amex developed an international cash management system that was expected to yield cash gains—increased investments or reduced borrowing—of about $35 million in Europe alone. About half of these savings were projected to come from accelerated receipts and better control of disbursements. The other half of projected gains represented improved bank-balance control, reduced bank charges, improved value-dating, and better control of foreign exchange.

The components of the system are collection and disbursement methods, bank-account architecture, balance targeting, and foreign exchange management. The worldwide system is controlled on a regional basis, with some direction from the corporate treasurer's office

[8]Sidney Robbins and Robert B. Stobaugh, *Money in the Multinational Enterprise* (New York: Basic Books, 1973), p. 113.

[9]This section is adapted from Lars H. Thunell, "The American Express Formula," *Euromoney,* March 1980, pp. 121–127.

in New York. A regional treasurer's office in Brighton, England, controls cash, financing, and foreign exchange transactions for Europe, the Middle East, and Africa.

The most advantageous collection and disbursement method for every operating division in each country was found by analyzing the timing of mail and clearing floats. This analysis involved

- Establishing what payment methods were used by customers in each country because checks are not necessarily the primary method of payment in Europe
- Measuring the mail time between certain sending and receiving points
- Identifying clearing systems and practices, which vary considerably among countries
- Analyzing for each method of payment the value-dating practice, the times for processing check deposits, and the bank charges per item

Using these data, Amex changed some of its collection and disbursement methods. For example, it installed interception points in Europe to minimize the collection float.

Next, Amex centralized the management of all its bank accounts in Europe on a regional basis. Allowing each subsidiary to set up its own independent bank account has the merit of simplicity, but it leads to a costly proliferation of different pools of funds. Amex restructured its bank accounts, eliminating some and ensuring that funds could move freely among the remaining accounts. By pooling its surplus funds, Amex can invest them for longer periods and also cut down on the chance that one subsidiary will be borrowing funds while another has surplus funds. Conversely, by combining the borrowing needs of various operations, Amex can use term financing and dispense with more expensive overdrafts. Reducing the number of accounts made cash management less complicated and also reduced banking charges.

The particular form of bank-account architecture used by Amex is a modular account structure that links separate accounts in each country with a master account. Management, on a daily basis, has only to focus on the one account through which all the country accounts have access to borrowing and investment facilities.

Balance targeting is used to control bank-account balances. The target is an average balance set for each account that reflects compensating balances, goodwill funds kept to foster the banking relationship, and the accuracy of cash forecasting. Aside from the target balance, the minimum information needed each morning to manage an account by balance targeting is the available opening balance and expected debits and credits.

Foreign exchange management in Amex's international cash management system focuses on its transaction exposure. This exposure, which is due to the multicurrency denomination of traveler's checks and credit card charges, fluctuates on a daily basis.

Procedures to control these exposures and to coordinate foreign exchange transactions center on how Amex finances its working capital from country to country, as well as the manner in which interaffiliate debts are settled. For example, if increased spending by cardholders creates the need for more working capital, Amex must decide whether to raise funds in local currency or in dollars. As a general rule, day-to-day cash is obtained at the local level through overdrafts or overnight funds.

To settle indebtedness among divisions, Amex uses interaffiliate settlements. For example, if a French cardholder uses her card in Germany, the French credit card office pays the German office, which in turn pays the German restaurant or hotel in Deutsche marks. Amex uses netting, coordinated by the regional treasurer's office in Brighton, to reduce settlement charges. For example, suppose that a German cardholder used his card in France at the same time the French cardholder charged with her card in Germany. Instead of two transactions, one foreign exchange transaction settles the differences between the two offices.

■ 14.5 ■
SUMMARY AND CONCLUSIONS

This chapter has examined the diverse elements involved in international cash, accounts receivable, and inventory management. We saw that although the objectives of cash management are the same for the MNC as for the domestic firm—to accelerate the collection of funds and optimize their use—the key ingredients to successful management differ. The wider investment options available to the multinational firm were discussed, as were the concepts of multilateral netting, cash pooling, and multinational cash mobilization. As multinational firms develop more efficient and comprehensive information-gathering systems, the international cash management options available to them will increase. Accompanying these options will be even more sophisticated management techniques than currently exist.

Similarly, we saw that inventory and receivable management in the MNC involve the familiar cost-minimizing strategy of investing in these assets up to the point at which the marginal cost of extending another dollar of credit or purchasing one more unit of inventory is just equal to the additional expected benefits to be derived. These benefits accrue in the form of maintaining or increasing the value of other current assets—such as cash and marketable securities— increasing sales revenue, or reducing inventory stock-out costs.

We have also seen that most of the inventory and receivables management problems that arise internationally have close parallels in the purely domestic firm. Currency changes have effects that are similar to those of inflation, and supply disruptions are not unique to international business. The differences that do exist are more in degree than in kind.

The major reason why inflation, currency changes, and supply disruptions generally cause more concern in the multinational rather than the domestic firm is that multinationals are often restricted in their ability to deal with these problems because of financial market constraints or import controls. Where financial markets are free to reflect anticipated economic events, there is no need to hedge against the loss of purchasing power by inventorying physical assets; financial securities or forward contracts are cheaper and more-effective hedging media. Similarly, there is less likelihood of government policies disrupting the flow of supplies among regions within a country than among countries.

■ QUESTIONS ■

1. Today's high interest rates put a premium on careful management of cash and marketable securities.

    a. What techniques are available to an MNC with operating subsidiaries in many countries to economize on these short-term assets?

b. What are the advantages and disadvantages of centralizing the cash management function?

c. What can the firm do to enhance the advantages and reduce the disadvantages described in part b?

2. Standard advice given to firms exporting to soft currency countries is to invoice in their own currency. Critically analyze this recommendation and suggest a framework that will help a financial manager to decide whether or not to stipulate hard-currency invoicing in export contracts.

a. Under what circumstances does this advice make sense?

b. Are these circumstances consistent with market efficiency?

c. Are there any circumstances under which importer and exporter will mutually agree on an invoicing currency?

3. Suppose a subsidiary is all-equity financed and, hence, has no interest expenses. Does it still make sense to charge local managers for the working capital tied up in their operations? Explain.

■ PROBLEMS ■

1. A $1.5 billion Italian multinational manufacturing company has a total of $600 million in intercompany trade flows and settles accounts in 13 currencies. It also has about $400 million in third-party trade flows. Intercompany settlements are all made manually, there are no predefined remittance channels for either intercompany or third-party payments, and the methods and currencies of payment are determined by each unit independently of the other units. Payment terms for both intercompany and third-party accounts are identical. What techniques might help this company better manage its affairs?

2. A major U.S. conglomerate operates eight large, independent subsidiaries in France that regularly trade with each other on an arm's length basis. Some of the units are relatively mature and are net generators of cash; others are growing rapidly and need cash. In addition, these units trade with a number of other units located in other countries. They all have dealings with third parties in other countries as well. A recent audit revealed that these units maintained eight separate accounts at the same bank. What potential areas of improvement are there in this company's cash management?

3. SmithKline Beckman, the health-care products multinational, has 105 affiliates worldwide. There is a great deal of intercompany sales, dividend flows, and fee and royalty payments. Each unit makes its intercompany credit, payments, and hedging decisions independently. What advantages might SKB realize from centralizing international cash management and foreign exchange management?

4. Pfizer, the pharmaceutical company, generates approximately 52% of its sales overseas. A consulting study of treasury management revealed that the international division had its own treasury group that reported to the president of the international division. Both the domestic and the international treasury groups managed sizable cash portfolios. Moreover, Pfizer Inc. was significantly increasing its issues of U.S. commercial paper, and Pfizer International had cash surpluses. Intercompany sales were made on an arm's length basis, with no coordination of payments or credit terms. Each foreign unit would report monthly on what its bank balances were. All banking relations were managed locally. What profitable opportunities has Pfizer overlooked?

5. A major food and beverage manufacturer with three major divisions, 150 countries of operation, and international revenues accounting for 15% of total revenues of $6 billion conducted a treasury audit. It gathered data in the following areas: (a) local reports put out by the subsidiaries; (b) cross-border reports prepared by regional headquarters; (c) the system's organization; (d) transmission of data between subsidiaries, regional headquarters, and parent headquarters; (e) possible computerization of local reporting systems; (f) local-bank-balance reports; and (g) the accuracy of cash forecasts. What information should the company be looking for in each of these areas and why?

6. Twenty different divisions of Union Carbide sell to thousands of customers in more than 50 countries throughout the world. The proceeds are received in the form of drafts, checks, and letters of credit. Controlling the flow of funds from each transaction is an extremely complex task. Union Carbide wants to reduce the collection float to improve its cash flow. What are some techniques that might help to achieve this objective?

7. RJR Nabisco, the tobacco and consumer products company, sells in more than 160 countries around the world. RJR collects, disburses, or invests more than $50 million each day in up to 80 different currencies. Much of the fund flows involve interaffiliate flows. In the mid-1980s, RJR's Corporate Treasury group discovered that combined borrowing of all RJR units totaled approximately $120 million to $130 million on a daily basis. Simultaneously, short-term investments entered into by RJR units ranged from $90 million to $100 million daily. Moreover, there was no central management of the fund flows. What are your recommendations to improve RJR's international cash management? Where and how might savings be achieved?

8. Newport Circuits is trying to decide whether to shift production overseas of its relatively expensive integrated circuits (they average around $11 each). Offshore assembly would save about 11.1 cents per chip in labor costs. But by producing offshore, it would take about five weeks to get the parts to customers, in contrast to one week with domestic manufacturing. Thus, offshore production would force Newport to carry another four weeks of inventory. In addition, offshore production would entail combined shipping and customs duty costs of 3.2 cents. Suppose Newport's cost of funds is 15 percent. Will it save money by shifting production offshore?

9. Tiger Car Corp., a leading Japanese automaker, is considering a proposal to locate a factory abroad in Tennessee. Although labor costs would rise by ¥33,000 per car, the time in transit for the cars (to be sold in the United States) would be reduced by 65 days. Tigers sell for ¥825,000, and TCC's cost of funds is 12.5 percent. Should TCC locate the plant in Tennessee?

■ APPENDIX 14A ■
ELECTRONIC MEANS OF INTERNATIONAL FUNDS TRANSFERS

CHIPS (Clearing House Interbank Payments System) is a computerized network developed by the New York Clearing House Association for transfer of international dollar payments, linking about 140 depository institutions that have offices or affiliates in New York City. Currently, CHIPS handles about 105,000 interbank transfers daily valued at $350 billion. The transfers represent about 90% of all interbank transfers relating to international dollar payments.

Under an agreement signed in August 1981, the New York Fed established a settlement account for member banks into which debit settlement payments are sent and from which credit settlement payments are disbursed. Transfers between member banks are netted out and settled at the close of each business day by sending or receiving FedWire transfers through the settlement account.

The FedWire system is operated by the Federal Reserve and is used for domestic money transfers. FedWire allows almost instant movement of balances, as well as the transfer of government securities, between institutions that have accounts at the Federal Reserve Banks. A transfer takes place when an order to pay is transmitted from an originating office to a Federal Reserve Bank. The account of the paying bank is charged, and the receiving bank's account is credited.

For example, suppose a London bank wants to transfer $1 million from its account at New York City correspondent bank A to an account at a bank outside New York City through New York correspondent bank B. Banks A and B are both members of CHIPS.

Bank A receives the London bank's transfer message by telex or through the SWIFT system. Bank A verifies the London bank's message and enters the message into its CHIPS terminal, providing the identifying codes for the sending and receiving banks and the identity of the account at bank B that will receive the funds and the amount. The message is then stored in the CHIPS central computer.

As soon as bank A approves and releases the "stored" transaction, the message is transmitted from the CHIPS computer to bank B. The CHIPS computer also makes a permanent record of the transaction and makes appropriate debits and credits in the CHIPS accounts of bank A and bank B. When correspondent bank B receives its credit message, it notifies the bank outside New York City that the funds have been credited to its account. Immediately following the closing of the CHIPS network at 4:30 P.M. (Eastern Standard Time), the CHIPS computer produces a settlement report showing the net debit or credit position of each participant.

A separate settlement report shows the net position of each settling participant. The net position of a nonsettling participant is netted against the position of its correspondent settling participant. Each settling participant has a set period to determine whether it will settle the net position of its participant respondents. After that time, if no settling participant refuses to settle, the settling participants with net debit positions have until 5:45 P.M. (Eastern Standard Time) to transfer their debit amounts through Fedwire to the CHIPS settlement account on the books of the New York Fed. The Clearing House then transfers those funds via FedWire out of the settlement account to those settling participants with net creditor positions. The process usually is completed by 6:00 P.M. (Eastern Standard Time).

■ BIBLIOGRAPHY ■

Goeltz, Richard K. "Managing Liquid Funds Internationally." *Columbia Journal of World Business,* July–August 1972, pp. 59–65.

Prindl, Andreas R. "International Money Management II: Systems and Techniques." *Euromoney,* October 1971.

Robbins, Sidney, and Robert B. Stobaugh. *Money in the Multinational Enterprise.* New York: Basic Books, 1973.

Shapiro, Alan C. "International Cash Management: The Determination of Multicurrency Cash Balances." *Journal of Financial and Quantitative Analysis,* December 1976, pp. 893–900.

———. "Payments Netting in International Cash Management." *Journal of International Business Studies,* Fall 1978, pp. 51–58.

▪ 15 ▪

Managing the Multinational Financial System

An injudicious tax offers a great temptation to smuggling. But the penalties of smuggling must rise in proportion to the temptation. The law, contrary to all the ordinary principles of justice, first creates the temptation, and then punishes those who yield to it.

—Adam Smith (1776)—

▪ The multinational corporation possesses a unique characteristic: the ability to shift funds and accounting profits among its various units through internal financial transfer mechanisms. Collectively, these mechanisms make up the *multinational financial system.* As we saw in Chapter 1, *internal financial transactions* are inherent in the MNC's global approach to international operations, specifically the highly coordinated international interchange of goods (material, parts, subassemblies, and finished products), services (technology, management skills, trademarks, and patents), and capital (equity and debt) that is the hallmark of the modern multinational firm. Indeed, almost 40% of U.S. imports and exports are transactions between U.S. firms and their foreign affiliates or parents.

The purpose of this chapter is to analyze the benefits, costs, and constraints associated with the multinational financial system. This analysis includes (1) identifying the conditions under which use of this system will increase the value of the firm relative to what it would be if all financial transactions were made at arm's length through external financial channels, (2) describing and evaluating the various channels for moving money and profits internationally, and (3) specifying the design principles for a global approach to managing international fund transfers. We will examine the objectives of such an approach and the various behavioral, informational, legal, and economic factors that help determine its degree of success.

■ 15.1 ■

THE VALUE OF THE MULTINATIONAL FINANCIAL SYSTEM

The value of the MNC's network of financial linkages stems from the wide variations in national tax systems and significant costs and barriers associated with international financial transfers. Exhibit 15.1 summarizes the various factors that enhance the value of internal, relative to external, financial transactions. These restrictions are usually imposed to allow nations to maintain artificial values (usually inflated) for their currencies. In addition, capital controls are necessary when governments set the cost of local funds at a lower-than-market rate when currency risks are accounted for—that is, when government regulations do not allow the international Fisher effect or interest rate parity to hold.

Consequently, the ability to transfer funds and to reallocate profits internally presents multinationals with three different types of arbitrage opportunities.

1. *Tax arbitrage*: MNCs can reduce their tax burden by shifting profits from units located in high-tax nations to those in lower-tax nations. Or, they may shift profits from units in a taxpaying position to those with tax losses.
2. *Financial market arbitrage*: By transferring funds among units, MNCs may be able to circumvent exchange controls, earn higher risk-adjusted yields on excess funds, reduce

■ **EXHIBIT 15.1**   Market Imperfections That Enchance the Value of Internal Financial Transactions

---

Formal Barriers to International Transactions
    Quantitative restrictions (exchange controls) and direct taxes on international movements of funds
    Differential taxation of income streams according to nationality and global tax situation of the owners
    Restrictions by nationality of investor and/or investment on access to domestic capital markets

Informal Barriers to International Transactions
    Costs of obtaining information
    Difficulty of enforcing contracts across national boundaries
    Transaction costs
    Traditional investment patterns

Imperfections in Domestic Capital Markets
    Ceilings on interest rates
    Mandatory credit allocations
    Limited legal and institutional protection for minority shareholders
    Limited liquidity due to thinness of markets
    High transaction costs due to small market size and/or monopolistic practices of key financial institutions
    Difficulty of obtaining information needed to evaluate securities

SOURCE: Donald R. Lessard, "Transfer Prices, Taxes, and Financial Markets: Implications of Internal Financial Transfers Within the Multinational Firm," in Robert G. Hawkins, ed., *The Economic Effects of Multinational Corporations* (Greenwich, Conn.: JAI Press, 1979). Reprinted by permission of the publisher.

their risk-adjusted cost of borrowed funds, and tap previously unavailable capital sources.

3. *Regulatory system arbitrage*: When subsidiary profits are a function of government regulations (for example, when a government agency sets allowable prices on the firm's goods) or union pressure, rather than the marketplace, the ability to disguise true profitability by reallocating profits among units may give the multinational firm a negotiating advantage.[1]

A fourth possible arbitrage opportunity is the ability to permit an affiliate to negate the effect of credit restraint or controls in its country of operation. If a government limits access to additional borrowing locally, then the firm able to draw on external sources of funds not only can achieve greater short-term profits but also may be able to attain a more powerful market position over the long term.

■ 15.2 ■
INTERCOMPANY FUND-FLOW MECHANISMS: COSTS AND BENEFITS

The MNC can be visualized as *unbundling* the total flow of funds between each pair of affiliates into separate components that are associated with resources transferred in the form of products, capital services, and technology. For example, dividends, interest, and loan repayments can be matched against capital invested as equity or debt; fees, royalties, or corporate overhead can be charged for various corporate services, trademarks, or licenses.

The different channels available to the multinational enterprise for moving money and profits internationally include transfer pricing, fee and royalty adjustments, leading and lagging, intercompany loans, dividend adjustments, and investing in the form of debt versus equity. This section examines the costs, benefits, and constraints associated with each of these methods: It begins by sketching out some of the tax consequences for U.S.-based MNCs of interaffiliate financial transfers.

Tax Factors

Total tax payments on intercompany fund transfers are dependent on the tax regulations of both the host and the recipient nations. The host country ordinarily has two types of taxes that directly affect tax costs: corporate income taxes and withholding taxes on dividend, interest, and fee remittances. In addition, several countries, such as Germany and Japan, tax retained earnings at a different (usually higher) rate than earnings paid out as dividends.

Many recipient nations, including the United States, tax income remitted from abroad at the regular corporate tax rate. Where this rate is higher than the foreign tax rate, dividend

---

[1]See Donald R. Lessard, in "Transfer Prices, Taxes, and Financial Markets: Implications of Internal Financial Transfers Within the Multinational Firm," in *The Economic Effects of Multinational Corporations,* Robert G. Hawkins, ed. (Greenwich, Conn.: JAI Press, 1979); and David P. Rutenberg, "Maneuvering Liquid Assets in a Multinational Company," *Management Science,* June 1970, pp. B–671–684.

and other payments will normally entail an incremental tax cost. There are a number of countries, however—such as Canada, the Netherlands, and France— that do not impose any additional taxes on foreign-source income.

As an offset to these additional taxes, most countries, including the United States, provide tax credits for affiliate taxes already paid on the same income. For example, if a subsidiary located overseas has $100 in pretax income, pays $30 in local tax, and then remits the remaining $70 to its U.S. parent in the form of a dividend, the U.S. Internal Revenue Service (IRS) will impose a $34 tax (0.34 × $100), but will then provide a dollar-for-dollar *foreign tax credit* (FTC) for the $30 already paid in foreign taxes, leaving the parent with a bill for the remaining $4. Foreign tax credits from other remittances can be used to offset these additional taxes. For example, if a foreign subsidiary earns $100 before tax, pays $45 in local tax, and then remits the remaining $55 in the form of a dividend, the parent will wind up with an FTC of $11, the difference between the $34 U.S. tax owed and the $45 foreign tax paid.

Transfer Pricing

The pricing of goods and services traded internally is one of the most sensitive of all management subjects, and executives are typically reluctant to discuss it. Each government normally presumes that multinationals use *transfer pricing* to its country's detriment. For this reason, a number of home and host governments have set up policing mechanisms to review the transfer pricing policies of MNCs.

The most important uses of transfer pricing include (1) reducing taxes, (2) reducing tariffs, and (3) avoiding exchange controls. Transfer prices may also be used to increase the MNC's share of profits from a joint venture and to disguise an affiliate's true profitability.

Tax Effects.   To illustrate the tax effects associated with a change in transfer price, suppose that affiliate A produces 100,000 circuit boards for $10 apiece and sells them to affiliate B. Affiliate B, in turn, sells these boards for $22 apiece to an unrelated customer. As shown in Exhibit 15.2, pretax profit for the consolidated company is $1 million regardless of the price at which the goods are transferred from affiliate A to affiliate B.

Nevertheless, because affiliate A's tax rate is 30% while affiliate B's tax rate is 50%, consolidated after-tax income will differ depending on the transfer price used. Under the low-markup policy, in which affiliate A sets a unit transfer price of $15, affiliate A pays taxes of $120,000 and affiliate B pays $300,000, for a total tax bill of $420,000 and a consolidated net income of $580,000. Switching to a high-markup policy (a transfer price of $18), affiliate A's taxes rise to $210,000 while affiliate B's decline to $150,000, for combined tax payments of $360,000 and consolidated net income of $640,000. The result of this transfer price increase is to lower total taxes paid by $60,000 and raise consolidated income by the same amount.

In effect, profits are being shifted from a higher to a lower tax jurisdiction. In the extreme case, an affiliate may be in a loss position because of high start-up costs, heavy depreciation charges, or substantial investments that are expensed. Consequently, it has a zero effective tax rate, and profits channeled to that unit can be received tax free. The basic rule of thumb to follow if the objective is to minimize taxes is as follows: If affiliate A is selling goods to

■ **EXHIBIT 15.2**   Tax Effect of High Versus Low Transfer Price ($ Thousands)

	Affiliate A	Affiliate B	Affiliates A + B
Low-Markup Policy			
Revenue	1,500	2,200	2,200
Cost of goods solds	1,000	1,500	1,000
Gross profit	500	700	1,200
Other expenses	100	100	200
Income before taxes	400	600	1,000
Taxes (30%/50%)	120	300	420
Net income	280	300	580
High-Markup Policy			
Revenue	1,800	2,200	2,200
Cost of goods sold	1,000	1,800	1,000
Gross profit	800	400	1,200
Other expenses	100	100	200
Income before taxes	700	300	1,000
Taxes (30%/50%)	210	150	360
Net income	490	150	640

affiliate B, and t_A and t_B are the marginal tax rates of affiliate A and affiliate B, respectively, then

> If $t_A > t_B$, set the transfer price as low as possible.
> If $t_A < t_B$, set the transfer price as high as possible.

Tariffs. The introduction of tariffs complicates this decision rule. Suppose that affiliate B must pay *ad valorem* import duties—tariffs that are set as a percentage of the value of the imported goods—at the rate of 10%. Then, raising the transfer price will increase the duties that affiliate B must pay, assuming that the tariff is levied on the invoice (transfer) price. The combined tax-plus-tariff effects of the transfer price change are shown in Exhibit 15.3.

Under the low-markup policy, import tariffs of $150,000 are paid. Affiliate B's taxes will decline by $75,000 because tariffs are tax-deductible. Total taxes plus tariffs paid are $495,000. Switching to the high-markup policy raises import duties to $180,000 and simultaneously lowers affiliate B's income taxes by half that amount, or $90,000. Total taxes plus tariffs rise to $450,000. The high-markup policy is still desirable, but its benefit has been reduced by $15,000 to $45,000. In general, the higher the ad valorem tariff relative to the income tax differential, the more likely it is that a low transfer price is desirable.

There are some costs associated with using transfer prices for tax reduction. If the price is too high, tax authorities in the purchaser's (affiliate B's) country will see revenues forgone; if the price is too low, both governments might intervene. Affiliate A's government may view low transfer prices as tax evasion at the same time that the tariff commission in affiliate B's country sees dumping and/or revenue forgone. These costs must be paid for in the form of legal fees, executive time, and penalties.

Most countries have specific regulations governing transfer prices. For instance, *Section 482* of the U.S. Revenue Code calls for *arm's-length prices*—prices at which a willing buyer and a willing unrelated seller would freely agree to transact. The four alternative methods for establishing an arm's length price, in order of their general acceptability to tax authorities, are as follows.

1. *Comparable uncontrolled price method*: Under this method, the transfer price is set by direct references to prices used in comparable bona fide transactions between enterprises that are independent of each other or between the multinational enterprise (MNE) group and unrelated parties. In principle, this method is the most appropriate to use; in theory, it is the easiest. In practice, however, it may be impractical or difficult to apply. For example, differences in quantity, quality, terms, use of trademarks or brand names, time of sale, level of the market, and geography of the market may be grounds for claiming that the sale is not comparable. There is a gradation: Adjustments can be made easily for freight and insurance, but cannot be made accurately for trademarks.

2. *Resale price method*: Under this method, the arm's length price for a product sold to an associate enterprise for resale is determined by reducing the price at which it is resold to an independent purchaser by an appropriate markup (that is, an amount that covers the

■ **EXHIBIT 15.3**   Tax-Plus-Tariff-Effect of High Versus Low Transfer Price ($ Thousands)

	Affiliate A	Affiliate B	Affiliates A + B
Low-Markup Policy			
Revenue	1,500	2,200	2,200
Cost of goods solds	1,000	1,500	1,000
Import duty (10%)	—	150	150
Gross profit	500	550	1,050
Other expenses	100	100	200
Income before taxes	400	450	850
Taxes (30%/50%)	120	225	345
Net income	280	225	505
High-Markup Policy			
Revenue	1,800	2,200	2,200
Cost of goods sold	1,000	1,800	1,000
Import duty	—	180	180
Gross profit	800	220	1,020
Other expenses	100	100	200
Income before taxes	700	120	820
Taxes (30%/50%)	210	60	270
Net income	490	60	550

reseller's costs and profit). This method is probably most applicable to marketing operations. However, determining an appropriate markup can be difficult, especially where the reseller adds substantially to the value of the product. Thus, there is often quite a bit of leeway in determining a standard markup.

3. *Cost-plus method*: This method adds an appropriate profit markup to the seller's cost to arrive at an arm's length price. This method is useful in specific situations, such as where semifinished products are sold between related parties or where one entity is essentially acting as a subcontractor for a related entity. However, ordinarily it is difficult to assess the cost of the product and to determine the appropriate profit markup. In fact, no definition of full cost is given, nor is there a unique formula for prorating shared costs over joint products. Thus, the markup over cost allows room for maneuver.

4. *Another appropriate method*: In some cases, it may be appropriate to use a combination of the above methods, or use still other methods (e.g., comparable profits and net yield methods) to arrive at the transfer price. In addition, the treasury regulations are quite explicit that while a new market is being established, it is legitimate to charge a lower transfer price.

In light of Section 482, and the U.S. government's willingness to use it, and similar authority by most other nations, current practice by MNCs appears to be setting standard prices for standardized products. However, the innovative nature of the typical multinational ensures a continual stream of new products for which no market equivalent exists. Hence, some leeway is possible on transfer pricing. In addition, although finished products do get traded among affiliates, trade between related parties increasingly is in high-tech, custom-made components and subassemblies (for example, automobile transmissions and circuit boards) where there are no comparable sales to unrelated buyers. Firms also have a great deal of latitude in setting prices on rejects, scrap, and returned goods.

Exchange Controls.   Another important use of transfer pricing is to avoid currency controls. For example, in the absence of offsetting foreign tax credits, a U.S. parent will wind up with $0.66Q_0$ after tax for each dollar increase in the price at which it sells Q_0 units of a product to an affiliate with blocked funds (based on a U.S. corporate tax rate of 34%). Hence, a transfer price change from P_0 to P_1 will lead to a shift of $0.66(P_1 - P_0)Q_0$ dollars to the parent. The subsidiary, of course, will show a corresponding reduction in its cash balances and taxes, due to its higher expenses.

In fact, bypassing currency restrictions appears to explain the seeming anomaly whereby subsidiaries operating in less-developed countries (LDCs) with low tax rates are sold overpriced goods by other units. In effect, companies appear to be willing to pay a tax penalty to access otherwise unavailable funds.

Joint Ventures.   Conflicts over transfer pricing often arise when one of the affiliates involved is owned jointly by one or more other partners. The outside partners are often suspicious that transfer pricing is being used to shift profits from the joint venture, where they must be shared, to a wholly owned subsidiary. Although there is no pat answer to this problem, the determination of fair transfer prices should be resolved before the establishment of a joint venture. Continuing disputes may still arise, however, over the pricing of new products introduced to an existing venture.

Disguising Profitability.   Many LDCs erect high tariff barriers in order to develop import-substituting industries. However, because they are aware of the potential for abuse, many host governments simultaneously attempt to regulate the profits of firms operating in such a protected environment. When confronted by a situation where profits depend on government regulations, the MNC can use transfer pricing (buying goods from sister affiliates at a higher price) to disguise the true profitability of its local affiliate, enabling it to justify higher local prices. Lower reported profits may also improve a subsidiary's bargaining position in wage negotiations. It is probably for this reason that several international unions have called for fuller disclosure by multinationals of their worldwide accounting data.

Evaluation and Control.   Transfer price adjustments will distort the profits of reporting units and create potential difficulties in evaluating managerial performance. In addition, managers evaluated on the basis of these reported profits may have an incentive to behave in ways that are suboptimal for the corporation as a whole.

Reinvoicing Centers

One approach used by some multinationals to disguise profitability, avoid the scrutiny of governments, and coordinate transfer pricing policy is to set up reinvoicing centers in low-tax nations. The reinvoicing center takes title to all goods sold by one corporate unit to another affiliate or to a third-party customer, although the goods move directly from the factory or warehouse location to the purchaser. The center pays the seller and, in turn, is paid by the purchasing unit.

With price quotations coming from one location, it is easier and quicker to implement decisions to have prices reflect changes in currency values. The reinvoicing center also provides a firm with greater flexibility in choosing an invoicing currency. Affiliates can be ordered to pay in other than their local currency if required by the firm's external currency obligations. In this way, the MNC can avoid the costs of converting from one currency to another and then back again.

Having a reinvoicing center can be expensive, however. There are increased communications costs due to the geographical separation of marketing and sales from the production centers. In addition, tax authorities may be suspicious of transactions with an affiliated trading company located in a tax haven.

Before 1962, many U.S. multinationals had reinvoicing companies located in low- or zero-tax countries. By buying low and selling high, most of the profit on interaffiliate sales could be siphoned off with little or no tax liability because the U.S. government at that time did not tax unremitted foreign earnings. As we have already seen, this situation changed with passage of the U.S. Revenue Act of 1962, which declared that reinvoicing-center income is Subpart F income and, hence, is not exempt from U.S. taxation. For most U.S.-based multinationals, this situation negated the tax benefits associated with a reinvoicing center.

A 1977 ruling by the IRS, however, has increased the value of tax havens in general and reinvoicing centers in particular. That ruling, which allocates to a firm's foreign affiliates certain parent expenses that previously could be written off in the United States, has generated additional foreign tax credits that can be utilized only against U.S. taxes owed on foreign-source income, increasing the value of tax haven subsidiaries.

A reinvoicing center, by channeling profits overseas, can create Subpart F income to offset these excess FTCs. In effect, foreign tax credits can be substituted for taxes that would otherwise be owed to the United States or to foreign governments. Suppose a firm shifts $100 in profit from a country with a 50% tax rate to a reinvoicing center where the tax rate is only 10%. If this $100 is deemed Subpart F income by the IRS, the U.S. parent will owe an additional $24 in U.S. tax (based on the U.S. tax rate of 34% and the $10 foreign tax credit). However, if the company has excess foreign tax credits available, then each $100 shift in profits can reduce total tax payments by $24, until the excess FTCs are all expended.

Fees and Royalties

Management services such as headquarters advice, allocated overhead, patents, and trademarks are often unique and, therefore, are without a reference market price. The consequent difficulty in pricing these corporate resources makes them suitable for use as additional routes for international fund flows by varying the *fees* or *royalties* charged for using these intangible factors of production.

Transfer prices for services have the same tax and exchange control effects as those for transfer prices on goods. However, host governments often look with more favor on payments for industrial know-how than for profit remittances. Where restrictions do exist, they are more likely to be modified to permit a fee for technical knowledge than to allow for dividends.

For MNCs, these charges have assumed a somewhat more important role as a conduit for funneling remittances from foreign affiliates. To a certain extent, this trend reflects the fact that many of these payments are tied to overseas sales or assets that grew very rapidly during the 1960s and early 1970s, as well as the growing importance of tax considerations and exchange controls. For example, by setting low transfer prices on intangibles to manufacturing subsidiaries in low-tax locations like Puerto Rico or Singapore, multinationals can receive profits essentially tax free. This possibility explains why the IRS now carefully scrutinizes the pricing of intangibles.

The most common approach to setting fee and royalty charges is for the parent to decide on a desired amount of total fee remittances from the overseas operations, usually based on an allocation of corporate expenses, and then to apportion these charges according to subsidiary sales or assets. This method, which sometimes involves establishing identical licensing agreements with all units, gives these charges the appearance of a legitimate and necessary business expense, thereby aiding in overcoming currency restrictions.

Governments typically prefer prior agreements and steady and predictable payment flows; a sudden change in licensing and service charges is likely to be looked at with suspicion. For this reason, firms try to avoid abrupt changes in their remittance policies. However, where exchange controls exist or are likely, or if there are significant tax advantages, many firms will initially set a higher level of fee and royalty payments while still maintaining a stable remittance policy.

Special problems exist with joint ventures because the parent company will have to obtain permission from its partner(s) to be able to levy charges for its services and licensing contributions. These payments ensure the parent of receiving at least some compensation for the resources it has invested in the joint venture, perhaps in lieu of dividends over which it may have little or no control.

Leading and Lagging

A highly favored means of shifting liquidity among affiliates is an acceleration (leading) or delay (lagging) in the payment of interaffiliate accounts by modifying the credit terms extended by one unit to another. For example, suppose affiliate A sells goods worth $1 million monthly to affiliate B on 90-day credit terms. Then, on average, affiliate A has $3 million of accounts receivable from affiliate B and is, in effect, financing $3 million of working capital for affiliate B. If the terms are changed to 180 days, there will be a one-time shift of an additional $3 million to affiliate B. Conversely, reducing credit terms to 30 days will create a flow of $2 million from affiliate B to affiliate A, as shown in Exhibit 15.4.

Shifting Liquidity. The value of leading and lagging depends on the opportunity cost of funds to both the paying unit and the recipient. When an affiliate already in a surplus position receives payment, it can invest the additional funds at the prevailing local lending rate; if it requires working capital, the payment received can be used to reduce its borrowings at the borrowing rate. If the paying unit has excess funds, it loses cash that it would have invested at the lending rate; if it is in a deficit position, it has to borrow at the borrowing rate. To assess the benefits of shifting liquidity among affiliates, these borrowing and lending rates must be calculated on an after-tax dollar (HC) basis.

■ **EXHIBIT 15.4**   Fund-Transfer Effects of Leading and Lagging

Affiliate A Sells $1 Million in Goods Monthly to Affiliate B

	Credit Terms		
Balance-Sheet Accounts	Normal (90 days)	Leading (30 days)	Lagging (180 days)
Affiliate A			
Accounts receivable from B	$3,000,000	$1,000,000	$6,000,000
Affiliate B			
Accounts payable to A	$3,000,000	$1,000,000	$6,000,000
Net Cash Transfers			
From B to A		$2,000,000	—
From A to B		—	$3,000,000

Suppose, for example, that a multinational company faces the following effective, after-tax dollar borrowing and lending rates in Germany and the United States:

	Borrowing Rate (%)	Lending Rate (%)
United States	3.8	2.9
Germany	3.6	2.7

Both the U.S. and German units can have either a surplus (+) or deficit (–) of funds. The four possibilities, along with the domestic interest rates (U.S./German) and interest differentials (U.S. rate – German rate) associated with each state, are as follows:

		Germany	
		+	–
United States	+	2.9%/2.7% (0.2%)	2.9%/3.6% (–0.7%)
	–	3.8%/2.7% (1.1%)	3.8%/3.6% (0.2%)

For example, if both units have excess funds, then the relevant opportunity costs of funds are the U.S. and German lending rates of 2.9% and 2.7%, respectively, and the associated interest differential (in parentheses) is 0.2%. Similarly, if the U.S. unit requires funds while the German affiliate has a cash surplus, then the relevant rates are the respective U.S. borrowing and German lending rates of 3.8% and 2.7% and the interest differential is 1.1%.

If the interest rate differential is positive, the corporation as a whole—by moving funds to the United States—will either pay less on its borrowing or earn more interest on its investments. This move can be made by leading payments to the United States and lagging payments to Germany. Shifting money to Germany—by leading payments to Germany and lagging them to the United States—will be worthwhile if the interest differential is negative.

Based on the interest differentials in this example, all borrowings should be done in Germany, and surplus funds should be invested in the United States. Only if the U.S. unit has excess cash and the German unit requires funds should money flow into Germany.

For example, suppose the German unit owes $2 million to the U.S. unit. The timing of this payment can be changed by up to 90 days in either direction. Assume the U.S. unit is borrowing funds, and the German unit has excess cash available. According to the prevailing interest differential of 1.1%, given the current liquidity status of each affiliate, the German unit should speed up, or lead, its payment to the U.S. unit. The net effect of these adjustments is that the U.S. firm can reduce its borrowing by $2 million, and the German unit has $2 million less in cash—all for 90 days. Borrowing costs for the U.S. unit are pared by $19,000 ($2,000,000 × 0.038 × 90/360), and the German unit's interest income is reduced by $13,500 ($2,000,000 × 0.027 × 90/360). There is a net savings of $5,500. The savings could be computed more directly by using the relevant interest differential of 1.1% as follows: $2,000,000 × 0.011 × 90/360 = $5,500.

Advantages.   Leading and lagging has several advantages over direct intercompany loans.

1. No formal note of indebtedness is needed, and the amount of credit can be adjusted up or down by shortening or lengthening the terms on the accounts. Governments do not always allow such freedom on loans.
2. Governments are less likely to interfere with payments on intercompany accounts than on direct loans.
3. Section 482 allows intercompany accounts up to six months to be interest free. In contrast, interest must be charged on all intercompany loans. The ability to set a zero interest rate is valuable if the host government does not allow interest payments on parent company loans to be tax deductible or if there are withholding taxes on interest payments.

Government Restrictions.   As with all other transfer mechanisms, government controls on intercompany credit terms are often tight and given to abrupt changes. While appearing straightforward on the surface, these rules are subject to different degrees of government interpretation and sanction. For example, in theory Japan permits firms to employ leads and lags. However, in reality leading and lagging is very difficult because regulations require that all settlements be made in accordance with the original trade documents unless a very good reason exists for an exception. On the other hand, Sweden, which prohibits import leads, will often lift this restriction for imports of capital goods.

Intercompany Loans

A principal means of financing foreign operations and moving funds internationally is to engage in intercompany lending activities. The making and repaying of *intercompany loans* is often the only legitimate transfer mechanism available to the MNC.

Intercompany loans are more valuable to the firm than arm's length transactions only if at least one of the following market distortions exist: (1) credit rationing (due to a ceiling on local interest rates), (2) currency controls, or (3) differential tax rates among countries. This list is not particularly restrictive because it is the rare MNC that faces none of these situations in its international operations.

Although a variety of types of intercompany loans exist, the most important methods at present are direct loans, back-to-back financing, and parallel loans. *Direct loans* are straight extensions of credit from the parent to an affiliate or from one affiliate to another. The other types of intercompany loans typically involve an intermediary.

Back-to-Back Loans.   *Back-to-back loans,* also called *fronting loans* or *link financing,* are often employed to finance affiliates located in nations with high interest rates or restricted capital markets, especially when there is a danger of currency controls or when different rates of withholding tax are applied to loans from a financial institution. In the typical arrangement, the parent company deposits funds with a bank in country A that in turn lends the money to a subsidiary in country B. These transactions are shown in Exhibit 15.5. By contrasting these transactions with a direct intercompany loan, the figure reveals that, in

■ **EXHIBIT 15.5**   Structure of a Back-to-Back Loan

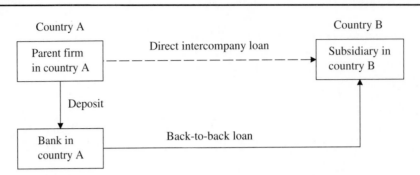

effect, a back-to-back loan is an intercompany loan channeled through a bank. From the bank's point of view, the loan is risk free because the parent's deposit fully collateralizes it. The bank simply acts as an intermediary or a front; compensation is provided by the margin between the interest received from the borrowing unit and the rate paid on the parent's deposit.

A back-to-back loan may offer several potential advantages when compared with a direct intercompany loan. Two of the most important advantages are as follows:

1. Certain countries apply different withholding-tax rates to interest paid to a foreign parent and interest paid to a financial institution. A cost saving in the form of lower taxes may be available with a back-to-back loan.
2. If currency controls are imposed, the government will usually permit the local subsidiary to honor the amortization schedule of a loan from a major multinational bank; to stop payment would hurt the nation's credit rating. Conversely, local monetary authorities would have far fewer reservations about not authorizing the repayment of an intercompany loan. In general, back-to-back financing provides better protection than does a parent loan against expropriation and/or exchange controls.

Some financial managers argue that a back-to-back loan conveys another benefit: The subsidiary seems to have obtained credit from a major bank on its own, possibly enhancing its reputation. However, this appearance is unlikely to be significant in the highly informed international financial community.

The costs of a back-to-back loan are evaluated in the same way as any other financing method (i.e., by considering relevant interest and tax rates and the likelihood of changes in currency value). To illustrate how these calculations should be made, assume the parent's opportunity cost of funds is 10%, and the parent's and affiliate's marginal tax rates are 34% and 40%, respectively. Then, if the parent earns 8% on its deposit, the bank charges 9% to lend dollars to the affiliate, and the local currency devalues by 11% during the course of the loan, the effective cost of this back-to-back loan equals

$$\underset{\text{to parent}}{\text{Interest cost}} - \underset{\text{to parent}}{\text{Interest income}} + \underset{\text{to subsidiary}}{\text{Interest cost}} - \underset{\text{exchange loss}}{\text{Tax gain on}}$$

$$0.10(0.66) - 0.08(0.66) + 0.09(0.6) - 0.4(0.11) = 2.08\%$$

Variations on the back-to-back loan include the parent depositing dollars while the bank lends out local currency or a foreign affiliate placing the deposit in any of several currencies with the bank loan being denominated in the same or a different currency. To calculate the costs of these variations would require some modification to the methodology shown previously, but the underlying rationale is the same: Include all interest, tax, and currency effects that accrue to both the borrowing and the lending units and convert these costs to the home currency.

Users of the fronting technique include U.S. companies that have accumulated sizable amounts of money in "captive" insurance firms and holding companies located in low-tax nations. Rather than reinvesting this money overseas (assuming that is the intent) by first paying dividends to the parent company and incurring a large tax liability, some of these companies attempt to recycle their funds indirectly via back-to-back loans.

For example, suppose affiliate A, wholly owned and located in a tax haven, deposits $2 million for one year in a bank at 7%; the bank, in turn, lends this money to affiliate B at 9%. Assuming no currency changes, if B has an effective tax rate of 50%, then its after-tax interest expense equals $90,000 ($2,000,000 × 0.09 × 0.5). The return to A equals $140,000 ($2,000,000 × 0.07), assuming that A pays no taxes. The net result of this transaction has been to shift $140,000 from B to A at a cost to B of only $90,000 after tax.

Back-to-back arrangements can also be used to access blocked currency funds without physically transferring them. Suppose Xerox wishes to use the excess funds being generated by its Brazilian operation to finance a needed plant expansion in Colombia, where long-term money is virtually unobtainable. Xerox prefers not to invest additional dollars in Colombia because of the high probability of a Colombian peso devaluation. Because of stringent Brazilian exchange controls, though, this movement of cruzeiros cannot take place directly. However, Xerox may be able to use the worldwide branching facilities of an international bank as a substitute for an internal transfer. For example, suppose the Brazilian branch of Chase Manhattan Bank needs cruzeiro deposits to continue funding its loans in a restrictive credit environment. Chase may be willing to lend Xerox long-term pesos through its branch in Colombia in return for a cruzeiro deposit of equivalent maturity in Brazil.

In this way, Xerox gets the use of its funds in Brazil and at the same time receives locally denominated funds in Colombia. Protection is provided against a peso devaluation, although the firm's cruzeiro funds are, of course, still exposed. The value of this arrangement is based on the relative interest rates involved, anticipated currency changes, and the opportunity cost of the funds being utilized. Given the exchange and credit restrictions and other market imperfections that exist, it is quite possible that both the bank and its client can benefit from this type of arrangement. Negotiation between the two parties will determine how these benefits are to be shared.

Parallel Loans.   A *parallel loan* is a method of effectively repatriating blocked funds (at least for the term of the arrangement), circumventing exchange control restrictions, avoiding a premium exchange rate for investments abroad, financing foreign affiliates without incurring additional exchange risk, or obtaining foreign currency financing at attractive rates. As shown in Exhibit 15.6, it consists of two related but separate—that is, parallel— borrowings and usually involves four parties in at least two different countries. In Exhibit 15.6a, a U.S. parent firm wishing to invest in Spain lends dollars to the U.S. affiliate of a Spanish firm that wants to invest in the United States. In return, the Spanish parent lends pesetas in Spain to the U.S. firm's Spanish subsidiary. Drawdowns, payments of interest, and repayments of principal are made simultaneously. The differential between the rates of interest on the two loans is determined, in theory, by the cost of money in each country and anticipated changes in currency values.

Exhibit 15.6b shows how a parallel loan can be used to access blocked funds. In this instance, the Brazilian affiliate of ITT is generating cruzeiros that it is unable to repatriate. It lends this money to the local affiliate of Dow; in turn, Dow lends dollars to ITT in the United States. Hence, ITT would have the use of dollars in the United States while Dow would obtain cruzeiros in Brazil. In both cases, the parallel transactions are the functional equivalent of direct intercompany loans.

■ **EXHIBIT 15.6**   Structure of a Parallel Loan

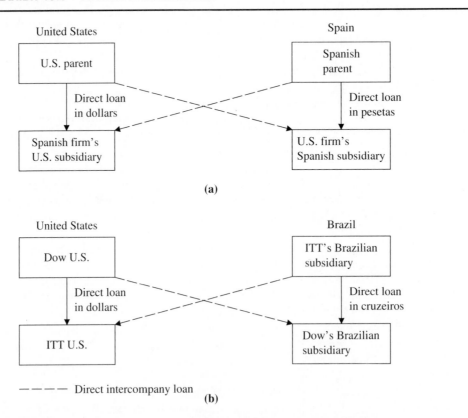

Fees to banks brokering these arrangements usually run from 0.25% to 0.5% of the principal for each side. (Chapter 23 discusses currency swaps, which are an outgrowth of parallel loans.)

Dividends

Dividends are by far the most important means of transferring funds from foreign affiliates to the parent company, typically accounting for over 50% of all remittances to U.S. firms. Among the various factors that MNCs consider when deciding on dividend payments by their affiliates are taxes, financial statement effects, exchange risk, currency controls, financing requirements, availability and cost of funds, and the parent's dividend payout ratio. Firms differ, though, in the relative importance they place on these variables, as well as in how systematically the variables are incorporated in an overall remittance policy.

The parent company's *dividend payout ratio* often plays an important role in determining the dividends to be received from abroad. Some firms require the same payout percentage as the parent's rate for each of their subsidiaries; others set a target payout rate as a percentage of overall foreign-source earnings without attempting to receive the same percentage from each subsidiary. The rationale for focusing on the parent's payout ratio is that the subsidiaries should contribute their share of the dividends paid to the stockholders. Thus, if the parent's payout rate is 60%, then foreign operations should contribute 60% of their earnings toward meeting this goal. Establishing a uniform percentage for each unit, rather than an overall target, is explained as an attempt to persuade foreign governments, particularly those of less-developed countries, that these payments are necessary rather than arbitrary.

Tax Effects.   A major consideration behind the dividend decision is the effective tax rate on payments from different affiliates. By varying payout ratios among its foreign subsidiaries, the corporation can reduce its total tax burden.

Once a firm has decided on the amount of dividends to remit from overseas, it can then reduce its tax bill by withdrawing funds from those locations with the lowest transfer costs. To take a highly simplified example, suppose a U.S. company, International Products, wishes to withdraw $1 million from abroad in the form of dividends. Its three foreign subsidiaries—located in Germany, the Republic of Ireland, and France—have each earned $2 million before tax this year and, hence, are all capable of providing the funds. The problem for International Products is to decide on the dividend strategy that will minimize the firm's total tax bill.

The German subsidiary is subject to a split corporate tax rate of 50% on retained earnings and 36% on dividends as well as a dividend withholding tax of 10%. As an export incentive, the Republic of Ireland grants a 15-year tax holiday on all export profits. Since the Irish unit receives all its profits from exports, it pays no taxes. There are no dividend withholding taxes. The French affiliate is taxed at a rate of 45% and must also pay a 10% withholding tax on its dividend remittances. It is assumed there are no excess foreign tax credits available and that any credits generated cannot be used elsewhere. Exhibit 15.7 summarizes the relevant tax consequences of remitting $1 million from each affiliate in turn.

These calculations indicate that it would be cheapest to remit dividends from Germany. In fact, by paying this $1 million dividend with its associated tax cost of $1.86 million,

■ **EXHIBIT 15.7**   Tax Effects of Dividend Remittances from Abroad

Location of Foreign Affiliate	Dividend Amount	Host Country Income Tax If Dividend Paid	Host Country Withholding Tax	U.S. Income Tax	Total Taxes If Dividend Paid	Host Country Income Tax If No Dividend Paid	Worldwide Tax Liability If Dividend Paid*
Germany	$1,000,000	$360,000 500,000 $860,000	$100,000	0[1]	$ 960,000	$1,000,000	$1,860,000
Republic of Ireland	$1,000,000	0	0	$340,000	$ 340,000	0	$2,240,000
France	$1,000,000	$900,000	$100,000	0	$1,000,000	$900,000	$2,000,000

[1]Computation of U.S. tax owed

Profit before tax	$2,000,000		Included in U.S. income:	
Tax = $1,000,000 × 0.50 + $1,000,000 × 0.36 =	860,000		Gross dividend received	$1,000,000
Profit after tax	1,140,000		Foreign indirect tax deemed paid	842,105
Dividend paid to U.S. parent company	1,000,000		U.S. gross dividend included	$1,842,105
Less withholding tax @ 10%	100,000		U.S. tax @ 34%	626,316
Net dividend received in United States	$ 900,000		Less foreign tax credit[2]	942,105
			Net U.S. tax cost (credit)	$ (315,789)
			U.S. tax payable	0

[2]Foreign tax credit
  (a) Direct credit for withholding tax   100,000
  (b) Indirect foreign tax credit

$$\frac{\text{Dividend paid}}{\text{Profit after tax}} \times \text{Foreign tax} = \frac{1,000,000}{1,140,000} \times 960,000 = \underline{842,105}$$

Total tax credit $942,105

*Worldwide tax liability if dividend paid equals tax liability for foreign affiliate paying the dividend plus tax liabilities of non-dividend-paying affiliates plus any U.S. taxes owed.

International Products is actually reducing its worldwide tax costs by $40,000—compared with its total tax bill of $1.9 million in the absence of any dividend. This result is due to the tax penalty that the German government imposes on retained earnings.

Financing Requirements.   In addition to their tax consequences, dividend payments lead to liquidity shifts. The value of moving these funds depends on the different opportunity costs of money among the various units of the corporation. For instance, an affiliate that must borrow funds will usually have a higher opportunity cost than a unit with excess cash available. Moreover, some subsidiaries will have access to low-cost financing sources, while others have no recourse but to borrow at a relatively high interest rate.

All else being equal, a parent can increase its value by exploiting yield differences among its affiliates—that is, setting a high dividend payout rate for subsidiaries with relatively low opportunity costs of funds while requiring smaller dividend payments from those units facing high borrowing costs or having favorable investment opportunities.

Exchange Controls. Exchange controls are another major factor in the dividend decision. Nations with balance-of-payments problems are apt to restrict the payment of dividends to foreign companies. These controls vary by country, but in general they limit the size of dividend remittances, either in absolute terms or as a percentage of earnings, equity, or registered capital.

Many firms try to reduce the danger of such interference by maintaining a record of consistent dividends. The record is designed to show that these payments are part of an established financial program, rather than an act of speculation against the host country's currency. Dividends are paid every year, whether they are justified by financial and tax considerations or not, just to demonstrate a continuing policy to the local government and central bank. Even when they cannot be remitted, dividends are sometimes declared for the same reason, namely, to establish grounds for making future payments when these controls are lifted or modified.

Some companies even set a uniform dividend payout ratio throughout the corporate system to set a global pattern and maintain the principle that affiliates have an obligation to pay dividends to their stockholders. If challenged, the firm can then prove that its French or Brazilian or Italian subsidiaries must pay an equivalent percentage dividend. MNCs are often willing to accept higher tax costs to maintain the principle that dividends are a necessary and legitimate business expense. Many executives believe that a record of paying dividends consistently (or at least declaring them) helps in getting approval for further dividend disbursements.

Joint Ventures.   The presence of local stockholders may constrain an MNC's ability to adjust its dividend policy in accordance with global factors. In addition, to the extent that multinationals have a longer-term perspective than their local partners, conflicts might arise with local investors demanding a shorter payback period and the MNC insisting on a higher earnings retention rate.

Equity Versus Debt

Corporate funds invested overseas, whether they are called debt or equity, require the same rate of return, namely, the firm's marginal cost of capital. Nonetheless, MNCs generally prefer to invest in the form of loans rather than equity for several reasons.

First, a firm typically has wider latitude to repatriate funds in the form of interest and loan repayments than as dividends or reductions in equity because the latter fund flows are usually more closely controlled by governments. In addition, a reduction in equity may be frowned on by the host government and is likely to pose a real problem for a firm trying to repatriate funds in excess of earnings. Withdrawing these funds by way of dividend payments will reduce the affiliate's capital stock, whereas applying this money toward repayment of a loan will not affect the unit's equity account. Moreover, if the firm ever desired to increase its equity investment, it can relatively easily convert the loan into equity.

A second reason for the use of intercompany loans over equity investments is the possibility of reducing taxes. The likelihood of a tax benefit is due to two factors: (1) Interest paid on a loan is ordinarily tax-deductible in the host nation, whereas dividend payments are not; and (2) unlike dividends, loan repayments do not normally constitute taxable income to the parent company.

For example, suppose General Foods Corporation (GFC) is looking for a way to finance a $1 million expansion in working capital for its Danish affiliate, General Foods Denmark (GFD). The added sales generated by this increase in working capital promise to yield 20% after local tax (but before interest payments), or $200,000 annually, for the foreseeable future. GFC has a choice between investing the $1 million as debt, with an interest rate of 10%, or as equity. GFD pays corporate income tax at the rate of 50% as well as a 10% withholding tax on all dividend and interest payments. Other assumptions are that the parent expects all available funds to be repatriated and that any foreign tax credits generated are unusable.

If the $1 million is financed as an equity investment, the Danish subsidiary will pay the full return as an annual dividend to GFC of $200,000—of which GFC will receive $180,000 net of the withholding tax. Alternatively, if structured as a loan, the investment will be repaid in ten annual installments of $100,000 each with interest on the remaining balance. Because interest is tax-deductible, the net outflow of cash from GFD is only half the interest payment. It is assumed that the parent does not have to pay additional tax to the United States on dividends received because of the high tax rate on GFD's income. In addition, the interest is received tax-free due to the availability of excess foreign tax credits. All funds remaining after interest and principal repayments are remitted as dividends. In year 5, for example, $100,000 of the $200,000 cash flow is sent to GFC as a loan repayment and $60,000 as interest (on a balance of $600,000). The $30,000 tax saving on the interest payment and the remaining $40,000 on the $200,000 profit are remitted as dividends. Hence, GFC winds up with $217,000 after the withholding tax of $13,000 (on total dividend plus interest payments of $130,000).

The evaluation of these financing alternatives is presented in Exhibit 15.8. Assuming a 15% discount rate, the present value of cash flows under the debt financing plan is $1,102,695. This amount is $199,275 more over the first ten years of the investment's life than the $903,420 present value using equity financing. The reason for this disparity is the absence of withholding tax on the loan repayments and the tax-deductibility of interest expenses. It is apparent that the higher the interest rate that can be charged on the loan, the larger the cash flows will be. After ten years, of course, the cash flows are the same under debt and equity financing because all returns will be in the form of dividends.

Alternatively, suppose the same investment and financing plans are available in a country having no income or withholding taxes. This situation increases annual project returns to $400,000. Because no excess foreign tax credits are available, the U.S. government will impose a tax of 34% on all remitted dividends and interest payments. The respective cash flows are presented in Exhibit 15.9. In this situation, the present value under debt financing is $170,650 more (1,495,660 – 1,325,010) than with equity financing.

Firms do not have complete latitude in choosing their debt-to-equity ratios abroad, though. This subject is frequently open for negotiation with the host governments. In addition, dividends and local borrowings are often restricted to a fixed percentage of equity. A small equity base can also lead to a high return on equity, exposing a company to charges of exploitation.

Another obstacle to taking complete advantage of parent company loans is the U.S. government. The IRS may treat loan repayments as constructive dividends and tax them if

■ **EXHIBIT 15.8** Dollar Cash Flows Under Debt and Equity Financing

	Debt					Equity		
	(1)	(2)	(3)	(4)	(5)	(6)	(7)	(8)
Year	Principal Repayment	Interest	Dividend	Withholding Tax	Cash Flow to Parent (1 + 2 + 3 − 4)	Dividend	Withholding Tax	Cash Flow to Parent (6 − 7)
1	100,000	100,000	50,000	15,000	235,000	200,000	20,000	180,000
2	100,000	90,000	55,000	14,500	230,500	200,000	20,000	180,000
3	100,000	80,000	60,000	14,000	226,000	200,000	20,000	180,000
4	100,000	70,000	65,000	13,500	221,500	200,000	20,000	180,000
5	100,000	60,000	70,000	13,000	217,000	200,000	20,000	180,000
6	100,000	50,000	75,000	12,500	212,500	200,000	20,000	180,000
7	100,000	40,000	80,000	12,000	208,000	200,000	20,000	180,000
8	100,000	30,000	85,000	11,500	203,500	200,000	20,000	180,000
9	100,000	20,000	90,000	11,000	199,000	200,000	20,000	180,000
10	100,000	10,000	95,000	10,500	194,500	200,000	20,000	180,000
Present Value Discounted at 15%					$1,102,695			$903,420

it believes the subsidiary is too thinly capitalized. Many executives and tax attorneys feel that the IRS is satisfied as long as the debt-to-equity ratio does not exceed four to one.

Firms normally use guidelines such as 50% of total assets or fixed assets in determining the amount of equity to provide their subsidiaries. These guidelines usually lead to an equity position greater than that required by law, causing MNCs to sacrifice flexibility and pay higher taxes than necessary.

■ **EXHIBIT 15.9** Dollar Cash Flows Under Debt and Equity Financing

	Debt					Equity		
	(1)	(2)	(3)	(4)	(5)	(6)	(7)	(8)
Year	Principal Repayment	Interest	Dividend	U.S. Tax (2 + 3) × .34	Cash Flow to Parent (1 + 2 + 3 − 4)	Dividend	U.S. Tax (6 × .34)	Cash Flow to Parent (6 − 7)
1	100,000	100,000	200,000	102,000	298,000	400,000	136,000	264,000
2	100,000	90,000	210,000	102,000	298,000	400,000	136,000	264,000
3	100,000	80,000	220,000	102,000	298,000	400,000	136,000	264,000
4	100,000	70,000	230,000	102,000	298,000	400,000	136,000	264,000
5	100,000	60,000	240,000	102,000	298,000	400,000	136,000	264,000
6	100,000	50,000	250,000	102,000	298,000	400,000	136,000	264,000
7	100,000	40,000	260,000	102,000	298,000	400,000	136,000	264,000
8	100,000	30,000	270,000	102,000	298,000	400,000	136,000	264,000
9	100,000	20,000	280,000	102,000	298,000	400,000	136,000	264,000
10	100,000	10,000	290,000	102,000	298,000	400,000	136,000	264,000
Present Value Discounted at 15%					$1,495,660			$1,325,010

Invoicing Intercompany Transactions

Firms often have the option of selecting the currencies in which to invoice interaffiliate transactions. The choice of invoicing currency has both tax and currency control implications.

Tax Effects.   The particular currency or currencies in which intercompany transactions are invoiced can affect after-tax profits if currency fluctuations are anticipated. For example, suppose a firm's Swedish subsidiary is selling subassemblies to a German affiliate. Assume the firm's effective tax rate in Sweden is t_S while in Germany, it is t_G. Should the transaction be invoiced in Deutsche marks or kronor if the Deutsche mark is expected to rise with respect to the krona and dollar?

If the invoice is in Deutsche marks, the German subsidiary will be unaffected (in terms of DM), but the Swedish subsidiary will show a foreign exchange gain. It will retain $1 - t_S$ of the gain after Swedish taxes, which is directly consolidated into the U.S. parent's account if the dollar:krona rate is assumed to remain unchanged.

If the invoice is in kronor, the Swedish subsidiary will be unaffected, but the German subsidiary will use fewer Deutsche marks to pay the invoice. After making more German profit, it will pay more tax, and so it will retain $1 - t_G$ of its foreign exchange gain denominated in dollars. Therefore, to reduce taxes if t_G is greater than t_S, invoice in Deutsche marks; otherwise invoice in kronor. A numerical example is provided in Exhibit 15.10.

■ **EXHIBIT 15.10**   Invoicing Intercompany Transactions

Assume: German affiliate G has a tax rate of 50%
                 Swedish affiliate S has a tax rate of 40%
                 S sells $1,000,000 in goods to G

Base Case: DM 1 = $0.50, SEK 1 = $0.20

Invoice in Kronor	**Invoice in Deutsche Marks**
Goods	Goods
$S \longrightarrow G$	$S \longrightarrow G$
SEK 5,000,000	DM 2,000,000

Currency Change: DM 1 = $0.55, SEK 1 = $0.20

Invoice in Kronor	**Invoice in Deutsche Marks**
Goods	Goods
$S \longrightarrow G$	$S \longrightarrow G$
SEK 5,000,000 = DM 1,818,182	DM 2,000,000 = SEK 5,500,000

Prechange cost to G = DM 2,000,000	Prechange revenue to S = SEK 5,000,000
Postchange cost to G = DM 1,818,182	Postchange revenue to S = SEK 5,500,000
Taxable gain to G = DM 181,818	Taxable gain to S = SEK 500,000
Increased tax @ 50% = DM 90,909	Increased tax @ 40% = SEK 200,000
= $50,000	= $40,000

Tax Savings by Invoicing in Deutsche Marks: $10,000

Now suppose the subassemblies were flowing from Germany to Sweden (or from Sweden to Germany but with prepayment). If the invoice is in kronor, the Swedish subsidiary will be unaffected, but the German subsidiary will receive fewer Deutsche marks. On an after-tax basis, though, its dollar loss is only $1 - t_G$ of the original foreign exchange loss. Had the invoice been in Deutsche marks, the Swedish subsidiary would have incurred a loss after tax equal to just $1 - t_S$ of the before-tax loss. To minimize taxes, therefore, if t_G is greater than t_S, invoice in kronor; otherwise, invoice in Deutsche marks. The general rule is to denominate intracorporate transactions so that gains are taken in low-tax nations and losses in high-tax ones. Note finally that on a pretax consolidated basis, the parent's books would show a net gain of zero from these transactions (i.e., intracorporate transactions net out on a before-tax basis but not after tax, unless effective tax rates are equal).

Exchange Controls.   The choice of invoicing currency can also enable a firm to remove some blocked funds from a country that has currency controls. Suppose a subsidiary is located in a country that restricts profit repatriation. A forecasted local currency devaluation can provide this firm with an opportunity to shift excess funds to where they will earn a higher rate of return. This shift can be accomplished by invoicing exports from that subsidiary to the rest of the corporation in the local currency at a contracted price. As the local currency deteriorates, profit margins are squeezed in the subsidiary (compared to what they would have been with hard-currency billing) but improved elsewhere in the system. In effect, cost savings from the devaluation will be shifted elsewhere in the system. If that subsidiary were exporting $1 million worth of goods monthly to its parent, for example, then a 10% LC devaluation would involve a monthly shift of $100,000 to the parent.

Conversely, funds can be moved into a country such as Germany that imposes controls on capital inflows. They can be moved by invoicing exports to the German affiliate in a weak currency and invoicing exports from the German affiliate in a strong currency.

■ 15.3 ■
DESIGNING A GLOBAL REMITTANCE POLICY

The task facing international financial executives is to coordinate the use of the various financial linkages in a manner consistent with value maximization for the firm as a whole. This task requires the following four interrelated decisions: (1) how much money (if any) to remit; (2) when to do so; (3) where to transmit these funds; and (4) which transfer method(s) to use.

In order to take proper advantage of its internal financial system, the firm must conduct a systematic and comprehensive analysis of the available remittance options and their associated costs and benefits. It must also compare the value of deploying funds in affiliates other than just the remitting subsidiary and the parent. For example, rather than just deciding whether to keep earnings in Germany or remit them to the U.S. parent, corporate headquarters must consider the possibility and desirability of moving those funds to, say, Italy or France via leading and lagging or transfer price adjustments. In other words, the key question to be answered is, Where and how in the world can available funds be deployed most profitably? Most multinationals, however, make their dividend remittance decision independently of, say, their royalty or leading and lagging decision, rather than considering what mix of transfer mechanisms would be best for the company overall.

In part, the decision to "satisfice" rather than optimize is due to the complex nature of the financial linkages in a typical multinational corporation. For instance, if there are ten financial links connecting each pair of units in a multinational enterprise, then a firm consisting of a parent and two subsidiaries will have 30 intercompany links, three times as many as a parent with just one affiliate. A parent with three subsidiaries will have 60 links; a company with n units will have $10n(n + 1)/2$ financial linkages.

Since a real-life firm will have many more than three affiliates, the exponential growth of potential intercompany relationships means that unless the options are severely limited, system optimization will be impossible. It is not surprising, therefore, that surveys by Zenoff and by Robbins and Stobaugh found that few firms seemed to think in terms of a worldwide pool of funds to be allocated in accordance with global profit maximization.[2] Instead, most parents allowed their affiliates to keep just enough cash on hand to meet their fund requirements, with the rest sent back home.

This limited approach to managing international financial transactions is understandable in view of the tangled web of interaffiliate connections that has already been depicted. Still, compromising with complexity ought not to mean ignoring the system's profit potential. A hands-off policy is not the only alternative to system optimization. Instead, the MNC should search for relatively high-yield uses of its internal financial system. This task is often made easier by choices that are generally more limited in practice than in theory.

First of all, many of the potential links will be impossible to use because of government regulations and the specifics of the firm's situation. For example, two affiliates may not trade with each other, eliminating the transfer pricing link. Other channels will be severely restricted by government controls.

Furthermore, in many situations, it is not necessary to develop an elaborate mathematical model to figure out the appropriate policy. For example, where a currency is blocked and investment opportunities are lacking or local tax rates are quite high, it will normally be in the company's best interest to shift its funds and profits elsewhere. Where credit rationing exists, a simple decision rule usually suffices: Maximize local borrowing. Moreover, most MNCs already have large staffs for data collection and planning, as well as some form of computerized accounting system. These elements can form the basis for a more complete overseas planning effort.

The more limited, although still numerous, real-life options facing a firm and the existing nucleus of a planning system can significantly reduce the costs of centralizing the management of a firm's intercompany transactions. In addition, for most multinationals, fewer than ten affiliates account for an overwhelming majority of intercompany fund flows. Recognizing this situation, several firms have developed systems to optimize flows among this limited number of units. The lack of global optimization (interactions with other affiliates are taken as given, rather than treated as decision variables) is not particularly costly

---

[2]David B. Zenoff, "Remitting Funds from Foreign Affiliates," *Financial Executive,* March 1968, pp. 46–63; and Sidney M. Robbins and Robert B. Stobaugh *Money in the Multinational Enterprise,* (New York: Basic Books, 1973), p. 86.

because most of the major fund flows are already included. Realistically, the objective of such an effort should be profit improvement rather than system optimization.

Prerequisites

A number of factors strongly impact on an MNC's ability to benefit from its internal financial transfer system. These include the (1) number of financial links, (2) volume of interaffiliate transactions, (3) foreign affiliate ownership pattern, (4) degree of product and service standardization, and (5) government regulations.

Because each channel has different costs and benefits associated with its use, the wider the range of choice, the greater a firm's ability to achieve specific goals. For example, some links are best suited to avoiding exchange controls, while others are most efficiently employed in reducing taxes. In this vein, a two-way flow of funds will give a firm greater flexibility in deploying its money than if all links are only in one direction. Of course, the larger the volume of flows through these financial arteries, the more funds that can be moved by a given adjustment in intercompany terms. A 1% change in the transfer price on goods flowing between two affiliates will have a ten times greater absolute effect if annual sales are $10 million rather than just $1 million. Similarly, altering credit terms by 30 days will become a more effective means of transferring funds as the volume of intercompany payables and receivables grows.

A large volume of intercompany transactions is usually associated with the worldwide dispersal and rationalization of production activities. As plants specialize in different components and stages of production, interaffiliate trade increases, as do the accompanying financial flows. Clearly, 100% ownership of all foreign affiliates removes a major impediment to the efficient allocation of funds worldwide. The existence of joint ventures is likely to confine a firm's transfer activities to a set of mutually agreed-upon rules, eliminating its ability to react swiftly to changed circumstances.

Also, the more standardized are its products and services, the less latitude an MNC has to adjust its transfer prices and fees and royalties. Conversely, a high-technology input, strong product differentiation, and short product life cycle enhance a company's ability to make use of its mechanisms for transfer pricing and fee adjustments. Because the latter situation is more typical of the MNC, it is not surprising that the issue of transfer pricing is a bone of contention between multinationals and governments.

Last, and most importantly, government regulations exert a continuing influence on international financial transactions. It is interesting to consider that government tax, credit allocation, and exchange control policies provide the principal incentives for firms to engage in international fund maneuvers at the same time that government regulations most impede these flows.

Information Requirements

In order to take full advantage of its global financial system, a multinational firm needs detailed information on affiliate financing requirements, sources and costs of external credit, local investment yields, available financial channels, the volume of interaffiliate transactions, all relevant tax factors, and government restrictions and regulations on fund flows.

Without belaboring the points already made, it is clear that the costs and benefits of operating an integrated financial system depend on the funds and transfer options available, as well as on the opportunity costs of money for different affiliates and the tax effects associated with these various transfer mechanisms. Hence, the implementation of centralized decision making requires information concerning all these factors.

Behavioral Consequences

Manipulating transfer prices on goods and services, adjusting dividend payments, and leading and lagging remittances lead to a reallocation of profits and liquidity among a firm's various affiliates. Although the aim of this corporate intervention is to boost after-tax global profits, the actual result may be to destroy incentive systems based on profit centers and to cause confusion and computational chaos. Subsidiaries may rebel when asked to undertake actions that will benefit the corporation as a whole, but will adversely affect their own performance evaluations. To counter this reaction, the rules must be clearly spelled out, and profit center results adjusted to reflect true affiliate earnings rather than the distorted remnants of a global profit-maximizing exercise.

■ 15.4 ■
ILLUSTRATION: TRANSFER PRICING AND TAX EVASION

On September 19, 1983, the Swiss-based commodities trading firm Marc Rich & Co. AG, its U.S. unit, and its two principal officers, Marc Rich and Pincus Green, were indicted by the U.S. government for allegedly evading over $100 million in U.S. taxes, making it the biggest tax-evasion case in history. The U.S. government charged that Marc Rich, his companies, and Pincus Green had the U.S. unit transfer profit to the Swiss parent by having the U.S. affiliate pay the Swiss company artificially high prices for oil.

In 1982, the United States subpoenaed from the Swiss parent documents that it thought would buttress its case—and that would make public a great deal of information about the company. Despite its size—annual revenue exceeding $10 billion—Marc Rich & Co. has a penchant for secrecy. Because of its refusal to give the documents to a grand jury, Marc Rich was cited in contempt of court and subject to a $50,000-a-day fine while it appealed a federal judge's refusal to vacate the contempt order. In September 1983, Marc Rich's internal documents were seized by the Swiss government on the ground that releasing them to U.S. authorities would violate Swiss secrecy laws.

Marc Rich settled with the U.S. government in October 1984. The back taxes plus interest, penalties, fines, and seized assets made the settlement worth almost $200 million— the most ever recovered in a criminal tax-evasion case.

But except for its magnitude, the Rich case isn't unique. Since the late 1960s, the Department of Justice has been cracking down on the use of transfer pricing to evade U.S. taxes. One case was U.S. Gypsum Co. Strange things were happening to the price of gypsum rock that the company mined in Canada and shipped to the United States. The rock was sold by the company's Canadian unit at a low price, keeping Canadian profit and taxes down, and was resold to the U.S. unit at a high price, keeping U.S. profit and taxes down. The profit was siphoned into another U.S. Gypsum subsidiary that owned the rock only while it fell through the air from the Canadian conveyor belt down to the hold of a U.S. ship. This intermediate subsidiary was a paper company and was in a low tax bracket. The Department of Justice challenged this arrangement in court and won in a civil case.

In June 1983, the American sales subsidiary of Toyota Motor Co. was ordered by a federal judge to turn over to the Internal Revenue Service information about the prices its parent firm charged its car dealers in Japan. The IRS maintained that the Japanese data were necessary for it to determine whether the transfer prices it charged Toyota Motor Sales U.S.A. for Toyota products in the United States were being used to reduce its U.S. tax liability. The IRS claimed that the U.S. sales unit of Toyota trimmed its taxable U.S. income by paying its Japanese parent higher than reasonable prices for the vehicles sold in the United States. This case and a similar one brought against Nissan Motor Co. were settled in late 1987 when the U.S. sales units of both companies paid undisclosed amounts of additional income taxes to the IRS. Reportedly, the combined payments exceeded $600 million. These taxes were offset by tax refunds of an equivalent (though lesser) amount received from Japan's national tax agency for taxes paid on the income previously recorded in Japan but now reallocated to the United States. Currently, the IRS has cases pending against a number of Japanese and South Korean companies, including Hitachi, Mitsubishi Electric, Tokai Bank, and Daewoo.

Sometimes it is not the U.S. government that feels cheated. Amway of Canada and its U.S. parent, Amway Corp., were fined $25 million in November 1983 after pleading guilty in Ontario Supreme Court to using a complex transfer pricing scheme to undervalue goods they were exporting to Canada, defrauding the Canadian government of more than $28 million in customs duties and sales tax.

■ 15.5 ■
SUMMARY AND CONCLUSIONS

This chapter examined a variety of different fund-shifting mechanisms. Corporate objectives associated with the use of these techniques include financing foreign operations, reducing interest costs, reducing tax costs, and removing blocked funds.

It is apparent after examining these goals that there are trade-offs involved. For instance, removing blocked funds from a low-tax nation is likely to raise the firm's worldwide tax bill. Similarly, reducing exchange risk often results in higher interest expenses and adds to the financing needs of affiliates in soft-currency nations. The realistic weight that should be assigned to each of these goals depends on the individual impact of each goal on corporate profitability. Focusing on just one or two of these goals, such as avoiding exchange risk or minimizing taxes, to the exclusion of all others will probably lead to suboptimal decisions.

The recommended global approach to managing fund transfers is best illustrated by the creative use of financial linkages, whereby one unit becomes a conduit for the movement of funds elsewhere. For example, requiring affiliate A to remit dividends to its parent while financing this withdrawal by lowering transfer prices on goods sold to affiliate A by affiliate B will reduce income taxes and/or customs duties in the process. Or cash can be shifted from A to B through leading and lagging, with these same funds moved on to affiliate C by adjusting royalties or repaying a loan. Taking advantage of being multinational means remitting funds to the parent and other affiliates via royalties and licensing fees from some countries, dividend payments from other nations, and loan repayments from still others; all these maneuvers are to be coordinated with an eye toward maximizing corporate benefits.

It is apparent that the major benefit expected from engaging in these various maneuvers comes from government actions that distort the risk-return trade-offs associated with borrowing or lending in different currencies or that alter after-tax returns because of tax asymmetries. The fact that a particular action is legal and profitable, however, does not necessarily mean it should be undertaken. When devising currency, credit, and tax regulations, governments obviously have other goals in mind besides creating profitable arbitrage opportunities for multinational firms. A company that consistently attempts to apply a "sharp pencil" and take maximum advantage of these arbitrage opportunities may optimize short-run profits, but this "penciling" is likely to be done at the expense of long-run profits.

The notion of being a good corporate citizen may be an amorphous concept, but firms that are perceived as being short-run profit oriented may face questions regarding their legitimacy. More and more, multinationals are dependent on the good will of home and host governments, and actions that undermine this key factor may reduce the viability of their foreign operations.

Thus, it may well be worthwhile to pass up opportunities to make higher profits today if these profits are gained at the expense of the corporation's long-run international existence. As in all business decisions, of course, it is important to evaluate the costs and benefits associated with particular actions, which has been the goal of this chapter in the area of intercompany fund flows.

■ QUESTIONS ■

1. Where does the value of an MNC's multinational financial system reside?

2. California, like several other states, applies the unitary method of taxation to firms doing business within the state. Under the unitary method a state determines the tax on a company's worldwide profit through a formula based on the share of the company's sales, assets, and payroll falling within the state. In California's case, the share of worldwide profit taxed is calculated as the average of these three factors.

   a. What are the predictable corporate responses to the unitary tax?

   b. What economic motives might help explain why Oregon, Florida, and several other states have eliminated their unitary tax schemes?

3. Under what circumstances is leading and lagging likely to be of most value?

4. What are the principal advantages of investing in foreign affiliates in the form of debt instead of equity?

5. When comparing a multinational firm's reported foreign profits with domestic profits, caution must be exercised. This same caution must also be applied when analyzing the reported profits of the firm's various subsidiaries. Only coincidentally will these reported profits correspond to actual profits.

   a. Describe five different means that MNCs use to manipulate reported profitability among their various units.

    b. What adjustments to its reported figures would be required to compute the true profitability of a firm's foreign operations so as to account for these distortions?

    c. Describe at least three reasons that might explain some of these manipulations.

6. In 1987, the most recent year for which aggregate information is available, U.S.-controlled companies earned an average 2.09% return on assets, nearly four times their foreign-controlled counterparts. A number of American politicians have used these figures to argue that there is widespread tax cheating by foreign-owned multinationals.

    a. What are some economically plausible reasons (other than tax evasion) that would explain the low rates of return earned by foreign-owned companies in the United States? Consider the consequences of the debt-financed U.S.-investment binge that foreign companies went on during the 1980s and the dramatic depreciation of the U.S. dollar beginning in 1985.

    b. What are some of the mechanisms that foreign-owned companies can use to reduce their tax burden in the United States?

    c. The corporate tax rate in Japan is 60%, whereas it is 34% in the United States. Are these figures consistent with the argument that big Japanese companies are overcharging their U.S. subsidiaries in order to avoid taxes? Explain.

■ PROBLEMS ■

1. Suppose Navistar's Canadian subsidiary sells 1,500 trucks monthly to the French affiliate at a transfer price of $27,000 per unit. Assume the Canadian and French marginal tax rates on corporate income equal 45% and 50%, respectively.

    a. Suppose the transfer price can be set at any level between $25,000 and $30,000. At what transfer price will corporate taxes paid be minimized? Explain.

    b. Suppose the French government imposes an ad valorem tariff of 15% on imported tractors. How would this affect the optimal transfer pricing strategy?

    c. If the transfer price of $27,000 is set in French francs and the French franc revalues by 5%, what will happen to the firm's overall tax bill? Consider the tax consequences both with and without the 15% tariff.

    d. Suppose the transfer price is increased from $27,000 to $30,000 while credit terms are extended from 90 days to 180 days. What are the fund-flow implications of these adjustments?

2. Suppose a U.S. parent owes $5 million to its English affiliate. The timing of this payment can be changed by up to 90 days in either direction; assume the following effective annualized after-tax dollar borrowing and lending rates in England and the United States.

	Lending (%)	Borrowing (%)
United States	3.2	4.0
England	3.0	3.6

    a. If the U.S. parent is borrowing funds while the English affiliate has excess funds, should the parent speed up or slow down its payment to England?

    b. What is the net effect of the optimal payment activities in terms of changing the units' borrowing costs and/or interest income?

3. Suppose that covered after-tax lending and borrowing rates for three units of Eastman Kodak—located in the United States, France, and Germany—are

	Lending (%)	Borrowing (%)
United States	3.1	3.9
France	3.0	4.2
Germany	3.2	4.4

Currently, the French and German units owe $2 million and $3 million, respectively, to their U.S. parent. The German unit also has $1 million in payables outstanding to its French affiliate. The timing of these payments can be changed by up to 90 days in either direction. Assume that Kodak U.S. is borrowing funds while both the French and German subsidiaries have excess cash available.

a. What is Kodak's optimal leading and lagging strategy?

b. What is the net profit impact of these adjustments?

c. How would Kodak's optimal strategy and associated benefits change if the U.S. parent has excess cash available?

4. Suppose that in the section on dividends, International Products has $500,000 in excess foreign tax credits available. How will this situation affect its dividend remittance decision?

5. Suppose affiliate A sells 10,000 chips monthly to affiliate B at a unit price of $15. Affiliate A's tax rate is 45%, and affiliate B's tax rate is 55%. In addition, affiliate B must pay an ad valorem tariff of 12% on its imports. If the transfer price on chips can be set anywhere between $11 and $18, how much can the total monthly cash flow of A and B be increased by switching to the optimal transfer price?

6. Suppose GM France sells goods worth $2 million monthly to GM Denmark on 60-day credit terms. A switch in credit terms to 90 days will involve a one-time shift of how much money between the two affiliates?

7. Suppose that DMR SA, located in Switzerland, sells $1 million worth of goods monthly to its affiliate DMR Gmbh, located in Germany. These sales are based on a unit transfer price of $100. Suppose the transfer price is raised to $130 at the same time that credit terms are lengthened from the current 30 days to 60 days.

a. What is the net impact on cash flow for the first 90 days? Assume that the new credit terms apply only to new sales already booked but uncollected.

b. Assume the tax rate is 25% in Switzerland and 50% in Germany and that revenues are taxed and costs deducted upon sale or purchase of goods, not upon collection. What is the impact on after-tax cash flows for the first 90 days?

8. Suppose a firm earns $1 million before tax in Spain. It pays Spanish tax of $0.52 million and remits the remaining $0.48 million as a dividend to its U.S. parent. Under current U.S. tax law, how much U.S. tax will the parent owe on this dividend?

9. Suppose a French affiliate repatriates as dividends all the after-tax profits it earns. If the French income tax rate is 50% and the dividend withholding tax is 10%, what is the effective tax rate on the French affiliate's before-tax profits, from the standpoint of its U.S. parent?

10.* Merck Mexicana SA, the wholly owned affiliate of the U.S. pharmaceutical firm, is considering alternative financing packages for its increased working capital needs resulting from growing market penetration. Ps 250 million are needed over the next six months and can be financed as follows:

*Contributed by Laurent Jacque.

- From the Mexican banking system at the semiannual rate of 50%.
- From the U.S. parent company at the semiannual rate of 6%.

The parent company loan would be denominated in dollars and would have to be repaid through the floating-exchange-rate tier of the Mexican exchange market. The exchange loss would, thus, be fully incurred by the Mexican subsidiary. The exchange rate as of March 1, 1984, was Ps 250 = $1 and widely expected to depreciate further.

    a. If interest payments can be made through the stabilized tier of the Mexican exchange market where the dollar is worth Ps 125, what is the break-even exchange rate on the floating tier that would make Merck Mexicana indifferent between dollar and peso financing?

    b. Merck Mexicana imports from its U.S. parent $500,000 worth of chemical compounds monthly, payable on a 90-day basis. Suppose that the parent adjusts its transfer prices so that Merck Mexicana must now pay $700,000 monthly for its chemical supplies. All payments for imports of chemicals involved in the manufacture of pharmaceuticals are transacted through the stabilized tier of the exchange market. At the current exchange rate of Ps 250 = $1, what is the net before-tax annual benefit to Merck of this transfer price increase?

11. A well-known U.S. firm has a reinvoicing center located in Geneva. The reinvoicing center handles an annual sales volume of $1.2 billion—$700 million in interaffiliate sales and the rest in third-party sales. The RC buys goods manufactured by the parent company or other subsidiaries and reinvoices the product to other affiliates or third parties. Many of these trades are with "low-volume, highly complex countries." When buying the goods, the RC takes title to them, but it does not take actual possession of the goods. The RC pays the selling company in its own currency and receives payment from the purchasing company in its own currency. What benefits can such a center provide?

■ APPENDIX 15A ■
MANAGING BLOCKED CURRENCY FUNDS

    A common policy of host governments facing balance-of-payments difficulties is to impose exchange controls that block the transfer of funds to nonresidents. As this chapter makes clear, the principal target of many of these controls is the multinational corporation with local operations. There are numerous types of currency controls, some more ingenious than others, but all with the goal of allocating foreign exchange via nonprice means. Often these exchange rate restrictions go hand in hand with substantial deviations from purchasing power parity and the international Fisher effect. Thus, currency controls are a major source of market imperfection, posing opportunities as well as risks for the multinational firm.

    The purpose of this appendix is to identify and evaluate the major strategies, and associated tactics, that MNCs use to cope with actual, as well as potential, restrictions.

    The management of blocked funds can be considered a three-stage process: (1) preinvestment planning, including analyzing the effects of currency controls on investment returns and structuring the operation so as to maximize the company's ability to access its funds, (2) developing a coordinated approach to repatriating blocked funds from an ongoing operation, and (3) maintaining the value of those funds that, despite all efforts, cannot be removed.

■ 15A.1 ■ PREINVESTMENT PLANNING

    To formulate an effective management plan, it is necessary to (1) know what is at risk and (2) devise a means to facilitate the use of blocked funds before their accumulation. These two elements form the nucleus of preinvestment planning.

In assessing the risks associated with currency controls, the firm must take into account the fact that the impact of these controls is unlikely to be uniform over the life of an investment. Rather, these effects are often favorable initially, gradually turning unfavorable in the later stages of a project's life. For instance, a firm may be able to import capital goods at a very favorable exchange rate if this equipment is assigned a high priority. Many governments, in effect, subsidize the importation of certain "essential" products through the use of multiple exchange rates. Another advantage from exchange controls is that the company's affiliate may be able to arrange local currency financing at attractive (subsidized) rates by borrowing the blocked funds being held by subsidiaries of other multinationals. These effects of currency controls are particularly beneficial early on, when the project is a net user of funds. Later on, though, when the investment becomes a net generator of cash, or a cash cow, the imposition of remittance controls has an onerous impact. In other words, it is only when a project is throwing off excess cash that restrictions on profit repatriation are likely to be onerous. Until that time, controls may be advantageous.

Once a parent company has committed funds to another country, it has largely determined its ability to remit or utilize any resultant project cash flows. Thus, many firms have found it highly useful to structure their investments in advance, in a way that maximizes future remittance flexibility. The principal components of such a strategy include

- Establishing trading links with other units
- Charging separate fees for the use of trademarks, licenses, and other corporate services
- Employing local currency borrowing
- Utilizing special financing arrangements
- Investing parent company funds as debt rather than equity
- Negotiating special agreements with host governments

By establishing as many trading links as possible with other affiliates, multinationals can enhance their ability to repatriate funds via transfer price adjustments. Extensive intercompany transactions also allow for the leading and lagging of payments.

Charging affiliates for the use of corporate patents, licenses, trademarks, and other headquarters services has enabled many firms to continue receiving income from abroad in the form of fees and royalties, even when dividend remittances are controlled.

Companies normally borrow locally when investing in countries with currency controls, thereby reducing the amount of funds that is at risk. Cash flows that would otherwise remain blocked can be used to service local currency debt. Moreover, the greater the amount of local financing, the fewer profits that must be remitted to the parent company to ensure it a reasonable return on its investment. However, local credit restrictions often go hand in hand with exchange controls, requiring firms to explore alternative sources of funds. As we have previously seen, special financing arrangements such as currency swaps, back-to-back loans, and parallel loans provide an indirect means of borrowing locally. The ratio of parent company loans to parent equity can also affect its ability to withdraw funds from abroad and the cost of doing so.

Last, but not least, a company investing in a high-priority industry such as pharmaceuticals or computers may be able to bargain with the host government for authorization to repatriate a greater percentage of earnings if controls are currently in effect, or for an exemption from anticipated future controls. To be effective, these negotiations should take place before the investment.

■ 15A.2 ■ REPATRIATING BLOCKED FUNDS

Firms operating in a country that has imposed exchange controls can transfer the funds being generated either directly as cash or else indirectly via special financial arrangements or in the form of goods and services purchased locally for use elsewhere. Direct transfer methods include

- Transfer price adjustments
- Fee and royalty charges
- Leads and lags in making payments abroad
- Dividends

Tactics for transferring funds indirectly include

- Parallel or back-to-back loans
- Purchase of commodities for transfer abroad
- Purchase of capital goods for corporate-wide use
- Purchase of local services for worldwide use (e.g., engineering and architectural design services)
- Conducting corporate research and development
- Hosting corporate conventions, vacations, and so on

Most of these methods have already been discussed. But note that although paying dividends is the most-used means of repatriating earnings, it is also the most restricted. Two methods of increasing dividend payments in the face of these restrictions are becoming increasingly popular. Both involve increasing the value of the local investment base because the level of profit remittance often depends on the amount of a company's capital. One way to augment a unit's registered capital is to buy used equipment at artificially inflated values. A related technique is for an affiliate to acquire a bankrupt firm at a large discount from book value. The acquisition is then merged with the affiliate on the basis of the failed firm's original book value, thereby raising the affiliate's equity base.

One innovative use of blocked currencies is to create export equivalents by purchasing services locally, which can aid the firm in other countries. For example, an MNC with operations in Brazil might establish research and development facilities there and pay for them with blocked funds. Key research personnel would be transferred to Brazil to supplement local employees, with all salaries and expenses paid in cruzeiros. Similarly, Brazilian architectural and engineering firms can be engaged to design plants and buildings in California or Colombia, with their services paid for in cruzeiros.

A related, though more common, technique is to host conventions or business meetings in, say, Rio de Janeiro. In addition, employees can be sent on vacations in Brazil and provided with cruzeiros that would otherwise remain blocked. Similarly, employees of the firm may be asked, where possible, to fly Varig, the Brazilian national airline, with the tickets to be purchased with cruzeiros in Brazil by the local Brazilian affiliate. These activities benefit Brazil as well as the MNC because they help to create export-oriented jobs.

■ 15A.3 ■ MAINTAINING THE VALUE OF BLOCKED FUNDS

Despite all efforts, a company may wind up with significant hoards of cash that cannot be repatriated. The company then has the choice of placing these funds in either long-term, illiquid investments such as new plant and equipment or else in fairly liquid, short-term assets such as local-currency-denominated securities.

Notwithstanding the similarity of goals (namely, to maintain or increase the value of inconvertible funds), these short- and long-term investments are not necessarily substitutes for each other. Each form of investment is predicated on certain assumptions. Short-term placements implicitly assume at least one of the following:

1. The funds are either not necessary or yield too low a return in the current business.
2. There are no reasonable business opportunities in other fields.

3. Long-run prospects in the country are not favorable and so divestment is the best course.

4. Exchange controls are expected to be temporary.

Whatever the case may be, the firm is holding its funds in a liquid form, ready to repatriate them as soon as it is able to do so.

The situation is different with long-term investments. Here the premise is that the company intends to remain in the country and that, at some point, it will be able to repatriate the cash flows generated by its reinvested funds. Alternatively, it may be that because so much cash is available, there are not enough short-term investment possibilities, thereby forcing the company to seek out less-liquid repositories for its money.

■ BIBLIOGRAPHY ■

Arpan, Jeffrey S. *International Intracorporate Pricing.* New York: Praeger, 1972.

Lessard, Donald R. "Transfer Prices, Taxes, and Financial Markets: Implications of International Financial Transfers within the Multinational Firm." In *The Economic Effects of Multinational Corporations,* Robert G. Hawkins, ed. Greenwich, Conn.: JAI Press, 1979.

Obersteiner, Erich. "Should the Foreign Affiliate Remit Dividends or Reinvest?" *Financial Management,* Spring 1973, pp. 88–93.

Robbins, Sidney M., and Robert B. Stobaugh. *Money in the Multinational Enterprise.* New York: Basic Books, 1973.

Rutenberg, David P. "Maneuvering Liquid Assets in a Multinational Company." *Management Science,* June 1970, pp. B–671–684.

Zenoff, David B. "Remitting Funds from Foreign Affiliates." *Financial Executive,* March 1968, pp. 46–63.

■ PART III ■
■ Case Study ■

■ Case III.1
Mobex Inc.

Mobex Inc., a U.S.-based firm engaged in the manufacture of instrument gauges for automobiles, was founded in 1949 by three former employees of Ford. The company began operations in Detroit, producing conventional mechanical instruments for major U.S. auto companies. The product line utilizes standard internal mechanisms with customized bezel (frontface) design to meet dashboard requirements of individual customers.

In 1971, the firm began design and testing of a new generation of instruments and gauges, utilizing custom, integrated circuits to perform functions heretofore performed by complex mechanical devices. The resulting product was cheaper to manufacture and had greater customer marketing appeal due to the digital readout feature. Mobex gained considerable competitive advantage by being the first to offer this new line in late 1975. The first of these products was installed in the 1977 luxury models.

The advent of the microprocessor marked another milestone in the evolution of Mobex. In 1983, Mobex began incorporating these so-called "smart chips" in a range of new products designed to continuously monitor certain performance attributes (e.g., fuel consumption and engine heat) and external conditions (e.g., temperature and altitude) and automatically adjust operating characteristics (e.g., the leanness of the fuel mixture and the timing of the spark-plug firing). These microprocessor-based products first appeared in the 1984-model cars and were an immediate success.

III 1.1 INTERNATIONAL OPERATIONS

Mobex set up a small manufacturing plant in West Germany in 1963 to supply Ford Europe with instrument gauges for its European models. Horst Stoffel, a native Bavarian and former employee of Beyrische Motor Werk (producers of BMW cars), had been hired to set up and manage Mobex AG (the new German subsidiary). Herr Stoffel's connections within the West German auto industry resulted in contracts with Opel and BMW by the end of 1967.

Results for 1967 showed foreign sales representing 6% of Mobex Inc.'s consolidated sales of $31 million. By 1970, as a result of Herr Stoffel's aggressive pursuit of new markets in Sweden and Switzerland (and a slump in the U.S. auto industry), Mobex AG accounted for 11% of total revenues of $43 million. In addition, productivity in the German subsidiary was higher than in the Detroit plant, causing foreign profits to represent 14% of the consolidated total.

These figures, plus informed opinions within the European auto industry, caused Mobex to commission a consulting study of the West European market. The company engaged the international project consulting group of Coopers & Lybrand, its certified public accountants, to perform the study. The group considered economic and psychological factors affecting auto sales, plus business environmental aspects, in England, France, Belgium, Spain, Switzerland, Italy, and Sweden.

The consultants identified two highly favored markets. Switzerland characterized a rapidly growing consumer market for automobiles, and it was believed that the new solid-state line of

SOURCE: This case was originally prepared by Carolyn Stevens, under the supervision of Alan C. Shapiro and Laurent Jacque. Revision and copyright © 1985 by Alan C. Shapiro.

instruments Mobex offered would be in high demand. (Although Switzerland has no auto producers of its own, local dealers install many of the gauges and instruments manufactured by Mobex as optional equipment or as part of the special-performance packages.) Mobex AG already exported the conventional line to that country. In addition, Switzerland offered an industrious work force as well as a favorable tax environment.

Italy also presented a unique opportunity to Mobex. Labor problems in southern Italy had severely hampered deliveries by domestic suppliers to Fiat, the large Italian auto producer. Industry sources believed that the company could be induced to change suppliers to achieve a reliable delivery pattern. In addition, the promise of the new Mobex line of instruments was bound to hold high appeal for Fiat. It was further believed that Alfa Romeo would soon follow Fiat's lead, in order to obtain Mobex's high quality product. The consultants recommended a manufacturing plant in northern Italy, where the labor force was considered to be more favorable.

Mobex had acted upon both recommendations, first locating and engaging foreign nationals with both technical and sales experience in the industry, and then providing the needed managerial assistance in start-up of operations. The Swiss subsidiary, Mobex Suisse, began operations in September 1971. A contract was signed by Fiat, leading to the start-up of operations in Italy (Mobex SpA) in February 1972. Shortly thereafter, Alfa Romeo also signed with Mobex SpA. Capital equipment for both of the subsidiaries was obtained in the United States, with local borrowing (using parent company guarantees) to finance start-up costs and to supply working capital.

Typical of practices within the local instrumentation industry, orders are placed annually for a 12-month supply, with delivery occurring every 90 days. Payment falls due 90 days following each delivery for the quantity supplied. This schedule enabled the company to engage in financial and production planning on a quarterly basis.

Growth in international operations continued to be rapid, due to Mobex's superior quality line, aggressive pricing, and strong marketing efforts by local managers. Foreign managers supplied a regular flow of information to the parent on product needs, thereby enabling the parent to maintain a centralized design and R & D effort in Detroit. Other than this centralized function, each subsidiary remained relatively autonomous. Local managers were free to hire local nationals, and parent management provided appropriate training. This policy of decentralization was maintained to encourage maximum adaptation to and penetration of local markets.

International production was rationalized in part during 1975, when it became clear that savings could be obtained by sourcing the flexible steel cable, fittings, plastic housings, and aluminum (deep-drawn) cups in Germany and assembling these for shipment to Switzerland and Italy. Savings were also possible by purchasing the silk-screen painted faceplates and clear glass covers in Switzerland for all three plants. Production of the line of instruments utilizing integrated circuits began at foreign locations in late 1978. The integrated circuits were sourced in the United States initially, but by 1982, about 80% of the circuits were being sourced in Europe. Manufacture of microprocessor-based products in Europe began in 1984. The microprocessors would have to be sourced in the United States for some time to come. Parts and subassemblies transferred among the foreign subsidiaries were priced at cost plus labor and handling, and payment was generally made upon delivery. No attempt had been made to determine if overall savings could be obtained by altering the transfer prices or payment schedules on these transactions.

III 1.2 INTERNATIONAL FINANCIAL PLANNING

By 1984, the coordination of international financial planning activities had become such a heavy burden on the parent's treasury staff that a special Assistant Treasurer in charge of international activities was hired. Kathryn Lee, formerly an Assistant Vice President in Northern Bank & Trust

Company's international division, was selected for this position. Her role was to take charge of international financial planning activities.

Ms. Lee was introduced at the annual planning meeting in June 1984. Anticipating reluctance on the part of local managers and treasurers to relinquish control and flexibility, she scheduled an additional one-day session to highlight the need for coordination. In addition, she was sure that savings could be achieved by looking at the system as a whole rather than allowing each subsidiary to act independently. Now seemed to be an opportune time to conduct such a review because operations would be expanding due to the growth supplied by the new products. In addition, Mobex intended to further rationalize its European production. The result was sure to be an increase in interaffiliate sales, in both absolute and relative terms, and, hence, greater advantages to rationalizing financial policy.

During this meeting, each of the foreign treasurers submitted projections for the relevant financing rates during the first two quarters of 1985 plus expected intersubsidiary purchases at present transfer price levels. This information is summarized in Exhibit III 1.1.

Exhibit III 1.1 also presents expected exchange rate changes based upon weighted probability estimates. The lira is expected to depreciate 1% during each of the first two quarters in 1985, while the Deutsche mark is expected to appreciate 0.75% during the first quarter and 0.50% during the second quarter. The Swiss franc:dollar exchange rate is expected to remain constant throughout the first half of 1985.

Pro forma balance sheets, shown in Exhibit III 1.2, were prepared to highlight financing needs and exposure to exchange rate fluctuations. Interaffiliate payables and receivables are nonexistent because current payment terms are cash on delivery. Exhibit III 1.2 is expressed in U.S. dollar terms and separates out exposed and nonexposed transactions from a system standpoint. This means that if, contrary to current policy, Mobex SpA had an account payable denominated in Deutsche marks to

■ **EXHIBIT III 1.1** Financing and Hedging Costs (Annualized) and Amounts ($ Millions)

	Affiliate Quarter											
	Mobex SpA—Italy				Mobex AG—West Germany				Mobex Suisse—Switzerland			
	1st		2nd		1st		2nd		1st		2nd	
	Limit	Cost	Limit	Cost	Limit	Cost	Limit	Cost	Limit	Cost	Limit	Cost
Overdraft	2.0	14%	2.0	15%	3.0	8%	3.0	10%	3.0	11%	3.0	12%
Two-quarter local loan	2.5	12	2.5	12	1.5	8	1.5	8	2.0	12	2.0	12
One-quarter Eurodollar loan*	2.0	10	2.0	12	3.0	10	3.0	12	2.0	10	2.0	12
Two-quarter Eurodollar loan*	2.0	10	2.0	10	3.0	10	3.0	10	2.0	10	2.0	10
Export financing	—	—	—	—	2.0	7	2.0	8	1.0	9	0.5	10
	Forward Discount				Forward Premium							
One-quarter forward premium (discount)	6%		6%		2.5%		2.5%		0%		0%	
Two-quarter forward premium (discount)			10%				2%		0%		0%	
Expected exchange rate changes	–1%		–1%		+0.75%		+0.50%		0%		0%	

*The overall limit on Eurodollar borrowing is $5.0 million.

■ EXHIBIT III 1.2   Balance-Sheet Forecasts ($ Millions)

Affiliate Quarter

	Mobex SpA—Italy						Mobex AG—West Germany						Mobex Suisse—Switzerland					
	1st			2nd			1st			2nd			1st			2nd		
	Total	Exposed	Not Exposed	Total	Exposed	Not Exposed	Total	Exposed	Not Exposed	Total	Exposed	Not Exposed	Total	Exposed	Not Exposed	Total	Exposed	Not Exposed
Assets																		
Cash	$1.0	$1.0	$—	$1.0	$1.0	$—	$1.5	$1.5	$—	$2.0	$2.0	$—	$1.5	$1.5	$—	$1.5	$1.5	$—
Receivables	3.5	2.0	1.5	4.0	3.5	0.5	4.0	2.0	2.0	4.5	2.5	2.0	3.0	2.5	0.5	3.0	2.5	0.5
Intersubsidiary receivables*	—	—	—	—	—	—	—	—	—	—	—	—	—	—	—	—	—	—
Inventories	2.0	1.5	0.5	2.5	2.0	0.5	3.0	1.0	2.0	3.0	1.5	1.5	2.5	0.5	2.0	3.0	1.0	2.0
Plant and equipment	3.5	—	3.5	3.5	—	3.5	4.0	—	4.0	4.0	—	4.0	3.5	—	3.5	3.5	—	3.5
	$10.0	$4.5	$5.5	$11.0	$6.5	$4.5	$12.5	$4.5	$8.0	$13.5	$6.0	$7.5	$10.5	$4.5	$6.0	$11.0	$5.0	$6.0
Liabilities																		
Notes/loans	$—	$—	$—	$—	$—	$—	$—	$—	$—	$—	$—	$—	$—	$—	$—	$—	$—	$—
Taxes payable	1.5	1.5	—	1.5	1.5	—	0.5	0.5	—	0.5	0.5	—	0.5	0.5	—	0.5	0.5	—
Accounts payable	0.5	0.5	—	1.0	0.5	0.5	2.0	1.5	0.5	2.0	2.0	—	1.5	1.5	—	1.5	1.5	—
Intersubsidiary payables*	—	—	—	—	—	—	—	—	—	—	—	—	—	—	—	—	—	—
Capital stock	2.5	—	2.5	2.5	—	2.5	3.0	—	3.0	3.0	—	3.0	2.0	—	2.0	2.0	—	2.0
Retained earnings	2.0	—	2.0	2.0	—	2.0	2.5	—	2.5	2.5	—	2.5	2.0	—	2.0	2.0	—	2.0
	$6.5	$1.5	$5.0	$7.0	$2.0	$5.0	$7.5	$1.5	$6.0	$8.0	$2.5	$5.5	$6.0	$2.0	$4.0	$6.0	$2.0	$4.0
Financing needs	$3.5			$4.0			$5.0			$5.5			$4.5			$5.0		
Exposure		$3.0			$4.5			$3.0			$3.5			$2.5			$3.0	
Tax rate		40%			40%			45%			45%			35%			35%	

*No interaffiliate credit is currently extended. However, purchase plans for the next two quarters include

A buys 0.5 from B in period 1   C buys 1.0 from B in period 1
A buys 0.5 from B in period 2   C buys 1.0 from B in period 2
A buys 0.5 from C in period 1   B buys 1.0 from C in period 1
A buys 0.5 from C in period 2   B buys 1.0 from C in period 2

All intersubsidiary sales are denominated in seller's currency.

Mobex AG, it would appear as a nonexposed item, even though it represents a foreign currency transaction, because it would be offset by a DM-denominated account receivable held by Mobex AG. From a system standpoint, therefore, it would not represent a foreign currency transaction exposure. Mobex's policy is to fully cover its estimated transaction exposure.

Based upon these figures, each subsidiary treasurer had come up with a tentative plan to finance working-capital needs and cover its transaction exposure. These formulations were based upon selection of the financing methods involving the lowest nominal cost and are shown in Exhibit III 1.3.

Ms. Lee suggested that savings might be achieved through a more rigorous examination of costs, considering the impact of currency changes and tax effects, in addition to the level of nominal interest rates. She proposed that an analysis of these additional factors be performed to determine the actual cost of the proposed financing methods. Two additional areas were also cited for investigation: (1) lagging of payments on intersubsidiary transactions and (2) adjusting the transfer prices on these transactions. With the exception of Italy, no country placed restrictions on leading or lagging of payments. Italy was primarily concerned with variations of 120 days or more. The treasurers themselves decided to limit lagging for 90 days, so Italy's restriction was not considered to be limiting (especially since the normal billing period within the industry was 90 days). The corporate tax counsel then expressed his opinion that transfer prices can be raised or lowered by 5% from their currently planned values, without provoking the attention of tax authorities in the various countries. Managers of the individual subsidiaries generally agreed that 5% was a conservative amount. To play it safe, it was decided to limit consideration of transfer pricing changes to the ± 5% range.

The meeting concluded with an agreement to review possible savings through implementation of a system-financing approach at the final budgeting review session in November. In the interim, Ms. Lee's staff would be responsible for developing the cost formulations and taking an initial cut at determining the optional financing/transfer-pricing solution, taking into account the costs and benefits and the constraints involved.

■ **EXHIBIT III 1.3**   Affiliate Financial Plans for 1985 ($ Millions)

| | Affiliate Quarter | | | | | |
| | Mobex SpA | | Mobex AG | | Mobex Suisse | |
	1st	2nd	1st	2nd	1st	2nd
Working-capital requirements	$3.5	$4.0	$5.0	$5.5	$4.5	$5.0
Proposed financing:						
2-quarter Lit loan	2.0	2.0				
2-quarter DM loan			1.5	1.5		
Export financing			2.0	2.0	1.0	0.5
Overdraft		0.5	1.5	2.0		0.5
1-quarter Eurodollar loan					1.5	2.0
2-quarter Eurodollar loan	1.5	1.5			2.0	2.0
Total	$3.5	$4.0	$5.0	$5.5	$4.5	$5.0
Projected exposure	3.0	4.5	3.0	3.5	2.5	3.0
To be eliminated by						
Local currency loan(s)	2.0	2.0	5.0	5.5	1.0	1.0
Forward contracts	$1.0	$2.5	$(2.0)	$(2.0)	$1.5	$2.0

QUESTIONS

1. What are the expected after-tax dollar costs of the different financing alternatives facing each of Mobex's foreign affiliates?

2. What are the costs and benefits associated with lagging payments between each pair of affiliates?

3. What are the tax and financing consequences associated with adjusting transfer prices between each pair of affiliates?

4. What are the interactions between modifying the credit terms and changing the transfer prices on transactions?

5. Which currencies should the interaffiliate transactions be denominated in, given the anticipated currency changes and tax considerations?

6. What is the optimal (i.e., the cost-minimizing) solution to the overall financing/transfer-pricing problem faced by Mobex's European subsidiaries, given the actual or self-imposed constraints they face? *Hint:* This is a linear programming problem, and you can find the values of the dual variables, which will tell you how much it would be worth to Mobex to relax each of the constraints it faces.

PART IV

Foreign Investment Analysis

▪16▪

International Portfolio Investment

Capital now flows at the speed of light across national borders and into markets once deemed impregnable.

—Citicorp Annual Report—

▪ There was a time when investors treated national boundaries as impregnable barriers, limiting their reach and financial options to predominantly domestic and regional markets. Times have changed. Just as companies and consumers are going global, so are increasing numbers of investors. American investors are buying foreign stocks and bonds and foreign investors are purchasing U.S. securities. The purpose of this chapter is to examine the nature and consequences of international portfolio investing. Although the chapter focuses on international investing from an American perspective, its lessons are applicable to investors from around the world.

▪ 16.1 ▪
MEASURING THE TOTAL RETURN FROM FOREIGN INVESTING

Before proceeding further, it is necessary to determine how we are going to measure the return associated with investing in securities issued in different markets and denominated in a variety of currencies. In general, the *total dollar return* on an investment can be decomposed into three separate elements: dividend/interest income, capital gains (losses), and currency gains (losses).

Bonds

The one-period total dollar return on a foreign bond investment $r_\$$ can be calculated as follows:

$$\begin{matrix} \text{Dollar} \\ \text{return} \end{matrix} = \begin{matrix} \text{Local currency} \\ \text{return} \end{matrix} \times \begin{matrix} \text{Currency} \\ \text{gain (loss)} \end{matrix}$$

$$1 + r_\$ = \left[1 + \frac{B(1) - B(0) + C}{B(0)} \right](1 + g) \tag{16.1}$$

where $B(t)$ = local currency (LC) bond price at time t
        C = local currency coupon income
        g = percent change in dollar value of the local currency

For example, suppose the initial bond price is LC 95, the coupon income is LC 8, the end-of-period bond price is LC 97, and the local currency appreciates by 3% against the dollar during the period. Then, according to Equation 16.1, the total dollar return is 13.8%:

$$\begin{aligned} r_\$ &= [1 + (97 - 95 + 8)/95](1 + 0.03) - 1 \\ &= (1.105)(1.03) - 1 \\ &= 13.8\% \end{aligned}$$

Note that the currency gain applies to both the local currency principal and to the local currency return.

Stocks

The one-period total dollar return on a foreign stock investment $R_\$$ can be calculated as follows:

$$\begin{matrix} \text{Dollar} \\ \text{return} \end{matrix} = \begin{matrix} \text{Local currency} \\ \text{return} \end{matrix} \times \begin{matrix} \text{Currency} \\ \text{gain (loss)} \end{matrix}$$

$$1 + R_\$ = \left[1 + \frac{P(1) - P(0) + DIV}{P(0)} \right](1 + g) \tag{16.2}$$

where $P(t)$ = local currency stock price at time t
        DIV = local currency dividend income

For example, suppose the beginning stock price is LC 50, the dividend income is LC 1, the end-of-period stock price is LC 48, and the local currency depreciates by 5% against the dollar during the period. Then according to Equation 16.2, the total dollar return is –6.9%:

$$\begin{aligned} R_\$ &= [1 + (48 - 50 + 1)/50](1 - 0.05) - 1 \\ &= (0.98)(0.95) - 1 \\ &= -6.9\% \end{aligned}$$

In this case, the investor suffered both a capital loss on the LC principal and a currency loss on the investment's dollar value.

■ 16.2 ■

THE BENEFITS OF INTERNATIONAL EQUITY INVESTING

The advantages of *international investing* are several. For one thing, an international focus offers far more opportunity. Over two-thirds of the world's stock market capitalization is in non-U.S. companies, and this fraction has been increasing over time (see Exhibit 16.1). In fact, if you want to invest in certain products with huge global markets, you'll find that most of the big, highly profitable manufacturers are overseas. For example, videotape recorders are the world's best-selling consumer electronics product, and 95% of them are made in Japan, over 80% of all cars are made abroad, 85% of all stereo systems, and 99% of all 35mm cameras. The Japanese dominance of these and other consumer product markets helps explain why in recent years Japanese market capitalization actually exceeded that of the United States. The 40% plunge in the Tokyo Stock Exchange during 1990 has evened up market capitalizations.

International Diversification

The expanded universe of securities available internationally suggests the possibility of achieving a better *risk-return trade-off* than by investing solely in U.S. securities: That is, expanding the universe of assets available for investment should lead to higher returns for the same level of risk or less risk for the same level of expected return. This follows from the basic rule of portfolio diversification: *The broader the diversification, the more stable the returns and the more diffuse the risks.*

Prudent investors know that diversifying across industries leads to a lower level of risk for a given level of expected return. Ultimately, though, the advantages of such diversification are limited because all companies in a country are more or less subject to the same cyclical economic fluctuations. Through *international diversification*—that is, by diversifying across nations whose economic cycles are not perfectly in phase—investors should be able to reduce still further the variability of their returns. In other words, risk that is systematic in the context of the U.S. economy may be unsystematic in the context of the global economy. For example, an oil price shock that hurts the U.S. economy helps the economies of oil-exporting nations, and vice versa. Thus, just as movements in different

■ **EXHIBIT 16.1**   Stock Market Capitalizations as Percent of World Total (20 Main Markets)

	March 1966	December 1970	December 1980	December 1989	November 1990
Japan	3%	5%	15%	39%	32%
United States	71	66	53	31	32
Europe	19	20	20	24	31
Rest of world	7	9	12	6	5

SOURCE: *Morgan Stanley Capital International*, various issues.

stocks partially offset one another in an all-U.S. portfolio, so also movements in U.S. and non-U.S. stock portfolios cancel out each other somewhat.

The value of international equity diversification appears to be significant. Bruno Solnik and Donald Lessard, among others, have both presented evidence that national factors have a strong impact on security returns relative to that of any common world factor.[1] They also found that returns from the different national equity markets have relatively low correlations with one another.

Exhibit 16.2 contains some data on correlations between the U.S. and non-U.S. stock markets. Foreign market betas, which are a measure of market risk derived from the capital

■ **EXHIBIT 16.2** How Foreign Markets Correlate with the U.S. Market, 1974–1983

Country	Correlation with U.S. Market	Standard Deviation of Returns (%)	Market Risk (Beta) from U.S. Perspective
United States	1.00	18.2	1.00
Canada	0.60	21.9	0.72
United Kingdom	0.33	34.4	0.62
France	0.25	28.8	0.40
West Germany	0.31	19.4	0.33
Switzerland	0.46	23.5	0.59
Italy	0.19	31.5	0.33
Netherlands	0.60	22.6	0.75
Belgium	0.36	22.0	0.44
Austria	0.21	15.0	0.17
Spain	0.06	20.9	0.07
Sweden	0.30	21.7	0.36
Norway	0.25	35.5	0.49
Japan	0.38	20.5	0.43
Hong Kong	0.34	45.5	0.85
Singapore	0.39	41.1	0.88
Australia	0.43	29.3	0.69
EAFE Index[1]	0.47	17.2	0.44
World Index[2]	0.91	17.1	0.86

NOTE: The table is based on data appearing in *Morgan Stanley Capital International,* various issues.

[1]The Morgan Stanley Capital International Europe, Australia, Far East (EAFE) Index is the non-American part of the world index and consists of stock markets from these parts of the world.

[2]The Morgan Stanley Capital International World Index has a combined market value of $2.1 trillion, covers 19 countries including the United States, and includes about 1600 of the largest companies worldwide.

[1]Bruno H. Solnik, "Why Not Diversify Internationally Rather Than Domestically?" *Financial Analysts Journal,* July–August 1974, pp. 48–54; and Donald R. Lessard, "World, Country, and Industry Relationships in Equity Returns: Implications for Risk Reduction Through International Diversification," *Financial Analysts Journal,* January–February 1976, pp. 32–38.

asset pricing model (see Chapter 19), are calculated relative to the U.S. market in the same way that individual asset betas are calculated:

$$\frac{\text{Foreign market}}{\text{beta}} = \frac{\text{Correlation with}}{\text{U.S. market}} \times \frac{\text{Standard deviation of foreign market}}{\text{Standard deviation of U.S. market}}$$

For example, the Canadian market beta is $0.60 \times 21.9/18.2 = 0.72$.

Measured for the ten-year period 1974–1983, foreign markets correlated with the U.S. market from a high of 0.60 for Canada and the Netherlands to a low of 0.06 for Spain. The relatively high correlations for Canada and the Netherlands reveal that these markets tracked the U.S. market's ups and downs. Spain's low correlation, on the other hand, indicates that the Spanish and U.S. markets have tended to move largely independently of each other.

Notice also that the investment risks associated with these different markets can be quite different—with the Hong Kong market showing the highest level and the Austrian market the lowest. Indeed, all but the Austrian market had a higher level of risk, as measured by the standard deviation of returns, than the U.S. market. Yet the internationally diversified Morgan Stanley Capital International World Index had the next-lowest level of risk—lower even than the U.S. market. The reason, of course, is that much of the risk associated with markets in individual countries is unsystematic and so can be eliminated by diversification, as indicated by the relatively low betas of these markets.

These results imply that international diversification may significantly reduce the risk of portfolio returns. In fact, the standard deviation of an internationally diversified portfolio appears to be as little as 11.7% of that of individual securities. In addition, as shown in Exhibit 16.3, the benefits from international diversification are significantly greater than those that can be achieved solely by adding more domestic stocks to a portfolio.

Moreover, from 1961 through 1990, the compound annual return for the Morgan Stanley Capital International Europe, Australia, Far East (EAFE) Index (which reflects all major stock markets outside of North America) was 13.7% compared with 9.6% for the U.S. market. Further, the EAFE Index outpaced the U.S. market 19 times during the 30-year period 1961–1990. Just between 1980 and 1988, the EAFE Index rose 450%, in comparison to a 150% rise for the S&P 500 (see Exhibit 16.4). Even more astounding, from 1949 to 1990, the Japanese market soared an incredible 25,000%. The obvious conclusion is that international diversification pushes out the *efficient frontier*—the set of portfolios that has the smallest possible standard deviation for its level of expected return and has the maximum expected return for a given level of risk—allowing investors simultaneously to reduce their risk and increase their expected return. The effect of international diversification on the efficient frontier is illustrated by Exhibit 16.5.

One way to estimate the benefits of international diversification is to consider the expected return and standard deviation of return for a portfolio consisting of a fraction a invested in U.S. stocks and the remaining fraction, $1 - a$, invested in foreign stocks. Define r_{us} and r_{rw} to be the expected returns on the U.S. and rest-of-world stock portfolios. Similarly, let σ_{us} and σ_{rw} be the standard deviations of the U.S. and rest-of-world portfolios. The expected return r_p can be calculated as

$$r_p = ar_{us} + (1 - a)r_{rw}$$

■ **EXHIBIT 16.3**   The Potential Gains from International Diversification

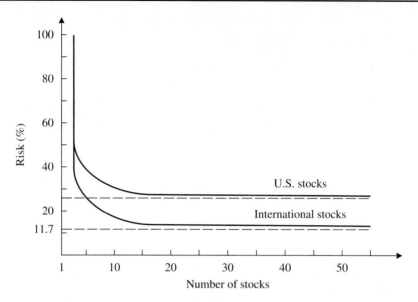

SOURCE: Bruno H. Solnik, "Why Not Diversify Internationally Rather Than Domestically?" *Financial Analysts Journal,* July–August 1974, p. 51. Reprinted by permission of the publisher.

To calculate the standard deviation of this portfolio, it helps to know that the general formula for the standard deviation of a two-asset portfolio with weights w_1 and w_2 ($w_1 + w_2 = 1$) is

$$\text{Portfolio standard deviation} = \left[w_1^2 \sigma_1^2 + w_2^2 \sigma_2^2 + 2 w_1 w_2 \sigma_{12} \sigma_1 \sigma_2 \right]^{1/2} \qquad \textbf{(16.3)}$$

where σ_1^2 and σ_2^2 are the respective variances of the two assets, σ_1 and σ_2 are their standard deviations, and σ_{12} is their correlation. We can apply Equation 16.3 to our internationally diversified portfolio by treating the domestic and foreign portfolios as separate assets. This yields a portfolio standard deviation σp equal to

$$\sigma_p = \left[a^2 \sigma_{us}^2 + (1-a)^2 \sigma_{rw}^2 + 2a(1-a) \sigma_{us} \sigma_{rw} \sigma_{us,rw} \right]^{1/2} \qquad \textbf{(16.4)}$$

where $\sigma_{us,rw}$ is the correlation between the returns on the U.S. and foreign stock portfolios.

To see the benefits of international diversification, assume that the portfolio is equally invested in U.S. and foreign stocks, where the EAFE Index represents the foreign stock portfolio. Using data from Exhibit 16.2, we see that $\sigma_{us} = 18.2\%$, $\sigma_{rw} = 17.1\%$, and $\sigma_{us,rw} = 0.47$. According to Equation 16.4, these figures imply that the standard deviation of the internationally diversified portfolio is

■ **EXHIBIT 16.4**   How Foreign Stock Markets Have Performed Relative to the U.S. Market, 1980–1988

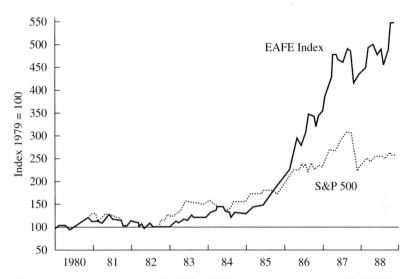

■ **EXHIBIT 16.5**   International Diversification Pushes Out the Efficient Frontier

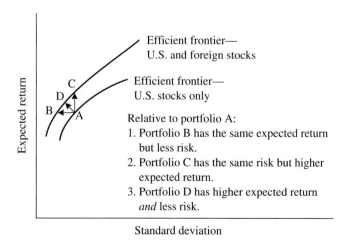

$$\sigma_p = [0.5^2(18.2)^2 + 0.5^2(17.1)^2 + 0.5^2 \times 2 \times 18.2 \times 17.1 \times 0.47]^{1/2}$$
$$= 0.5(912.57)^{1/2}$$
$$= 15.1\%$$

Here the risk of the internationally diversified portfolio is considerably below the risk of the U.S. portfolio. Moreover, as indicated earlier, the expected return is much higher as well.

Surprisingly, it is often the developing countries, with volatile economic and political prospects that offer the greatest degree of diversification and the highest expected returns.[2] Exhibit 16.6 shows how some of these "emerging markets" performed in the year ending September 30, 1990. Historically, no other stock markets so lavishly rewarded investors. Gains of 50% to 100% and more a year were not unusual.

But the high returns possible in these markets are matched by some breathtaking risks. In February 1990, when the newly elected Brazilian president froze most personal bank

■ **EXHIBIT 16.6**   The Emerging Stock Markets (September 28, 1989–September 30, 1990)

Country	Listed Companies	P/E	Total Dollar Return
Turkey	98	41	872.4%
Greece	128	29	267.5
Venezuela	66	17	246.8
India	2,450	24	62.2
Thailand	202	16	59.1
Colombia	80	12	48.8
Chile	216	6	46.8
Mexico	205	11	28.9
Argentina	174	−0.4	15.1
Malaysia	265	23	13.3
Portugal	183	17	8.6
Pakistan	471	10	6.7
Jordan	105	8	0.8
Brazil	587	10	−27.4
Philippines	151	16	−33.7
Korea	660	19	−40.5
Taiwan	193	27	−60.8
Indonesia	114	39	n/a
U.S. (S&P 500)		15	− 4.3
Japan (Nikkei)		34	−27.4
Britain (FT 100)		11	11.7

SOURCES: International Finance Corp. and *Morgan Stanley Capital International*

[2]See, for example, Vihang R. Errunza, "Gains from Portfolio Diversification into Less Developed Countries," *Journal of International Business Studies,* Fall–Winter 1977, pp. 83–99, and Warren Bailey and Rene M. Stulz, "Measuring the Benefits from International Diversification with Daily Data: The Case of Pacific Basin Stock Markets," Ohio State University working paper, April 1990.

accounts, the Sao Paulo exchange plummeted 70% in a few days. Similarly, Taiwan's market rose more than 1,000% from January 1987 to its peak in February 1990. It then gave back most of these gains, falling nearly 80% by October 1990. Despite their high investment risks, however, emerging markets can reduce portfolio risk because of their low correlations with returns elsewhere.

Barriers to International Diversification

The benefits to international diversification will be limited, however, to the extent that there are barriers to investing overseas. Such barriers do exist. They include legal, informational, and economic impediments that serve to segment national capital markets, deterring investors seeking to invest abroad. The lack of *liquidity*—the ability to buy and sell securities efficiently—is a major obstacle on some overseas exchanges. Other barriers include currency controls, specific tax regulations, relatively less-developed capital markets abroad, exchange risk, and the lack of readily accessible and comparable information on potential foreign security acquisitions. The lack of adequate information can significantly increase the perceived riskiness of foreign securities, giving investors an added incentive to keep their money at home.

Some of these barriers are apparently being eroded. Money invested abroad by both large institutions and individuals is growing dramatically (see Exhibit 16.7 for recent growth in U.S. pension fund investing overseas). For the world as a whole, a recent study by the investment bank Salomon Brothers estimated that *cross-border equity trading*—investors in one country buying stocks in another—was about $1.4 trillion in 1989 (see Exhibit 16.8).[3]

■ **EXHIBIT 16.7**   Growth of International Investing by U.S. Pension Funds

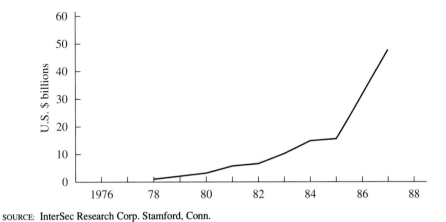

SOURCE: InterSec Research Corp. Stamford, Conn.

---

[3]Salomon's study was reported by Michael R. Sesit, "Foreign Investing Makes a Comeback," *The Wall Street Journal*, September 1, 1989, pp. C1 and C14.

■ **EXHIBIT 16.8**   International Stock Trading

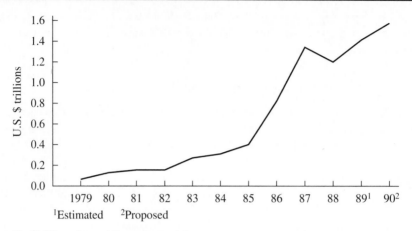

Salomon also estimated that at year end 1988, investors worldwide held about $640 billion in foreign stocks, or 6.7% of global equity markets.

Despite this growth in the level of foreign investing, however, these holdings still represent a relatively minor degree of international diversification (for example, about 4% of U.S. pension fund assets are invested in foreign equities), certainly when compared to MNCs with over half of their earnings coming from overseas. Nonetheless, discussions with U.S. institutional investors indicate that many intend to have 20%–25% of their funds invested overseas by the year 2000.[4]

There are several ways in which U.S. investors can diversify into foreign securities. A small number of foreign firms—fewer than 100—have listed their securities on the New York Stock Exchange (NYSE) or the American Stock Exchange. Historically, a major barrier to foreign listing has been the NYSE requirements for substantial disclosure and audited financial statements. For firms that wished to sell securities in the United States, the U.S. Securities and Exchange Commission's (SEC) disclosure regulations have also been a major obstruction. However, the gap between acceptable NYSE and SEC accounting and disclosure standards and those acceptable to European multinationals has narrowed substantially. Moreover, Japanese and European multinationals that raise funds in international capital markets have been forced to conform to stricter standards. This change may encourage other foreign firms to list their securities and gain access to the U.S. capital market.

Investors can always buy foreign securities in their home markets. One problem with buying stocks listed on foreign exchanges is that it can be expensive, primarily because of steep brokerage commissions. Owners of foreign stocks also face the complications of foreign tax laws and the nuisance of converting dividend payments into dollars.

[4]These discussions were reported by Michael R. Sesit, "Foreign Investing Makes a Comeback."

Instead of buying foreign stocks overseas, investors can buy foreign equities traded in the United States in the form of

1. *American Depository Receipts* (ADRs): These receipts are certificates of ownership issued by a U.S. bank as a convenience to investors in lieu of the underlying shares it holds in custody. The investors in ADRs absorb the handling costs through transfer and handling charges. ADRs for about 825 companies from 33 foreign countries are currently traded on U.S. exchanges.
2. *American shares*: These shares are securities certificates issued in the United States by a transfer agent acting on behalf of the foreign issuer. The foreign issuer absorbs part or all of the handling expenses involved.

The easiest approach to investing abroad is to buy shares in an internationally diversified mutual fund, of which a growing number are available. There are four basic categories of mutual fund that invests abroad:

1. *Global funds* can invest anywhere in the world, including the United States.
2. *International funds* invest only outside the United States.
3. *Regional funds* focus on specific geographic areas overseas, such as Asia or Europe.
4. *Single-country funds* invest in individual countries, such as Germany or Taiwan.

The greater diversification of the global and international funds reduces the risk for investors, but it also lessens the chances of a high return if one region (for example, Asia) or country (for example, Germany) suddenly gets hot. The problem with this approach is that forecasting returns is essentially impossible in an efficient market. This suggests that most investors would be better off buying an international-diversified mutual fund. Of course, it is possible to construct one's own internationally diversified portfolio by buying shares in several different regional or country funds.

■ 16.3 ■
INTERNATIONAL BOND INVESTING

The benefits of international diversification extend to bond portfolios as well. Barnett and Rosenberg started with a portfolio fully invested in U.S. bonds and then replaced them, in increments of 10%, with a mixture of foreign bonds from seven markets.[5] They then calculated for the period 1973–1983 the risk and return of the ten portfolios they created. Their conclusions, which can be seen in Exhibit 16.9, were as follows:

1. As the proportion of U.S. bonds fell, the portfolio return rose. This result reflects the fact that foreign bonds outperformed U.S. bonds over this ten-year period.
2. As the proportion of U.S. bonds fell from 100% to 70%, the volatility of the portfolio fell. This fact reflects the low correlation between U.S. and foreign bond returns.

---

[5]G. Barnett and M. Rosenberg, "International Diversification in Bonds," *Prudential International Fixed Income Investment Strategy,* Second Quarter 1983.

■ **EXHIBIT 16.9**   Risk-Return Trade-Off of an Internationally Diversified Bond Portfolio,
January 1973 to March 1983

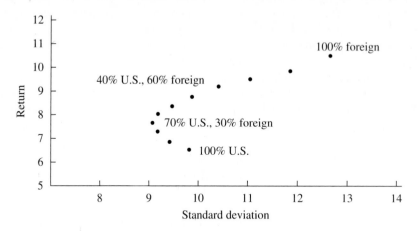

SOURCE: G. Barnett and M. Rosenberg, "International Diversification in Bonds," *Prudential International Fixed
Income Investment Strategy,* Second Quarter 1983. Reprinted by permission.

3. By investing up to 60% of their funds in foreign bonds, U.S. investors could have raised
   their return substantially while not increasing risk above the level associated with
   holding only U.S. bonds.

Other studies examining different time periods and markets have similarly found that
an internationally diversified bond portfolio delivers superior performance.

■ 16.4 ■
OPTIMAL INTERNATIONAL ASSET ALLOCATION

The evidence clearly indicates that both international stock diversification and international bond diversification pays off. Not surprisingly, expanding the investment set to include
stock and bonds, both domestic and foreign, similarly pays off in terms of an improved
risk-return trade-off.

The most detailed study to date of the advantages of international stock and bond
diversification is by Solnik and Noetzlin.[6] They compared the performances of various
investment strategies over the period 1970–1980. Exhibit 16.10 shows the outcome of their
analysis. The right-hand curve is the efficient frontier when investments are restricted to
stocks only. The left-hand curve is the efficient frontier when investors can buy both stocks
and bonds. All returns are calculated in U.S. dollars.

---

[6]Bruno H. Solnik and Bernard Noetzlin, "Optimal International Asset Allocation," *Journal of Portfolio Management,* Fall 1982, pp. 11–21.

The conclusions of their study were as follows:

1. International stock diversification yields a substantially better risk-return trade-off.
2. International diversification combining stock and bond investments results in substantially less risk than international stock diversification alone.
3. A substantial improvement in the risk-return trade-off can be realized by investing in internationally diversified stock and bond portfolios whose weights don't conform to relative market capitalizations. In other words, the various market indexes used to measure world stock and bond portfolios (e.g., Capital International's EAFE Index and World Index) don't lie on the efficient frontier.

As indicated by Exhibit 16.9, optimal *international asset allocation* makes it possible to double or even triple the return from investing in an index fund without taking on more risk. Although Solnik and Noetzlin had the advantage of hindsight in constructing their efficient frontier, they concluded that the opportunities for increased risk-adjusted returns are sizable and that the performance gap between optimal international asset allocations and passive investing in simple index funds is potentially quite large.

■ **EXHIBIT 16.10**   Efficient Frontiers, December 1970 to December 1980

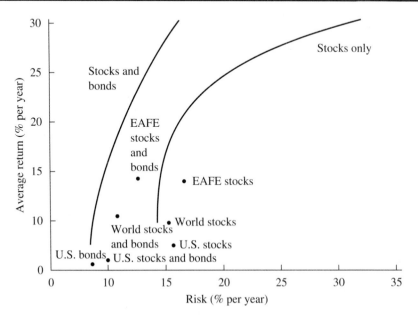

SOURCE: Bruno H. Solnik and Bernard Noetzlin, "Optimal International Asset Allocation," *Journal of Portfolio Management,* Fall 1982. Reprinted by permission.

■ 16.5 ■
SUMMARY AND CONCLUSIONS

As the barriers to international capital flows come down and improved communications and data processing technology provide low-cost information about foreign securities, investors are starting to realize the enormous potential in international investing. We saw in this chapter that international stock and bond diversification can provide substantially higher returns with less risk than investment in a single market. A major reason is that international investment offers a much broader range of opportunities than domestic investment alone, even in a market as large as the United States. An investor restricted to the U.S. stock market, for example, is cut off, in effect, from over two-thirds of the available investment opportunities.

Even though a passive international portfolio—one invested in an index fund based on market capitalization weights—improves risk-adjusted performance, an active strategy can do substantially better. The latter strategy bases the portfolio proportions of domestic and foreign investments on their expected returns and their correlations with the overall portfolio.

■ QUESTIONS ■

1. As seen in Exhibit 16.2, Hong Kong stocks are about 2.5 times more volatile than U.S. stocks. Does that mean that risk-averse American investors should avoid Hong Kong equities? Explain.

2. What characteristics of foreign securities lead to diversification benefits for American investors?

3. Will increasing integration of national capital markets reduce the benefits of international diversifications?

4. Mexican bonds are currently yielding over 100% annually. Does this make them suitable for American investors looking to raise the return on their portfolios? Explain.

5. The Brazilian stock market rose by 165% during 1988. Are American investors likely to be pleased with that performance? Explain.

6. Comment on the following statement: "On October 19, 1987, the U.S. stock market crashed. As the globe turned the following day, the devastation spread from New York to Tokyo, Hong Kong, Sydney, and Singapore, and on to Frankfurt, Paris, and London, then back to New York. The domino-style spread of the crash from one market to the next accelerated as international investors attempted to outrun the wave of panic selling from Tokyo to London and back to New York. It is difficult to imagine that some investors thought they had been able to diversify their investment risks by spreading their money across different stock markets around the world, when in fact their downside risks were actually multiplying as one market followed another into decline."

7. Persian Gulf countries receive virtually all their income from oil revenues denominated in dollars. At the same time, they buy substantial amounts of goods and services from Japan and Western Europe. Their investment portfolios are heavily weighted towards short-term U.S. Treasury bills and other dollar-denominated money market instruments. Comment on their asset allocation.

8. Investors should avoid Hong Kong, given its problematic outlook after Britain surrenders the colony to China in 1997. Comment.

9. In deciding where to invest your money, you read that Germany looks like it's well-positioned to capitalize on the opening of Eastern Europe. But Britain is troubled by weak growth and high inflation and interest rates. Which of these countries would it make sense to invest in? Explain.

10. As noted in the chapter, from 1949 to 1990, the Japanese market rose 25,000%.

   a. Given these returns, does it make sense for Japanese investors to diversify internationally?

   b. What arguments would you use to persuade a Japanese investor to invest overseas?

   c. Why might Japanese (and other) investors still prefer to invest in domestic securities despite the potential gains from international diversification?

■ PROBLEMS ■

1. During the year the price of British gilts (government bonds) went from £102 to £106, while paying a coupon of £9. At the same time, the exchange rate went from £1.76 to £1.62. What was the total dollar return, in percent, on gilts for the year?

2. During the first half of 1990, Swiss government bonds yielded a local-currency return of −1.6%. However, the Swiss franc rose by 8% against the dollar over this six-month period. Corresponding figures for France were 1.8% and 2.6%. Which bond earned the higher U.S. dollar return? What was the return?

3. During the year Toyota Motor Company shares went from ¥9,000 to ¥11,200, while paying a dividend of ¥60. At the same time, the exchange rate went from $1 = ¥145 to $1 = ¥120. What was the total dollar return, in percent, on Toyota stock for the year?

4. During 1989, the Mexican stock market climbed 112% in peso terms while the peso depreciated by 28.6% against the U.S. dollar. What was the dollar return on the Mexican stock market during the year?

5. Here are some data on stock market returns and exchange rate changes during 1988 for some of the world's stock markets. Determine the dollar return on each of these markets.

Country	Return in Local Currency(%)	Currency Units per Dollar	
		12/31/87	12/31/88
Australia	14.5	1.41	1.17
Belgium	56.3	35.10	38.80
Canada	10.9	1.29	1.20
France	56.8	5.65	6.31
West Germany	27.9	1.68	1.85
Holland	42.8	1.88	2.09
Italy	26.2	1230.00	1357.00
Japan	44.8	129.00	128.00
Spain	25.0	114.00	116.00
Sweden	60.5	6.03	6.30
Switzerland	31.9	1.37	1.58
United Kingdom	9.1	0.56	0.57

6. A portfolio manager is considering the benefits of increasing his diversification by investing overseas. He can purchase shares in individual country funds with the following characteristics:

	United States (%)	United Kingdom (%)	Spain (%)
Expected return	15	12	5
Standard deviation of return	10	9	4
Correlation with the United States	1.0	0.33	0.06

a. What is the expected return and standard deviation of return of a portfolio with 25% invested in the United Kingdom and 75% in the United States?

b. What is the expected return and standard deviation of return of a portfolio with 25% invested in Spain and 75% in the United States?

c. Calculate the expected return and standard deviation of return of a portfolio with 50% invested in the United States and 50% in the United Kingdom. With 50% invested in the United States and 50% invested in Spain.

d. Calculate the expected return and standard deviation of return of a portfolio with 25% invested in the United States and 75% in the United Kingdom. With 25% invested in the United States and 75% invested in Spain.

e. Plot the two sets of risk-return combinations (parts a through d) as in Exhibit 16.5. Which leads to a better set of risk-return choices, Spain or the United Kingdom?

f. How can you achieve an even better risk-return combination?

■ BIBLIOGRAPHY ■

Ibbotson, Roger C., Richard C. Carr, and Anthony W. Robinson. "International Equity and Bond Returns." *Financial Analysts Journal,* July–August 1982, pp. 61–83.

Lessard, Donald R. "World, Country, and Industry Relationships in Equity Returns: Implications for Risk Reduction Through International Diversification." *Financial Analysts Journal,* January–February 1976, pp. 32–38.

Solnik, Bruno H. "Why Not Diversify Internationally Rather Than Domestically?" *Financial Analysts Journal,* July–August 1974, pp. 48–54.

———. *International Investments.* Reading, Mass.: Addison-Wesley, 1988.

———, and Bernard Noetzlin. "Optimal International Asset Allocation." *Journal of Portfolio Management,* Fall 1982, pp. 11–21.

17

Corporate Strategy and Foreign Direct Investment

Luck. There isn't any. Just winners and losers.

—The Silver Fox —

■ Although investors are buying an increasing amount of foreign stocks and bonds, most still invest overseas indirectly, by holding shares of multinational corporations. MNCs create value for their shareholders by investing overseas in projects that have positive *net present values* (NPVs)—returns in excess of those required by shareholders. To continue to earn excess returns on foreign projects, multinationals must be able to transfer abroad their sources of domestic competitive advantage. This chapter discusses how firms create, preserve, and transfer overseas their competitive strengths.

The focus here on competitive analysis and value creation stems from the view that generating projects that are likely to yield *economic rent*—excess returns that lead to positive net present values—is a critical part of the capital budgeting process. This is the essence of corporate strategy—creating and then taking best advantage of imperfections in product and factor markets that are the precondition for the existence of economic rent.

The purpose of this chapter is to examine the phenomenon of *foreign direct investment* (FDI)—the acquisition abroad of plant and equipment—and identify those market imperfections that lead firms to become multinational. Only if these imperfections are well understood can a firm determine which foreign investments are likely ex ante to have positive NPVs. The chapter also analyzes corporate strategies for international expansion and presents a normative approach to global strategic planning and foreign investment analysis.

■ 17.1 ■
THEORY OF THE MULTINATIONAL CORPORATION

It has long been recognized that all MNCs are oligopolists (although the converse is not true), but it is only recently that oligopoly and multinationality have been explicitly linked via the notion of *market imperfections*. These imperfections can be related to product and factor markets or to financial markets.

Product and Factor Market Imperfections

The most promising explanation for the existence of multinationals relies on the theory of *industrial organization* (IO), which focuses on imperfect product and/or factor markets. *IO theory* points to certain general circumstances under which each approach—exporting, licensing, or local production—will be the preferred alternative for exploiting foreign markets.

According to this theory, multinationals have *intangible capital* in the form of trademarks, patents, general marketing skills, and other organizational abilities.[1] If this intangible capital can be embodied in the form of products without adaptation, then exporting will generally be the preferred mode of market penetration. Where the firm's knowledge takes the form of specific product or process technologies that can be written down and transmitted objectively, then foreign expansion will usually take the licensing route.

Often, however, this intangible capital takes the form of organizational skills that are inseparable from the firm itself. A basic skill involves knowing how best to service a market through new-product development and adaptation, quality control, advertising, distribution, after-sales service, and the general ability to read changing market desires and translate them into salable products. Because it would be difficult, if not impossible, to unbundle these services and sell them apart from the firm, this form of market imperfection often leads to corporate attempts to exert control directly via the establishment of foreign affiliates. But internalizing the market for an intangible asset by setting up foreign affiliates makes economic sense if—and only if—the benefits from circumventing market imperfections outweigh the administrative and other costs of central control.

A useful means to judge whether a foreign investment is desirable is to consider the type of imperfection that the investment is designed to overcome.[2] *Internalization,* and hence FDI, is most likely to be economically viable in those settings where the possibility of contractual difficulties make it especially costly to coordinate economic activities via arm's length transactions in the marketplace.

Such "market failure" imperfections lead to both vertical and horizontal direct investment. *Vertical integration*—direct investment across industries that relate to different stages of production of a particular good—enables the MNC to substitute internal production and distribution systems for inefficient markets. For instance, vertical integration might allow a firm to install specialized cost-saving equipment in two locations without the worry and risk that facilities may be idled by disagreements with unrelated enterprises. *Horizontal direct investment*—investment that is cross-border but within an industry—enables the MNC to utilize an advantage such as know-how or technology and avoid the contractual difficulties of dealing with unrelated parties. Examples of contractual difficulties are the MNC's

[1]Richard E. Caves, "International Corporations: The Industrial Economics of Foreign Investment," *Economica,* February 1971, pp. 1–27.

[2]These considerations are discussed by William Kahley, "Direct Investment Activity of Foreign Firms," *Economic Review,* Federal Reserve Bank of Atlanta, Summer 1987, pp. 36–51.

inability to price know-how or to write, monitor, and enforce use restrictions governing technology transfer arrangements. Thus, foreign direct investment makes most sense when a firm possesses a valuable asset and is better off directly controlling use of the asset rather than selling or licensing it.

Yet the existence of market failure is not sufficient to justify FDI. Because local firms have an inherent cost advantage over foreign investors (who must bear, for example, the costs of operating in an unfamiliar, and possibly hostile, environment), multinationals can succeed abroad only if the production or marketing edge that they possess cannot be purchased or duplicated by local competitors. Eventually, though, all barriers to entry erode, and the firm must find new sources of competitive advantage or be driven back to its home country. Thus, to survive as multinational enterprises, firms must create and preserve effective barriers to direct competition in product and factor markets worldwide.

Financial Market Imperfections

An alternative, though not necessarily competing, hypothesis for explaining foreign direct investment relies on the existence of financial market imperfections. We have already seen in Chapter 15 that the ability to reduce taxes and circumvent currency controls may lead to greater project cash flows and a lower cost of funds for the MNC than for a purely domestic firm.

An even more important financial motivation for foreign direct investment is likely to be the desire to reduce risks through international diversification. This motivation may be somewhat surprising because the inherent riskiness of the multinational corporation is usually taken for granted. Exchange rate changes, currency controls, expropriation, and other forms of government intervention are some of the risks that are rarely, if ever, encountered by purely domestic firms. Thus, the greater a firm's international investment, the riskier its operations should be.

Yet, there is good reason to believe that being multinational may actually reduce the riskiness of a firm. Much of the systematic or general market risk affecting a company is related to the cyclical nature of the national economy in which the company is domiciled. Hence, the diversification effect due to operating in a number of countries whose economic cycles are not perfectly in phase should reduce the variability of MNC earnings. Several studies indicate that this result, in fact, is the case.[3] Thus, since foreign cash flows are generally not perfectly correlated with those of domestic investments, the greater riskiness of individual projects overseas can well be offset by beneficial portfolio effects. Furthermore, because most of the economic and political risks specific to the multinational corporation are unsystematic, they can be eliminated through diversification.

The value of international diversification was made clear in Chapter 16. Thus, the ability of multinationals to supply an indirect means of international diversification should be

---

[3]See, for example, Benjamin I. Cohen, *Multinational Firms and Asian Exports* (New Haven, Conn.: Yale University Press, 1975); and Alan Rugman, "Risk Reduction by International Diversification," *Journal of International Business Studies,* Fall 1976, pp. 75–80.

advantageous to investors. But this *corporate international diversification* will prove beneficial to shareholders only if there are barriers to direct *international portfolio investment* by individual investors. These barriers do exist and were described in Chapter 16. However, we also saw that many of these barriers are eroding.

Our present state of knowledge does not allow us to make definite statements about the relative importance of financial and nonfinancial market imperfections in stimulating foreign direct investment. Most researchers who have studied this issue, however, would probably agree that the latter market imperfections are much more important than the former ones. In the remainder of this chapter, therefore, we will concentrate on the effects of nonfinancial market imperfections on overseas investment.

■ 17.2 ■
THE STRATEGY OF MULTINATIONAL ENTERPRISES

An understanding of the strategies followed by MNCs in defending and exploiting those barriers to entry created by product and factor market imperfections is crucial to any systematic evaluation of investment opportunities. For one thing, it would suggest those projects that are most compatible with a firm's international expansion. This ranking is useful because time and money constraints limit the investment alternatives that a firm is likely to consider. More importantly, a good understanding of multinational strategies should help to uncover new and potentially profitable projects; only in theory is a firm fortunate enough to be presented, with no effort or expense on its part, with every available investment opportunity. This creative use of knowledge about global corporate strategies is as important an element of rational investment decision making as is the quantitative analysis of existing project possibilities.

Some MNCs rely on product innovation, others on product differentiation, and still others on cartels and collusion to protect themselves from competitive threats. We will now examine three broad categories of multinationals and their associated strategies.[4]

Innovation-Based Multinationals

Firms such as IBM (United States), N.V. Philips (Netherlands), and Sony (Japan) create barriers to entry by continually introducing new products and differentiating existing ones, both domestically and internationally. Firms in this category spend large amounts of money on R&D and have a high ratio of technical to factory personnel. Their products are typically designed to fill a need perceived locally that often exists abroad as well.

But technological leads have a habit of eroding. In addition, even the innovative multinationals retain a substantial proportion of standardized product lines. As the industry matures, other factors must replace technology as a barrier to entry; otherwise, local competitors may succeed in replacing foreign multinationals in their domestic markets.

---

[4]These categories are described by Raymond Vernon, *Storm Over the Multinationals* (Cambridge, Mass.: Harvard University Press, 1977); and Ian H. Giddy, "The Demise of the Product Cycle Model in International Business Theory," *Columbia Journal of World Business,* Spring 1978, p. 93.

The Mature Multinationals

What strategies have enabled the automobile, petroleum, paper and pulp, and packaged foods industries, among others, to maintain viable international operations long after their innovative leads have disappeared and their products have become standardized? Simply put, these industries have maintained international viability by erecting the same barriers to entry internationally as those that allowed them to remain domestic oligopolists. A principal barrier is the presence of *economies of scale,* which exist whenever a given increase in the scale of production, marketing, or distribution results in a less-than-proportional increase in cost. The existence of scale economies means that there are inherent cost advantages to being large. The more significant these scale economies are, therefore, the greater will be the cost disadvantage faced by a new entrant to the market.

Some companies, such as Coca-Cola and Procter & Gamble, take advantage of enormous advertising expenditures and highly developed marketing skills to differentiate their products and keep out potential competitors that are wary of the high marketing costs of new product introduction. By selling in foreign markets, these firms can exploit the premium associated with their strong brand names. Other firms, such as Alcan and Exxon, fend off new market entrants by exploiting economies of scale in production and transportation.

Economies of scale also explain why so many firms are currently investing in Western Europe in preparation for 1992, when cross-border barriers to the movement of goods, services, labor, and capital are supposed to be removed. Their basic rationale for moving now is that once Europe becomes a single market, the opportunities to exploit economies of scale will be greatly expanded. Companies that are not well positioned in the key European markets fear that they will be at a cost disadvantage relative to multinational rivals that are better able to exploit these scale economies.

Still other firms take advantage of economies of scope. *Economies of scope* exist whenever the same investment can support multiple profitable activities less expensively in combination than separately. Examples abound of the cost advantages to producing and selling multiple products related by a common technology, set of production facilities, or distribution network. For example, Honda has leveraged its investment in small-engine technology in the automobile, motorcycle, lawn mower, marine engine, chain saw, and generator businesses. Similarly, Matsushita has leveraged its investment in advertising and distribution of Panasonic products in a number of consumer and industrial markets, ranging from personal computers to VCRs. Each dollar invested in the Panasonic name or distribution system aids sales of dozens of different products.

Production economies of scope are becoming more prevalent as flexible manufacturing systems allow the same equipment to produce a variety of products more cheaply in combination than separately. The ability to manufacture a wide variety of products—with little cost penalty relative to large-scale manufacture of a single product—opens up new markets, customers, channels of distribution, and with them, new routes to competitive advantage.

A strategy that is followed by Texas Instruments, Sony, and others, is to take advantage of the *learning curve* in order to reduce costs and drive out actual and potential competitors. This latter concept is based on the old dictum that you improve with practice. As production experience accumulates, costs can be expected to decrease because of improved production methods, product redesign and standardization, and the substitution of cheaper materials or practices. Thus, there is a competitive payoff from rapid growth. By acquiring a larger share of the world market, a firm can lower its production costs and gain a competitive advantage over its rivals.

The consequences of disregarding these economic realities are illustrated by U.S. television manufacturers, which (to their sorrow) ignored the growing market for color TVs in Japan in the early 1960s. The failure of the U.S. manufacturers to preempt Japanese color-TV development spawned a host of Japanese competitors—such as Sony, Matsushita, and Hitachi—that not only came to dominate their own market but eventually took most of the U.S. market. The moral seems to be that to remain competitive at home, it is often necessary to attack potential rivals in their local markets.

The high fixed costs that serve as barriers to entry for these mature oligopolists also ensure that average marketing or production costs are well above their marginal costs. Because this situation can lead to price cutting and other destabilizing behavior when demand slackens, members of the international oligopoly tend to follow strategies that are designed to reduce instability and foster cooperation in the industry. These strategies are follow-the-leader, joint ventures, and pricing conventions and cross-investment.

Follow-the-Leader Behavior. A major threat to the stability of any oligopoly is that one firm will gain a cost advantage by finding a low-cost production site or a major new market with attendant learning-curve effects, thereby putting it in a position to cut prices with fewer harmful consequences to itself. One way to ensure that all members of the industry have a similar cost structure is to follow the leader overseas (quickly, before the first firm has the opportunity to petition the local government to impose barriers to future trade or investment).

Joint Ventures. Another approach is to engage in joint ventures with competitors. This strategy is particularly prevalent in the raw material oligopolies (copper, iron ore, nickel, oil, aluminum). A side benefit to these alliances is that firms can diversify their sources of supply and, sometimes, their markets to a greater extent than if they each followed a policy of going it alone. Not only does this strategy reduce risk directly, it also provides each individual company with greater leverage over host governments and labor unions. With greater diversification, production can more easily be shifted elsewhere if excessive demands are made by any one country.

Pricing Conventions and Cross-Investment. Pricing conventions are useful sometimes, but they have a way of being ignored when demand decreases or flattens out. To counter the danger that a foreign multinational will use high home-country prices to subsidize marginal cost pricing overseas, firms will often invest in one another's domestic markets. This strategy is known as cross-investment. The implied threat is that "if you undercut me in my home market, I'll do the same in your home market." Firms with high domestic market share, and minimal sales overseas, are especially vulnerable to the strategic dilemma illustrated by the example of Fiat.

■ ───

ILLUSTRATION

Fiat's Strategic Dilemma. Suppose Toyota, the Japanese auto company, cuts prices in order to gain market share in Italy. If Fiat, the dominant Italian producer with minimal foreign sales, responds with its own price cuts, it will lose profit on most of its sales. In contrast, only a small fraction of Toyota's sales and profits are exposed. Fiat is effectively boxed in: If it responds to the competitive intrusion with a price cut of its own, the response will damage it more than Toyota.

The correct competitive response is for the local firm (Fiat) to cut price in the intruder's (Toyota's) domestic market (Japan). Having such a capability will deter foreign competitors from using high home-country prices to subsidize marginal cost pricing overseas. But this necessitates investing in the domestic markets of potential competitors. The level of market share needed to pose a credible retaliatory threat depends on access to distribution networks and the importance of the market to the competitor's profitability. The easier distribution access is and the more important the market is to competitor profitability, the smaller the necessary market share.[5]

─── ■

The Senescent Multinationals

Eventually, product standardization is far enough advanced or organizational and technological skills sufficiently dispersed that all barriers to entry erode. What strategies do large multinationals follow when the competitive advantages in their product lines or markets become dissipated?

One possibility is to enter new markets where little competition currently exists. For example, Crown Cork & Seal, the Philadelphia-based maker of bottle tops and cans, reacted to slowing growth and heightened competition in its U.S. business by expanding overseas. It set up subsidiaries in such countries as Thailand, Malaysia, Zambia, Peru, and Ecuador, guessing—correctly, as it turned out—that in those developing and urbanizing societies, people would eventually switch from home-grown produce to food in cans and drinks in bottles. However, local firms are soon capable of providing stiff competition for those foreign multinationals that are not actively developing new sources of differential advantage.

One strategy often followed when senescence sets in is to use the firm's *global-scanning capability* to seek out lower cost production sites. Costs can then be minimized by combining production shifts with *rationalization* and *integration* of the firm's manufacturing facilities worldwide. This strategy usually involves plants specializing in different stages of production—for example, in assembly or fabrication as well as in particular components or products. Yet the relative absence of market imperfections confers a multinational production network with little, if any, advantage over production by purely local enterprises. For example, many U.S. electronics and textile firms shifted production facilities to Asian locations, such as Taiwan and Hong Kong, to take advantage of lower labor costs there. However, as more firms took advantage of this cost-reduction opportunity, competition in

───

[5]The notion of undercutting competitors in their home market is explored in Gary Hamel and C.K. Prahalad, "Do You Really Have a Global Strategy?" *Harvard Business Review,* July–August 1985, pp. 139–148.

U.S. consumer electronics and textile markets—increasingly from Asian firms—intensified, causing domestic prices to drop and excess profits to be dissipated.

In general, the excess profits due to processing new information are temporary. Once new market or cost-reduction opportunities are recognized by other companies, the profit rate declines to its normal level. Hence, few firms rely solely on cost minimization or entering new markets to maintain competitiveness.

The more common choice is to drop old products and turn corporate skills to new products. Companies that follow this strategy of continuous product rollover are likely to survive as multinationals. Those who are unable to transfer their original competitive advantages to new products or industries must plan on divesting their international operations and returning home. But firms that withdraw from overseas operations because of a loss of competitive advantage should not count on a very profitable homecoming.

ILLUSTRATION

The U.S. Tire Industry Gets Run Over.   The U.S. tire industry illustrates the troubles faced by multinational firms that have lost their source of differential advantage. Although Europe had once been a profitable market for the Big Four U.S. tiremakers—Goodyear, Firestone, Goodrich, and Uniroyal—each of these firms has, by now, partially or completely eliminated its European manufacturing operations. The reason is the extraordinary price competition resulting from a lack of unique products or production processes and the consequent ease of entry into the market by new firms. Moreover, these firms then faced well-financed challenges in the U.S. market by, among others, the French tiremaker Michelin, the developer of the radial tire and its related production technology. Uniroyal responded by selling off its European tire-manufacturing operation and reinvesting its money in businesses that were less competitive there (and, hence, more profitable) than the tire industry. This reinvestment includes its chemical, plastics, and industrial products businesses in Europe. Similarly, Goodrich stopped producing tires for new cars and expanded its operations in polyvinyl chloride resin and specialty chemicals. In 1986, Uniroyal and Goodrich merged their tire units to become Uniroyal Goodrich Tire, selling only in North America. Late in 1989, its future in doubt, Uniroyal Goodrich sold out to Michelin. The previous year, in early 1988, Firestone sold out to the Japanese tiremaker Bridgestone.

Foreign Direct Investment and Survival

Thus far we have seen how firms are capable of becoming and remaining multinationals. However, for many of these firms, becoming multinational is not a matter of choice but, rather, one of survival.

Cost Reduction.   It is apparent, of course, that if competitors gain access to lower-cost sources of production abroad, following them overseas may be a prerequisite for domestic survival. One strategy that is often followed by firms for which cost is the key consideration is to develop a global-scanning capability to seek out lower-cost production sites or production technologies worldwide. In fact, firms in competitive industries have to continually seize new nonproprietary cost reduction opportunities, not to earn excess returns but to make normal profits and survive.

Economies of Scale.   A somewhat less-obvious factor motivating foreign investment is the effect of economies of scale. In a competitive market, prices will be forced close to marginal costs of production. Hence, firms in industries characterized by high fixed costs relative to variable costs must engage in volume selling just to break even. A new term describes the size that is required in certain industries to compete effectively in the global marketplace: *world-scale*. These large volumes may be forthcoming only if the firms expand overseas. For example, companies manufacturing products such as computers that require huge R&D expenditures often need a larger customer base than that provided by even a market as large as the United States in order to recapture their investment in knowledge. Similarly, firms in capital-intensive industries with enormous production economies of scale may also be forced to sell overseas in order to spread their overhead over a larger quantity of sales.

L.M. Ericsson, the highly successful Swedish manufacturer of telecommunications equipment, is an extreme case. The manufacturer is forced to think internationally when designing new products because its domestic market is too small to absorb the enormous R&D expenditures involved and to reap the full benefit of production scale economies. Thus, when Ericsson developed its revolutionary AXE digital switching system, it geared its design to achieve global market penetration.

These firms may find a foreign market presence necessary in order to continue selling overseas. Local production can expand sales by providing customers with tangible evidence of the company's commitment to service the market. It also increases sales by improving a company's ability to service its local customers. Domestic retrenchment can thus involve not only the loss of foreign profits but also an inability to price competitively in the home market because it no longer can take advantage of economies of scale.

ILLUSTRATION

U.S. Chipmakers Produce in Japan.   Many U.S. chipmakers have set up production facilities in Japan. One reason is that the chipmakers have discovered they can't expect to increase Japanese sales from halfway around the world. It can take weeks for a company without testing facilities in Japan to respond to customer complaints. A customer must send a faulty chip back to the maker for analysis. That can take up to three weeks if the maker's facilities are in the United States. In the meantime, the customer will have to shut down its assembly line, or part of it. With testing facilities in Japan, however, the wait can be cut to a few days.

But a testing operation alone would be inefficient; testing machines cost millions of dollars. Because an assembly plant needs the testing machines, a company usually moves in an entire assembly operation. Having the testing and assembly operations also reassures procurement officials about quality: They can touch, feel, and see tangible evidence of the company's commitment to service the market.

Multiple Sourcing.   Once a firm has decided to produce abroad, it must determine where to do so. Although cost minimization will often dictate concentrating production in one or two plants, fear of strikes and political risks usually lead firms to follow a policy of multiple sourcing. For example, a series of strikes against British Ford in the late 1960s and early 1970s caused Ford to give lower priority to rationalization of supplies. It went for safety instead, by a policy of double sourcing. Ford has since modified this policy, but many other firms still opt for several smaller plants in different countries instead of one large plant that can take advantage of scale economies but that would be vulnerable to disruptions.

The costs of multiple sourcing are obvious; the benefits, less apparent. One benefit is the potential leverage that can be exerted against unions and governments by threatening to shift production elsewhere. For example, to reach settlement in the previously mentioned strikes against British Ford, Henry Ford II used the threat of withholding investments from England and placing them in Germany. Another, more obvious, benefit is the additional safety achieved by having several plants capable of supplying the same product.

Similarly, Dow Chemical of Midland, Michigan, uses multiple sourcing of supplies to reduce the risk of being overly dependent on one or two producers. Without a link to any oil company, Dow—a major user of petroleum in its petrochemical business—has always had to shop around for its feedstock. The company has developed multiple sourcing to a fine art. To feed its cracking facilities in Terneuzen, Netherlands, and Tarragona, Spain, Dow Europe buys naptha from the Total refinery near Terneuzen, but it also buys on the Rotterdam spot market and under long-term contracts from Saudi Arabia and other supplier countries, including the Soviet Union.

Multiple facilities also give the firm the option of switching production from one location to another to take advantage of transient unit cost differences arising from, say, real exchange rate changes or new labor contracts. This option is enhanced, albeit at a price, by building excess capacity into the plants.

Knowledge Seeking.   Some firms enter foreign markets for the purpose of gaining information and experience that is expected to prove useful elsewhere. For instance, the English firm Beecham deliberately set out to learn from its U.S. operations how to be more competitive, first in consumer products and, later, in pharmaceuticals. This knowledge proved to be highly valuable in France and Germany.

In 1983, three South Korean concerns—the Samsung Group, the Hyundai Group, and the Lucky-Gold Star Group—set up operations in Silicon Valley. The Korean companies are trying to bring their technology up to U.S. levels by working in proximity to the top electronics producers in Silicon Valley, and with access to some of the best technicians. They also hope to gain respectability in the global electronics trade by establishing a presence in the region.

The flow of ideas is not all one way, however. As Americans have demanded better-built, better-handling, and more fuel-efficient small cars, Ford of Europe has become an important source of design and engineering ideas and management talent for its U.S. parent.

In industries characterized by rapid product innovation and technical breakthroughs by foreign competitors, it is imperative to track overseas developments constantly. Most firms have found that a local market presence aids in this process of gathering information. For example, Data General's Japanese affiliate is giving the company a close look at Japanese advances in manufacturing technology and product development, enabling it to quickly pick up and transfer back to the United States new information on Japanese innovations in the areas of computer design and manufacturing. Data General has already adopted some Japanese manufacturing techniques and quality-control procedures that will improve its competitive position worldwide.

More firms are building labs in Japan and hiring its scientists and engineers to absorb Japan's latest technologies. For example, Texas Instruments works out production of new chips in Japan first because, an official says, "production technology is more advanced and Japanese workers think more about quality control."[6] A firm that remains at home can be "blind sided" by current or future competitors with new products, manufacturing processes, or marketing procedures.

Tough competition in a foreign market is a valuable experience in itself. For many industries, a competitive home marketplace has proved to be as much of a comparative advantage as cheap raw materials or technical talent. Fierce domestic competition is one reason the U.S. telecommunications industry has not lost its huge lead in technology, R&D, design, software, quality, and cost. Japanese and European firms are at a disadvantage in this business because they don't have enough competition in their home markets. U.S. companies have been able to engineer a great leap forward because they saw firsthand what the competition could do. Thus, for telecommunications firms like Germany's Siemens, Japan's NEC, and France's Alcatel, a position in the U.S. market has become mandatory.

Similarly, it is slowly dawning on consumer electronics firms that to compete effectively elsewhere, they must first compete in the toughest market of all: Japan. What they learn in the process—from meeting the extraordinarily demanding standards of Japanese consumers and battling a dozen relentless Japanese rivals—is invaluable and will possibly make the difference between survival and extinction.

Although it may be stating the obvious to note that operating in a competitive marketplace is an important source of competitive advantage, this viewpoint appears to be a minority one today. Many companies are preparing for Europe 1992 by seeking mergers, alliances, and collaboration with competitors. Some go further and petition their governments for protection from foreign rivals and assistance in R&D. But to the extent companies succeed in sheltering themselves from competition, they endanger the basis of true competitive advantage: dynamic improvement, which derives from continuous effort to enhance existing skills and learn new ones.

Keeping Domestic Customers.   Suppliers of goods or services to multinationals will often follow their customers abroad in order to guarantee them a continuing product flow. Otherwise, the threat of a potential disruption to an overseas supply line—for example, a dock strike or the imposition of trade barriers—can lead the customer to select a local supplier, which may be a domestic competitor with international operations. Hence, comes the dilemma: Follow your customers abroad or face the loss of not only their foreign but also their domestic business. A similar threat to domestic market share has led many banks, advertising agencies, and accounting, law, and consulting firms to set up foreign practices in the wake of their multinational clients' overseas expansion.

---

[6]*The Wall Street Journal,* August 1, 1986, p. 6.

■ ───

ILLUSTRATION

Bridegestone Buys Firestone. As noted earlier, in March 1988, Bridgestone, the largest
Japanese tiremaker, bought Firestone and its worldwide tire operations. Like other Japanese
companies that preceded it to the United States, Bridgestone was motivated by a desire to
circumvent potential trade barriers and soften the impact of the strong yen. The move also
greatly expanded Bridgestone's customer base, allowing it to sell its own tires directly to
U.S. automakers, and strengthened its product line. Bridgestone excelled in truck and
heavy-duty-vehicle tires, while Firestone's strength was in passenger-car tires. But beyond
these facts, a key consideration was Bridgestone's wish to reinforce ties with Japanese auto
companies that had set up production facilities in the United States. By 1992, these
companies, either directly or in joint ventures with U.S. firms, are scheduled to produce
about 2 million vehicles annually in the United States.

Firestone also contributed plants in Spain, France, Italy, Portugal, Argentina, Brazil,
and Venzuela. Thus, Bridgestone's purchase of Firestone has firmly established the company
not only in North America, but in Europe and South America as well. Formerly, it had been
primarily an Asian firm, but had come to acknowledge the need to service Japanese
automakers globally by operating closer to their customers' production facilities. The
increasing globalization of the automobile market has prompted vehicle producers and
tiremakers alike to set up production facilities in each of the three main markets: North
America, Western Europe, and Japan.

Two main factors have been responsible for this trend toward globalization: transport
costs are high for tires and, as a result, exporting has ceased to be a viable long-term strategy
for supplying distant markets. For another, shifting manufacturing overseas was the only
way for the tire companies to meet the logistic challenges posed by the adoption of
"just-in-time" manufacturing and inventory systems by automakers.

A series of combinations in the tire industry—including Sumitomo Rubber's purchase
of Dunlop Tire's European and U.S. operations, Pirelli's acquisition of Armstrong Tire and
Rubber, and Continental AG's acquisition of General Tire and Rubber and its subsequent
joint venture with two Japanese tiremakers—practically forced Bridgestone to have a major
presence in the important American market if it were to remain a key player in the United
States and worldwide. Absent such a move, its Japanese competitors may have taken
Bridgestone's share of the business of Japanese firms producing in the United States and
Europe. This result would have affected its competitive stance in Japan as well.

A similar desire to increase its presence in the vital North American market was behind
Michelin's 1989 acquisition of Uniroyal Goodrich. For Michelin, the addition of Uniroyal
Goodrich provided entry into private-label and associate-label tire markets from which it
had been absent, as well as added sales to U.S. automakers.
─── ■

By now it should be apparent that a foreign investment may be motivated by considerations other than profit maximization and that its benefits may accrue to an affiliate far
removed from the scene. Moreover, these benefits may take the form of a reduction in risk
or an increase in cash flow, either directly or indirectly. Direct cash flows would include
those based on a gain in revenues or a cost savings. Indirect flows include those resulting

from a competitor's setback or the firm's increased leverage to extract concessions from various governments or unions (for example, by having the flexibility to shift production to another location). In computing these indirect effects, a firm must consider, of course, what would have been the company's worldwide cash flows in the absence of the investment.

■ 17.3 ■
DESIGNING A GLOBAL EXPANSION STRATEGY

Although a strong competitive advantage today in, say, technology or marketing skills may give a company some breathing space, these competitive advantages will eventually erode, leaving the firm susceptible to increased competition both at home and abroad. The emphasis must be on systematically pursuing policies and investments congruent with worldwide survival and growth. This approach involves five interrelated elements.

1. It requires an awareness of those investments that are likely to be most profitable. As we have previously seen, these investments are ones that capitalize on and enhance the differential advantage possessed by the firm; that is, an investment strategy should focus explicitly on building competitive advantage. This strategy could be geared to building volume where economies of scale are all important or to broadening the product scope where economies of scope are critical to success. Such a strategy is likely to encompass a sequence of tactical projects; several may yield low returns when considered in isolation, but together they may either create valuable future investment opportunities or allow the firm to continue earning excess returns on existing investments. To properly evaluate a sequence of tactical projects designed to achieve competitive advantage, the projects must be analyzed jointly, rather than incrementally.

For example, if the key to competitive advantage is high volume, the initial entry into a market should be assessed on the basis of its ability to create future opportunities to build market share and the associated benefits thereof. Alternatively, market entry overseas may be judged according to its ability to deter a foreign competitor from launching a market-share battle by posing a credible retaliatory threat to the competitor's profit base. By reducing the likelihood of a competitive intrusion, foreign market entry may lead to higher future profits in the home market.

In designing and valuing a strategic investment program, a firm must be careful to consider the ways in which the investments interact. For example, where scale economies exist, investment in large-scale manufacturing facilities may only be justified if the firm has made supporting investments in foreign distribution and brand awareness. Investments in a global distribution system and a global brand franchise, in turn, are often economical only if the firm has a range of products (and facilities to supply them) that can exploit the same distribution system and brand name.

Developing a broad product line usually requires and facilitates (by enhancing economies of scope) investment in critical technologies that cut across products and businesses. Investments in R&D also yield a steady stream of new products that raises the return on the investment in distribution. At the same time, a global distribution capability may be critical in exploiting new technology.

The return to an investment in R&D is largely determined by the size of the market in which the firm can exploit its innovation and the durability of its technological advantage. As the technology imitation lag shortens, a company's ability to fully exploit a technological advantage may depend on its being able to quickly push products embodying that technology through distribution networks in each of the world's critical national markets.

Individually or in pairs, investments in large-scale production facilities, worldwide distribution, a global brand franchise, and new technology are likely to be negative net present value projects. Together, however, they may yield a highly positive NPV by forming a mutually supportive framework for achieving global competitive advantage.

2. This global approach to investment planning necessitates a systematic evaluation of individual entry strategies in foreign markets, a comparison of the alternatives, and selection of the optimal mode of entry. For example, in the absence of strong brand names or distribution capabilities but with a labor-cost advantage, Japanese television manufacturers entered the U.S. market by selling low-cost, private-label, black-and-white TVs.

3. A key element is a continual audit of the effectiveness of current entry modes, bearing in mind that a market's sales potential is at least partially a function of the entry strategy. As knowledge about a foreign market increases or sales potential grows, the optimal market penetration strategy will likely change. By the late 1960s, for example, the Japanese television manufacturers had built a large volume base by selling private-label TVs. Using this volume base, they invested in new process and product technologies, from which came the advantages of scale and quality. Recognizing the transient nature of a competitive advantage built on labor and scale advantages, Japanese companies, such as Matsushita and Sony, strengthened their competitive position in the U.S. market by investing throughout the 1970s to build strong brand franchises and distribution capabilities. The new-product positioning was facilitated by large-scale investments in R&D. By the 1980s, the Japanese competitive advantage in TVs and other consumer electronics had switched from being cost based to one based on quality, features, strong brand names, and distribution systems.[7]

4. A systematic investment analysis requires the use of appropriate evaluation criteria. Nevertheless, despite the complex interactions between investments or corporate policies and the difficulties in evaluating proposals (or perhaps because of them), most firms still use simple rules of thumb in selecting projects to undertake. Analytical techniques are used only as a rough screening device or as a final checkoff before project approval. While simple rules of thumb are obviously easier and cheaper to implement, there is a danger of obsolescence and consequent misuse as the fundamental assumptions underlying their applicability change. On the other hand, the use of the theoretically sound and recommended present value analysis is anything but straightforward. The strategic rationale underlying many investment proposals can be translated into traditional capital budgeting criteria, but it is necessary to look beyond the returns associated with the project itself to determine its true impact on corporate cash flows and riskiness. For example, an investment made to save a market threatened by competition or trade barriers must be judged on the basis of the sales that would otherwise have been lost. Also, export creation and direct investment often go

---

[7]For an excellent discussion of Japanese strategy in the U.S. TV market and elsewhere, see Hamel and Prahalad, "Do You Really Have a Global Strategy?"

hand in hand. In the case of ICI, the British chemical company, its exports to Europe were enhanced by its strong market position there in other product lines, a position due mainly to ICI's local manufacturing facilities.

We saw earlier that some foreign investments are designed to improve the company's competitive posture elsewhere. For example, Air Liquide, the world's largest industrial-gas maker, opened a facility in Japan because Japanese factories make high demands of their gas suppliers and keeping pace with them ensures that the French company will stay competitive elsewhere. In the words of the Japanese unit's president, "We want to develop ourselves to be strong wherever our competitors are."[8] Similarly, a spokesperson says that Air Liquide has expanded its U.S. presence because the United States is "the perfect marketing observatory."[9] U.S. electronics companies and papermakers have found new uses for the company's gases, and Air Liquide has brought back the ideas to European customers.

Applying this concept of evaluating an investment on the basis of its global impact will force companies to answer tough questions: How much is it worth to protect our reputation for prompt and reliable delivery? What effect will establishing an operation here have on our present and potential competitors or on our ability to supply competitive products, and what will be the profit impact of this action? One possible approach is to determine the incremental costs associated with, say, a defensive action such as building multiple plants (as compared with several larger ones) and then use that number as a benchmark against which to judge how large the present value of the associated benefits (e.g., greater bargaining leverage vis-à-vis host governments) must be to justify the investment.

5. The firm must estimate the longevity of its particular form of competitive advantage. If this advantage is easily replicated, both local and foreign competitors will not take long to apply the same concept, process, or organizational structure to their operations. The resulting competition will erode profits to a point where the MNC can no longer justify its existence in the market. For this reason, the firm's competitive advantage should be constantly monitored and maintained to ensure the existence of an effective barrier to entry into the market. Should these entry barriers break down, the firm must be able to react quickly and either reconstruct them or build new ones. But no barrier to entry can be maintained indefinitely; to remain multinational, firms must continually invest in developing new competitive advantages that are transferable overseas and that are not easily replicated by the competition.

■ 17.4 ■
ILLUSTRATION: THE JAPANESE STRATEGY FOR GLOBAL EXPANSION

In 1945, Japan was a bombed-out wreck of a nation, humiliated and forced into unconditional surrender. All through the 1950s, Japanese exports were hampered by a low-quality image. Yet less than 20 years later, Japanese companies such as Sony, Hitachi, Seiko, Canon, and Toyota had established worldwide reputations equal to those of Zenith, Kodak, Ford, Philips, and General Electric.

[8]*The Wall Street Journal*, November 12, 1987, p. 32.

[9]*The Wall Street Journal*, February 23, 1988, p. 20.

Here are some lessons about international strategy to be learned from the Japanese, who arguably are the most successful global expansionists in history. To begin, it should be pointed out that the Japanese have invested a great deal of money and effort in quality, ever since quality gurus W. Edwards Deming and J.M. Juran crossed the Pacific in the 1950s to teach them how to manage for quality—an approach often called *Total Quality Control* (TQC). Few U.S. companies paid much heed to Deming or Juran and TQC, but the Japanese avidly embraced their ideas. In fact, the Deming Prize is now Japan's most prestigious award for industrial quality control.

Beyond quality, the Japanese have followed a simple strategy—repeated time and again—for penetrating world markets. Whether in cars, TVs, motorcycles, or photocopiers, the Japanese have started at the low end of the market. In each case, this market segment had been largely ignored by U.S. firms focusing on higher margin products. At the same time, the Japanese firms invested money in process technologies and simpler product design to cut costs and expand market share. Japan's lower-cost products sold in high volume, giving the manufacturers production economies of scale that other contenders could not match.

U.S. companies retreated to the high-end segment of each market, believing that the Japanese could not challenge them there. The incumbents' willingness to surrender the low end of the market was not entirely irrational. In each case, the incumbents had successful, established products that would be cannibalized by a vigorous response. General Motors, for example, believed that if it came up with high-quality smaller cars, sales of these cars would come at the expense of its bigger, higher-margin cars. So, it chose to hold back in responding to competitive attacks by the Japanese.

But the Japanese weren't content to remain in the low-end segment of the market. Over time, they invested in new-product development, built strong brand franchises and global distribution networks, and moved up-market. They amortized the costs of these investments by rapid expansion across contiguous product segments and by acceleration of the product life cycle. Here, *contiguous* refers to products that share a common technology, brand name, or distribution system. In this way, the Japanese managed to take full advantage of the economies of scope inherent in core technologies, brand franchises, and distribution networks. Simultaneously, global expansion allowed them to build up production volume and garner available scale economies.

■ ───

ILLUSTRATION

Canon Doesn't Copy Xerox. The tribulations of Xerox illustrate the dynamic nature of Japanese competitive advantage.[10] Xerox dominates the U.S. market for large copiers. Its competitive strengths—a large direct sales force that constitutes a unique distribution channel, a national service network, a wide range of machines using custom-made components, and a large installed base of leased machines—have defeated attempts by IBM and Kodak to replicate its success by creating matching sales and service networks. Canon's strategy, by contrast, was simply to sidestep these barriers to entry by (1) creating low-end copiers that it sold through office-product dealers, thereby avoiding the need to set up a

---

[10]This example appears in Gary Hamel and C.K. Prahalad, "Strategic Intent," *Harvard Business Review,"* May–June 1989, pp. 63–76.

national sales force; (2) designing reliability and serviceability into its machines, so users or nonspecialist dealers could service them; (3) using commodity components and standardizing its machines to lower costs and prices and boost sales volume; and (4) selling rather than leasing its copiers. By 1986, Canon and other Japanese firms had over 90% of copier sales worldwide. And having ceded the low end of the market to the Japanese, Xerox soon found those same competitors flooding into its stronghold sector in the middle and upper ends of the market.

Canon's strategy points out an important distinction between *barriers to entry* and *barriers to imitation.*[11] Competitors like IBM that tried to imitate Xerox's strategy had to pay a matching entry fee. Through competitive innovation, Canon avoided these costs and, in fact, stymied Xerox's response. Xerox realized that the quicker it responded—by downsizing its copiers, improving reliability, and developing new distribution channels—the quicker it would erode the value of its leased machines and cannibalize its existing high-end product line and service revenues. Hence, what were barriers to entry for imitators became barriers to retaliation for Xerox.

■

■ 17.5 ■
SUMMARY AND CONCLUSIONS

For many firms, becoming multinational was the end result of an apparently haphazard process of overseas expansion. But, as international operations provide a more important source of profit and as competitive pressures increase, these firms are trying to develop global strategies that will enable them to maintain their competitive edge both at home and abroad.

The key to the development of a successful strategy is to understand and then capitalize on those factors that led to success in the past. In this chapter, we saw that the rise of the multinational firm can be attributed to a variety of market imperfections that prevent the completely free flow of goods and capital internationally. These imperfections include government regulations and controls, such as tariffs and capital controls, that impose barriers to free trade and private portfolio investment. More significant as a spawner of multinationals are market failures in the areas of firm-specific skills and information. There are various transactions, contracting, and coordinating costs involved in trying to sell a firm's managerial skills and knowledge apart from the goods it produces. To overcome these costs, many firms have created an internal market, one in which these firm-specific advantages can be embodied in the services and products they sell.

Searching for and utilizing those sources of differential advantage that have led to prior success is clearly a difficult process. This chapter sketched some of the key factors involved in conducting an appropriate global investment analysis. Essentially, such an analysis requires the establishment of corporate objectives and policies that are congruent with each other and with the firm's resources and that lead to the continual development of new sources of differential advantage as the older ones obsolesce.

---

[11]This distinction is emphasized by Hamel and Prahalad, "Strategic Intent."

Clearly, such a comprehensive investment approach requires large amounts of time, effort, and money; yet, competitive pressures and increasing turbulence in the international environment are forcing firms in this direction. Fortunately, the supply of managers qualified to deal with such complex multinational issues is rising to meet the demand for their services.

■ QUESTIONS ■

1. Why do firms from each category below become multinational? Identify the competitive advantages that a firm in each category must have to be a successful multinational.

   a. Raw-materials seekers

   b. Market seekers

   c. Cost minimizers

2. What factors help determine whether a firm will export its output, license foreign companies to manufacture its products, or set up its own production or service facilities abroad? Identify the competitive advantages that lead companies to prefer one mode of international expansion over another.

3. Warner Brothers is trying to decide whether to license foreign companies to produce its films and records or to set up foreign sales affiliates to sell its products directly. What factors might determine whether it expands abroad via licensing or by investing in its own sales force and distribution network?

4. What are the important advantages of going multinational? Consider the nature of global competition.

5. Given the added political and economic risks that appear to exist overseas, are multinational firms more or less risky than purely domestic firms in the same industry? Consider whether a firm that decides not to operate abroad is insulated from the effects of economic events that occur outside the home country.

6. How does the nature of IBM's competitive advantages relate to its becoming a multinational firm?

7. Goodyear Tire and Rubber Company, the world's number-one tire producer before Michelin's acquisition of Uniroyal Goodrich, is competing in a global tire industry. To maintain its leadership, Goodyear has invested over $1 billion to build the most automated tire-making facilities in the world and is aggressively expanding its chain of wholly owned tire stores to maintain its position as the largest retailer of tires in the United States. It has also invested heavily in R&D to produce tires that are recognized as being at the cutting edge of world-class performance. Based on product innovation and high advertising expenditures, Goodyear dominates the high-performance segment of the tire market; it has captured nearly 90% of the market for high-performance tires sold as original equipment on American cars and is well represented on sporty imports. Geography has given Goodyear and other American tire manufacturers a giant assist in the U.S. market. Heavy and bulky, tires are expensive to ship overseas.

   a. What barriers to entry has Goodyear created or taken advantage of?

   b. Goodyear has production facilities throughout the world. What competitive advantages might global production provide Goodyear?

   c. How do tire-manufacturing facilities in Japan fit in with Goodyear's strategy to create shareholder value?

   d. How will Bridgestone's acquisition of Firestone affect Goodyear? How might Goodyear respond to this move by Bridgestone?

8. Black & Decker, the maker of small, hand-held power tools, finds that when it builds a plant in a foreign country, sales of both its locally manufactured products and its exports to that country grow. What could account for this boost in sales? Consider the likely reactions of customers, distributors, and retailers to the fact that Black & Decker is producing there.

9. OPEC nations have obviously preferred portfolio investments abroad to direct foreign investment. How does the theory of market imperfections explain this preference?

10. What was the Japanese strategy for penetrating the TV market? What similarities are there between it and the Japanese strategy for entering the U.S. car market? The photocopier market?

11. What are the benefits of having a global distribution capability?

12. How sustainable is a competitive advantage based on technology? On low-cost labor? On economies of scale? Explain.

13. The value of a particular foreign subsidiary to its parent company may bear little relationship to the subsidiary's profit-and-loss statement. In addition to the manipulations described in Chapter 15, the strategic purpose or nature of a foreign unit may dictate that some of the value of the unit will show up in the form of higher profits in other affiliates.

    a. Describe three ways, aside from profit manipulations, in which the incremental cash flows associated with a foreign unit can diverge from its actual cash flows.

    b. Describe two strategic rationales for establishing and maintaining a foreign subsidiary that will lead to higher profits elsewhere in the corporation, but will not be reflected in the subsidiary's profit-and-loss statement.

14. Politicians, business executives, and the media lament the sale of corporate America to foreign buyers. Recent foreign acquisitions include Firestone Tire, Pillsbury, and CBS Records. A persistent theme sounded by executives and the business press is that the depreciated dollar offers a significant financial advantage to foreign bidders for American companies. According to this argument, if the dollar has depreciated relative to, say, the yen, a Japanese company can buy a U.S. company at a discount. Evaluate this argument.

15. In 1989, the British company Beecham Group merged with the U.S. company SmithKline Beckman. What economic advantages might the two drug companies be expecting from their marriage? More generally, what economic forces underlie the ongoing process of consolidation and globalization in the world pharmaceutical industry? Consider the merger's impact in the areas of R&D, marketing, and production.

■ PROBLEMS ■

1. Suppose the worldwide profit breakdown for General Motors is 85% in the United States, 3% in Japan, and 12% in the rest of the world. Its principal Japanese competitors earn 40% of their profits in Japan, 25% in the United States, and 35% in the rest of the world. Suppose further that through diligent attention to productivity and substitution of enormous quantities of capital for labor (for example, Project Saturn), GM manages to get its automobile production costs down to the level of the Japanese.

    a. Who is likely to have the global competitive advantage? Consider, for example, the ability of GM to respond to a Japanese attempt to gain U.S. market share through a sharp price cut.

    b. How might GM respond to the Japanese challenge?

    c. Which competitive response would you recommend to GM's CEO?

2. More and more Japanese companies are moving in on what once was an exclusive U.S. preserve: making and selling the complex equipment that makes semiconductors. World sales are between $3 billion and $5 billion annually. The U.S. equipment makers already have seen their share of the Japanese market fall to 30% recently from a dominant 70% in the late 1970s. Because sales in Japan are expanding as rapidly as 50% a year, Japanese concerns have barely begun attacking the U.S. market. But U.S. experts consider it only a matter of time.

    a. What are the possible competitive responses of U.S. firms?

    b. Which one(s) would you recommend to the head of a U.S. firm? Why?

3. Airbus Industrie, the European consortium of aircraft manufacturers, buys jet engines from U.S. companies. According to a recent story in *The Wall Street Journal,* "as a result of the weaker dollar, the cost of a major component (jet engines) is declining for Boeing's biggest competitor." The implication is that the lower price of engines for Airbus gives it a competitive advantage over Boeing. Will Airbus now be more competitive relative to Boeing? Explain.

4. Nordson Co. of Amherst, Ohio, a maker of painting and glue equipment, exports nearly half its output. Customers value its reliability as a supplier. Because of an especially sharp run-up in the value of the dollar against the French franc, Nordson is reconsidering its decision to continue supplying the French market. What factors are relevant in reaching a decision?

5. Tandem Computer, a U.S. maker of fault-tolerant computers, is thinking of shifting virtually all the labor-intensive portion of its production to Mexico. What risks is Tandem likely to face if it goes ahead with this move?

6. Germany's $28 billion electronics giant, Siemens AG, sells medical and telecommunications equipment, power plants, automotive products, and computers. Siemens has been operating in the United States since 1952, but its U.S. revenues account for only about 10% of worldwide revenues. It intends to expand further in the U.S. market.

    a. According to the head of its U.S. operation, "The United States is a real testing ground. If you make it here, you establish your credentials for the rest of the world." What does this statement mean? How would you measure the benefits flowing from this rationale for investing in the United States?

    b. What other advantages might Siemens realize from a larger American presence?

7. Kao Corporation is a highly innovative and efficient Japanese company that has managed to take on and beat Proctor & Gamble in Japan. Two of Kao's revolutionary innovations include disposable diapers with greatly enhanced absorption capabilities and concentrated laundry detergent. However, Kao has had difficulty in establishing the kind of market-sensitive foreign subsidiaries that P&G has built.

    a. What competitive advantages might P&G derive from its global network of market-sensitive subsidiaries?

    b. What competitive disadvantages does Kao face if it is unable to replicate P&G's global network of subsidiaries?

■ APPENDIX 17A ■
CORPORATE STRATEGY AND JOINT VENTURES

The multinational strategies discussed in the chapter are reflected in the ownership policies of these firms. In particular, a company's ownership strategy appears to be related systematically to the benefits and costs of having local partners. Exhibit 17A.1 lists some of the costs and benefits of entering into joint ventures.

■ 17A.1 ■ JOINT VENTURE BENEFITS

International *joint ventures* are cropping up everywhere. By merging their sometimes divergent skills and resources, companies can quickly establish themselves in new markets and gain access to technology that might not otherwise be available. Thus, it's not unusual to see a company such as Burroughs using various partnerships to access Hitachi's technology, to package Fujitsu's high-speed facsimile machines, and to manufacture Nippon Electric's optical readers. General Motors has teamed up with Toyota and Isuzu of Japan and with Daewoo of South Korea to manufacture and sell autos and has joined with Fujitsu Fanuc of Japan to manufacture and sell robots. Similarly, AT&T has entered joint ventures with Olivetti (Italy) and N.V. Philips (Netherlands). Whatever the industry—be it chemicals, autos, pharmaceuticals, telecommunications, electronics, or even aerospace—companies find themselves in tangled webs of international consortia.

Joint ventures, however, typically face unusually complex problems. Maintaining them requires a daunting amount of work. With representatives of both companies sitting on the board of directors, forging a consensus can be difficult, especially when the firms involved have different expectations for the venture. Nevertheless, the advantages in terms of access to markets, low manufacturing costs, technology, and the economies of scale in product development and production have proved irresistible to many firms.

Market Access

A company with a product that it thinks might be useful to overseas markets may find formidable barriers to local entry. Such obstacles include unfamiliar language, culture, and business practice. In the case of Japan, there is also the difficulty in breaking into that nation's "Byzantine" distribution network.

■ EXHIBIT 17A.1   Joint-Venture Considerations

Advantages	Disadvantages
Obtain:	**Disagreements over:**
Local capital	Marketing programs
Local management	Dividend policy
Assured source of raw	Reinvestment of earnings
materials	
Trained labor	Exports to third countries
Marketing capabilities	Sources of materials and components
Established distribution	Transfer pricing
network	
Technology	Management selection and
Aid in obtaining:	remuneration, expansion
Government approvals	**Share profits based on monopoly rents from:**
Local currency loans	Technology, marketing, and managerial
Tax incentives	capabilities
Assurances of imports	**Give up technology**
Reduce nationalistic sentiments	

In 1983, Armco (U.S.) and Mitsubishi (Japan) formed a joint venture to sell (and eventually manufacture) Armco's lightweight plastic composites in Japan. For Armco the venture was a way into an otherwise impenetrable Japanese market. For Mitsubishi the venture was a way to get Armco's materials technology. Similarly, Fuji Photo Film Co. (Japan) and Hunt Chemical Co. (U.S.) teamed up to make and sell—in Japan—photoresists, which are sensitive coatings used in the semiconductor and microelectronics industries.

Japanese firms have also found joint ventures to be of value in penetrating foreign markets. For example, Japanese drug firms have found that their lack of a significant local marketing presence is their greatest hindrance to expanding in the United States. Marketing drugs in the United States requires considerable political skill in maneuvering through the U.S. regulatory process, as well as great rapport with U.S. researchers and doctors. The latter requirement means that pharmaceutical firms must develop extensive sales forces to maintain close contact with their customers. There are economies of scale here; the cost of developing such a sales force is the same whether a firm sells one product or one hundred. Thus, only firms with extensive product lines can afford a large sales force, raising a major entry barrier to Japanese drug firms trying to go it alone in the United States.

One way the Japanese drug firms have found to get around this entry barrier is to form joint ventures with U.S. drug firms, with the Japanese supplying the patents and the U.S. firms supplying the distribution network. This same strategy was followed by Novo Industri, a Danish biotechnology firm, when it linked up with Squibb Corp. of New York to sell its insulin in the United States.

In many cases, joint ventures are not just advisable for getting into foreign markets—they are mandatory. Countries such as India and Mexico require joint ventures in order to promote technology transfer from foreign to domestic firms. Union Carbide's ill-fated venture in Bhopal, India, was a result of such a requirement. Similarly, Hewlett-Packard, Apple Computer, and other U.S. computer companies have formed Mexican joint ventures because they were not allowed to ship products into Mexico without such partnerships.

In recent years, many Japanese firms have set up joint ventures in the United States and Western Europe as an insurance policy against possible U.S. and European trade barriers and as a way to ease political tensions. For example, Honda Motor Co. teamed up with BL in Great Britain to design and produce cars for local sale. Similarly, Toyota formed its joint venture with GM to produce cars in California as a way to forestall tougher quotas on Japanese cars.

Technology

Improved access to technology is a powerful incentive for joint ventures. Traditionally, U.S. firms have traded technology for access to Japanese and other foreign markets. Examples cited earlier include Armco and Philip Hunt. In recent years, the trend has reversed somewhat. Kawasaki, initially weak in the technology of automation equipment, has invested to catch up with its partner, Unimation of Cincinnati, Ohio. And Elxsi, a California manufacturer of general-purpose computers, is taking advantage of foreign technology via a joint venture. Elxsi joined with Tata, a large Indian conglomerate, and the Singapore government in a start-up manufacturing and marketing firm in Singapore. Tata contributed its expertise in software engineering to the partnership.

Joint ventures are a means to make use of each other's technical strengths. Joint ventures between U.S. and Japanese firms are especially useful in linking U.S. product innovation with low-cost Japanese design and manufacturing technology. For instance, Xerox used its long-standing joint venture with Fuji Photo Film Co.—Fuji Xerox—to develop a low-cost copier equal to the competition from Ricoh and Canon.

GM set up United Motor Mfg. (Fremont, California) to build subcompacts, a 50–50 joint production venture with Toyota Motor Corp. For GM, one of the attractions of this joint venture was Japanese expertise in low-cost manufacturing. GM also hopes to learn Japanese inventory and quality control methods. Based on the lessons it has already learned, especially the importance of worker participation to quality and productivity, GM has revamped its multibillion-dollar factory automation program.

In the biotechnology industry, the Japanese have entered into numerous joint ventures with U.S. R&D companies—for example, Biogen, Damon, and Genentech. The American firms supply the basic science while the Japanese firms—particularly in the liquor, food, and chemical businesses—bring to the joint ventures their skills in brewing, fermentation, or chemical processing. These techniques are needed to make genetically engineered substances in volume.

Economies of Scale

Companies are teaming up on product development because costs have become enormous—over a billion dollars for the design of a central-office switching system or a new mainframe computer. An example is the joint venture between AT&T and N.V. Philips, the Dutch electronics giant, to develop, manufacture, and market sophisticated telecommunications equipment outside the United States. Or, companies are turning to marketing arrangements to ensure sufficient sales worldwide to justify these investments. More recently, they have been teaming up in production to gain scale advantages. In part, that's why Alfa-Romeo and Nissan Motors are jointly producing car engines in southern Italy. Similarly, Renault and International Harvester (now Navistar) agreed on joint production of parts for farm tractors as a way to cut costs and boost sales.

■ 17A.2 ■ CORPORATE STRATEGY AND THE OPTIMUM OWNERSHIP PATTERN

Despite the potential benefits of joint ventures, the strategies of some firms mitigate against such partnerships. Those firms that require tight control to coordinate their pricing, marketing, quality control, and production policies worldwide typically shun joint ventures. The resources that a local partner can provide (capital, for example, or marketing skills) are in abundant supply in this type of multinational and, hence, the dilution of control makes little sense. We now examine the implications for the optimum ownership pattern of four broad strategies that MNCs follow.[1]

Product Differentiation

Where marketing is used to create barriers to entry, then control over the various elements of marketing strategy is considered vital. For firms such as Pepsi, Heinz, or Coca Cola, bringing in local partners would likely lead to conflicts over the large advertising expenditures, channels of distribution, and pricing policies deemed optimum by headquarters. Many of these firms, however, have found that they are able to participate in joint ventures at the manufacturing stage, provided that the parent company can control quality standards, and have separate wholly owned sales affiliates market the output.

Production Rationalization

The strategy of production *rationalization* entails the concentration of production in large plants—in order to take advantage of economies of scale—and the specialization of plants in different countries in manufacturing different parts and engaging in different stages of production. This strategy requires central planning and coordination; production decisions cannot be left to individual affiliates. Having a joint-venture partner is bound to cause conflicts over transfer pricing, the allocation of

---

[1]See Raymond Vernon and Louis T. Wells, Jr., *Manager in the International Economy,* 3d ed. (Englewood Cliffs, N.J.: Prentice-Hall, 1976), Chapter 2.

products and markets to each plant, and the maintenance of quality control. The Canadian farm machinery manufacturer Massey-Ferguson, for example, found that its joint ventures competed with its other affiliates for export markets. Ford eventually bought out its minority shareholders in Ford of England because of their resistance to production shifts and other necessary elements of cost minimization.

Control of Raw Materials

Firms in extractive industries typically attempt to maintain control of raw materials in order to keep them out of the hands of potential entrants into the oligopoly and to assure themselves of supplies. The high fixed and low marginal costs of production encourage the formation of joint ventures among competitors. This joint ownership creates a common cost structure in the industry and a common exposure to risk, reducing the likelihood that any one competitor will cut prices during periods of slack demand. Cutting prices would just lead to a reallocation of the market rather than an increase in total sales and revenues because demand for most raw materials is relatively price inelastic. On the other hand, the desire to stabilize demand for the output of company-owned wells, mines, and refineries encourages wholly owned downstream facilities, such as gasoline stations and metal-working operations.

Research and Development

Some firms, such as IBM, invest heavily in research and new-product development within a fairly narrow product line. These companies need to maintain tight control over their marketing organizations and logistics networks in order to extract the maximum profit from their organizational capabilities; therefore, they resist joint ventures. Other firms, such as Union Carbide, follow a strategy of using high R&D expenditures to generate a diversified and innovative line of new products. Since each new product line requires a different marketing strategy and, therefore, a large investment in acquiring this know-how, these firms are more willing to trade their technology for royalty payments and equity in a joint venture with local partners. Their shortage of the management personnel and marketing skills necessary to carry their product lines to new countries makes them value the marketing capabilities and other resource contributions of their local partners more than control.

■ 17A.3 ■ JOINT VENTURE ANALYSIS

In deciding whether to go through with a joint venture, a firm must systematically analyze the likelihood of the joint venture's success. Not all partnerships work out as planned. Some of the casualties include ventures by Ampex and Toshiba, Sterling Drug and Niigata Engineering, Pentax and Honeywell, Canon and Bell & Howell, Hitachi and Singer, and Avis and Mitsubishi. However, there are also winners: Dow Chemical and Asahi, CBS and Sony, and Xerox and Fuji.

Even if a joint venture works on paper, careful advance planning is necessary for it to work in practice. Both companies must subscribe to a "prenuptial agreement" that spells out the ground rules of the partnership and their future plans and expectations. In effect, the proposed venture should be viewed as a marriage between two partners, with each partner having needs to be fulfilled by the venture and contributions to make to the venture. Before venturing into such an arrangement, it helps to see if there is a proper match. An initial step can involve listing the business objectives and contributions of each partner, as shown in Exhibit 17A.2.

The objectives can include gaining a distribution network, managerial expertise, or government contracts; contributions might include capital and technology. However, the match-up may not work for various reasons. For example, many Japanese-U.S. joint ventures in Japan have failed because of conflicting objectives. The U.S. firms entered into these joint ventures in hopes of using their partners'

■ **EXHIBIT 17A.2**   Joint-Venture Analysis

Us	New Venture	Them
We want (business objectives): — — —	⟶ ⟵	They have to offer (resources): — — —
We offer (resources): — — —	⟶ ⟵	They want (business objectives): — — —

SOURCE: Adapted from David B. Zenoff, presentation at the University of Hawaii Advanced Management Program, Honolulu, August 1978.

distribution networks to increase their market shares in Japan. Their Japanese partners, on the other hand, expected to gain access to U.S. technology in order to export to third-country markets, a policy at odds with U.S. corporate objectives.

Perhaps the most important lesson we can learn from the history of joint ventures is that alliances and cooperative research activity are no panacea for corporate failure to develop internally the critical skills and assets they need to compete—the *core competencies* that spawn new generations of products and enable companies to adapt quickly to changing opportunities.[2] For example, 3M has applied its skills in adhesives and coatings across a broad range of products and markets—bandages and dental restoratives in health care, Post-it notes and Scotch tape in office supplies, reflective highway signs, diskettes and optical disks for personal computers, and videocassettes and audiocassettes in consumer electronics. What seems to be a highly diversified portfolio of businesses turns out to rest on a few shared competencies.

Unlike physical assets, which diminish with use, core skills are enhanced as they are applied; they wither with disuse. Thus, to sustain leadership in core competencies, firms should manufacture inhouse the core products—like laser "engines" in printers or engines in cars—that embody those core competencies and provide high value added to the end products. A key advantage of in-house manufacturing is that by working with the production process on a daily basis, the firm has a better sense of the wider potential of the technology, of possible applications that it would not otherwise consider. The history of the videocassette recorder shows how production know-how can yield important technical advances.

Unfortunately, the growth options associated with investments in core products and competencies tend to be undervalued using the standard discounted cash flow analysis (Chapter 18 discusses growth

[2]The concept and implications of core competence appear in Gary Hamel and C.K. Prahalad, "The Core Competence of the Corporation," *Harvard Business Review,* May–June 1990, pp. 79–91.

options further). To compensate for this bias, firms must use an expanded net present rule that considers the costs of *not* making such investments. Otherwise, as many American firms have discovered, they will wake up one day to find that their "partners"—who have invested in core skills and products— have metamorphosed into rivals, who now control the product and process technologies necessary to compete. To avoid this fate, companies entering collaborative arrangements must rethink their strategic goals.

Many companies enter alliances to share investment risk, or to reduce the costs and risks of entering new businesses or markets on their own. Although laudable, these goals are too limiting. Rather, the primary objective should be to emerge from the alliance more competitive than upon entry.[3] This means learning new skills and capabilities from the partner. But too many strategic alliances— especially those between Western companies and their Asian rivals—are little more than sophisticated outsourcing arrangements.

Unfortunately, as noted above, those who rent competencies from other firms instead of developing their own tend to lose control over the key value-creating activities. The immediate gain in cost savings from outsourcing can be fatal in the long term.

Collaboration can also quash innovative design and produce indistinguishable "me-too" products. For example, to deal with Japanese car makers after 1992, European producers are engaged in a variety of collaborative efforts. The danger is that this will blunt competition and remove much of the pressure for innovation.

Forced Marriages

Joint ventures that are forced on firms can be successful in foreign markets separated by trade barriers from other markets. Since the affiliate operates on a stand-alone basis, coordination with the parent company's activities elsewhere is of much less importance.

In several highly publicized cases, large U.S. multinationals have chosen to pull out of foreign countries rather than comply with government regulations that require joint ventures. Both IBM and Citibank, for example, have withdrawn from Nigeria, and IBM has also pulled out of India. Looked at on an individual country basis, these companies might have been better off complying with the joint-venture requirements. Apparently, however, IBM and Citibank felt that to give in just once would lead a number of other nations to demand similar equity-sharing arrangements.

An alternative to foreign direct investment (other than licensing) is to sell managerial expertise in the form of a management contract. This unbundling of services, with its attendant reduction in political and economic risks, has become more attractive to some firms. The best example would be the current sale of various types of management skills to OPEC nations.

Nevertheless, despite the risk-reducing advantages provided by management contracts and the pressure placed on them by many host governments, particularly in the third world, to divest themselves of their foreign operations, most MNCs appear to be quite reluctant to unbundle and sell their services directly. Clearly, firms believe they can take better advantage of market imperfections and earn higher returns through direct investment.

The low price offered by host governments may reflect the fact that these services are worth less in an unbundled form. As we have already seen, much of the value of management expertise lies in its interactions with the various organizational skills available to the firm. Unbundling these services destroys that synergy, thereby reducing their value.

---

[3]For a discussion of how to properly structure collaborative arrangements, see Gary Hamel, Yves L. Doz, and C.K. Prahalad, "Collaborate with Your Competitors—and Win," *Harvard Business Review,* January–February 1989, pp. 133–139.

QUESTIONS

1. Multinational corporations use many different entry strategies abroad, including 100% ownership of all subsidiaries, majority-owned joint ventures, minority participation in joint ventures, and the licensing of foreign companies to produce the firm's products. Discuss the characteristics of a firm and its products, that might lead it to prefer 100% ownership of all of its overseas subsidiaries.

2. Motorola, the number-two U.S. chipmaker, signed an agreement in 1986 with Toshiba of Japan to jointly manufacture memories and microprocessors in a new Japanese plant. The pact gives Toshiba access to Motorola's popular 32-bit microprocessor technology; Motorola gets a share in a highly efficient manufacturing facility, a source of chips, and access to the Japanese market.

   a. How can Motorola maximize the advantages of this joint venture?

   b. What are some of the risks Motorola faces?

   c. What can it do to control these risks?

■ APPENDIX 17B ■
STRATEGIC IMPLICATIONS OF EUROPE 1992

By December 1992, the last of some 300 directives designed to create a single European market for goods and services is set to be implemented.[1] The objective of Europe 1992 is to tear down barriers to trade and commerce within Europe so that European nations can achieve economic prosperity.

The economic unification of Europe contains a mix of good news and bad news for corporations—including those outside as well as inside the European Community. On the one hand, companies can cash in on the purchasing power of 320 million potential customers—a market larger than the United States and Canada combined. On the other hand, they will have to comply with new laws and regulations, some of which have protectionist overtones.

■ 17B.1 ■ LESSONS FROM U.S. DEREGULATION

Despite the enormous uncertainty surrounding Europe 1992, corporate management can look to the recent American experience with deregulation for guidance in entering uncharted territory. That experience shows clearly the competitive changes that take place when new entrants are allowed into once restricted markets. As such, it provides valuable lessons for managers seeking to position their companies for the opening of the European market.[2]

Since 1975, the United States has deregulated various aspects of the securities industry, banking, airlines, trucking, railroads, and telecommunications. In all the industries, we can see the same set of competitive dynamics at work:

   1. *The industry becomes more competitive and profitability deteriorates rapidly as strong firms expand into formerly protected markets, while many new, low-cost suppliers enter the market.* Falling profits spur staff reductions and other cost-cutting measures. In addition, the weak get weaker and many of them fail, but the strong do not get more profitable—not right away, at least. For example,

---

[1]This appendix is based on Alan C. Shapiro, "Economic Import of Europe 1992," *Journal of Applied Corporate Finance,* Winter 1991, pp. 25–36.

[2]These lessons are elaborated in Joel A. Bleeke, "Strategic Choices for Newly Opened Markets," *Harvard Business Review,* September–October 1990, pp. 158–165.

trade barriers have allowed European banks to remain highly inefficient. Deregulation will shrink bank margins dramatically.

2. *The most profitable market segments come under severe price pressure as competitors flock to them.* Conversely, the least profitable segments before deregulation, which were typically cross-subsidized to hold down prices, become more attractive as the cross-subsidies are ended and many firms exit these markets. For example, the biggest changes in the banking industry will come in retail banking, which provides as much as two-thirds of European bank profits and has served to cross-subsidize expansion into deregulated wholesale and investment banking.

3. *Merger and acquisition activity accelerates.* Initially, weaker firms combine to gain the size needed to compete with the giants of the industry. But the anticipated scale economies often don't materialize—and a wave of divestitures of at least some of the unwanted pieces obtained in these mergers typically follows. Later on, some of the strongest firms in the industry merge with each other. They also make selected acquisitions—and divestitures—to fill out gaps in their product portfolio or customer segments and to focus better on their core business.

4. *Only a handful of firms survive as broad-based competitors.* Those that succeed are companies that achieve, among other things, a precise understanding of their cost structures and pricing. With such understanding, they were able to eliminate hidden cross-subsidies and create new price/service trade-offs for their customers. The rest are forced to narrow their product range to those in which they have a competitive advantage and spin off noncore activities to survive. The result is much greater segmentation within the industry.

In short, the early years of deregulation are characterized by shakeouts, restructuring, and the consolidation of position among survivors. There is an important difference, however, between Europe 1992 and U.S. deregulation: Many of the new entrants are already mighty international competitors like American Airlines and Toyota. Thus, the shakeout and consolidation phases are likely to be even bloodier than they were in the United States during the 1980s. And, because low industry profitability often forecloses the option of going to the capital markets, the biggest mistake many companies can make during this period is to spend too much money on acquisitions, entry into new markets, or major capital investments—thus leaving themselves with too little cash to weather the profit drought.

U.S. multinationals stand to benefit from their experience in highly competitive markets. As a result of such experience, they have acquired a greater readiness to organize their European activities along the most economically efficient lines and to redeploy assets aggressively across national boundaries. This willingness stems in part from the painful decisions many American managers had to make during the wave of corporate restructuring in the 1980s—along with the knowledge that these decisions were the more painful for having been so long delayed. Westinghouse, for example, is cutting back on mature products such as electrical equipment that it has decided it cannot add more value to and focusing its resources instead on such growth areas as refrigerated trucking, defense electronics, and environmental controls. In so doing, Westinghouse has reduced its European work force by about 50% since 1980.

■ 17B.2 ■ BUSINESS STRATEGY FOR EUROPE 1992

Although there remains considerable uncertainty about what agreements will survive the current negotiations over Europe 1992, companies inside and outside the European Community are acting on the assumption that the single market will be established and that it will mean stronger competition. In response, companies in industries as diverse as electrical engineering, packaged food, and insurance are entering into cross-border alliances, merging with competitors, and otherwise restructuring their operations. Most such strategies, however, represent nothing more substantial than managerial "leaps of faith"—investments of corporate time and capital whose principal aim at this point seems to be to provide companies with the flexibility to respond to whatever surprises 1992 may yield.

Many of the moves are obvious ones. Those companies like IBM and Ford that have acted for three decades as if Europe were one market will realize large savings from market integration. They will no longer have to make alterations in their products to meet local standards, and transportation will be quicker and cheaper.

■ ───

ILLUSTRATION

The Case of N.V. Philips. European firms will also benefit from new opportuntities for production efficiencies. Consider N.V. Philips, the Dutch electronics firm that has long operated without much regard to national borders. Giant assembly plants take in components from Philips factories across Europe and dispatch finished products to distribution centers by way of a vast trucking network. A TV factory in Belgium, for example, gets tubes from Germany, transistors from France, and plastics from Italy. In theory Philips' system of centralized manufacturing should be a model of efficiency; in practice frontiers have made it cumbersome and expensive. Trucks spend 30% of their travel time idling in lines at customs posts. To avoid shutting down assembly lines when shipments are late, factories keep extra stock on hand. By eliminating delays at customs posts, Philips will be able to cut inventories, close warehouses, and reduce clerical staff and save several hundred million dollars a year. Also, as local standards vanish, Philips intends to shrink its vast range of washing machines, fluorescent light bulbs, and above all TV sets (Europe currently has two standards for TV reception).

─── ■

Besides opportunities for greater efficiencies in production and distribution, established multinationals may also be able to cut costs by centralizing and coordinating administrative and marketing functions. In dealing with a fragmented Europe, many multinationals have evolved into collections of unrelated national subsidiaries, each serving its own local market. But to serve pan-European customers, these companies must develop organizations that can coordinate production, marketing, and logistics across subsidiary boundaries so as to present a common face to their customers. For example, IBM organizes its production by continent, but its sales by country. This structure may not suffice after 1992 because of customers' increased scope for arbitrage. Perhaps, as in the U.S., customers will buy where prices and sales taxes are lowest and then ship their computers in. In general, companies redesigning their organizational structures to cope with post–1992 Europe must reckon with their customers' responses to the expanded choices they will have in an integrated European market.

Those U.S. firms that are currently operating in a few protected local markets, such as medical supplies, may find that when regulatory barriers fall, they will face new competitors from other European countries. Companies like Philips, Siemens, and Thomson are committed to transforming themselves from "national champions" to global competitors. In responding to such competition, the choices available to U.S. firms include expansion in Europe through acquisition of the moderate-sized European companies that appear to be for sale; the formation of strategic alliances, such as joint ventures or cooperation agreements, for joint R&D or cross marketing of products; or sale to a competitor and withdrawal from Europe. The last may be the best option for those companies that don't realize much in the way of economies of scale. But for those businesses that exhibit scale economies, the greater the growth potential and the weaker the current ties between supplier and customer, the greater the opportunity to expand outward into a multinational position.

Those U.S. companies that are currently exporting to Europe may wish to consider producing there. The argument for manufacturing at home is that U.S. labor costs are generally lower and the cheap dollar makes American-made goods competitive. Yet, simply staying home may be risky if a large share of the company's sales are in Europe, and 1992 brings greater protectionism and competition from stronger European firms. Establishing production facilities abroad—through a start-up, acquisition, or joint venture—can improve relations with European customers, as well with U.S. customers now producing aboard, by demonstrating a deeper commitment to Europe. And producing abroad also provides a hedge against exchange risk.

Finally, U.S. companies that have focused exclusively on the domestic market should reconsider their options. The thrust of Europe 1992 is to allow European companies to build a market base that gives them the scale to compete globally. Ready or not, U.S. companies in many industries are going to face aggressive competition in the U.S. market from European multinationals like Siemens and Philips. At the same time, U.S. companies that have stayed out of Europe because the EC market was too fragmented or the local producers too well protected may find that 1992 will create new opportunities for them. For example, deregulation has given American companies in industries like telecommunications and trucking years of valuable experience with innovative product and service concepts—experience that their European counterparts lack. An integrated EC market may also provide opportunities for U.S. retailers like Circuit City, Toys "R" Us, or Wal-Mart Stores to create new international distribution networks.

■ 17B.3 ■ THE MYTH OF SCALE ECONOMIES

Underlying much of the planning for a single market is the conventional wisdom—shared by many corporate executives and European governments—that, come 1992, bigger will be better. In post–1992 Europe, national markets will become more like American states, and the companies that prosper will be those that learn to compete according to the time-honored American formula for success: Exploit economies of scale and build up regional brands. This view has touched off a wave of cross-border mergers, as companies seek to gain the size necessary to compete in a borderless Europe.

But if national differences across Europe run as deep as some observers maintain, 1992 will pose a much more complex challenge to management than learning to think as big as Americans. For example, in both the United States and Japan the white-goods business (large appliances like refrigerators and washing machines) is dominated by single brands that have economies of scale in both marketing and production. Europe, by contrast, has many national brands. Although the industry appears ripe for restructuring and consolidation, national brands continue to predominate. So far, widely varying national preferences, combined with the complexity of creating so many different machines, have overwhelmed economies of scale.

These difficulties are exemplified by the experiences of Philips and Sweden's Electrolux, the first firms to try to create European-wide white-goods firms. Although they have operations in most countries, neither firm dominates any national market, except for their small home markets and Italy (where Electrolux bought the leading local supplier, Zanussi). In recent years, the two companies have been among the least profitable European producers of washing machines. Much more profitable have been those local firms that have tenaciously defended their dominance of a single national market. Both Philips and Electrolux have found it difficult to realize scale economies through international expansion because of differences in languages, retail systems, and consumer tastes.

Moreover, the newest technologies—flexible manufacturing, faster computers, and better telecommunications—have reduced the optimal size of many businesses, and will probably continue to do so. Computer-controlled flexible manufacturing, producing batches tailored to changing customer needs, can now be just as profitable as mass production. Indeed, smaller runs may be necessary to keep up with fast-changing and increasingly specialized markets. For example, Electrolux has developed a flexible manufacturing system that can retool quickly enough to produce its entire range of 1,000 different types of refrigerators within a week.

The view that economies of scale are less important today will not surprise those who have seen GM, with its legendary economies of scale, lose the lead in profitability not only to much smaller Japanese companies but to smaller U.S. companies like Ford and Chrysler as well. Indeed, the restructuring of corporate America during the 1980s indicates that many companies are too large—that there are, in fact, significant diseconomies of scale after a certain point. Such diseconomies stem from several sources: the growth of large bureaucracies that slow decision making, the increased likelihood of *cross-subsidization* in larger companies, and the greater administrative costs (including weakened management incentives) associated with managing unrelated businesses.

For example, Philips has cross-subsidized its ventures in computers and semiconductors with profits from its protected consumer electronics and lighting divisions. Such unprofitable businesses are prime candidates for restructuring or divestiture. Philips also spawned a bloated bureaucracy, weak marketing, and operations that are highly inefficient compared to its Japanese and American rivals. Its sales per employee in 1989 were $100,000, roughly half Matsushita's and Sony's and 25% below General Electric's.

The appropriate response is to weed out unprofitable products, production facilities, and activities. This means breaking down the business into the activities involved—purchasing, manufacturing, sales, distribution, R&D—and then figuring out how much each costs and how much value each adds. It also means examining every aspect of the business—product lines, customers, organizational structure—to identify those that create value and those that destroy it.

Despite growing skepticism about the benefits of size, and the generally dismal experience of large mergers in the United States, Western European mergers totaled a record $55 billion in 1989. Many of these mergers will likely fail because of the inability to bridge corporate culture differences and to make tough decisions on cost-cutting and strategy.

In short, companies should be highly selective in their pursuit of scale economies. Some computer makers, for example, have found that they can reap large economies only in R&D and component purchasing; so linking with other firms' R&D or purchasing divisions might be the best strategy. Automakers, by contrast, benefit from size in the centralized development of new engines, which explains why companies like Renault, Peugeot, and Volvo now develop their engines jointly.

Similarly, since many of the differences between the machines sold across Europe can be achieved by combining the same parts in different ways, companies have found they can achieve economies of scale in component production, although not in producing and selling the end product. Electrolux, for example, wants to create a world-scale business in white-goods components, such as pumps and engines, as well as in the appliances themselves. It is also centralizing component purchasing and pooling research.

In sum, the surest route to pan-European efficiency is for corporate managements to subject every part of their business to a test of "critical mass." Since each activity—R&D, purchasing, manufacturing, assembly, marketing, and distribution—has its own optimal size, a merger that requires bigness across the board can be very inefficient. Megamerged firms—joined together, lock, stock and barrel—may find that they are too big in some areas—and not large enough in others. Rather, firms should focus on growing only those areas where scale economies predominate. Finally, corporate executives who associate size with competitive advantage may well have it backwards: Companies become large because they are competitive, and not vice versa.

Where economies of scale do exist, it may be preferable to realize them from worldwide sales rather than from expansion in a protected home market. Foreign competition tends to toughen companies and increase their competitiveness, improving their chances of becoming world-class competitors.

■ BIBLIOGRAPHY ■

Caves, Richard E. "International Corporations: The Industrial Economics of Foreign Investment." *Economica,* February 1971, pp. 1–27.

Hamel, Gary, and C.K. Prahalad. "Do You Really Have a Global Strategy?" *Harvard Business Review,* July–August 1985, pp. 139–148.

———. "Strategic Intent." *Harvard Business Review,"* May–June 1989, pp. 63–76.

Rugman, Alan M. "Motives for Foreign Investment: The Market Imperfections and Risk Diversification Hypothesis." *Journal of World Trade Law,* September–October 1975, pp. 567–573.

Shapiro, Alan C. "Capital Budgeting and Corporate Strategy." *Midland Corporate Finance Journal,* Spring 1985, pp. 22–36.

———. "Economic Import of Europe 1992." *Journal of Applied Corporate Finance,* Winter 1991, pp. 25–36.

◾ 18 ◾

Capital Budgeting for the Multinational Corporation

Nobody can really guarantee the future. The best we can do is size up the chances, calculate the risks involved, estimate our ability to deal with them, and then make our plans with confidence.

—Henry Ford II—

◼ Multinational corporations evaluating foreign investments find their analyses complicated by a variety of problems that are rarely, if ever, encountered by domestic firms. This chapter examines several such problems, including differences between project and parent company cash flows, foreign tax regulations, expropriation, blocked funds, exchange rate changes and inflation, project-specific financing, and differences between the basic business risks of foreign and domestic projects. The purpose of this chapter is to develop a framework that allows measuring, and reducing to a common denominator, the consequences of these complex factors on the desirability of the foreign investment opportunities under review. In this way, projects can be compared and evaluated on a uniform basis. The major principle behind methods proposed to cope with these complications is to maximize the use of available information while reducing arbitrary cash flow and cost of capital adjustments.

◼ 18.1 ◼
BASICS OF CAPITAL BUDGETING

Once a firm has compiled a list of prospective investments, it must then select from among them that combination of projects that maximizes the company's value to its shareholders. This selection requires a set of rules and decision criteria that enables managers to determine, given an investment opportunity, whether to accept or reject it. It is generally agreed that the criterion of net present value is the most appropriate one to use since its consistent application will lead the company to select the same investments the shareholders would make themselves, if they had the opportunity.

Net Present Value

The *net present value* (NPV) is defined as the present value of future cash flows discounted at an appropriate rate minus the initial net cash outlay for the project. Projects with a positive NPV should be accepted; negative NPV projects should be rejected. If two projects are mutually exclusive, the one with the higher NPV should be accepted. The discount rate, known as the *cost of capital,* is the expected rate of return on projects of similar risk. For now, we take its value as given. Section 18.6 discusses its derivation in detail.

In mathematical terms, the formula for net present value is

$$NPV = -I_0 + \sum_{t=1}^{n} \frac{X_t}{(1+k)^t}$$ (18.1)

where I_0 = the initial cash investment
    X_t = the net cash flow in period t
    k = the project's cost of capital
    n = the investment horizon

To illustrate the NPV method, consider a plant expansion project with the following stream of cash flows and their present values:

Year	Cash Flow	×	Present Value Factor (10%)	=	Present Value	Cumulative Present Value
0	-$4,000,000		1.0000		-$4,000,000	-$4,000,000
1	1,200,000		0.9091		1,091,000	- 2,909,000
2	2,700,000		0.8264		2,231,000	- 678,000
3	2,700,000		0.7513		2,029,000	1,351,000

Assuming a 10% cost of capital, the project is acceptable.

The most desirable property of the NPV criterion is that it evaluates investments in the same way the company's shareholders do; the NPV method properly focuses on cash rather than on accounting profits and emphasizes the opportunity cost of the money invested. Thus, it is consistent with shareholder wealth maximization.

Another desirable property of the NPV criterion is that it obeys the *value additivity principle*. That is, the NPV of a set of independent projects is just the sum of the NPVs of the individual projects. This property means that managers can consider each project on its own. It also means that when a firm undertakes several investments, its value increases by an amount equal to the sum of the NPVs of the accepted projects. Thus, if the firm invests in the previously described plant expansion, its value should increase by $1,351,000, the NPV of the project.

Incremental Cash Flows

The most important and also the most difficult part of an investment analysis is to calculate the cash flows associated with the project: the cost of funding the project; the cash inflows during the life of the project; and the terminal, or ending value, of the project. Shareholders are interested in how many additional dollars they will receive in the future for the dollars they lay out today. Hence, what matters is not the project's total cash flow per period, but the *incremental cash flows* generated by the project.

The distinction between total and incremental cash flows is a crucial one. Incremental cash flow can differ from total cash flow for a variety of reasons. We now examine some of these reasons.

Cannibalization. When Honda introduced its Acura line of cars, some customers switched their purchases from the Honda Accord to the new models. This example illustrates the phenomenon known as *cannibalization,* a new product taking sales away from the firm's existing products. Cannibalization also occurs when a firm builds a plant overseas and winds up substituting foreign production for parent company exports. To the extent that sales of a new product or plant just replace other corporate sales, the new project's estimated profits must be reduced by the earnings on the lost sales.

The previous examples notwithstanding, it is often difficult to assess the true magnitude of cannibalization because of the need to determine what would have happened to sales in the absence of the new product or plant. Consider the case of Motorola building a plant in Japan to supply chips to the Japanese market previously supplied via exports. In the past, Motorola got Japanese business whether it manufactured in Japan or not. But now Japan is a chip-making dynamo whose buyers no longer have to depend on U.S. suppliers. If Motorola had not invested in Japan, it might have lost export sales anyway. But instead of losing these sales to local production, it would have lost them to one of its rivals. The incremental effect of cannibalization—which is the relevant measure for capital-budgeting purposes—equals the lost profit on lost sales that would not otherwise have been lost had the new project not been undertaken. Those sales that would have been lost anyway should not be counted a casualty of cannibalization.

Sales Creation. Black & Decker, the U.S. power tool company, significantly expanded its exports to Europe after investing in European production facilities that gave it a strong local market position in several product lines. Similarly, GM's auto plants in England use parts made by its U.S. plants, parts that would not otherwise be sold if GM's English plants disappeared.

In both cases, an investment either created or was expected to create additional sales for existing products. Thus, *sales creation* is the opposite of cannibalization. In calculating the project's cash flows, the additional sales and associated incremental cash flows should be attributed to the project.

Opportunity Cost. Suppose IBM decides to build a new office building in Sao Paulo on some land it bought ten years ago. IBM must include the cost of the land in calculating the value of undertaking the project. Also, this cost must be based on the current market value of the land, not the price it paid ten years ago.

This example demonstrates a more general rule. Project costs must include the true economic cost of any resource required for the project, regardless of whether the firm already owns the resource or has to go out and acquire it. This true cost is the *opportunity cost,* the cash the asset could generate for the firm should it be sold or put to some other productive use. It would be foolish for a firm that acquired oil at $3/barrel and converted it into petrochemicals to sell those petrochemicals based on $3/barrel oil if the price of oil has risen to $30/barrel. So, too, it would be foolish to value an asset used in a project at other than its opportunity cost, regardless of how much cash changes hands.

Transfer Pricing.   By raising the price at which a proposed Ford plant in Dearborn will sell engines to its English subsidiary, Ford can increase the apparent profitability of the new plant, but at the expense of its English affiliate. Similarly, if Matsushita lowers the price at which its Panasonic division buys microprocessors from its microelectronics division, the latter's new semiconductor plant will show a decline in profitability.

It is evident from these examples that the transfer prices at which goods and services are traded internally can significantly distort the profitability of a proposed investment. Where possible, the prices used to evaluate project inputs or outputs should be market prices. If no market exists for the product, then the firm must evaluate the project based on the cost savings or additional profits to the corporation of going ahead with the project. For example, when Atari decided to switch most of its production to Asia, its decision was based solely on the cost savings it expected to realize. This approach was the correct one to use because the stated revenues generated by the project were meaningless, an artifact of the transfer prices used in selling its output back to Atari in the United States.

Fees and Royalties.   Often companies will charge projects for various items such as legal counsel, power, lighting, heat, rent, research and development, headquarters staff, management costs, and the like. These charges appear in the form of fees and royalties. They are costs to the project, but are a benefit from the standpoint of the parent firm. From an economic standpoint, the project should be charged only for the additional expenditures that are attributable to the project; those overhead expenses that are unaffected by the project should not be included when estimating project cash flows.

In general, incremental cash flows associated with an investment can be found only by subtracting worldwide corporate cash flows without the investment from postinvestment corporate cash flows. In performing this incremental analysis, the key question that managers must ask is, What will happen if we *don't* make this investment? Failure to heed this question led General Motors during the 1970s to slight investment in small cars despite the Japanese challenge; small cars looked less profitable than GM's then-current mix of cars. As a result, Toyota, Nissan, and the other Japanese automakers were able to expand and eventually threaten GM's base business. Similarly, many U.S. companies that thought overseas expansion too risky today find their worldwide competitive positions eroding. They didn't adequately consider the consequences of *not* building a strong global position.

■ ──

ILLUSTRATION

Investing in Memory Chips.   Since 1984, the intense competition from Japanese firms has caused most U.S. semiconductor manufacturers to lose money in the memory chip business.

The only profitable part of the chip business for them is in making microprocessors and other specialized chips. Why do they continue investing in facilities to produce memory chips despite their losses in this business?

U.S. companies care so much about memory chips because of their importance in fine-tuning the manufacturing process. Memory chips are manufactured in huge quantities and are fairly simple to test for defects, which makes them ideal vehicles for refining new production processes. Having worked out the bugs by making memories, chip companies apply an improved process to hundreds of more complex products. Without manufacturing some sort of memory chip, most chipmakers believe, it is very difficult to keep production technology competitive. Thus, making profitable investments elsewhere in the chip business may be contingent on producing memory chips.   ∎

Clearly, although the principle of incremental analysis is a simple one to state, its rigorous application is a tortuous undertaking. However, this rule at least points executives responsible for estimating cash flows in the right direction. Moreover, when estimation shortcuts or simplifications are made, it provides those responsible with some idea of what they are doing and how far they are straying from a thorough analysis.

Alternative Capital-Budgeting Frameworks

As we have just seen, the standard capital-budgeting analysis involves first calculating the expected after-tax values of all cash flows associated with a prospective investment, and then discounting those cash flows back to the present, using an appropriate discount rate. Typically, the discount rate used is the *weighted average cost of capital* (WACC), where the weights are based on the proportion of the firm's capital structure accounted for by each source of capital.

An Adjusted Present Value Approach. The weighted cost of capital is simple in concept and easy to apply. A single rate is appropriate, however, only if the financial structures and commercial risks are similar for all investments undertaken. Projects with different risks are likely to possess differing debt capacities with each project, therefore, necessitating a separate financial structure. Moreover, the financial package for a foreign investment often includes project-specific loans at concessionary rates or higher-cost foreign funds due to home country exchange controls, leading to different component costs of capital.

The weighted cost of capital figure can be modified, of course, to reflect these deviations from the firm's typical investment. But for some companies, such as those in extractive industries, there is no norm. Project risks and financial structure vary by country, raw material, production stage, and position in the life cycle of the project. An alternative approach is to discount cash flows at a rate that reflects only the business risks of the project and abstracts from the effects of financing. This rate, called the *all-equity rate,* would apply directly if the project were financed entirely by equity.

The all-equity rate k^* can be used in capital budgeting by viewing the value of a project as being equal to the sum of the following components: (1) the present value of project cash flows after taxes but before financing costs, discounted at k^*; (2) the present value of the tax savings on debt financing; and (3) the present value of any savings (penalties) on interest costs associated with project-specific financing.[1] This latter differential would generally be due to government regulations and/or subsidies that caused interest rates on restricted funds to diverge from domestic interest payable on unsubsidized, arm's length borrowing. The *adjusted present value* (APV) with this approach is

$$
\text{APV} = \begin{array}{c} \text{Present value} \\ \text{of investment} \\ \text{outlay} \end{array} + \begin{array}{c} \text{Present value} \\ \text{of operating} \\ \text{cash flows} \end{array} + \begin{array}{c} \text{Present value} \\ \text{of interest} \\ \text{tax shield} \end{array} + \begin{array}{c} \text{Present value} \\ \text{of interest} \\ \text{subsidies} \end{array}
$$

$$
APV = -I_0 + \sum_{t=1}^{n} \frac{X_t}{(1+k^*)^t} + \sum_{t=1}^{n} \frac{T_t}{(1+i_d)^t} + \sum_{t=1}^{n} \frac{S_t}{(1+i_d)^t} \tag{18.2}
$$

where T_t = tax savings in year t due to the specific financing package

S_t = before-tax dollar value of interest subsidies (penalties) in year t due to project-specific financing

i_d = before-tax cost of dollar debt

The last two terms are discounted at the before-tax cost of dollar debt to reflect the relatively certain value of the cash flows due to tax shields and interest savings (penalties).

It should be emphasized that the all-equity cost of capital equals the required rate of return on a specific project—that is, the riskless rate of interest plus an appropriate risk premium based on the project's particular risk. Thus, k^* varies according to the risk of the specific project.

According to the capital asset pricing model (CAPM), the market prices only *systematic* risk relative to the market rather than total corporate risk. In other words, only interactions of project returns with overall market returns are relevant in determining project riskiness; interactions of project returns with total corporate returns can be ignored. Thus, each project has its own required return and can be evaluated without regard to the firm's other investments. If a project-specific approach is not used, the primary advantage of the CAPM is lost—the concept of value additivity, which allows projects to be considered independently.

■ 18.2 ■
ISSUES IN FOREIGN INVESTMENT ANALYSIS

The analysis of a foreign project raises two additional issues other than those dealing with the interaction between the investment and financing decisions. The two issues are

1. Should cash flows be measured from the viewpoint of the project or the parent?
2. Should the additional economic and political risks that are uniquely foreign be reflected in cash-flow or discount rate adjustments?

---

[1] This material is based on Donald R. Lessard, "Evaluating Foreign Projects: An Adjusted Present Value Approach," in Donald R. Lessard, ed., *International Financial Management,* 2nd ed. (Boston: Warren, Graham & Lamont), 1985.

Parent Versus Project Cash Flows

A substantial difference can exist between the cash flow of a project and the amount that is remitted to the parent firm because of tax regulations and exchange controls. In addition, project expenses such as management fees and royalties are returns to the parent company. Furthermore, the incremental revenue contributed to the parent MNC by a project can differ from total project revenues if, for example, the project involves substituting local production for parent company exports or if transfer price adjustments shift profits elsewhere in the system.

Given the differences that are likely to exist between parent and project cash flows, the question arises as to the relevant cash flows to use in project evaluation. Economic theory has the answer to this question. According to economic theory, the value of a project is determined by the net present value of future cash flows back to the investor. Thus, the parent MNC should value only those cash flows that are, or can be, repatriated net of any transfer costs (such as taxes) because only accessible funds can be used for the payment of dividends and interest, for amortization of the firm's debt, and for reinvestment.

A Three-Stage Approach.   To simplify project evaluation, a three-stage analysis is recommended. In the first stage, project cash flows are computed from the subsidiary's standpoint, exactly as if the subsidiary were a separate national corporation. The perspective then shifts to the parent company. This second stage of analysis requires specific forecasts concerning the amounts, timing, and form of transfers to headquarters, as well as information about what taxes and other expenses will be incurred in the transfer process. Finally, the firm must take into account the indirect benefits and costs that this investment confers on the rest of the system, such as an increase or decrease in export sales by another affiliate.

Estimating Incremental Project Cash Flows.   Essentially, the company must estimate a project's true profitability. *True profitability* is an amorphous concept, but basically it involves determining the marginal revenue and marginal costs associated with the project. In general, as mentioned earlier, incremental cash flows to the parent can be found only by subtracting worldwide parent company cash flows (without the investment) from postinvestment parent company cash flows. This estimating entails the following:

1. Adjust for the effects of transfer pricing and fees and royalties.
   —Use market costs/prices for goods, services, and capital transferred internally
   —Add back fees and royalties to project cash flows since they are benefits to the parent
   —Remove the fixed portions of such costs as corporate overhead
2. Adjust for global costs/benefits that are not reflected in the project's financial statements. These costs/benefits include
   —Cannibalization of sales of other units
   —Creation of incremental sales by other units
   —Additional taxes owed when repatriating profits
   —Foreign tax credits usable elsewhere
   —Diversification of production facilities
   —Market diversification
   —Provision of a key link in a global service network

The second set of adjustments involves incorporating the project's strategic purpose and its impact on other units. These strategic considerations embody the factors that were discussed in Chapter 17.

Although the principle of valuing and adjusting incremental cash flows is itself simple, it can be complicated to apply. Its application is illustrated in the case of taxes.

Tax Factors.   Because only after-tax cash flows are relevant, it is necessary to determine when and what taxes must be paid on foreign-source profits. To illustrate the calculation of the incremental tax owed on foreign-source earning, suppose an affiliate will remit after-tax earnings of $150,000 to its U.S. parent in the form of a dividend. Assume the foreign tax rate is 25%, the withholding tax on dividends is 4%, and excess foreign tax credits are unavailable. The marginal rate of additional taxation is found by adding the withholding tax that must be paid locally to the U.S. tax owed on the dividend. Withholding tax equals $6,000 (150,000 × 0.04), while U.S. tax owed equals $12,000. This latter tax is calculated as follows. With a before-tax local income of $200,000 (200,000 × 0.75 = 150,000), the U.S. tax owed would equal $200,000 × 0.34, or $68,000. The firm then receives foreign tax credits equal to $56,000—the $50,000 in local tax paid and the $6,000 dividend withholding tax—leaving a net of $12,000 owed the IRS. This calculation yields a marginal tax rate of 12% on remitted profits, as follows:

$$\frac{6,000 + 12,000}{150,000} = 0.12$$

If excess foreign tax credits are available, then the marginal tax rate on remittances is just the dividend withholding tax rate of 4%.

Political and Economic Risk Analysis

All else being equal, firms prefer to invest in countries with stable currencies, healthy economies, and minimal political risks, such as expropriation. But all else is usually not equal, so firms must assess the consequences of various political and economic risks for the viability of potential investments.

The three main methods for incorporating the additional political and economic risks, such as the risks of currency fluctuation and expropriation, into foreign investment analysis are (1) shortening the minimum payback period, (2) raising the required rate of return of the investment, and (3) adjusting cash flows to reflect the specific impact of a given risk.

Adjusting the Discount Rate or Payback Period.   The additional risks confronted abroad are usually described in general terms instead of being related to their impact on specific investments. This rather vague view of risk probably explains the prevalence among multinationals of two unsystematic approaches to account for the added political and economic risks of overseas operations. One is to use a higher discount rate for foreign operations; another, to require a shorter payback period. For instance, if exchange restrictions are anticipated, a normal required return of 15% might be raised to 20%, or a five-year payback period may be shortened to three years.

Neither of the aforementioned approaches, however, lends itself to a careful evaluation of the actual impact of a particular risk on investment returns. Thorough risk analysis requires an assessment of the magnitude and timing of risks and their implications for the projected cash flows. For example, an expropriation five years hence is likely to be much less threatening than one expected next year, even though the probability of it occurring later may be higher. Thus, using a uniformly higher discount rate just distorts the meaning of the present value of a project by penalizing future cash flows relatively more heavily than current ones, without obviating the necessity for a careful risk evaluation. Furthermore, the choice of a risk premium is an arbitrary one, whether it is 2% or 10%. Instead, adjusting cash flows makes it possible to fully incorporate all available information about the impact of a specific risk on the future returns from an investment.

Adjusting Expected Values.   The recommended approach is to adjust the cash flows of a project to reflect the specific impact of a given risk, primarily because there is normally more and better information on the specific impact of a given risk on a project's cash flows than on its required return. The cash-flow adjustments presented in this chapter employ only expected values; that is, the analysis reflects only the first moment of the probability distribution of the impact of a given risk. While this procedure does not assume that shareholders are risk neutral, it does assume either that risks such as expropriation, currency controls, inflation, and exchange rate changes are unsystematic or that foreign investments tend to lower a firm's systematic risk. In the latter case, adjusting only the expected values of future cash flows will yield a lower bound on the value of the investment to the firm.

Although the suggestion that cash flows from politically risky areas should be discounted at a rate that ignores those risks is contrary to current practice, the difference is more apparent than real: Most firms evaluating foreign investments discount most likely (modal) rather than expected (mean) cash flows at a risk-adjusted rate. If an expropriation or currency blockage is anticipated, then the mean value of the probability distribution of future cash flows will be significantly below its mode. From a theoretical standpoint, of course, cash flows should always be adjusted to reflect the change in expected values caused by a particular risk; however, only if the risk is systematic should these cash flows be further discounted.

Exchange Rate Changes and Inflation

The present value of future cash flows from a foreign project can be calculated using a two-stage procedure: (1) Convert nominal foreign currency cash flows into nominal home currency terms, and (2) discount those nominal cash flows at the nominal domestic required rate of return. Let C_t be the nominal expected foreign currency cash flow in year t, e_t the nominal exchange rate in t, and k^* is the nominal required rate of return. Then $C_t e_t$ is the nominal HC value of this cash flow in year t and $C_t e_t /(1 + k^*)^t$ is its present value.

In order to properly assess the effect of exchange rate changes on expected cash flows from a foreign project, one must first remove the effect of offsetting inflation and exchange rate changes. It is worthwhile to analyze each effect separately because different cash flows may be differentially affected by inflation. For example, the *depreciation tax shield* will not rise with inflation, while revenues and variable costs are likely to rise in line with inflation.

Or local price controls may not permit internal price adjustments. In practice, correcting for these effects means first adjusting the foreign currency cash flows for inflation and then converting the projected cash flows back into HC using the forecast exchange rate.

■ ──

ILLUSTRATION

Factoring in Currency Depreciation and Inflation. Suppose that with no inflation the cash flow in year 2 of a new project in France is expected to be FF 1 million, and the exchange rate is expected to remain at its current value of FF 1 = $0.20. Converted into dollars, the FF 1 million cash flow yields a projected cash flow of $200,000. Now suppose that French inflation is expected to be 6% annually, but project cash flows are expected to rise only 4% annually because the depreciation tax shield will remain constant. At the same time, because of purchasing power parity, the franc is expected to devalue at the rate of 6% annually— giving rise to a forecast exchange rate in year 2 of $0.20 \times (1 - 0.06)^2 = \$0.1767$. Then the forecast cash flow in year 2 becomes FF $1,000,000 \times 1.04^2 =$ FF 1,081,600, with a forecast dollar value of $191,119 ($0.1767 \times 1,081,600$).

── ■

■ 18.3 ■
FOREIGN PROJECT APPRAISAL: THE CASE OF INTERNATIONAL DIESEL CORPORATION

This section illustrates how to deal with some of the complexities involved in foreign project analysis by considering the case of a U.S. firm with an investment opportunity in England. International Diesel Corporation (IDC-U.S.), a U.S.-based multinational firm, is trying to decide whether to establish a diesel manufacturing plant in the United Kingdom (IDC-U.K.). IDC-U.S. expects to significantly boost its European sales of small diesel engines (40–160 hp) from the 20,000 it is currently exporting there. At the moment, IDC-U.S. is unable to increase exports because its domestic plants are producing to capacity. The 20,000 diesel engines it is currently shipping to Europe are the residual output that it is not selling domestically.

IDC-U.S. has made a strategic decision to significantly increase its presence and sales overseas. A logical first target of this international expansion is the European Community (EC). Market growth seems assured by recent large increases in fuel costs, and the market opening expected in 1992. IDC-U.S. executives believe that manufacturing in England will give the firm a key advantage with customers both in England and throughout the rest of the EC.

England is the most likely production location because IDC-U.S. can acquire a 1.4-million-square-foot plant in Manchester from BL, which used it to assemble gasoline engines before its recent closing. As an inducement to locate in this vacant plant and, thereby, ease unemployment among auto workers in Manchester, the National Enterprise Board (NEB) will provide a five-year loan of £5 million ($10 million) at 8% interest, with interest paid annually at the end of each year and the principal to be repaid in a lump sum at the end of the fifth year. Total acquisition, equipment, and retooling costs for this plant are estimated to equal $50 million.

Full-scale production can begin six months from the date of acquisition because IDC-U.S. is reasonably certain it can hire BL's plant manager and about 100 other former employees. In addition, conversion of the plant from producing gasoline engines to producing diesel engines should be relatively simple.

The parent will charge IDC-U.K. licensing and overhead allocation fees equal to 7% of sales in pounds sterling. In addition, IDC-U.S. will sell its English affiliate valves, piston rings, and other components that account for approximately 30% of the total amount of materials used in the manufacturing process. IDC-U.K. will be billed in dollars at the current market price for this material. The remainder will be purchased locally. IDC-U.S. estimates that its all-equity nominal required rate of return for the project will equal 15%, based on an estimated 8% U.S. rate of inflation and the business risks associated with this venture. The debt capacity of such a project is judged to be about 20%—that is, a debt/equity ratio for this project of about 1:4 is considered reasonable.

To simplify its investment analysis, IDC-U.S. uses a five-year capital budgeting horizon and then calculates a terminal value for the remaining life of the project. If the project has a positive net present value for the first five years, there is no need to engage in costly and uncertain estimates of future cash flows. If the initial net present value is negative, then IDC-U.S. can calculate a break-even terminal value at which the net present value will just be positive. This break-even value is then used as a bench mark against which to measure projected cash flows beyond the first five years.

We now apply the three-stage investment analysis outlined in Section 18.2: (1) Estimate project cash flows; (2) forecast the amounts and timing of cash flows to the parent; and (3) add to, or subtract from, these parent cash flows the indirect benefits or costs that this project provides the remainder of the multinational firm.

Estimation of Project Cash Flows

A principal cash outflow associated with the project is the initial investment outlay, consisting of the plant purchase, equipment expenditures, and working-capital requirements. Other cash outflows include operating expenses, later additions to working capital as sales expand, and taxes paid on its net income.

IDC-U.K. has cash inflows from its sales in England and other EC countries. It also has cash inflows from three other sources:

- The tax shield provided by depreciation and interest charges
- Interest subsidies
- The terminal value of its investment, net of any capital gains taxes owed upon liquidation

Recapture of working capital is not assumed until eventual liquidation because this working capital is necessary to maintain an ongoing operation after the fifth year.

Initial Investment Outlay.   Total plant acquisition, conversion, and equipment costs for IDC-U.K. were previously estimated at $50 million. Part of this $50 million is accounted for by equipment valued at $15 million, which is required for retooling. Approximately $10 million worth of this equipment will be purchased locally, with the remaining $5 million imported as used equipment from the parent. Although this used equipment has a book value of zero, it will be transferred at its market value of $5 million. The parent will be taxed at a rate of 25% on this gain over book value. If the equipment were transferred at other than its market value, say at $7 million, the stated value on IDC-U.K.'s books ($7 million) would differ from its capital budgeting value ($5 million), which is based solely on its opportunity cost (normally its market value). Both the new and used equipment will be depreciated on a straight-line basis over a five-year period, with a zero salvage value.

Of the $50 million in net plant and equipment costs, $10 million will be financed by NEB's loan of £5 million at 8%. The remaining $40 million will be supplied by the parent, $20 million as equity and $20 million as debt. The debt carries a fair market rate of 12%, and the principal is repayable in ten equal installments, commencing at the end of the first year.

Working-capital requirements—comprising cash, accounts receivable, and inventory—are estimated at 30% of sales, but this amount will be partially offset by accounts payable to local firms, which are expected to average 10% of sales. Therefore, net investment in working capital will equal approximately 20% of sales. The transfer price on the material sold to IDC-U.K. by its parent includes a 25% contribution to IDC-U.S.'s profit and overhead. That is, the variable cost of production equals 75% of the transfer price. Lloyds Bank is providing an initial working-capital loan of £1.5 million ($3 million). All future working-capital needs will be financed out of internal cash flow. Exhibit 18.1 summarizes the initial investment.

Financing IDC-U.K. Based on the information just provided, IDC-U.K.'s initial balance sheet, both in pounds and dollars, is presented in Exhibit 18.2. The debt ratio for IDC-U.K. is 15/25, or 60%. Note that this debt ratio could vary from 20%, if the parent's total investment was in the form of equity, to 100%, if the parent provided all of its $40 million investment for plant and equipment as debt. In other words, an affiliate's capital structure is not independent; rather, it is a function of its parent's investment policies. (Chapter 24 elaborates on subsidiary capital structure.)

■ **EXHIBIT 18.1** Initial Investment Outlay in IDC-U.K. (£1 = $2)

	£ (Millions)	$ (Millions)
Plant purchase and retooling expense	17.5	35
Equipment		
Supplied by parent (used)	2.5	5
Purchased in the United Kingdom	5	10
Working capital		
Bank financing	1.5	3
Total initial investment	£26.5	$53

■ **EXHIBIT 18.2**   Initial Balance Sheet of IDC-U.K. (£1 = $2)

	£ (Millions)	$ (Millions)
Assets		
Current assets	1.5	3
Plant and equipment	25	50
Total assets	26.5	53
Liabilities		
Loan payable (to Lloyds)	1.5	3
Total current liabilities	1.5	3
Loan payable (to NEB)	5	10
Loan payable (to IDC-U.S.)	10	20
Total liabilities	16.5	33
Equity	10	20
Total liabilities plus equity	£26.5	$53

As discussed in the previous section, the tax shield benefits of interest write-offs are represented separately. Assume that IDC-U.K. contributes $10.6 million to its parent's debt capacity (0.2 × $53 million), the market rate of interest for IDC-U.K. is 12%, and the U.K. tax rate is 40%. This calculation translates into a cash flow in the first and subsequent years equal to $10,600,000 × 0.12 × 0.40, or $509,000. Discounted at 12%, this cash flow provides a benefit equal to $1.8 million over the next five years.

Interest Subsidies.   Based on an 11% anticipated rate of inflation in England and on an expected annual 3% depreciation of the pound relative to the dollar, the market rate on the pound loan to IDC-U.K. would equal about 15%. Thus, the 8% interest rate on the loan by the National Enterprise Board represents a 7% subsidy to IDC-U.K. The cash value of this subsidy equals £350,000 (5,000,000 × 0.07), or approximately $700,000 annually for the next five years, with a present value of $2,500,000.[2]

Sales and Revenue Forecasts.   At a profit-maximizing price of $500 per unit (£250) in current dollars, demand for diesel engines in England and the other Common Market countries is expected to increase by 10% annually, from 60,000 units in the first year to 88,000 units in the fifth year. It is assumed here that purchasing power parity holds with no lag and that real prices remain constant in both absolute and relative terms. Hence, the

---

[2]The exact present value of this subsidy is given by the difference between the present value of debt service on the 8% loan discounted at 15% and the face value of the loan.

sequences of nominal pound prices and exchange rates, reflecting anticipated annual rates of inflation equaling 11% and 8% for the pound and dollar, respectively, are

	Year				
	1	2	3	4	5
Price (pounds)	250	278	308	342	380
Exchange rate (dollars)	2.00	1.95	1.89	1.84	1.79

It is also assumed here that purchasing power parity holds with respect to the currencies of the various EC countries to which IDC-U.K. exports. These exports account for about 60% of total IDC-U.K. sales. Disequilibrium conditions in the currency markets or relative price changes can be dealt with using an approach similar to that taken in the exposure measurement example (Spectrum Manufacturing) in Chapter 10.

In the first year, although demand is at 60,000 units, IDC-U.K. can produce and supply the market with only 30,000 units (due to the six-month start-up period). Another 20,000 units are exported by IDC-U.S. to its English affiliate at a unit transfer price of $500, leading to no profit for IDC-U.K. Since these units would have been exported anyway, IDC-U.K. is not credited from a capital budgeting standpoint with any profits on these sales. IDC-U.S. ceases its exports of finished products to England and the EC after the first year. From year 2 on, IDC-U.S. is counting on an expanding U.S. market to absorb the 20,000 units. Based on these assumptions, IDC-U.K.'s projected sales and revenues are shown in Exhibit 18.3.

■ **EXHIBIT 18.3**   Sales and Revenue Projections for IDC-U.K.

	Year				
	1	2	3	4	5
A. Sales in U.K.					
1. Diesel units	15,000	26,000	29,000	32,000	35,000
2. Price per unit (£)	250	278	308	342	380
3. U.K. sales revenue (millions)	3.8	7.2	8.9	10.9	13.3
B. Sales in EEC					
1. Diesel units	15,000	40,000	44,000	48,000	53,000
2. Price per unit (£)	250	278	308	342	380
3. EEC sales revenue (£ millions)	3.8	11.1	13.6	16.4	20.1
C. Total revenue (A3 + B3 in £ millions)	£7.5	£18.4	£22.5	£27.4	£33.4
D. Exchange rate ($)	2.00	1.95	1.89	1.84	1.79
E. Total revenue (C × D in $ millions)	$15.00	$35.8	$42.5	$50.3	$59.9

In nominal terms, IDC-U.K.'s pound sales revenues are projected to rise at a rate of 22% annually, based on a combination of the 10% annual increase in unit demand and the 11% annual increase in unit price ($1.10 \times 1.11 = 1.22$). Dollar revenues will increase at about 19% annually, due to the anticipated 3% annual pound devaluation.

Production Cost Estimates.   Based on the assumption of constant relative prices and purchasing power parity holding continually, variable costs of production, stated in real terms, are expected to remain constant, whether denominated in pounds or dollars. Hence, the pound prices of both labor and material sourced in England and components imported from the United States are assumed to increase by 11% annually. Unit variable costs in the first year are expected to equal £140, including £30 ($60) in components purchased from IDC-U.S.

In addition, the license fees and overhead allocations, which are set at 7% of sales, will rise at an annual rate of 22% because pound revenues are rising at that rate. With a full year of operation, initial overhead expenses would be expected to equal £1,100,000. Actual overhead expenses incurred, however, are only £600,000 because the plant does not begin operation until midyear. Since these expenses are partially fixed, their rate of increase should be about 13% annually.

The plant and equipment, valued at £25 million, can be written off over five years, yielding an annual depreciation charge against income of £5 million. The cash flow associated with this tax shield remains constant in nominal pound terms but declines in nominal dollar value by 3% annually. With an 8% rate of U.S. inflation, its real value is, therefore, reduced by 11% annually, the same as its loss in real pound terms.

Annual production costs for IDC-U.K. are estimated in Exhibit 18.4. It should be realized, of course, that some of these expenses are, like depreciation, a noncash charge or, like licensing fees, a benefit to the overall corporation.

Total production costs rise less rapidly each year than the 22% annual increase in nominal revenue. This situation is due both to the fixed depreciation charge and to the semifixed nature of overhead expenses. Thus, the profit margin should increase over time.

Projected Net Income.   In Exhibit 18.5, net income for years 1 through 5 is estimated based on the sales and cost projections in Exhibits 18.3 and 18.4. The effective tax rate on corporate income faced by IDC-U.K. in England is estimated to be 40%. The $5.8 million loss in the first year is applied against income in years 2, 3, and 4, reducing corporate taxes owed in these years.

Additions to Working Capital.   One of the major outlays for any new project is the investment in working capital. IDC-U.K. begins with an initial investment in working capital of £1.5 million ($3 million). Working-capital requirements are projected at a constant 20% of sales. Thus, the necessary investment in working capital will increase by 22% annually, the rate of increase in pound sales revenue. Translated into dollars, this means a 19% yearly increase in dollar working capital, as shown in Exhibit 18.6.

Terminal Value.   Calculating a terminal value is a complex undertaking, given the various possible ways to treat this issue. Three different approaches are pointed out. One

■ **EXHIBIT 18.4**   Production Cost Estimates for IDC–U.K.

	Year				
	1	**2**	**3**	**4**	**5**
A. Production volume (units)	30,000	66,000	73,000	80,000	88,000
B. Variable costs					
1. Labor and material purchased in U.K.					
a. Unit price (£)	110.0	122.1	135.5	150.4	167.0
b. Total cost (£ millions)	3.3	8.1	9.9	12.0	14.7
2. Components purchased from IDC-U.S.					
a. Unit price ($)	60.0	64.8	70	75.6	81.6
b. Unit price (£)	30.0	33.2	37.0	41.0	45.6
c. Total cost (£ millions)	0.9	2.2	2.7	3.3	4.0
3. Total variable costs (B1b + B2c in £ millions)	£ 4.2	£10.3	£12.6	£15.3	£18.7
C. License and overhead allocation fees					
1. Total revenue (from Exhibit 18.3, line C in £ millions)	7.5	18.4	22.5	27.4	33.4
a. License fees at 5% of revenue (£ millions)	0.4	0.9	1.1	1.4	1.7
b. Overhead allocation at 2% of revenue (£ millions)	0.2	0.4	0.5	0.6	0.7
2. Total licensing and overhead allocation fees (C1a + C1b in £ millions)	£ 0.6	£ 1.3	£ 1.6	£ 2.0	£ 2.4
D. Overhead expenses (£ millions)	0.6*	1.3	1.5	1.7	1.9
E. Depreciation (£ millions)	5.0	5.0	5.0	5.0	5.0
F. Total production costs (B3 + C2 + D + E in £ millions)	£10.4	£17.9	£20.7	£24.0	£28.0
G. Exchange rate ($)	2.00	1.95	1.89	1.84	1.79
H. Total production costs (F × G in $ millions)	$20.8	$34.9	$39.1	$44.2	$50.1

*Represents overhead expenses for less than one full year.

approach is to assume the investment will be liquidated after the end of the planning horizon and to use this value. However, this approach just takes the question one step further: What would a prospective buyer be willing to pay for this project? The second approach is to estimate the market value of the project, assuming that it is the present value of remaining

■ **EXHIBIT 18.5** Projected Net Income for IDC-U.K. ($ Millions)

	Year				
	1	2	3	4	5
A. Revenue (from Exhibit 18.3, line E)	$15.0	$35.8	$42.5	$50.3	$59.9
B. Total production costs (from Exhibit 18.4, line H)	20.8	34.9	39.1	44.2	50.1
C. Profit before tax	$(5.8)	$ 0.9	$ 3.4	$ 6.1	$ 9.8
D. Corporate income taxes paid to England @ 40% (0.4 × C)	0	0[1]	0[2]	1.8[3]	3.9
E. Net profit after tax (C – D)	$(5.8)	$ 0.9	$ 3.4	$ 4.3	$ 5.9

[1]Loss carryforward from year 1 of 0.9.

[2]Loss carryforward from year 1 of 3.4.

[3]Loss carryforward from year 1 of remaining 1.5 (5.8 – 0.9 – 3.4).

cash flows. Again, though, the value of the project to an outside buyer may differ from its value to the parent firm, due to parent profits on sales to its affiliate, for instance. The third approach is to calculate a break-even terminal value at which the project is just acceptable to the parent, and then use that as a bench mark against which to judge the likelihood of the present value of future cash flows exceeding that value.

Most firms try to be quite conservative in estimating terminal values. IDC-U.K. calculates a terminal value based on the assumption that the nominal dollar value of future income remains constant from years 6 through 10, and equals net income in year 5, except for adjustments to depreciation charges. In real terms, dollar income declines by 8% per year. It is assumed that this decline is due to the higher maintenance expenditures associated with aging plant and equipment. Nominal dollar revenue is expected to increase at the yearly

■ **EXHIBIT 18.6** Projected Additions to IDC-U.K.'s Working Capital ($ Millions)

	Year					
	0	1	2	3	4	5
A. Revenue (from Exhibit 18.3, line E)	$0	$15.0	$35.8	$42.5	$50.3	$59.9
B. Working-capital investment at 20% of revenue	0	3.0	7.2	8.5	10.1	12.0
C. Initial working-capital investment	3.0	—	—	—	—	—
D. Required addition to working capital (line B for year i – line B for year i – 1; $i = 2, \ldots, 5$)	—	0	4.2	1.3	1.6	1.9

rate of inflation (i.e., real sales remain constant). To support the higher level of sales, nominal working-capital needs also increase by 8% annually. All working capital is recaptured at the end of year 10, when the project is expected to cease. The calculation of terminal value for IDC-U.K. appears in Exhibit 18.7. As of the end of year 5, the terminal value has a present value of $42.6 million.

Estimated Project Present Value.   We are now ready to estimate the net present value of IDC-U.K. from the viewpoint of the project. As shown in Exhibit 18.8, the NPV of project cash flows equals –$2.4 million. Adding to this amount the $2.5 million value of interest subsidies and the $1.8 million present value of the tax shield on interest payments yields an overall positive project net present value of $1.9 million. The estimated value of the tax shield would be correspondingly greater if this analysis were to incorporate benefits derived over the full ten-year assumed life of the project, rather than including benefits from the first five years only. Over ten years, the present value of the tax shield would equal $2.9 million, bringing the overall project net present value to $3 million. The latter approach is the conceptually correct one.

Despite the favorable net present value for IDC-U.K., it is unlikely a firm would undertake an investment that had a positive value only because of interest subsidies or the interest tax shield provided by the debt capacity of the project. However, this is exactly what

■ **EXHIBIT 18.7**   Calculation of Terminal Value for IDC-U.K. ($ Millions)

	Year					
	6	**7**	**8**	**9**	**10**	**10+**
A. Net income after tax	$11.2[1]	$11.2	$11.2	$11.2	$11.2	
B. Required addition to working capital	1.0[2]	1.0	1.1	1.2	1.3	
C. Recapture of working capital	—	—	—	—	—	17.6
D. Total cash flow (A – B + C)	10.2	10.2	10.1	10.0	9.9	17.6
E. Present value factor at 15%	0.870	0.756	0.658	0.572	0.497	0.497
F. Present value[3] (D × E)	8.9	7.7	6.6	5.7	4.9	8.8
G. Cumulative present value[3]	$ 8.9	$16.6	$23.2	$28.9	$33.8	$42.6

[1]Profit before tax in year 5 is 9.8. Add back depreciation of 8.9 (5×1.79), since book value of fixed assets is zero in year 6. Thus, profit before tax is 18.7 and profit after tax is 18.7×0.6, or 11.2.

[2]Calculated as in Exhibit 18.6, assuming an 8% annual increase in required working capital (based on 8% increase in dollar sales volume).

[3]Present values are calculated as of the end of year 5.

■ **EXHIBIT 18.8** Present Value of IDC-U.K.: Project Viewpoint ($ Millions)

				Year			
	0	1	2	3	4	5	5+
A. Cash inflows							
1. Net income after tax (from (Exhibit 18.5, line E)	—	(5.8)	0.9	3.4	4.3	5.9	—
2. Depreciation*	—	10.0	9.8	9.4	9.2	8.9	—
3. Terminal value	—	—	—	—	—	—	42.6
4. Total	—	4.2	10.7	12.8	13.5	14.8	42.6
B. Cash outflows							
1. Initial investment in fixed assets	50	—	—	—	—	—	—
2. Additions to working capital	3	0	4.2	1.3	1.6	1.9	—
3. Total cash outflow	53	0	4.2	1.3	1.6	1.9	
C. Net cash flow (A4 − B3)	$(53)	$ 4.2	$ 6.5	$11.5	$11.9	$12.9	$42.6
D. Present value factor at 15%	1.0	0.870	0.756	0.658	0.572	0.497	0.497
E. Present value (C × D)	(53)	3.7	4.9	7.6	6.8	6.4	21.2
F. Cumulative present value	$(53)	$(49.3)	$(44.4)	$(36.8)	$(30.0)	$(23.6)	$(2.4)

*Equals depreciation charge of £5 million multiplied by the current exchange rate.

most firms do if they accept a marginal project, using a weighted cost of capital. Based on the debt capacity of the project and its subsidized financing, IDC-U.K. would have a weighted cost of capital of approximately 13%. At this discount rate, IDC-U.K. would be marginally profitable.

It would be misleading, however, to conclude the analysis at this point without recognizing and accounting for differences between project and parent cash flows and their impact on the worth of investing in IDC-U.K. Ultimately, shareholders in IDC-U.S. will benefit from this investment only to the extent that it generates cash flows that are, or can be, transferred out of England. The value of this investment is now calculated from the viewpoint of IDC-U.S.

Estimation of Parent Cash Flows

From the parent's perspective, additional cash outflows are recorded for any taxes paid to England or the United States on remitted funds. In addition, IDC-U.S. must pay tax to the U.S. Internal Revenue Service on gains associated with the sale for $5 million of equipment having a book value of zero. The effective tax rate on these gains is assumed to be 25%. But because IDC-U.S. had planned to sell this equipment anyway, its opportunity cost for transferring it to IDC-U.K. is only 75% of $5 million, or $3,750,000. This figure is the after-tax amount it would have received from a sale to a third party.

IDC-U.S. has additional cash inflows as well. It receives licensing and overhead allocation fees each year for which it incurs no additional expenses. If it did, the expenses would have to be charged against the fees. IDC-U.S. also profits from exports to its English affiliate.

Loan Payments.   IDC-U.K. will first make all necessary loan repayments before paying dividends. These include principal repayments to the parent on its loan of $20 million, at the rate of $2 million annually for the first ten years. The interest payments of 12% each year on the remaining loan balance are netted out, because they involve a simultaneous decrease in IDC-U.K.'s cash flow and increase in IDC-U.S.'s cash flow. Tax effects are minimal and are, therefore, ignored. In addition, IDC-U.K. will repay the £1.5 million working-capital loan from Lloyds at the end of year 2 and NEB's loan of £5 million at the end of the fifth year. Their dollar repayment costs are estimated at $2.8 million and $9 million, respectively, based on the forecasted exchange rates. These latter two loan repayments are counted as parent cash inflows because they reduce the parent's outstanding consolidated debt burden and increase the value of its equity by an equivalent amount. Assuming that the parent would repay these loans regardless, having IDC-U.K. borrow and repay funds is equivalent to IDC-U.S. borrowing the money, investing it in IDC-U.K., and then using IDC-U.K.'s higher cash flows (because it no longer has British loans to service) to repay IDC-U.S.'s debts. Exhibit 18.9, line D, shows the relevant cash flows associated with the loan repayments.

■ **EXHIBIT 18.9**   Loan Repayments by IDC-U.K. ($ Millions)

	Year					
	1	2	3	4	5	5+
A. Working-capital loan repayment	—	2.8	—	—	—	—
B. Principal repayments to IDC-U.S.	2.0	2.0	2.0	2.0	2.0	6.7*
C. Principal repayment to NEB	—	—	—	—	9.0	—
D. Total loan repayments	$2.0	$4.8	$2.0	$2.0	$11.0	$6.7

*Present value of loan repayments from years 6–10, discounted at 15%.

U.S. and U.K. Taxes on Remittances to IDC-U.S. IDC-U.K. is projected to pay dividends equal to 100% of its remaining net cash flows after making all necessary loan repayments. It also pays licensing and overhead allocation fees equal, in total, to 7% of gross sales. On both these forms of transfer, the English government will collect a 10% withholding tax. IDC-U.S. will also have to pay U.S. corporate income taxes on the dividends and fees it receives, less any credits for foreign income and withholding taxes already paid. These tax calculations are shown in Exhibits 18.10 and 18.11.

Although England's 40% tax rate exceeds the U.S. tax rate of 34%, IDC-U.S. owes taxes on its initial dividend remittances because the U.S. taxes owed exceed the English taxes paid by IDC-U.K. However, U.S. taxes owed on dividends from years 3 and 4 are offset by the excess foreign tax credits carried back from years 5 through 10. It is assumed that IDC-U.S. does not have excess FTCs from elsewhere.

With respect to fee remittances, IDC-U.S. owes U.S. tax for each year. However, for years 6 through 10, these taxes are offset by the excess FTCs associated with dividend payments.[3]

It is apparent that the more cash that can be remitted as principal repayments, rather than dividends, the fewer additional transfer taxes need be paid to England and the United States. One way to avoid these transfer taxes here would be for IDC-U.S. to make more of its investment in the form of debt and less as equity.

Earnings on Exports to IDC-U.K. With a 20% margin on its exports, and assuming it has sufficient spare-parts manufacturing capacity, IDC-U.S. has incremental earnings on sales to IDC-U.K. equaling 20% of the value of these shipments. After U.S. corporate tax of 34%, IDC-U.S. generates cash flows valued at 13.2% (20% × 66%) of its exports to IDC-U.K. These cash flows are presented in Exhibit 18.12.

Estimated Present Value of Project to IDC-U.S. In Exhibit 18.13, all the various cash flows are added up, net of tax and interest subsidies on debt; and their present value is calculated at $12.2 million. Adding the $5.4 million in debt-related subsidies ($2.9 million for the interest tax shield and $2.5 million for the NEB loan subsidy) brings this value up to $17.6 million. It is apparent that, despite the additional taxes that must be paid to England and the United States, IDC-U.K. is more valuable to its parent than it would be to another owner on a stand-alone basis. This situation is primarily due to the various licensing and overhead allocation fees received and the incremental earnings on exports to IDC-U.K.

Lost Sales. There is a circumstance, however, that can reverse this conclusion. This discussion has assumed that IDC-U.S. is now producing at capacity and that the 20,000 diesels currently being exported to the EC can be sold in the United States, starting in year 2. Should this assumption not be the case (that is, should 20,000 units of IDC-U.K. sales just replace 20,000 units of IDC-U.S. sales), then the project would have to be charged with the incremental cash flow that IDC-U.S. would have earned on these lost exports. We now see how to incorporate this effect in a capital-budgeting analysis.

---

[3]Since all the remittances are paid out of operating income, IDC-U.S. gets full credit for the income taxes paid by IDC-U.K.

■ **EXHIBIT 18.10**   Net Dividends Received by IDC-U.S. ($ Millions)

	Year					
	1	2	3	4	5	5+
A. Net cash flow to IDC-U.K. (from Exhibit 18.8, line C)	4.2	6.5	11.5	11.9	12.9	42.6
B. Loan repayments by IDC-U.K. (from Exhibit 18.9, line D)	2.0	4.8	2.0	2.0	11.0	6.7
C. Dividend paid to IDC-U.S. (A – B)	$2.2	$1.7	$ 9.5	$ 9.9	$ 1.9	$35.9
D. Withholding tax paid to England @ 10% (0.10 × C)	0.2	0.2	1.0	1.0	0.2	3.6
E. Net dividend received by IDC-U.S. (C – D)	$2.0	$1.5	$ 8.5	$ 8.9	$ 1.7	$32.3
F. Foreign Tax Credit						
1. Net income to IDC-U.K. (from Exhibit 18.5, line E)	(5.8)	0.9	3.4	4.3	5.9	37.5[1]
2. English income tax paid (from Exhibit 18.5, line D)	0	0	0	1.8	3.9	25.0[2]
3. Deemed-paid credit for income taxes paid by IDC-U.K. ((C/F1) × F2)	0[3]	0[3]	03	1.8[3]	1.3	23.9
4. Withholding tax paid (D)	0.2	0.2	1.0	1.0	0.2	3.6
5. Total foreign tax credit (F3 + F4)	0.2	0.2	1.0	2.8	1.5	27.5
G. *Additional* U.S. tax owed						
1. Included in U.S. income (E + F5)	2.2	1.7	9.5	11.7	3.2	59.8
2. U.S. tax owed @ 34% (0.34 × G1)	0.7	0.6	3.2	4.0	1.1	20.3
3. Less foreign tax credit (F5)	0.2	0.2	1.0	2.8	1.5	27.5
4. Net U.S. tax owed (G2 – G3)	0.5	0.4	0[4]	0[4]	0[4]	(4.2)[4]
H. After-tax value of dividend to IDC-U.S. (E – G4)	$1.5	$1.1	$ 8.5	$ 8.9	$ 1.7	$32.3

[1]Present value of an annuity of $11.2 million for five years, discounted at 15%.

[2]Present value of an annuity of $7.5 million (18.7 × 0.4) for five years, discounted at 15%.

[3]Deemed-paid credit is limited to foreign income taxes paid.

[4]Figures reflect the carryback of excess FTCs for the two-year maximum allowable period.

Suppose the incremental after-tax cash flow per unit to IDC-U.S. on its exports to the EC equals $180 at present and that this contribution is expected to maintain its value in current dollar terms over time. Then, in nominal dollar terms, this margin grows by 8% annually. Assuming lost sales of 20,000 units per year, beginning in year 2 and extending

■ **EXHIBIT 18.11**   Net Licensing and Overhead Allocation Fees Received by IDC-U.S.
($ Millions)

	Year					
	1	**2**	**3**	**4**	**5**	**5+**
A. Net sales revenue to IDC-U.K. (from Exhibit 18.3, line E)	15.0	35.8	42.5	50.3	59.9	245.8[1]
B. Licensing fees at 5% $(0.5 \times A)$	0.8	1.8	2.1	2.5	3.0	12.3
C. Overhead allocation at 2% $(0.02 \times A)$	0.3	0.7	0.9	1.0	1.2	4.9
D. Total fees (B + C)	$ 1.1	$ 2.5	$ 3.0	$ 3.5	$ 4.2	$17.2
E. Withholding taxes @ 10% $(0.10 \times D)$	0.1	0.3	0.3	0.4	0.4	1.7
F. Net fees received by IDC-U.S. (D − E)	$ 1.0	$ 2.2	$ 2.7	$ 3.1	$ 3.8	$15.5
G. U.S. income tax @ 34% $(0.34 \times D)$	0.4	0.9	1.0	1.2	1.4	5.8
H. Net U.S. tax owed (G − E)	0.3	0.6	0.7	0.8	1.0	0[2]
I. After-tax value of fees to IDC-U.S. (F − H)	$ 0.7	$ 1.6	$ 2.0	$ 2.3	$ 2.8	$15.5

[1]Calculated in terms of its present value.

[2]Application of $3.8 million in excess FTCs from dividend payments.

■ **EXHIBIT 18.12**   Net Cash Flows from Exports to IDC-U.K. ($ Millions)

	Year					
	1	**2**	**3**	**4**	**5**	**5+**
A. Production volume	30,000	66,000	73,000	80,000	88,000	88,000
B. Components purchased from IDC-U.S.						
1. Unit price (from Exhibit 18.4, line B2a)	60	64.8	70	75.6	81.6	81.6*
2. Total export revenues (A × B1)	1.8	4.3	5.1	6.0	7.2	7.2
C. After-tax cash flow $(0.132 \times B2)$	$ 0.2	$ 0.6	$ 0.7	$ 0.8	$ 1.0	$ 1.0

*In constant year-5 dollar terms.

■ **EXHIBIT 18.13**   Present Value of IDC-U.K.: Parent Viewpoint ($ Millions)

	Year						
	0	**1**	**2**	**3**	**4**	**5**	**5+**
A. Cash inflows							
1. Loan repayments (from (Exhibit 18.9, line D)[1]	—	2.0	4.8	2.0	2.0	11.0	6.7
2. Dividends (from (Exhibit 18.10, line H)	—	1.5	1.1	8.5	8.9	1.7	32.3
3. Fees (from Exhibit 18.11, line I)	—	0.7	1.6	2.0	2.3	2.8	15.5
4. Net cash flows from exports (from Exhibit 18.12, line C)	—	0.2	0.6	0.7	0.8	1.0	4.1[2]
5. Total cash inflows	—	4.4	8.1	13.2	14.0	16.5	58.6
B. Cash outflows							
1. Plant purchase and retooling	35	—	—	—	—	—	—
2. Equipment							
a. Supplied by parent	3.8[3]	—	—	—	—	—	—
b. Purchased in United Kingdom	10.0	—	—	—	—	—	—
3. Working capital	3	—	—	—	—	—	—
4. Total cash outflows	51.8	—	—	—	—	—	—
C. Net cash flow (A5 – B4)	$(51.8)	$ 4.4	$ 8.1	$13.2	$14.0	$16.5	$58.6
D. Present value factor at 15%	1.0	0.870	0.756	0.658	0.572	0.497	0.497
E. Present value (C × D)	(51.8)	3.9	6.1	8.7	8.0	8.2	29.1
F. Cumulative present value	$(51.8)	$(47.9)	$(41.8)	$(33.1)	$(25.1)	$(16.9)	$12.2

[1]Loan payments count as cash inflows because they reduce the parent's total liabilities.

[2]Present value of an annuity of $1 million annually for five years, discounted at 7%. The 7% rate is the real risk-adjusted rate since the $1 million annuity is expressed in constant year-5 dollar terms.

[3]After-tax cost of $5 million is used equipment supplied by parent ($0.75 \times \$5$ million).

through year 10, and a discount rate of 15%, the present value associated with these lost sales equals $20.6 million. The calculations are presented in Exhibit 18.14. Subtracting the present value of lost sales from the previously calculated present value of $17.6 million yields a net present value of IDC-U.K. to its parent equal to –$3 million (–$8.4 million ignoring the interest tax shield and subsidy).

This example points up the importance of looking at incremental cash flows generated by a foreign project, rather than total cash flows. An investment that would be marginally profitable on its own, and quite profitable when integrated with parent activities, becomes unprofitable when taking into account earnings on lost sales.

■ **EXHIBIT 18.14**   Value of Lost Export Sales ($ Millions)

	Year								
	2	3	4	5	6	7	8	9	10
A. Lost unit sales	20,000	20,000	20,000	20,000	20,000	20,000	20,000	20,000	20,000
B. Cash flow per unit	194.4*	209.95	226.8	244	264.4	285.6	308.4	333.2	359.8
C. Total cash flow from exports (A × B)	3.8	4.2	4.6	4.8	5.2	5.6	6.2	6.6	7.2
D. Present value factor at 15%	0.756	0.658	0.572	0.497	0.432	0.376	0.327	0.284	0.247
E. Present value (C × D)	2.8	2.8	2.6	2.4	2.2	2.2	2.0	1.8	1.8
F. Cumulative present value	$ 2.8	$ 5.6	$ 8.2	$10.6	$12.8	$15.0	$17.0	$18.8	$20.6

*The figures in this row grow by 8% each year. Thus, 194.4 = 180(1.08), and so on.

■ 18.4 ■
POLITICAL RISK ANALYSIS

It is apparent from the figures in Exhibit 18.13 that IDC-U.S.'s English investment is quite sensitive to the potential political risks of currency controls and expropriation. The net present value of the project does not turn positive until well after its fifth year of operation (assuming there are no lost sales). Should expropriation occur or exchange controls be imposed at some point during the first five years, it is unlikely that the project will ever be viable from the parent's standpoint. Only if compensation is sufficiently great in the event of expropriation, or if unremitted funds can earn a return reflecting their opportunity cost to IDC-U.S. with eventual repatriation in the event of exchange controls, can this project still be viable in the face of these risks.

The general approach recommended previously for incorporating political risk in an investment analysis usually involves adjusting the cash flows of the project (rather than its required rate of return) to reflect the impact of a particular political event on the present value of the project to the parent. This section shows how these cash flow adjustments can be made for the cases of expropriation and exchange controls.

Expropriation

The extreme form of political risk is *expropriation*. Expropriation is an obvious case where project and parent company cash flows diverge. The approach suggested here examines directly the impact of expropriation on the present value of the project to the parent. In this section, we examine the technique of adjusting expected cash flows to show how expropriation and currency controls affect the value of specific projects.

- **EXHIBIT 18.15**   United Fruit Company's Choices (U.S. $ Millions)

	Expropriation	No Expropriation	Expected Present Value
Sell out now	128	128	128
Wait	100	300	$[100p + 300(1-p)]/1.22$

-

ILLUSTRATION

United Fruit Compay Calculates the Consequences of Expropriation. Suppose that United Fruit Company (UFC) is worried that its banana plantation in Honduras will be expropriated during the next 12 months.[4] The Honduran government has promised, however, that compensation of $100 million will be paid at the year's end if the plantation is expropriated. UFC believes that this promise would be kept. If expropriation does not occur this year, it will not occur anytime in the foreseeable future. The plantation is expected to be worth $300 million at the end of the year. A wealthy Honduran has just offered UFC $128 million for the plantation. If UFC's risk-adjusted discount rate is 22%, what is the probability of expropriation at which UFC is just indifferent between selling now or holding onto its plantation?

Exhibit 18.15 displays UFC's two choices and their consequences. If UFC sells out now, it will receive $128 million today. Alternatively, if it chooses to hold onto the plantation, its property will be worth $300 million if expropriation doesn't occur and worth only $100 million in the event the Honduran government expropriates its plantation and compensates UFC. If the probability of expropriation is p, then the expected end-of-year value of the plantation to UFC (in millions of dollars) is $100p + 300(1-p) = 300 - 200p$. The present value of the amount, using UFC's discount rate of 22%, is $(300 - 200p)/1.22$. Setting this equal to the $128 million offer by the wealthy Honduran yields a value of $p = 72\%$. In other words, if the probability of expropriation is at least 72%, UFC should sell out now for $128 million. If the probability of expropriation is less than 72%, it would be more worthwhile for UFC to hold on to its plantation.

-

Blocked Funds

The same method of adjusting expected cash flows can be used to analyze the effects of various exchange controls. In discussing blocked funds, it must be pointed out that if all funds are expected to be blocked in perpetuity, then the value of the project is zero.

-

ILLUSTRATION

Brascan Calculates the Consequences of Currency Controls. On January 1, 1981, the Indonesian electrical authority expropriated a power-generating station owned by Brascan,

---

[4]Illustration suggested by Richard Roll.

■ **EXHIBIT 18.16**   Cash Flows to Brascan (C$ Millions)

	Cash Flow at Year End		
	1981	**1982**	**1983 and On**
Currency controls	50.0	50.0	37.5
No currency controls	50.0	50.0	50.0

Inc., a Canadian operator of foreign electric facilities.[5] In compensation, a perpetuity of C$50 million will be paid annually at the end of each year. Brascan believes, however, that the Indonesian Central Bank may block currency repatriations during the calendar year 1983, allowing only 75% of each year's payment to be repatriated (and no repatriation of reinvestments from the other 25%). Assuming a cost of capital of 20% and a probability of currency blockage of 40%, what is the current value (on January 1, 1981) of Indonesia's compensation?

Exhibit 18.16 displays the two possibilities and their consequences for the cash flows Brascan expects to receive. If currency controls are not imposed, Brascan will receive C$50 million annually, with the first payment due December 31, 1981. The present value of this stream of cash equals C$250 million (50/0.2). Alternatively, if controls are imposed, Brascan will receive C$50 million at the end of the first two years and C$37.5 million (50 × 0.75) on each December 31 thereafter. The present value of these cash flows is C$206.6 million $[50/1.2 + 50/(1.2)^2 + (37.5/0.2)/(1.2)^2]$.[6] Weighting these present values by the probability that each will come to pass yields an expected present value (in millions of Canadian dollars) of 0.6 × 250 + 0.4 × 206.6 = C$232.6 million.

■

■ 18.5 ■
GROWTH OPTIONS AND PROJECT EVALUATION

The discounted cash flow (DCF) analysis presented so far treats a project's expected cash flows as given at the outset. This approach presupposes a static approach to investment decision making: It assumes that all operating decisions are set in advance. In reality, though, the opportunity to make decisions contingent on information to become available in the future is an essential feature of many investment decisions.

Consider the decision of whether to reopen a gold mine. The cost of doing so is expected to be $1 million. There are an estimated 40,000 ounces of gold remaining in the mine. If the mine is reopened, the gold can be removed in one year at a variable cost of $390 per ounce. Assuming an expected gold price in one year of $400/ounce, the expected profit per ounce mined is $10. Clearly, the expected cash inflow (ignoring taxes) of $400,000 next year ($10 × 40,000) is far below that necessary to recoup the $1 million investment in reopening the

[5]Illustration suggested by Richard Roll.

[6]As of the end of year 2 the $37.5 million annuity beginning in year 3 has a present value equal to 37.5/0.2. The present value of this annuity as of today equals $[37.5/0.2]/(1.2)^2$.

mine, much less to pay the 15% yield required on such a risky investment. But intuition—which suggests a highly negative project NPV of –$652,174 (–$1,000,000 + 400,000/1.15)—is wrong in this case. The reason is that the cash flow projections underlying the classical DCF analysis ignore the option *not* to produce gold if it is unprofitable to do so.

Here is a simple example that demonstrates the fallacy of always using expected cash flows to judge an investment's merits. Suppose there are only two possible gold prices next year: $300/ounce and $500/ounce, each with probability 0.5. The expected gold price is $400/ounce, but this expected price is irrelevant to the optimal mining decision rule: Mine gold if, and only if, the price of gold at year's end is $500/ounce. Exhibit 18.17 shows the cash flow consequences of that decision rule. Closure costs are assumed to be zero.

Incorporating the mine owner's option *not* to mine gold when the price falls below the cost of extraction reveals a positive net present value of $913,043 for the decision to reopen the gold mine:

$$\text{NPV of gold mine investment} = -\$1,000,000 + \frac{\$2,200,000}{1.15}$$

$$= \$913,043$$

As the example of the gold mine demonstrates, the ability to alter decisions in response to new information may contribute significantly to the value of a project. Such investments bear the characteristics of options on securities and should be valued accordingly. As we saw in the case of foreign exchange, a call option gives the holder the right, but not the obligation, to buy a security at a fixed, predetermined price (called the exercise price) on or before some fixed future date. By way of analogy, the opportunities a firm may have to invest capital to increase the profitability of its existing product lines and benefit from expanding

■ **EXHIBIT 18.17**   The Gold Mine-Operating Decision

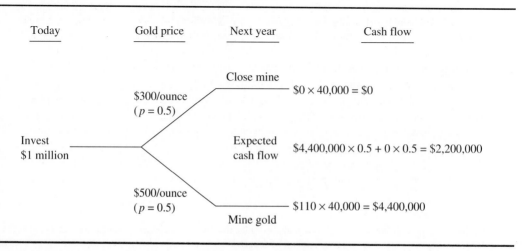

Today	Gold price	Next year	Cash flow

Close mine
$0 × 40,000 = $0

$300/ounce
($p = 0.5$)

Invest
$1 million

Expected
cash flow $4,400,000 × 0.5 + 0 × 0.5 = $2,200,000

$500/ounce
($p = 0.5$)

$110 × 40,000 = $4,400,000

Mine gold

into new products or markets may be thought of as *growth options.*[7] Similarly, a firm's ability to capitalize on its managerial talent, experience in a particular product line, its brand name, technology, or its other resources may provide valuable but uncertain future prospects.

Growth options are of great importance to multinational firms. Consider the value of IDC-U.K.'s production and market positions at the end of its planning horizon. IDC-U.S. may increase or decrease the diesel plant's output depending on current market conditions, expectations of future demand, and relative cost changes, such as those due to currency movements. The plant can be expanded; it can be shut down, then reopened when production and market conditions are more favorable; or it can be abandoned permanently. Each decision is an option from the viewpoint of IDC-U.S. The value of these options, in turn, affects the value of the investment in IDC-U.K.

Moreover, by producing locally, IDC-U.S. will have an enhanced market position in the EC that may enable the company to expand its product offerings at a later date. The ability to exploit this market position depends on the results of IDC-U.S.'s R&D efforts and the shifting pattern of demand for its products. In all these cases, the optimal operating policy depends on outcomes that are not known at the project's inception.

Similarly, the investments that many Western firms are now considering in Eastern Europe can also be thought of as growth options. Some view investments there as a way to gain entre into a potentially large market. Others see Eastern Europe as an underdeveloped area with educated and skilled workers but low wages and view such investments as a low-cost backdoor to Western European markets. In either case, companies who invest there are buying an option that will pay off in the event that Eastern European markets boom or that Eastern European workers turn out to be much more productive with the right technology and incentives than they have been under communism. By failing to take into account the benefits of operating flexibility and potentially valuable add-on projects, the traditional DCF will tend to understate project values.

The problem of undervaluing investment projects using the standard DCF analysis is particularly acute for strategic investments. Many strategically important investments, such as investments in R&D, factory automation, a brand name, or a distribution network, provide growth opportunities because they are often but the first link in a chain of subsequent investment decisions.

Valuing investments that embody discretionary follow-up projects requires an expanded net present value rule that considers the attendant options. More specifically, the value of an option to undertake a follow-up project equals the expected project NPV using the conventional discounted cash-flow analysis plus the value of the discretion associated with undertaking the project. This relation is shown in Exhibit 18.18. Based on the discussion of currency options in Chapter 3, the latter element of value (the discretion to invest or not invest in a project) depends on the following.

1. *The length of time the project can be deferred*: The ability to defer a project gives the firm more time to examine the course of future events and to avoid costly errors if

---

[7]A good discussion of growth options is contained in W. Carl Kester, "Today's Options for Tomorrow's Growth," *Harvard Business Review,* March–April 1984, pp. 153–160.

■ **EXHIBIT 18.18**   Valuing a Growth Option to Undertake a Follow-Up Project

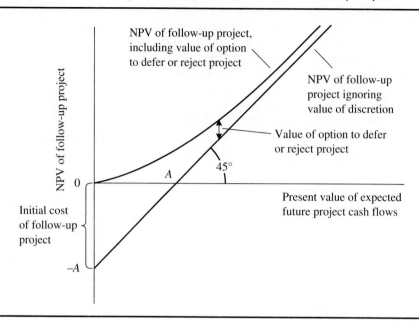

unfavorable developments occur. A longer time interval also raises the odds that a positive turn of events will dramatically boost the project's profitability and turn even a negative NPV project into a positive one.

2. *The risk of the project*: Surprisingly, the riskier the investment, the more valuable is an option on it. The reason is the asymmetry between gains and losses. A large gain is possible if the project's NPV becomes highly positive, whereas losses are limited by the option not to exercise when the project NPV is negative. The riskier the project, the greater the odds of a large gain without a corresponding increase in the size of the potential loss. Thus, growth options are likely to be especially valuable for MNCs because of the large potential variation in costs and the competitive environment.

3. *The level of interest rates*: Although a high discount rate lowers the present value of a project's future cash flows, it also reduces the present value of the cash outlay needed to exercise an option. The net effect is that high interest rates generally raise the value of projects that contain growth options.

4. *The proprietary nature of the option*: An exclusively owned option is clearly more valuable than one that is shared with others. The latter might include the chance to enter a new market or to invest in a new production process. Shared options are less valuable because competitors can replicate the investments and drive down returns. For the multinational firm, though, most growth options arise out of its intangible assets. These assets, which take the form of skills, knowledge, brand names, and the like, are difficult to replicate and so are likely to be more valuable.

■ ──

ILLUSTRATION

Ford Gives Up on Small Car Development. In late 1986, Ford gave up on small-car development in the United States and handed over the job to Japan's Mazda. Although seemingly cost effective in the short run (Ford should save about $500 million in development costs for one car model alone), such a move—which removed a critical mass from Ford's own engineering efforts—could prove dangerous in the longer term. Overcoming engineering obstacles unique to subcompact cars—for example, the challenges of miniaturization—enhances engineers' skills and allows them to apply innovations to all classes of vehicles. By eroding its technological base, Ford may have yielded the option of generating ideas that can be applied elsewhere in its business. Moreover, the cost of reentering the business of in-house design can be substantial. The abandonment option is not one to be exercised lightly.

Some American consumer-electronics companies, for example, are learning the penalties of ceding major technologies and the experiences that come from working with these technologies on a day-to-day basis. Westinghouse Electric, after quitting the development and manufacture of color television tubes in 1976, recently decided to get back into the color-video business. But, because it had lost touch with the product, Westinghouse has been able to reenter only by way of a joint venture with Japan's Toshiba.

Similarly, RCA and other U.S. manufacturers several years ago conceded to the Japanese development of videocassette recorders and laser video disk players. Each technology has since spawned entirely new, popular product lines—from video cameras to compact disk players—in which U.S. companies are left with nothing to do beyond marketing Japanese-made goods. Even those companies that merely turn to outside partners for technical help could nevertheless find their skills atrophying over the years as their partners handle more of the complex designing and manufacturing. Such companies range from Boeing, which has enlisted three Japanese firms to help engineer a new plane, to Honeywell, which is getting big computers from NEC. The corresponding reduction in in-house technological skills decreases the value of the option these firms have to develop and apply new technologies in novel product areas.   ■

■ 18.6 ■
SUMMARY AND CONCLUSIONS

Capital budgeting for the multinational corporation presents many elements that rarely, if ever, exist in domestic capital budgeting. The primary thrust of this chapter has been to adjust project cash flows instead of the discount rate to reflect the key political and economic risks that MNCs face abroad. Tax factors are also incorporated via cash-flow adjustments. Cash-flow adjustments are preferred on the pragmatic grounds that there is available more and better information on the effect of such risks on future cash flows than on the required discount rate. Furthermore, adjusting the required rate of return of a project to reflect incremental risk does not usually allow for adequate consideration of the time pattern and magnitude of the risk being evaluated. Using a uniformly higher discount rate to reflect additional risk involves penalizing future cash flows relatively more heavily than present ones.

This chapter showed how these cash-flow adjustments can be carried out by presenting a lengthy numerical example. It also discussed the significant differences that can exist between project and parent cash flows and showed how these differences can be accounted for when estimating the value to the parent firm of a foreign investment.

The chapter also pointed out that failure to take into account the options available to managers to adjust the scope of a project will lead to a downward bias in estimating project cash flows. These options include the possibility of expanding or contracting the project or abandoning it, the chance to employ radical new process technologies by utilizing skills developed from implementing the project, and the possibility of entering the new lines of business to which a project may lead.

■ QUESTIONS ■

1. A foreign project that is profitable when valued on its own will always be profitable from the parent firm's standpoint. True or false. Explain.

2. What are the principal cash outflows associated with the IDC-U.K. project?

3. What are the principal cash inflows associated with the IDC-U.K. project?

4. In what ways do parent and project cash flows differ on the IDC-U.K. project? Why?

5. Suppose the real value of the pound declines. How would this decline likely affect the economics of the IDC-U.K. project?

6. Describe the alternative ways to treat the interest subsidy provided by the British government.

7. Suppose England raised its corporate tax rate by one percentage point. How would this affect the economics of the IDC-U.K. project?

8. Why are IDC-U.S. earnings on exports to IDC-U.K. credited to the project?

9. Why are loan repayments by IDC-U.K. to Lloyds and NEB treated as a cash inflow to the parent company?

10. Under what circumstances should IDC-U.S. earnings on lost export sales to the United Kingdom and the rest of the EC countries be treated as a cost of the project?

11. Under what circumstances should these lost export earnings be ignored when evaluating the project?

12. How sensitive is the value of the project to the threat of currency controls and expropriation? How can the financing be structured so as to make the project less sensitive to these political risks?

13. What options does investment in the new British diesel plant provide to IDC-U.S.? How can these options be accounted for in the traditional capital budgeting analysis?

14. Early results on the Lexus, Toyota's upscale car, showed it was taking the most business from customers changing from either BMW (15%), Mercedes (14%), Toyota (14%), General Motors' Cadillac (12%), and Ford's Lincoln (6%). With what in the auto business is considered a high percentage of sales coming from its own customers, how badly is Toyota hurting itself with the Lexus?

15. Comment on the following statement that appeared in *The Economist* (August 20, 1988, p. 60): Those oil producers that have snapped up overseas refineries—Kuwait, Venezuela, Libya and, most recently, Saudi Arabia—can feed the flabbiest of them with dollar-a-barrel crude and make a profit . . . . The

majority of OPEC's existing overseas refineries would be scrapped without its own cheap oil to feed them. Both Western European refineries fed by Libyan oil (in West Germany and Italy) and Kuwait's two overseas refineries (in Holland and Denmark) would almost certainly be idle without it.

16. Some economists have stated that too many companies aren't calculating the cost of *not* investing in new technology, world-class manufacturing facilities, or market position overseas. What are some of these costs? How do these costs relate to the notion of growth options discussed in the chapter?

17. In December 1989, General Electric spent $150 million to buy a controlling interest in Tungsram, the Hungarian state-owned light bulb maker. Even in its best year, Tungsram earned less than a 4% return on equity (based on the price GE paid).

   a. What might account for GE's decision to spend so much money to acquire such a delapidated, inefficient manufacturer?

   b. A Hungarian lighting worker earns about $170 a month in Hungary, compared with about $1,700 a month in the United States. Do these figures indicate that Tungsram will be a low-cost producer?

■ PROBLEMS ■

1. Suppose a firm projects a $5 million perpetuity from an investment of $20 million in Spain. If the required return on this investment is 20%, how large does the probability of expropriation in year 4 have to be before the investment has a negative NPV? Assume that all cash inflows occur at the end of each year and that the expropriation, if it occurs, will occur just prior to the year-4 cash inflow or not at all. There is no compensation in the event of expropriation.

2. Suppose a firm has just made an investment in France that will generate $2 million annually in depreciation, converted at today's spot rate. Projected annual rates of inflation in France and in the United States are 7% and 4%, respectively. If the real exchange rate is expected to remain constant and the French tax rate is 50%, what is the expected real value (in terms of today's dollars) of the depreciation charge in year 5, assuming that the tax write-off is taken at the end of the year?

3. Jim Toreson, chairman and CEO of Xebec Corporation, a Sunnyvale, California, manufacturer of disk-drive controllers, is trying to decide whether to switch to offshore production. Given Xebec's well-developed engineering and marketing capabilities, Toreson could use offshore manufacturing to ramp up production, taking full advantage of both low-wage labor and a grab bag of tax holidays, low-interest loans, and other government largess. Most of his competitors seem to be doing it. The faster he follows suit, the better off Xebec would be according to the conventional discounted cash-flow analysis, which showed that switching production offshore was clearly a positive NPV investment. However, Toreson is concerned that such a move would entail the loss of certain intangible strategic benefits associated with domestic production.

   a. What might be some strategic benefits of domestic manufacturing for Xebec? Consider the fact that its customers are all U.S. firms and that manufacturing technology—particularly automation skills—is key to survival in this business.

   b. What analytic framework can be used to factor these intangible strategic benefits of domestic manufacturing (which are intangible costs of offshore production) into the factory location decision?

   c. How would the possibility of radical shifts in manufacturing technology affect the production location decision?

   d. Xebec is considering producing more-sophisticated drives that require substantial customization. How does this possibility affect its production decision?

e. Suppose the Taiwan government is willing to provide a loan of $10 million at 5% to Xebec to build a factory there. The loan would be paid off in equal annual installments over a five-year period. If the market interest rate for such an investment is 14%, what is the before-tax value of the interest subsidy?

f. Projected before-tax income from the Taiwan plant is $1 million annually, beginning at the end of the first year. Taiwan's corporate tax rate is 25%, and there is a 20% dividend withholding tax. However, Taiwan will exempt the plant's income from corporate tax (but not withholding tax) for the first five years. If Xebec plans to remit all income as dividends back to the United States, how much is the tax holiday worth?

g. An alternative sourcing option is to shut down all domestic production and contract to have Xebec's products built for it by a foreign supplier in a country such as Japan. What are some of the potential advantages and disadvantages of foreign contracting vis-à-vis manufacturing in a wholly owned foreign subsidiary?

■ BIBLIOGRAPHY ■

Lessard, Donald R. "Evaluating Foreign Projects: An Adjusted Present Value Approach." In *International Financial Management*, 2nd. ed. Donald R. Lessard, ed. New York: John Wiley & Sons, 1985.

Shapiro, Alan C. "Capital Budgeting for the Multinational Corporation." *Financial Management*, Spring 1978, pp. 7–16.

———. "International Capital Budgeting." *Midland Journal of Corporate Finance*, Spring 1983, pp. 26–45.

◾ 19 ◾

The Cost of Capital for Foreign Investments

Traders and other undertakers may, no doubt, with great propriety, carry on a very considerable part of their projects with borrowed money. In justice to their creditors, however, their own capital ought to be, in this case, sufficient to ensure, if I may say so, the capital of those creditors; or to render it extremely improbable that those creditors should incur any loss, even though the success of the project should fall very short of the expectations of the projectors.

—Adam Smith (1776)—

◾ A central question for the multinational corporation (MNC) is whether the required rate of return on foreign projects should be higher, lower, or the same as that for domestic projects. To answer this question, we must examine the issue of cost of capital for multinational firms, one of the most complex in international financial management. Yet, it is an issue that must be addressed because the foreign investment decision cannot be made properly without knowledge of the appropriate cost of capital.

In this chapter we will seek to determine the cost-of-capital figure(s) that should be used in appraising the profitability of foreign investments. By definition, the cost of capital for a given investment is the minimum risk-adjusted return required by shareholders of the firm for undertaking that investment. As such, it is the basic measure of financial performance. Unless the investment generates sufficient funds to repay suppliers of capital, the firm's value will suffer. This return requirement is met only if the net present value of future project cash flows, using the project's cost of capital as the discount rate, is positive.

The development of appropriate cost-of-capital measures for multinational firms is closely bound up with how those measures will be used. Since they are to be used as discount rates to aid in the global resource allocation process, the rates must reflect the value to firms of engaging in specific activities. Thus, the emphasis here is on the cost of capital or required rate of return for a specific foreign project rather than for the firm as a whole. Unless the financial structures and commercial risks are similar for all projects engaged in, the use of a single overall cost of capital for project evaluation is incorrect. Different discount rates should be used to value projects that are expected to change the risk complexion of the firm.

■ 19.1 ■
THE COST OF EQUITY CAPITAL

The *cost of equity capital* for a firm is the minimum rate of return necessary to induce investors to buy or hold the firm's stock. This required return equals a basic yield covering the time value of money plus a premium for risk. Because owners of common stock have only a residual claim on corporate income, their risk is the greatest, and so also are the returns they demand.

Alternatively, the cost of equity capital is the rate used to capitalize total corporate cash flows. As such, it is just the weighted average of the required rates of return on the firm's individual activities. From this perspective, the corporation is a mutual fund of specified projects, selling a compound security to capital markets. According to the principle of value additivity, the value of this compound security equals the sum of the individual values of the projects.

Although both definitions are equivalent, the latter view is preferred from a conceptual standpoint because it focuses attention on the most important feature of the cost of equity capital; namely, that this cost is not an attribute of the firm per se, but is a function of the riskiness of the activities it engages in. Thus, the cost of equity capital for the firm as a whole can be used to value the stream of future equity cash flows—that is, to set a price on equity shares in the firm. It cannot be used as a measure of the required return on equity investments in future projects unless these projects are of a similar nature to the average of those already being undertaken by the firm.

One approach to determining the project-specific required return on equity is based on modern capital market theory. According to this theory, an equilibrium relationship exists between an asset's required return and its associated risk, which can be represented by the capital asset pricing model (CAPM):

$$r_i = r_f + \beta_i(r_m - r_f) \tag{19.1}$$

where r_i = equilibrium expected return for asset i
   r_f = rate of return on a risk-free asset, usually measured as the yield on a 30-day U.S. government Treasury bill
   r_m = expected return on the market portfolio consisting of all risky assets
   β_i = cov $(r_i, r_m)/\sigma^2(r_m)$, where cov (r_i, r_m) refers to the covariance between returns on security i and the market portfolio and $\sigma^2(r_m)$ is the variance of returns on the market portfolio

The CAPM is based on the notion that intelligent risk-averse shareholders will seek to diversify their risks, and as a consequence, the only risk that will be rewarded with a risk premium will be systematic risk. As can be seen from Equation 19.1, the risk premium associated with a particular asset i is assumed to equal $\beta_i(r_m - r_f)$, where β_i is the *systematic* or *nondiversifiable* risk of the asset. In effect, β measures the correlation between returns on a particular asset and returns on the market portfolio. The term $r_m - r_f$ is known as the *market risk premium.*

Where the returns and financial structure of an investment are expected to be similar to those of the firm's typical investment, the corporate-wide cost of equity capital may serve as a reasonable proxy for the required return on equity of the project. In this case, estimates of the value of the project's β can be found either by direct computation using the CAPM or through professional investment companies that keep track of company βs.

One check on the required return derived from the CAPM is to compare it with the cost of equity capital obtained from the dividend valuation model. According to this model,

$$P_0 = \frac{DIV_1}{k_e - g} \tag{19.2}$$

where k_e = company's cost of equity capital
  DIV_1 = expected dividend in year 1
  P_0 = current stock price
  g = average expected annual dividend growth rate

From Equation 19.2, we can estimate the cost of the equity capital as

$$k_e = \frac{DIV_1}{P_0} + g \tag{19.3}$$

The dividend growth rate, g, can be estimated using either historical data or, if the past is not considered a reliable indicator of future performance, expectations of future earnings and resulting dividends.

It should be emphasized again that estimates of the required return on equity capital, using either of these methods, apply only at the corporate level or to investments with financial characteristics typical of the "pool" of projects represented by the corporation. These cost of equity capital estimates are useless in calculating project-specific required returns on equity when the characteristics of the project diverge from the corporate norm.

■ 19.2 ■
THE WEIGHTED COST OF CAPITAL
FOR FOREIGN PROJECTS

As commonly used, the required return on equity for a particular investment assumes that the financial structure and risk of the project is similar to that for the firm as a whole. This cost of equity capital, k_e, is then combined with the after-tax cost of debt, $i_d(1 - t)$, to yield a weighted cost of capital (WACC) for the parent and the project, k_0, computed as

$$k_0 = (1 - L)k_e + Li_d(1 - t) \tag{19.4}$$

where L is the parent's debt ratio (debt/total assets). This cost of capital is then used as the discount rate in evaluating the specific foreign investment. It should be stressed that k_e is the required return on the firm's stock given the particular debt ratio selected.

Two caveats in employing the weighted average cost of capital are appropriate here. First, the weights must be based on the proportion of the firm's capital structure accounted for by each source of capital using *market,* not *book,* values. Second, in calculating the WACC the firm's historical debt-equity mix is not relevant. Rather, the weights must be marginal weights that reflect the firm's *target capital structure,* that is, the proportions of debt and equity the firm plans to use in the future.

■ ───

ILLUSTRATION

Estimating the Weighted Average Cost of Capital. Suppose a company is financed with 60% common stock, 30% debt, and 10% preferred stock, with respective after-tax costs of 20%, 6%, and 14%. Based on the financing proportions and the after-tax costs of the various capital components, and employing Equation 19.4, the WACC for this firm is calculated as 15.2% $(0.6 \times 0.20 + 0.3 \times 0.06 + 0.1 \times 0.14)$. If the net present value of those cash flows—discounted at the weighted average cost of capital—is positive, the investment should be undertaken; if negative, the investment should be rejected.

─── ■

However, both project risk and project financial structure can vary from the corporate norm. It is necessary, therefore, to adjust the various costs and weights of the different cost components to reflect their actual values.

Costing Various Sources of Funds

Suppose a foreign subsidiary requires *I* dollars to finance a new investment to be funded as follows: *P* dollars by the parent; E_f dollars by the subsidiary's retained earnings; and D_f dollars by foreign debt, with $P + E_f + D_f = I$. To compute the project's weighted cost of capital, it is first necessary to compute the individual cost of each component.

Parent Company Funds. The required rate of return on parent company funds is the firm's marginal cost of capital, k_0. Hence, parent funds invested overseas should yield the parent's marginal cost of capital provided that the foreign investments undertaken do not change the overall riskiness of the MNC's operations. (The effect of risk will be addressed later.)

Retained Earnings. The cost of retained earnings overseas, k_s, is a function of dividend withholding taxes, tax deferral, and transfer costs. In general, if T equals the incremental taxes owed on earnings repatriated to the parent, then $k_s = k_e(1 - T)$.

Local Currency Debt. The after-tax dollar cost of borrowing locally, r_f, equals the sum of the after-tax interest expenses plus the exchange gain or loss. Appendix 19A shows how this cost can be calculated explicitly, given particular assumptions concerning the future course of the exchange rate.

Computing the Weighted Cost of Capital

With no change in risk characteristics, the parent's after-tax cost of debt and equity remain at $i_d(1 - t)$ and k_e, respectively. As introduced above, the subsidiary's cost of retained earnings equals k_s and its expected after-tax dollar cost of foreign debt equals i_f.

Under these circumstances the weighted cost of capital for the project equals

$$k_I = k_0 - a(k_e - k_s) - b[i_d(1 - t) - i_f] \tag{19.5}$$

where $a = E_f/I$ and $b = D_f/I^1$. If this investment changes the parent's risk characteristics in such a way that its cost of equity capital is k_e', rather than k_e, Equation 19.5 becomes instead

$$k_I = k_0 + (1 - L)(k_e' - k_e) - a(k_e' - k_s) - b[i_d(1 - t) - i_f] \tag{19.6}$$

■ ───

ILLUSTRATION

Estimating a Foreign Project's Weighted Average Cost of Capital. Suppose that a new foreign investment requires $100 million in funds. Of this total, $20 million will be provided by parent company funds, $25 million by retained earnings in the subsidiary, and $55 million through the issue of new debt by the subsidiary. The parent's cost of equity equals 14%, and its after-tax cost of debt is 5%. If the firm's current debt ratio, which is considered to be optimal, is 0.3, then k_0 equals 11.3% ($0.14 \times 0.7 + 0.05 \times 0.3$). However, this project has higher systematic risk than the typical investment undertaken by the firm, thereby requiring a rate of return of 16% on new parent equity and 6% on new parent debt. Based on an incremental tax of 8% on repatriated earnings, the cost of retained earnings is estimated to be 14.7% [$0.16 \times (1 - 0.08)$]. Let the nominal LC rate of interest be 20%, with an anticipated average annual devaluation of 7%. Then with a foreign tax rate of 40%, the expected after-tax dollar cost of the LC debt is 4.2% [$0.20 \times (1 - 0.4)(1 - 0.7) - 0.07$].

Applying Equation 19.6, the project's weighted cost of capital is

$$k_I = 0.113 + 0.7(0.16 - 0.14) - [25/100(0.16 - 0.147) - 55/100(0.06 - 0.042)] = 0.114$$

The parent's weighted cost of capital for this project would have been 13% ($0.16 \times 7 + 0.06 \times 0.3$) in the absence of the retained earnings and foreign debt financing. ─── ■

■ 19.3 ■
THE ALL-EQUITY COST OF CAPITAL FOR FOREIGN PROJECTS

The various adjustments needed to go from the weighted average cost of capital for the firm to the weighted average cost of capital for the project makes it a somewhat awkward technique to use at times. An alternative (suggested in Chapter 18) is the use of an all-equity

───────────────

[1]See Alan C. Shapiro, "Financial Structure and the Cost of Capital in the Multinational Corporation," *Journal of Financial and Quantitative Analysis,* June 1978, pp. 211–226.

discount rate, k^*, that abstracts from the project's financial structure and that is based solely on the riskiness of the project's anticipated cash flows.

To calculate the all-equity rate, we rely on the CAPM introduced earlier as Equation 19.1:

$$k^* = r_f + \beta^*(r_m - r_f) \tag{19.7}$$

where β^* is the all-equity beta—that is, the beta associated with the unleveraged cash flows.

■ ───

ILLUSTRATION

Estimating a Foreign Project's Cost of Capital. Suppose that a foreign project has a beta of 1.15, the risk-free return is 13%, and the required return on the market is estimated at 21%. Then based on Equation 19.7, the project's cost of capital is

$$k^* = 0.13 + 1.15(0.21 - 0.13)$$
$$= 22.2\%$$

─── ■

In reality, of course, the firm will not be able to estimate β^* with the degree of precision implied here. Instead, it will have to use guesswork based on theory. The considerations involved in the estimation process are discussed in the following section.

If the project is of similar risk to the average project selected by the firm, it is possible to estimate β^* by reference to the firm's stock price beta, β_e. In other words, β_e is the beta that appears in the estimate of the firm's cost of equity capital, k_e:

$$k_e = r_f + \beta_e[E(r_m) - r_f] \tag{19.8}$$

To transform β_e into β^*, we must separate out the effects of debt financing. This is known as unlevering, or converting a levered equity beta to its unlevered or all-equity value. Unlevering can be accomplished by using the following approximation:

$$\beta^* = \beta_e/[1 + (1 - t)D/E] \tag{19.9}$$

where t is the firm's marginal tax rate, and D/E is its current debt/equity ratio. Thus, for example, if a firm has a stock price beta of 1.1, a debt/equity ratio of 0.6, and a marginal tax rate of 34%, its all-equity beta equals 0.79 [$1.1/(1 + 0.66 \times 0.6)$].

It turns out that the case of similar risk characteristics is an important one in estimating the foreign project cost of capital.

■ 19.4 ■
DISCOUNT RATES FOR FOREIGN INVESTMENTS

The importance of the CAPM for the international firm is that the relevant component of risk in pricing a firm's stock is its systematic risk—that is, that portion of return variability that cannot be eliminated through diversification. Evidence suggests that most of the economic and political risk faced by MNCs is unsystematic risk, which therefore can be eliminated through diversification on the level of the individual investor. While these risks may be quite large, they should not affect the discount rate to be used in valuing foreign projects.

On the other hand, much of the systematic or general market risk affecting a company, at least as measured using a domestic stock index such as the Standard and Poor's 500 or the New York Stock Exchange index, is related to the cyclical nature of the national economy in which the company is domiciled. Consequently, the returns on a project located in a foreign country whose economy is not perfectly synchronous with the home country's economy should be less highly correlated with domestic market returns than the returns on a comparable domestic project. If this is the case, then the systematic risk of a foreign project actually could be lower than the systematic risk of its domestic counterpart.

Paradoxically, it is the less developed countries (LDCs), where political risks are greatest, that are likely to provide the greatest diversification benefits. This is because the economies of LDCs are less closely tied to the United States, or to any other Western economy. By contrast, the correlation among the economic cycles of developed countries is considerably stronger, so the diversification benefits from investing in industrialized countries, from the standpoint of a Western investor are proportionately less.

It should be noted, however, that the systematic risk of projects even in relatively isolated LDCs is unlikely to be far below the average for all projects because these countries are still tied into the world economy. The important point about projects in LDCs, then, is that their ratio of systematic to total risk generally is quite low; their systematic risk, while perhaps slightly lower, is probably not significantly less than that of similar projects located in industrialized countries.

Even if a nation's economy is not closely linked to the world economy, the systematic risk of a project located in that country might still be rather large. For example, a foreign copper mining venture probably will face systematic risk very similar to that faced by an identical extractive project in the United States, whether the foreign project is located in Canada, Chile, or Zaire. The reason is that the major element of systematic risk in any extractive project is related to variations in the price of the mineral being extracted, which is set in a world market. The world market price in turn depends on worldwide demand, which itself is systematically related to the state of the world economy. By contrast, a market-oriented project in an LDC, whose risk depends largely on the evolution of the domestic market in that country, is likely to have a systematic risk that is small both in relative and absolute terms.

An example of the latter would be a Ford plant in Brazil whose profitability is closely linked to the state of the Brazilian economy. The systematic risk of the project, therefore, largely depends on the correlation between the Brazilian economy and the U.S. economy. While positive, this correlation is much less than one.

Thus, *corporate international diversification* should prove beneficial to shareholders, particularly where there are barriers to international portfolio diversification. To the extent that multinational firms are uniquely able to supply low-cost international diversification, investors may be willing to accept a lower rate of return on shares of MNCs than on shares of single-country firms. By extension, the risk premium applied to foreign projects may be lower than the risk premium for domestic ones; that is, the required return on foreign projects may be less than the required return on comparable domestic projects. The net effect may be to enable MNCs to undertake overseas projects that would otherwise be unattractive.

But if *international portfolio diversification* can be accomplished as easily and as cheaply by individual investors, then although required rates of return on MNC securities would be lower to reflect the reduced covariability of MNC returns caused by international diversification, the discount rate would not be reduced further to reflect investors' willingness to pay a premium for the indirect diversification provided by the shares of MNCs. In fact, though, we saw in Chapter 16 that American investors actually undertake very little foreign portfolio investment. The lack of widespread international portfolio diversification has an important implication for estimating the beta coefficient.

Estimating Project Betas

A major issue when selecting a discount rate for foreign investments is the relevant market portfolio for estimating a project's beta coefficient. Is the relevant base portfolio against which beta is measured the domestic portfolio of the investor or the world market portfolio? Selecting the appropriate portfolio matters because a risk that is systematic in the context of the home country market portfolio may well be diversifiable in the context of the world portfolio. If this is the case, using the domestic market portfolio to calculate beta will result in a higher required return—and a less desirable project—than if beta were calculated using the world market portfolio.

The appropriate market portfolio to use in measuring a *project beta* depends on one's view of world capital markets. More precisely, it depends on whether or not capital markets are globally integrated. If they are, then the world portfolio is the correct choice; if they are not, the correct choice is the domestic portfolio. The test of capital market integration depends on whether these assets are priced in a common context; that is, capital markets are integrated to the extent that security prices offer all investors worldwide the same trade-off between systematic risk and real expected return.

The truth probably lies somewhere in between. Capital markets are now integrated to a great extent, and they can be expected to become ever more so with time. However, because of various government regulations and other market imperfections, that integration is not complete. Unfortunately, it is not currently within our power, if indeed it ever will be, to empirically determine the relevant market portfolio and, hence, the correct beta to use in project evaluation. (This problem also arises domestically as well as internationally.)

A pragmatic recommendation to American managers is to measure the betas of international projects against the U.S. market portfolio. This recommendation is based on the following two reasons:

1. It ensures comparability of foreign with domestic projects, which are evaluated using betas that are calculated relative to a U.S. market index.
2. The relatively minor amount of international diversification attempted (as yet) by American investors suggests that the relevant portfolio from their standpoint is the U.S. market portfolio.

This reasoning suggests that the required return on a foreign project may well be lower, and is unlikely to be higher, than the required return on a comparable domestic project. Thus, applying the same discount rate to an overseas project as to a similar domestic project probably will yield a conservative estimate of the relative systematic riskiness of the project.

Using the domestic cost of capital to evaluate overseas investments also is likely to understate the benefits that stem from the ability of foreign activities to reduce the firm's total risk. As we saw in Chapter 1, reducing total risk can increase a firm's cash flows. By confining itself to its domestic market, a firm would be sensitive to periodic downturns associated with the domestic business cycle and other industry-specific factors. By operating in a number of countries, the MNC can trade off negative swings in some countries against positive ones in others. This option is especially valuable for non-American firms, whose local markets are small relative to the efficient scale of operation.

Evidence from the Stock Market

The most careful study to date of the effects of foreign operations on the cost of equity capital is by Ali Fatemi.[2] That study compared the performance of two carefully constructed stock portfolios: a portfolio of 84 MNCs, each with at least 25% of its annual sales generated from international operations; and a portfolio of 52 purely domestic firms. Monthly performance comparisons were made over the five-year period January 1976–December 1980.

Although the validity of the study is limited by the relatively short time period involved, the difficulty in properly matching MNCs with their purely domestic counterparts (most firms do business in more than one industry), and in calculating the degree of sales from abroad (consider the transfer pricing problem, for example), its conclusions are nonetheless of interest.

1. The rates of return on the two portfolios are statistically identical. Ignoring risk, MNCs and uninational (purely domestic) corporations (UNCs) provide shareholders the same returns.
2. Consistent with our expectations, the rates of return on the MNC portfolio fluctuate less than those on the UNC portfolio. Thus, corporate international diversification seems to reduce shareholder total risk and may do the same for the firm's total risk.
3. The betas of the multinational portfolio are significantly lower and more stable than are those of the purely domestic portfolio, indicating that corporate international diversification reduces the degree of systematic risk, at least if systematic risk is calculated relative to the domestic portfolio. It was also found that the higher the degree of international involvement, the lower the beta.

Despite the apparent benefits of corporate international diversification for shareholders, research by Jacquillat and Solnik concluded that although multinational firms do provide some diversification for investors, they are poor substitutes for international portfolio diversification.[3] Their results indicate that an internationally diversified portfolio leads to a

[2]Ali M. Fatemi, "Shareholder Benefits from Corporate International Diversification," *Journal of Finance*, December 1984, pp. 1325–1344.

[3]Bertrand Jacquillat and Bruno H. Solnik, "Multinationals Are Poor Tools for Diversification," *Journal of Portfolio Management*, Winter 1978, pp. 8–12.

much greater reduction in variance than does one comprised of firms with internationally diversified activities. Thus, the advantages of international portfolio diversification remain.

■ 19.5 ■
COMPARING THE COST OF CAPITAL IN THE UNITED STATES AND JAPAN

According to conventional wisdom, U.S. companies have a much higher cost of capital than Japanese companies, up to twice as high. Many economists and business executives often cite these differences in the cost of capital to explain why Japanese companies outspend their U.S. competitors in plant modernization and research and development.[4] The argument is that capital in the United States is too expensive to justify huge investments in automated equipment, new factories, and cutting-edge research with longer-term payoffs. Conversely, Japanese companies with their lower cost of capital logically focus less on short-term profits and emphasize investments, even riskier ones, that are designed to promote the creation of dominant positions in the marketplace.

The evidence to support these contentions includes the short-term focus of U.S. executives and markets, higher U.S. interest rates, high debt ratios in Japan that allow Japanese companies to substitute cheap debt for equity, and sky-high Japanese price/earnings (P/E) ratios. However, there may be less here than meets the eye.

Short-Term Orientation

Current thinking by many business leaders is that the best way to boost the stock price is to boost short-term earnings by cutting back on capital spending and research and development. Accordingly, U.S. companies that dare to undertake long-term investments that improve their longer-term prospects but hurt short-term profits are penalized by the stock market. By contrast, Japanese companies, it is said, have more patient investors and are, therefore, better able to take a long-run view and make the expensive investments in R&D and factory automation that will improve their long-term competitive position.

But the notion that the way to lift a company's stock price is to pump up short-term earnings by skipping attractive long-term investments assumes that the market systematically undervalues future earnings. Fortunately for U.S. competitiveness, the evidence overwhelmingly supports the ability of investors to peer far into the future and discern the effect of current management actions on the firm's true economic status over time. There is also strong evidence that the stock market takes a long-run view of capital expenditures and investments in R&D. McConnell and Muscarella studied the stock market's responses to public announcements of changes in corporate capital budgets.[5] They found that stock prices rose when companies increased their capital budgets and dropped when companies cut their

---

[4]See, for example, the comments in Louis S. Richman, "How Capital Costs Are Crippling America," *Fortune*, August 14, 1989, pp. 50–54.

[5]John J. McConnell and Chris J. Muscarella, "Corporate Capital Expenditure Decisions and the Market Value of the Firm," *Journal of Financial Economics*, September 1985, pp. 399–422.

capital budgets. Similarly, Jarrell, Lehn, and Marr studied the market's reaction to public announcements that companies were embarking on new R&D projects. They found that stock prices increased by an average of 1%–2% when companies increased their R&D spending.[6]

In short, managers may be shortsighted; markets are not. The basic problem is that most executive reward systems stress current period profits rather than shareholder wealth creation. Only a minority of firms use return to shareholders as one of the measures of financial performance. Thus, while some managers are underpaid and others overpaid, most are mispaid—with pay and bonus tied to accounting profits instead of the value they create for shareholders.

High U.S. Interest Rates

Although interest rates are higher in the United States than in Japan, this difference is deceptive since it is based on nominal and not real interest rates. The differential largely disappears once allowance is made for inflation and taxes. One cost of capital study found that during the second half of the 1980s, real after-tax debt costs were virtually identical for the United States (1.85%), Japan (1.82%), and Britain (1.82%).[7] Exhibit 19.1 shows the convergence of real U.S. and Japanese interest rates over the period 1973–1989.

The evidence provided by Exhibit 19.1 is consistent with the behavior of Japanese companies during the 1980s, when they raised over $125 billions overseas—behavior that would be inexplicable if more attractive terms were available at home. And, if yen debt was really less expensive than dollar debt, why would U.S. companies not borrow yen? Indeed, taking into account currency changes, dollars have been much less expensive to borrow than yen during the 1980s.

High Japanese Leverage

Many observers point to high Japanese leverage as another source of their capital cost advantage. Because the tax deductibility of interest makes debt cheaper than equity, Japanese companies are said to have a lower weighted average cost of capital. However, this conclusion suffers from three basic problems. First, the measurement of debt/equity (D/E) ratios is usually done with book values, instead of market values. Book values are especially tricky things to use for cross-country comparisons. Different accounting conventions and other practices distort them. For example, Japanese companies value land on their balance sheet at cost. The phenomenal rise in Tokyo property prices in recent years can mean that

[6]Gregg A. Jarrell, Kenneth Lehn, and Wayne Marr, "Institutional Ownership, Tender Offers, and Long-Term Investments," The Office of the Chief Economist, Securities and Exchange Commission, April 19, 1985. Additional evidence of the market's positive response to value-creating capital investments is provided by J. Randall Woolridge, "Competitive Decline: Is a Myopic Stock Market to Blame?" *Journal of Applied Corporate Finance,* Spring 1988, pp. 26–36.

[7]Robert N. McCauley and Steven A. Zimmer, "Explaining International Differences in the Cost of Capital," *FRBNY Quarterly Review,* Summer 1989, pp. 7–27.

■ **EXHIBIT 19.1**   Japanese and U.S. Government Bond Yields, 1973–1989

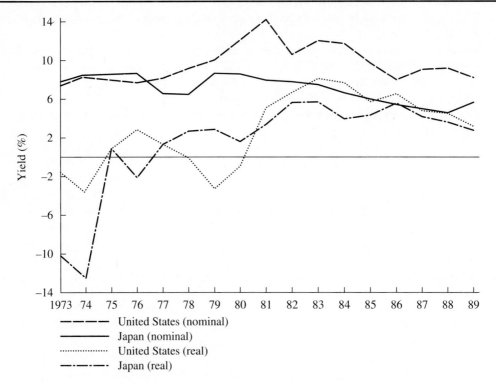

SOURCE: Based on Niso Abuaf and Kathleen Carmody, "The Cost of Capital in Japan and the United States: A Tale of Two Markets," Salomon Brothers, July 1990, p. 4.

the market value is up to 100 times the book value, seriously understating the debt-to-equity ratios of Japanese companies on a replacement cost basis.

Using market value weights, Japanese leverage has systematically fallen and U.S. leverage systematically risen during the past decade. Exhibit 19.2 illustrates this phenomenon with aggregate data for the period 1971–1989. By 1989, the U.S. D/E ratio had surpassed the Japanese ratio. Even though the plunge in the Tokyo Stock Exchange during 1990 has raised Japanese leverage on a market value basis, the trend is clearly moving in the opposite direction.[8]

Second, the measurement of leverage must adjust for the excess cash that many Japanese firms hold. According to Michael Jensen, "Many of Japan's public companies are flooded with free cash flow far in excess of their opportunities to invest in profitable internal growth.

---

[8]Two studies found that Japanese firms are no more highly levered than American firms when equity is valued at market instead of book. See Allen Michel and Israel Shaked, "Japanese Leverage: Myth or Reality," *Financial Analysts Journal,* Winter 1985, pp. 61–67; and Carl W. Kester, "Capital and Ownership Structure: A Comparison of United States and Japanese Manufacturing Corporations," *Financial Management,* Spring 1986, pp. 17–24.

In 1987, more than 40% of Japan's large public companies had no net bank borrowings—that is, cash balances larger than their short- and long-term borrowings."[9] In addition, Japanese firms give banks "compensating balances" in the form of deposits in order to borrow from them. On average, a Japanese firm wanting to borrow ¥100 will have to borrow ¥160 and place ¥60 on deposit with its bank. This practice boosts the Japanese corporate sector's measured debt ratio while leaving unchanged its actual degree of financial risk.

To estimate leverage, excess cash must be subtracted from debt. This procedure is employed in Exhibit 19.3 to estimate leverage ratios for selected large U.S. and Japanese multinationals. Note that four of the nine Japanese firms have negative leverage when excess cash is subtracted. And the 50% difference in leverage between Kodak and Fuji Photo underscores the importance of comparing leverage between direct competitors as opposed to market aggregates.

Third, as pointed out earlier, the appropriate weights in the WACC must reflect the target capital structure, not historical figures. As Exhibit 19.2 shows, since the late 1970s, U.S. companies have taken on more and more debt whereas Japanese firms have been deleverag-

■ **EXHIBIT 19.2**   Japanese and U.S. Debt-to-Equity Ratios, 1971–1989

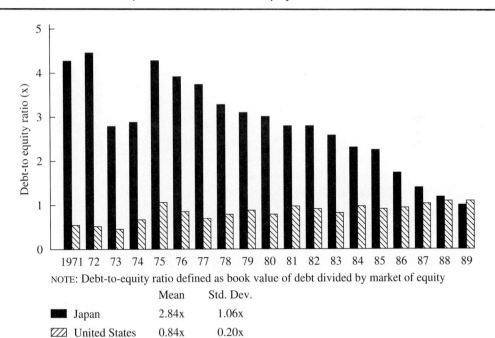

NOTE: Debt-to-equity ratio defined as book value of debt divided by market of equity

	Mean	Std. Dev.
■ Japan	2.84x	1.06x
▨ United States	0.84x	0.20x

SOURCE: Niso Abuaf and Kathleen Carmody, "The Cost of Capital in Japan and the United States: A Tale of Two Markets," Salomon Brothers, July 1990, p. 7.

---

[9]Michael C. Jensen, "Eclipse of the Public Corporation," *Harvard Business Review,* September–October 1989, p. 73.

■ **EXHIBIT 19.3**   Comparing Leverage for Selected U.S. and Japanese Companies, 1989

	Unadjusted Book Leverage*	Adjusted Market Leverage**
Japanese Companies		
TDK	28%	2%
Sony	25%	5%
Pioneer	20%	−1%
NEC	61%	24%
Matsushita	33%	3%
Kyocera	17%	−20%
Hitachi	37%	−3%
Fuji Photo	14%	−13%
Canon	50%	5%
9 Company Average	32%	0%
U.S. Companies		
IBM	25%	15%
DEC	2%	−13%
HP	12%	5%
NCR	18%	0%
Intel	21%	−3%
Kodak	56%	36%
Polaroid	63%	3%
Xerox	58%	55%
Westinghouse	34%	18%
GE	24%	9%
10 Company Average	31%	12%
U.S. Industrials	42%	25%

*Leverage defined as interest bearing debt (IBD) + book equity

**Adjusted for excess cash and market value of equity

SOURCE: Value-line and Marakon Associates

ing. It appears that target weights for debt are now lower for Japanese firms than for American firms.

To the extent that Japanese firms do have a leverage advantage, it stems in part from the way in which each nation's firms relate to the banking system. Almost all big Japanese companies have one main bank that is their primary source of long-term loans. The main bank will have access to information about the company and have a say in its management that in most other countries would be unacceptable. Moreover, Japanese banks, unlike their U.S. counterparts, can hold industrial shares. So, the main bank often holds a sizable amount of the equity of its borrowers. For example, until recently, Japanese banks owned nearly 40% of the outstanding stock of Japanese manufacturing companies. Thus, for Japanese companies, the strong relation with one main bank is their main method of minimizing the risk of financial distress. In the United States, where corporate bank relations are less intimate, companies rely primarily on equity as a shock absorber.

■ ───

ILLUSTRATION

Toyo Kogyo and Chrysler Experience Financial Distress. The contrasting experiences of Toyo Kogyo (producer of Mazda cars) and Chrysler during recent periods of financial distress illustrate the unusual features of the Japanese financial system. In 1973, Toyo Kogyo (TK) was a successful producer of light and medium-sized cars. The energy crisis of 1974 precipitated a crisis at TK because of the high energy consumption of its rotary-engine Wankel powered Mazda models. Worldwide sales plunged 19%. To weather the storm, TK required a massive infusion of funds to develop new product offerings. Sumitomo Bank, its main bank, had the resources to rescue TK. Based on its thorough knowledge of TK's operations, Sumitomo decided that the company could be profitable with new product offerings and massive cost cutting. But because it lacked confidence in TK's senior management, Sumitomo replaced them. With its own hand-picked executives in place, Sumitomo then financed the simultaneous development of three new models and the overhaul of TK's production system. The new models were highly successful and labor productivity grew by 118% over the next seven years.

In contrast to the situation at TK, Chrysler was able to persist with poor performance for over two decades because its investors had no effective remedies. Chrysler could ignore the need to restructure its operations due to its continued ability to borrow money (because it still had a substantial, though dwindling, amount of shareholders' equity to support these loans). Despite the activities of some dissident shareholders, Chrysler continued under a self-perpetuating management until the crisis of 1979. Although Chrysler faced bankruptcy, its banks refused to lend it more money. In contrast to TK's Japanese banks, Chrysler's banks had an incomplete understanding of its plight and no way to obtain all the essential information. Even if they had, they could not have sent in the same type of rescue team that Sumitomo sent into TK. In the end, Chrysler was rescued by the U.S. government, which offered loan guarantees sufficient for the company's survival at about half its former size.

─── ■

The price that Japanese and German companies pay for their heavy reliance on bank debt is less freedom of action. As the cost of accessing the capital markets directly has dropped, the main-bank relationship is gradually eroding in Japan and Germany, and Japanese and German companies are looking more to the equity market as their cushion against financial distress. The pace of change has accelerated in Japan because of a new law that forced Japanese banks to reduce their shareholdings in individual companies to 5% or less by December 1987.

High Japanese Price/Earnings Ratios

Finally, the high Japanese P/E ratios shown in Exhibit 19.4. are said to "prove" that Japanese firms have a lower cost of equity capital. Having peaked at over 60 times, Japanese

■ **EXHIBIT 19.4**   Price-to-Earnings Ratios, January 1973–April 1990

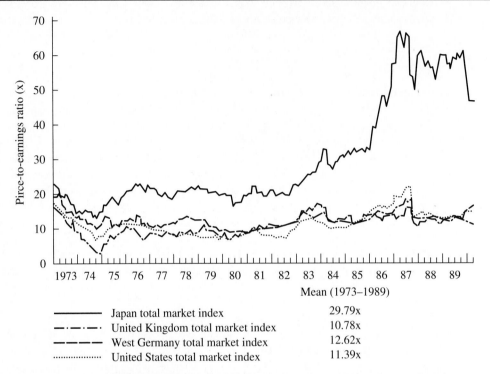

	Mean (1973–1989)
——— Japan total market index	29.79x
—·—·—· United Kingdom total market index	10.78x
— — — West Germany total market index	12.62x
·············· United States total market index	11.39x

SOURCE: Niso Abuaf and Kathleen Carmody, "The Cost of Capital in Japan and the United States: A Tale of Two Markets," Salomon Brothers, July 1990, p. 8.

P/E multiples in the mid-40s are still much higher than those in other major countries despite the sharp decline in the Japanese market during 1990.

Assuming a zero growth rate in profits, and a 100% dividend payout rate, Equation 19.3 shows that a P/E ratio of 40 implies a 2.5% cost of equity capital, while a P/E ratio of 12 (the average for U.S. firms) implies that $k_e = 8.33\%$. Taken at face value, therefore, the high Japanese P/E ratios do suggest a low cost of equity capital. But this conclusion ignores the role of growth in pricing stocks. To the extent that the profits of Japanese firms are expected to grow more rapidly than those of U.S. companies, Japanese companies should have higher P/E ratios even with an identical cost of equity capital. But even after adjusting for higher Japanese earnings growth, Japanese companies still appear to have a lower cost of equity capital.

The use of unadjusted P/E ratios also fails to take into account the extensive crossholding—ownership by affiliated companies—of Japanese shares and consequent understatement of corporate earnings. This understatement arises because a Japanese firm that owns less than a 20% share of another company does not include the latter company's retained earnings in its own reported earnings.

An alternative approach to estimating the Japanese cost of equity capital is based on modern finance theory, which relies on the CAPM and observed returns. The observed returns, taken over a 15- to 20-year period are assumed to approximate expected returns, and so can be used to infer the market risk premium that enters the CAPM. Based on the high returns historically from investing in the Japanese market, the estimated equity risk premium is substantially higher for Japan than for the United States. After deleveraging the Japanese market to put it on a comparable basis with the U.S. market (using the formula provided in Equation 19.9), one study found that the equity risk premiums appear to be about the same in both markets (3.44% in Japan versus 3.45% in the United States).[10] With U.S. and Japanese real interest rates approximately the same, this should give Japanese and U.S. companies the same cost of capital.

Where does that leave us? Three separate studies that made various combinations of these adjustments all concluded that Japanese companies have a cost of capital advantage on the order of 1.5% to 3%.[11] They also concluded that this gap is closing. That is not surprising, considering that it would be foolish for Japanese investors to continue investing in Japanese securities expected to earn several percentage points less than U.S. securities when they can easily invest in the United States.

Nonetheless, it does appear that American companies face a cost of capital disadvantage, at least in the near future. And although this differential is much lower than those that are based on unadjusted data, there are situations where a small cost of capital differential can have a large strategic impact.

A cost of capital disadvantage is most harmful in capital intensive industries where companies compete primarily on price. For example, a cost of capital differential is much more important in the auto industry than in the software business. Moreover, capital cost differences are more important for the economy car segment of the market than for the luxury car segment.

Companies have several ways to deal with a cost of capital disadvantage. First, companies can attempt to reduce the capital intensity of the business. This can often be accomplished by reducing working capital and changing the production process. Second, as with currency risk management, companies can attempt to increase product differentiation and, thereby, reduce the price sensitivity of its output.

Perhaps the most important advice to U.S. companies is to recognize both the costs of not undertaking investments in factory modernization and new technology as well as the growth options that these investments often create. Many financial economists now believe that undervaluing such growth options is a major reason why U.S. corporations often underinvest in new products and processes. As we saw in Chapter 18, such follow-up projects, which create options on investments in other products, markets, or production processes, are sometimes referred to as *growth options* and may be an important component

---

[10]See Niso Abuaf and Kathleen Carmody, "The Cost of Capital in Japan and the United States: A Tale of Two Markets," Salomon Brothers, Financial Strategy Group, July 1990.

[11]These studies include McCauley and Zimmer, "Explaining International Differences in the Cost of Capital;" Abouf and Carmody, "The Cost of Capital in Japan and the United States: A Tale of Two Markets;'' and Ronald K. Langford, "The Cost of Capital in the U.S. and Japan: Comparisons and Implications," *Commentary,* Marakon Associates, Fall 1989, pp. 11–20.

of firm value. For example, an auto company may give up on ceramic engines because they seem technically infeasible. Meanwhile, a Japanese rival who makes ordinary ceramic parts with the aim of one day using that knowledge to build a ceramic engine can quickly change the competitive balance.

■ 19.6 ■
ILLUSTRATION: INTERNATIONALIZING THE COST OF CAPITAL OF NOVO INDUSTRI

Capital market segmentation implies that the same firm raising debt or equity funds in different national capital markets may face a different cost of capital as a result of diverging investor perceptions between domestic and foreign shareholders or of asymmetry in tax policies, exchange controls, and political risks. Indeed, a firm based in a fully segmented capital market is likely to have a higher cost of capital due to a relatively depressed price for its stock than if it had access to fully integrated capital markets. A good illustration of how a company can overcome such segmentation barriers in order to effectively reduce its cost of capital is provided by Novo Industri, the Danish multinational firm that is a recognized industry leader in the manufacturing of industrial enzymes and pharmaceuticals (mostly insulin) in Western Europe.[12]

Novo perceived it had a high cost of capital relative to its foreign competitors for several reasons. First, Danish investors were prohibited from investing in foreign stocks. Since Danish stock price movements are closely correlated with each other, Danish investors bore a great deal of systematic risk, raising their required returns. Second, Denmark taxed capital gains on stocks at prohibitive rates, reducing stock turnover and hence liquidity. These effects combined to greatly increase the pre-tax return required by Danish investors. Finally, foreign investors were quite unfamiliar with the Danish market, thereby reducing their incentive to arbitrage away the high returns available on Danish stocks.

In 1977, Novo embarked on an ambitious strategy aimed at internationalizing its cost of capital in order to be in a position to better compete with its major multinational rivals such as Eli Lilly (United States), Miles Laboratory (United States-based but a subsidiary of the giant chemical conglomerate Bayer, headquartered in West Germany), and Gist Brocades (the Netherlands).

The first step was for Novo to float a $20 million convertible Eurobond issue (1978). In connection with this offering, it listed its shares on the London Stock Exchange (1979) to facilitate conversion and to gain visibility among foreign investors. Next, Novo decided to capitalize on the emerging interest among U.S. investors for biotechnology companies. It ran a seminar in New York (1980) and then sponsored an American Depository Receipts system and listed its shares on the U.S. over-the-counter market (NASDAQ, in 1981).

Having gained significant visibility among both the London and New York investment communities, Novo was ready to take the final and most difficult step—floating an equity issue on the New York Stock Exchange. Under the guidance of Goldman Sachs, a prospectus

---

[12]Adapted from *Internationalizing the Cost of Capital* by Arthur I. Stonehill and Kare B. Dullum (New York: Wiley, 1982) by Laurent L. Jacque and Alan C. Shapiro.

was prepared for SEC registration of a U.S. stock offering and eventual listing on the NYSE. On July 8, 1981, Novo became the first Scandinavian firm to successfully sell stock through a public issue in the United States.

Exhibit 19.5 illustrates how the price of Novo's B shares increased dramatically between the issue of the convertible Eurobond (1978) and the equity issue on the New York Stock Exchange (1981). This gain in share price correlates highly with, and is probably a result of, steady foreign buying. Indeed by July 1981, foreign ownership of Novo's B shares exceeded 50% as Danish investors were more than willing to sell a stock that many considered to be grossly and increasingly overvalued; at the same time, foreign investors—mostly from the United States—were ready to step up their investment in a stock that they considered to be either grossly undervalued or a suitable vehicle for international diversification. As its P/E ratio had more than tripled from 9 to 31, Novo was successful in sourcing much needed capital to better compete with its foreign rivals.[13]

■ **EXHIBIT 19.5**   Novo's B Share Prices Compared to Stock Market Indexes, 1977–1982

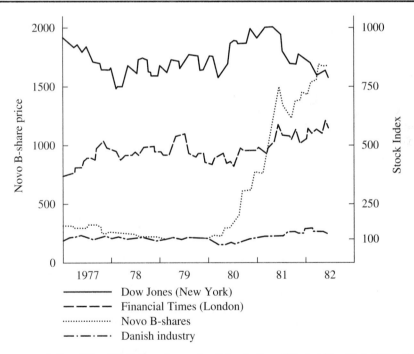

SOURCE: A. Stonehill and K. Dullum, *Internationalizing the Cost of Capital* (New York: Wiley, 1982). Copyright © 1982. Reproduced by permission of John Wiley and Sons Limited.

[13]This is, of course, an illustration, and not a proof, of how selling securities to foreign investors can effect the cost of capital for a firm.

■ 19.7 ■
SUMMARY AND CONCLUSIONS

Analysis of the available evidence on the impact of foreign operations on firm riskiness suggests that if there is an effect, that effect is generally to reduce both actual and perceived riskiness. These results indicate that corporations should continue investing abroad as long as there are profitable opportunities there. Retrenching because it is believed that investors desire smaller international operations is likely to lead to the foregoing of profitable foreign investments that would be rewarded, instead of penalized, by the firm's shareholders. At the very least, executives of multinational firms should seriously question the use of a risk premium to account for the added political and economic risks of overseas operations, when evaluating prospective foreign investments.

The use of any risk premium ignores the fact that the risk of an overseas investment in the context of the firm's other investments, domestic as well as foreign, will be less than the project's total risk. How much less depends on how highly correlated are the outcomes of the firm's different investments. Thus, the automatic inclusion of a premium for risk when evaluating a foreign project is not a necessary element of conservatism; rather, it is a management short cut that is unlikely to benefit the firm's shareholders. Some investments, however, are more risk-prone than are others, and these risks must be accounted for. Chapter 18, on capital budgeting, presented a method for conducting the necessary risk analysis for foreign investments when the foreign risks were unsystematic. This chapter showed how the necessary adjustments in project discount rates can be made, using the capital asset pricing model, when those additional foreign risks are systematic in nature.

■ QUESTIONS ■

1. Should the cost of capital for the IDC-U.K. project presented in Chapter 18 be higher, lower, or the same as the cost of capital for a similar project to manufacture and sell diesel engines in the United States? Explain.

2. Comment on the following statement: "There is a curious contradiction in corporate finance theory: Since equity is more expensive than debt, highly leveraged subsidiaries should be assigned a low hurdle rate. But when the highly leveraged subsidiaries are in risky nations, country risk dictates just the opposite: a high hurdle rate."

3. Comment on the following statement: "Our conglomerate recognizes that foreign investments have a very low covariance with our domestic operations and, thus, are a good source of diversification. We do not 'penalize' potential foreign investments with a high discount rate but, rather, use a discount rate just 3% above the prevailing riskless rate."

4. Major Tokyo Stock Exchange issues sell for an average 60 times earnings, more than four times the 13.8 price-earnings ratio for the S&P 500. According to *Business Week* (February 12, 1990, p. 76), "Since p-e ratios are a guide to a company's cost of equity capital, this valuation gap implies that raising new equity costs Japanese companies less than 2% a year, vs. an average 7% for the U.S." Comment on this statement.

■ PROBLEMS ■

1. A firm with a corporate-wide debt/equity ratio of 1:2, an after-tax cost of debt of 7%, and a cost of equity capital of 15% is interested in pursuing a foreign project. The debt capacity of the project is the same as for the company as a whole, but its systematic risk is such that the required return on equity is estimated to be about 12%. The after-tax cost of debt is expected to remain at 7%.

   a. What is the project's weighted average cost of capital? How does it compare with the parent's WACC?

   b. If the project's equity beta is 1.21, what is its unlevered beta?

2. Suppose that a foreign project has a beta of 0.85, the risk-free return is 12%, and the required return on the market is estimated at 19%. What is the cost of capital for the project?

■ APPENDIX 19A ■

CALCULATING LONG-TERM DEBT COSTS

Chapter 12 showed that the after-tax expected dollar cost to a foreign affiliate of a one-year foreign currency loan equals $r_f(1-d)(1-t)-d$, where r_f is the interest rate, d is the expected foreign currency devaluation relative to the dollar, and t is the local tax rate. The after-tax cost of borrowing dollars at an interest rate of r_{us} was similarly shown to equal $r_{us}(1-t)-dt$, assuming foreign exchange losses are tax deductible locally. When $r_{us} = r_f(1-d)-d$, the company is indifferent between borrowing dollars or the foreign currency.

This appendix shows how to calculate the dollar costs of long-term debt, both before and after tax. While the tax factor is often crucial, governments and other nontaxpaying borrowers are important users of Eurobonds and Eurocredits, and taxation is not relevant in their case.[1]

■ 19A.1 ■ NO TAXES

Assume a firm can borrow dollars or the local (foreign) currency for n years at fixed interest rates of r_{us} and r_f, respectively. Interest is to be paid at the end of each year, and the principal will be repaid in a lump sum at the end of year n. If P is the principal amount in local currency of the foreign currency loan and e_i is the dollar value of the foreign currency at the end of year i, then the effective dollar cost of the foreign currency debt, in the absence of taxes, is the solution, r, to Equation 19A.1:

$$-Pe_0 + \sum_{i=1}^{n} \frac{r_f P e_i}{(1+r)^i} + \frac{P e_i}{(1+r)^n} = 0 \qquad (19A.1)$$

In other words, r is the internal rate of return, or yield, on the foreign currency-denominated bond. The yield on the dollar debt remains at r_{us}. With flotation costs of s per dollar's worth of foreign currency, the first term in Equation 19A.1 would become $-Pe_0(1-s)$. In general, the equation can be solved for r only by using techniques of numerical analysis (unless you happen to have a calculator with an internal rate of return function). Its application is illustrated in the following example.

---

[1] The equations in this appendix are elaborated in Alan C. Shapiro, "The Impact of Taxation on the Currency-of-Denomination Decision for Long-Term Borrowing and Lending," *Journal of International Business Studies,* Spring–Summer 1984, pp. 15–25.

■ ───

ILLUSTRATION

Evaluating DMR's Long-Term Financing Choices. Suppose DMR Inc. is planning to float a seven-year, $30 million bond issue. It has the choice of having its Swiss subsidiary borrow dollars at a coupon rate of 9.625% or Swiss francs at 3.5%. Both bond issues are sold at par. The flotation costs are 3% for the Swiss franc issue and 1.2% for the dollar issue, leading to an effective rate of 4% for the Swiss franc debt and 9.87% for the dollar debt. Repayment is in a lump sum at the end of year seven.

The current exchange rate is 1.75 Swiss francs to the dollar. Thus, DMR can either borrow $30 million or SFr 52,500,000. If the following exchange rates and dollar servicing requirements listed in Exhibit 19A.1 are forecast for the coming seven years, which issue is preferable?

Using Equation 19A.1 (and adjusting for flotation costs), the effective cost of the Swiss franc issue, given the expected dollar depreciation of approximately 6.1% compounded annually, turns out to equal 10.31%. The effective cost of the dollar debt remains at 9.87%. To minimize expected dollar costs, therefore, DMR should issue dollar debt. The break-even rate of annual dollar decline at which DMR should just be indifferent between borrowing dollars or Swiss francs equal 5.64%. ■

Annual Revaluation

Making such detailed currency projections is generally not done, given the uncertainties involved. Instead, it is simpler to project an average rate of currency change over the life of the debt and to calculate effective dollar costs on that basis. For example, suppose the foreign currency is expected to revalue (devalue) relative to the dollar at a steady rate of g per annum (i.e., one dollar's worth of foreign currency today will be worth $(1 + g)^i$ dollars at the end of i years). Then, the interest expense in year i per dollar's worth of foreign currency borrowed today equals $r_f(1 + g)^i$ while the principal repayment is $(1 + g)^n$.

The present value of the cash flow per dollar of foreign currency financing discounted at r equals

$$-1 + \sum_{i=1}^{n} \frac{r_f(1 + g)^i}{(1 + r)^i} + \frac{(1 + g)^n}{(1 + r)^n} = 0 \qquad \textbf{(19A.2)}$$

■ **EXHIBIT 19A.1**   Cash Flows Associated with Swiss Franc Debt

Year	Cash-Flow Category	Swiss Franc Cash Flow (1)	÷	Rate of Exchange (2)	=	Dollar Cash Flow (3)
0	Bond sale	−52,500,000		1.75		−30,000,000.00
	Flotation charge	1,575,000		1.75		900,000.00
1	Interest	1,837,500		1.665		1,103,603.60
2	Interest	1,837,500		1.580		1,162,974.68
3	Interest	1,837,500		1.495		1,229,097.00
4	Interest	1,837,500		1.410		1,303,191.49
5	Interest	1,837,500		1.325		1,386,792.45
6	Interest	1,837,500		1.240		1,481,854.84
7	Interest	1,837,500		1.155		1,590,909.09
	Principal repayment	SFr 52,500,000		1.155		$45,454,545.45

The effective yield, r, equals $r_f(1 + g) + g$. This is the same as the cost of a one-period foreign currency loan that devalues by an amount g during the period. Thus, in order for the yield on the foreign currency-denominated bond to equal r_{us}, it is necessary that

$$r_{us} = r_f(1 + g) + g \qquad \text{(19A.3)}$$

For instance, if $r_{us} = 9\%$ and the currency is expected to appreciate at a rate of 3% annually (i.e., $g = 3\%$), then the break-even value of r_f is 5.83%. In other words, if r_f is greater than 5.83%, it would be cheaper to borrow dollars, and vice versa if r_f is less than 5.83%. If $r_f = 5.83\%$, the firm should be indifferent between the two currencies.

■ 19A.2 ■ TAXES

Chapter 2 demonstrated that international covered interest arbitrage normally ensures that the annualized forward exchange premium or discount equals the nominal yield differential between debt denominated in different currencies. Moreover, in an efficient market, the forward premium or discount should equal the expected rate of change of the exchange rate (adjusted for risk). Therefore, in the absence of taxes, corporations willing to base decisions solely on expected costs should be indifferent between issuing debt in one currency or another.

The presence of taxes, however, distorts the interest arbitrage relationships that have already been developed, since interest rates that were at parity before tax may no longer be so after tax. This presents a new decision problem for international financial executives. The discussion now turns to some of the alternative tax treatments of exchange gains and losses arising from foreign currency loans and how these tax effects can be integrated into the computation of effective after-tax differences in the costs of borrowing in different currencies.

In general, using the same notation as before and letting t be the foreign tax rate, the after-tax yield on a foreign currency-denominated bond issued by a local affiliate can be found as the solution, r, to Equation 19A.4:

$$-Pe_0 + \sum_{i=1}^{n} \frac{r_f Pe_i(1-t)}{(1+r)^i} + \frac{Pe_i}{(1+r)^n} = 0 \qquad \text{(19A.4)}$$

Similarly, the effective after-tax cost of dollar debt is the solution, k, to Equation 19A.5:

$$-L + \sum_{i=1}^{n} \frac{r_{us}L(1-t)}{(1+k)^i} + \frac{L + t(Le_i/e_0 - L)}{(1+k)^n} = 0 \qquad \text{(19A.5)}$$

where $L = Pe_0$ is the dollar equivalent of the foreign currency loan. The final term in Equation 19A.5, $t(Le_i/e_0 - L)$, equals the tax on the LC gain on repaying the dollar loan if the currency appreciates (because it now costs fewer units of LC to repay a given dollar principal) or tax deduction on the LC loss if the LC depreciates. As before, with flotation costs of s per dollar, the first term in Equations 19A.4 and 19A.5 would be multiplied by $(1 - s)$.

Equations 19A.4 and 19A.5 (adjusted for flotation costs) can be applied to the previous example of dollar versus Swiss franc debt. Assume the tax rate is 45%, all flotation costs are tax deductible as soon as they are incurred, and the debt is issued by DMR's Swiss affiliate. Exhibits 19A.2 and 19A.3 contain the year-by-year Swiss franc cash flows and dollar cash flows associated with both issues.

The effective after-tax yield on the Swiss franc issue is now 8.40% and, on the dollar debt issue, is 8.02%. These contrast with the respective no-tax yields of 10.31% and 9.87%.

■ EXHIBIT 19A.2   After-Tax Cash Flows Associated with Swiss Franc Debt

Year	Cash-Flow Category	Swiss Franc Cash Flows (1)	÷	Rate of Exchange (2)	×	After-Tax Factor (3)	=	After-Tax Dollar Cash Flows (4)
0	Bond sale	−52,500,000		1.75		1		−30,000,000.00
	Flotation charge	1,575,000		1.75		0.55		495,000.00
1	Interest	1,837,500		1.665		0.55		606,981.98
2	Interest	1,837,500		1.580		0.55		639,636.09
3	Interest	1,837,500		1.495		0.55		676,003.35
4	Interest	1,837,500		1.410		0.55		716,755.33
5	Interest	1,837,500		1.325		0.55		762,735.88
6	Interest	1,837,500		1.240		0.55		815,020.14
7	Interest	1,837,500		1.155		0.55		875,000.01
	Principal repayment	SFr 52,500,000		1.155		1		$45,454,545.45

Annual Revaluation

If a steady appreciation of the foreign currency at a rate of g per annum is anticipated, then the effective after-tax dollar yield on the foreign currency bond issued by a local affiliate can be found by solving Equation 19A.6:

$$-1 + \sum_{i=1}^{n} \frac{r_f(1+g)^i(1-t)}{(1+r)^i} + \frac{(1+g)^n}{(1+r)^n} = 0 \qquad \textbf{(19A.6)}$$

■ EXHIBIT 19A.3   After-Tax Cash Flows Associated with Dollar Debt

Year	Cash-Flow Category	Dollar Cash Flows (1)	×	After-Tax Factor (2)	=	After-Tax Dollar Cash Flow (3)
0	Bond sale	−30,000,000		1		−30,000,000.00
	Flotation charge	360,000		0.55		198,000.00
1	Interest	2,887,500		0.55		1,588,125.00
2	Interest	2,887,500		0.55		1,588,125.00
3	Interest	2,887,500		0.55		1,588,125.00
4	Interest	2,887,500		0.55		1,588,125.00
5	Interest	2,887,500		0.55		1,588,125.00
6	Interest	2,887,500		0.55		1,588,125.00
7	Interest	2,887,500		0.55		1,588,125.00
	Principal repayment	$30,000,000		1		$30,000,000.00
	Capital gain recognized by Swiss tax authorities (SFr 17,850,000 at $0.87)	$15,454,545		0.45		$ 6,954,545.30

The solution to Equation 19A.6 is $r = r_f(1 + g)(1 - t) + g$, the same as in the single-period case.

Assuming that $r_f = 6\%$, $t = 45\%$, and $g = 3\%$, the effective cost of foreign currency borrowing equals $0.06 \times 1.03 \times 0.55 + 0.03$, or 6.4%. In the absence of taxes, this cost would equal 9.18% ($0.06 \times 1.03 + 0.03$).

England does not allow the tax deductibility of exchange losses on foreign currency debt. In other words, the term $t(Le_i/e_0 - L)$ in Equation 19A.5 goes to zero. It can be shown that if debt is issued in the United Kingdom, and assuming the pound sterling will devalue relative to the dollar, there is a simple after-tax equilibrium relationship between the dollar interest rate, r_{us}, and the pound sterling rate, r_{uk}:

$$r_{us}(1 - t) = r_{uk}(1 - u)(1 - t) - u \qquad (19A.7)$$

where u is the anticipated annual devaluation of the pound relative to the dollar. When Equation 19A.7 holds, the after-tax dollar costs of borrowing pounds and dollars are the same.

To illustrate Equation 19A.7, suppose $r_{us} = 9\%$, $t = 40\%$, and the pound is expected to devalue by 2% annually. According to Equation 19A.7 then, the equilibrium pound interest rate is $r_{uk} = 12.59\%$.

PROBLEMS

1. Multicountry, Inc. has a $200 million principal value Eurobond with two more 10% coupon interest payments due at the end of the next two years. Multicountry would like to switch currencies on the bond. The issue is currently denominated in yen, but Multicountry feels the Deutsche mark would be more advantageous. Given the following current and expected currency rates, what should Multicountry do, assuming it wishes to minimize its expected financing cost? The interest rate will remain at 10%.

	$/DM	$/¥
Current exchange rate	0.654	0.00761
Expected, one year	0.665	0.00772
Expected, two year	0.685	0.00799

2. Suppose the current rate of exchange between the U.S. dollar and the pound sterling is £1 = $2. The English affiliate of Global Industries, GI Ltd, is contemplating raising $12 million by issuing bonds denominated either in dollars or pounds sterling. The dollar bonds would carry a coupon rate of 10% and the pound sterling bonds would carry a coupon rate of 13%. In either case, the bonds would have annual interest payments and mature in five years.

   a. Suppose GI Ltd is interested only in minimizing its expected financing costs. In the absence of taxes, what annual rate of pound devaluation or revaluation would leave GI Ltd indifferent between borrowing either pounds or dollars? What would be the expected exchange rate at the end of year 5, given these currency changes?

   b. Suppose the British tax rate is 45% and exchange losses on foreign currency principal repayments are not tax deductible, but all interest expenses, including exchange losses, are tax deductible. Rework part a on an after-tax basis.

   c. Suppose the international Fisher effect holds on an after-tax basis. Which currency should GI Ltd borrow, given the tax scenario in part b? Explain your answer.

   d. What other factors besides expected borrowing costs might the parent corporation be concerned about in deciding whether to approve GI Ltd's currency selection for this bond issue?

■ BIBLIOGRAPHY ■

Adler, Michael. "The Cost of Capital and Valuation of a Two-Country Firm." *Journal of Finance,* March 1974, pp. 119–132.

Adler, Michael, and Bernard Dumas. "Optimal International Acquisitions." *Journal of Finance,* March 1975, pp. 1–19.

———. "International Portfolio Choice and Corporation Finance: A Synthesis." *Journal of Finance,* June 1983, pp. 925–984.

Agmon, Tamir, and Donald R. Lessard. "Investor Recognition of Corporate International Diversification." *Journal of Finance,* September 1977, pp. 1049–1056.

Black, Fischer. "International Capital Market Equilibrium with Investment Barriers." *Journal of Financial Economics,* December 1974, pp. 337–352.

Grauer, Frederick L.A., Robert H. Litzenberger, and Richard E. Stehle. "Sharing Rules and Equilibrium in an International Capital Market Under Uncertainty." *Journal of Financial Economics,* June 1976, pp. 233–257.

Hughes, John S., Dennis E. Logue, and Richard J. Sweeney. "Corporate International Diversification and Market Assigned Measures of Risk and Diversification." *Journal of Financial and Quantitative Analysis,* November 1975, pp. 627–637.

Jacquillat, Bertrand, and Bruno H. Solnik. "Multinationals Are Poor Tools for Diversification." *Journal of Portfolio Management,* Winter 1978, pp. 8–12.

Mikhail, Azmi D., and Hany A. Shawkey. "Investment Performance of U.S.-Based Multinational Corporations," *Journal of International Business Studies,* Spring–Summer 1979, pp. 53–66.

Senbet, Lemma W. "International Capital Market Equilibrium and the Multinational Firm Financing and Investment Policies." *Journal of Financial and Quantitative Analysis,* September 1979, pp. 455–480.

Shapiro, Alan C. "Financial Structure and the Cost of Capital in the Multinational Corporation." *Journal of Financial and Quantitative Analysis,* June 1978, pp. 211–226.

———. "The Impact of Taxation on the Currency-of-Denomination Decision for Long-Term Borrowing and Lending." *Journal of International Business Studies,* Spring–Summer 1984, pp. 15–25.

Solnik, Bruno H. "Testing International Asset Pricing: Some Pessimistic Views." *Journal of Finance,* May 1977, pp. 503–512.

Stonehill, Arthur I., and Kare B. Dullum. *Internationalizing the Cost of Capital.* New York: Wiley, 1982.

Stulz, Rene M. "A Model of International Asset Pricing." *Journal of Financial Economics,* December 1981, pp. 383–406.

◾ 20 ◾

The Measurement and Management of Political Risk

People say they want clarification of the rules of the game, but I think it isn't very clear what isn't clear to them.

—Adolfo Hegewisch Fernandez,—
Mexico's Subsecretary for Foreign Investment

Potential investors don't want flexibility, they want fixed rules of the game.

—John Gavin, U.S. Ambassador to Mexico—

◾ In recent years, there has been a significant increase in developing and developed countries alike in the types and magnitudes of political risks that multinational companies have historically faced. Currency controls, expropriation, changes in tax laws, and requirements for additional local production are just some of the more visible forms of political risk. The common denominator of such risks, however, is not hard to identify: government intervention into the workings of the economy that affects, for good or ill, the value of the firm. While the consequences are usually adverse, changes in the political environment can provide opportunities. The imposition of quotas on autos from Japan, for example, was undoubtedly beneficial to U.S. automobile manufacturers.

The purpose of this chapter is to provide a framework that can facilitate a formal assessment of political risk and its implications for corporate decision making. Both international banks and nonbank multinationals analyze political risk, but from different perspectives. This chapter takes the perspective of nonbank MNCs, who analyze political risk in order to determine the investment climate in various countries. Political risk assessments may be used in investment analyses to screen out countries that are excessively risky or to monitor countries in which the firm is currently doing business to determine whether new policies are called for.

503

The focus is on forecasting and managing the extreme form of political risk, expropriation.[1] Some risks, such as currency controls, have already been dealt with; others, such as tax changes, have been discussed indirectly or, like local content requirements, are too firm-specific to provide meaningful general guidelines. However, the same strategies that reduce a firm's exposure to expropriation are also likely to strengthen its bargaining position in any confrontation with new governmental policies.

The basic approach to managing political risk presented here involves three steps: (1) identifying political risk and its likely consequences; (2) developing policies in advance to cope with the possibility of political risk; and (3) in the event of expropriation, developing measures to maximize compensation. The experiences in Chile of Kennecott and of Anaconda, detailed in Section 20.5, illustrate this approach.

■ 20.1 ■
MEASURING POLITICAL RISK

Despite the near-universal recognition among multinational corporations, political scientists, and economists of the existence of *political risk,* there is no unanimity yet as to what constitutes that risk and how to measure it. The two basic approaches to viewing political risk are from a country-specific perspective and a firm-specific perspective. The former perspective depends on *country risk analysis,* whereas the latter depends on a more micro approach.

A number of commercial and academic political risk forecasting models are available today. These models normally supply country risk indexes that attempt to quantify the level of political risk in each nation. Most of these indexes rely on some measure(s) of the stability of the local political regime.

Political Stability

Measures of political stability may include the frequency of changes of government, the level of violence in the country (for example, violent deaths per 100,000 population), number of armed insurrections, conflicts with other states, and so on. The basic function of these stability indicators is to determine how long the current regime will be in power and whether that regime also will be willing and able to enforce its foreign investment guarantees. Most companies believe that greater political stability means a safer investment environment.

A basic problem in many Third World countries is that the local actors have all the external trappings of genuine nation-states—United Nations-endorsed borders, armies, foreign ministries, flags, currencies, national airlines. But they are nothing of the kind. They lack social cohesion, political legitimacy, and the institutional infrastructures that are necessary for economic growth.

---

[1]The terms *expropriation* and *nationalization* are used interchangeably in this book and refer specifically to the taking of foreign property, with or without compensation.

■ ───

ILLUSTRATION

Threats to the Nation-State. From Canada to Czechoslovakia, from India to Ireland, and from South Africa to the Soviet Union, political movements centered around ethnicity, national identity, and religion are reemerging to contest some of the most fundamental premises of the modern nation-state. In the process, they are reintroducing ancient sources of conflict so deeply submerged by the Cold War that they seemed almost to have vanished from history's equation.

The implications of this resurgence of national, ethnic, and religious passions are profound.

- A host of modern nation-states—from Canada to Lebanon to Iraq to Yugoslavia—are beginning to crumble because the concept of the "melting pot," the idea that diverse and even historically hostile peoples could readily be assimilated under larger political umbrellas in the name of modernization and progress, has failed them. Even in the strongest nations, including the United States, the task of such assimilation has proved difficult and the prognosis is for even greater tension in the years ahead.

- Turmoil in the Soviet Union and parts of China threaten to blow apart the last remnants of an imperial age that began more than 500 years ago. The turbulent dismantling of 19th Century European empires after World War II may be matched by new waves of disintegration within the Soviet and Chinese Communist empires, with incalculable consequences for the rest of the world. Stretching from the Gulf of Finland to the mountains of Tibet and beyond, the sheer scale of the potential instability would tax the world's capacity to respond. Ethnic unrest could spill into neighboring countries, old border disputes could reignite and, if the central governments tried to impose order with force, civil wars could erupt within two of the world's largest nuclear powers.

- Around the world, fundamentalist religious movements have entered the political arena in a direct challenge to one of the basic principles of the modern age: that governments and other civic institutions should be predominantly secular and religion confined to the private lives of individuals and groups. Since the end of the Middle Ages, when religion dominated not just government but every aspect of society, the pervasive trend in the past 500 years has been to separate church and state. Now, in many parts of the world, powerful movements—reacting against the secular quality of modern public culture and the tendency of traditional values to be swept aside in periods of rapid change—are insisting on a return to God-centered government. One consequence of this trend is to make dealings between states and groups more volatile. As the United States learned with the Arab-Israeli conflict, the Iranian revolution, and the Persian Gulf war, disputes are far harder to manage when governments root their positions in religious principle.

At the same time that many states and societies are fragmenting over religion, ethnicity, and national culture, their people nourish hopes of achieving economic progress by allying themselves with one or another of the new trade blocs—Europe, North America, Pacific

Rim—now taking shape. Yet in many cases such dreams will not materialize. Civil strife and dogmatic politics hold little allure for foreign investors; bankers lend money to people whose first priority is money, not religion or ethnic identity. The challenge for business is to create profitable opportunities in a world that is simultaneously globalizing and localizing.

■

Economic Factors

Other frequently used indicators of political risk include various economic factors, such as inflation, balance-of-payments deficits or surpluses, and the growth rate of per capita GNP. The intention behind these measures is to determine whether the economy is in good shape or requires a quick fix, such as expropriation to increase government revenues or currency inconvertibility to improve the balance of payments. In general, the better a country's economic outlook, the less likely it is to face political and social turmoil that will inevitably harm foreign companies.

Subjective Factors

More subjective measures of political risk are based on a general perception of the country's attitude toward private enterprise: whether private enterprise is considered a necessary evil to be eliminated as soon as possible or is actively welcomed. The attitude toward multinationals is particularly relevant and may differ from the feeling regarding local private ownership. Consider, for example, the Soviet Union and other Eastern European countries that have actively sought products, technology, and even joint ventures with Western firms while refusing to tolerate (until recently) domestic free enterprise. In general, most countries probably view foreign direct investment in terms of a cost/benefit trade-off and are not either for or against it in principle.

An index that tries to incorporate all these various economic, social, and political factors into an overall measure of the business climate, including the political environment, is the Business Environment Risk Index (BERI), shown in Exhibit 20.1. The scores of countries listed on the BERI scale are based on an aggregation of the subjective assessments of a panel of experts.

Political Risk and Uncertain Property Rights   Models, such as BERI, are useful insofar as they provide an indication of the general level of political risk in a country. From an economic standpoint, political risk refers to uncertainty over *property rights*. If the government can expropriate either legal title to property or the stream of income it generates, then political risk exists. Political risk also exists if property owners may be constrained in the way they use their property. This definition of political risk encompasses government actions ranging from outright expropriation to a change in the tax law that alters the government's share of corporate income to laws that change the rights of private companies to compete against state-owned companies. Each action affects corporate cash flows and hence the value of the firm.

■ **EXHIBIT 20.1**   BERI Rankings, November 1987

Low Risk	Category*	High Risk	Category*
Switzerland	82	Greece	54
Japan	80	Israel	54
Germany	78	Thailand	54
United States	78	South Africa	52
Singapore	74	Turkey	50
Taiwan	70	Ecuador	49
Medium Risk		Italy	49
Netherlands	69	Colombia	48
Belgium	68	Côte d'Ivoire	48
United Kingdom	68	Hungary	48
Canada	67	Brazil	46
Sweden	67	Chile	46
Norway	66	India	46
France	64	Portugal	46
Ireland	64	Indonesia	42
Australia	62	Argentina	40
Denmark	62	Kenya	40
Korea (South)	61	Mexico	40
Saudi Arabia	58	Pakistan	40
Spain	57	Venezuela	40
Malaysia	56	**Prohibitive Risk**	
		Egypt	39
		Peru	39
		Philippines	39
		Iraq	38
		Morocco	38
		Nigeria	38
		Iran	34
		Zaire	28

*BERI Categories:

100–86   Unusually stable and superior business environment for the foreign investor.

85–70   Typical for an industrialized economy. Any tendency toward nationalism is offset in varying degrees by the country's efficiency, market opportunities, financial entities, etc.

69–56   Moderate-risk countries with complications in day-to-day operations. Usually the political structure is sufficiently stable to permit business without serious disruption.

55–41   High risk for foreign-owned businesses. Only special situations should be considered (e.g., scarce raw materials).

Below 41   Unacceptable business conditions.

SOURCE: Business Environment Risk Information, Geneva, 1987.

■ ──

ILLUSTRATION

Political Risk in Venezuela. According to *The Wall Street Journal* (December 31, 1980, p. 10), when Venezuela's oil income quadrupled in 1973, a high government official declared, "Now we have so much money that we won't need any new foreign investment." President Carlos Perez calculated that the country was rich enough to buy machinery from abroad and set up factories without any foreign participation. He overlooked the fact that Venezuela didn't have enough skilled technicians to run and maintain sophisticated equipment. Despite an orgy of buying foreign-made machinery, economic growth stalled as companies were left with equipment they couldn't operate.

By 1980, President Luis Herrera, who succeeded Perez, recognized the mistake and invited foreigners back. But once shunned, foreigners didn't rush back, particularly since the Herrera administration sent out such mixed signals that investors couldn't be certain how sincere the welcome was or how long it would last.

Consider the uncertainty faced by a foreign investor trying to decipher government policy from the following statements. On the one hand, the Superintendent of Foreign Investment insisted that the government had had "a change of heart" and declared that the country needed "new capital and new technology in manufacturing, agro-industry, and construction of low-cost housing." On the other hand, the head of the powerful Venezuelan Investment Fund, which invests much of the country's oil income, was downright hostile to foreign investors. He said, "Foreign investment is generally unfavorable to Venezuela. Foreign investors think Venezuela is one big grab bag, where they can come and pick out whatever goodies they want." Still another official, the president of the Foreign Trade Institute, said, "It is a grave error to think that foreign investment can contribute to the transfer of technology, capital formation, the development of managerial capacity, and equilibrium in the balance of payments."

── ■

Capital Flight   One good indicator of the degree of political risk is the seriousness of capital flight. *Capital flight* refers to the export of savings by a nation's citizens because of fears about the safety of their capital. By its nature, capital flight is difficult to measure accurately because it is not directly observed in most cases. Nevertheless, one can usually infer the capital outflows, using balance-of-payments figures—particularly the entry labeled "errors and omissions." These estimates indicate that capital flight represents an enormous outflow of funds from developing countries.

Between 1974 and 1982, Argentina borrowed $32.6 billion. Estimates of the level of capital flight from Argentina over the same period range from $15 billion to over $27 billion.[2] These estimates would mean that capital flight amounted to between half and four-fifths of the entire inflow of foreign capital to Argentina. For Venezuela, the inflow was $27 billion over the same period, with capital flight estimated at between $12 billion and $22 billion. The inflow for Mexico was $79 billion between 1979 and 1984; the outflow has been

──

[2]These figures come from Steven Plaut, "Capital Flight and LDC Debt," *FRBSF Weekly Letter,* Federal Reserve Bank of San Francisco, January 8, 1988.

estimated at between $26 billion and $54 billion for the same period. Other debtor countries, such as Nigeria and the Philippines, have also had large capital outflows.

Capital flight is continuing. As of the end of 1987, Morgan Guaranty estimates that Latin Americans held $243 billion in assets abroad, far exceeding the amount of loans to the region held by U.S. banks. And this excludes assets taken abroad before 1977. Exhibit 20.2 shows the breakdown of the $243 billion figure by country.

Capital flight occurs for several reasons, most of which have to do with inappropriate economic policies. These reasons include government regulations, controls, and taxes that lower the return on domestic investments. In countries where inflation is high and domestic inflation hedging is difficult or impossible, investors may hedge by shifting their savings to foreign currencies deemed less likely to depreciate. They may also make the shift when domestic interest rates are artificially held down by their governments, or when they expect a devaluation of an overvalued currency.

Perhaps the most powerful motive for capital flight is political risk. In unstable political regimes (and in some stable ones) wealth is not secure from government seizure, especially when changes in regime occur. Savings may be shifted overseas to protect them. For example, the citizens of Hong Kong, which will be turned over to communist China in 1997, have responded to the anticipated change in regime by sending much of their money abroad.

Common sense dictates that if a nation's own citizens don't trust the government, then investment there is unsafe. After all, residents presumably have a better feel for conditions and governmental intentions than do outsiders. Thus, when analyzing investment or lending opportunities, multinationals firms and international banks must bear in mind the apparent unwillingness of the nation's citizens to invest and lend in their own country.

What's needed to halt capital flight are tough-minded economic policies—the kind of policies that make investors want to put their money to work instead of taking it out. As we

■ **EXHIBIT 20.2** Latin American Flight Capital: Estimated Assets Held Abroad at Year-End, 1988

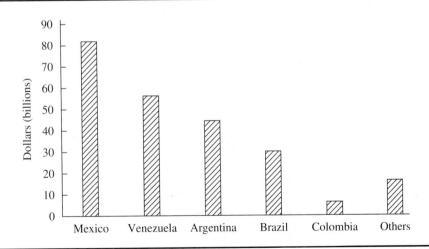

shall see in the next section, these policies include cutting budget deficits and taxes, removing barriers to investment by foreigners, selling off state-owned enterprises, allowing for freer trade, and avoiding currency overvaluations that virtually invite people to ship their money elsewhere before the official exchange rate falls.

The Micro Approach

Despite the increased sophistication of political risk models such as BERI, however, their usefulness remains problematic. For one thing, political instability by itself does not necessarily contribute to political risk. Changes of government in Latin America, for example, are quite frequent; yet most multinationals continue to go about their business undisturbed.

The most important weakness of these indices, however, lies in their assumption that each firm in a country is facing the same degree of political risk. This is manifestly untrue, as is indicated by the empirical evidence on the post–World War II experiences of American and British MNCs. The data clearly show that except in those countries that went communist, companies differ in their susceptibilities to political risk depending on their industry, size, composition of ownership, level of technology, and degree of vertical integration with other affiliates.[3] For example, expropriation or creeping expropriation is more likely to occur in the extractive, utility, and financial service sectors of an economy than in the manufacturing sector. Exhibit 20.3 shows corporate susceptibility to expropriation by industry. Moreover,

■ **EXHIBIT 20.3** Expropriation by Industry Group, 1960–1974

Industry	Number of Expropriations	Percent of Total
Oil	84	12.0
Extraction	38	18.0
Utilities and transportation	17	4.0
Insurance and banking	33	4.0
Manufacturing	30	1.2
Agriculture	19	*
Sales and service	16	*
Land, property, and construction	23	*

*Data unavailable

SOURCE: David Bradley, "Managing Against Expropriation," *Harvard Business Review,* July–August 1977, pp. 75–83. Reprinted by permission of the *Harvard Business Review,* Copyright © 1977 by the President and Fellows of Harvard College; all rights reserved.

[3]See, for example, studies by J. Frederick Truitt, "Expropriation of Foreign Investment: Summary of the Post–World War II Experience of American and British Investors in Less Developed Countries," *Journal of International Business Studies,* Fall 1970, pp. 21–34; Robert G. Hawkins, Norman Mintz, and Michael Provissiero, "Government Takeovers of U.S. Foreign Affiliates," *Journal of International Business Studies,* Spring 1976, pp. 3–15; and David Bradley, "Managing Against Expropriation," *Harvard Business Review,* July–August, 1977, pp. 75–83.

some firms may benefit from the same event that harms other firms. For instance, a company that relies on imports will be hurt by trade restrictions, whereas an import-competing firm may well be helped.

Because political risk has a different meaning for, and impact on, each firm, it is doubtful that any index of generalized political risk will be of much value to a company selected at random. The specific operating and financial characteristics of a company will largely determine its susceptibility to political risk and, hence, the effects of that risk on the value of its foreign investment.

In terms of the large majority of countries, expropriation appears to be used as a fairly selective instrument of policy, with the actions taken both limited in scope and, from the government's perspective, rational. Rarely do governments, even revolutionary ones, expropriate foreign investments indiscriminately. In general, the greater the perceived benefits to the host economy and the more expensive its replacement by a purely local operation, the smaller the degree of risk to the MNC. This selectivity suggests that firms can take actions to control their exposure to political risk.

■ 20.2 ■
COUNTRY RISK ANALYSIS

We now examine in more detail some of the economic and social factors that contribute to the general level of risk in the country as a whole—termed *country risk*. The primary focus here is on how well the country is doing economically. As noted earlier, the better a nation's economic performance, the lower the likelihood that its government will take actions that adversely affect the value of companies operating there.

Fiscal Irresponsibility

To begin, fiscal irresponsibility is one sign of a country likely to be politically risky since it will probably have an insatiable appetite for money. Thus, one country risk indicator is the government deficit as a percentage of gross national product. The higher this figure, the more the government is promising to its citizens relative to the resources it is extracting in payment. This gap lowers the possibility that the government can meet its promises without resorting to expropriations of property.

Controlled Exchange Rate System

The economic problems presented by a fiscally irresponsible government are compounded by having a *controlled exchange rate system,* where the government uses currency controls to fix the exchange rate. A controlled rate system goes hand in hand with an overvalued local currency, which is the equivalent of taxing exports and subsidizing imports. The risk of tighter currency controls and the ever-present threat of a devaluation encourage capital flight. Similarly, multinational firms will try to repatriate their local affiliates' profits rather than reinvest them. A controlled rate system also leaves the economy with little flexibility to respond to changing relative prices and wealth positions, exacerbating any unfavorable trend in the nation's terms of trade.

Wasteful Government Spending

Another indicator of potential political risk is the amount of unproductive spending in the economy. To the extent that capital from abroad is used to subsidize consumption or is wasted on showcase projects, the government will have less wealth to draw on to repay the nation's foreign debts and is more likely to resort to exchange controls, higher taxes, and the like. Additionally, funds diverted to the purchase of assets abroad (capital flight) will not add to the economy's dollar-generating capacity unless investors feel safe in repatriating their overseas earnings.

Resource Base

The resource base of a country consists of its natural, human, and financial resources. Others things equal, a nation with substantial natural resources, such as oil or copper, is a better economic risk than is one without those resources. But typically, all is not equal. Hence, nations such as South Korea or Taiwan turn out to be better risks than resource-rich Argentina or Brazil. The reason has to do with the quality of human resources and the degree to which these resources are allowed to be put to their most efficient use.

A nation with highly skilled and productive workers, a large pool of scientists and engineers, and ample management talent will have many of the essential ingredients needed to pursue a course of steady growth and development. Two further factors are necessary: (1) a stable political system that encourages hard work and risk taking by allowing entrepreneurs to reap the rewards (and bear the losses) from their activities, and (2) a free-market system that ensures that the prices people respond to correctly signal the relative desirability of engaging in different activities. In this way, the nation's human and natural resources will be put to their most efficient uses. The evidence by now is overwhelming that free markets bring wealth, and that endless state meddling brings waste. The reason is simple: Unlike a government-controlled economy, free markets do not tolerate and perpetuate mistakes.

Country Risk and Adjustment to External Shocks

Recent history shows that the impact of external shocks is likely to vary from nation to nation, however, with some countries dealing successfully with these shocks and others succumbing to them. The evidence suggests that domestic policies play a critical role in determining how effectively a particular nation will deal with external shocks. Asian nations, for example, successfully coped with falling commodity prices, rising real interest rates, and rising exchange rates because their policies promoted timely internal and external adjustment, as is manifest in relatively low inflation rates and small current-account deficits.

The opposite happened in Latin America where most countries accepted the then-prevalent ideology that growth is best promoted by an *import-substitution development strategy* characterized by extensive state ownership, controls, and policies to encourage import substitution. Many of these countries took over failing private businesses, nationalized the banks, protected domestic companies against imports, ran up large foreign debts, and heavily regulated the private sector. Whereas the "East Asian Tigers"—Hong Kong, South Korea, Taiwan, and Singapore—tested their ability to imitate and innovate in the international marketplace, Latin American producers were content with the exploitation of the internal market, charging prices that were typically several times the international price for their goods. The lack of foreign competition has contributed to long-term inefficiency among Latin American manufacturers.

In addition, by raising the cost of imported materials and products used by the export sector, the Latin American import-substitution development strategies worsened their international competitive position, leaving the share of exports in GNP far below that of other LDCs. Moreover, state expenditures on massive capital projects diverted resources from the private sector and exports. Much of the investment went to inefficient state enterprises, leading to wasted resources and large debts.

The decline in commodity prices and the simultaneous rise in real interest rates should have led to reduced domestic consumption. But fearing that spending cuts would threaten social stability, the Latin American governments delayed cutting back on projects and social expenditures. The difference between consumption and production was made up by borrowing overseas, thereby enabling their societies to temporarily enjoy artificially high standards of living.

Latin American governments also tried to stimulate their economies by increasing state spending, fueled by high rates of monetary expansion. This response exacerbated their difficulties because the resulting high rates of inflation combined with their fixed exchange rates to boost real exchange rates substantially and resulted in higher imports and lower exports. Moreover, the overvalued exchange rates, interest rate controls, and political uncertainties triggered massive capital flight from the region—estimated at up to $100 billion during the two-year period of 1981 and 1982. The result was larger balance-of-payments deficits that necessitated more foreign borrowing and higher debt service requirements. Moreover, in an attempt to control inflation, the Latin American governments imposed price controls and interest rate controls. These controls led to further capital flight and price rigidity. Distorted prices gave the wrong signals to the residents, sending consumption soaring and production plummeting.

Many of these countries are finally rejecting earlier policies and trying to stimulate the private sector and individual initiative. The slow progress in countries that are reforming their economies—including the Soviet Union, China, and India, as well as several Latin American nations—illustrates that it is far easier to regulate and extend the state's reach than to deregulate and retrench. When the state becomes heavily involved in the economy, many special interests from the state bureaucracy, business, labor, and consumer groups come to rely on state benefits. Of course, they actively oppose reforms that curtail their subsidies.

The process of reform is greatly complicated by egalitarian ideologies that deprecate private success while justifying public privilege and by the pervasiveness of the state, which distorts the reward pattern and makes it easier to get rich by politics than by industry, by connections than by performance.

The message is clear. In evaluating a nation's riskiness, it is not sufficient to identify factors—such as real interest shocks or world recession—that would systematically affect the economies of all foreign countries to one extent or another. It is necessary also to determine the susceptibility of the various nations to these shocks. This determination requires a focus on the financial policies and development strategies pursued by the different nations.

Based on the preceding discussion, some of the common characteristics of country risk include the following:

- A large government deficit relative to GNP
- A high rate of money expansion, especially if it is combined with a relatively fixed exchange rate
- Substantial government expenditures yielding low rates of return
- Price controls, interest rate ceilings, trade restrictions, and other government-imposed barriers to the smooth adjustment of the economy to changing relative prices
- Vast state-owned firms run for the benefit of their managers and workers
- A citizenry that demands, and a political system that accepts, government responsibility for maintaining and expanding the nation's standard of living through public sector spending and regulations (The less stable the political system, the more important this factor will likely be.)

Alternatively, indicators of a nation's long-run economic health include the following:

- *A structure of incentives that rewards risk taking in productive ventures*: People have clearly demonstrated that they respond rationally to the incentives they face, given the information and resources available to them. This statement is true whether we are talking about shopkeepers in Nairobi or bankers in New York.
- *A legal structure that stimulates the development of free markets*: The resulting price signals are most likely to contain the data that are essential to making efficient use of the nation's resources.
- *Minimal regulations and economic distortions*: Complex regulations are costly to implement and waste management time and other resources.
- *Clear incentives to save and invest*: In general, when there are such incentives, when the economic rules of the game are straightforward and stable, and when there is political stability, a nation's chances of developing are maximized.
- *An open economy*: Not only does free trade increase competition and permit the realization of comparative advantage, it also constrains government policies and makes them conform more closely to those conducive to increases in living standards and rapid economic growth.

The sorry economic state of Eastern Europe dramatically illustrates the consequences of pursuing policies that are the exact opposite of those recommended. Thus, the ability of the Eastern European countries to share in the prosperity of the Western world depends critically on their reversing the policies they have followed under communist rule.

ILLUSTRATION

The 1948 West German Erhard Reforms. At the end of World War II, the German economy lay in ruins. Industrial output in 1948 was one-third its 1936 level because of a massive disruption in production and trade patterns. Aside from the devastation caused by the war, economic disruption was aggravated by wartime money creation, price controls, and uncertainty about economic policy. Each day vast, hungry crowds traveled to the countryside to barter food from farmers; an extensive black market developed; and cigarettes replaced currency in many transactions.

In June 1948, Ludwig Erhard, West Germany's economic czar, announced an extensive reform package. This package created a new currency, the Deutsche mark, and dismantled most price controls and rationing ordinances. It also implemented a restrictive monetary policy, lowered tax rates, and provided incentives for investment.

Erhard's reforms almost immediately established sound and stable macroeconomic conditions and led to the German "economic miracle." Consumer prices initially rose by 20%, but inflation then subsided to an average annual rate of about 1% between 1949 and 1959. Goods that had been hoarded or sold only in the black market flooded the market. Industrial production increased 40% in the second half of 1948 and then tripled over the next ten years. Real GNP and productivity also grew rapidly. Although unemployment rose from 3% in the first half of 1948 to more than 10% in the first half of 1950, it then disappeared over the next eight years. In 1958, the DM became convertible.

Economic reform could not have produced such dramatic results if West Germany had not had key structural elements already in place. It had the legal framework necessary for a market economy, many intact businesses, and skilled workers and managers. Marshall Plan money helped, but absent the reforms, any aid would have been wasted.   ∎

As the West German example illustrates, realism demands that nations—especially those in the Third World and Eastern Europe—come to terms with their need to rely more on self-help. The most successful economies, such as South Korea and Taiwan, demonstrate the importance of aligning domestic incentives with world market conditions. Like it or not, nations must make their way in an increasingly competitive world economy that puts a premium on self-help and has little time for the inefficiency and pretension of *statism*—that is, the substitution of state-owned or state-guided enterprises for the private sector—as the road to economic success. This recognition—that they cannot realize the benefits of capitalism without the institutions of capitalism—is dawning in even the most socialist countries of Europe, Asia, and Latin America.

Market-oriented reform of Eastern European and LDC economic policies lies at the heart of any credible undertaking to secure these nations' economic and financial rehabilitation. The first and most critical step is to cut government spending. In practical terms, cutting government spending means reducing the bloated public sectors that permeate most Latin American and communist countries. Chile and Colombia have embarked on fairly comprehensive reform programs, and despite some backsliding, Mexico has made surprisingly good headway (see Exhibit 20.4 for a summary of the changes in Mexico's economic policies). Argentina has also announced a series of steps intended to improve public sector management, although it has not yet taken the logical next steps of *privatizing*—returning to the private sector from the public sector—major activities and galvanizing the private sector by deregulation and the elimination of protectionism. And Poland has instituted a radical set of market reforms.

Yet in the best of circumstances, structural reform meets formidable political obstacles: labor unions facing job and benefit losses, bureaucrats fearful of diminished power and influence (not to mention their jobs), and local industrialists concerned about increased

■ **EXHIBIT 20.4** Mexico's Economic Policies: Then and Now

Old Mexican Model	New Mexican Model
Large budget deficits	Fiscal restraint
Rapid expansion of money supply	Monetary discipline
Nationalization	Privatizations
Restrict foreign direct investment	Attract FDI
High tax rates	Tax reform
Import substitution	Trade liberalization
Controlled currency	End currency controls
Price and interest rate controls	Prices and interest rates set by market
Government dominates economy	Reduced size and scope of government

competition and reduced profitability. All are well aware that the benefits of restructuring are diffuse and materialize only gradually, while they must bear the costs immediately.

Despite these obstacles, reducing state subsidies on consumer goods and to inefficient industries, removing trade barriers and price controls, and freeing interest rates and the exchange rate to move to market levels is probably the most straightforward and workable solution to economic stagnation. These actions, if implemented, can increase output by making the economy more efficient, can reduce consumption, and, thereby, can increase the quantity of goods available for export. They will also discourage capital flight and stimulate domestic savings and investment.

■ ────────────────────────

ILLUSTRATION

Strategies for Eastern European Economic Success. Eastern Europe has the basic ingredients for successful development: an educated work force, low wages, and proximity to large markets. However, the key to creating a dynamic market economy is to mobilize the energies and savings of the populace on the broadest possible scale, without whose support any reform package is doomed to failure. Unfortunately, under communism, people had no incentive to take risks, and, thus, took no initiative. The result was no innovation, no consumer orientation, and low quality merchandise. Based on these considerations, here is a thumbnail sketch of the factors that will influence its chances of economic success.

- *Prerequisites*: Privatization of bloated state enterprises to force efficiency and customer responsiveness; market prices to signal relative scarcity and opportunity cost; private property, to provide incentives; and a complete revamping of the legal, financial, and administrative institutions that govern economic activity to permit enforceable contracts and property rights.
- *Economic reforms*: Decontrolling prices; eliminating subsidies and restrictions on international trade; creating strong, convertible currencies, so that people can receive something for their efforts; permitting bankruptcy, so that assets and people can be

redeployed; doing away with regulations of small businesses; introducing a free capital market; and demonopolizing state enterprises through privatization to introduce competition.

These are not mere details. Completing such tasks will embroil the region in all the wrangles about wealth distribution and the size and role of the state that Western countries have spent generations trying to resolve. And there's another complicating factor. For those born since 1945, the habits that constitute the tradition of private property, markets, and creativity have been blotted out. Two generations in Eastern Europe have never experienced private property, free contracts, markets, or inventive enterprise; the skills are gone. Whether and how fast these skills and habits can be resurrected remains an open question. Nonetheless, given the prerequisites and reforms outlined above, here are four strategies aimed at getting Eastern Europe off to a fast start.

1. *Deregulating agriculture* (especially farmers' access to markets, ownership of land, and decontrol of prices) offers the best hope for quickly easing food shortages and for containing food price increases as subsidies are eliminated. Communal ownership of land stifles initiative. Raising efficiency in agriculture is critical to successful development.

2. *Privatizing small businesses,* on the broadest possible scale, is desperately needed in order to create new job opportunities for workers displaced by the inevitable restructuring of heavy industry. Small businesses have the greatest potential for harnessing individual initiative and creating new jobs quickly and are an indispensable part of the infrastructure of any dynamic market economy.

3. *Manufacturing low-technology goods* plays a key role in increasing skill levels and in disseminating technology throughout the economy. The region's current comparative advantage lies in low-technology manufactured goods. East Europeans cannot be expected immediately to produce cars, computers, and consumer electronics of sufficient quality to compete with the West; moving up the ladder to more sophisticated products will take considerable time and lots of Western investment and expertise.

4. *Direct investment in local production* is a preferred strategy since none of the countries in the region can afford a huge influx of imports. Western companies should target relatively cheap, everyday products of less than premium quality. Living standards in Eastern Europe and the Soviet Union are too low to warrant mass purchases of anything but the most basic Western goods.

■ 20.3 ■
MANAGING POLITICAL RISK

Once the firm has analyzed the political environment of a country and assessed its implications for corporate operations, it must then decide whether to invest there and, if so, how to structure its investment to minimize political risk. The key point remains that political risk is not independent of the firm's activities; the configuration of the firm's investments will, in large measure, determine its susceptibility to changing government policies.

Preinvestment Planning

Given the recognition of political risk, an MNC has at least four separate, though not necessarily mutually exclusive, policies that it can follow: (1) avoidance, (2) insurance, (3) negotiating the environment, and (4) structuring the investment.

Avoidance.   The easiest way to manage political risk is to avoid it, and many firms do so by screening out investments in politically uncertain countries. However, inasmuch as all governments make decisions that influence the profitability of business, all investments, including those made in the United States, face some degree of political risk. For example, U.S. steel companies have had to cope with stricter environmental regulations requiring the expenditure of billions of dollars for new pollution control devices, while U.S. oil companies have been beleaguered by so-called windfall profit taxes, price controls, and mandatory allocations. Thus, risk avoidance is impossible.

The real issue is the degree of political risk a company is willing to tolerate and the return required to bear it. A policy of staying away from countries considered to be politically unstable ignores the potentially high returns available and the extent to which a firm can control these risks. After all, companies are in business to take risks, provided these risks are recognized, intelligently managed, and provide compensation.

Insurance.   An alternative to risk avoidance is insurance. By insuring assets in politically risky areas, firms can concentrate on managing their businesses and forget about political risk—or so it appears. Most developed countries sell *political risk insurance* to cover the foreign assets of domestic companies. The coverage provided by the U.S. government through the *Overseas Private Investment Corporation* (OPIC) is typical. Although its future has been in doubt several times—some U.S. citizens believe it is an instrument of U.S. imperialism, and others feel the government has no right to subsidize a service that would otherwise be provided by private enterprise—OPIC has managed to survive because of the general belief that this program, by encouraging U.S. direct investment in less-developed countries, helps these countries to develop.

The OPIC program provides U.S. investors with insurance against loss due to the specific political risks of expropriation, currency inconvertibility, and political violence—that is, war, revolution, or insurrection. To qualify, the investment must be a new one or a substantial expansion of an existing facility and must be approved by the host government. Coverage is restricted to 90% of equity participation. For very large investments or for projects deemed especially risky, OPIC coverage may be limited to less than 90%. The only exception is institutional loans to unrelated third parties, which may be insured for the full amount of principal and interest.

Similar OPIC political risk protection is provided for leases. OPIC's insurance provides lessors with coverage against loss due to various political risks, including the inability to convert into dollars local currency received as lease payments.

OPIC also provides business income coverage (BIC), which protects a U.S. investor's income flow if political violence causes damage that interrupts operation of the foreign enterprise. For example, an overseas facility could be bombed and partially or totally destroyed. It may take weeks or months to rebuild the plant. But during the rebuilding process the company still must meet its interest and other contractual payments and pay skilled workers in order to retain their services pending the reopening of the business. BIC allows a business to meet its continuing expenses and to make a normal profit during the period its operations are suspended. This is similar to the business interruption insurance available from private insurers for interruptions caused by nonpolitical events.

Another special program run by OPIC provides coverage for U.S. exporters of goods and services. OPIC insures against arbitrary drawings by a government buyer of bid, performance, advance payment and other guaranties (usually issued in the form of standby letters of credit). An arbitrary drawing is one not justified by the terms of the contract. OPIC will also insure a contractor's assets against loss due to political violence or confiscation. Protection in the event of contractual disputes is offered as well.

Premiums are computed for each type of coverage on the basis of a contractually stipulated maximum insured amount and a current insured amount that may, within the limits of the contract, be elected by the investor on a yearly basis. The current insured amount represents the insurance actually in force during any contract year.

The difference between the current insured amount and maximum insured amount for each coverage is called the standby amount. The major portion of the premium is based on the current insured amount, with a reduced premium rate being applicable to the standby amount. For expropriation and war coverage, the insured must maintain current coverage at a level equal to the amount of investment at risk.

The cost of the coverage varies by industry and risk insured. These costs, which are listed in Exhibit 20.5, are not based solely on objective criteria; they also reflect subsidies geared to achieving certain political aims, such as fostering development of additional energy supplies.

The only private insurer of consequence against expropriation risks is Lloyd's of London. There are several possible reasons why a large-scale private market for expropriation insurance has failed to develop. One major barrier to entry is the magnitude of the potential expropriation losses. A $1 billion claim may bankrupt a private insurer, unless that loss is only a small percentage of its total operations. However, the large loss factor can be dealt with by reinsuring most of the risks with other insurance firms and private investors. This reinsuring is routinely done in the insurance field.

Other possible obstacles to private insurers contemplating the sale of expropriation insurance are the problems of adverse selection and adverse incentives. *Adverse selection* refers to the possibility that only high-risk multinationals will seek insurance. This problem can be dealt with in several ways. The ways include adjusting premiums in accord with the perceived risks, screening out certain high-risk applicants, and providing premium reductions for firms engaged in activities that are likely to reduce expropriation risks.

The problem of *adverse incentives* is that by reducing the riskiness of certain activities, insurance may prompt firms to engage in activities with a higher probability of expropriation. Firms may undertake investments that were previously too risky and neglect certain policies responsive to the host country's needs. If the local affiliate is in financial difficulty, the parent can also take actions that would increase the possibility of expropriation or else collude with the host government to expropriate the affiliate—in much the same way that the owner of a failing business might commit arson to collect on the fire insurance. In effect, purchasing political risk insurance is equivalent to purchasing a put option on the project. The MNC

■ **EXHIBIT 20.5**   OPIC Insurance Fees: Annual Base Rates per $100 of Coverage

Coverage	Manufacturing/ Services Projects		Natural Resource Projects Other Than Oil and Gas		Oil and Gas Projects		Institutional Loans		Business Income Coverage		Contractors and Exporters Guaranty Coverage	
	Current	(Standby)	Current	(Standby)	Exploration	Production	Current	(Unused Commitment)	Current	(Standby)	Current	(Standby)
Inconvertibility	$0.30	$(0.25)	$0.30	$(0.25)	$0.30	$0.30	$0.25	$(0.20)	—	—	$0.30	$(0.25)
Expropriation	0.60	(0.25)	0.90	(0.25)	0.40	1.50	0.30	(0.20)	—	—	0.60	(0.25)
Political violence	0.50	(0.25)	0.50	(0.25)	0.60	0.60	0.60	(0.20)	0.25	(0.25)	0.50	(0.25)
With civil strife	0.60	(0.30)	0.60	(0.30)	0.75	(0.75)	—	—	—	—	0.60	(0.30)
Interference with operations	—	—	—	—	0.55	0.55	—	—	—	—	—	—
With civil strife	—	—	—	—	0.075	0.25	—	—	—	—	—	—
Inconvertibility and expropriation*	—	—	—	—	0.0075	0.0075	0.50	(0.30)	—	—	—	—
Inconvertibility, expropriation, and political violence*	—	—	—	—	—	—	0.90	(0.50)	—	—	—	—
With civil strife	—	—	—	—	—	—	1.00	(0.52)	—	—	—	—
Disputes	—	—	—	—	—	—	—	—	—	—	0.80	(0.25)
Bid, performance, and advance payment guaranties	—	—	—	—	—	—	—	—	—	—	0.60	(0.25)
Primary standby (per coverage)	—	—	—	—	0.075	(0.25)	—	—	—	—	—	—
With civil strife	—	—	—	—	0.09	(0.30)	—	—	—	—	—	—
Secondary standby (per coverage)	—	—	—	—	0.75	(0.75)	—	—	—	—	—	—

*Combined coverage

SOURCE: *Investment Insurance Handbook*, Overseas Private Investment Corporation, March 1988.

will seek to exercise this put option—which effectively involves selling its foreign project to the insurance company for the amount of coverage—whenever the market value of the project falls below the insurance claim.

The problem of adverse incentives can be coped with to a certain extent by *coinsurance*—forcing the purchaser to self-insure part of the losses—and by refusing to pay off on a claim if it can be shown that the insured firm caused the expropriation. While these are not ideal solutions, the problems of adverse selection and adverse incentives should not pose major deterrents to the establishment of a viable market for expropriation insurance.

The most important barrier preventing private competition with Lloyd's is likely to be the existence of OPIC and other government-operated expropriation schemes. By offering subsidized insurance, these government plans have made private expropriation insurance unprofitable. As in other instances of market distortion, it is in the MNC's best interest to buy insurance when it is priced at a below-market rate. Since the rate is uniform across countries (for example, 0.6% for manufacturing operations), it clearly pays to insure in risky nations (mostly LDCs) and not insure in low-risk nations. Thus, government plans are faced with the aforementioned problem of adverse selection.

Even with subsidized rates, there are two fundamental problems with relying on insurance as a protection from political risk. First, there is an asymmetry involved. If an investment proves unprofitable, it is unlikely to be expropriated. Since business risk is not covered, any losses must be borne by the firm itself. On the other hand, if the investment proves successful and is then expropriated, the firm is compensated only for the value of its assets. This result relates to the second problem: Whereas the economic value of an investment is the present value of its future cash flows, only the capital investment in assets is covered by insurance. Thus, although insurance can provide partial protection from political risk, it falls far short of being a comprehensive solution.

Negotiating the Environment.   In addition to insurance, therefore, some firms try to reach an understanding with the host government before undertaking the investment, defining rights and responsibilities of both parties. Also known as a *concession agreement,* such an understanding specifies precisely the rules under which the firm can operate locally.

These concession agreements were quite popular among firms investing in less-developed countries, especially in colonies of the home country. They often were negotiated with weak governments. In time, many of these countries became independent or their governments were overthrown. Invariably, the new rulers repudiated these old concession agreements, arguing that they were a form of exploitation.

Concession agreements are still being negotiated today, but they seem to carry little weight among Third World countries. Their high rate of obsolescence has led many firms to pursue a more active policy of political risk management.

Structuring the Investment.   Once a firm has decided to invest in a country, it can then try to minimize its exposure to political risk by increasing the host government's cost of interfering with company operations. This action involves adjusting the operating policies (in the areas of production, logistics, exporting, and technology transfer) and the financial policies so as to closely link the value of the foreign project to the multinational firm's continued control. In effect, the MNC is trying to raise the cost to the host government of exercising its ever-present option to expropriate or otherwise reduce the local affiliate's value to its parent.[4]

One key element of such a strategy is keeping the local affiliate dependent on sister companies for markets and/or supplies. Chrysler, for example, managed to hold on to its Peruvian assembly plant even though other foreign property was being nationalized. Peru ruled out expropriation because of Chrysler's stranglehold on the supply of essential components. Only 50% of the auto and truck parts were manufactured in Peru. The remainder—including engines, transmissions, sheet metal, and most accessories—were supplied from Chrysler plants in Argentina, Brazil, and Detroit. In a similar instance of vertical integration, Ford's Brazilian engine plant generates substantial exports, but only to other units of Ford. Not surprisingly, the data reveal no expropriations of factories that sell more than 10% of their output to the parent company.[5]

Similarly, by concentrating R&D facilities and proprietary technology, or at least key components thereof, in the home country, a firm can raise the cost of nationalization. To be effective, it is necessary that other multinationals with licensing agreements not be permitted to service the nationalized affiliate. Another element of this strategy is establishing a single, global trademark that cannot be legally duplicated by a government. In this way, an expropriated consumer products company would sustain significant losses by being forced to operate without its recognized brand name.

Control of transportation—including shipping, pipelines, and railroads—has also been used at one time or another by the United Fruit Company and other multinationals to gain leverage over governments. Likewise, sourcing production in multiple plants reduces the government's ability to hurt the worldwide firm by seizing a single plant and, thereby, changes the balance of power between government and firm.

Another defensive ploy is to develop external financial stakeholders in the venture's success. This defense involves raising capital for a venture from the host and other governments, international financial institutions, and customers (with payment to be provided out of production) rather than employing funds supplied or guaranteed by the parent company. In addition to spreading risks, this strategy will elicit an international response to any expropriation move or other adverse action by a host government.

A last approach, particularly for extractive projects, is to obtain unconditional host government guarantees for the amount of the investment that will enable creditors to initiate legal action in foreign courts against any commercial transactions between the host country and third parties if a subsequent government repudiates the nation's obligations. Such guarantees provide investors with potential sanctions against a foreign government, without having to rely on the uncertain support of their home governments.

---

[4]Arvind Mahajan, "Pricing Expropriation Risk," *Financial Management,* Winter 1990, pp. 77–86, points out that when a multinational firm invests in a country, it is effectively writing a call option to the government on its property. The aim of political risk management is to reduce the value to the government of exercising this option.

[5]Bradley, "Managing Against Expropriation," pp. 75–83.

Operating Policies

Once the multinational has invested in a project, its ability to further influence its susceptibility to political risk is greatly diminished but not ended. It still has at least five different policies that it can pursue with varying chances of success: (1) planned divestment, (2) short-term profit maximization, (3) changing the benefit/cost ratio of expropriation, (4) developing local stakeholders, and (5) adaptation.

Planned Divestment.   Several influential authors, notably Raul Prebisch and Albert Hirschman, have suggested that multinational firms phase out their ownership of foreign investments over a fixed time period by selling all or a majority of their equity interest to local investors.[6] Such *planned divestment,* however, may be difficult to conclude to the satisfaction of all parties involved. If the buyout price were set in advance and the investment is unprofitable, the government would probably not honor the purchase commitment. Moreover, with the constant threat of expropriation present during the bargaining, it is unlikely a fair price can be negotiated.

Short-Term Profit Maximization.   Confronted with the need to divest itself wholly or partially of an equity position, the multinational corporation may respond by attempting to withdraw the maximum amount of cash from the local operation. By deferring maintenance expenditures, cutting investment to the minimum necessary to sustain the desired level of production, curtailing marketing expenditures, producing lower-quality merchandise, setting higher prices, and eliminating training programs, cash generation will be maximized for the short term, regardless of the effects of such actions on longer-run profitability and viability. This policy, which almost guarantees that the company will not be in business locally for long, is a response of desperation. Of course, the behavior is likely to accelerate expropriation if such was the government's intention—perhaps even if it were not the government's intention originally.

Hence, the firm must select its time horizon for augmenting cash outflow and consider how this behavior will affect government relations and actions. Surprisingly, most politicians do not seem to appreciate how strongly their rhetoric affects corporate decisions. In effect, government rhetoric about the evils of multinationals becomes a self-fulfilling prophecy because these threats induce more and more myopic corporate behavior.

The secondary implications of the short-term profit maximization strategy must be evaluated as well. The unfriendly government can be replaced by one more receptive to foreign investment (as occurred in Chile), or the multinational firm may want to supply the local market from affiliates in other countries. In either case, an aggressive tactic of withdrawing as much as possible from the threatened affiliate will probably be considered a hostile act and will vitiate all future dealings between the MNC and the country. Moreover, it is unlikely that a firm can get away with this behavior for long. Other governments will

---

[6]Raul Prebisch, "The Role of Foreign Private Investment in the Developing of Latin America," Sixth Annual Meeting of the IA-ECOSOC, June 1969; and Albert O. Hirschman, "How to Divest in Latin America, and Why," *Essays in International Finance,* No. 76, Princeton University, November 1969.

be put on notice and begin taking closer and more skeptical looks at the company's actions in their countries.

One alternative to this indirect form of divestment is to do nothing and hope that even though the local regime can take over an affiliate (with minor cost), it will choose not to do so. This wish is not necessarily in vain because it rests on the premise that the country needs foreign direct investment and will be unlikely to receive it if existing operations are expropriated without fair and full compensation. However, this strategy is essentially passive, resting on a belief that other multinationals will hurt the country (by withholding potential investments) if the country nationalizes local affiliates. Whether or not this passive approach will succeed is a function of how dependent the country is on foreign investment to realize its own development plans and the degree to which economic growth will be sacrificed for philosophical or political reasons.

■ _____

ILLUSTRATION

Beijing Jeep. After the United States restored diplomatic relations with China in 1979, Western businesses rushed in to take advantage of the world's largest undeveloped market. Among them was American Motors Corporation (AMC). In 1983, AMC and Beijing Automotive Works formed a joint venture called the Beijing Jeep Company to build and sell jeeps in China.[7] The aim of Beijing Jeep was to first modernize the old Chinese jeep, the BJ212, and then replace it with a "new, second-generation vehicle" for sale domestically and overseas. Because it was one of the earliest attempts to combine Chinese and foreign forces in heavy manufacturing, Beijing Jeep became the "flagship" project other U.S. firms watched to asses the business environment in China. Hopes were high.

AMC viewed this as a golden opportunity: Build jeeps with cheap labor and sell them in China and the rest of the Far East. The Chinese government wanted to learn modern automotive technology and earn foreign exchange. Most importantly, the People's Liberation Army wanted a convertible-top, four-door jeep, so that Chinese soldiers could jump in and out and open fire from inside the car.

That the army had none of these military vehicles when they entered Tienanmen Square in 1989 has to do with the fact that this jeep could not be made from any of AMC's existing jeeps. But in signing the initial contracts, the two sides glossed over this critical point. They also ignored the realities of China's economy. For managers and workers, productivity was much lower than anybody at AMC had ever imagined. Equipment maintenance was minimal. Aside from windshield solvents, spare-tire covers, and a few other minor parts, no parts could be manufactured in China. The joint venture, thus, had little choice but to turn the new Beijing jeep into the Cherokee Jeep, using parts kits imported from the United States. The Chinese were angry and humiliated not to be able to manufacture any major jeep components locally.

They got even madder when Beijing Jeep tried to force its Chinese buyers to pay half of the Cherokee's $19,000 sticker price in U.S. dollars. With foreign exchange in short supply, the Chinese government ordered its state agencies, the only potential customers, not

_____

[7]This example is adapted from Jim Mann, *Beijing Jeep: The Short, Unhappy Romance of American Business in China* (New York: Simon and Shuster, 1989).

to buy any more Cherokees and refused to pay the $2 million that various agencies owed on 200 Cherokees already purchased.

The joint venture would have collapsed right then had Beijing Jeep not been such an important symbol of the government's modernization program. After deciding it could not let the venture fail, China's leadership arranged a bailout. The Chinese abandoned their hopes of making a new military jeep. And AMC gained the right to convert renminbi (the Chinese currency) into dollars at the official (and vastly overvalued) exchange rate. With this right, AMC realized it could make more money by replacing the Cherokee with the old, and much cheaper to build, BJ212s. The BJ212s were sold in China for renminbi and these profits were converted into dollars.

It was the ultimate irony: An American company that originally expected to make huge profits by introducing modern technology to China and by selling its superior products to the Chinese found itself surviving, indeed thriving, by selling the Chinese established Chinese products. AMC succeeded because its venture attracted enough attention to turn the future of Beijing Jeep into a test of China's open-door policy.

A more active strategy is based on the premise that expropriation is basically a rational process—that governments generally seize property when the economic benefits outweigh the costs. This premise suggests two maneuvers characteristic of active political risk management: Increase the benefits to the government if it does not nationalize a firm's affiliate, and increase the costs if it does.

Changing the Benefit/Cost Ratio.   If the government's objectives in an expropriation are rational—that is, based on the belief that economic benefits will more than compensate for the costs—the multinational firm can initiate a number of programs to reduce the perceived advantages of local ownership and, thereby, diminish the incentive to expel foreigners. These steps include establishing local R&D facilities, developing export markets for the affiliate's output, training local workers and managers, expanding production facilities, and manufacturing a wider range of products locally as substitutes for imports. It should be recognized that many of the foregoing actions lower the cost of expropriation and, consequently, reduce the penalty for the government. A delicate balance must be observed.

Realistically, however, it appears that those countries most liable to expropriation view the benefits—real, imagined, or both—of local ownership as more important than the cost of replacing the foreign investor. Although the value of a subsidiary to the local economy can be important, its worth may not be sufficient to protect it from political risk. Thus, one aspect of a protective strategy must be to engage in actions that raise the cost of expropriation by increasing the negative sanctions it would involve. These actions include control over export markets, transportation, technology, trademarks and brand names, and components manufactured in other nations. Some of these tactics may not be available once the investment has been made, but others may still be implemented. However, an exclusive focus on providing negative sanctions may well be self-defeating by exacerbating the feelings of dependence and loss of control that often lead to expropriation in the first place. Where expropriation appears inevitable, with negative sanctions only buying more time, it may be more productive to prepare for negotiations to establish a future contractual-based relationship.

Developing Local Stakeholders. A more positive strategy is to cultivate local individuals and groups who have a stake in the affiliate's continued existence as a unit of the parent MNC. Potential stakeholders include consumers, suppliers, the subsidiary's local employees, local bankers, and joint-venture partners.

Consumers worried about a change in product quality or suppliers concerned about a disruption in their production schedules (or even a switch to other suppliers) brought about by a government takeover may have an incentive to protest. Similarly, well-treated local employees may lobby against expropriation.[8] Local borrowing could help give local bankers a stake in the health of the MNC's operations if any government action threatened the affiliate's cash flows and, thereby, jeopardized loan repayments.

Having local private investors as partners seems to provide protection. One study finds that joint ventures with local partners have historically suffered only a 0.2% rate of nationalization, presumably because this arrangement establishes a powerful local voice with a vested interest in opposing government seizure.[9]

The shield provided by local investors may be of limited value to the MNC, however. The partners will be deemed to be tainted by association with the multinational. A government probably would not be deterred from expropriation or enacting discriminatory laws because of the existence of local shareholders. Moreover, the action can be directed solely against the foreign investor. And the local partners can be the genesis of a move to expropriate to enable them to acquire the whole of a business at a low or no cost.

Adaptation. Today, some firms are trying a more radical approach to political risk management. Their policy entails adapting to the inevitability of potential expropriation and trying to earn profits on the firm's resources by entering into licensing and management agreements. For example, oil companies whose properties were nationalized by the Venezuelan government received management contracts to continue their exploration, refining, and marketing operations. These firms have recognized that it is not necessary to own or control an asset such as an oil well to earn profits. This form of arrangement may be more common in the future as countries develop greater management abilities and decide to purchase from foreign firms only those skills that remain in short supply at home. Those firms that are unable to surrender control of their foreign operations due to the integration of these operations in a worldwide production planning system or some other form of global strategy are also those least likely to be troubled by the threat of property seizure, as was pointed out in the aforementioned Chrysler example.

■ 20.4 ■
POSTEXPROPRIATION POLICIES

Only rarely does expropriation occur without warning. Usually, the threatened firm has some advance notice of the government's intentions. Upon receiving this notice, the firm

---

[8]French workers at U.S.-owned plants, satisfied with their employers' treatment of them, generally stayed on the job during the May 1968 student-worker riots in France, even though most French firms were struck.

[9]Bradley, "Managing Against Expropriation," pp. 75–83.

can open discussions with the government in an attempt to dissuade it from proceeding further. Often, however, the combination of threats and promises will not work, and preconfiscation discussions will turn into postconfiscation negotiations. William Hoskins identifies four basic phases of confrontation between government and firm in the postconfiscation period; each successive phase involves increased hostility: (1) rational negotiation, (2) applying power, (3) legal remedies, and (4) management surrender.[10]

Rational Negotiation

Once expropriation occurs, the value of further negotiation sharply diminishes. The aim during this phase is to maintain contact with the host government in an effort to persuade it that confiscation was a mistake. The firm can cite the future economic benefits that it will provide or the disastrous consequences of not returning corporate property. Presumably, however, the government has assessed the advantages and disadvantages of its action and has decided that the consequences are acceptable. Only if confiscation was just a bargaining ploy to gain company concessions is this approach likely to be successful.

Applying Power

If these concessions do not restore its property, the firm can direct its economic power at the host government, using the tactics discussed previously. These tactics would include cutting off vital components, export markets, technology, and management skills. However, it is likely that the government has already assessed these possibilities before confiscation and has decided that they are not sufficiently harmful. Otherwise, it probably would not have expropriated the company's operation in the first place.

Legal Remedies

During or after phases 1 and 2, the firm will begin to seek legal redress. Although the home country government may pursue certain legal remedies, the experience of U.S. investors has generally been that this support is unreliable at best. Thus, the MNC will ordinarily have to rely on its own initiative for legal satisfaction.

A basic rule of law is that legal relief must first be sought in the courts of the host country. Only after this avenue has been exhausted can the firm proceed to espouse its case in home country or international courts. Where host courts are independent and relatively impartial, seeking local redress of grievances is likely to be cheaper and quicker than the alternatives.

Where local remedies are obviously inadequate or the judiciary is subservient to the government, the firm can bypass the local courts and take legal action in home country courts. This action might involve seeking judgments against the host country's property in the home country or in a third country.

---

[10]William R. Hoskins, "How to Counter Expropriation," *Harvard Business Review,* September–October 1970, pp. 102–112.

However, investors who petition U.S. courts for legal aid and indemnification are faced with two impediments:

1. The *doctrine of sovereign immunity* says that a sovereign state may not be tried in the courts of another state without its consent.
2. The *act of state doctrine* states that a nation is sovereign within its own borders, and its domestic actions may not be questioned in the courts of another nation, even if these actions violate international law.

Arbitration of investment disputes is another alternative, made more concrete by the establishment in 1966 of the *International Center for Settlement of Investment Disputes*. Under the auspices of the World Bank, the Center's purpose is to encourage foreign direct investment by providing an international forum to which private investors can turn in investment disputes with a foreign nation. Once both parties have consented to the jurisdiction of the Center, usually as part of the initial investment agreement, neither party may unilaterally withdraw. The Center provides conciliation or binding arbitration, depending on the desires of the disputants. The Center's practical influence is small, however, as may be expected when its judgments are being brought against sovereign nations.

Management Surrender

Given the general lack of success during the first three phases, most firms eventually surrender to reality and try to salvage what they can of their investment. Some may simply settle for whatever insurance payments are due them. From an economic perspective, however, legal ownership of property is largely irrelevant; what really matters is the ability to generate cash flow from that property. Through contractual arrangements, continuing value can be received from a confiscated enterprise in at least three ways:

- Handling exports as in the past, but under a commission arrangement
- Furnishing technical and management skills under a management contract
- Selling raw materials and components to the foreign state

Although the MNC no longer has legal title to its foreign property, it can still engage in profitable business with the foreign country under arrangements such as these. This option assumes, of course, that during the previous three phases, relations with the government were not completely poisoned and that the firm does have valuable nonmonetary contributions to make to the host country.

■ 20.5 ■
ILLUSTRATION: KENNECOTT AND ANACONDA IN CHILE

Most raw material seekers active in the Third World have found themselves under considerable pressure either to divest or to enter into minority joint ventures in order to avoid outright expropriation by host governments submerged by the tidal wave of economic nationalism. The tale of the involvement of two U.S. copper MNCs in Chile illustrates how political risk can be managed ex ante through a policy of multilateral entrapment.[11]

Both Kennecott and Anaconda had long held and operated substantial copper mines in Chile, but had radically different outlooks on Chile's future. Kennecott relied on the giant mine of El Teniente for 30% of its world output, but invested minimally above depreciation to keep production slightly increasing. Between 1945 and 1965 it did not attempt to develop any new mining sites. But in 1964, under pressure from President Frei to expand and modernize its operation at El Teniente, Kennecott initiated an ambitious capital expenditures plan aimed at increasing copper production from 180,000 metric tons to 280,000 metric tons per year. The expansion plan was to be financed by selling a 51% interest in the mine for $80 million to the Chilean government in exchange for a ten-year management contract. In addition, further financing was sourced from the U.S. Eximbank ($110 million to be paid back over a period of 10–15 years) and the Chilean Copper Corporation ($24 million). In exchange for agreeing to a minority position in the newly created joint venture, Kennecott obtained a special reassessment of the book value of the El Teniente property (from $69 million to $286 million) and a dramatic reduction in taxes from 80% to 44% on its share of the profits.

Not only did Kennecott not commit one cent to the new mine, but it also developed a multinational web of stakeholders in the project. Kennecott began by insuring its equity sale to the Chilean government (reinvested in the mine) with the U.S. Agency for International Development (AID) and ensured that the Eximbank loan be unconditionally guaranteed by the Chilean state. In addition, any disputes between Kennecott and Chile would be submitted to the law of the state of New York. Kennecott also raised $45 million for the new joint venture by writing long-term contracts for the future output (literally mortgaging copper still in the ground) with European and Asian customers. Finally, collection rights on these contracts were sold to a consortium of European banks ($30 million) and Mitsui & Co., the Japanese trading company ($15 million).

Anaconda, by contrast, had been bullish on Chile all along. Having invested heavily in its own name from 1945 to 1965 in new mines and the modernization of old ones, it refused voluntary divestiture and was eventually forced to sell 51% of its Chilean holdings to the state in 1969. Although it had partial coverage of its holdings with AID prior to its forced divestiture, Anaconda had allowed the policy to lapse after 1969.

The real test of these different strategies came in 1971, when the defiant new Marxist government of President Allende assumed power. Both firms shortly fell prey to Chilean vengeance as Allende fulfilled his pledge to expropriate without compensation the foreign interests in Chilean copper. Kennecott received compensation from OPIC (the successor organization to AID) of $80 million plus interest—an amount that surpassed the book value of its pre-1964 holdings and that was eventually reimbursed to the U.S. government by Chile as a condition for rolling over the Chilean debt. Kennecott, on its own, was using the unconditional guarantee initially extracted from the Frei government for the original sale amount to obtain a writ of attachment in the U.S. federal courts against all Chilean property

---

[11]Adapted from Theodore H. Moran, *The Politics of Dependence: Copper in Chile* (Princeton, N.J.: Princeton University Press, 1974), by Laurent L. Jacque and Alan C. Shapiro.

within the courts' jurisdiction, including the jets of Lanchile when they landed in New York. Faced with these actions, the Allende government assumed all debt obligations that the joint venture had contracted with Eximbank and the consortium of European banks and Mitsui. In effect, Kennecott had been freed from any further international obligations, financial and otherwise.

Anaconda was expropriated without compensation from either the Chilean government—because it had no leverage being the sole investor—or from OPIC—because it had failed to insure against political risk. The only recourse left to Anaconda's board of directors was to fire its entire management—which the board did.

■ 20.6 ■
SUMMARY AND CONCLUSIONS

Country risk analysis is the assessment of factors that influence the likelihood that a country will have a healthy investment climate. To summarize, a favorable political risk environment depends on the existence of a stable political and economic system in which entrepreneurship is encouraged and free markets predominate. Under such a system, resources are most likely to be allocated to their highest valued uses and people will have the greatest incentive to take risks in productive ventures.

Regardless of whether a nation has a high or low country risk rating, however, individual foreign investments are typically subject to differing degrees of political risk, based on their time pattern of benefits. The major benefits to a host country from a foreign investment usually appear at the beginning. Over time, the added benefits become smaller and the costs more apparent. Unless the firm is continually renewing these benefits—by introducing more products, say, or by expanding output and developing export markets—it is likely to be subject to increasing political risks. The common attitude of government is to ignore the past and ask what a firm will do for it in the future. In a situation where the firm's future contributions are unlikely to evoke a favorable government reaction, the firm had best concentrate on protecting its foreign investments by raising the costs of nationalization.

■ QUESTIONS ■

1. When investing in a copper mine in Peru, how can a U.S. mining firm such as Kennecott reduce its political risk?

2. Generally speaking, what is the most appropriate means of managing expropriation risk?

3. Can avoiding politically risky countries eliminate a company's political risk? Explain.

4. What factors affect the degree of political risk faced by a firm operating in a foreign country?

5. How might a government budget deficit lead to inflation?

6. What political realities underlie a government budget deficit?

7. What are some indicators of country risk? Of country health?

8. What obstacles do Third World countries like Argentina, Brazil, and Ghana face in becoming developed nations with strong economies?

9. What can we learn about economic development and political risk from the contrasting experiences of East and West Germany, North and South Korea, and communist China and Taiwan, Hong Kong and Singapore?

10. What role do property rights and the price system play in national development and economic efficiency?

11. What indicators would you look for in assessing the political riskiness of an investment in Eastern Europe?

12. Exhibit 20.3 describes some economic changes that have been instituted by Mexico in recent years.

   a. What are the likely consequences of those changes?

   b. Who are the winners and the losers from these economic changes?

13. What is the link between a controlled exchange rate system and political risk?

14. Milton Friedman has suggested that public sector firms in Latin American countries should simply be given away, possibly to their employees. How do you think workers would feel about being given (for free) ownership of the public sector firms that employ them? Why?

■ PROBLEMS ■

1. Comment on the following statement discussing Mexico's recent privatization. "Mexican state companies are owned in the name of the people, but are run and now privatized to benefit Mexico's ruling class."

2. Between 1981 and 1987, direct foreign investment in the Third World plunged by over 50%. The World Bank is concerned about this decline and wants to correct it by improving the investment climate in Third World countries. Its solution: Create a Multilateral Investment Guarantee Agency (MIGA) that will guarantee foreign investments against expropriation at rates to be subsidized by Western governments.

   a. Assess the likely consequences of MIGA on both the volume of Western capital flows to Third World nations and the efficiency of international capital allocation.

   b. How will MIGA affect the probability of expropriation and respect for property rights in Third World countries?

   c. Is MIGA likely to improve the investment climate in Third World nations?

   d. According to a senior World Bank official (*The Wall Street Journal,* December 22, 1987, p. 20), "There is vastly more demand for political risk coverage than the sum total available." Is this a valid economic argument for setting up MIGA? Explain.

   e. Assess the following argument made on behalf of MIGA by a State Department memo: "We should avoid penalizing a good project [by not providing subsidized insurance] for bad government policies over which they have limited influence .... Restrictions on eligible countries [receiving insurance subsidies because of their doubtful investment policies] will decrease MIGA's volume of business and spread of risk, making it harder to be self-sustaining." (Quoted in *The Wall Street Journal,* December 22, 1987, p. 20.)

3. You have been asked to head up a special presidential commission on the Soviet economy. Your first assignment is to assess the economic consequences of the following seven policies and suggest alternative policies that may have more favorable consequences.

   a. Under the current Soviet system, any profits realized by a state enterprise are turned over to the state to be used as the state sees fit. At the same time, shortfalls of money don't constrain enterprises from consuming resources. Instead, the state bank automatically advances needy enterprises credit, at a zero interest rate, to buy the inputs they need to fulfill the state plan and to make any necessary investments.

   b. The Soviet fiscal deficit had risen from 2.5% of GNP when Mikhail Gorbachev assumed power in 1985 to an estimated 13.1% of GNP in 1989. This deficit has been financed almost exclusively by printing rubles. At the same time, prices are controlled for most goods and services.

   c. Soviet enterprises are allocated foreign exchange to buy goods and services necessary to accomplish the state plan. Any foreign exchange earned must be turned over to the state bank.

   d. In an effort to introduce a more market-oriented system, some Soviet enterprises have been allowed to set their own prices on goods and services. However, other features of the system have not been changed: Each enterprise is still held accountable for meeting a certain profit target; only one state enterprise can produce each type of good or service; and individuals are not permitted to compete against state enterprises.

   e. Given the disastrous state of Soviet agriculture, the Soviet government has permitted some private plots on which anything grown can be sold at unregulated prices in open-air markets. Because of their success, the government has recently expanded this program, giving Soviet farmers access to much more acreage. At the same time, a number of Western nations are organizing massive food shipments to the Soviet Union to cope with the current food shortages.

   f. The United States and other Western nations are considering instituting a Marshall Plan for Eastern Europe that would involve massive loans to the Soviet Union and other Eastern Bloc nations in order to prop up Gorbachev and the reform governments.

   g. In order to strip the country's powerful black marketeers of their operating capital, driving as many as possible out of business, and to reduce inflation, which has been running at about 80% a year, Mr. Gorbachev has decreed that all 50- and 100-ruble notes would be banned. Each person could exchange one month's salary, up to a maximum of 1,000 rubles, for small-denomination notes. In addition, savings accounts will be frozen, with people allowed to withdraw only 500 rubles a month from their bank accounts for the next six months. The official Soviet news agency Tass reported that the government had "clearly decided that the confiscation version of monetary reform was the most efficient and least expensive version at its disposal."

4. The president of Mexico has asked you to advise him on the likely economic consequences of the following five policies designed to improve Mexico's economic environment. Describe the consequences of each policy, and evaluate the extent to which these proposed policies will achieve their intended objective.

   a. Expand the money supply to drive down interest rates and stimulate economic activity.

   b. Increase the minimum wage so as to raise the incomes of poor workers.

   c. Impose import restrictions on most products so as to preserve the domestic market for local manufacturers and, thereby, increase national income.

   d. Raise corporate and personal tax rates from 50% to 70% to boost tax revenues and reduce the Mexican government deficit.

   e. Fix the nominal exchange rate at its current level in order to hold down the cost to Mexican consumers of imported necessities (assume that inflation is currently 100% annually in Mexico).

5.* The president of Brazil has just appointed you to work with the country's cabinet ministers to launch a radical restructuring of the Brazilian economy. Inflation is running at over 1,000% annually, and the federal government is running a deficit in excess of 10% of GNP (the U.S. deficit is about 3% of GNP). To finance the deficit, the government has incurred huge debts, both internally and externally.

In your initial discussions with the cabinet ministers, you realize that there is considerable disagreement about a number of specific program proposals. Your job is to assess the issues and the relative merits of the proposed policies.

a. The Governor of the Banco do Brasil, Brazil's central bank, wants to cease its purchases of government bonds issued by the Ministry of Finance to fund the ongoing federal budget deficit. The Banco do Brasil has acquired 50% to 60% of all government bonds issued in the past several years with money expressly created for that purpose. In other words, it has been monetizing the deficit. Other cabinet ministers are afraid that this policy will lead to higher interest rates and wonder how the deficit can be financed otherwise.

b. The Minister of Infrastructure has proposed that his ministry will begin privatizing the hundreds of state-owned enterprises under his administration. These enterprises include virtually all of Brazil's steel industry, mining industry, electric utilities, the telephone company, national oil company, chemical companies, and a wide range of manufacturing companies. Opponents claim that this move will lead to massive unemployment and the bankruptcy of vital national industries.

c. The Minister of Political Economy has proposed that Brazil enter into free trade agreements with its Latin American neighbors. This would involve eliminating all tariffs, duties, and fees on imports. A number of other government leaders oppose this move, since the Brazilian market is larger and generally more protected than those of its neighbors. They feel that opening the border would expose Brazil to rapid growth in imports that exceed any incremental export activity.

d. The Minister of Finance has proposed creating a new tax on consumption and lowering income tax rates. His concern is that Brazil's personal savings rate has been close to zero over the past several years. He believes that increased savings will help to dampen inflation, lower interest rates on the federal debt, and promote exports. Critics of this proposal argue that the vast majority of Brazil's population are living very near the poverty line and that a consumption tax would be highly regressive (hit the poor relatively harder than the rich). It would also tend to dampen domestic demand, the principal engine of economic growth in Brazil.

e. The Minister of Labor has proposed raising the minimum wage so as raise the income of poor workers and, thereby, offset the effects of restructuring on them. Other cabinet members are concerned about the effects this policy will have on employment and competitiveness.

f. The Central Bank has proposed that it replace the current fixed exchange rate system with a freely floating exchange rate system. Critics of this proposal argue that floating the cruzeiro will devalue the currency and raise the cost of living (by boosting the price of imported necessities) for Brazilians.

g. In order to reduce the money supply and, thereby, suppress inflation, the Minister of Finance has proposed freezing all bank accounts. Depositors will be able to withdraw only the cruzeiro equivalent of about $1,000. However, other cabinet ministers are concerned about possible adverse consequences of such a freeze.

* Developed by William H. Davidson and Alan C. Shapiro.

■ BIBLIOGRAPHY ■

Bradley, David. "Managing Against Expropriation." *Harvard Business Review,* July–August 1977, pp. 75–83.

Kobrin, Stephen J. "Political Risk: A Review and Reconsideration." *Journal of International Business Studies,* Spring–Summer 1979, pp. 67–80.

Krueger, Anne O. "Asian Trade and Growth Lessons." *American Economic Review,* May 1990, pp. 108–112.

Landes, David S. "Why Are We So Rich and They So Poor?" *American Economic Review,* May 1990, pp. 1–13.

Shapiro, Alan C. "The Management of Political Risk." *Columbia Journal of World Business,* Fall 1981, pp. 45–56.

Stobaugh, Robert B. "How to Analyze Foreign Investment Climates." *Harvard Business Review,* September–October 1969, pp. 100–108.

Van Agtamael, A.W. "How Business Has Dealt with Political Risk." *Financial Executive,* January 1976, pp. 26–30.

■ 21 ■

International Tax Management

There is no art which one government sooner learns of another, than that of draining money from the pockets of people.

—Adam Smith (1776)—

It ought to be remembered that when the wisest government has exhausted all the proper subjects of taxation, it must, in cases of urgent necessity, have recourse to improper ones.

—Adam Smith (1776)—

■ As can be seen throughout this book, taxes have a significant impact on areas as diverse as making foreign investment decisions, managing exchange risk, planning capital structures, determining financing costs, and managing interaffiliate fund flows. Consequently, the international financial executive must be knowledgeable about the broad outlines of the international tax environment and its impact on various corporate decisions.

International tax planning involves using the flexibility of the multinational corporation in structuring foreign operations and remittance policies in order to maximize global after-tax cash flows. Tax management is difficult because the ultimate tax burden on a multinational firm's income is the result of a complex interplay between the heterogeneous tax systems of home and host governments, each with its own fiscal objectives. These complexities, which have been exacerbated by the Tax Reform Act of 1986, have led several multinationals to develop elaborate computer simulation models in an attempt to facilitate their tax planning.

This chapter presents an overview of international taxation, including tax treatment of foreign-source earnings, tax credits, effects of bilateral tax treaties for avoiding double taxation, tax havens, special incentives to reduce taxes, and advantages of organizing overseas operations in the form of a branch or a subsidiary. Although the focus here is on U.S. tax laws, the first section discusses some of the relevant tax theory behind the home country taxation of foreign-source income.

■ 21.1 ■
THE THEORETICAL OBJECTIVES OF TAXATION

There are two concepts of taxation that are characteristic of most tax systems: neutrality and equity. Each is oriented toward achieving a status of equality within the tax system. The economic difference between the two concepts lies in their effect on decision making. Whereas tax neutrality is achieved by ensuring that decisions are unaffected by the tax laws, tax equity is accomplished by ensuring that equal sacrifices are made in bearing the tax burdens.

Tax Neutrality

A *neutral tax* is one that would not influence any aspects of the investment decision, such as the location of the investment or the nationality of the investor. The basic justification for tax neutrality is economic efficiency. World welfare will be increased if capital is free to move from countries where the rate of return is low to those where it is high. Therefore, if the tax system distorts the after-tax profitability between two investments, or between two investors, leading to a different set of investments being undertaken, then gross world product will be reduced. Tax neutrality can be separated into domestic and foreign neutrality.

Domestic neutrality encompasses the equal treatment of U.S. citizens investing at home and U.S. citizens investing abroad. The key issues to consider here are whether the marginal tax burden is equalized between home and host countries and whether such equalization is desirable. This form of neutrality involves (1) uniformity in both the applicable tax rate and the determination of taxable income and (2) equalization of all taxes on profits.

The lack of uniformity in setting tax rates and determining taxable income stems from differences in accounting methods and governmental policies. There are no universal principles to follow in accounting for depreciation, allocating expenses, and determining revenue. Therefore, different levels of profitability for the same cash flows are possible. Moreover, governmental policy in the areas of tax allocation and incentives is not uniform. Some capital expenditures are granted investment credits while others are not, and the provisions for tax-loss carrybacks and carryforwards vary in leniency as well. Thus, in many cases, equal tax rates do not lead to equal tax burdens.

The incidence of indirect taxation is also an important issue. The importance of this issue, particularly for U.S. multinationals, stems from the fact that foreign countries levy heavier indirect taxes than does the United States, especially in the form of value-added taxes (VAT). If these indirect taxes are borne out of profits rather than being shifted to consumers or other productive factors, then domestic tax neutrality will be violated, even if direct tax rates are equal.

It is the practice of the United States to tax foreign income at the same rate as domestic income, with a credit for any taxes paid to a foreign government in accordance with basic domestic tax neutrality. However, there are several important departures from the theoretical norm of tax neutrality.

1. The United States has never allowed an investment tax credit on foreign investments. The rules for carrybacks and carryforwards are also less liberal on foreign operations.
2. The tax credit for taxes paid to a foreign government is limited to the amount of tax that would have been due if the income had been earned in the United States. There is no additional credit if the tax rate in the foreign country is higher than that of the United States.
3. There are special tax incentives for U.S. exports sold through a Foreign Sales Corporation (FSC).
4. The United States defers taxation of income earned in foreign subsidiaries (except Subpart F income, to be discussed in a later section) until it is returned to the United States in the form of a dividend. This deferral becomes important only if the effective foreign tax is below that of the United States.

Both the theory and the actual practice give a good indication of the influence domestic tax neutrality has on U.S. tax policy. This influence, however, is limited with regard to foreign neutrality.

The theory behind *foreign neutrality* in taxation is that the tax burden placed on the foreign subsidiaries of U.S. firms should equal that imposed on foreign-owned competitors operating in the same country. There are basically two types of foreign competitors that the U.S. subsidiary faces: the firm owned by residents of the host country and the foreign subsidiary of a non-U.S. corporation. Since other countries gear their tax systems to benefit domestic firms, the United States would have to modify its tax system to that of other countries to achieve foreign neutrality. This modification would mean foregoing taxation of income from foreign sources. In other words, the corporation's foreign affiliate would be impacted by taxes only in the country of operation. Foreign neutrality cannot be a principal guide for tax policy because its achievement would be impossible in light of present U.S. tax policies and objectives. Certainly it is inconsistent with the principle of domestic neutrality.

Most major capital exporting countries—including the United States, Germany, Japan, Sweden, and Great Britain—follow a mixed policy of foreign and domestic tax neutrality whereby the home government currently taxes foreign branch profits but defers taxation of foreign subsidiary earnings until those earnings are repatriated. Host taxes on branch or subsidiary earnings may be credited against the home tax; the credit is limited by the home tax or host tax, whichever is lower. However, this latter provision violates domestic neutrality.

Several home countries—including France, Canada, and the Netherlands—fully or partially exempt foreign subsidiary and/or branch earnings from domestic taxation. Other countries—such as Italy, Switzerland, and Belgium—exclude a portion of foreign income when calculating the domestic tax liability. The policy of equity in taxation is also justified on many of the same grounds as neutrality in taxation.

Tax Equity

The basis of *tax equity* is the criterion that all taxpayers in a similar situation be subject to the same rules. All U.S. corporations should be taxed on income, regardless of where it is earned. Thus, the income of a foreign branch should be taxed in the same manner that the income of a domestic branch is taxed. This form of equity should neutralize the tax consideration in a decision on foreign location versus domestic location. The basic consideration here is that all similarly situated taxpayers should help pay the cost of operating a government. The key to the application of this concept lies in the definition of similarly situated. According to the U.S. Department of the Treasury, the definition encompasses all entities and income of U.S. corporations. Opponents of the position advocate that the definition should limit taxation only to sources within the United States. (The effect of this difference in interpretation will be seen when Subpart F taxation is discussed later in the chapter.)

Tax Treaties

The general tax policies toward the multinational firm outlined here are modified somewhat by a bilateral network of tax treaties designed to avoid double taxation of income by two taxing jurisdictions. Although foreign tax credits help to some extent, the treaties go further in that they allocate certain types of income to specific countries and also reduce or eliminate withholding taxes.

These tax treaties should be considered when planning foreign operations because under some circumstances, they can provide for full exemption from tax in the country in which a minor activity is carried on (one that does not require a permanent establishment in the country). The general pattern of the treaties is for the two treaty countries to grant reciprocal reductions in withholding taxes on dividends, royalties, and interest.

■ 21.2 ■
U.S. TAXATION OF MULTINATIONAL CORPORATIONS

The overriding criterion of U.S. tax law historically has been *juridic domicile*—in the country of incorporation. Domestic corporations are taxed on their income earned in the United States. A *domestic corporation* is defined simply as one incorporated within the United States; a *foreign corporation* is one incorporated outside the United States. Juridic domicile means that if the foreign-based affiliate of a U.S. company is not a branch, but a separate incorporated entity under the host country's law, its profit would generally not be subject to U.S. taxation unless, and until, that profit is transferred to the parent company in this country or distributed as dividends to its stockholders.

U.S. tax laws distinguish between branches and subsidiaries. Foreign activity undertaken as a *branch* is regarded as part of the parent's own operation. The result is that earnings realized by a branch of a U.S. corporation are fully taxed as foreign income in the year in which they are earned, even though they may not be remitted to the U.S. parent company. In contrast, taxes on earnings of a foreign *subsidiary* can be deferred until the year they are transferred to the U.S. parent as dividends or payments for corporate services (for example, fees and royalties). This deferral permits the parent company to enjoy foreign tax advantages as long as it reinvests foreign income in operations abroad. Branch losses, however, may be written off immediately against U.S. taxes owed, whereas subsidiary losses will be recognized from a U.S. perspective only when the affiliate is liquidated. Hence, if a foreign investment is expected to show initial losses, it may pay to first operate it as a branch. When the operation turns profitable, it can then be reorganized as a subsidiary, with a possible deferral of U.S. taxes owed. (The issue of taxation and corporate organization is discussed in Section 21.5.)

Foreign Tax Credit

In order to eliminate double taxation of foreign-source earnings, the United States and other home countries grant a credit against domestic income tax for foreign income taxes already paid. In general, if the foreign tax on a dollar earned abroad and remitted to the United States is less than or equal to the U.S. rate of 34%, then that dollar will be subject to additional tax in order to bring the total tax paid up to 34 cents. If the foreign tax rate is in excess of 34%, the United States will not impose additional taxes and, in fact, will allow the use of these excess taxes paid as an offset against U.S. taxes owed on other foreign-source income. These *foreign tax credits* (FTCs) are either direct or indirect.

Direct Foreign Tax Credit.   A direct tax is one imposed directly on a U.S. taxpayer. Direct taxes include the tax paid on the earnings of a foreign branch of a U.S. company and any foreign withholding taxes deducted from remittances to a U.S. investor. Under Section 901 of the U.S. Internal Revenue Code, a *direct foreign tax credit* can be taken for these direct taxes paid to a foreign government.

Taxes that are allowable in computing foreign tax credits must be based on income. These taxes would include foreign income taxes paid by an overseas branch of a U.S. corporation and taxes withheld from passive income (i.e., dividends, rents, and royalties). Credit is not granted for nonincome-based taxes such as a sales tax or VAT.

Indirect Foreign Tax Credit.   U.S. corporate shareholders owning at least 10% of a foreign corporation are also permitted under Section 902 to claim an *indirect foreign tax credit*—or *deemed paid credit*—on dividends received from that foreign unit, based on an appointment of the foreign income taxes already paid by the affiliate. This indirect credit is in addition to the direct tax credit allowed for any dividend withholding taxes imposed.

The formula for computing the indirect tax credit is

$$\text{Indirect tax credit} = \frac{\text{Dividend (including withholding tax)}}{\text{Earnings net of foreign income taxes}} \times \text{Foreign tax}$$

The foreign dividend included in U.S. income is the dividend received *grossed up* to include both withholding and deemed paid taxes.

The calculation of both direct and indirect tax credits for a foreign branch and a foreign subsidiary is shown in Exhibit 21.1. In no case can the credit for taxes paid abroad in a given year exceed the U.S. tax payable on total foreign-source income for the same year. This rule is called the *overall limitation* on tax credit.

In calculating the overall limitation, total credits are limited to the U.S. tax attributable to foreign-source income (interest income is excluded). Losses in one country are set off against profits in others, thereby reducing foreign income and the total tax credit permitted. Thus,

$$\begin{array}{l}\text{Maximum total} \\ \text{tax credit}\end{array} = \frac{\begin{array}{c}\text{Consolidated foreign} \\ \text{profits and losses}\end{array}}{\text{Worldwide taxable income}} \times \begin{array}{l}\text{Amount of} \\ \text{tax liability}\end{array}$$

If the overall limitation applies, the excess foreign tax credit may be carried back two years and forward five years. The result of the carryback and carryforward provisions is that taxes paid by an MNC to a foreign country may be averaged over an eight-year period in calculating the firm's U.S. tax liability.

■ **EXHIBIT 21.1**   U.S. Foreign Tax Credit Calculations

Branch				Subsidiary		
20	40	50	Foreign tax rates	20	40	50
			Withholding tax 10% dividends			
			0% branch			
100	100	100	Pretax profits	100	100	100
(20)	(40)	(50)	Foreign corporate tax	(20)	(40)	(50)
80	60	50	Net available for dividends	80	60	50
—	—	—	Withholding tax	(8)	(6)	(5)
80	60	50	Net cash to U.S. shareholder	72	54	45
			Dividend income—gross	80	60	50
			Gross-up for foreign taxes paid by			
			subsidiary	20	40	50
100	100	100	U.S. taxable income	100	100	100
34	34	34	U.S. tax @ 34% before foreign tax credit	34	34	34
			Less U.S. foreign tax credit:			
(20)	(40)	(50)	Direct credit—withholding, branch	(8)	(6)	(5)
			taxes			
			Indirect credit	(20)	(40)	(50)
—	—	—				
14	(6)	(16)	Net U.S. tax cost—all credits used	6	(12)	(21)
34	34	34	Total tax cost—all credits used	34	34	34
34	40	50	Total tax cost—excess credits not used	34	46	55

Additional Limitations on the Foreign Tax Credit

In the past, MNCs could average low-tax income with high-tax income to create a lower overall tax rate. The Tax Reform Act of 1986, however, creates five new and distinct *baskets,* or limitations for which separate tax credits will now be calculated. These basket limitations are in addition to the overall limitation discussed above. The first four baskets apply to controlled foreign corporations. A foreign corporation is a *controlled foreign corporation* (CFC) if more than 50% of the voting power of its stock is owned by U.S. shareholders (i.e., U.S. citizens, residents, partnerships, trusts, or domestic corporations). For the purpose of arriving at the percentage of control, only shareholders controlling (directly or indirectly) 10% or more of the voting power are counted. Thus, a foreign corporation in which six unrelated U.S. citizens each own 9% would not be a CFC; nor would a foreign corporation in which U.S. shareholders own exactly 50% be so construed.

The four baskets are passive income, financial services income, shipping income, and high withholding-tax interest income. The fifth is a separate basket for dividends from minority foreign subsidiaries—the so-called 10–50 companies. Each 10–50 subsidiary is subject to its own separate limitation. The foreign tax credit on each basket of income is limited to the U.S. tax on that income. Other income goes into the "overall" basket, with its own limitation.

This new approach prevents averaging the rates on highly taxed and low-taxed classes of income. In particular, it isolates classes of income that can be shifted to foreign sources without attracting much (or any) foreign tax. The purpose is to prevent foreign taxes paid in high-tax nations to be used to offset U.S. tax owed on certain types of low-tax income. The result is higher U.S. taxes.

With respect to remittances (or deemed remittances) from controlled foreign corporations to a related U.S. company, the 1986 tax act introduces a new method—called *look thru*—that takes into account the nature of the underlying income of the CFC out of which the item of income in question was paid. *Thru* is the spelling in the statute, and it is the only simplification in the foreign tax area. The look-thru rules recharacterize remittances from a CFC and place them into the separate FTC limitation baskets—depending on whether the underlying income of the CFC is operating income, passive income or the like. The look-thru rules do not apply to remittances from noncontrolled foreign corporations.

Under the look-thru rules, if all of a CFC's income is operating income, all its payments to its U.S. parent will be deemed operating income (i.e., the overall basket)—regardless of whether the remittances are dividends, interest, rents, or royalties. Thus high-taxed dividends (deemed-paid taxes plus withholding tax) can be averaged with low (or no) taxed interest and royalties.

On the other hand, if the payer is not a CFC (i.e., 10% to 50% owned), its dividends will be in a separate per-corporation basket. This rule means that any excess credits on deemed-paid dividends and dividend withholding will be lost forever except in the (unlikely) event that they can be carried forward or carried back. With foreign corporate tax rates generally in the 40% to 50% range, plus withholding taxes of at least 5%, the disallowance hurts.

■ ──

ILLUSTRATION

How Look-Thru Raises an MNC's Tax Bill. Here's how these FTC limitations act to raise an MNC's tax bill: A $550,000 dividend from a French subsidiary to a U.S. parent implies $1 million in pretax earnings. That is, $1 million in earnings, less tax at France's 45% corporate tax rate ($450,000 deemed paid), nets to a $550,000 dividend. The same $1 million earned in the United States and taxed at 34% would result in a tax bill of $340,000. The French tax of $450,000 less the $340,000 creates a tax credit of $110,000.

At the same time, France also has a 10% withholding tax on royalty payments. A royalty of $1 million paid to the U.S. parent in the same year would result in French withholding taxes of $100,000. With a U.S. tax rate of 34%, the royalty would attract an additional U.S. tax bill of $240,000 ($1,000,000 × 0.34 – 100,000 deemed paid).

Under the old rules, the $110,000 foreign tax credit from the dividend could be used to offset the additional U.S. tax on the royalty paid to the parent. Instead of paying the full $240,000, the firm's tax would be reduced by the $100,000 FTC to $140,000.

But under the new rules, only the percentage of the dividend attributable to royalty income—as prescribed in the look-thru rules—could be used to offset the withholding tax. Assume that only 5% of the French subsidiary's pretax income was attributable to royalties. Throwing the royalty earnings (now part of the dividend) and the royalty payment into their own basket, only 5% (or $5,500) of the tax credit could be applied. The result: a net excess FTC of $104,500.

── ■

Allocation of Income Rules

One of the most important features of the foreign tax credit calculation is that it is based on ratios of *taxable* income—that is, gross income minus deductions—rather than on ratios of gross income. Disputes abound between taxpayers and the IRS as to which expenses are deductible in general. It is beyond the scope and purpose of this chapter, however, to deal with the complexities of such disputes. Assuming a taxpayer corporation and the IRS are agreed as to the total amount of worldwide deductions, what then becomes important is the *allocation* of deductions between foreign-source and domestic-source income.

According to both the U.S. Internal Revenue Code and generally accepted accounting principles, a dollar that was spent on earning income in India should be allocated to, and deducted against, dollars of income from India, whether the dollar of expense was actually spent in India, New York, or any other place. Suppose a corporation has worldwide operations with a head office in New York, for example. Obviously a certain percentage of salary and other head-office expenses in New York should properly be deducted against income abroad because work is done at the head office that in effect "earns" the foreign-source income.

The U.S. source of income rules are important to U.S. companies because foreign-source taxable income is a key element in calculating the foreign tax credit (the higher the better from the taxpayer's point of view). Current tax law obliges companies to transfer certain interest, R&D, and general and administrative expenses incurred in the United States to the books of foreign subsidiaries.

Allocation of Interest Expense.   Under prior law, interest expenses on U.S. borrowing was allocated against U.S. income. Thus, a U.S. parent could borrow (incurring interest expense) and then inject foreign operations with an equity investment (using the borrowed funds). The 1986 tax act allocates interest expense, no matter where incurred, on the basis of assets. For example, if interest expense is $100 and foreign assets account for 30% of total assets, then $30 of that interest is allocated against foreign-source income—even if all the interest is paid in the United States by the parent—thereby reducing the FTC limitation. This rule also eliminates the U.S. tax deduction for that part of interest expense allocated abroad. Here, only $70 of the $100 in U.S. interest expense is deductible in the United States.

Research and Development Expenses.   Under current tax law, 50% of all U.S.-based R&D expenses are apportioned to U.S.-source income. The remaining 50% can then be apportioned between U.S.-source and foreign-source income on the basis of either sales or gross income.

Expenses Other Than Interest and R&D.   Expenses not directly allocable to a specific income producing activity are to be allocated based on either assets or gross income.

Allocating more expenses incurred in the United States against foreign-source income lowers the FTC limitation—the maximum amount of foreign tax credits that can be applied against U.S. taxes—and, therefore, the deductibility of foreign taxes paid.

The impact that such reallocations can have on the calculation of the foreign tax credit can readily be seen by returning to the tax credit calculation of the overall limitation:

$$\frac{\text{A. Taxable income from foreign sources}}{\text{B. Taxable income from all sources}} = \frac{\text{C. Maximum foreign tax credit}}{\text{D. U.S. tax liability before foreign tax credit}} \qquad (21.1)$$

In this equation, the B figure will remain unchanged no matter what allocation is used because

Total income – Total deductions = Total taxable income

and allocations among countries have no impact on the net total figure. Since B is constant in a given year, D will also be constant and will equal a flat 34% of B. The figure that will be affected by allocations is A.

As dollars of head-office expense are allocated abroad, they are deducted from gross foreign-source income, thereby reducing the net taxable foreign-source income, A. As A is reduced and B and D remain constant, C must also be reduced in order to maintain the equality. Thus, it is in the interest of the IRS to allocate head-office expenses abroad because by doing so, the IRS reduces the maximum foreign tax credit available to the domestic corporation.

Such allocations by the IRS would not work a hardship on U.S. corporations if the IRS allocations were binding on foreign taxing authorities. This, however, is not the case. A U.S. corporation would not object to a reduced foreign tax credit limitation if its actual foreign taxes were being reduced as well, and so long as it were able to credit all eligible foreign taxes paid. A serious problem arises when the IRS allocates certain head-office expenses to income earned in France, for example, but the French tax authorities refuse to recognize such expenses as deductions for purposes of reducing the French income-tax liability (or, alternatively, the deductibility of the expenses is recognized but not the propriety of the allocation to French-source income). In this case, the expenses are not deductible anywhere and, yet, the foreign tax credit limitation has been reduced by the allocation of these expenses to foreign sources.

For example, assume

U.S. income	$100
Country X income	$100
U.S. tax rate	34%
Country X tax rate	50%
Head-office expenses (HOE)	$10

Using the foreign tax credit (FTC) calculation set forth earlier in Equation 21.1 (A/B = C/D), we can examine three possible cases:

Case 1: Head-office expense allocable to the United States

U.S. income	100
Less HOE	10
U.S. taxable income	90
Country X income	100
Country X tax at 50%	50

FTC calculation

$$\frac{A}{B} = \frac{100}{190} = \frac{34}{64.6} = \frac{C}{D}$$

Thus, $50 in taxes is paid to X; and a maximum tax credit, C, of $34 is permitted.

Case 2: Head-office expense allocable to X and head-office expense deductible in X

Country X income	100
Less HOE	10
Country X taxable income	90
Country X tax at 50%	45
U.S. taxable income	100

FTC calculation

$$\frac{A}{B} = \frac{90}{190} = \frac{30.6}{64.6} = \frac{C}{D}$$

Thus, $45 is paid to X; and a maximum tax credit, C, of $30.60 is permitted.

Case 3: Head-office expense allocable to X but head-office expense not deductible in X

U.S. Perspective	
Country X income	100
Less HOE	10
Country X taxable income	90
U.S. taxable income	100

Country X Perspective	
Country X taxable income	100
Country X tax at 50%	50

FTC calculation

$$\frac{A}{B} = \frac{90}{190} = \frac{30.6}{64.6} = \frac{C}{D}$$

Thus, A equals 90 rather than 100 because the foreign tax credit is calculated under IRS regulations and allocations rather than by the liabilities imposed under foreign law. According to the IRS, the $10 of HOE should be deducted from $100 gross income in Country X before taxable income from Country X (A) is determined. The result is that $50 in taxes is paid to X and a maximum tax credit, C, of $30.60 is permitted.

The U.S. corporation here has been forced, by an IRS reallocation and a foreign government's refusal to permit a deduction, into an excess foreign tax credit position. The net result is to raise taxes on corporate profits, leading to tax avoidance behavior. The latter includes shifting expenses from the United States to foreign subsidiaries, especially those in high-tax countries, and developing more creative tax management strategies. It can easily be seen in the third case that by shifting an additional $10 overseas to a zero-tax subsidiary, $3.40 in foreign tax credits can be created and used.

It is interesting to note that although the maximum foreign tax credits available are reduced by an IRS reallocation, actual FTCs can be increased. Again returning to the third case, if the affiliate declares a dividend of $36, then its foreign tax credit equals

$$\frac{\text{Dividends}}{\text{Net earnings from U.S. perspective}} \frac{36}{40} \times (\text{Foreign tax}) \, 50 = \$45$$

Without the reallocation of the $10 in head-office expense, the affiliate's income from a U.S. perspective would equal $50, leading to a foreign tax credit of $36:

$$\frac{36}{50} \times 50 = \$36$$

Hence, despite a reduction in the maximum allowable FTC, the actual credit has been increased from $36 to $45. But because of the FTC limitation, the firm winds up with an excess foreign tax credit of $14.40 (45 − 30.60).

Under the new tax rules, the low 34% statutory rate will generate more FTCs for multinationals. At the same time, the proliferation of income baskets will isolate many FTCs from a company's pool of low-tax income, making it harder to use them up. With the low U.S. corporate tax rate, the basic planning ploy of U.S. multinationals must be to reduce foreign income taxes. An obvious approach is to (1) shift expenses from the United States to higher-tax countries (e.g., by borrowing abroad instead of in the United States) and (2) maximize remittances by foreign subsidiaries that are deductible in the foreign country (e.g., interest, rents, royalties, and management fees) rather than nondeductible dividends. These types of payments also typically incur less withholding tax than dividends under most tax treaties. Simultaneously, firms should try to increase income in low-tax countries to offset as many remaining FTCs as possible.

One approach is to establish a management and financing center (MFC) that charges out financial and other services to sister operating subsidiaries. By locating the MFC in a low-tax nation, the income earned from these services—in the form of management fees, interest payments, and royalties—will be minimally taxed. Moreover, when the MFC's income is remitted to the United States and averaged in with other, higher-taxed income, it effectively reduces FTCs.

A closer look at the technicalities of the FTC regulations explains why the MFC approach works. When a company computes its FTC limitation, it looks at each foreign-sourced income stream to determine if it goes into a separate basket or into the overall limitation basket. Because MFC service income is considered passive, it comes under Subpart F (described shortly) of the tax code. Not only is Subpart F income taxable immediately, but it is generally allocated to a separate basket. This allocation would render the whole MFC strategy ineffective because FTCs will generally accumulate in the overall basket, not in the separate baskets.

However, thanks to the look-thru rules of the FTC provisions, this income does not wind up in the passive-income basket. Instead, much of it will be allocable to the overall basket, where most high-tax income ends up. The look-thru rules maintain that even though the income is passive to the MFC, the IRS must look through to see what sort of income the paying subsidiary had. If the operating company—the user of services or borrower of money—has passive income, then part of its income is tainted. But if it had operating income, then the passive income paid to the MFC is deemed to be operating income that enters the overall basket, and so the income is averageable.

■ ──

ILLUSTRATION

How One Firm Coped With Subpart F. A U.S. firm with extensive global operations implemented a creative strategy to cope with the Subpart F provisions of the 1986 Tax Reform Act. It was forced to act because Subsidiary A, domiciled in a low-tax European country, was cash-rich and generating large sums of passive income from short-term investments.

By lowering the threshold for the amount of income that is exempt from Subpart F, the tax bill raised Subsidiary A's taxes. As noted above, not only is Subpart F income taxable when realized, but it is allocated to a separate basket, making it more difficult for many firms to utilize their excess foreign tax credits.

One of Subsidiary A's activities was to add value to a product input owned by Subsidiary B, domiciled in a high-tax European nation. Subsidiary B was cash-poor and relied on an expensive overdraft to buy the product and to pay Subsidiary A for its services.

Having Subsidiary A lend money to Subsidiary B would have lowered Subsidiary B's interest costs but would still have left Subsidiary A with passive, Subpart F interest income. Instead, the company implemented a solution that simultaneously reduced the Subpart F income accumulating at Subsidiary A and transferred more manufacturing income to the low-tax jurisdiction.

Under the new setup, Subsidiary A uses its excess cash to purchase the product input directly. Thus, Subsidiary A reduces its investment income, and Subsidiary B no longer needs an overdraft to buy the product from the third party. Because Subsidiary A, in its new role, adds more value to the end product, its legitimate arm's-length share of Subsidiary B's trading income is increased. In effect, by investing money in Subsidiary B and getting it back as low-tax manufacturing income in Subsidiary A, the company converted Subpart F income into trading income.

■

Intercompany Transactions

In recent years, both amendments to and applications of tax legislation show a significant departure from the principle of juridic domicile. Such departures are particularly prevalent in the case of *intercompany transactions*—that is, transactions between members of the same MNC. One example is the authority of the U.S. Internal Revenue Service to recalculate parent-subsidiary income and expenses in certain circumstances. Because U.S. operations have historically been more heavily taxed than foreign operations, there has been a tendency for the parent firm to minimize its overall tax bill by assigning deductible costs, where possible, to itself rather than to its affiliates. As we have just seen, however, U.S. MNCs now have an incentive to shift more expenses overseas.

Generally, when transactions between related parties are adjusted by the IRS, the result is to make these transactions arm's length. As a general principle, the IRS regards the price (or cost) in an *arm's-length transaction* as that price that would be reached by two independent firms in normal dealings. Chapter 15 discussed the allowable methods for calculating arm's length transfer prices.

Examples of transactions between related companies that would usually be adjusted include the following.

1. *Noninterest-bearing loans*: Generally, the Internal Revenue Service imputes interest at a rate of 6% per annum.
2. *Performance of services by one related corporation for another at no charge or at a charge that would be less than an arm's-length charge*: This category would also include an allocation of cost between a related group of companies for services rendered by an

unrelated company. Generally, the cost is allocated based on the services received by each related company.

3. *Transfer of machinery or equipment without charge*: Generally, a factor equal to the normal rental charge for such equipment is imputed as income to the transferor and as expense to the transferee.

4. *Transfer of intangible property*: A cost factor is generally imputed based on the income received from the use of intangible property such as patents, trademarks, formulas, or licenses by the receiving corporation. Moreover, under the superroyalty provision of the 1986 tax act, the IRS can use the benefit of hindsight to retroactively adjust the transfer price on intangibles transferred to foreign affiliates to reflect the income the intangible generates—even though the price was arm's length when the deal was made. For example, a company licenses its German affiliate at a low fee to produce a new drug with uncertain uses. But if, three years down the road, the drug turns out to be a cure for cancer, the IRS can reset the royalty at a higher level to reflect the higher value of the license. The odds are, however, that the German tax authorities will disallow the revalued royalty for tax purposes.

5. *Sale of inventory*: The basis for adjustment is generally the arm's-length price charged by the manufacturer (related corporations) to unrelated customers. The tax regulations specifically note that a reduced price to a related corporation cannot be justified by selling a quantity of the same product at the reduced price to an unrelated customer.

Subpart F

More recent amendments to the tax law have emphasized the domestic neutrality and equity criteria and have, therefore, converted the test of juridic domicile to a rather hollow formality. The most critical damage to this test was done by Subpart F of the 1962 Revenue Act. Subpart F subjects U.S. company affiliates that are incorporated abroad to U.S. tax obligations whenever they engage in intercompany international trade in goods, factors, or services—and regardless of where their profits originate or accumulate. Subpart F only applies to U.S. shareholders of controlled foreign corporations.

To determine the taxable amount, the income of the controlled foreign corporation must be analyzed and the items constituting Subpart F income distinguished. When each item of such income has been identified and quantified, there are several relief provisions available to reduce or eliminate income taxable to U.S. shareholders. Amounts that are finally taxed under Subpart F are treated as if they were distributed as a dividend to the U.S. shareholders.

The kinds of CFC income taxable under Subpart F include the following:

- Foreign base company income
- Income from the insurance of U.S. risks
- Increase in earnings invested in U.S. property
- Income earned during participation in, or cooperation with, international boycotts
- Sum of illegal foreign bribes

Foreign base company income includes the following.

1. *Foreign holding company income*: This income includes dividends, interest, royalties, rents, and distributions received from the ownership of stock or other securities in foreign enterprises, such as subsidiaries of affiliates.
2. *Foreign base company sales income*: This income is derived from purchase-and-sales transactions between affiliated firms or related parties where goods being traded are both produced and sold outside the host country of the affiliate. For example, if a Finnish subsidiary of a U.S. company bought goods from its sister subsidiary in Switzerland and sold them to an Italian buyer, the Finnish subsidiary would have earned base company income.
3. *Foreign base company service income*: This income is derived from services rendered to an affiliated firm in another country. It is derived along the same lines as sales income.

A controlled foreign corporation's Subpart F income includes the net income from premiums received for the insurance of U.S. risks (for example, property, life, or health of U.S. citizens). If a CFC invests any of its earnings in certain property or rights in the United States or in a U.S. corporation, the increase in the amount of earnings invested over the preceding year is Subpart F income.

The three categories of foreign base company income are identified and isolated in their gross amounts. In the case of sales income, the amount is gross income or gross profit on sales; in the case of manufactured goods, the amount is gross income or gross profit after deducting manufacturing costs. The following relief provisions are then applied, if appropriate:

1. If Subpart F income is less than the lesser of either 5% of gross income or $1 million, no part of base company income is treated as foreign base company income for that year; if gross foreign base company income exceeds 70% of total gross income, the entire gross income will be treated as foreign base company income, subject to further possible limitations enumerated below.
2. Subpart F does not apply (other than to oil-related income) if the foreign tax rate is at least 90% of the maximum U.S. corporate rate.
3. Foreign base company income excludes certain income from shipping and aircraft operations.
4. While foreign base company income is identified by reference to gross income for purposes of the 5–70 rule (and so forth), all appropriate expenses allocable to such income are deducted in arriving at the net foreign base company income that is taxable under Subpart F.

If foreign income is blocked because of foreign currency restrictions, it is excluded from the earnings and profits of a controlled foreign corporation for Subpart F purposes.

If a CFC's earnings remain abroad, the Subpart F income is deemed to be distributed to the parent company and must be included in its taxable income on an annual basis as if it were actually received. Thus, by simply labeling the affiliate earnings as deemed-paid dividends, the law compels the parent to pay taxes on income that in reality never has entered the United States.

■ 21.3 ■
U.S. TAX INCENTIVES FOR FOREIGN TRADE

Over the years, a number of *tax incentives* designed to encourage certain types of business activity in different regions of the world have been added to the U.S. tax code. To take advantage of these incentives, firms usually find it necessary to assign certain activities to a separate corporate entity. It is important that managers carefully compare the various possible methods of carrying out a particular activity in order to select the most advantageous form of organization. The most important U.S. tax incentives currently available include those for export operations (foreign sales corporation) and for operations in U.S. possessions (possessions corporation).

The Foreign Sales Corporation (FSC)

The *Foreign Sales Corporation* (FSC), created by the Tax Reform Act of 1984, is the U.S. government's primary tax incentive for exporting U.S.-produced goods overseas. The FSC is a corporation incorporated, and maintaining an office, in a possession of the United States or in a foreign country that has an IRS-approved exchange-of-tax-information program with the United States. Possessions of the United States for purposes of the FSC include Guam, American Samoa, the Commonwealth of Northern Mariana Islands, and the U.S. Virgin Islands; the Commonwealth of Puerto Rico, which is treated as part of the United States, is excluded. Because Puerto Rico is considered as part of the United States for these purposes, goods manufactured there will qualify as export property eligible for FSC benefits.

To qualify for tax benefits under the law, the FSC must meet the following criteria:

1. There must be 25 or fewer shareholders at all times.
2. There can be no preferred stock.
3. The FSC must maintain certain tax and accounting records at a location within the United States
4. The Board of Directors must have at least one member who is not a U.S. resident.
5. An election to be treated as an FSC must be filed within the 90-day period immediately preceding the beginning of a taxable year.

An FSC must generate foreign trading gross receipts (FTGR), either as a commission agent or as a principal. *Foreign trading gross receipts* are gross receipts derived from

- Sale, exchange, or other disposition of export property
- Lease or rental of export property for use outside the United States by unrelated parties
- Performance of services related, and subsidiary to, the sale or lease of export property
- Performance of managerial services for unrelated FSCs, provided at least 50% of the FSC's gross receipts are derived from the first three activities above

Export property includes property manufactured, produced, grown, or extracted in the United States by a person other than the FSC. The property must be held primarily for sale, lease, or rental in the ordinary course of business and for ultimate use, consumption, or disposition outside the United States. Furthermore, up to 50% of the fair market value of the property may be attributable to imported materials.

In order to derive FTGR, there are foreign management and foreign economic process requirements that the FSC must fulfill. The thrust of these requirements is that a measurable degree of FSC activity and business be accomplished outside the United States.

To determine the FSC's income from the sale or other disposition of export property, the normal arm's-length transfer pricing rules need not be applied. The transfer price between the producer and the FSC may be set so that the income earned by the FSC is the greater of

- 1.83% of the FTGR derived from the export transactions involved
- 23% of the combined taxable income of the FSC and the related supplier derived from the export transactions involved
- Taxable income that would arise under the arm's-length pricing methods of Section 482

For example, if the combined taxable income from the manufacture and sale of a product is $100 with associated revenue of $1,000, then the FSC's income can be recorded as either $18.30 (0.0183 × $1,000) or $23.00 (0.23 × $100). Due to the tax exemption on a portion of the FSC's income, the second method of income allocation will be selected in this case.

The 1.83% gross receipts method and the 23% combined taxable income method are referred to as the *administrative pricing rules*. In order to use the administrative pricing rules, the FSC must perform all the activities related to the solicitation (other than advertising), negotiation, and making of the sales contracts involved in its business and must itself (or its agent) perform all the following five activities: advertising and sales promotion; processing orders and arranging for delivery; handling transportation; billing and collecting; and the assumption of credit risk. Exhibit 21.2 illustrates the three transfer pricing methods available to an FSC and its related supplier.

Once the determination of the FSC's profit or taxable income is made, the FSC's income from the export sale must be segregated into exempt and nonexempt pools. This segregation requires determining the FSC's gross income attributable to FTGR. The FSC's gross income is called *foreign-trade income* (FTI). If an arm's-length transfer price is used, the resulting profit becomes the FSC's FTI. On the other hand, where one of the administrative pricing methods is used, FTI can be calculated by adding back all costs and expenses of the FSC to the taxable income, except for the FSC's cost of goods sold. The amount of exempt foreign-trade income for a transaction is

- 30% of the foreign trade income derived from transactions in which the arm's-length pricing method is used
- 15/23 (62.21739%) of the foreign-trade income derived from transactions in which one of the two administrative pricing methods is used

Exhibit 21.2 illustrates the exempt and nonexempt income calculations for a corporate shareholder and its FSC. The example shows that the nonexempt portion of an FSC's taxable income determined under the arm's-length pricing method is potential Subpart F income.

■ **EXHIBIT 21.2**   Example of FSC Transfer Pricing and Exempt Income Calculations

Gross receipts from the export sale	$1,000
Related supplier cost of manufacture	(600)
FSC marketing expenses	(200)
Related supplier allocated expenses	(100)
Combined taxable income (CTI): FSC-supplier	$100

	Transfer Pricing Method		
	1.83% of Gross Receipts	**23% of CTI**	**Arm's-Length Pricing**
Foreign trading gross receipts	$1,000.0	$1,000.0	$1,000.0
FSC selling expense	(200.0)	(200.0)	(200.0)
FSC profit	(18.3)	(23.0)	(50.0)
Transfer price to FSC	781.7	777.0	750.0
Cost of manufacture	(600.0)	(600.0)	(600.0)
Related supplier expenses	(100.0)	(100.0)	(100.0)
Related supplier's taxable income	$ 81.7	$ 77.0	$ 50.0
Foreign trading gross receipts	$1,000.0	$1,000.0	$1,000.0
Transfer price to FSC	(781.7)	(777.0)	(750)
Foreign trade income (FTI)	218.3	223.0	250.0
Exempt FTI	(142.4)[1]	(145.4)[1]	(75.0)[2]
Nonexempt FTI	$ 75.9	$ 77.6	$ 175.0
FSC profit	$ 18.3	$ 23.0	$ 50.0
FSC exempt profit	(11.9)[3]	(15.0)[3]	(15.0)[3]
FSC taxable income—Subpart-F income	$ 6.4[4]	$ 8.0[4]	$ 35.0[4]
Total taxable income	$ 88.1[5]	$ 85.0[5]	$ 85.0[5]
Total U.S. tax @ 34 percent	$ 30.0	$ 28.9	$ 28.9
Total tax savings from $34 tax on $100 of CTI	$ 4.0	$ 5.1	$ 5.1

[1]15/23 of FTI.

[2]30% of FTI.

[3]Exempt FTI/FTI × FSC profit.

[4]Nonexempt FTI/FTI × FSC profit—arm's length pricing taxed as Subpart-F income

[5]Related supplier's taxable income plus FSC taxable income.

The income qualifying as exempt foreign-trade income is treated as foreign-source income not effectively connected with a U.S. trade or business. Thus, exempt foreign-trade income is not subject to U.S. income tax. Moreover, domestic corporate shareholders receive a 100% dividends-received deduction with respect to distributions from an FSC out of foreign-trade income (except for the nonexempt portion of foreign-trade income determined under the arm's-length method).

The Small FSC

An alternative to an FSC is a small FSC. The small FSC is generally the same as an FSC except that a small FSC does not have to meet the foreign management or foreign economic process requirements. The tax benefits are the same as for an FSC but they are limited to $5 million worth of foreign trading gross receipts for every taxable year of a small FSC.

U.S. Possessions Corporation

A domestic operation may be taxed as a *U.S. possessions corporation* (Section 936 of Internal Revenue Code) if it meets the following requirements:

1. At least 80% of its gross income has been derived from sources in a U.S. possession or possessions (excluding the Virgin Islands).
2. At least 75% of gross income is derived from the active conduct of trade.

In both cases, the requirements must be met for three years preceding the close of the taxable year that the corporation is to become a U.S. possessions corporation. The possessions corporation is entitled to the following tax benefits:

- No U.S. tax on income from sources outside the United States (if received outside the United States) except for passive income from nonpossession sources
- No U.S. tax on income from sources outside the United States from the active conduct of a trade or business within a possession—even if the income is received in the United States—if it is received from an unrelated party
- Possible exemption from Puerto Rican taxation if it engages in manufacturing operations in certain areas
- Tax-free repatriation of earnings to the U.S. parent corporation
- More liberal intercompany transfer pricing rules

For all practical purposes, the benefits described here apply almost exclusively to Puerto Rican activities.

■ 21.4 ■
TAX HAVENS AND THE MULTINATIONAL CORPORATION

A perennial charge against the multinational corporation is its use (or misuse) of *tax havens* to shield income from the local tax collector. Tax-haven countries include those countries whose moderate level of taxation and liberal tax incentives enable the multinational corporation to substantially reduce or defer taxation on income channeled through these countries. Although the Subpart F regulations in the Revenue Act of 1962 have substantially reduced the effectiveness of the tax haven, there are still some viable possibilities available in this area.

Before selecting the type of tax haven to use, the MNC must develop a framework to evaluate its projected needs against the advantages of the various tax havens. Factors that are usually considered in choosing a tax haven include the following:

- The political and economic stability of the country and the integrity of its government
- The attitude of the country toward tax-haven business
- The other taxes, aside from income taxes, it imposes
- Tax treaties (Some tax havens owe their very existence to the fact that they are parties to advantageous tax treaty arrangements. Other tax-haven countries are party to few, if any, tax treaties.)
- The lack of exchange controls (Although some tax havens have exchange controls, most offshore companies organized by nonresidents are granted relative freedom from such controls.)
- Liberal incorporation laws that minimize both the cost of incorporation and the length of time it takes to incorporate
- Banking facilities
- Transportation facilities and telephone, cable, and telex communications with the rest of the world
- The long-range prospects for continued freedom from taxation

After the selection of a tax haven, the next relevant consideration is the form of organization outside the United States. This choice entails the branch versus subsidiary decision, as well as the use of any tax incentive organization (for example, a possessions corporation). There are three key factors underlying this decision about the form of organization.

The first factor is the projected cash flows in the country under consideration. A forecast of several years of initial operating losses in any country would be significant in weighing the desirability of operating initially as a branch. Branch operation would allow the deduction of those losses on the U.S. tax return.

The second factor is the attitude of the U.S. parent corporation toward repatriation of funds. The tax-free use of funds can be an important factor in the determination of working-capital needs. Also, by allowing earnings to accumulate offshore, they may be repatriated tax free if certain forms of organization that allow for tax-free liquidation are undertaken.

The third factor to consider is alternative uses for funds. If the U.S. parent company has other offshore facilities, the earnings from some facilities can provide cash flows for other subsidiaries. This factor is especially important for a U.S. parent that is constantly seeking out and developing new foreign investment opportunities.

With the preceding considerations and factors in mind, the MNC can make a selective examination of possible locations. The focus here is on the relative advantages and disadvantages of each country based on its tax laws. The objective of tax planning is to interpret laws correctly to legally avoid paying unnecessary taxes, rather than to escape corporate obligations under the law.

The various tax havens of the world can be grouped into four types:

- Type 1: Tax havens that have no income or capital gains tax or gift and estate tax
- Type 2: Tax havens that do impose taxes, but whose rate is very low
- Type 3: Tax havens that tax income from domestic sources, but exempt all income from foreign sources
- Type 4: Countries that allow special tax privileges and are suitable for tax havens only for selected purposes

The first group encompasses many of the tax havens in the Caribbean, such as the Bahamas, Bermuda, and the Cayman Islands. The Bahamas levies a small tax of $100 per year on all Bahamian companies. It has no tax treaty with any country requiring it to furnish information to other countries. Since 1960, manufacturing companies have been getting long-term guarantees against taxes. Bermuda has no tax treaties and has moderate corporate and incorporation fees. In the Cayman Islands, foreign-owned companies are guaranteed against taxes for 20 years. As well, the Cayman Islands has no tax treaties and has moderate corporate and incorporation fees.

A country representative of the second group would be the British Virgin Islands because of its 12% income tax rate. However, the British Virgin Islands usefulness as a tax haven in relation to other countries is somewhat diminished by its 12% withholding tax on dividends. Another major tax haven is the Netherlands Antilles, a colony of the Netherlands located a few miles off the coast of Venezuela. Most business is centered in Curaçao. Income taxes are very low, and there are special tax privileges to shipping, aviation, and holding companies.

A country whose tax benefits are characteristic of the third group is Hong Kong. Although Hong Kong imposes a nominal tax of 15% on Hong Kong-sourced income, foreign-source income is completely exempt. Nor is there any tax on capital, capital gains, or dividends remitted to foreign shareholders. Another popular country under this group is Panama, which has a tax on domestically sourced income but none on foreign-source income of companies located in Panama. It also has no income tax treaties and encourages incorporation in Panama through very liberal incorporation laws that allow the articles of incorporation to be written in any language. Panama's role as a secure tax haven, however, has been diminished by the political unrest in that country.

The fourth group mainly includes those countries that are trying to promote development in certain regions or encourage industrialization within the country. The most notable example here is the Republic of Ireland, which exempts from taxation the export earnings of corporations that set up manufacturing operations in certain regions. Also included in this group is Puerto Rico, which grants tax exemption for up to 17 years for firms to set up operations in certain less-developed zones. As noted previously, under Section 936 of the U.S. Internal Revenue Code, the funds generated from these corporations can now be repatriated to the United States tax free.

There are a few European tax-haven countries that should be mentioned: Switzerland, the Netherlands, and Liechtenstein.

Switzerland has some unique enticements for the tax avoider. First, it does not tax profits that locally incorporated businesses earn outside the country. However, Switzerland has a decentralized government consisting of 25 sovereign cantons, and most direct taxes are levied by the cantons and not the federal government. The cantons do impose a nominal tax on capital. Second, Swiss laws allow corporations extraordinary freedom from official surveillance. Tax evasion is not a criminal offense in Switzerland, and even the Swiss federal tax authorities know that local banks will refuse their requests for information.

The Netherlands is a favorite tax haven for holding companies. A holding company in the Netherlands does not pay any tax on income and capital gains emanating from its direct (not portfolio) participations in either domestic or foreign subsidiaries. Moreover, the tax treaties that the Netherlands has with other countries almost eliminate the withholding tax on dividend distributions to the parent company.

Liechtenstein is a tiny principality that is tucked picturesquely in the Alpine scenery; it has 20,000 people, 7,000 cows, and about 15,000 "foreign legal entities." These entities are companies, partnerships, and other vehicles through which foreigners can hide their money, free of virtually all taxes and safe from anybody's curiosity. The most famous Liechtenstein corporate device is the Anstalt—a company that can be used for virtually any purpose. Its only visibility is on the public register, which merely gives the Anstalt's name, capital at formation, and the name of its Liechtenstein representative—by law there must be at least one resident Liechtensteiner on the board.

■ 21.5 ■
TAXATION AND CORPORATE ORGANIZATION

The determination of the form of organization to use abroad demands a careful analysis that involves many complex issues. At the heart of such an analysis is the objective of the firm and the cash flow of the particular unit under consideration. From this base, the firm can then begin to examine the tax systems in the United States and abroad—and their interaction.

The basic decision about the form of organization hinges on whether the use of a branch or an incorporated subsidiary would best suit the intended project. The key consideration here would be the alternative uses of excess tax credits. The examples indicate that if the sum of the foreign tax rates exceeds the U.S. tax rate and if the excess tax credits cannot be used, then a branch may be preferred to a subsidiary. The reverse appears to be true if the U.S. rate exceeds the foreign rates. However, there are many factors that can quickly change these conclusions. First, there can be alternative uses for the excess tax credits, especially now that the overall, rather than per country, method of calculating the tax credit must be used. Second, the cash flow and tax situations change from country to country. The deductibility of losses with a branch operation is important, along with the ability to carry back and carry forward tax losses and credits. This once-permanent advantage, however, has been reduced to a tax deferral by the 1976 Tax Reform Act, which requires that foreign losses sustained after 1976 be recaptured when operations turn profitable. Also of importance here is the allocation of income by the IRS (based on its allocation of expenses). Third, there might be problems if part of the cash flows of the subsidiary include any taint of income of a controlled foreign corporation under Subpart F of the Revenue Act of 1962.

The other possible forms of organization hinge around the special corporations pre-viously discussed: the FSC, U.S. possessions corporation, and tax-haven corporations. An illustration of the operation of many of these organizations can be seen in the following example, that traces the activities of Alpha, Inc. as it expands its overseas business.

Alpha first decides to establish branches in those Latin American countries in which it intends to start its selling and marketing operations. The start-up costs are to be substantial for the first four years of these operations. Because the high start-up costs are liable to result in operating losses, branches would allow Alpha (the U.S. parent company) to credit these losses against its other income. This tax write-off generates additional cash flows available for the Latin American operations.

After each branch begins to operate profitably, Alpha turns the business and all of its assets over to its wholly owned U.S. Virgin Islands corporation Beta. Alpha sells its products to Beta, which in turn sells them in Latin America. Because Beta conducts all of its business outside the United States, it is allowed a deduction as a FSC. Alpha can also include Beta in its consolidated tax return and to claim credit for all foreign taxes paid, including those incurred by Beta. There is no income tax liability for property transferred from Alpha to Beta in return for stock of Beta.

As its Latin American operations grow, Alpha decides to organize a wholly owned Bermuda corporation, Gamma, to operate its Latin American business. Gamma buys semifinished products from Beta and uses them to produce goods for sale to its Latin American customers. Although Gamma pays taxes in Latin America, there is no income tax in Bermuda. No U.S. tax will be paid on Gamma's income until it is repatriated to Alpha as a dividend. The deferment of dividend payments by Gamma, and consequent deferment of the payment of U.S. tax on Gamma's income, will leave funds in Gamma's hands for plant expansion and other business purposes. Note here the lack of Subpart F income, even though Gamma is a controlled foreign corporation. The absence of Subpart F income is due to the nature of the goods sold to Gamma, which are only semifinished. Since Gamma engages in a significant amount of manufacturing activity in its country of incorporation, its products may be sold to customers anywhere, without leading to foreign base company sales income.

Alpha is now considering the manufacture and sale of its products in Europe, especially in the Common Market. To accomplish this end, Alpha organizes an Irish corporation, Phi, to operate a factory in the Republic of Ireland. Alpha sells semifinished goods to Phi, which in turn uses them to produce finished goods for sale in Europe. The Republic of Ireland provides for a 100% tax exemption for all profits arising from export-related business. The maximum rate on manufacturing profits through the year 2,000 is only 10%.

Because the Republic of Ireland is a member of the Common market, manufacturers in that country enjoy access to a large, somewhat unified market with limited trade and tariff barriers. Phi can also obtain nonrepayable cash grants from the Republic of Ireland toward the cost of plant and equipment and training employees (even in the United States). There will be no duties on imported machinery and materials used in producing goods for export in the Republic of Ireland, nor is there any duty on the shipment of those exports into Great Britain or other Commonwealth countries.

Because manufacture of the finished product is conducted in the Republic of Ireland, neither Phi nor its parent Alpha is subject to U.S. income tax on Phi's income from the sale of its products until that income is received by Alpha as dividends. This is the case even if

Phi sells its products to Alpha or to affiliated corporations. Moreover, income realized by an affiliated firm on the resale of Phi's products in such a circumstance is not taxed by the United States, provided that the resales of such goods are made to unrelated customers for use, consumption, or disposition in the foreign country in which the affiliated reseller is incorporated.

As long as more than 90% of Phi's gross income is from the sale of its products, for every $0.90 of such income it earns, it can realize $0.05 of other income (up to $1 million)—normally classified as Subpart F income—without any of its undistributed income being taxed to Alpha as imagined (deemed) dividends from Phi. Phi can use its accumulation of funds resulting from its tax-free income to expand its plant and working capital and to make investments outside the United States. These investments can include stock of other foreign corporations selling Phi's products in the countries in which they are incorporated.

Eventually, when Phi distributes dividends to Alpha, the U.S. Treasury will collect the tax that the Republic of Ireland waived on Phi's foreign income. However, the use of those temporarily tax-free dollars has allowed a foreign subsidiary to develop and expand faster than it would have been able to do otherwise.

■ 21.6 ■
ILLUSTRATION: BEEHIVE INTERNATIONAL

Beehive International (BI), founded in 1968 and taken public in 1970, is a small manufacturer of computer terminals and peripherals. Located in Salt Lake City, it began marketing its terminals abroad in 1972, using foreign distributors; by the late 1970s, BI was doing about 35% of its sales overseas. By 1979, however, it had become obvious that what had sufficed in the past wouldn't succeed in the future. According to Warren B. Clifford, president of Beehive, "We realized that in order to deal with the increasingly nationalistic attitudes of the European Community and to bring the manufacturing closer to the market-place, we'd have to set up a European company."

After a lengthy search process, Beehive decided to locate a plant in the Republic of Ireland. "Frankly, it resolved into incentives and taxes," says Clifford. After lengthy and hard-nosed negotiations, the Republic of Ireland offered the company an outright grant covering 40% of the cost of building and equipping the new plant, a separate grant to cover employee training expenses, and tax-free operation until 1990, with a maximum corporate tax thereafter of 10% through the year 2000.

The tax situation was made even sweeter by Beehive's decision not to operate its Irish facility as a wholly owned subsidiary. Instead, it set up a separate corporation in the Cayman Islands—Beehive International Ltd.—with which it paired its stock, to serve as the parent. Stock pairing involved issuing stock on a share-for-share basis in Beehive International Ltd. as a dividend to Beehive International shareholders. Because the stock had no value at the time (the Irish plant had yet to be built), the dividend wasn't taxable to shareholders. The stock of the two sister companies now trade in tandem; for each share of Beehive International issued and outstanding, there is an identical share of Beehive International Ltd. (The stock, in fact, is printed on opposite sides of the same certificate.)

BI and BI Ltd. share the same list of stockholders and three officers of each; but they are otherwise separate entities, both legally and operationally—an important point in the eyes of the Internal Revenue Service, which might otherwise challenge the paired status.

As a result of their separateness, BI Ltd. has virtually eliminated the corporate income tax. It enjoyed a tax holiday in Ireland through 1990; repatriates the profits from Ireland to the Cayman Islands, which is a tax-free nation; and avoids the U.S. corporate income tax entirely. The ability to avoid U.S. corporate taxes is based on a quirk in U.S. tax law: If five or fewer U.S. shareholders own 50% or more of the stock of a foreign company, then that company may be considered a U.S. corporation and is taxable. In the case of Beehive International Ltd., however, there are about 1,800 stockholders, none of whom owns more than 8%—which means no tax. Only the dividends paid to shareholders are taxable as personal income. Some companies have found that the "paired advantage" can help give them a profit margin nearly twice as high overseas. Half a dozen U.S. firms—among them Sea Containers Inc. (ship and container leasing), Ralph M. Parsons Co. (construction), and L. E. Meyers Co. (electrical construction)—are taking advantage of the tactic.

■ 21.7 ■
SUMMARY AND CONCLUSIONS

One of the key areas in which financial management can have a major impact on increasing the firm's value is tax planning. While the complexities involved in tax planning for the multinational corporation are greater than for the domestic firm, so are the possible payoffs. The major decisions that must be made in global tax planning include

- Determining the legal form of organization for the firm's foreign operations
- Deciding when, how, and from where to bring back funds
- Arranging for the optimal use of tax havens, bilateral tax treaties, and special corporate tax incentive vehicles such as the Foreign Sales Corporation (FSC)

The appropriate decisions, in turn, are influenced by home and host country policies concerning taxation of foreign-source income and the allocation of expenses among corporate units; bilateral tax treaties in effect; the various relevant tax rates and tax differentials; corporate investment policies and sources of financing; the distribution of required and available funds; and the existence of other corporate goals besides tax minimization, such as accessing blocked currencies. These decisions also depend on likely changes in current tax laws.

In making these decisions, managers need to understand the international tax environment and the basic principles that have helped to shape it. In this chapter, we examined some of these principles—including domestic and foreign tax neutrality and tax equity—and saw how they have influenced U.S. tax policy toward foreign-source earnings and U.S. multinationals.

In addition, specific U.S. tax regulations concerning MNCs were described and then analyzed in terms of their impact on corporate decision making. We also analyzed the various types of tax havens and incentives that exist, as well as how they might be used in international tax management.

The material in this chapter will not make anyone an international tax expert. Nor will it remain correct for long. The objective, however, is not to develop international tax lawyers but, instead, to acquaint financial managers of multinational firms with some of the basic tax parameters they should know about in order to better understand how taxes might influence corporate policy. Even more importantly, the material can help financial managers to know the kinds of questions they should ask of their corporate tax counsel. Without this basic background, managers might miss opportunities to reduce taxes because they did not know that such opportunities even existed.

■ BIBLIOGRAPHY ■

Benjamin, Robert Weld. "Tax Aspects of Operating a Possessions Corporation in Puerto Rico." *The International Tax Journal,* Spring 1976, pp. 197–221.

Bischel, Jon E., and Robert Feinschreiber. *Fundamentals of International Taxation.* New York: Practicing Law Institute, 1977.

Gifford, William C., and William P. Streng. *International Tax Planning,* 2d ed. Washington, D.C.: Tax Management, Inc., 1979.

Price Waterhouse. *International Tax Review.* New York: Price Waterhouse, various issues.

———. *Foreign Sales Corporation,* July 1984.

———. *Guide to the New Tax Law.* New York: Bantam Books, 1986.

Sato, Mitsuo, and Richard M. Bird. "International Aspects of the Taxation of Corporations and Shareholders." *IMF Staff Papers,* July 1975, pp. 384–455.

■ PART IV ■
■ Case Study ■

■ Case IV.1
The International Machine Corporation

The International Machine Corporation (IMC) is a large, well-established manufacturer of a wide variety of food processing and packaging equipment. Total revenue for last year was $12 billion, of which 45% was generated outside of the United States. IMC has subsidiaries in 23 different countries, with licensing arrangements in 8 others.

The management of IMC is currently contemplating the establishment of a subsidiary in Mexico. IMC has been exporting products to Mexico for several years, and its international division believes there is sufficient demand for the product and that a Mexican investment might be appropriate at this time. More importantly, management believes that the Mexican market is expanding, that the economy is growing, and that producing such products locally appears to be consistent with the national aspirations of the Mexican government.

Mexican inflation is projected to be 20% annually while the U.S. inflation rate is expected to be 10% annually. The current exchange rate is $1 = Ps 2,200 and is expected to remain fixed in real terms over the life of the investment. The following list contains details of the contemplated investment.

A. Initial investment
1. It is estimated that it would take one year to purchase and install plant and equipment.
2. Imported machinery and equipment will cost $9 million. No import duties will be levied by the Mexican government. With a small allowance for banking fees, the bill will come to Ps 20 billion.
3. The plant would be set up on government-owned land that will be sold to the project for Ps 2 billion.
4. IMC plans to maintain effective control of the subsidiary with ownership of 60% of equity. The remaining 40% is to be distributed widely among Mexican financial institutions and private investors. Accordingly, IMC needs to invest U.S. $6 million in the project.

B. Working capital
1. The company plans to maintain 5% of annual sales as a minimum cash balance.
2. Accounts receivable are estimated to be 73 days of annual sales.
3. Inventory is estimated to be 20% of annual sales.
4. Accounts payable are estimated to be 10% of annual sales.
5. Other payables are estimated to be 5% of annual sales.
6. Licensing and overhead allocation fees are paid annually at the end of the year.

C. Sales volume
1. Sales volume for the first year is estimated to be 200 units.
2. Selling price in the first year will be Ps 140 million per unit.

SOURCE: This is an edited version of "The International Machine Corporation: An Analysis of Investment in Mexico," by Vinod B. Bavishi, University of Connecticut, and Haney A. Shawkey, State University of New York at Albany. Permission to use this case was provided by Professors Bavishi and Shawkey.

     3. Sales growth of 10% is expected during the project life.

     4. An annual price increase of 20% is expected.

D. Cost of goods sold

     1. The U.S. parent company is expected to provide parts and components adding up to Ps 18 million per unit in the first year of operation. These costs (in U.S. dollars) are expected to rise on an average of 10% annually, in line with the projected U.S. inflation rate.

     2. Local material and labor costs are expected to be Ps 42 million per unit, with an annual rate of increase of 20%.

     3. Manufacturing overhead (without depreciation) is expected to be Ps 2.8 billion the first year of operation. An average rate of increase of 15% is expected.

     4. Depreciation of manufacturing equipment is to be computed on a straight-line basis, with a projected life of ten years and zero salvage value to be assumed.

E. Selling and administrative costs

     1. Selling and administrative costs are expected to equal 10% of annual sales. These costs will all be incurred within Mexico and will rise at 20% annually.

     2. Semifixed selling costs are expected to equal 5% of annual sales. These costs will rise at 15% annually.

F. Licensing and overhead allocation fees

     1. The parent company will levy Ps 7 million per unit as licensing and overhead allocation fees, payable at year-end in U.S. dollars.

     2. This fee will increase 20% per year to compensate for Mexican inflation.

G. Interest expense

     1. Local borrowings can be obtained for working capital purposes at 15%. Borrowing will occur at the end of the year with the full year's interest budgeted in the following year.

     2. Any excess funds can be invested in Mexican marketable securities with an annual rate of return of 15%. Investment will be made at the end of the year, with the full year's interest to be received in the following year.

H. Income taxes

     1. Corporate income taxes in Mexico are 42% of taxable income.

     2. Withholding taxes on licensing and overhead allocation fees are 20%.

     3. The parent company's effective U.S. tax rate is 34%, which is the rate used in analyzing investment projects. It can be assumed that the parent company can take appropriate credits for taxes paid to, or withheld by, the Mexican government.

I. Dividend payments

     1. No dividends will be paid for the first three years.

     2. Dividends equal to 70% of earnings will be paid to the shareholders, beginning in the fourth year.

J. Terminal payment

It is assumed that, at the end of the tenth year of operation, IMC's share of net worth in the Mexican subsidiary will be remitted in the form of a terminal payment.

K. Parent company's capital structure

     1. Domestic debt equals U.S. $1 billion with an average before-tax cost of 12%. The cost of new long-term debt is estimated at 14% before tax.

     2. An amount equivalent to $600 million of parent debt is denominated in various foreign currencies and after adjusting for previous exchange gains/losses the cost (or effective cost) of this debt has averaged 16%.

3. Shareholder equity (capital, surplus, and retained earnings) equals U.S. $1.5 billion. The company plans to pay U.S. $3.20 in dividends per share during the coming year. Over the last ten years, earnings and dividends have grown at a compounded rate of 7%. The market price of common stock was $40, and number of shares outstanding were 60 million as of last December 31.

L. Exports lost

At present IMC is exporting about 25 units per year to Mexico. If IMC decides to establish the Mexican subsidiary, it is expected that the after-tax effects on income due to the lost exports sales would be $648,000, $742,000, and $930,000 in the first three years of operation, respectively. IMC assumes it cannot count on these export sales for more than three years because the Mexican government is determined to see that such machinery is manufactured locally in the near future.

QUESTIONS

1. Should IMC make this investment?
2. What is IMC's required rate of return for this project?
3. What factors and assumptions are critical to your project analysis?

Part V

Financing Foreign Operations

◾ 22 ◾

International Financing and International Financial Markets

Money, like wine, must always be scarce with those who have neither wherewithal to buy it nor credit to borrow it.

—Adam Smith (1776) —

◾ The growing internationalization of capital markets and the increased sophistication of companies means that the search for capital no longer stops at the water's edge. This reality is particularly true for multinational corporations. A distinctive feature of the financial strategy of MNCs is the wide range of external sources of funds that they use on an ongoing basis. General Motors packages car loans as securities and sells them in Europe and Japan. British Telecommunications offers stock in London, New York, and Tokyo, while Beneficial Corporation issues Euroyen notes that may not be sold in either the United States or Japan. Swiss Bank Corporation—aided by Italian, Belgian, Canadian, and German banks, as well as other Swiss banks—helps RJR Nabisco sell Swiss franc bonds in Europe and then swap the proceeds back into U.S. dollars.

This chapter explores the MNC's external medium- and long-term financing alternatives. While many of the sources are internal to the countries in which the MNCs operate, more of their funds are coming from offshore markets, particularly the Eurocurrency and Eurobond markets. We will, therefore, study both national and international capital markets in this chapter and the links between the two. We begin by discussing trends in corporate financing patterns.

◾ 22.1 ◾
CORPORATE SOURCES AND USES OF FUNDS

Firms have three general sources of funds available: internally generated cash, short-term external funds, and long-term external funds. External finance can come from investors or lenders. Investors give a company money by buying the securities it issues in the financial markets. These securities, which are generally *negotiable* (tradeable), usually take the form of debt or equity.

The main alternative to issuing public debt securities directly in the open market is to obtain a loan from a specialized financial intermediary that issues securities (or deposits) of its own in the market. These alternative debt instruments usually are commercial bank loans—for short-term and medium-term credit—or privately placed bonds—for longer-term credit. Unlike *publicly issued bonds, privately placed bonds* are sold directly to only a limited number of sophisticated investors, usually life insurance companies and pension funds. Moreover, privately placed bonds are generally nonnegotiable and have complex, customized loan agreements—called *covenants.* The restrictions in the covenants range from limits on dividend payments to prohibitions on asset sales and new debt issues. They provide a series of checkpoints that permit the lender to review actions by the borrower that have the potential to impair the lender's position. These agreements have to be regularly renegotiated prior to maturity. As a result, privately placed bonds are much more like loans than publicly issued and traded securities.

National Financing Patterns

Companies in different countries have different financial appetites. Companies in Great Britain get an average of 60% to 70% of their funds from internal sources. German companies get about 40% to 50% of their funds from external suppliers. In Japan, when their profitability has been low, companies have relied heavily on external finance. As recently as 1975, Japanese companies got almost 70% of their money from outside sources. The shortfall of funds reflected the Japanese strategy of making huge industrial investments and pursuing market share at the expense of profit margins. In 1985, by contrast, almost 70% of Japanese corporate funds came from internal sources. The switch from external to internal financing since 1975 is one demonstration of the maturity of Japanese industry.

In Europe and the United States, there has been no comparable transformation. Internal finance has consistently supplied the lion's share of financial requirements. The percentage of external finance fluctuates more or less in line with the business cycle; when profits are high, firms are even less reliant on external finance. Moreover, the predominance of internal financing is not accidental. After all, companies could pay out internal cash flow as dividends and issue additional securities to cover their investment needs.

Another empirical regularity about financing behavior relates to the composition of external finance. Regardless of the country studied, debt accounts for the overwhelming share of external funds. By contrast, new stock issues play a relatively small and declining role in financing investment.

Financial Markets Versus Financial Intermediaries

Industry's sources of external finance also differ widely from country to country. Historically, German and Japanese companies have relied heavily on bank borrowing, while U.S. and British industry raised much more money directly from financial markets by the sale of securities. In all these countries, however, bank borrowing is on the decline. There is a growing tendency for corporate borrowing to take the form of negotiable securities issued in the public capital markets rather than in the form of commercial bank loans.

This process, termed *securitization,* is most pronounced among the Japanese companies. Securitization largely reflects a reduction in the cost of using financial markets at the same time that the cost of bank borrowing has risen. Until recently, various regulatory restrictions enabled banks to attract low-cost funds from depositors. With *financial deregulation,* which began in the United States in 1981 and in Japan in 1986, banks must now compete for funds with a wide range of institutions at market rates. In addition, regulatory demands for a stronger capital base have forced U.S. banks to use more equity financing, raising their cost of funds. Inevitably, these changes have pushed up the price of bank loans. Any top-flight company can now get money more cheaply by issuing commercial paper than it can from its banks. As a result, banks now have a smaller share of the short-term business credit market.

At the same time, the cost of accessing the public markets is coming down, especially for smaller and less well known companies. Historically, these companies found it more economical simply to obtain a loan from a bank or to place a private bond issue with a life insurance company. These *private placements* proved cheaper because banks and life insurance companies specialize in credit analysis and assume a large amount of a borrower's debt. Consequently, they could realize important cost savings in several functions, such as gathering information about the condition of debtor firms, monitoring their actions, and renegotiating loan agreements.

Recent technological improvements in such areas as data manipulation and telecommunications have greatly reduced the costs of obtaining and processing information about the conditions that affect the creditworthiness of potential borrowers. Any analyst now has computerized access to a wealth of economic and financial information at a relatively low cost, along with programs to store and manipulate this information. Thus, investors are now more likely to find it cost-effective to lend directly to companies, rather than indirectly through *financial intermediaries,* such as commercial banks.

Globalization of Financial Markets

These same advances in communications and technology, together with financial deregulation abroad—the lifting of regulatory structures that inhibit competition and protect domestic markets—have blurred the distinction between domestic and foreign financial markets. As the necessary electronic technology has been developed and the cost of transactions has plummeted, the world has become one vast, interconnected market. Markets for U.S. government securities and certain stocks, foreign exchange trading, interbank borrowing and lending—to cite a few examples—operate continuously around the clock and around the world and in enormous size. The *globalization of financial markets* has brought about an unprecedented degree of competition among key financial centers and financial institutions that has further reduced the costs of issuing new securities.

Deregulation is hastened by the process of *regulatory arbitrage,* whereby the users of capital markets issue and trade securities in financial centers with the lowest regulatory standards and, hence, the lowest costs. In order to win back business, financial centers around the world are throwing off obsolete and costly regulations.

The combination of freer markets with widely available information has laid the foundation for global growth. Cross-border securities trading was estimated in 1990 to be $12 trillion.[1] Fund raising is also global now as well. In 1989, some $360 billion was raised in international capital markets, using the various financing categories shown in Exhibit 22.1. Treasurers are not confined to domestic markets for their source of funding and are now quick to exploit any attractive opportunity that occurs anywhere in the world.

Whereas competition drives the international financial system, innovation is its fuel. *Financial innovation* segments, transfers, and diversifies risk. It also enables companies to tap previously inaccessible markets and permits investors and issuers alike to take advantage of tax loopholes. Because of financial innovation, international capital mobility has increased dramatically.

As in the domestic case, cross-border financial transfers can take place through international securitization or international financial intermediation. The hypothetical case depicted in Exhibit 22.2 illustrates the distinction between these two mechanisms for international fund flows. A Belgian corporation with surplus funds seeks an investment outlet, while a Japanese corporation requires additional funds. International securitization

■ **EXHIBIT 22.1**   Borrowing on International Capital Markets, 1983–1989

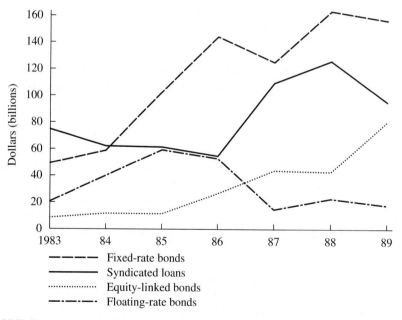

SOURCE: *OECD Financial Statistics Monthly,* various issues.

[1]This figure was cited in "A Survey of the International Capital Markets," *The Economist,* July 21, 1990, p. 7.

■ **EXHIBIT 22.2**   Securitization Versus Intermediation

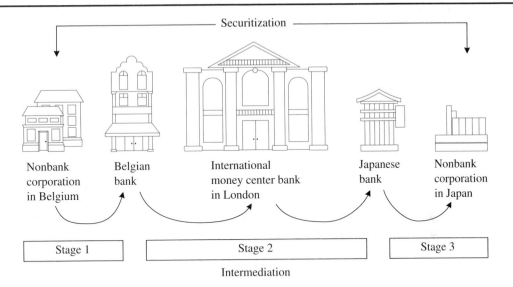

SOURCE: Anthony Saunders, "The Eurocurrency Interbank Market: Potential for International Crises?" *Business Review,* Federal Reserve Bank of Philadelphia, January/February 1988, p. 19. Used with permission.

might involve the Japanese firm issuing new bonds and selling them directly to the Belgian firm.

Alternatively, the Belgian firm's surplus funds could be transferred to the Japanese firm through international financial intermediation. This intermediation could involve three (or more) stages. First, the Belgian firm deposits its funds with a local Belgian bank. Second, the Belgian bank redeposits the money with an international money center bank in London that turns around and lends those funds to a Japanese bank. In stage three, the Japanese bank lends those funds to the Japanese corporation.

Whether international fund flows take place through financial intermediation or securitization depends on the relative costs and risks of the two mechanisms. The key determinant here is the cost of gathering information on foreign firms. As these costs continue to come down, international securitization should become increasingly more cost-effective.

■ 22.2 ■
NATIONAL CAPITAL MARKETS AS INTERNATIONAL FINANCIAL CENTERS

The principal functions of a financial market are to transfer current purchasing power (in the form of money) from savers to borrowers in exchange for the promise of greater future purchasing power and to allocate those funds among the potential users on the basis of risk-adjusted returns. The consequences of well-functioning financial markets is that more and better projects get financed, and individuals are able to select their preferred time pattern of consumption. Not surprisingly, most of the major financial markets attract both investors and fund raisers from abroad. That is, these markets are also *international financial markets* where foreigners can both borrow and lend money.

International Financial Markets

International financial markets can develop anywhere, provided that local regulations permit the market and that the potential users are attracted to it. The most important international financial centers are London, Tokyo, and New York. All the other major industrial countries have important domestic financial markets as well but only some, such as Germany and—recently—France, are also important international financial centers. On the other hand, some countries that have relatively unimportant domestic financial markets are important world financial centers. The markets of those countries—which include Switzerland, Luxembourg, Singapore, Hong Kong, the Bahamas, and Bahrain—serve as financial *entrepots,* or channels through which foreign funds pass. That is, these markets serve as financial intermediaries between nonresident suppliers of funds and nonresident users of funds.

Political stability and minimal government intervention are prerequisites for becoming and remaining an important international financial center, especially an entrepot center. Historically, London's preeminance as an entrepot for international finance comes from its being a lightly regulated offshore market in a world of financial rigidites. That is why it became home to the Euromarkets some 30 years ago. As financial markets deregulate, London's strength has shifted to its central location and financial infrastructure—its access to information by dint of its position astride huge international capital flows, its pool of financial talent, its well-developed legal system, and its telecommunications links.

Foreign Access to Domestic Markets

Despite the increasing liberalization of financial markets, governments are usually unwilling to rely completely on the market to perform the functions of gathering and allocating funds. Foreigners particularly are often hampered in their ability to gain access to domestic capital markets because of government-imposed or government-suggested restrictions relating to the maturities and amounts of money that they can raise. They are hampered as well by the government-legislated extra costs, such as special taxes (for example, the U.S. interest equalization tax (IET) that was in effect from 1963 to 1974) that they must bear on those funds that they can raise. Nonetheless, the financial markets of many countries are open wide enough to permit foreigners to borrow or invest.

As a citizen of many nations, the multinational firm has greater leeway in tapping a variety of local money markets than does a purely domestic firm, but it too is often the target of restrictive legislation aimed at reserving local capital for indigenous companies or the local government. The capital that can be raised is frequently limited to local uses through the imposition of exchange controls. As we have seen previously, however, multinationals are potentially capable of transferring funds, even in the presence of currency controls, by using a variety of financial channels. To the extent, therefore, that local credits substitute for parent- or affiliate-supplied financing, the additional monies are available for removal.

The Foreign Bond Market. The *foreign bond market* is an important part of the international financial markets. It is simply that portion of the domestic bond market that represents issues floated by foreign companies or governments. As such, foreign bonds are subject to local laws and must be denominated in the local currency. At times, these issues face additional restrictions as well. For example, foreign bonds floated in Switzerland, Germany, and the Netherlands are subject to a queuing system, where they must wait for their turn in line.

The United States and Switzerland contain the most important foreign bond markets. Major foreign bond markets are also located in Japan and Luxembourg. Data on the amounts of foreign bond issues are presented in Exhibit 22.3.

The Foreign Bank Market. The *foreign bank market* represents that portion of domestic bank loans supplied to foreigners for use abroad. As in the case of foreign bond issues, governments often restrict the amounts of bank funds destined for foreign purposes.

The importance of foreign banks, particularly Japanese banks, as a funding source is obvious from the roster of the world's ten largest banks ranked by assets as of December 31, 1989, as shown in Exhibit 22.4. All of the top seven banks are Japanese. The only U.S. bank,

■ **EXHIBIT 22.3** Foreign Bond Market (U.S. $ Millions)

Market	1985	%	1986	%	1987	%	1988	%	1989	%	1990	%
Austria	72	0.2	84	0.2	99	0.2			319		595	1.2
Belgium	282	0.9	345	0.9	672	1.7	114	0.2	106	0.2	2308	4.5
Canada	147	0.5					119	0.2				
Finland			49	0.1	66	0.2	276	0.6			302	0.6
France	417	1.3	539	1.4	674	1.7	578	1.2	729	1.7	927	1.8
Germany	1741	5.6							754	1.7		
Ireland	18	0.1					38	0.1	133	0.3		
Italy	257	0.8	210	0.5	147	0.4	340	0.7	146	0.3	642	1.2
Japan	6255	20.0	5223	13.3	4071	10.2	6720	13.9	8156	18.6	7452	14.4
Luxembourg	400	1.3	816	2.1	1380	3.4	1774	3.7	1674	3.8	4422	8.6
Netherlands	979	3.1	1724	4.4	1008	2.5	750	1.6	274	0.6	119	0.2
Portugal							35	0.1	62	0.1	1360	2.6
Spain					240	0.6	728	1.5	2225	5.1	1434	2.8
Switzerland	14873	47.6	23213	59.0	24301	60.6	26318	54.6	18624	42.5	23152	44.8
United Kingdom	873	2.8	394	1.0			355	0.7	1155	2.6		
United States	4917	15.7	6782	17.2	7416	18.5	10051	20.9	9440	21.6	8932	17.3
Total	31229	100.0	39359	100.0	40074	100.0	48196	100.0	43797	100.0	51645	100.0

SOURCE: *OECD Financial Statistics Monthly,* December 1990.

■ **EXHIBIT 22.4**   The World's Ten Largest Banking Concerns (Ranked by Assets; Converted into U.S. Dollars as of December 31, 1989)

Bank	Country	Assets (U.S. $ Billions)
1. Dai-Ichi Kangyo Bank	Japan	$357.4
2. Mitsui Taiyo Kobe Bank	Japan	350.5
3. Sumitomo Bank	Japan	346.7
4. Fuji Bank	Japan	336.0
5. Mitsubishi Bank	Japan	324.4
6. Sanwa Bank	Japan	321.9
7. Industrial Bank of Japan	Japan	246.8
8. Credit Agricole	France	242.5
9. Banque Nationale de Paris	France	231.9
10. Citicorp	United States	227.0

SOURCE: Excerpted from *The Wall Street Journal,* September 21, 1990, p. R29.

Citicorp, is tenth in size. (Of the world's 100 largest banks, only 13 are American; 28 are Japanese.) The minimal representation by American banks owes primarily to prohibitions on interstate banking in the United States, as well as the high Japanese savings rate.

The Foreign Equity Market.   The idea of placing stock in foreign markets has long attracted corporate finance managers. One attraction of the *foreign equity market* is the diversification of equity funding risk: A pool of funds from a diversified shareholder base insulates a company from the vagaries of a single national market. For large companies located in small countries, foreign sales may be a necessity. When KLM, the Dutch airline, issued 50 million shares in 1986 to raise $304 million, it placed 7 million shares in Europe, 7 million in the United States, and 1 million in Japan. According to a spokesman for the company, "The domestic market is too small for such an operation."[2]

Selling stock overseas also increases the potential demand for the company's shares, and hence its price, by attracting new shareholders. In addition, for a firm that wants to project an international presence, an international stock offering can spread the firm's name in local markets.

Selling stock overseas can also increase the potential demand for the company's shares, and hence its price, by attracting new shareholders. For example, a study by Gordon Alexander, Cheol Eun, and S. Janakiramanan found that foreign companies that listed their shares in the United States experienced a decline in their expected return.[3] This evidence is

[2]"International Equities: The New Game in Town," *Business International Money Report,* September 29, 1987, p. 306.

[3]Gordon J. Alexander, Cheol S. Eun, and S. Janakiramanan, "International Listings and Stock Returns: Some Empirical Evidence," working paper, University of Minnesota, May 1986.

consistent with the theoretical work of Robert Merton, who shows that a company can lower its cost of equity capital and, thereby, increase its market value by expanding its investor base.[4]

For a firm that wants to project an international presence, an international stock offering can spread the firm's name in local markets. In the words of a London investment banker, "If you are a company with a brand name, it's a way of making your product known and your presence known in the financial markets, which can have a knock-off effect on your overall business. A marketing exercise is done; it's just like selling soap."[5]

■ ──

ILLUSTRATION

Waste Management Lists Its Stock in Australia. Chicago-based Waste Management has been operating in Australia since 1984 and has gained a leading share of the garbage collection market through expansion and acquisition. In 1986, the firm issued shares in Australia and then listed these shares on the Australian exchanges. A principal reason for the listing was to enhance its corporate profile. According to a Waste Management spokesman, "We view Australia as a growth market, and what we really wanted was to increase our visibility."[6]

Listing gets Waste Management better known in the financial community as well. This visibility in turn aids the expansion program, which hinges largely on mergers and acquisitions, by increasing contacts with potential joint venture or acquisition candidates. Listing also facilitates stock-for-stock swaps.

An Australian listing also enhances the local profit-sharing package. Waste Management uses an employee stock program as an integral feature of its compensation. By listing locally, the prominence of the firm's shares is increased, and the program becomes more attractive to employees. ──────────── ■

Despite these advantages, the advent of stock issues specifically structured for, and directed toward, foreign markets has occurred only in the past few years. Today, a growing number of American and non-American companies are selling stock issues overseas. See Exhibit 22.5 for the announcement of a $512 million international equity offering by Hong Kong Telecommunications.

Not only are foreign companies issuing stock in the United States, many U.S. companies—which until recently issued stock almost exclusively in the United States—are now selling part of their issues overseas. For example, when Black & Decker issued 4.5 million shares in 1983, Europe was never brought up as a potential market. But when the company

[4]Robert C. Merton, "A Simple Model of Capital Market Equilibrium with Incomplete Information," *Journal of Finance,* July 1987, pp. 483–510.

[5]"International Equities: The New Game in Town," *Business International Money Report,* September 29, 1987, p. 306.

[6]"Waste Management Who? Why One U.S. Giant Is Now Listed Down Under," *Business International Money Report,* December 22, 1986, p.403.

■ **EXHIBIT 22.5**   The International Equity Offering by Hong Kong Telecommunications Limited

All of these securities having been sold, this announcement appears as a matter of record only and is neither an offer to sell nor a solicitation of an offer to buy these securities in Hong Kong Telecommunications Limited.

877,500,000 Shares

Hong Kong Telecommunications Limited
香 港 電 訊 有 限 公 司

Hong Kong Offering
607,500,000 Shares
The undersigned acted as underwriters in connection with the Hong Kong Offering.
Price HK$4.55 Per Share

Prudential-Bache Capital Funding

Baring Brothers & Co., Limited

Wardley Corporate Finance Limited

United States Offering
6,024,793 American Depositary Shares
Representing 180,743,790 Shares
These shares have been distributed in the United States by the undersigned.
Price US$17.50 Per American Depositary Share

Prudential-Bache Capital Funding

Baring Securities Inc.

Goldman, Sachs & Co.

Merrill Lynch Capital Markets

Bear, Stearns & Co. Inc.	The First Boston Corporation	Alex. Brown & Sons	Dillon, Read & Co. Inc.	Donaldson, Lufkin & Jenrette
Hambrecht & Quist	Kidder, Peabody & Co.		Lazard Frères & Co.	Montgomery Securities
PaineWebber Incorporated	Robertson, Colman & Stephens		Salomon Brothers Inc	Shearson Lehman Hutton Inc.
Smith Barney, Harris Upham & Co.	S.G. Warburg Securities		Wertheim Schroder & Co.	Dean Witter Capital Markets
Arnhold and S. Bleichroeder, Inc.	Bateman Eichler, Hill Richards	Blunt Ellis & Loewi	Dain Bosworth	A. G. Edwards & Sons, Inc.
Robert Fleming Inc.	Legg Mason Wood Walker		Oppenheimer & Co., Inc.	Piper, Jaffray & Hopwood
The Robinson-Humphrey Company, Inc.	Rothschild Inc.		Thomson McKinnon Securities Inc.	Wheat, First Securities, Inc.
Robert W. Baird & Co.	Sanford C. Bernstein & Co., Inc.		Butcher & Singer Inc.	Cable, Howse & Ragen
Cowen & Co.	Furman Selz Mager Dietz & Birney		Janney Montgomery Scott Inc.	Ladenburg, Thalmann & Co. Inc.
C.J. Lawrence, Morgan Grenfell Inc.	Mabon, Nugent & Co.		McDonald & Company	Needham & Company, Inc.
First Albany Corporation	Gabelli & Company, Inc.		Gruntal & Co., Incorporated	Howard, Weil, Labouisse, Friedrichs

International Offering
89,256,210 Shares
These shares have been distributed outside of Hong Kong and the United States by the undersigned.
Price US$.5834 Per Share

Prudential-Bache Capital Funding

Baring Brothers & Co., Limited

CL-Alexanders Laing & Cruickshank	Credit Suisse First Boston Limited	Goldman Sachs International Limited	Merrill Lynch International & Co.
Nomura International Limited	NM Rothschild & Sons Limited		SBCI Swiss Bank Corporation Investment banking
Algemene Bank Nederland N.V.	Amsterdam-Rotterdam Bank N.V.	Banca Commerciale Italiana	Banque Bruxelles Lambert S.A.
Banque Indosuez	Banque Paribas Capital Markets Limited	Daiwa Europe Limited	Dresdner Bank
Société Générale	Swiss Volksbank		Union Bank of Switzerland (Securities) Limited

In connection with this offering the sellers of the shares of Hong Kong Telecommunications Limited were advised by the undersigned.

Cable and Wireless (Far East) Limited
by
Prudential Asia Capital Limited

The Financial Secretary Incorporated
(a Hong Kong Government entity)
by
Baring Brothers & Co., Limited

December 19, 1988

SOURCE: Used by permission.

issued another 8.5 million shares in late 1985, it sold 2 million shares in Europe. The increasing number of multiple syndications is reflected in more and more securities ads (called "tombstones" because of their appearance) for equity issues, looking like the one for First Brands that is shown in Exhibit 22.6.

International equity placements generally fall into one of two categories. U.S. companies typically do *dual syndicate equity offerings,* such as the First Brands issue, where the offering is split into two *tranches*—domestic and overseas—and each tranche is handled by a separate lead manager. In contrast, European companies most often do *Euroequity issues*—single tranche, syndicated equity offerings placed throughout Europe and handled

■ **EXHIBIT 22.6**   The First Brands Dual Syndicate Equity Offering

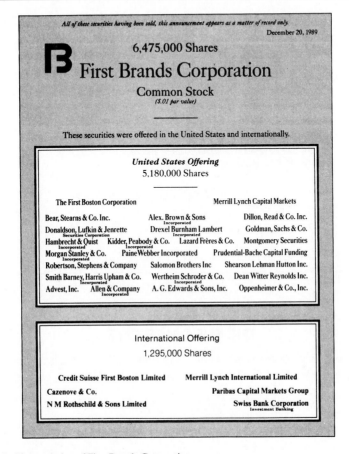

SOURCE: Used with permission of First Brands Corporation.

by one lead manager. The offering by Hong Kong Telecommunications, appearing in Exhibit 22.5, illustrates a Euroequity issue.

Most major stock exchanges permit sales of foreign issues provided the issue satisfies all the listing requirements of the local market. Some of the major stock markets list large numbers of foreign stocks. For example, Union Carbide, Black & Decker, Caterpillar, and General Motors are among the more than 200 foreign stocks listed on the German stock exchanges. Similarly, over 500 foreign stocks—including ITT, Hoover and Woolworth—are listed on the British exchanges. More companies are also seeking to be listed on the Tokyo Stock Exchange. Exhibit 22.7 announces Bell Atlantic's listing on the Tokyo exchange.

■ **EXHIBIT 22.7**   Announcement of Bell Atlantic's Listing on the Tokyo Stock Exchange

本日 東京証券市場へ上場！
ベル・アトランテック

🔔 **Bell Atlantic**™
LISTED TODAY ON THE TOKYO STOCK EXCHANGE

> Today, Bell Atlantic's shares will be listed on the
> Tokyo Stock Exchange. This step is in recognition of the
> internationalization of capital markets and of Japan's increasingly
> important role in international trade.
>
> Bell Atlantic™ is currently listed on the following
> stock exchanges:
> New York, Boston, Mid-West, Pacific, Philadelphia, London,
> Zurich, Geneva, Basel.

SOURCE: Used with permission of Bell Atlantic Network Services, Inc.

■ 22.3 ■
THE EUROMARKETS

This section discusses the Eurocurrency and Eurobond markets. It describes the functioning of these markets and then shows how each can be used to meet the multinational firm's financing requirements.

The Eurocurrency Market

A *Eurocurrency* is a dollar or other freely convertible currency deposited in a bank outside its country of origin. Thus, U.S. dollars on deposit in London become *Eurodollars*. These deposits can be placed in a foreign bank or in the foreign branch of a domestic U.S. bank.[7] The *Eurocurrency market* then consists of those banks—called *Eurobanks*—that accept deposits and make loans in foreign currencies.

The Eurobond and Eurocurrency markets are often confused with each other, but there is a fundamental distinction between the two. In the *Eurobond market, Eurobonds,* which are bonds sold outside the countries in whose currencies they are denominated, are issued directly by the final borrowers; whereas the Eurocurrency market enables investors to hold short-term claims on commercial banks, which then act as intermediaries to transform these deposits into long-term claims on final borrowers. However, banks do play an important role in placing these bonds with the final investors.

---

[7]The term foreign is relative to the operating unit's location, not to its nationality.

The dominant Eurocurrency is the U.S. dollar. But the importance of the Eurodollar waxes and wanes with the strength of the U.S. dollar. With dollar weakness in the latter parts of both the 1970s and 1980s, other currencies—particularly the Deutsche mark and the Swiss franc—increased in importance (see Exhibit 22.8).

Modern Origins.   The origin of the post–World War II Eurodollar market is often traced to the fear of Soviet Bloc countries that their dollar deposits in U.S. banks might be attached by U.S. citizens with claims against Communist governments. Therefore, they left their dollar balances with banks in France and England.

Whatever its postwar beginnings, the Eurocurrency market has thrived for one reason: government regulation. By operating in Eurocurrencies, banks and suppliers of funds are able to avoid certain regulatory costs that would otherwise be imposed. The following series of U.S. government policies provided a major impetus for the rapid development of the Eurodollar market.

1. Regulation Q set interest rate ceilings on deposits in the United States. These ceilings imposed by the Federal Reserve allowed overseas banks to attract dollar deposits whenever equilibrium rates rose above the Regulation Q limit.
2. Federal Reserve Regulation M in the United States mandated fractional reserves on dollar deposits taken in, whereas Eurobanks were not required to maintain reserves against the dollar deposits.
3. The interest equalization tax (IET) introduced in 1963 taxed interest on foreign debt sold in the United States, thereby raising significantly the cost of borrowing in U.S. capital markets by non-U.S. corporations and governments. Borrowers had to look outside the United States for funds, often turning to the Eurodollar market.
4. Regulations in 1968 from the U.S. Office of Foreign Direct Investment (OFDI) restricted U.S. companies in their use of domestic dollars overseas. Future expansion had to be financed overseas, greatly increasing the demand for external dollars, or Eurodollars.

Although the IET and OFDI regulations and Regulation Q have been abolished, the Eurodollar market still exists. Despite its ups and downs, it will continue to exist as long as

■ **EXHIBIT 22.8**   Eurocurrency Market Size, Measured by Liabilities, End of Period ($ Billion)

	1977	1978	1979	1980	1981	1982	1983	1984	1985	1986	1987
Gross market size	740	949	1233	1524	1861	2168	2278	2386	2846	3579	4461
By Denomination											
U.S. dollars	76%	74%	72%	75%	78%	80%	81%	82%	75%	71%	66%
Other currencies	24%	26%	28%	25%	22%	20%	19%	18%	25%	29%	34%
Net market size	379	478	578	705	859	1285	1382	1430	1676	1979	2377
Rate of growth of net market size	21%	26%	21%	22%	22%	50%	8%	3%	17%	18%	20%

SOURCE: *World Financial Markets,* Morgan Guaranty Trust Company, various issues.

there are profitable opportunities to engage in offshore financial transactions. These opportunities persist because of continuing government regulations and taxes that raise costs and lower returns on domestic transactions.

Eurodollar Creation.   The creation of Eurodollars can be illustrated by using a series of T-accounts to trace the movement of dollars into and through the Eurodollar market.

First, suppose that Leksell AB, a Swedish firm, sells medical diagnostic equipment worth $1 million to a U.S. hospital. It receives a check payable in dollars drawn on Citibank in New York. Initially, Leksell AB deposits this check in its Citibank checking account for dollar-working-capital purposes. This transaction would be represented on the firm's and Citibank's accounts as follows:

Citibank		Leksell AB	
	Demand deposit due Leksell AB +$1M	Demand deposit in Citibank +$1M	

In order to earn a higher rate of interest on the $1 million account (U.S. banks cannot pay interest on corporate checking accounts), Leksell decides to place the funds in a time deposit with Barclays Bank in London. This transaction is recorded as follows:

Citibank		Barclays	
	Demand deposit due Leksell AB −$1M Demand deposit due Barclays +$1M	Demand deposit in Citibank +$1M	Time deposit owed Leksell +$1M

Leksell AB	
Demand deposit in Citibank −$1M Demand deposit in Barclays +$1M	

One million Eurodollars have just been created by substituting a dollar account in a London bank for a dollar account held in New York. Notice that no dollars have left New York, although ownership of the U.S. deposit has shifted from a foreign corporation to a foreign bank.

Barclays can leave those funds idle in its account in New York, but the opportunity cost would be too great. If it cannot immediately loan those funds to a government or commercial borrower, Barclays will place the $1 million in the London interbank market. This involves loaning the funds to another bank active in the Eurodollar market. The interest rate at which such interbank loans are made is called the *London interbank offer rate* (LIBOR). In this case, however, Barclays chooses to loan these funds to Ronningen SA, a Norwegian importer of fine wines. The loan is recorded as follows:

Citibank		
Demand deposit due Barclays		
		−$1M
Demand deposit due Ronningen SA		
		+$1M

Barclays	
Demand deposit in Citibank	Time deposit owed Leksell
−$1M	$1M
Loan to Ronningen SA	
+$1M	

Ronningen SA	
Demand deposit in Citibank	Eurodollar loan from Barclays
+$1M	+$1M

We can see from this example that the Eurocurrency market involves a chain of deposits and a chain of borrowers and lenders, not buyers and sellers. One does not buy or sell Eurocurrencies. Ordinarily, an owner of dollars will place them in a time-deposit or demand-deposit account in a U.S. bank, and the owner of a French franc deposit will keep it in an account with a French bank. Until the dollar (or franc) deposit is withdrawn, control over its use resides with the U.S. (or French) bank. In fact, the majority of Eurocurrency transactions involve transferring control of deposits from one Eurobank to another Eurobank. Loans to nonEurobanks account for fewer than half of all Eurocurrency loans. The data in Exhibit 22.8 show that the net market size (subtracting off interEurobank liabilities) is much smaller than the gross market size; in 1987, for example, the gross market size was about $4.4 trillion, while the net market size was about $2.4 trillion.

The example and data presented indicate that Eurocurrency operations differ from the structure of domestic banking operations in two ways:

1. There is a *chain of ownership* between the original dollar depositor and the U.S. bank.
2. There is a *changing control over the deposit* and the use to which the money is put.

It should be noted, however, that despite the chain of transactions, the total amount of foreign dollar deposits in the United States remains the same. Moreover, on the most fundamental level—taking in deposits and allocating funds—the Eurocurrency market operates much as does any other financial market, except for the absence of government regulations on loans that can be made and interest rates that can be charged. This section now examines some of the particular characteristics of Eurocurrency lending.

Eurocurrency Loans.   The most important characteristic of the Eurocurrency market is that loans are made on a floating-rate basis. Interest rates on loans to governments and their agencies, corporations, and nonprime banks are set at a fixed margin above LIBOR for the given period and currency chosen. At the end of each period, the interest for the next period is calculated at the same fixed margin over the new LIBOR. For example, if the margin is 0.75% and the current LIBOR is 13%, then the borrower is charged 13.75% for the upcoming period. The period normally chosen is six months, but shorter periods such as one month or three months are possible. The LIBOR used corresponds to the maturity of the rollover period.

The *margin,* or spread between the lending bank's cost of funds and the interest charged the borrower, varies a good deal among borrowers and is based on the borrower's perceived riskiness. Typically, such spreads have ranged from slightly below 0.5% to over 3%, with the median being somewhere between 1% and 2%.

The *maturity* of a loan can vary from approximately three to ten years. Maturities have tended to lengthen over time, from a norm of about five years originally to a norm of eight to ten years these days for prime borrowers. Lenders in this market are almost exclusively banks. In any single loan, there will normally be a number of participating banks that form a syndicate. The bank originating the loan will usually manage the syndicate. This bank, in turn, may invite one or two other banks to comanage the loan.

The managers charge the borrower a once-and-for-all fee of 0.25% to 1% of the loan value, depending on the size and type of the loan. Part of this fee is kept by the managers, and the rest is divided up among all the participating banks (including the managing banks) according to the amount of funds each bank supplies.

The *drawdown*—the period over which the borrower may take down the loan—and the repayment period vary in accordance with the borrower's needs. A commitment fee of about 0.5% per annum is paid on the unused balance, and prepayments in advance of the agreed-upon schedule are permitted but are sometimes subject to a penalty fee.

Multicurrency Clauses.   Borrowing can be done in many different currencies, although the dollar is still the dominant currency. Increasingly, Eurodollars have a multicurrency clause. This clause gives the borrower the right (subject to availability) to switch from one currency to another on any rollover date. The multicurrency option enables the borrower to match currencies on cash inflows and outflows (a potentially valuable exposure management technique as we saw in Chapter 9). Equally important, the option allows a firm to take advantage of its own expectations regarding currency changes (if they differ from the market's expectations) and shop around for those funds with the lowest effective cost.

An example of a typical multicurrency loan is a $100 million, ten-year revolving credit arranged by the Dutch firm Thyssen Bornemisza NV with nine Dutch, German, U.S., and Swiss banks, led by Amsterdam-Rotterdam Bank. Rates are fixed, at the company's discretion, at three-month, six-month, or 12-month intervals. At each rollover date, the firm can choose from any freely available Eurocurrency except Eurosterling, but only four different Eurocurrencies may be outstanding at any one time.

Relationship Between Domestic and Eurocurrency Money Markets.   The presence of arbitrage activities ensures a close relationship between interest rates in national and international (Eurocurrency) money markets. Interest rates in the U.S. and Eurodollar markets, for example, can differ only to the extent that there are additional costs, controls, or risks associated with moving dollars between, say, New York and London. Otherwise, arbitrageurs would borrow in the low-cost market and lend in the high-return market, quickly eliminating any interest differential between the two.

Since the cost of shifting funds is relatively insignificant, we must look to currency controls or risk to explain any substantial differences between domestic and external rates. To the extent that exchange controls are effective, the national money market can be isolated or segmented from its international counterpart. In fact, the difference between internal and external interest rates can be taken as a measure of the effectiveness of the monetary authorities' exchange controls.

Interest differentials can also exist if there is a danger of future controls. The possibility that at some future time either the lender or borrower will not be able to transfer funds across a border—also known as sovereign risk—can help sustain persistent differences between domestic and external money market rates.

In general, Eurocurrency spreads (a spread is the margin between lending and deposit rates) are narrower than in domestic money markets. Lending rates can be lower for the following reasons:

1. The lack of reserve requirements increases a bank's earning asset base (that is, a larger percentage of deposits can be lent out).
2. Regulatory expenses, such as the requirement to pay Federal Deposit Insurance Corporation fees, are lower or nonexistent.
3. Eurobanks are not forced to lend money to certain borrowers at concessionary rates, thereby raising the return on their assets.
4. Most borrowers are well known, reducing the cost of information gathering and credit analysis.
5. Eurocurrency lending is characterized by high volumes, allowing for lower margins; transactions costs are reduced because most of the loan arrangements are standardized and conducted by telephone or telex.
6. Eurocurrency lending can and does take place out of tax-haven countries, providing for higher after-tax returns.

Eurocurrency deposit rates are higher than domestic rates for the following reasons:

1. They must be higher to attract domestic deposits.
2. Eurobanks can afford to pay higher rates based on their lower regulatory costs.
3. Eurobanks are able to pay depositors higher interest rates because they are not subject to the interest rate ceilings that prevail in many countries.
4. A larger percentage of deposits can be lent out.

Euromarket Trends.   In recent years, the London interbank offer rate has started to fade as a benchmark for lending money in the Eurocurrency market, in much the same way that the prime rate is no longer the all-important benchmark in the U.S. bank loan market. In a trend that shows no sign of abating, a growing number of creditworthy borrowers— including Denmark, Sweden, several major corporations, and some banks—are obtaining financing in the Euromarkets at interest rates well below LIBOR.

This trend largely reflects the fact that because many international bank loans soured in the early 1980s, banks lost much of their appeal to investors. As a result, banks' ability to impose themselves as the credit yardstick by which all other international borrowers are measured has faltered drastically. What the Euromarket is saying in effect is that borrowers such as Denmark are considered better credit risks than are most banks.

Moreover, investor preferences for an alternative to bank Eurodollar certificates of deposit (whereby banks substitute their credit risk for their borrowers') have enabled investment banks to transform usual bank syndicated lending into securities offerings, such as floating-rate notes (FRNs). This preference for the ultimate borrower's credit risk, rather than the bank's credit risk, has led to rapid growth in the Eurobond market, particularly the floating-rate segment of the market.

Eurobonds

Eurobonds are similar in many respects to the public debt sold in domestic capital markets. Unlike domestic bond markets, however, the Eurobond market is almost entirely free of official regulation, but instead is self-regulated by the Association of International Bond Dealers. The prefix Euro indicates that the bonds are sold outside the countries in whose currencies they are denominated. For example, the General Motors issue shown in Exhibit 22.9 is a Eurobond. You can tell that because the tombstone says, "These securities have not been registered under the United States Securities Act of 1933 and may not be offered or sold in the United States or to United States persons as part of the distribution."

Until recently, the Eurobond market has been substantially smaller than the Eurocurrency market. Borrowers in the Eurobond market must be well known and must have impeccable credit ratings (for example, developed countries, international institutions, and large multinational corporations). Even then the amounts raised in the Eurobond market have historically been far less than those in the Eurocurrency market.

As can be seen in Exhibit 22.10, however, the Eurobond market has grown dramatically over the past decade and its size now rivals that of the Eurocurrency market. But Exhibit 22.10 also shows that the Eurobond market has had its ups and downs.

Swaps.   The major catalyst for growth in the Eurobond market over the last few years has been the emergence of a technique known as the *swap,* a financial transaction in which two counterparties agree to exchange streams of payments over time. It is now estimated that 70% of Eurobond issues are "swap-driven." Swaps allow borrowers to raise money in one market and to swap one interest rate structure for another (for example, from fixed to floating), or to go further and to swap principal and interest from one currency to another. These swaps allow the parties to the contract to arbitrage their relative access to different currency markets; a borrower whose paper is much in demand in one currency can obtain a cost saving in another currency sector by raising money in the former and swapping the funds into the latter currency. Chapter 23 discusses swaps in detail.

Links Between the Domestic and Eurobond Markets.   The growing presence of sophisticated investors willing to arbitrage between the domestic dollar and Eurodollar bond markets—in part because the United States no longer imposes withholding taxes on foreign

■ **EXHIBIT 22.9**   Announcement of a GMAC Eurobond Issue

These securities have not been   ...ered under the United States Securities Act of 1933 and may not be
o'fered or sold in the Ui   States or to United States persons as part of the distribution.

General Motors Acceptance Corporation
(Incorporated in the State of New York, United States of America)

U.S.$200,000,000

7⅝ per cent. Notes due September 3, 1991

Swiss Bank Corporation International Limited

Credit Suisse First Boston Limited	**Deutsche Bank Capital Markets Limited**
Merrill Lynch Capital Markets	**Morgan Stanley International**
Nomura International Limited	**Salomon Brothers International Limited**

Union Bank of Switzerland (Securities) Limited

Algemene Bank Nederland N.V.	BankAmerica Capital Markets Group
Bankers Trust International Limited	Banque Bruxelles Lambert S.A.
Banque Générale du Luxembourg S.A.	Banque Nationale de Paris
Banque Paribas Capital Markets Limited	Commerzbank Aktiengesellschaft
Crédit Lyonnais	Creditanstalt-Bankverein
Daiwa Europe Limited	IBJ International Limited
Leu Securities Limited	The Nikko Securities Co., (Europe) Ltd.
Shearson Lehman Brothers International	Société Générale
Sumitomo Trust International Limited	Swiss Volksbank
S.G. Warburg Securities	Wood Gundy Inc.

Yamaichi International (Europe) Limited

New Issue   This announcement appears as a matter of record only.   September 1986

SOURCE: Used with permission of General Motors Acceptance Corporation.

investors—has eliminated much of the interest disparity that used to exist between Eurobonds and domestic bonds. Despite the closer alignment of the two markets, though, the Eurobond issuer may at any given time take advantage of Eurobond "windows" when a combination of domestic regulations, tax laws, and expectations of international investors enable the issuer to achieve a lower all-in financing cost—often involving currency and interest swaps—than is available in domestic markets.[8] In addition to the possibility of reduced borrowing costs, the Eurobond issuer may diversify its investor base and funding sources by having access to the international Eurocapital markets of Western Europe, North America, and the Far East.

[8]The existence of such windows is documented by Yong-Cheol Kim and Rene M. Stulz in "The Eurobond Market and Corporate Financial Policy: A Test of the Clientele Hypothesis," *Journal of Financial Economics* 22, 1988, pp. 189–205, and "Is There Still a Global Market for Convertible Bonds?" working paper, Ohio State University, April 1990.

■ **EXHIBIT 22.10**   Eurobond New Issues, 1979–1990

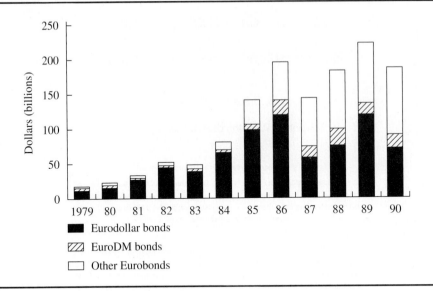

Placement.   Issues are arranged through an underwriting group, often with a hundred or more underwriting banks involved for an issue as small as $25 million. A growing volume of Eurobonds is being placed privately because of the simplicity, speed, and privacy with which private placements can be arranged.

Currency Denomination.   Historically, about 75% of Eurobonds have been dollar denominated. During the late 1970s, however, when the dollar was in a downward spiral, other currencies (particularly the Deutsche mark) became more important in the Eurobond market. The sharp increase in the share of dollar-denominated Eurobonds in the period up to mid-1985, shown in Exhibit 22.10, largely reflects the surging value of the dollar. The subsequent drop in the dollar's value again led to a rise in nondollar issues, particularly yen and Deutsche mark issues. The absence of Swiss franc Eurobonds is due to the Swiss Central Bank's ban on using the Swiss franc for Eurobond issues.

As an alternative to issuing dollar, Deutsche-mark, or other single-currency-denominated Eurobonds, several borrowers in recent years have offered bonds whose value is a weighted average or "basket" of several currencies. The most successful of these currency "cocktails" is the European Currency Unit (ECU).

ECU bonds offer advantages to both investors and borrowers, including the following:

1. *Access to markets that might not otherwise be available*: The markets for some individual European currencies are not very liquid and certain European capital markets—such as the Belgian franc, French franc, Italian lira, and Danish krone bond markets—are difficult to tap directly for funds because of remaining capital controls. Using the ECU lowers transaction costs, enables indirect access to currencies otherwise unavailable, and allows wider market diversification.

2. *Diversification of currency risk, especially for investors and borrowers within the European Monetary System*: The effect of weakening currencies will—to some degree—be offset by strengthening currencies within the basket. Although the currency percentage contained in an ECU bond is probably suboptimal in terms of its risk-return trade-off, investors and borrowers dealing in ECUs may face lower transaction costs than if they were to tailor their own currency baskets.

3. *A hedge against the dollar*: Because the ECU basket excludes the dollar, the value of the ECU in terms of any of its component currencies is generally unaffected by changes in the dollar's value.

Eurobond Secondary Market. Historically, there has been a lack of depth in the Eurobond *secondary market* (the market where investors trade securities already bought). However, the growing number of institutions carrying large portfolios of Eurobonds for trading purposes has increased the depth and sophistication of this market, making it second only to the U.S. domestic bond market in liquidity—where liquidity refers to the ease of trading securities at close to their quoted price. Until recently, the liquidity of Eurobonds has not mattered because investors were usually willing to purchase and lock such issues away. But because of heightened volatility in bond and currency markets, investors increasingly want assurance that they can sell Eurobonds before maturity at bid-ask spreads (the difference between the buy and the sell rate, which is a major determinant of liquidity) comparable to those in other capital markets.

One problem is that there is no central trading floor where dealers post prices. Hence, buyers sometimes have difficulty getting price quotes on Eurobonds. However, many commercial banks, investment banks, and securities trading firms act as *market makers* in a wide range of issues by quoting two-way prices (buy and sell) and being prepared to deal at those prices. Another factor adding liquidity to the market is the presence of bond brokers. They act as middlemen, taking no positions themselves but transacting orders when a counterparty is found to match a buy or sell instruction. Brokers deal only with market makers and never with the ultimate investor.

Eurobond Retirement. Sinking funds or purchase funds are usually required if a Eurobond is of more than seven years' maturity. A *sinking fund* requires the borrower to retire a fixed amount of bonds yearly after a specific number of years. By contrast, a *purchase fund* often starts in the first year, and bonds are retired only if the market price is below the issue price. The purpose of these funds is to support the market price of the bonds as well as reduce bondholder risk by assuring that not all the firm's debt will come due at once.

The desire for price support is reinforced by the fact that, historically there has been a lack of depth in the secondary market. However, as noted above, the growing number of institutions carrying large portfolios of Eurobonds for trading purposes has greatly enhanced the liquidity of the Eurobond market.

Most Eurobond issues carry *call provisions,* giving the borrower the option of retiring the bonds prior to maturity should interest rates decline sufficiently in the future. As with domestic bonds, Eurobonds with call provisions require both a call premium and higher interest rates relative to bonds without call provisions.

Rationale for Existence of Eurobond Market.   The Eurobond market survives and thrives because, unlike any other major capital market, it remains largely unregulated and untaxed. Thus, big borrowers, such as Texaco, IBM, and Sears Roebuck, can raise money more quickly and more flexibly than they can at home. And because the interest investors receive is tax free, these companies have historically been able to borrow at a rate that is below the rate at which the U.S. Treasury could borrow.

The tax-free aspect of Eurobonds relates to the notice in the tombstone for the GMAC Eurobond issue that it may not be offered to the U.S. public. U.S. tax law requires that for interest and principal to be payable in the United States, bonds must be in registered form. Eurobonds, however, are issued in bearer form, meaning they are unregistered, with no record to identify the owners. (Money can be considered to be a zero-coupon bearer bond.) This feature allows investors to collect interest in complete anonymity and, thereby, evade taxes. Although U.S. law discourages the sale of such bonds to U.S. citizens or residents, bonds issued in bearer form are common overseas. As expected, investors are willing to accept lower yields on bearer bonds than on nonbearer bonds of similar risk.

Highly rated American firms have long taken advantage of this opportunity to reduce their cost of funds by selling overseas Eurobonds in bearer form. Often corporations could borrow abroad below the cost at which the U.S. government could borrow at home. Exxon's issue of zero-coupon Eurobonds shows how companies were able to exploit the arbitrage possibilities inherent in such a situation. Zero-coupon bonds pay no interest until maturity. Instead, they are sold at a deep discount from their par value.

■ _____

ILLUSTRATION

Exxon Engages in International Tax Arbitrage.   In the fall of 1984, Exxon sold $1.8 billion principal amount of zero-coupon Eurobonds due November 2004 at an annual compounded yield of 11.65%, realizing net proceeds of about $199 million:

$$\text{Bond value} = \$1,800,000,000/(1.1165)^{20}$$
$$= \$199,000,000$$

It then used part of the proceeds to buy $1.8 billion principal amount of U.S. Treasury bonds maturing in November 2004 from which the coupons had been removed and sold separately. The yield on these "stripped" Treasurys, which are effectively zero-coupon Treasury bonds, was around 12.20%.[9] At this yield, it would have cost Exxon $180 million to purchase the $1.8 billion in stripped Treasury bonds:

$$\text{Bond value} = \$1,800,000,000/(1.1220)^{20}$$
$$= \$180,000,000$$

_____

[9]This case is discussed at greater length in John D. Finnerty, "Zero Coupon Bond Arbitrage: An Illustration of the Regulatory Dialectic at Work," *Financial Management,* Winter 1985, pp. 13–17.

At this price, Exxon earned the difference of about $19 million.

A peculiar quirk in Japanese law is largely responsible for the big difference in yield between zero-coupon Eurobonds and stripped Treasurys: Japanese investors—who were the principal buyers of the Eurobonds—did not have to pay tax on a zero-coupon bond's accrued interest if they sold the bond prior to maturity. Because of this tax advantage, they were willing to pay a premium price for zeros (relative to coupon-bearing bonds). Although in principle the Japanese would have preferred to purchase the higher-yielding (and safer) stripped U.S. Treasury bonds, they are prohibited by Japanese law from doing so. The threatened taxation of the accrued interest on zeros in Japan has eliminated this arbitrage opportunity.

■

It is apparent that the Eurobond market, like the Eurocurrency market, exists because it enables borrowers and lenders alike to avoid a variety of monetary authority regulations and controls, as well as providing them with an opportunity to escape the payment of some taxes. As long as governments attempt to regulate domestic financial markets but allow a (relatively) free flow of capital among countries, the various external financial markets will survive. If tax and regulatory costs rise, these markets will grow in importance.

Recent years have seen a reversal of some of these tax and regulatory costs. In 1984, the United States repealed its withholding tax on interest paid to foreign bondholders. That made domestic bonds, particularly U.S. Treasurys, more attractive to foreign investors. Whereas yields on top-rated Eurodollar bonds were about 40 basis points *below* similar-maturing Treasurys in 1984, the same Eurobonds in 1988 yielded about 70 basis points more than did Treasurys (see Exhibit 22.11).

■ **EXHIBIT 22.11**   Eurodollar Bond Yields Relative to Ten-Year U.S. Treasury Bond Yields

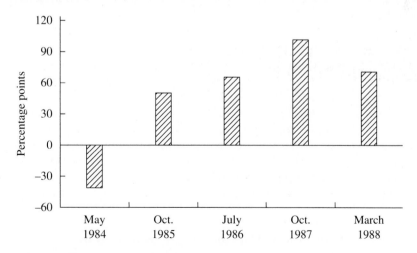

SOURCE: *The Wall Street Journal*, March 29, 1988, p. 22. Reprinted with permission of *The Wall Street Journal*, © Dow Jones & Company, Inc. 1988. All rights reserved worldwide.

At the same time, the United States began permitting well-known companies—precisely the ones that would otherwise have used the Eurobond market—to bypass complex securities laws when issuing new securities by using the *shelf registration* procedure. By lowering the cost of issuing bonds in the United States and dramatically speeding up the issuing process, shelf registration improved the competitive position of the U.S. capital market relative to the Eurobond market. More recently, the Securities and Exchange Commission (SEC) adopted *Rule 144A,* which allows qualified institutional investors to trade in unregistered private placements, making them a closer substitute for public issues. This deliberate relaxation of U.S. securities laws was designed to stimulate private placements, especially by foreign companies. Many such firms have been scared off in the past by the SEC's strict, expensive, and time-consuming disclosure requirements for public issues. Because of Rule 144A, companies can now issue bonds simultaneously in Europe and the United States, further blurring the distinction between the U.S. bond market and its Eurobond equivalent. Other nations, such as Japan and England, are also deregulating their financial markets.

With repeal of the withholding tax and financial market deregulation in the United States and elsewhere, the Eurobond market lost some of the cost advantage that lured corporate borrowers in the first place. Nonetheless, as long as Eurobond issuance entails low regulatory and registration costs relative to domestic bond issuance, the Eurobond market will continue to attract investors and borrowers from all over the world.

Despite several forecasts of imminent death, the Eurobond market has survived, largely because its participants are so fleet of foot. As demand for one type of bond declines, quick-witted investment bankers seem to find other opportunities to create value for their customers. When the demand for fixed-rate Eurobonds fell, the Eurobond market led the boom in floating-rate note issues. When the FRN market collapsed in 1986, this business was replaced by issues of Japanese corporate bonds with equity warrants attached. *Equity warrants* confer on their holder the option to buy a given issuer's shares at a specified price over a set period. In return for what is in effect a long-dated call option on the issuer's stock, the investor accepts a lower interest rate on the Eurobond to which the equity warrant is attached.

Demand for such issues soared as investors used the warrants to play Japan's rising stock market. In turn, Japanese companies found the Eurobond market easier and cheaper to use than the regulated domestic-yen market. However, the Tokyo stock market's plunge in 1990 triggered a 71.5% drop in the Japanese equity-warrant issue market and a 14.4% fall in the Eurobond market overall (see Exhibit 22.12).

The financial infrastructure in place in London should ensure the Eurobond market's survival. However, tax harmonization, financial deregulation, and the widespread loosening of capital controls mean that issuers have less incentive to borrow money offshore, and so are returning to their domestic markets to raise capital. If these trends persist, the Eurobond market may never regain its preeminence. But it can still preserve its basic role—as the nimblest intermediary for international capital flows between domestic markets.

Eurobonds Versus Eurocurrency Loans

Both Eurocurrency and Eurobond financing have their advantages and disadvantages. Although many of these factors are reflected in the relative borrowing costs, not all factors

■ **EXHIBIT 22.12**   Eurobond Issues by Type

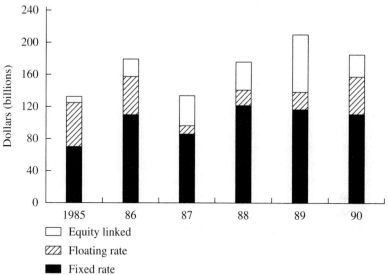

SOURCE: Euromoney Bondware, *OECD Financial Statistics Monthly,* various issues.

are so reflected. For a given firm, therefore, and for a specific set of circumstances, one method of financing may be preferred to the other. The differences are categorized in five ways.

1. *Cost of borrowing*: Eurobonds are issued in both fixed-rate and floating-rate forms. Fixed-rate bonds are an attractive exposure management tool since known long-term currency inflows can be offset with known long-term outflows in the same currency. By contrast, the interest rate on a Eurocurrency loan is variable, making Eurocurrency loans better hedges for noncontractual currency exposures. The variable interest rate benefits borrowers when rates decline but hurts them when rates rise. Arbitrage between Eurobonds and Eurocurrencies, however, should not provide a certain cost advantage to one or the other form of borrowing.

2. *Maturity*: While the period of borrowing in the Eurocurrency market has tended to lengthen over time, Eurobonds still have longer maturities.

3. *Size of issue*: Until recently, the amount of loanable funds available at any one time has been much greater in the interbank market than in the bond market. In 1983, for the first time, the volume of Eurobond offerings exceeded voluntary global bank lending (those loans not forced by debt reschedulings). In many instances, borrowers have discovered that the Eurobond market can easily accommodate financings of a size and at a price not previously thought possible. When Digital Equipment, Texas Instruments, International Paper, and Illinois Power brought out $475 million worth of Eurodollar bonds over two days in February 1984, they saved as much as 0.45% on the cost of issuing debt in the United States. This translates into millions of dollars of interest savings. Moreover, although in the past the flotation costs of a Eurocurrency loan have been much lower than on a Eurobond (about 0.5% of the total loan amount versus about 2.25% of the face value of a Eurobond issue), competition has worked to lower Eurobond flotation costs.

4. *Flexibility*: In the case of a Eurobond issue, the funds must be drawn down in one sum on a fixed date and repaid according to a fixed schedule unless the borrower pays an often substantial prepayment penalty. By contrast, the drawdown in a floating-rate loan can be staggered to suit the borrower's needs with a fee of about 0.5% per annum paid on the unused portion (normally much cheaper than drawing down and redepositing) and can be prepaid in whole or in part at any time, often without penalty. Moreover, a Eurocurrency loan with a multicurrency clause enables the borrower to switch currencies on any rollover date, whereas switching the denomination of a Eurobond from currency A to currency B would require a costly combined refunding and reissuing operation. A much cheaper and comparable alternative, however, would be to sell forward for currency B an amount of currency A equal to the value of the Eurobond issue still outstanding. There is a rapidly growing market in such currency swaps that enable the proceeds from bonds issued in one currency to be converted into money in another currency.

5. *Speed*: Internationally known borrowers can raise funds in the Eurocurrency market very quickly, often within two to three weeks of first request. A Eurobond financing generally takes more time to put together, although here again the difference is becoming less significant.

Note Issuance Facilities

Eurobanks have responded to the competition from the Eurobond market by creating a new instrument: the *note issuance facility* (NIF). The NIF, which is a low-cost substitute for syndicated credits, allows borrowers to issue their own short-term notes that are then placed or distributed by the financial institutions providing the NIF. NIFs—sometimes also called *short-term note issuance facilities* or SNIFs—have some features of the U.S. commercial paper market and some features of U.S. commercial lines of credit. Like commercial paper, notes under NIFs are unsecured short-term debt generally issued by large corporations with excellent credit ratings. Indeed, NIFs are sometimes referred to as Eurocommercial paper. Like loan commitments in the United States, NIFs generally include multiple pricing components for various contract features, including a market-based interest rate and one or more fees known as participation, facility, and underwriting fees. Participation fees are paid when the contract is formalized and are generally about 10 basis points (100 basis points equals 1%) times the facility size. Other fees are paid annually and are sometimes based on the full size of the facility, sometimes on the unused portions thereof.

Many NIFs include underwriting services as part of the arrangements. When they are included, the arrangement generally takes the form of a *revolving underwriting facility* (RUF). The RUF gives borrowers long-term continuous access to short-term money under-written by banks at a fixed margin.

NIFs are more flexible than floating-rate notes and usually cheaper than syndicated loans. Banks eager to beef up their earnings without fattening their loan portfolios (which would then require them to add expensive equity capital) made NIFs an important new segment of the Euromarket. As in the case of floating-rate notes, the popularity of NIFs benefits from the market's current preference for lending to high-grade borrowers through securities rather than bank loans.

Here's how the basic facility works (although alternate methods exist in abundance in the marketplace). A syndicate of banks underwrites an amount—usually about $50–200 million—for a specified period, typically for five to seven years. A LIBOR-based underwriting margin is set, determined by the credit rating of the borrower, the size of the issue, and market conditions. When the borrower decides to draw on the facility, the borrower can choose to issue promissory notes, called Euronotes, with one-month, three-month, six-month, or 12-month maturities. A tender panel of banks is then established, whose members submit competitive bids. Any bids above the agreed underwriting margin are not accepted but are automatically purchased by the underwriters at the agreed-upon margin over LIBOR.

In effect, NIFs are put options. They give borrowers the right to sell their paper to the bank syndicate at a price that yields the prearranged spread over LIBOR. Borrowers will exercise this right only if they cannot place their notes at a better rate elsewhere, a plight most likely to occur if their creditworthiness deteriorates. The primary risk to the banks, therefore, is that they might someday have to make good on their pledge to buy paper at a spread that is too low for the credit risks involved. Although Euronote issuers generally are firms with sound credit standing, a NIF may oblige the banks to keep rolling the notes over for five to ten years—time enough for even the best credit risk to turn into a nightmare.

Most Euronotes are denominated in U.S. dollars and are issued with high face values (often $500,000 or more). They are intended for professional or institutional investors rather than private individuals.

Note Issuance Facilities Versus Eurobonds

In addition to their lower direct costs, NIFs offer several other benefits to the issuer relative to floating rate notes, their most direct competitor.

1. *Drawdown flexibility*: Note issuers can usually opt to draw down all or part of their total credit whenever their need arises, and they can roll over portions at will. This option is especially valuable for borrowers with seasonal or cyclical needs.

2. *Timing flexibility*: With FRNs, the borrower must live with the prevailing rate for the period's duration. By contrast, a Euronote borrower who thinks rates are going to fall can wait a month or so to issue. However, unless the financial director is better able to forecast interest rates, this option to wait is a dubious advantage.

3. *Choice of maturities*: FRN issuers are generally locked into one maturity setting—three months or six months—over the life of the deal. NIFs, on the other hand, give borrowers the choice of issuing notes with different maturities whenever they choose to draw down new debt or roll over old.

4. *Secondary market*: The secondary market for Euronotes is relatively undeveloped compared to the market for FRNs. This condition makes Euronotes less liquid, limiting Euronote investors to those who want to hold them to maturity.

The Asiacurrency Market

Although dwarfed by its European counterpart, the Asiacurrency (or Asiadollar) market has been growing rapidly in terms of both size and range of services provided. Located in Singapore because of the lack of restrictive financial controls and taxes there, the Asiadollar market was founded in 1968 as a satellite market to channel to and from the Eurodollar market the large pool of offshore funds, mainly U.S. dollars, circulating in Asia. Its primary economic functions these days are to channel investment dollars to a number of rapidly growing Southeast Asian countries and to provide deposit facilities for those investors with excess funds.

■ 22.4 ■
DEVELOPMENT BANKS

To help provide the huge financial resources required to promote the development of economically backward areas, the United States and other countries have established a variety of *development banks* whose lending is directed to investments that would not otherwise be funded by private capital. These investments include dams, roads, communication systems, and other infrastructure projects whose economic benefits cannot be completely captured by private investors, as well as projects such as a steel mill or chemical plant whose value lies in perceived political and social advantages to the nation (or at least to its leaders). The loans generally are medium-term to long-term and carry concessionary rates. Even though most lending is done directly to a government, this type of financing has two implications for the private sector. First, the projects require goods and services, which corporations can provide. Second, by establishing an infrastructure, new investment opportunities become available for multinational corporations.

There are three different types of development banks: the World Bank Group, regional development banks, and national development banks.

The World Bank Group

The *World Bank Group* is a multinational financial institution established at the end of World War II to help provide long-term capital for the reconstruction and development of member countries. It comprises three related financial institutions: the *International Bank for Reconstruction and Development* (IBRD), also known as the *World Bank;* the *International Development Association* (IDA); and the *International Finance Corporation* (IFC). The Group is important to multinational corporations because it provides much of the planning and financing for economic development projects involving billions of dollars for which private businesses can act as contractors and as suppliers of goods and engineering-related services.

IBRD. The IBRD, or World Bank, makes loans at nearly conventional terms for projects of high economic priority. To qualify for financing, a project must have costs and revenues that can be estimated with reasonable accuracy. A government guarantee is a necessity for World Bank funding. The bank's main emphasis has been on large infrastructure projects such as roads, dams, power plants, education, and agriculture. However, in recent years the bank more and more has emphasized quick loans to help borrower countries alleviate their balance-of-payments problems. These loans are tied to the willingness of the debtor nations to adopt economic policies that will spur growth: freer trade, more open investment, and a more vigorous private sector. Besides its members' subscriptions, the World Bank raises funds by issuing bonds to private sources.

IFC.   The purpose of the IFC is to finance various projects in the private sector through loans and equity participations. In contrast to the World Bank, the IFC does not require government guarantees; it emphasizes providing risk capital for manufacturing firms that have a reasonable chance of earning the investors' required rate of return and that will provide economic benefits to the nation.

IDA.   The World Bank concentrates on projects that have a high probability of being profitable; consequently, many of the poorest of the less-developed countries (LDCs) were unable to access its funds. IDA was founded in 1960 to remedy this shortcoming. As distinguished from the World Bank, IDA is authorized to make soft (highly concessionary) loans (for example, 50-year maturity with no interest). It does require a government guarantee, however. The establishment of IDA illustrates a major unresolved issue for the World Bank Group: Should its emphasis be on making sound loans to developing countries, or should it concentrate on investing in those projects most likely to be of benefit to the host country? These goals are not necessarily in conflict, although many of a project's benefits may not be captured by the project itself but instead will appear elsewhere in the economy (for example, the benefits of an educational system).

Regional and National Development Banks

The past two decades have seen a proliferation of development banks. The functions of a development bank are to provide debt and equity financing to aid in the economic development of underdeveloped areas. This financing includes extending intermediate-term to long-term capital directly, strengthening local capital markets, and supplying management consulting services to new companies. The professional guidance helps to safeguard, and thereby encourage, investments in a firm.

Regional Development Banks.   Regional development banks provide funds for the financing of manufacturing, mining, agricultural, and infrastructure projects considered important to development. They tend to support projects that promote regional cooperation and economic integration. Repayment terms for the loans, in most cases, are over a 5-year to 15-year period at favorable interest rates. Some of the leading regional development banks include the following.

1. *European Investment Bank* (EIB): The EIB offers funds for certain public and private projects in European and other nations associated with the Common Market. It emphasizes loans to the lesser-developed regions in Europe and to associated members in Africa.
2. *Inter-American Development Bank* (IADB): The IADB is one of the key sources of long-term capital in Latin America. It lends to joint ventures, both minority and majority foreign-owned.

3. *Atlantic Development Group for Latin America* (ADELA): ADELA is an international private investment company dedicated to the socioeconomic development of Latin America. Its objective is to strengthen private enterprise by providing capital and entrepreneurial and technical services.

4. *Asian Development Bank* (ADB): The ADB guarantees or makes direct loans to private ventures in Asian/Pacific countries and helps to develop local capital markets by underwriting securities issued by private enterprises.

5. *African Development Bank* (ADB): The bank makes or guarantees loans and provides technical assistance to member states for various development projects. Beneficiaries of ADB loans and activities are normally governments or government-related agencies.

6. *Arab Fund for Economic and Social Development* (AFESD): The AFESD is a multilateral Arab fund that actively searches for projects (restricted to Arab League countries) and then assumes responsibility for project implementation by conducting feasibility studies, contracting, controlling quality, and supervising the work schedule.

7. *European Bank for Reconstruction and Development* (EBRD). The EBRD, which was founded in 1990 with an initial capital of about $13 billion, is supposed to finance the privatization of Eastern Europe. Many are skeptical of its chances, however, since the person appointed to head it is a French socialist who masterminded the most sweeping program of nationalizations in French history.

National Development Banks.   Some national development banks concentrate on a particular industry or region; others are multipurpose. Although most are public institutions, there are several privately controlled development banks as well. The characteristics for success, however, are the same: They must attract capable, investment-oriented management; and they must have a large enough supply of economically viable projects to enable management to select a reasonable portfolio of investments.

The Proper Role of Development Banks

Critics of development banks claim that they tend to perpetuate economic stagnation by financing statist solutions, rather than free-market solutions. By giving money to governments, rather than providing capital to private firms, these banks support bureaucratic planning over private enterprise. This support builds up the public sector at the expense of the private sector. In the absence of funds from development banks, governments might have to grant more freedom to the private sector. Since the marketplace is a far more efficient mechanism for supplying goods and services, any policy that hampers the private sector will retard economic growth.

■ ——

ILLUSTRATION

The World Bank's Role in Africa's Agricultural Failure.   The decline of African agriculture throughout the 1970s and 1980s is now widely understood to be due primarily to African governments' penchant for state marketing boards. These set the "official" and only price at which farmers may sell, and the government is frequently the sole legal buyer. To guarantee cheap food to urban populations—the politically important constituency—the rule of the African marketing boards has been: Buy low, sell low (or lower). Most have run up large deficits for decades. Price conscious farmers responded by selling their produce in black markets, smuggling it across the border, reverting to subsistence agriculture, or leaving the land entirely to join the urban swell. At the same time, low food prices led to increased demand and shortages.

The World Bank had a pivotal role in this. From 1974 to 1986 the bank channeled $5.5 billion into African agriculture—an eightfold increase in the lending rate over the previous period. Much of this money was used to set up and finance—that is, subsidize—state marketing boards.

■

During its 30-year history, the IDB has lent more than $35 billion, much of it to underwrite a development strategy that concentrated investment decisions in the hands of hugely unsuccessful parastatal companies. In short, the IDB has financed inefficient state monopolies at the expense of private, competitive development.

Because they are government-owned and government-controlled institutions doing business with other governments, it is perhaps not surprising that development banks have been hostile in general to enforcing stringent free-market principles as conditions for receiving loans. Thus, they have been unable—and unwilling—to foster the prime conditions for development: sound economic policies and stable political environments. Economic success stories such as the United States, post–World War II Japan and West Germany, modern Taiwan, South Korea, Hong Kong, and Singapore all have a common factor: reliance on private enterprise to organize most economic activity.

If one accepts the view that a vigorous private sector is key to economic growth, then development banks could play an important role in LDC development if they would condition their loans on the elimination in Third World economies of price controls, nationalized industries, high tax rates, government subsidies, state monopolies, trade restrictions, and impediments to private capital flows.

The Reagan administration recognized this role and tried to turn these banks into positive forces for LDC development. In 1985, Treasury Secretary James Baker outlined the so-called Baker Plan. The *Baker Plan* called for parceling out development aid only if borrowers pursue free-market reforms to encourage private enterprise. For example, the United States vetoed a concessional IADB loan to Guyana, which wanted a subsidized loan to aid its ailing rice farmers. The U.S. Treasury pointed out that rice farmers would be better served by eliminating Guyana's government price controls, a major cause of the poor rice production.

But the Baker Plan and others like it face hostility from less market-oriented major members such as France, Canada, and Japan. Moreover, many of the banks' staffs are hostile to marketplace solutions and tend to emphasize capital flows from their banks as the key factor in development.

■ 22.5 ■
SUMMARY AND CONCLUSIONS

Although there are significant differences among countries in their methods and sources of finance, corporate practice appears to be converging. Most significantly, more firms are bypassing financial intermediaries, mainly commercial banks, and going directly to the financial markets for funds. The convergence of corporate financing practice largely reflects the globalization of financial markets, the inextricable linkage—through arbitrage—of financial markets worldwide. In line with this trend, firms are finding that it pays to seek capital on a global basis, rather than restricting their search to any one nation or capital market.

We saw that the growth of the international capital markets, specifically the Eurocurrency and Eurobond markets, is largely a response to the various restrictions and regulations that governments impose on domestic financial transactions. At the same time, capital flows between the international capital markets and domestic markets have linked domestic markets in a manner that increasingly makes such government intervention irrelevant.

We also saw that while some sources of funds are readily accessible (for example, the Eurocurrency market), others (such as government-subsidized export credits) are strictly limited in terms of availability. It is, of course, just this latter type of financing that is so appealing to corporate financial executives.

■ QUESTIONS ■

1. What are some basic differences between the financing patterns of U.S. and Japanese firms? What might account for some of these differences?

2. How and why has the Japanese pattern of finance changed over time?

3. What is securitization? What forces underlie it and how has it affected the financing policies of multinational corporations?

4. Why is bank lending on the decline worldwide? How have banks responded to their loss of market share?

5. What is meant by the globalization of financial markets? How has technology affected the process of globalization?

6. How has globalization affected government regulation of national capital markets?

7. What is the difference between a Eurocurrency loan and a Eurobond?

8. What is the difference between a foreign bond and a Eurobond?

9. Why might investors and borrowers be attracted to an ECU bond?

10. What is the basic reason for the existence of the Eurodollar market? What factors have accounted for its growth over time?

11. Suppose the French government imposes an interest rate ceiling on French bank deposits. What is the likely effect on Eurofranc interest rates of this regulation?

12. List some reasons why a U.S.-based corporation might issue debt denominated in a foreign currency.

13. What factors account for the rise and recent decline of the Eurobond market as a source of financing for American companies?

14 a. What factors account for the growth of note issuance facilities?

    b. In what sense is the NIF part of the process of securitization?

    c. Why is the NIF described as a put option?

■ PROBLEMS ■

1. Suppose that the current 180-day interbank Eurodollar rate is 9% (all rates are stated on an annualized basis). If next period's rate is 9.5%, what will a Eurocurrency loan priced at LIBOR plus 1% cost?

2. Refer to the example of Exxon's zero-coupon Eurobond issue in Section 22.3.

   a. How much would Exxon have earned if the yield on the stripped Treasurys had been 12.10%? 12.25%?

   b. Suppose the Japanese government taxed the accretion in the value of zero-coupon bonds at a rate of 15%. Assuming the same 11.65% after-tax required yield, how would this tax have affected the price Japanese investors were willing to pay for Exxon's Eurobond issue? What would the pre-tax yield be at this new price? Would any arbitrage incentive still exist for Exxon?

   c. Suppose Exxon had sold its zero-coupon Eurobonds to yield 11.5% and bought stripped Treasury bonds yielding 12.30% to meet the required payment of $1.8 billion. How much would Exxon have earned through its arbitrage transaction?

3. A European company issues common shares that pay taxable dividends and bearer shares that pay an identical dividend but offer an opportunity to evade taxes. (Bearer shares come with a large supply of coupons that can be redeemed anonymously at banks for the current value of the dividend.)

   a. Suppose taxable dividends are taxed at the rate of 10%. What is the ratio between market prices of taxable and bearer shares? If a new issue is planned, should taxable or bearer shares be sold?

   b. Suppose, in addition, that it costs 10% of proceeds to issue a taxable dividend, whereas it costs 20% of the proceeds to issue bearer stocks because of the expense of distribution and coupon printing. What type of share will the corporation prefer to issue?

   c. Suppose now that individuals pay 10% taxes on dividends, and corporations pay no taxes, but bear an administrative cost of 10% of the value of any bearer dividends. Can you determine the relative market prices for the two types of shares?

■ APPENDIX 22A ■
A EUROCURRENCY LOAN AGREEMENT
IN PLAIN ENGLISH

4th October 19XX

Mr. Al Yx
The State Mining Co.
Ruritania

Dear Al,

Please pardon me for writing this on the back of an envelope. It's all I had on the plane back to London.

As I said, we and the syndicate can let you have the U.S. $100,000,000 for your big new hole in the ground.

This is how we see the deal:

SOURCE: Anonymous

1. *Send us a telex*

    You can have the money any time up to 12 months from now. Just send us a telex. In good time please, say, five banking days. Big round amounts only, we don't deal in peanuts. We will each chip in our bit and no more.

2. *We've got shareholders too*

    Pay us back our money. Eight equal lots, one every six months starting 30 months from now.

3. *You want out*

    If you want to pay back early, that's fine, but you must call us up 30 days ahead and pay us 1/4% consolation fee. Big rounded amounts only. Early payback means a shorter deal.

4. *Milk of human kindness*

    As I explained to you, we unfortunately have to charge for this money. I congratulate you on beating us down to 1% over LIBOR. Charity runs in our blood.

    We will fix a new interest rate every three or six months at your choice (five banking days again, please). You pay the interest at the end of each period. I hope you took on board my explanation of how we work out interest periods, the 11:00 a.m. (London time) routine, etc. Remember? Anyway, just leave the mechanics to us as we always do it.

    If you don't pay on the nail, we can add the extra 1% to the usual rate till you pay up.

5. *That's your problem*

    I know it's very difficult for you to understand, Al, but we don't carry the $100,000,000 around in our pockets. We have to get it elsewhere in London. If we can't, naturally, we'll get round a table with you and talk about other ways and means. But if we don't see eye to eye after, say, 30 days, you pay us back. And that's the end. It's too bad that you may not be able to get the money either; that's your problem.

6. *The taxman*

    You pay us in spendable dollars of the U.S. of A. at our New York agent in Clearing House Funds. And we want the full amount (i.e., you pay the taxman and top up our money).

7. *Extras*

    So far, the authorities have left us alone. Cost to us is cost to you plus spread. But we have to face facts. Some central bank, taxman, or other like person may decide to poke his nose into our business. The deal could become more pricey for one of us. Reserves, different taxes, that sort of thing. If that happens, you pay us the extra. We will tell you how much and you can't argue. But if any of us ups the cost, then you can take him out.

8. *We don't want to go to jail*

    If our side of the deal runs foul of the law, no more money from the bank affected and you take him out straightaway. Plus the unwinds.

9. *The paperwork*

    You can't have any money until your directors, the central bank, and our lawyers have given us their O.K. the way we like it.

10. *Promises, promises*

    You promise us

    (a) Your company is there in good shape.

    (b) Your company can do this deal and you, Al, can sign.

    (c) It's all legal.

    (d) The authorities have given their thumbs-up.

    (e) No mistakes in your last financials. Things haven't got worse since then.

    (f) Nobody's suing you for big money.

    (g) You are sticking by the terms of your other deals.

    (h) The fact-sheet we sent round about you sets it out like it is.

11. *Do's and don'ts*

    (a) Don't put your assets in hock.

    (b) If the balloon goes up, we get equal payout with your other deals.

    (c) Send us your fiscals within 90 days of year-end.

    (d) Send us other info when we ask for it.

    (e) Dig the hole ASAP.

12. *The plug*

Our money back straightaway and not another cent if

    (a) You don't comply.

    (b) You have told us a lie.

    (c) You don't stick by the terms of your other deals.

    (d) You go bust.

    (e) You vanish.

    (f) You close up shop or sell out in a big way.

    (g) Your other creditors move in.

    (h) We don't like the way things are going for you financially.

    (i) Your hole in the ground doesn't get dug like you said or fills up with water, etc.

13. *No stabs in the back*

Al, this bit is between us and the banks.

You, colleagues in the syndicate, appoint us as your leader to run this deal. We are delighted to be of assistance and value your esteemed confidence. But, just to avoid any unpleasant misunderstandings, we have to make some things clear. It's every man for himself. We don't have to tell you what we know; you check it out yourselves. If we have slipped from the very highest standards of veracity in order to get you into this deal, keep your eyes open next time. We can believe everything the lawyers or anybody else tells us. We can do other deals with the borrower and pocket the profit. If it's between us and you, we can look after No. 1. Naturally, we will do what most of you want within reason, but if we foul up, no liability. Sorry.

14. *Boilerplate*

You can mostly skip this part, Al, since it's the boilerplate.

    (a) You will pay us our out-of-pockets, including the lawyers. I much enjoyed eating out in Ruritania at your expense.

    (b) We could lose money if you don't pay when we say. You will see us whole, especially for the unwinds.

    (c) You pay the stamps.

    (d) If we turn a blind eye once, it doesn't mean we'll do so next time.

    (e) We don't have to write it all out here; we can still throw the book at you.

    (f) We can give other banks a slice of the action any time. We can switch to our other offices.

    (g) I'm a lousy linguist and I don't speak Ruritanian, beautiful language though it is. Please help us out with translations.

    (h) If the judge gives us dinarios, etc. you make up the difference.

    (i) If you don't pay, we can grab any money you left with us.

15. *The rules*

I was most touched by your patriotism, Al, but you must appreciate that if we play by your Ruritanian rules, His Most Majestic Excellency The Sun King of Ruritania can change the rules in the middle of the game. So, if you don't mind, we'll keep to the English rulebook.

16. *The judge*

    (a) English judge to sort out any problems. Or New York. Or anywhere else we care to name. We can send the invite c/o your offices in London and New York. Don't say it's inconvenient.

    (b) I have to speak in metaphors here. If you park your car on a yellow line, we can give you a ticket. And tow your car away. Even if it's marked CD.

Assuming you like this deal, Al, please say so.

Yours hopefully,

Joe Y. Zed
Moneybank

TO: Moneybank

It's O.K. by me.

Al Yx

TO: State Mining Co.

It's O.K. by us.

	Million U.S. Dollars
Moneybank	20
Manybanks	20
Muslimbank	20
Moltobanco	10
Magnifiquebanque	10
Misyomobank	10
Meanbank	8
Meanestbank	2

■ BIBLIOGRAPHY ■

Dufey, Gunter, and Ian H. Giddy. *The International Money Market.* Englewood Cliffs, N.J.: Prentice-Hall, 1978.

———. "Innovation in the International Financial Markets." *Journal of International Business Studies,* Fall 1981, pp. 35–51.

Financing Foreign Operations. Business International Corporation, various issues.

George, Abraham M., and Ian H. Giddy, eds. *International Finance Handbook.* New York: John Wiley & Sons, 1983.

Grabbe, Oren J. *International Financial Markets.* New York: Elsevier, 1986.

Kim, Yong-Cheol, and Rene M. Stulz. "The Eurobond Market and Corporate Financial Policy: A Test of the Clientele Hypothesis." *Journal of Financial Economics,* 22, 1988, pp. 189–205.

———. "Is There Still a Global Market for Convertible Bonds?" working paper, Ohio State University, April 1990.

Solnik, Bruno H. *International Investments.* Reading, Mass.: Addison-Wesley, 1987.

▪ 23 ▪

Special Financing Vehicles

Man is not the creature of circumstances, circumstances are the creatures of men.

—Benjamin Disraeli—

▪ The purpose of this chapter is to examine three special financing vehicles that multinational corporations can use to fund their foreign investments. These vehicles include interest rate and currency swaps, international leasing, and bank loan swaps. Each of them presents opportunities to the multinational firm to reduce financing costs and/or risk.

▪ 23.1 ▪
INTEREST RATE AND CURRENCY SWAPS

Corporate financial managers can use swaps to arrange complex, innovative financings that reduce borrowing costs and increase control over interest rate risk and foreign currency exposure. As a result of the deregulation and integration of national capital markets and extreme interest rate and currency volatility, the relatively new swaps market has experienced explosive growth, with outstanding swaps in early 1991 in excess of $2 trillion. In fact, few Eurobonds are issued without at least one swap behind them to give the borrower cheaper or in some way more desirable funds.

This section discusses the structure and mechanics of the two basic types of swaps—interest rate swaps and currency swaps—and shows how swaps can be used to achieve diverse goals. Swaps have had a major impact on the treasury function, permitting firms to tap new capital markets and to take further advantage of innovative products without an increase in risk. Through the swap, they can trade a perceived risk in one market or currency for a liability in another. The swap has led to a refinement of risk-management techniques, which in turn has facilitated corporate involvement in international capital markets.

Interest Rate Swaps

An *interest rate swap* is an agreement between two parties to exchange U.S. dollar interest payments for a specific maturity on an agreed upon notional amount. The term *notional* refers to the theoretical principal underlying the swap. Thus, the *notional principal* is simply a reference amount against which the interest is calculated. No principal ever changes hands. Maturities range from under a year to over 15 years; however, most transactions fall within a two-year to ten-year period. The two main types are coupon swaps and basis swaps. In a *coupon swap,* one party pays a *fixed rate* calculated at the time of trade as a spread to a particular Treasury bond, while the other side pays a *floating rate* that resets periodically throughout the life of the deal against a designated index. In a *basis swap,* two parties exchange floating interest payments based on different reference rates. Basically, using this relatively straightforward mechanism, interest rate swaps transform debt issues, assets, liabilities, or any cash flow from type to type and—with some variation in the transaction structure—from currency to currency.

The Classic Swap Transaction. Counterparty A in Exhibit 23.1 is an institution that invests in fixed-rate mortgages yielding 13.25%. Counterparty A is not an investment-grade credit. It is funding its assets through a floating-rate loan from a group of banks that is charging A the six-month London Interbank Offer Rate (LIBOR) plus 50 basis points (a basis point equals 0.01%). A's profitability depends on the actual level of the floating interest rate that is paid over the long run. Thus, a large upward swing in interest rates will burden A with large debt service expenses. And A will actually lose money whenever LIBOR exceeds 12.75% (13.25 − 0.50) on any reset date. Concerned that this risk may threaten the profitability and even solvency of the firm, the risk manager seeks a way to reduce it.

■ **EXHIBIT 23.1**   Situations Confronting Counterparties A and B Before the Swap

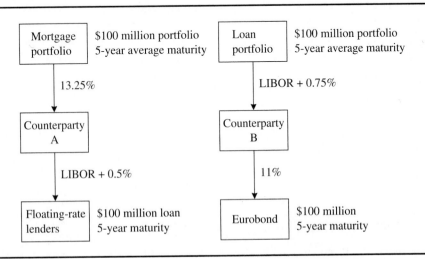

Suppose that a second firm, counterparty B in Exhibit 23.1, has also borrowed $100 million for five years, but at a fixed rate. B is a AAA-rated bank and is funding its loan portfolio with funds generated by a Eurobond carrying an 11% coupon. B's loan portfolio is yielding LIBOR plus 75 basis points. The profitability of B depends on the actual floating interest rate that is received on its loan portfolio. Whenever LIBOR is less than 10.25% (11 − 0.75) on any reset date, B is losing money.

In order to eliminate its interest rate risk, A enters into the following interest rate swap with BigBank, as diagrammed in Exhibit 23.2. A agrees that it will pay BigBank 11.35% for five years, with payments calculated by multiplying that rate by the $100 million notional principal amount. In return for this payment, BigBank agrees to pay A six-month LIBOR over five years, with reset dates matching the reset dates on its floating rate loan.

Counterparty A, through the swap with BigBank, has eliminated the volatility in its earnings due to interest rate fluctuations over the five-year horizon of the swap and should now earn a locked-in spread of 1.4% on its loan portfolio:

Receive on portfolio	13.25%
Pay BigBank	(11.35%)
Receive from BigBank	LIBOR
Pay on loan	(LIBOR + 0.50%)
Cost of funds	(11.85%)
Locked-in spread	1.40%

In a similar fashion, B enters into a swap with BigBank where it agrees to pay six-month LIBOR to BigBank on a notional principal amount of $100 million for five years in exchange for receiving payments of 11.25%. This swap is shown in Exhibit 23.3.

■ **EXHIBIT 23.2**   Counterparty A's Interest Rate Swap Agreement with BigBank

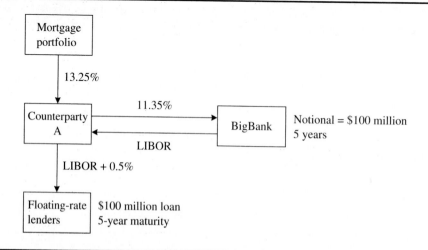

■ **EXHIBIT 23.3**   Counterparty B's Interest Rate Swap Agreement with BigBank

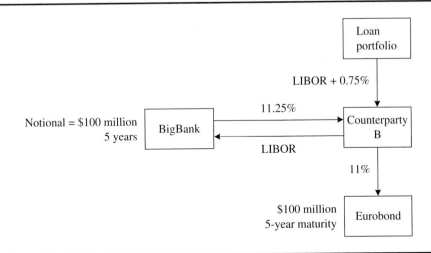

The net result to B is as follows:

Receive on portfolio	LIBOR + 0.75%
Pay BigBank	(LIBOR)
Receive from BigBank	11.25%
Pay on Eurobond	(11.00%)
Cost of funds	(LIBOR – 0.25%)
Locked-in spread	1.00%

Once the effect of the swap is netted against the payments on the Eurobond, it is clear that B has reduced its cost of funds to LIBOR less 25 basis points, resulting in a locked-in spread on its portfolio of 100 basis points.

Why would BigBank or any financial intermediary enter into such transactions? The net result in each of these transactions is that the risk of loss due to interest rate fluctuations has been transferred from the counterparty to BigBank. The reason BigBank is willing to enter into such contracts is more evident when looking at the transaction in its entirety. This classic swap structure is shown in Exhibit 23.4.

As a financial intermediary, BigBank puts together both transactions. The risks net out, and BigBank is left with a spread of 10 basis points:

Receive	11.35%
Pay	(11.25%)
Receive	LIBOR
Pay	(LIBOR)
Net	10 basis points

■ **EXHIBIT 23.4**   Classic Swap Structure

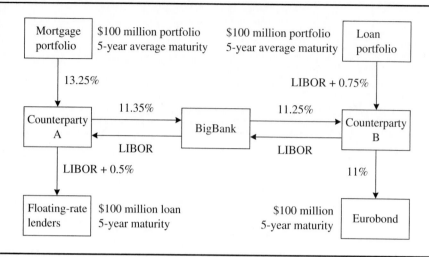

BigBank thus receives compensation equal to $100,000 annually for the next five years on the $100 million swap transaction:

$$\text{Swap profit to BigBank} = 0.001 \times \$100,000,000$$
$$= \$100,000$$

Cost Savings Associated with Swaps.   The example just discussed shows the risk-reducing potential of interest rate swaps. However, swaps may also be used to reduce costs. Their ability to do so depends on a difference in perceived credit quality across financial markets. In essence, interest rate swaps exploit the comparative advantages—if they exist—enjoyed by different borrowers in different markets, thereby increasing the options available to both borrower and investor.

Returning to the previous example, suppose that A is a company with a BBB rating, while B is a AAA-rated bank. Although A has good access to banks or other sources of floating-rate funds for its operations, it may have difficulty raising fixed-rate funds from bond issues in the capital markets at a price it finds attractive. By contrast, B can borrow at the finest rates in either market. Exhibit 23.5 outlines the cost to each party of accessing either the fixed-rate or the floating-rate market for a new five-year debt issue.

The basic point noted in Exhibit 23.5 is that there is an anomaly between the two markets: One judges that the difference in credit quality between a AAA-rated firm and a BBB-rated firm is worth 150 basis points; the other determines that this difference is worth only 50 basis points. Since both markets cannot simultaneously be correct, at least one of these markets is mispricing different quality credits. The bottom line is that there is a difference of 100 basis points that the interest rate swap has permitted the parties to share among themselves as follows:

■ **EXHIBIT 23.5**   Credit Costs in the Fixed-Rate and Floating-Rate Markets

Borrower	Fixed Rate (%)	Floating Rate (%)
Counterparty A = BBB-rated	12.50	LIBOR + 0.50
Counterparty B = AAA-rated	11.00	LIBOR
Difference	1.50	0.50
		Spread differential = 100 basis points

Party	Normal Funding Cost (%)	Cost After Swap (%)	Difference (%)
Counterparty A	12.50	11.85	0.65
Counterparty B	LIBOR	LIBOR − 0.25	0.25
BigBank	—	—	0.10
		Total	1.00

In this example, A lowers its fixed-rate costs by 65 basis points, B lowers its floating-rate costs by 25 basis points, and BigBank receives 10 basis points for arranging the transaction and bearing the credit risk of the counterparties.

You might expect that the process of financial arbitrage would soon eliminate any such cost savings opportunities associated with a mispricing of credit quality. Despite this efficient markets view, many players in the swaps market believe that such anomalies in perceived credit risk continue to exist. The explosive growth in the swaps market supports this belief. It may also indicate the presence of other factors, such as differences in information and risk aversion of lenders across markets, that are more likely to persist.

Currency Swaps

A swap contract can also be arranged across currencies. For example, a company that has borrowed Japanese yen at a fixed interest rate can "swap away" the exchange rate risk by setting up a contract whereby it receives yen at a fixed rate in return for dollars at either a fixed- or a floating-interest rate. Such contracts are known as *currency swaps* and can help manage both interest rate and exchange rate risk. Many financial institutions count the arranging of swaps, both domestic and foreign currency, as an important line of business.

Currency swaps achieve an economic purpose similar to the parallel loan arrangements discussed in Chapter 15. They have effectively displaced the use of parallel loans, however, because they solve two potential problems associated with parallel loans: (1) If there is no right of offset, default by one party does not release the other from making its contractually obligated payments; and (2) parallel loans remain on the balance sheet, even though they effectively cancel one another. With a currency swap, the *right of offset*, which gives each party the right to offset any nonpayment of principal or interest with a comparable nonpayment, is more firmly established. Moreover, because a currency swap is not a loan, it does not appear as a liability on the parties' balance sheets.

Although the structure of currency swaps differs from interest rate swaps in a variety of ways, the major difference is that with a currency swap, there is always an exchange of principal amounts at maturity at a predetermined exchange rate. Thus, the swap contract behaves like a long-dated forward foreign exchange contract, where the forward rate is the current spot rate.

The reason that there is always an exchange of principal amounts at maturity can be explained as follows. Assume the prevailing coupon rate is 8% in one currency and 5% in the other currency. What would convince an investor to pay 8% and receive 300 basis points less? The answer lies in the spot and long-term forward exchange rates and how currency swaps adjust to compensate for the differentials. According to interest rate parity theory, forward rates are a direct function of the interest rate differential for the two currencies involved. As a result, a currency with a lower interest rate has a correspondingly higher forward exchange value. It follows that future exchange of currencies at the present spot exchange rate would offset the current difference in interest rates. This *exchange of principals* is what occurs in every currency swap at maturity based on the original amounts of each currency and, by implication, done at the original spot exchange rate.

The following example illustrates an *interest rate/currency swap*. This swap is designed to convert a liability in one currency with a stipulated type of interest payment into one denominated in another currency with a different type of interest payment.

Kodak's Zero-Coupon Australian Dollar Interest Rate/Currency Swap

In late March 1987, Eastman Kodak Company, a AAA-rated firm, indicated to Merrill Lynch that it needed to raise U.S.$400 million.[1] Kodak's preference was to fund through nontraditional structures, obtaining U.S.$200 million for both five and ten years. Kodak stated that it would spend up to two weeks evaluating nondollar financing opportunities for the five-year tranche, targeting a minimum size of U.S.$75 million and an all-in cost of U.S. Treasurys plus 35 basis points. In contrast, a domestic bond issue by Kodak would have to be priced to yield an all-in cost equal to about 50 basis points above the rate on U.S. Treasurys. At the end of the two-week period, the remaining balance was to be funded with a competitive bid.

After reviewing a number of potential transactions, the Capital Markets group at Merrill Lynch decided that investor interest in nondollar issues was much stronger in Europe than in the United States and that Merrill Lynch should focus on a nondollar Euroissue for Kodak. The London Syndicate Desk informed the Capital Markets Desk that it was a co-lead manager of an aggressively priced five-year, Australian dollar (A$) zero-coupon issue that was selling very well in Europe. The London Syndicate believed it could successfully underwrite a similar five-year A$ zero-coupon issue for Kodak. It was determined that

---

[1]This example was supplied by Grant Kvalheim of Merrill Lynch, whose help is greatly appreciated. The actual interest rates and spot and forward rates have been disguised.

Merrill Lynch could meet Kodak's funding target if an attractively priced A$ zero-coupon swap could be found.

To meet Kodak's minimum issue size of U.S.$75 million, an A$200 million zero-coupon issue would be necessary, which was the largest A$ zero-coupon issue ever underwritten. Merrill Lynch then received a firm mandate on a five-year A$130 million zero-coupon swap with Australian Bank B at a semiannual interest rate of 13.39%. The remaining A$70 million was arranged through a long-dated forward foreign exchange contract with Australian Bank A at a forward rate of A$1 = U.S.$0.5286.

With the currency swap mandate and the long-dated forward contract, Merrill Lynch received final approval by Kodak for the transaction, and the five-year A$200 million zero-coupon issue was launched in Europe at a net price of 54 1/8%, with a gross spread of 1 1/8%. Net proceeds to Kodak were 53% of A$200 million, or A$106 million. Kodak converted this principal into U.S.$75 million at the spot rate of U.S.$0.7059. Simultaneously, Merrill Lynch entered into a currency swap with Kodak to convert the Australian dollar cash flows into U.S. dollar cash flows at 7.35% paid semiannually, or U.S. Treasurys plus 35 basis points (since five-year Treasury bonds were then yielding approximately 7%). As part of this swap, Merrill Lynch agreed to make semiannual interest payments of LIBOR less 40 basis points to Australian Bank B. Merrill Lynch then arranged an interest rate swap to convert a portion of the fixed-rate payments from Kodak into floating-rate payments to Bank B. Exhibit 23.6 contains an annotated schematic diagram of the currency and interest rate swaps and the long-dated foreign exchange purchase that appeared in a Merrill Lynch ad. Exhibit 23.7 summarizes the period-by-period cash flows associated with these transactions.

The final column of Exhibit 23.7 presents the net cash flows to Merrill Lynch from these transactions. The net present value of these flows discounted at $r\%$ compounded semiannually is

$$NPV = \sum_{t=1}^{10} \$968{,}250/(1 + r/2)^t - \$10{,}000{,}000/(1 + r/2)^{10}$$

Discounted at the then risk-free, five-year Treasury bond rate of 7% compounded semiannually, the NPV of these flows is $963,365. Using a higher discount rate, say 7.5%, to reflect the various risks associated with these transactions results in a net present value to Merrill Lynch of $1,031,826. The actual NPV of these cash flows falls somewhere in between these two extremes.

By combining a nondollar issue with a currency swap and interest rate swap, Merrill Lynch was able to construct an innovative, lower-cost source of funds for Kodak. The entire package involved close teamwork and a complex set of transactions on three continents. In turn, through its willingness to consider nontraditional financing methods, Kodak was able to lower its cost of funds by about 15 basis points, yielding an annual savings of approximately $112,500 (0.0015 × $75,000,000). The present value of this savings discounted at 7.5% compounded semiannually is

$$\sum_{t=1}^{10} 56{,}250/(1.0375)^t = \$461{,}969$$

■ **EXHIBIT 23.6**   Kodak's A$200 Million Zero-Coupon Eurobond and Currency Swap

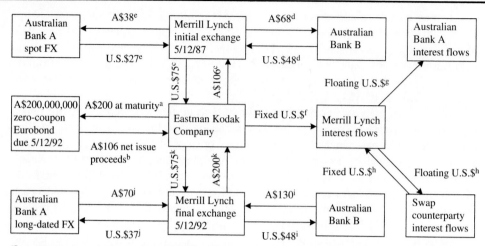

[a]Investors receive a single payment of A$200 million on 5/12/92, which represents both principal and interest.

[b]The bonds are priced at 54 1/8% less 1 1/8% gross spread. Net proceeds to Kodak at settlement on 5/12/87 are A$106 million.

[c]Kodak exchanges A$106 million with Merrill Lynch and receives U.S. $75 million at a fixed semiannual interest rate of 7.35%.

[d]Australian Bank B provides a 5-year A$130 million zero-coupon swap at a semiannual rate of 13.39%. In the currency swap's initial exchange on 5/12/87, Merrill Lynch pays Australian Bank B A$68 million $(A\$130,000,000 \times [1/(1 + (13.39\%/2))^{10}])$ and receives U.S. $48 million (A$68,000,000 × .7059) based on a spot exchange rate of U.S. $0.7059/A$1.

[e]Merrill Lynch sells the remaining A$38 million (A$106,000,000 − A$68,000,000) to Australian Bank A on 5/12/87 at a spot rate of U.S.$.7105/A$1, and receives U.S. $27 million.

[f]Kodak makes seminannual fixed-rate interest payments of U.S.$2,756,250 to Merrill Lynch ((7.35%/2) × U.S. $75,000,000)).

[g]Merrill Lynch makes semiannual floating-rate interest payments of LIBOR less 40 basis points on a notional principal amount of U.S.$48 million to Australian Bank B.

[h]Merrill Lynch makes semiannual interest payments of U.S. $1,884,000 based on a notional principal amount of U.S. $48 million and fixed interest rate of 7.85% and receives semiannual floating-rate interest payments of LIBOR flat in a fixed-floating rate swap with its book.

[i]Merrill Lynch receives A$130 million and pays U.S.$48 million in the Australian Bank B currency swap's final exchange on 5/12/92.

[j]In a long-dated forward foreign exchange transaction with Australian Bank A, Merrill Lynch purchases A$70 million on 5/12/92 for U.S.$37 million based on a forward exchange rate of U.S.$0.5286/A$1.

[k]On 5/12/92, Kodak pays U.S.$75 million to Merrill Lynch, receives A$200 million in return, and Kodak then pays the A$200 million to its zero-coupon bondholders.

■ EXHIBIT 23.7 MLCS Cash Flows—Eastman Kodak Transaction

Date	Cash-Flow Type	Kodak Currency Swap		Austalian Bank B Currency Swap		Foreign Exchange Market		Fixed/Floating U.S.$ Swap		Net U.S.$ Flows
		A$	U.S.$	A$	U.S.$	A$	U.S.$	Fixed	Floating	
12 May 87	Initial exchange	106,000,000	(75,000,000)[1]	(68,000,000)	48,000,000	38,000,000	27,000,000	—	—	—
12 Nov. 87	Interest	—	2,756,250	—	(LIBOR – 40BPS)	—	—	(1,884,000)[2]	LIBOR	968,250[3]
12 May 88	Interest	—	2,756,250	—	(LIBOR – 40BPS)	—	—	(1,884,000)	LIBOR	968,250
12 Nov. 88	Interest	—	2,756,250	—	(LIBOR – 40BPS)	—	—	(1,884,000)	LIBOR	968,250
12 May 89	Interest	—	2,756,250	—	(LIBOR – 40BPS)	—	—	(1,884,000)	LIBOR	968,250
12 Nov. 89	Interest	—	2,756,250	—	(LIBOR – 40BPS)	—	—	(1,884,000)	LIBOR	968,250
12 May 90	Interest	—	2,756,250	—	(LIBOR – 40BPS)	—	—	(1,884,000)	LIBOR	968,250
12 Nov. 90	Interest	—	2,756,250	—	(LIBOR – 40BPS)	—	—	(1,884,000)	LIBOR	968,250
12 May 91	Interest	—	2,756,250	—	(LIBOR – 40BPS)	—	—	(1,884,000)	LIBOR	968,250
12 Nov. 91	Interest	—	2,756,250	—	(LIBOR – 40BPS)	—	—	(1,884,000)	LIBOR	968,250
12 May 92	Interest	—	2,756,250	—	(LIBOR – 40BPS)	—	—	(1,884,000)	LIBOR	968,250
12 May 92	Final exchange	(200,000,000)	75,000,000	130,000,000	(48,000,000)	70,000,000	(37,000,000)	—	—	(10,000,000)

[1] (U.S.$75,000,000) × (0.0735) × (180 days/360 days)

[2] (U.S.$48,000,000) × (0.0785) × (180 days/360 days)

[3] U.S.$2,756,250 – U.S.$1,884,000 + [U.S.$48,000,000 × 0.004 × (180 days/360 days)]

Economic Advantages of Swaps

For swaps to provide a real economic benefit to both parties, a barrier generally must exist to prevent arbitrage from functioning fully. This impediment must take the form of legal restrictions on spot and forward foreign exchange transactions, different perceptions by investors of risk and creditworthiness of the two parties, appeal or acceptability of one borrower to a certain class of investor, tax differentials, and so forth.[2]

Swaps also allow firms to lower their cost of foreign exchange risk management. A U.S. corporation, for example, may want to secure fixed-rate funds in Deutsche marks in order to reduce its DM exposure, but is hampered in doing so because it is a relatively unknown credit in the German financial market. In contrast, a German company that is well established in its own country may desire floating-rate dollar financing, but is relatively unknown in the U.S. financial market.

In such a case, a bank intermediary familiar with the funding needs and "comparative advantages" in borrowing of both parties may arrange a currency swap. The U.S. company borrows floating-rate dollars, and the German company borrows fixed-rate DM. The two companies then swap both principal and interest payments. When the term of the swap matures, say, in five years, the principal amounts revert to the original holder. Both parties receive a cost savings because they borrow initially in the market where they have a comparative advantage and then swap for their preferred liability.

Currency swaps, thus, are often used to provide long-term financing in foreign currencies. This function is important because in many foreign countries, long-term capital and forward foreign exchange markets are notably absent or not well developed. Swaps are one type of vehicle providing liquidity to these markets.

In effect, swaps allow the transacting parties to engage in some form of tax, regulatory system, or financial market arbitrage. If the world capital market were fully integrated, the incentive to swap would be reduced because fewer arbitrage opportunities would exist. As noted above, however, even in the United States, where financial markets function freely, interest rate swaps are extremely popular and are credited with cost savings.

■ 23.2 ■
INTERNATIONAL LEASING

Cross-border or international leasing can be used to both defer and avoid tax. It can also be used to safeguard the assets of a multinational firm's foreign affiliates and avoid currency controls.

Operating Versus Financial Leases

Leases can be designated as either operating or financial leases. The tax advantages of international leasing typically turn on this distinction. An *operating lease,* sometimes called a *service lease,* is a true lease in that ownership and use of the asset are separated. The

---

[2]This explanation is provided in Clifford W. Smith, Jr., Charles W. Smithson, and Lee M. Wakeman, "The Evolving Market for Swaps," *Midland Corporate Finance Journal,* Winter 1986, pp. 20–32.

operating lease agreement typically covers only part of the useful life of the asset; it may be renewed on a period-by-period basis. By contrast, a *financial lease* is one that extends over most of the economic life of the asset and is noncancelable or is cancelable only upon payment of a substantial penalty to the lessor. Normally, the payments under a financial lease amortize most of the economic value of the asset.

Noncancelability means that the firm has a contractual obligation to make all the lease payments specified in the agreement, regardless of whether—at a later date—it needs or wants the asset. In effect, economic ownership in a financial lease resides with the lessee. The contractual nature of a financial lease means that entering into one is equivalent to borrowing money and buying the asset outright. Thus, although it is in form a lease, in substance the lessor in a financial lease is lending money to the lessee, with the loan secured by the asset. The equivalence between a financial lease and debt financing extends further: The lessor's profit comes from interest, while default by the lessee can lead to bankruptcy. Leasing and borrowing can and should be considered as alternative financing techniques and can be compared as such.

Tax Factors

Vital issues in any leasing transaction are the tax status of lease payments and who gets to deduct depreciation and to claim any investment tax credit. In the United States, the answer depends on whether the transaction is considered an operating lease (also called a true lease) or a financial lease. The IRS makes this distinction to ensure that the lease transaction is not a disguised installment sale. A lease that qualifies as a true lease for tax purposes is called a tax-oriented lease.

In a *tax-oriented lease,* the lessor receives the tax benefits of ownership, and the lessee gets to deduct the full value of lease payments. But if the lease is considered a financial lease, lease payments are treated as installments of the purchase price plus interest and, therefore, are not fully deductible by the lessee. As the stipulated owner, the lessee is allowed tax depreciation for the purchase price and a tax deduction for the interest factor. The lessor is taxed on the interest imputed to the lease payment and realizes none of the tax benefits of ownership.

Double-Dipping.   The principal tax advantage from international leasing arises when it is possible to structure a "double-dip" lease. In a *double-dip lease,* the disparate leasing rules of the lessor's and lessee's countries let both parties be treated as the owner of the leased equipment for tax purposes. Thus, both the lessee and the lessor are entitled to benefits such as fast depreciation and tax credits. This benefit to the lessor can be passed to the lessee in the form of lower rentals. In the absence of double dipping, the lessee's deductions would be limited to the rent paid.

An example of extraordinary benefits used to be U.K. lessors financing U.S. projects (especially aircraft acquisitions) through financial leases. The U.K. lessor could claim a 100% first-year depreciation write-off and pass its tax savings via reduced rentals to the U.S. lessee, who would also claim the U.S. investment tax credit and depreciation for its own account. Another popular arrangement involved structuring double-dip leases with the United Kingdom and Ireland to get 100% first-year write-offs in both countries. Although this route is now less attractive—the United Kingdom has scaled down its first-year depreciation write-off for assets used outside the U.K. to 10%—the principles remain and can be applied to other countries.

Double dipping is most often achieved with lessees in countries that look to the economic reality of the arrangement (e.g., the United States, Japan, Germany, and the Netherlands) and lessors in countries that characterize leases solely on the basis of legal ownership (e.g., Switzerland, France, Sweden, and the United Kingdom). Readily recognizable financial leases will achieve depreciation allowances in both countries when the lease is considered an operating lease in the lessor's country but a financial lease in the lessee's country.

For example, a double dip from Sweden to Germany is relatively straightforward. As long as the lease does not require the lessee to purchase the asset, the Swedish lessor will get the normal depreciation allowance. The German lessee will be entitled to German allowances if, for example, the leased asset is limited-use property.

However, fine tuning and considerable skill are needed to double dip between two countries that make the economic ownership distinction. In such a case, it is necessary to structure a lease that fits into the perhaps very narrow crack between what the lessor's country considers an operating lease and the lessee's country considers a finance lease. For example, the Dutch airline KLM leased planes from the United States in an arrangement that gave both the U.S. lessor and KLM depreciation write-offs in their home countries. In that deal, the planes were registered in both the United States and the Netherlands. U.S. registry of the aircraft made them eligible for fast write-offs and an investment tax credit, even though they were used outside the United States.

It can also be beneficial to double dip from a captive leasing company in a low-tax country. For example, a multinational firm's leasing company located in Switzerland can lease an asset to an affiliate located in the United Kingdom, under an arrangement that permits both lessor and lessee to receive the tax benefits of ownership. Both benefits are at the 35% (previously 52%) corporate tax rate. Until 1986, the U.K. subsidiary would get its 100% first-year allowance (it's now 25%) and a deduction for the interest factor in the lease payment. The Swiss leasing affiliate's taxable income from lease receipts will be reduced by its depreciation allowances, with the balance taxed at approximately 10%. The after-tax earnings remain within the multinational group.

Additional Dips.   Where additional parties are involved, it is possible that each will be entitled to capital allowances. For example, a triple dip can be achieved by arranging a lease with a Swiss lessor (always entitled to allowances), a U.K. lessee with a purchase option (qualifying it for the 25% depreciation allowance in the first year), and a German sublessee who satisfies German economic ownership rules (qualifying it for a depreciation deduction as well).

International Leasing Companies

By incorporating a captive international leasing company (for interaffiliate transactions) in an appropriate location, the MNC can shift income from high-tax to low-tax jurisdictions and reduce or eliminate withholding tax on lease payments. It may also be able to receive lease income tax free.

Multinationals can also reduce political risk by investing in politically risky countries via a captive international leasing company incorporated in an appropriate location. Lease financing limits the ownership of assets by subsidiaries in politically unstable countries. Leasing also enables the firm to more easily extract cash from affiliates located in countries where there are exchange controls; lease payments are often a more acceptable method of extracting funds than dividends, interest, or royalty payments. Similarly, there will be more chance of recovering assets (or at least obtaining compensation for them) in the case of nationalization if they are not owned by the local subsidiary.

The ideal characteristics of an international leasing company location include (1) no exchange control restrictions, (2) a stable currency, (3) political stability, and (4) a wide network of tax treaties to eliminate withholding tax on lease payments and payment of dividends by the leasing company to its parent. The end result, ideally, would be that profits arise in a low-tax country, tax-deductible expenses such as depreciation and lease payments arise in a high-tax country, and there are no withholding taxes on rent payments and on dividends to the parent of the leasing company.

Japanese Yen-Based Leasing

Because of Japan's huge trade surpluses, it has become a major source of international financing, including international lease financing. An important Japanese development in the international leasing business was the introduction in early 1981 of yen-based leases, known as Shoguns. *Shogun leases* allow leasing companies, usually with the help of U.S. banks, to bypass restrictions imposed by Japan's Ministry of Finance on long-term yen loans. Whereas (in principle at least) it is not possible to lend yen for more than ten years or for more than certain amounts, it is possible to provide both operating leases and conditional sale leases for longer periods and for greater amounts and, thus, accommodate big-ticket items such as planes and ships.

■ 23.3 ■
LDC DEBT-EQUITY SWAPS

In recent years, a market has developed that enables investors to purchase the external debt of less-developed countries (LDCs) to acquire equity or domestic currency in those same countries. The market for *LDC debt-equity swaps,* as the transactions are called, has grown rapidly over the past few years. Between 1985, when swapping began, and 1988, about $15 billion worth of LDC loans were swapped. Although the rate at which debt swaps are occurring is still small in relation to the $437 billion that the 15 most-troubled debtor nations owe the world's commercial banks, there are indications that the debt swaps market is poised for faster growth. Six major debtor nations—Chile, Brazil, Mexico, Venezuela, Argentina, and the Philippines—have initiated debt swaps programs, and more will likely follow.

Types of Debt Swaps and Their Rationale

Swaps can be quite complex, but the basics are fairly simple. For several years, European and regional U.S. commercial banks have been selling troubled LDC loans in the so-called secondary market—an informal network of large banks, big multinational corporations, and some Wall Street investment banks that trade loans of troubled debtor nations over the telephone and by telex. The trading, centered in New York, has grown steadily since the international debt crisis broke in 1982. Traders estimate that $15 billion or more in LDC debt changed hands in this market in 1988.

The loans trade at deep discounts to their face value, reflecting the market's opinion that they will not be repaid in full. For example, in mid-1987, Chilean debt sold at about 70% of its face value, or 70 cents on the dollar. Mexican loans traded at about 60% of par, Brazilian loans at 40%, and Bolivian debt at a mere 10%.

Usually, discount market quotations are cast in terms of bids and offers, not single market-clearing transaction prices. Exhibit 23.8 contains a set of bid-offer quotations for six Latin American countries from July 1985 to January 1989. The spread between bid and offered prices is frequently rather wide—one indication of a thin market—although it seems to have narrowed over time.

Regarding the level of prices quoted, it is clear that substantial variation can occur across countries. During January 1986, for example, average prices ranged from Venezuela at about 80 cents per dollar to Peru at about 20 cents. There has also been a tendency for prices to drift down over this time period, as the dimensions of the debt problem became clearer (see Exhibit 23.9). By mid-1990, with the international debt crisis heating up again, prices for several LDC loans were at or close to their lowest levels in recent history. Conversely, Chile, which has generally followed sound economic policies, and bought back substantial amounts of its debt, has seen the price of its debt rise in recent years.

In a typical deal, a multinational that wants to invest in, say, Chile hires an intermediary (usually a bank) to buy Chilean loans in the secondary market. The company (again through a middleman) presents the loans, denominated in dollars, to the Chilean central bank, which redeems them for pesos. The central banks pay less than face value, but more than the loans

■ **EXHIBIT 23.8**   Bid-Offer Quotations in the Secondary Market for Developing Country Debt (Percent of Face Value of Loans)

	Argentina	**Brazil**	**Chile**	**Mexico**	**Peru**	**Venezuela**
July 1985	60–65%	75–81%	65–69%	80–82%	45–50%	81–83%
January 1986	62–66	75–81	65–69	69–73	25–30	80–82
January 1987	62–65	74–76.5	65–68	54–57	16–19	72–74
January 1988	30–33	44–47	60–63	50–52	2–7	55–57
January 12, 1989	21–22	38–40	58–60	40–41	5–8	38–39
January 20, 1989	18–19	34–35	60–61	38–39	5–8	37–38

SOURCE: Leroy O. Laney, "The Secondary Market in Developing Country Debt," *Economic Review,* Federal Reserve Bank of Dallas, July 1987, p. 2. Data for 1988 and 1989 from Shearson Lehman Hutton, Inc.

■ **EXHIBIT 23.9**   Secondary Market Debt Prices (As Percent of Face Value)

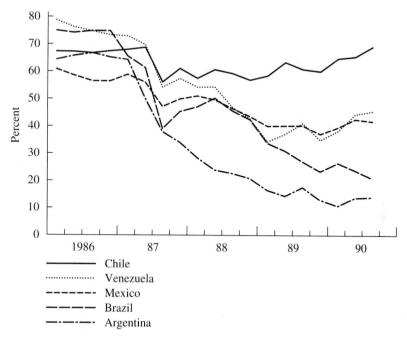

SOURCE: Salomon Brothers

trade for in the secondary market. Chile pays about 92 cents on the dollar, and Mexico an average of 88 cents.

Thus, a company that wants to expand in Chile can pick up $100 million of loans in the secondary market for $70 million and swap them for $92 million in pesos. Chile gets $100 million of debt off its books and doesn't have to part with precious dollars. The company gets $92 million of investment for $70 million, which amounts to a 24% subsidy (22/92).

■ ──

ILLUSTRATION

Citicorp Structures a Debt Swap for Nissan. In 1986, Citicorp learned that Nissan Motors wanted to invest the equivalent of $54 million to expand its truck factory in Mexico. When Citicorp offered to get them the $54 million in pesos for much less than $54 million through a debt-equity swap, Nissan liked the idea.

Citicorp went to the Mexican government and got their approval for the swap. The Mexican government agreed to pay $54 million in pesos for approximately $60 million of their external debt, a 10% discount. Citicorp went out and bought the $60 million in Mexican bank debt for about $38 million. Nissan wound up with the peso equivalent of $54 million at a price of only $40 million. Mexico retired about $60 million in bank debt. And Citicorp was paid about $2 million for structuring the deal and assuming the risk. ∎

The variations on this theme are endless. Chrysler has used some of the pesos it got in swaps to pay off local debt owed by its Mexican subsidiary. Kodak and Unisys have used swaps to expand their operations in Chile. Club Med is building a new beach resort in Mexico. Big U.S. banks usually act only as intermediaries in these deals, but a few have swapped for themselves, trading their LDC loans for equity in Latin businesses. In 1988, Manufacturers Hanover used a debt-equity swap to exchange some of its $2 billion in Brazilian debt for a 10% equity stake in Companhia Suzano de Papel e Celulose, a Brazilian paper and pulp company (see Exhibit 23.10 for details).

In addition to debt-equity swaps, there are also "debt-peso" swaps. *Debt-peso swaps* enable residents of a debtor country to purchase their country's foreign debt at a discount and to convert this debt into domestic currency. To finance these purchases, residents use funds held abroad or hard currency acquired from international trade or in the exchange market.

By arrangement with the debt country, domestic currency assets obtained via debt swaps are acquired at closer to the original face value of the debt. For example, in 1986, a purchaser who acquired Mexican debt for 57 cents on the dollar could obtain equity worth 82 cents. Even after accounting for fees and redemption discounts applied by debtor countries to convert the debt into domestic currency, debt-swaps allow investors to acquire the domestic currency of debtor countries much more cheaply than do official exchange markets. In effect, investors resorting to the debt swap market enjoy a preferential exchange rate.

Because the debt swap market offers a more favorable exchange rate than do official exchange markets, it creates an incentive for arbitrage. For example, a resident of a debtor country may exchange 100 pesos in domestic currency in the official exchange market to acquire a dollar. The resident may then use this dollar to acquire, via the debt swap market,

∎ **EXHIBIT 23.10**   How a Debt-Equity Swap Works

Manufacturers Hanover takes $115 million in Brazilian government loans to Multplic, a Sao Paulo broker. ⟶	The broker takes the loans to the Brazilian central bank's monthly debt auction, where they are valued at an average of 86¢ on the dollar.
With its cruzados, Manufacturers Hanover buys 10% of Companhia Suzano de Papel e Celulose's stock, and Suzano uses the ⟵ bank's cash to expand production and exports.	Through the broker, Manufacturers Hanover exchanges the loans at the central bank for $100 million worth of Brazilian cruzados.* It pays the broker a $150,000 commission. The central bank retires the loans.

*At the time of this transaction, the cruzado was the Brazilian currency.

---

125 pesos in domestic currency and, thus, gain a 25 peso profit. Exchange controls will not necessarily be effective in preventing this "round trip" process because domestic residents may elude exchange controls in a number of ways (for example, by overstating imports or understating exports).

Typically, access to swap programs involves wading through a lot of government red tape. For example, rules for foreign investors to participate in Mexico's swap program are outlined, in sometimes indecipherable language, in a 44-page *Manual Operativo*. Mexico also tailors its swap program to promote industrial policy goals. It does that by redeeming loans at different prices, depending on how the proceeds will be used. If a foreign investor wants to buy shares in a nationalized company that the government is trying to privatize, the central bank redeems loans at full face value. It pays as much as 95 cents on the dollar if the pesos will be invested in tourism and other businesses that help the trade balance. However, it pays only 75 cents on the dollar on deals that create no jobs, no exports, and no new technology.

Debt Swaps and Inflation

One problem with debt swaps is that there is no free lunch. All too frequently, governments finance their purchases of bank debt by simply printing more currency. Consider Brazil. Suppose it buys back $100 million of its debt during a particular month. If the government isn't running a surplus, which it rarely is, it must print money to pay for the debt. The net result is fewer dollars of foreign debt outstanding but higher inflation. In effect, the country has taxed its citizens (by means of the inflation tax) and turned over the proceeds to banks, which then use them to acquire local assets.

■ 23.4 ■
SUMMARY AND CONCLUSIONS

Multinational corporations can use creative financing to achieve various objectives. These include reducing their cost of funds, cutting taxes, and reducing political risk. This chapter focused on three such techniques—interest and currency swaps, international leasing, and LDC loan swaps.

Interest and currency swaps involve a financial transaction in which two counterparties agree to exchange streams of payments over time. In an interest rate swap, no actual principal is exchanged either initially or at maturity, but interest payment streams are exchanged according to predetermined rules and based on an underlying notional amount. The two main types are coupon swaps (or fixed rate to floating rate) and basis swaps (from floating rate against one reference rate to floating rate with another reference rate).

Currency swap refers to a transaction in which two counterparties exchange specific amounts of two currencies at the outset and repay over time according to a predetermined rule that reflects both interest payments and amortization of principal. A cross-currency interest rate swap involves swapping fixed-rate flows in one currency to floating-rate flows in another.

International lease transactions, or cross-border leasing, may provide certain tax and political risk management advantages. The principal tax advantage from international leasing arises when the disparate leasing rules of the lessor's and lessee's countries enable both parties to retain the tax advantages of ownership. This lease is known as a double-dip lease. International leasing also enables MNCs to reduce their assets at risk in politically unstable countries and may permit greater access to local profits. The latter benefit arises because host governments are more likely to permit lease payments than dividends or royalties.

Under a debt-equity program, a firm buys a country's dollar debt on the secondary loan market at a discount and swaps it into local equity. Although such programs are still in their infancy, debt-equity swaps can provide cheap financing for expanding plant and for retiring local debt in hard-pressed LDCs. However, debt swaps are not an unmixed blessing for the participating countries, since they tend to exacerbate already high rates of inflation.

■ QUESTIONS ■

1. What is the difference between a basis swap and a coupon swap?

2. What is a currency swap?

3. What factors underlie the economic benefits of swaps?

4. Comment on the following statement. "In order for one party to a swap to benefit, the other party must lose."

5. As noted in Chapter 22, the Swiss Central Bank bans the use of Swiss francs for Eurobond issues. Explain how currency swaps can be used to enable foreign borrowers who want to raise Swiss francs through a bond issue outside of Switzerland to get around this ban.

6. Comment on the following statement. "During the period 1987–1989, Japanese companies issued some $115 billion of bonds with warrants attached. Nearly all were issued in dollars. The dollar bonds usually carried coupons of 4% or less; by the time the Japanese companies swapped that exposure into yen (whose interest rate was as much as five percentage points lower than the dollar's), their cost of capital was zero or negative."

7. In May 1988, Walt Disney Productions sold to Japanese investors a 20-year stream of projected yen royalties from Tokyo Disneyland. The present value of that stream of royalties, discounted at 6% (the return required by the Japanese investors), was ¥93 billion. Disney took the yen proceeds from the sale, converted them to dollars, and invested the dollars in bonds yielding 10%. According to Disney's chief financial officer, Gary Wilson, "In effect, we got money at a 6% discount rate, reinvested it at 10%, and hedged our royalty stream against yen fluctuations—all in one transaction."

   a. At the time of the sale, the exchange rate was ¥124 = $1. What dollar amount did Disney realize from the sale of its yen proceeds?

   b. Demonstrate the equivalence between Walt Disney's transaction and a currency swap. (*Hint*: A diagram would help.)

   c. Comment on Gary Wilson's statement. Did Disney achieve the equivalent of a free lunch through its transaction?

8. How can international lease transactions enable multinational firms to reduce taxes and political risk?

9. Global Industries (GI) is looking for a place in which to locate its international leasing company. What factors should GI take into account in selecting the location? Explain.

10. Explain the benefits of a debt-equity swap program to

    a. A multinational firm seeking to expand its investment in the country.

    b. The host government.

    c. The bank that sells its LDC debt in the secondary market.

11. How can debt swaps cause inflation?

12. Jose Angel Gurria, Mexico's chief debt negotiator and the architect of its swap program, questions the gain to Mexico from its swap program: "The latest restructuring package on our debt gives us 20 years to repay principal, with no principal payments for seven years. So why are we giving money away? Why pay 88 cents for debt that is worth only 60 cents?" Comment on Señor Gurria's statement.

■ PROBLEMS ■

1. Company A, a low-rated firm, desires a fixed-rate, long-term loan. A presently has access to floating interest rate funds at a margin of 1.5% over LIBOR. Its direct borrowing cost is 13% in the fixed-rate bond market. In contrast, company B, which prefers a floating-rate loan, has access to fixed-rate funds in the Eurodollar bond market at 11% and floating-rate funds at LIBOR + 1/2%.

    a. How can A and B use a swap to advantage?

    b. Suppose they split the cost savings. How much would A pay for its fixed-rate funds? How much would B pay for its floating-rate funds?

2. Square Corp. has not tapped the Swiss franc public debt market because of concern about a likely appreciation of that currency and only wishes to be a floating-rate dollar borrower, which it can be at LIBOR + 3/8%. Circle Corp. has a strong preference for fixed-rate Swiss franc debt, but it must pay 1/2 of 1% more than the 5 1/4% coupon that Square Corp.'s notes would carry. Circle Corp., however, can obtain Eurodollars at LIBOR flat (a zero margin). What is the range of possible cost savings to Square from engaging in a currency swap with Circle?

3. In the Kodak Australian dollar swap example, suppose Merrill Lynch had been able to arrange a forward contract for the A$70 million at a rate of A$1 = U.S.$0.49.

    a. If Merrill Lynch retained full benefits from the better forward rate, what would have been the present value of its profit on the deal?

    b. If Merrill Lynch had passed these savings on to Kodak, what would have been Kodak's annualized all-in rate on the swap? (*Hint*: Take the internal rate of return on all of Kodak's cash flows.)

    c. Suppose the interest rate swap with Australian bank B had been at LIBOR – 20 basis points. If Merrill Lynch passed this higher cost along to Kodak, what would Kodak's all-in cost have been?

4. Chrysler has decided to make a $100 million investment in Mexico via a debt-equity swap. Of that $100 million, $20 million will go to pay off high-interest peso loans in Mexico. The remaining $80 million will go for new capital investment. The government will pay 86 cents on the dollar for debt used to pay off peso loans and 92 cents on the dollar for debt used to finance new investment. If Chrysler can buy Mexican debt in the secondary market for 60 cents on the dollar, how much will it cost Chrysler to make its $100 million investment?

■ BIBLIOGRAPHY ■

Fierman, Jaclyn. "Fast Bucks in Latin Loan Swaps." *Fortune,* August 3, 1987, pp. 91–99.

Moreno, Ramon. "LDC Debt Swaps." *FRBSF Weekly Letter,* Federal Reserve Bank of San Francisco, September 4, 1987.

Smith, Clifford W., Jr., Charles W. Smithson, and Lee M. Wakeman. "The Evolving Market for Swaps." *Midland Corporate Finance Journal,* Winter 1986, pp. 20–32.

◣ 24 ◢

Designing a Global Financing Strategy

Let us all be happy and live within our means, even if we have to borrow money to do it with.

—Artemus Ward—

■ In selecting an appropriate strategy for financing its worldwide operations, the multi-national corporation (MNC) must consider the availability of different sources of funds and the relative cost and effects of these sources on the firm's operating risks. Some of the key variables in the evaluation include the firm's capital structure (debt-equity mix), taxes, exchange risk, diversification of fund sources, the freedom to move funds across borders, and a variety of government credit and capital controls and subsidies. The eventual funding strategy selected must reconcile a variety of potentially conflicting objectives, such as minimizing expected financing costs, reducing economic exposure, providing protection from currency controls and other forms of political risk, and ensuring availability of funds in times of tight credit.

The choice of trade-offs to be made in establishing a worldwide financial policy requires an explicit analytical framework. The approach taken in this chapter separates the financing of international operations into three largely separable objectives:

1. Minimize expected after-tax financing costs.
2. Arrange financing to reduce the riskiness of operating cash flows.
3. Achieve an appropriate worldwide financial structure.[1]

---

[1]This chapter is based in part on Donald R. Lessard and Alan C. Shapiro, "Guidelines for Global Financing Choices," *Midland Corporate Finance Journal,* Winter 1984, pp. 68–80; and Alan C. Shapiro, *Modern Corporate Finance* (New York: Macmillan, 1990), especially Chapter 16.

■ 24.1 ■

MINIMIZE EXPECTED AFTER-TAX FINANCING COSTS

Sharp-eyed firms are always on the lookout for financing choices that are "bargains"—
that is, financing options priced at below-market rates. The value of arranging *below-market
financing* can be illustrated by examining a case involving Sonat, the energy and energy
services company based in Birmingham, Alabama. In late 1984, Sonat ordered from Daewoo
Shipbuilding, a South Korean shipyard, six drilling rigs that can be partly submerged.
Daewoo agreed to finance the $425 million purchase price with an 8.5-year loan at an annual
interest rate of 9% paid semiannually. The loan is repayable in 17 equal semiannual
installments. How much is this loan worth to Sonat? That is, what is its net present value?

At 9% interest paid semiannually, Sonat must pay interest equal to 4.5% of the loan
balance plus $25 million in principal repayment every six months for the next 8.5 years. In
return, Sonat receives $425 million today. Given these cash inflows and outflows, we can
calculate the loan's NPV just as we would for any project analysis. Note, however, that unlike
the typical capital-budgeting problem we looked at, the cash inflow occurs immediately and
the cash outflows later. But the principle is the same. All we need now is the required return
on this deal and Sonat's marginal tax rate.

The required return is based on the opportunity cost of the funds provided, that is, the
rate that Sonat would have to pay to borrow $425 million in the capital market. At the time
the loan was arranged, in late 1984, the market interest rate on such a loan would have been
about 16%. If the marginal tax rate at which the interest payments are written off is 50% (the
federal plus state corporate tax rate at that time), then the after-tax semiannual required return
is 4% (8% annually), and the after-tax semiannual interest payments are $0.0225 \times P_t$, where
P_t is the loan balance in period t and 2.25% is the after-tax interest rate ($0.5 \times 4.5\%$). Now
we can calculate the NPV of Sonat's financing bargain:

$$
\begin{aligned}
\text{NPV} &= \$425,000,000 - \sum_{t=1}^{17} 0.0225 P_t/(1.04)^t - \sum_{t=1}^{17} \$25,000,000/(1.04)^t \\
&= \$425,000,000 - \$372,210,000 \\
&= \$52,790,000
\end{aligned}
$$

These calculations are shown in Exhibit 24.1. You don't need a degree in financial
economics to realize that borrowing money at 9% when the market rate is 16% is a good
deal. But what the NPV calculations tell you is just how much a particular below-market
financing option is worth.

Raising funds at a below-market rate is easier said than done, however. A company
selling securities is competing for funds on a global basis, not only with other firms in its
industry but with all firms, foreign and domestic, and with numerous government units and
private individuals as well. The fierce competition for funds makes it much less likely that
the firm can find bargain-priced funds. But, as we shall see, the task is not impossible.
Financial market distortions arising from taxes, *government credit and capital controls,* and
government subsidies and incentives sometimes enable firms to raise funds at below-market
rates. Companies may also be able to raise low-cost money by devising securities for which
specific investors are willing to pay a higher price.

■ **EXHIBIT 24.1**   Calculating the Value of Sonat's Low-Cost Loan Arrangement
(U.S.$ Millions)

Period	Principal Balance (1)	Interest (1) × 0.0225 = (2)	+	Principal Repayment (3)	=	Total Payment (4)	×	PV Factor @ 4% (5)	=	Present Value (6)
1	$425	$9.56		$25		$34.56		0.962		$ 33.25
2	400	9.00		25		34.00		0.925		31.45
3	375	8.44		25		33.44		0.889		29.73
4	350	7.88		25		32.88		0.855		28.11
5	325	7.31		25		32.31		0.822		26.56
6	300	6.75		25		31.75		0.790		25.08
7	275	6.19		25		31.19		0.760		23.70
8	250	5.63		25		30.63		0.731		22.39
9	225	5.06		25		30.06		0.703		21.13
10	200	4.50		25		29.50		0.676		19.94
11	175	3.94		25		28.94		0.650		18.81
12	150	3.38		25		28.38		0.625		17.73
13	125	2.81		25		27.81		0.601		16.71
14	100	2.25		25		27.25		0.578		15.75
15	75	1.69		25		26.69		0.555		14.81
16	50	1.13		25		26.13		0.534		13.95
17	25	0.56		25		25.56		0.513		13.11
								Sum		$372.21

Taxes

The asymmetrical tax treatment of various components of financial cost—such as dividend payments versus interest expenses and exchange losses versus exchange gains—often means that equality of before-tax costs will lead to inequality in after-tax costs. This asymmetry holds out the possibility of reducing after-tax costs by judicious selection of securities. Yet, everything is not always what it seems.

For example, many firms consider debt financing to be less expensive than equity financing because interest expense is tax-deductible, whereas dividends are paid out of after-tax income. But this comparison is too limited. In the absence of any restrictions, the supply of corporate debt can be expected to rise. Yields will also have to rise in order to attract investors in higher and higher tax brackets. Companies will continue to issue debt up to the point at which the marginal investor tax rate will equal the marginal corporate tax rate.[2] At this point, the necessary yield would be such that there would no longer be a tax incentive for issuing more debt.

The tax advantage of debt can be preserved only if the firm can take advantage of some tax distortion, issue tax-exempt debt, or sell debt to investors in marginal tax brackets below 34%. The example of zero-coupon bonds illustrates all of these categories.

[2]This insight first appeared in Merton Miller, "Debt and Taxes," *Journal of Finance,* May 1977, pp. 261–276.

Zero-Coupon Bonds.   In 1982, PepsiCo issued the first long-term *zero-coupon bond*. Although they have since become a staple of corporate finance, zero-coupon bonds initially were a startling innovation. They don't pay interest, but are sold at a deep discount to their face value. For example, the price on PepsiCo's 30-year bonds was around $60 for each $1,000 face amount of the bonds. Investors gain from the difference between the discounted price and the amount they receive at redemption.

Between 1982 and 1985, investors paid $4 billion for $18.9 billion worth of zero-coupon bonds, about half of which were purchased by Japanese investors. The offerings were attractive in Japan because the government doesn't tax the capital gain on bonds sold prior to maturity. Catering to this tax break, a number of companies—including Exxon (see the illustration in Chapter 22) and IBM—were able to obtain inexpensive financing by targeting Japanese investors for zero-coupon bonds offered on international markets.

The ability to take advantage quickly of such tax windows is evident considering subsequent developments in Japan. Japan's Finance Ministry, embarrassed at this tax break, has effectively ended the tax exemption for zero-coupon bond gains; Japanese investors have accordingly demanded higher yields to compensate for their anticipated tax liability. The reaction by the Japanese government to the proliferation of zero-coupon debt illustrates a key point: If one devises a legal way to engage in unlimited tax arbitrage through the financial markets, the government will change the law.

This example also points out that even though the world's capital markets are highly integrated, companies can still profit from tax differentials and government restrictions on capital flows between countries. But the benefits go to those who are organized to quickly take advantage of such windows of opportunity.

Debt Versus Equity Financing.   Interest payments on debt extended by either the parent or a financial institution generally are tax-deductible by an affiliate, but dividends are not. In addition, principal repatriation is tax free, whereas dividend payments may lead to further taxation. Thus, parent company financing of foreign affiliates in the form of debt rather than equity has certain tax advantages. These and other factors are discussed in the section on financial structure.

Government Credit and Capital Controls

Governments intervene in their financial markets for a number of reasons: to restrain the growth of lendable funds, to make certain types of borrowing more or less expensive, and to direct funds to certain favored economic activities. In addition, corporate borrowing is often restricted in order to hold down interest rates (thereby providing the finance ministry with lower-cost funds to meet a budget deficit). When access to local funds markets is limited, interest rates in them are usually below the risk-adjusted equilibrium level. There is often an incentive to borrow as much as possible where nonprice credit rationing is used.

Restraints on, or incentives to promote, overseas borrowing are often employed as well. There are numerous examples of restraints and incentives affecting overseas borrowing. Certain countries have limited the amount of local financing the subsidiary of a multinational firm can obtain to that required for working-capital purposes; any additional needs will have to be satisfied from abroad. A prerequisite condition for obtaining official approval for a new investment or acquisition often is a commitment to inject external funds. Capital-exporting nations may attempt to control balance-of-payments deficits by restricting overseas investment flows—as the United States did from 1968 to 1974 under the Office of Foreign Direct Investment (OFDI) regulations.

Conversely, when a nation is concerned about excess capital inflows, a portion of any new foreign borrowing might have to be placed on deposit with the government, thereby raising the effective cost of external debt. Ironically, the effect of many of these government credit allocation and control schemes has been to hasten the development of the external financial markets—the Eurocurrency and Eurobond markets—further reducing government ability to regulate domestic financial markets.

The multinational firm with access to a variety of sources and types of funds and the ability to shift capital with its internal transfer system has more opportunities to secure the lowest risk-adjusted cost money and to circumvent credit restraints. These attributes should give it a substantial advantage over a purely domestic company.

Government Subsidies and Incentives

Despite the often hostile rhetoric directed against the multinational firm, many governments offer a growing list of incentives to MNCs to influence their production and export sourcing decisions. Direct investment incentives include interest rate subsidies, loans with long maturities, official repatriation guarantees, grants related to project size, favorable prices for land, and favorable terms for the building of plants. For example, new investments located in the Mezzogiorno region of Italy can qualify for cash grants that cover up to 40% of the cost of plant and equipment, in addition to low interest rate loans.

Governments sometimes will make the infrastructure investments as well by building the transportation, communication, and other links to support a new industrial project. Some indirect incentives include corporate income tax holidays, accelerated depreciation, and a reduction or elimination of the payment of other business taxes and import duties on capital equipment and raw materials.

In addition, all governments of developed nations have some form of export financing agency whose purpose is to boost local exports by providing loans with long repayment periods at interest rates below the market level and with low-cost political and economic risk insurance. These export credit programs can often be employed advantageously by multinationals. The use will depend on whether the firm is seeking to export or import goods or services, but the basic strategy remains the same: Shop around among the various export credit agencies for the best possible financing arrangement.

■ ———

ILLUSTRATION

Texas Instruments Searches for Low-Cost Capital. Texas Instruments (TI) is seeking to finance an aggressive capital spending program through a series of joint ventures and other cooperative arrangements with foreign governments and corporations. In Italy, TI received a package of development grants and low-cost loans from the government which will offset more than half of TI's investment in a state-of-the-art semiconductor plant there—an investment expected to total more than $1 billion over a multiyear period. TI was able to negotiate the incentive package because the Italian government was seeking to improve its technological infrastructure in the area selected by TI for the new plant.

In Taiwan, TI and a Taiwanese customer, Acer Computer Company, established a joint venture in which Acer's majority stake is financed with Taiwanese equity capital that would be unavailable to a U.S. company acting alone. In Japan, TI entered into a joint venture with Kobe Steel, a company seeking diversification. Here, too, TI relies on its foreign partner to supply a majority of the equity. In both Asian joint ventures, however, TI has an option to convert its initial minority stake into a majority holding.   ∎

Export Financing Strategy.   Massey-Ferguson (now Varity Corp.), the multinational Canadian farm-equipment manufacturer, illustrates how MNCs are able to generate business for their foreign subsidiaries at minimum expense and risk by playing off various national export credit programs against each other.

The key to this *export financing strategy* is to view the foreign countries in which the MNC has plants not only as markets, but also as potential sources of financing for exports to third countries. For example, in early 1978, Massey-Ferguson was looking to ship 7200 tractors (worth $53 million) to Turkey, but it was unwilling to assume the risk of currency inconvertibility.[3] Turkey at that time already owed $2 billion to various foreign creditors, and it was uncertain whether it would be able to come up with dollars to pay off its debts (especially since its reserves were at about zero).

Massey solved this problem by manufacturing the tractors at its Brazilian subsidiary, Massey-Ferguson of Brazil, and selling them to Brazil's Interbras—the trading-company arm of Petrobras, the Brazilian national oil corporation. Interbras, in turn, arranged to sell the tractors to Turkey and pay Massey in cruzeiros. The cruzeiro financing for Interbras came from Cacex, the Banco do Brazil department that is in charge of foreign trade. Cacex underwrote all the political, commercial, and exchange risks as part of the Brazilian government's intense export promotion drive. Before choosing Brazil as a supply point, Massey made a point of shopping around to get the best export credit deal available.

Import Financing Strategy.   Firms engaged in projects that have sizable import requirements may be able to finance these purchases on attractive terms. A number of countries, including the United States, make credit available to foreign purchasers at low (below-market) interest rates and with long repayment periods. These loans are almost always tied to procurement in the agency's country; thus, the firm must compile a list of goods and services required for the project and relate them to potential sources by country. Where there is overlap among the potential suppliers, the purchasing firm may have leverage to extract more favorable financing terms from the various export credit agencies involved. This strategy is illustrated by the hypothetical example of a copper mining venture in Exhibit 24.2.

---

[3] "Massey-Ferguson's No-Risk Tractor Deal," *Business International Money Report,* February 3, 1978, pp. 35–36.

■ **EXHIBIT 24.2** Alternative Sources of Procurement: Hypothetical Copper Mine
(U.S.$ Millions)

Item	Total Project	United States	France	Germany	Japan	United Kingdom	Sweden	Italy
Mine Equipment								
Shovels	$12	$12	$ 8	$12	$12	$12	$10	—
Trucks	20	20	—	20	20	10	20	12
Other	8	8	5	3	6	8	—	4
Mine Facilities								
Shops	7	7	7	7	3	7	5	6
Offices	3	3	3	3	2	3	3	2
Preparation Plant								
Crushers	11	11	8	11	11	11	—	—
Loading	15	15	10	10	15	12	15	7
Environmental	13	13	5	8	5	10	7	5
Terminal								
Ore handling	13	13	10	13	13	13	8	9
Shiploader	6	6	6	6	6	6	2	4
Bulk Commodities								
Steel	20	20	20	20	20	15	8	20
Electrical	17	17	12	14	10	15	5	8
Mechanical	15	15	8	—	12	10	6	—
Total potential foreign purchases	$160	$160	$92	$127	$135	$132	$89	$77

Perhaps the best-known application of this *import financing strategy* in recent years is the financing of the Soviet gas pipeline to Western Europe. The Soviet Union played off various European and Japanese suppliers and export financing agencies against each other and managed to get extraordinarily favorable credit and pricing terms.

Regional and International Development Banks. Organizations such as the World Bank and Inter-American Development Bank (which were discussed in Chapter 22) are potential sources of low-cost, long-term, fixed-rate funds for certain types of ventures. The time-consuming nature of arranging financing from them, however—in part due to their insistence on conducting their own in-house feasibility studies—usually leaves them as a secondary source of funds. Their participation may be indispensable, however, for projects that require heavy infrastructure investments such as roads, power plants, schools, communications facilities, and housing for employees. These infrastructure investments are the most difficult part of a project to arrange financing for because they generate no cash flow of their own. Thus, loans or grants from an international or regional development bank are often essential to fill a gap in the project financing plan.

Financial Innovation

The dizzying pace of securities innovation in recent years has created an overwhelming abundance of financing alternatives. To a person schooled in marketing, the reasons for such variety are obvious. The vast array of securities in the marketplace exists for the same reasons that M&Ms come in more than one color and that Fords, Chevrolets, and Volkswagens coexist with one another and with Mercedes-Benzes and Rolls-Royces. People have different tastes, preferences, and wealth levels. And whether the market is for cars or financial securities, the better designed the product is and the more closely it is tailored to the particular needs and desires of its potential customers, the higher the price it can command. Moreover, as the environment changes, whether in the form of higher oil prices, new tax laws, or more uncertain inflation, opportunities arise for astute managers to design new cars or securities that fit the new needs of the marketplace.

Furthermore, as Baskin-Robbins has successfully demonstrated, even though plain vanilla may be the most popular ice cream flavor, there's also a market out there for peanut butter ice cream. This suggests a potential source of value creation: To the extent that the firm can design a security that appeals to a special niche in the capital market, it can attract funds at a cost that is less than the market's required return on securities of comparable risk.

But as we saw in the case of zeros, such a rewarding situation is likely to be temporary, because the demand for a security that fits a particular niche in the market is not unlimited. On the other hand, the supply of securities designed to tap that niche is likely to increase dramatically once the niche is recognized. However, even though financial innovation may not be a sustainable form of value creation, it can nonetheless enable the initial issuers to raise money at a below-market rate.

■ ──

ILLUSTRATION

The Swedish Export Credit Corporation Innovates. The Swedish Export Credit Corporation (SEK) borrows about $2 billion annually. To keep its funding costs low, SEK relies heavily on financial innovation. For example, SEK recently issued a straight bond, stripped it down to its two components—an annuity consisting of the interest payments and a zero-coupon bond consisting of the principal repayment at maturity—and sold the pieces to different investors. The annuity cash flow was tailored to meet the demands of a Japanese insurance company that was looking for an interest-only security, while the zero-coupon portion appealed to European investors who desired earnings taxed as capital gains rather than interest income. By unbundling the bond issue into separate parts that appealed to distinct groups of investors, SEK created a financial transaction whose parts were more valuable than the whole.

── ■

■ 24.2 ■
REDUCING OPERATING RISKS

After taking advantage of the opportunities available to it to lower its risk-adjusted financing costs, the firm should then arrange its additional financing in such a way that the risk exposures of the company are kept at manageable levels. The profitability, and thus the market value, of any company depends to a large extent on its ability to compete. A key element of corporate competitiveness is the firm's ability to inspire sufficient trust and confidence such that customers, employees, and other stakeholders are willing to develop relationships with the firm. One prerequisite for such confidence is that the firm be seen as financially sound and viable over the long run.

Clearly, excessive risk taking—with a corresponding decrease in the firm's survival odds—could adversely affect the firm's relationships with its noninvestor stakeholders, thereby jeopardizing the firm-specific capital that has been accumulated over time. The result is that higher total risk can lead to a reduction in a company's operating cash flows by decreasing sales or increasing operating costs.[4]

Thus, to the extent that a particular element of risk contributes materially to the firm's total risk, management will want to lay off that risk as long as the cost of doing so is not too great. The risks and their relationship to financing arrangements that we examine here arise from four sources: currency fluctuations, political instability, sales uncertainty, and changing access to funds.

Since the political and economic changes that bring about these risks are impossible to predict—otherwise there would be no risk—the firm cannot expect to profit from financial arrangements that lay such risks off to others. Otherwise, arbitrage opportunities would present themselves, a condition inconsistent with financial market efficiency. Rather, these financial arrangements should be viewed as insurance against corporate risk.

Exchange Risk

We saw in Chapter 11 that if financing opportunities in various currencies are fairly priced, firms can structure their liabilities so as to reduce their exposure to foreign exchange risk at no added cost to shareholders. In the case of contractual items—those fixed in nominal terms—this structuring simply involves matching net positive positions (ones with net cash inflows) in each currency with borrowings of similar maturity. The goal here is to offset unanticipated changes in the dollar value of its cash flows with identical changes in the dollar cost of servicing its liabilities.

With noncontractual operating cash flows—those from future revenues and costs—the same financing principle applies: Finance assets that generate foreign currency cash flows with liabilities denominated in those same foreign currencies. Although it is impossible to perfectly hedge operating cash flows in this manner due to the many uncertainties concerning the effects of currency changes on operating flows, the hedging objective at least provides a clear-cut goal for firms to strive for.

Political Risk

The use of financing to reduce political risks typically involves mechanisms to avoid or at least reduce the impact of certain risks, such as those of exchange controls. It may also

---

[4]This point is elaborated on in Alan C. Shapiro and Sheridan Titman, "An Integrated Approach to Corporate Risk Management," *Midland Corporate Finance Journal,* Summer 1985, pp. 41–56.

involve financing mechanisms that actually change the risk itself, as in the case of expropriation or other direct political acts.

Firms can sometimes reduce the risk of currency inconvertibility by appropriately arranging their affiliates' financing. Strategies include investing parent funds as debt rather than equity, arranging back-to-back and parallel loans, and using local financing to the maximum extent possible. Of course, such arrangements will be most valuable when the banks or local investors face significantly fewer restrictions or smaller risks—especially if the risk in question involves possible discrimination against direct foreign investors. While local investors may often have an advantage in this regard, this advantage cannot be taken as a general rule. Even if a particular political risk cannot be modified by shifting it from one firm or investor to another, a firm with substantial exposure will benefit by laying off such risks to investors with less exposure.

Another approach used by multinational firms, especially those in the expropriation-prone extractive industries, is to finance their foreign investments with funds from the host and other governments, international development agencies, overseas banks, and from customers—with payment to be provided out of production—rather than supplying their own capital. Because repayment is tied to the project's success, the firm(s) sponsoring the project can create an international network of banks, government agencies, and customers with a vested interest in the faithful fulfillment of the host government's contract with the sponsoring firm(s). Any expropriation threat is likely to upset relations with customers, banks, and governments worldwide. As we saw in Chapter 20, this strategy was employed successfully by Kennecott to finance a major copper mine expansion in Chile. Despite the subsequent rise to power of Salvador Allende—a politician who promised to expropriate all foreign holdings in Chile with "ni un centavo" in compensation—Chile was forced to honor all prior government commitments to Kennecott.

International leasing is another financing technique that may help multinationals to reduce their political risk. As we saw in the previous chapter, international leasing allows multinationals to limit the ownership of assets by subsidiaries in politically unstable countries and to more easily extract cash from affiliates located in countries where there are exchange controls.

Product Market Risk

Some firms sell their project's or plant's expected output in advance to their customers on the basis of mutual advantage. The purchaser benefits from these so-called *"take-or-pay" contracts* by having a stable source of supply, usually at a discount from the market price. The seller also benefits by having an assured outlet for its product—which protects the firm against, *product market risk,* the risk of demand fluctuations—and a contract that it can then discount with a consortium of banks. That is, it sells collection rights on these contracts to the banks. As noted earlier, this technique, which is similar to factoring but on a far grander scale, was used to help finance Kennecott's Chilean copper mine expansion and the Soviet Union's natural gas pipeline to Western Europe. Similarly, Texas Instruments seeks to lower its risk by establishing long-term supply agreements in which customers make advance payments for purchases of semiconductors.

Securing Access to Funds

A multinational firm's operational flexibility is dependent in part on its ability to secure continual access to funds at a reasonable cost and without onerous restrictions. In this way, the firm can meet temporary shortfalls of cash and also take advantage of profitable investment opportunities without having to sell off assets or otherwise disrupt operations. The fear is that during some future period of monetary stringency, the quantity of credit available to them might be limited, while their competitors retain access to funds in a broader range of markets. In such conditions of uneven credit allocation, the market shares of their own business would be at risk because the scale of their operations would be limited by the scale of available finance. This potential problem creates demand among firms for access to an expanded range of credit sources.

The ability to marshal substantial financial resources also signals competitors, actual and potential, that the firm will not be an easy target. Consider the alternative: a firm that is highly leveraged with no excess lines of credit or cash reserves. A competitor can move into the firm's market and gain market share with less fear of retaliation. In order to retaliate—by cutting price, say, or by increasing advertising expenditures—the firm will need more money. Since it has no spare cash and can't issue additional debt at a reasonable price, it will have to go to the equity market. But firms issuing new equity are suspect because of the asymmetric information relationship between investors and management (Is the firm selling equity now because it knows the stock is overpriced?). The problem of information asymmetry will be particularly acute when the firm is trying to fend off a competitive attack. Thus, a firm that lacks financial reserves faces a Hobson's choice: Acquiesce in the competitive attack or raise funds on unattractive terms.

To ensure adequate financial reserves, an MNC can maintain substantial unused debt capacity and liquid assets. It can also diversify its fund sources and indirectly buy insurance through excess borrowing. Having these extra financial resources signals competitors, as well as customers and other stakeholders, that the firm is financially healthy and has staying power; temporary setbacks will not become permanent ones.

Diversification of Fund Sources.   A key element of any MNC's global financial strategy should be to gain access to a broad range of fund sources to lessen its dependence on any one financial market. An ancillary benefit to *diversification of fund sources* is that the firm broadens its sources of economic and financial information, providing a useful supplement to its domestic information sources and aiding in its financial decision-making process.

For example, in January 1985, Signal Cos. issued $125 million of Eurodollar bonds, even though it had $1.2 billion in cash and very little debt at the time. According to the chief financial officer, Signal "wanted access to a large capital market that's separate from the U.S. Next time, we may come to this market for $500 million and we'll know we can do a major offering at a substantial savings [to a comparable U.S. financing]."[5]

---

[5]*The Wall Street Journal,* January 23, 1985, p. 38.

Similarly, in 1977, Natomas sold a $30 million Eurobond even though it could have obtained funds at a lower cost by drawing on its existing revolving credit lines or by selling commercial paper. The key purpose of this Euroissue was to introduce the company's name to international investors as part of its global financial strategy.[6] Each lead underwriter was hand-picked by the company, with an eye to its overall financing needs. For example, a Swiss bank was picked as the issue's lead manager because Natomas felt that European banks, and Swiss banks in particular, have greater placing power with long-term investors than do U.S. underwriters operating in Europe. In addition, these European institutions were expected to serve Natomas as a source of market and economic information to counterbalance the input it already was receiving from U.S. banks.

This latter benefit of dealing with several financial institutions at once has been described by Richard K. Goeltz, Vice President, Finance, of Joseph E. Seagram & Sons, Inc., as follows:

[B]y being a major client at a number of high quality firms rather than only one, we are able to avail ourselves of the knowledge, ingenuity and expertise of different groups of skilled professionals. No one bank is omniscient and omnipotent; we must be able to draw on the resources of many organizations.[7]

The threat of domestic credit controls has accelerated the trend toward global diversification of financing sources. For example, after the Federal Reserve Board tightened credit in October 1979 and proposed a voluntary ceiling on loan growth in March 1980, many anxious corporate treasurers feared that mandatory credit controls might be close at hand. So, large numbers of them arranged to borrow abroad, far from the Fed's reach.

Monsanto, for example, negotiated a short-term credit line of nearly $200 million with eight European banks. Dow Chemical had about $1 billion in unused credit lines with foreign banks. Ford Motor opened a $1 billion credit line with a group of banks, including some European banks. In the event that the United States imposed formal controls, these firms planned to tap their foreign credit lines and repatriate the funds back home. According to John Rolls, Monsanto's treasurer, "To us, this credit line is insurance. We probably won't need it, but it's a good idea to have it."[8]

Similarly, Japanese firms such as Pioneer are issuing securities in the United States. By familiarizing American investors with their names, they can more easily raise funds in the United States in the future as a safeguard against one of the periodic credit controls imposed by the Bank of Japan, the Japanese central bank.

Excess Borrowing. Most firms have lines of credit with a number of banks that give them the right to borrow up to an agreed-upon credit limit. Unused balances carry a commitment fee, normally on the order of 0.5% per annum. In order not to tie up funds

[6]See "Diversifying Sources of Financing," *Business International Money Report,* September 23, 1977, pp. 297–298.

[7]Richard Karl Goeltz, "Citibank Treasurers' Conference," June 28, 1984, p. 5. This is the text of a speech by Mr. Goeltz.

[8]Anthony Ramirez, "Dodging the Fed," *The Wall Street Journal,* April 17, 1980, p. 44.

unnecessarily, most banks periodically review each credit limit to see whether the customer's account activity level justifies that credit line. Some firms are willing to borrow funds that they do not require (and then place them on deposit) in order to maintain their credit limit in the event of a tight money situation. In effect, they are buying insurance against the possibility of being squeezed out of the money market. One measure of the cost of this policy is the difference between the borrowing rate and the deposit rate, multiplied by the average amount of borrowed funds placed on deposit.

■ 24.3 ■
ESTABLISHING A WORLDWIDE CAPITAL STRUCTURE

In the two previous sections, we examined various motivations for using particular types of financing. However, while knowledge of the costs and benefits of each individual source of funds is helpful, it is not sufficient to establish an optimal global financial plan. This plan requires consideration not only of the component costs of capital, but also of how the use of one source affects the cost and availability of other sources. A firm that uses too much debt might find the cost of equity (and new-debt) financing prohibitive. The capital structure problem for the multinational enterprise, therefore, is to determine the mix of debt and equity for the parent entity and for all consolidated and unconsolidated subsidiaries that maximizes shareholder wealth.

The focus is on the consolidated, *worldwide financial structure* because suppliers of capital to a multinational firm are assumed to associate the risk of default with the MNC's worldwide debt ratio. This association stems from the view that bankruptcy or other forms of financial distress in an overseas subsidiary can seriously impair the parent company's ability to operate domestically. Any deviations from the MNC's target capital structure will cause adjustments in the mix of debt and equity used to finance future investments.

Another factor that may be relevant in establishing a worldwide debt ratio is the empirical evidence that earnings variability appears to be a decreasing function of foreign-source earnings. Because the risk of bankruptcy for a firm is dependent on its total earnings variability, the earnings diversification provided by its foreign operations may enable the multinational firm to leverage itself more highly than can a purely domestic corporation, without increasing its default risk.

Foreign Subsidiary Capital Structure

Once a decision has been made regarding the appropriate mix of debt and equity for the entire corporation, questions about individual operations can be raised. How should MNCs arrange the capital structures of their foreign affiliates? And what factors are relevant in making this decision? Specifically, the problem is whether *foreign subsidiary capital structures* should

- Conform to the capital structure of the parent company
- Reflect the capitalization norms in each foreign country
- Vary to take advantage of opportunities to minimize the MNC's cost of capital

Disregarding public and government relations and legal requirements for the moment, the parent company could finance its foreign affiliates by raising funds in its own country and investing these funds as equity. The overseas operations would then have a zero debt ratio (debt/total assets). Alternatively, the parent could hold only one dollar of share capital in each affiliate and require all to borrow on their own, with or without guarantees; in this case, affiliate debt ratios would approach 100%. Or the parent can itself borrow and relend the monies as intracorporate advances. Here again, the affiliates' debt ratios would be close to 100%. In all these cases, the total amount of borrowing and the debt/equity mix of the consolidated corporation are identical. Thus, the question of an optimal capital structure for a foreign affiliate is completely distinct from the corporation's overall debt/equity ratio.

Moreover, any accounting rendition of a separate capital structure for the subsidiary is wholly illusory *unless* the parent is willing to allow its affiliate to default on its debt.[9] As long as the rest of the MNC group has a legal or moral obligation or sound business reasons for preventing the affiliate from defaulting, the individual unit has no independent capital structure. Rather, its true debt/equity ratio is equal to that of the consolidated group. Exhibits 24.3 and 24.4 show the stated and the true debt-to-equity ratios for a subsidiary and its parent for four separate cases. In cases I, II, and III, the parent borrows $100 to invest in a foreign subsidiary, in varying portions of debt and equity. In case IV, the subsidiary borrows the $100 directly from the bank. Depending on what the parent calls its investment, the subsidiary's debt-to-equity ratio can vary from zero to infinity. Despite this variation, the consolidated balance sheet shows a debt-to-equity ratio following the foreign investment of 4:7 regardless of how the investment is financed and what it is called.

Exhibit 24.5 shows that the financing mechanism does affect the pattern of returns, whether they are called dividends or interest and principal payments. It also determines the initial recipient of the cash flows. Are the cash flows from the foreign unit paid directly to the outside investor (the bank) or are they first paid to the parent, which then turns around and repays the bank?

■ **EXHIBIT 24.3** Subsidiary Capital Structure

I.	**100% Parent Financed**			**II.**	**100% Parent Financed**	
	$100	D = $50			$100	D = $100
		E = 50				E = 0
	D/E = 1:1				D/E = Infinity	
III.	**100% Parent Financed**			**IV.**	**100% Bank Financed**	
	$100	D = $ 0			$100	D = $100
		E = 100				E = 0
	D/E = 0				D/E = Infinity	

[9]See, for example, Michael Adler, "The Cost of Capital and Valuation of a Two-Country Firm," *Journal of Finance,* March 1974, pp. 119–132; and Alan C. Shapiro, "Financial Structure and Cost of Capital in the Multinational Corporation," *Journal of Financial and Quantitative Analysis,* June 1978, pp. 211–226.

■ **EXHIBIT 24.4** Consolidated Parent Balance Sheet

Before Foreign Investment

$1,000	D = $300
	E = 700

D/E = 3:7

After Foreign Investment

Cases I, II, and III **Parent Financed with** **100% Bank Debt**			**Case IV** **Subsidiary Financed with** **100% Bank Debt**		
Domestic	$1,000	D = $400	Domestic	$1000	D = $400
Foreign	100	E = 700	Foreign	100	E = 700
	D/E = 4:7			D/E = 4:7	

The point of this exercise is to show that unlike the case for the corporation as a whole, an affiliate's degree of leverage does not determine its financial risk. Therefore, the first two options—having affiliate financial structures conform to parent or local norms—are unrelated to shareholder wealth maximization.

The irrelevance of subsidiary financial structures seems to be recognized by multinationals. In a 1979 survey by Business International of eight U.S.-based MNCs, most of the firms expressed little concern with the debt/equity mixes of their foreign affiliates.[10]

■ **EXHIBIT 24.5** Subsidiary Capital Structure Depends on What Its Funds Are Called

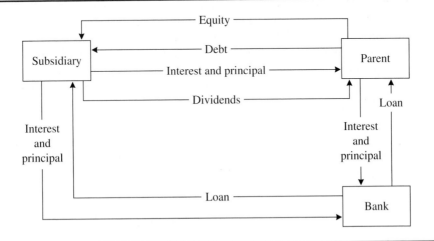

---

[10]"Policies of MNCs on Debt/Equity Mix," *Business International Money Report*, September 21, 1979, pp. 319–320.

(Admittedly, for most of the firms interviewed, the debt ratios of affiliates had not significantly raised the MNCs' consolidated indebtedness.) Their primary focus was on the worldwide, rather than individual, capital structure. The third option of varying affiliate financial structures to take advantage of local financing opportunities appears to be the appropriate choice. Thus, within the constraints set by foreign statutory or minimum equity requirements, the need to appear to be a responsible and good guest, and the requirements of a worldwide financial structure, a multinational corporation should finance its affiliates to minimize its incremental average cost of capital.

A subsidiary with a capital structure similar to its parent may forgo profitable opportunities to lower its cost of funds. For example, rigid adherence to a fixed debt/equity ratio may not allow a subsidiary to take advantage of government-subsidized debt or low-cost loans from international agencies. Furthermore, it may be worthwhile to raise funds locally if the country is politically risky. In the event the affiliate is expropriated, for instance, it would default on all loans from local financial institutions. Similarly, borrowing funds locally will decrease the company's vulnerability to exchange controls. Local currency (LC) profits can be used to service its LC debt. On the other hand, forcing a subsidiary to borrow funds locally to meet parent norms may be quite expensive in a country with a high-cost capital market or if the subsidiary is in a tax-loss-carryforward position. In the latter case, since the subsidiary can't realize the tax benefits of the interest write-off, the parent should make an equity injection financed by borrowed funds. In this way, the interest deduction need not be sacrificed.

Leverage and the Tax Reform Act of 1986. The choice of where to borrow to finance foreign operations has become more complicated with passage of the Tax Reform Act of 1986 because the distribution of debt between U.S. parents and their foreign subsidiaries affects the use of foreign tax credits. As we saw in Chapter 21, the Tax Reform Act has put many U.S.-based MNCs in a position of excess foreign tax credits. One way to use up these FTCs is to push expenses overseas—and thus lower overseas profits—by increasing the leverage of foreign subsidiaries. In the aforementioned example, the U.S. parent may have one of its taxpaying foreign units borrow funds and use them to pay a dividend to the parent. The parent can then turn around and invest these funds as equity in the nontaxpaying subsidiary. In this way, the worldwide corporation can reduce its taxes without being subject to the constraints imposed by the Tax Reform Act.

Leasing and the Tax Reform Act of 1986. As an alternative to increasing the debt of foreign subsidiaries, U.S. multinationals could expand their use of leasing in the United States. Although leasing an asset is economically equivalent to using borrowed funds to purchase the asset, the international tax consequences differ. Prior to 1986, U.S. multinationals counted virtually all their interest expense as a fully deductible U.S. expense. Under the new law, firms must allocate interest expense on general borrowings to match the location of their assets, even if all the interest is paid in the United States. This allocation has the effect of reducing the amount of interest expense that can be written off against U.S. income. Rental expense, on the other hand, can be allocated to the location of the leased property. Lease payments on equipment located in the United States, therefore, can be fully deducted.

At the same time, leasing equipment to be used in the United States, instead of borrowing to finance it, increases reported foreign income (since there is less interest expense to allocate against foreign income). The effect of leasing, therefore, is to increase the allowable foreign tax credit to offset U.S. taxes owed on foreign source income, thereby providing another tax advantage of leasing for firms that owe U.S. tax on their foreign source income.

Cost Minimizing Approach to Global Capital Structure. The cost-minimizing approach to determining foreign affiliate capital structures would be to allow subsidiaries with access to low-cost capital markets to exceed the parent company capitalization norm, while subsidiaries in higher-capital-cost nations would have lower target debt ratios. These costs must be figured on an after-tax basis, taking into account the company's worldwide tax position.

A counterargument is that a subsidiary's financial structure should conform to local norms.[11] Then because German and Japanese firms are more highly leveraged than, say, companies in the United States and France, the Japanese and German subsidiaries of a U.S. firm should have much higher debt/equity ratios than the U.S. parent or a French subsidiary. The problem with this argument, though, is that it ignores the strong linkage between U.S.-based multinationals and the U.S. capital market. Because most of their stock is owned and traded in the United States, it follows that the firms' target debt/equity ratios are dependent on U.S. shareholders' risk perceptions. Similar arguments hold for multinationals not based in the United States. Furthermore, the level of foreign debt/equity ratios is usually determined by institutional factors that have no bearing on foreign-based multinationals. For example, Japanese and German banks own much of the equity as well as the debt issues of local corporations. Combining the functions of stockholder and lender may reduce the perceived risk of default on loans to captive corporations and increase the desirability of substantial leverage. These institutional considerations would not apply to a wholly owned subsidiary. However, a joint venture with a corporation tied to the local banking system may enable an MNC to lower its local cost of capital by leveraging itself—without a proportional increase in risk—to a degree that would be impossible otherwise.

The basic hypothesis proposed in this section is that a subsidiary's capital structure is relevant only insofar as it affects the parent's consolidated worldwide debt ratio. Nonetheless, some companies have a general policy of "every tub on its own bottom." Foreign units are expected to be financially independent following the parent's initial investment. The rationale for this policy is to "avoid giving management a crutch." By forcing foreign affiliates to stand on their own feet, affiliate managers will presumably be working harder to improve local operations, thereby generating the internal cash flow that will help replace parent financing. Moreover, the local financial institutions will have a greater incentive to monitor the local subsidiary's performance because they can no longer look to the parent company to bail them out if their loans go sour. But companies that expect their subsidiaries to borrow locally had better be prepared to provide enough initial equity capital or subordinated loans. In addition, local suppliers and customers are likely to shy away from a new

---

[11]See, for example, Arthur I. Stonehill and Thomas Stitzel, "Financial Structure and Multinational Corporations," *California Management Review,* Fall 1969, pp. 91–96.

subsidiary operating on a shoestring if that subsidiary is not receiving financial backing from its parent. The foreign subsidiary may have to show its balance sheet to local trade creditors, distributors, and other stakeholders. Having a balance sheet that shows more equity demonstrates that the unit has greater staying power.

It also takes more staff time to manage a highly leveraged subsidiary in countries like Brazil and Mexico where government controls and high inflation make local funds scarce. One treasury manager complained, "We spend 75%–80% of management's time trying to figure out how to finance the company. Running around chasing our tails instead of attending to our basic business—getting production costs lower, sales up, and making the product better."[12]

Parent Company Guarantees and Consolidation

Multinational firms are sometimes reluctant to guarantee explicitly the debt of their subsidiaries, even when a more advantageous interest rate can be negotiated for several reasons.

1. Some companies argue that their affiliates should be able to stand alone. In the case of a joint venture when the other partner is unable or unwilling to provide a valuable counterguarantee, a penalty rate of interest may be accepted to avoid overfinancing other shareholders. A cost is incurred to maintain a principle and avoid a dangerous precedent.
2. The protection against expropriation provided by an affiliate's borrowing may be lost if the parent guarantees those debts.
3. Many firms believe lenders should be reasonable, requesting a guarantee when the affiliate is operating at a loss or with a debt-heavy capital structure and lending without one when the borrower itself is creditworthy.
4. Providing explicit support for one operation can lead to lenders' demands in other cases.
5. Many firms assume that nonguaranteed debt would not be included in the parent company's worldwide debt ratio, whereas guaranteed debt as a contingent liability would affect the parent's debt-raising capacity.

The issue of whether or not to issue guarantees may be more important in theory than in fact. It is likely that a parent company would keep lenders whole if a subsidiary defaulted, even if it had no legal obligation to do so. In a 1985 survey by Business International, most treasurers said that they would always assume the debt of a failed overseas subsidiary even if the parent had not guaranteed it.[13] This attitude reflects pragmatic business reasons, not benevolence or a sense of morality. A multinational firm relies on financial institutions in many countries. In a real sense, it could rarely, if ever, function without them. Any action, such as allowing an affiliate to become bankrupt, that

---

[12]"Determining Overseas Debt/Equity Ratios," *Business International Money Report,* January 27, 1986, p. 26.

[13]"Determining Overseas Debt/Equity Ratios," p. 26.

jeopardizes these relations has an extremely high cost. Multinational firms also may distinguish between international and local banks. The former could be kept whole and the latter directed to their own government for repayment if an affiliate were expropriated and were unable to pay its debts.

If an explicit guarantee will reduce a subsidiary's borrowing costs, it will usually be in the parent's best interest to give this support, provided there is an actual commitment to satisfy the subsidiary's obligations. It is likely that the market has already incorporated this practical commitment in its estimate of the parent's worldwide debt capacity. An overseas creditor, on the other hand, may not be as certain regarding the firm's intentions. The fact that the parent doesn't guarantee its subsidiaries' debt may then convey some information (i.e., commitment to subsidiary debt is not that strong).

In at least two cases, Raytheon in Sicily (1968) and Freeport Sulphur in Cuba (1960), firms did allow their foreign affiliates to go bankrupt. However, the publicity surrounding these events makes it clear how unusual they were. Moreover, a parent that once walks away from the debt of an affiliate will be unable to again borrow overseas unless it either guarantees its affiliates' debts or pays a higher interest rate to compensate lenders for the possibility of default.

The U.S. Internal Revenue Service argues that by guaranteeing foreign affiliates' debts, a U.S. corporation is providing a valuable service for which it should be compensated. The IRS, therefore, imputes income to the guarantor and levies a tax. This additional tax cost should be incorporated in the determination of whether the parent should guarantee a foreign subsidiary's borrowing.

Another factor may also influence corporate policy regarding parent guarantees. When a firm provides an affiliate with a loan guarantee, "you lose the bank as your partner in controls."[14] Since it will be repaid regardless of the affiliate's profitability, the bank will have less incentive to monitor the affiliate's activities. On the other hand, in the absence of a guarantee, the local bank will probably insist on inserting various restrictive covenants in its loan agreement with the subsidiary. The parent can prevent these restrictive covenants and the resulting loss in operational and financial flexibility by supplying loan guarantees. The relative magnitudes of these two costs will help determine whether the parent guarantees its affiliates' debts.

Related to the issue of parent-guaranteed debt is the belief among some firms that do not consolidate their foreign affiliates that unconsolidated (and nonguaranteed) overseas debt need not affect the MNC's debt ratio. But unless investors and analysts can be fooled permanently, unconsolidated overseas leveraging will not allow a firm to lower its cost of capital below the cost of capital for an identical firm that consolidates its foreign affiliates. Any overseas debt offering that is large enough to materially affect an MNC's degree of leverage would quickly come to the attention of financial analysts.

Some evidence of this form of market efficiency was provided by bond raters at Moody's and at Standard and Poor's. Individuals from both agencies said that they would closely

---

[14]Quote in Sidney M. Robbins and Robert B. Stobaugh, *Money in the Multinational Enterprise* (New York: Basic Books, 1973), p. 67.

examine situations where nonguaranteed debt issued by unconsolidated foreign affiliates would noticeably affect a firm's worldwide debt:equity ratio. In addition, parent-company-guaranteed debt is included in bond rater analyses of a firm's contingent liabilities, whether this debt is consolidated or not. Thus, it appears that the growing financial sophistication of MNCs has been paralleled by increased sophistication among rating agencies and investors.

Joint Ventures

Because many MNCs participate in joint ventures, either by choice or necessity, establishing an appropriate financing mix for this form of investment is an important consideration. The previous assumption that affiliate debt is equivalent to parent debt in terms of its impact on perceived default risk may no longer be valid. In countries such as Japan and Germany, increased leverage will not necessarily lead to increased financial risks, due to the close relationship between the local banks and corporations. Thus, debt raised by a joint venture in Japan, for example, may not be equivalent to parent-raised debt in terms of its impact on default risk. The assessment of the effects of leverage in a joint venture requires a qualitative analysis of the partner's ties with the local financial community, particularly with the local banks.

Unless the joint venture can be isolated from its partners' operations, there are likely to be some significant conflicts associated with this form of ownership. Transfer pricing, setting royalty and licensing fees, and allocating production and markets among plants are just some of the areas in which each owner has an incentive to engage in activities that will harm its partners. These conflicts explain why bringing in outside equity investors is generally such an unstable form of external financing.

Because of their lack of complete control over a joint venture's decisions and its profits, most MNCs will, at most, guarantee joint venture loans in proportion to their share of ownership. But where the MNC is substantially stronger financially than its partner, the MNC may wind up implicitly guaranteeing its weaker partner's share of any joint-venture borrowings, as well as its own. In this case, it makes sense to push for as large an equity base as possible; the weaker partner's share of the borrowings is then supported by its larger equity investment.

■ 24.4 ■
ILLUSTRATION: NESTLE

Nestle, the $17 billion Swiss foods conglomerate, is about as multinational as a company can be. About 98% of its sales take place overseas, and the group's diversified operations span 150 countries. Nestle's numerous (and generally wholly owned) subsidiaries are operationally decentralized. However, finances are centralized in Vevey, Switzerland. Staffed by just 12 people, the finance department makes all subsidiary funding decisions, manages the resulting currency exposures, determines subsidiary dividend amounts, sets the worldwide debt/equity structure, and evaluates subsidiary performance.

Nestle's centralized finance function plays the pivotal role in the firm's intricate web of subsidiary-to-headquarters profit remittances and headquarters-to-subsidiary investment flows. Profits and excess cash are collected by the treasury department in Vevey and then channeled back to overseas subsidiaries in the form of equity and debt investments. Nestle considers this approach to be the best possible investment for the group's wealth.

When a subsidiary is first established, its fixed assets—which form about half of the total investment—are financed by the Nestle group, generally with equity. Later on, the group may supply long-term debt as needed to support operations. The local subsidiary manager handles all the marketing and production decisions, but decisions regarding long-term debt and equity funding are managed solely by Vevey headquarters.

The other half of the investment—working capital—is then acquired locally, usually via bank credit or commercial paper. However, Nestle varies this general approach to suit each country. In certain countries—those that permit free transfers of funds—Nestle finances part of the working capital from Vevey instead of using local bank credits.

Central control over affiliate capital structures is facilitated by the policy of forcing local managers to dividend out almost 100% of their profits to Switzerland. The particular capital structure chosen for an affiliate depends on various considerations, including taxes, political risk, and currency risk.

To ensure that it borrows at the lowest possible cost, Nestle takes considerable care to structure its capital base to keep a top credit rating. The desire for a low-risk capital structure is also consistent with Nestle's business strategy. According to Senior Vice President, Finance, Daniel Regolatti, "Our basic strategy is that we are an industrial company. We have a lot of risks in a lot of countries, so we should not add high financial risks."[15]

■ 24.5 ■
SUMMARY AND CONCLUSIONS

This chapter has attempted to provide a framework for multinational firms to use in arranging their global financing. The primary emphasis is on taking advantage of distortions resulting from government intervention in financial markets or from differential national tax laws, either of which may cause differences to exist in the risk-adjusted after-tax costs of different sources and types of funds. Secondarily, this framework includes the possibility of reducing various operating risks resulting from political or economic factors. Last, it seeks to determine appropriate parent, affiliate, and worldwide capital structures—taking into account the unique attributes of being a multinational corporation.

■ QUESTIONS ■

1. What are the likely effects of the Japanese government's relaxing its restrictions on the ability of Japanese firms to raise funds in the Euromarkets on

   a. Japanese firms?

---

[15]"The Nestle Approach to Capital Markets and Innovation," *Business International Money Report,* October 27, 1986, p. 337.

    b. Their foreign competitors?

    c. Japanese investors who can now purchase Eurosecurities?

2. Low-cost export financing is often a bad sign. Explain.

3. Why do governments provide subsidized financing for some investments?

4. How can reducing operating risks increase corporate profitability?

5. Why have Eurobonds traditionally yielded less than comparable domestic issues?

6. What are some of the advantages and disadvantages of having highly leveraged foreign subsidiaries?

7. How has the Tax Reform Act of 1986 affected the capital structure choice for foreign subsidiaries?

8. What financing problems might be associated with joint ventures?

9. Under what circumstances does it make sense for a company to not guarantee the debt of its foreign affiliates?

10. How does government intervention in financial markets affect the choice of financing?

11. How can financial strategy be used to reduce political risk?

12. In order to develop large agricultural estates, the Republic of Coconutland offers the following financing deal: If an investor agrees to purchase a plantation and put up half the cost in U.S. dollars, the government will make a 20-year, zero-interest loan of U.S. dollars to cover the other half.

    a. What risks does the scheme entail?

    b. How can an investor use financing to reduce these risks?

13. Comment on the following statement. "Interest costs affect your ability to price competitively. If you're competing against a German or Japanese company that's paying 4% locally, and you're paying 9%, that's as if you had expensive labor. You can't be a low-cost producer that way."

■ PROBLEMS ■

1. Suppose that the cost of borrowing restricted French francs is 7% annually, whereas the market rate for these funds is 12%. If a firm can borrow FF 10 million of restricted funds, how much will it save annually in before-tax franc interest expense?

2. Suppose that one of the inducements provided by Taiwan to woo Xidex into setting up a local production facility is a ten-year, $12.5 million loan at 8% interest. The principal is to be repaid at the end of the tenth year. The market interest rate on such a loan is about 15%. With a marginal tax rate of 40%, how much is this loan worth to Xidex?

3. Compania Troquelados ARDA is a medium-sized Mexico City auto parts maker. It is trying to decide whether to borrow dollars at 9% or Mexican pesos at 75%. What advice would you give it? What information would you need before you gave the advice?

4. Boeing Commercial Airplane Co. manufactures all its planes in the United States and prices them in dollars, even the 50% of its sales destined for overseas markets. What financing strategy would you recommend for Boeing? What data do you need?

5. All-Nippon Airways, a Japanese airline, flies exclusively within Japan. It is looking to finance a recent purchase of Boeing 737s. The director of finance for All-Nippon is attracted to dollar financing because he expects the yen to keep appreciating against the dollar. What is your advice to him?

6. United Airlines recently inaugurated service to Japan and now wants to finance the purchase of Boeing 747s to service that route. The CFO for United is attracted to yen financing because the interest rate on yen is 300 basis points lower than the dollar interest rate. Although he doesn't expect this interest differential to be offset by yen appreciation over the ten-year life of the loan, he would like an independent opinion before issuing yen debt.

    a. What are the key questions you would ask in responding to UAL's CFO?

    b. Can you think of any other reason for using yen debt?

    c. What would you advise him to do, given his likely responses to your questions and your answer to part b?

7. The CFO of Eastman Kodak is thinking of borrowing Japanese yen because of their low interest rate, currently at 4.5%. The current interest rate on U.S. dollars is 9%. What is your advice to the CFO?

8. Rohm & Haas, a Philadelphia-based specialty chemicals company, traditionally finances its Brazilian operations from outside that country because it's "too expensive" to borrow local currency in Brazil. Brazilian interest rates vary from 50% to over 100%. Rohm & Haas is now thinking of switching to cruzeiro financing because of a pending cruzeiro devaluation. Assess Rohm & Haas's financing strategy.

9. Nord Resources's Ramu River property in Papua New Guinea contains one of the world's largest deposits of cobalt and chrome outside of the Soviet Union and South Africa. The cost of developing a mine on this property is estimated to be around $150 million.

    a. Describe three major risks in undertaking this project.

    b. How can Nord structure its financing so as to reduce these risks?

    c. How can Nord use financing to add value to this project?

10. United Carbon wants to take advantage of the current low interest rate, 9.5%, that the Japanese investment banks are offering on Eurodollar bonds. United would like to finance its $150 million borrowing needs with them rather than in the United States, where its borrowing rate is 12%. However, the company can borrow only at a ten-year maturity in the Eurodollar market, whereas the money is needed for 20 years. Thus, if United accepts the Japanese offer, in ten years it will have to roll over its borrowing for another ten years. Should United Carbon issue the Eurobonds? Assume that all principal payments are made at maturity. Ignore taxes. (*Hint*: What interest rate on a ten-year loan would have to prevail at the end of ten years in order to make the Japanese deal unattractive? How likely is it that interest rates will reach that level?)

■ BIBLIOGRAPHY ■

Adler, Michael. "The Cost of Capital and Valuation of a Two-Country Firm." *Journal of Finance,* March 1974, pp. 119–132.

Cornell, Bradford, and Alan C. Shapiro. "Corporate Stakeholders and Corporate Finance." *Financial Management,* Spring 1987, pp. 5–14.

Goeltz, Richard Karl. "The Corporate Borrower and the International Capital Markets." Manuscript dated March 6, 1984, p.5.

Hodder, James E., and Lemma W. Senbet. "International Capital Structure Equilibrium." *Journal of Finance*, forthcoming.

Lessard, Donald R., and Alan C. Shapiro. "Guidelines for Global Financing Choices." *Midland Corporate Finance Journal,* Winter 1984, pp. 68–80.

Shapiro, Alan C. "Financial Structure and Cost of Capital in the Multinational Corporation." *Journal of Financial and Quantitative Analysis,* June 1978, pp. 211–226.

Stobaugh, Robert B. "Financing Foreign Subsidiaries of U.S.-Controlled Multinational Enterprises," *Journal of International Business Studies,* Summer 1970, pp. 43–64.

■ PART V ■
■ Case Study ■

■ Case V.1
Multinational Manufacturing, Inc.

PART I

Multinational Manufacturing, Inc. (MMI) is a large manufacturing firm engaged in the production and sale of a widely diversified group of products in a number of countries throughout the world. Some product lines enjoy outstanding success in new fields developed on the basis of an active research and development program; other product lines, whose innovative leads have disappeared, face very severe competition.

Each domestic product line and foreign affiliate is a separate profit center. Headquarters influences these centers primarily by evaluating their managers on the basis of certain financial criteria, including return on investment, return on sales, and growth in earnings.

Division and affiliate executives are held responsible for planning and evaluating possible new projects. Each project is expected to yield at least 15%. Projects requiring an investment below $250,000 (about one-third of the projects) are approved at the division or affiliate level without formal review by headquarters management. The present cutoff rate was established three years ago as part of a formal review of capital budgeting procedures. The conclusion at that time was that the company's weighted average cost of capital was 15%, and it should be applied when calculating net present values of proposed projects. In announcing the policy, Mr. Thomas Black, Vice President-Finance, said, "It's about time that we introduced some modern management techniques in allocating our capital resources."

Now Mr. Black is concerned that the policy introduced three years ago is having some unintended consequences. Specifically, top management gets to review only obvious investment candidates. Low-risk, low-return projects and high-risk, high-return projects seem to be systematically screened out along the way. The basis for this screening is not entirely clear, but it appears to be related to the way in which managerial performance is evaluated. Local executives seem to be concerned that low-potential projects will hurt their performance appraisal, while high-potential projects can turn out poorly. The president of one foreign affiliate said privately when asked why he never submitted projects at the extremes of risk and return, "Why should I take any chances? When headquarters says it wants 15%, it means 15% and nothing less. My crystal ball isn't good enough to allow me to accurately estimate sales and costs in this country, especially when I never know what the government is going to do."

QUESTIONS: PART I

Make recommendations to Mr. Black concerning the following points:

1. Should MMI lower the hurdle rate in order to encourage the submission of more proposals, or should it drop the hurdle rate concept completely?
2. Should MMI invest in lower-return projects that are less risky and/or in high-risk projects that appear promising? What is the relevant measure of risk?
3. How should MMI factor in the additional political and economic risks it faces overseas in conducting these project analyses?

4. Why are projects at the extremes of risk and return not reaching top management for review?

5. What actions, if any, should Mr. Black take to correct the situation?

PART II

In line with this current review of capital budgeting procedures, Mr. Black is also reconsidering certain financial policies that he recently recommended to MMI's board of directors. These policies include the maintenance of a debt/total assets ratio of 35% and a dividend payout rate equal to 60% of consolidated earnings. In order to achieve these ratios for the firm overall, each affiliate has been directed to use these ratios as guidelines in planning its own capital structure and payout rate.

This directive has been controversial. The executives of several foreign affiliates have raised questions about the appropriateness of applying these guidelines at the local level. The general managers of some of the largest affiliates have been particularly vocal in their objections, stating that it simply was not possible for overall policies relative to capital structure proportions to be given much consideration in financial planning at the local level. They pointed out that differences in the economic and political environment in which the various affiliates operate are far too great to force them into a financial straitjacket designed by headquarters. In their view, they must be left free to respond to their own unique set of circumstances.

The executives of the Brazilian affiliate, for example, felt that their financing should not follow the same pattern as that of the overall firm because inflationary conditions made local borrowing especially advantageous in Brazil. Executives of other foreign affiliates stressed the need for varying capital structures in order to cope with the exchange risks posed by currency fluctuations. The general manager of the Mexican affiliate, which is owned on a 50–50 basis with local investors, has argued forcefully that, despite effective headquarters control over the policies of this operation, joint ventures such as his cannot and should not be financed in the same manner as firms wholly owned by MMI. In addition, the tax manager of MMI has expressed his concern that implementing a rigid policy of repatriating 60% of each affiliate's earnings in the form of dividends will impose substantial tax costs on MMI. Moreover, Mr. Black recently attended a seminar at which it was pointed out that overseas affiliates can sometimes be financed in such a way that their susceptibility to political and economic risks is diminished.

QUESTIONS: PART II

Make recommendations to Mr. Black concerning the policies that should be adopted as guides in planning the capital structure and dividend payout policies of foreign affiliates, taking into account the following key questions:

1. What are the pros and cons of using the following sources of funds to finance the operations of the foreign affiliates: equity funds versus loans from MMI, retained earnings of the affiliates, and outside borrowings? Consider cost, political and economic risks, and tax consequences in your answer.

2. Given these considerations, under what circumstances, if any, should the capital structure of foreign affiliates include more or less debt than the 35% considered desirable for the firm as a whole?

3. How will the resultant capital structures affect the required rates of return on affiliate projects? The actual rates of return?

4. How should MMI's dividend policy be implemented at the affiliate level?

PART VI

International Banking

◣ 25 ◥

International Banking Trends and Strategies

Whether we like it or not, the globalization of financial markets and institutions is a reality.

—E. Gerald Corrigan—
President, Federal Reserve
Bank of New York

■ The growth and increasing integration of the world economy since the end of World War II has been paralleled by expansion of global banking activities. Banks followed their customers overseas and lent to governments presiding over promising national economies. One indication of the worldwide scope of banking today is suggested by the fact that international bank loans extended by commercial banks located in major financial centers around the world have increased year after year over the past decade, reaching a total of $4.8 trillion outstanding by September 1987. Underneath the facade of unbroken growth, however, lie many divergent trends that have been profoundly influencing the direction of international banking activities over the past dozen years.

This chapter provides an overview of international banking. It focuses on recent trends in the expansion of international banking activities and the organizational forms and strategies associated with overseas bank expansion.

■ 25.1 ■
RECENT PATTERNS OF INTERNATIONAL BANKING ACTIVITIES

International banking has grown notably in both complexity and risk over the past two decades. Until recently, international banking was confined largely to providing foreign exchange and to financing specific export and import transactions through letters of credit and acceptances. This limitation is no longer the case.

International banking has grown steadily throughout the post–World War II period. Expansion of international trade in the 1950s and the effective emergence of the MNC in the 1960s sharply increased the demand for international financial services. Banks located in the traditional financial centers responded by extending loans and developing new, highly innovative financial techniques (such as the Eurocurrency markets) that laid the foundation for totally new approaches to the provision of international banking services. For many of these banks, their initial ventures overseas were defensive in nature, designed to retain the domestic business of customers who invested abroad by expanding and improving the scope of their activities abroad. In the words of an economist at Deutsche Bank, "In a global market, if you can't serve your multinational customers in all the major cities of the world, they won't need you even in their home country."[1] But it was the onset of the "energy crisis" that launched international banks into a period of phenomenal growth.

The Era of Growth

The energy crisis, brought about by the quadrupling of oil prices in late 1973, created a great need for global financial intermediation—for recycling *OPEC*'s (Organization of Petroleum Exporting Countries) surplus revenues back to deficit-plagued oil-importing countries. Without such *"petrodollar" recycling,* the balance-of-payments deficits of the oil-importing countries would not have been financed, threatening dire consequences for the entire world economy. The alternative would have entailed massive economic dislocation to speedily adapt to the changing relative price of oil.

International banks were able to recycle funds from oil-exporting to oil-importing nations because (1) they had broad experience in international lending, backed by capable staffs and worldwide facilities; and (2) they were the recipients of large shares of OPEC's surplus revenues in the form of deposits placed with them by OPEC's central bankers. These deposits rose from $16 billion in 1973 to $117 billion in 1979.

Flush with OPEC money, the banks embarked upon a rapid lending expansion, often with the active encouragement of their governments. The net claims outstanding of banks in the reporting area of the Bank for International Settlements (BIS)—which acts as the central bank for the industrial countries' central banks—increased from $155 billion at year-end 1973 to $665 billion at year-end 1979—a more than fourfold increase in loans to final borrowers in just six years.

Of this amount, $157 billion (24%) were loans to less-developed countries (LDCs) and $60 billion (9%) were loans to Communist countries. Thus, about one-third of these loans, aggregating $217 billion, were to nations that turned out to be very risky credits.

Banks located in major financial centers throughout the world participated in this expansion of international lending. The largest share of the total was booked by banks located in major European centers, particularly in London, where foreign branches of major banks throughout the world (including U.S. banks) were operating.

---

[1] Quoted in *Fortune,* February 26, 1990, p. 95.

Most of the loans being extended were denominated in U.S. dollars. The BIS data show over 82% of the total bank loans outstanding at the end of 1979 were loans denominated in dollars. DM-denominated loans represented the second largest category, at 12%.

Loans to the less-developed countries were the fastest growing category of international bank loans during the 1970s. A combination of sharply increased oil import bills and a recession in the industrial countries that cut into the LDCs' export earnings—compounded by unrealistic exchange rate policies (see the discussion in Chapter 20)—sharply raised these countries' aggregate balance-of-payments deficits from an annual average of about $7 billion in the 1970–1973 period to $21 billion in 1974 and $31 billion in 1975. The banks, replete with funds and faced with declining domestic loan demand, were willing and able to provide financing in the forms of direct government loans and development financing.

The International Banking Crisis of 1982

Bank lending to LDCs continued to grow rapidly during the early 1980s. In the summer of 1982, however, the international financial markets were shaken when a number of developing countries found themselves unable to meet payments to major banks around the world on debt amounting to several hundred billion dollars. With the onset of the debt crisis, lending to LDCs quickly dried up.

Confronted with interruptions in inflows of funds due to repayment problems on their past loans, with the drying up of new sources, and with the growing uncertainties as to the capacity of their borrowers to service their debt, the international banks pulled back sharply on their lending to LDCs. This pattern is evident in the data presented in Exhibits 25.1 to 25.3. New loans to the LDCs dropped from about $40 billion in 1981 to $20 billion in 1982 and to $12 billion in 1983. The pullback was actually much sharper than the figures indicate. A great majority of the new loans represented "involuntary" lending—loans made by banks

■ **EXHIBIT 25.1**   Total International Bank Lending, 1973–1983

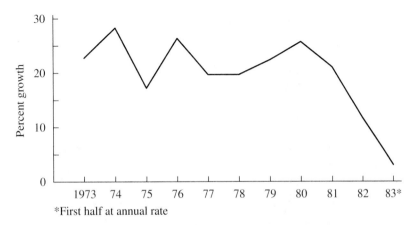

*First half at annual rate

SOURCE: *International Letter,* Federal Reserve Bank of Chicago, December 16, 1983, p. 1.

■ **EXHIBIT 25.2**   International Loans Extended by Banks in the Major Industrial Countries

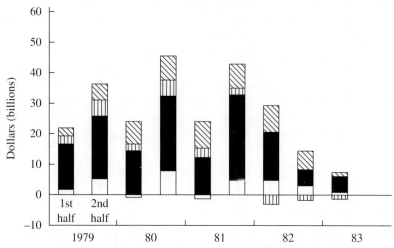

NOTE: Loans are new lending minus repayment of loans to residents of countries other than in the major industrial countries and offshore banking centers. Areas below the line indicate net repayment.

▨ Other developed countries

▥ Eastern Europe

■ Non-OPEC developing countries

▢ OPEC

SOURCE: *International Letter,* Federal Reserve Bank of Chicago, December 16, 1983, p. 2.

to facilitate both rescheduling of past loans and payment of interest by their creditors. Banks actually reduced their Latin loans starting in 1985.

The Present Climate

By late 1983, the intensity of the international debt crisis began to ease as the world's economic activities picked up—boosting the LDCs' export earnings—and as the orderly rescheduling of many overdue international loans was completed. However, although lending by international banks has picked up, it continues to be depressed compared to the high-growth period of the late 1970s. The major reason for the slowdown in international lending activity is the difficulty the LDC debtor nations are having in achieving sustained economic growth (see Exhibit 25.4).

International Risk-Based Capital Standards

One of the most important factors currently affecting international bank expansion is the new capital requirements set down under the Bank for International Settlements in Basel,

■ **EXHIBIT 25.3**   Changes in Bank Claims on Developing Countries

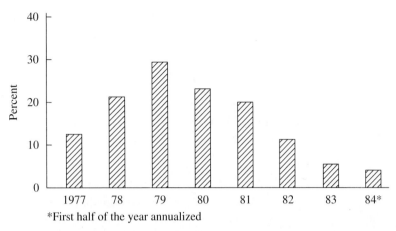

*First half of the year annualized

SOURCE: *International Letter,* Federal Reserve Bank of Chicago, November 16, 1984, p. 3.

Switzerland, and due to be in force by 1993. In late 1987, the BIS developed a risk-based framework for measuring the adequacy of *bank capital*—the equity capital and other reserves available to protect depositors against credit losses. Its objective was to strengthen the international banking system and to reduce competitive inequalities arising from differences in capital requirements across nations. In part, the BIS requirements were aimed at Japanese banks, since their reserves were so much smaller than those required by most

■ **EXHIBIT 25.4**   Dramatic Slowdown in Growth Rates of LDC Debtors

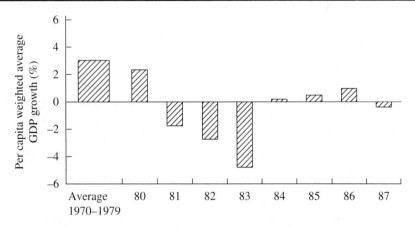

SOURCE: Data from IMF.

Western central banks. Under the Basel agreement, banks must achieve a minimum 8% risk-based ratio of capital to assets by the end of 1992.

There was disagreement in Basel on how to define bank capital, with a political compromise eventually producing a two-tier system. Core or Tier 1 capital consists of shareholders' funds and retained earnings. Supplemental or Tier 2 capital consists of internationally accepted noncommon equity items—such as hidden reserves, preferred shares, and subordinated debt—to add to core capital. However, Tier 2 capital can make up only 50% of a bank's capital. Thus, core capital must amount to at least 4% of risk-weighted assets.

To meet the capital standards, banks are focusing more on profits and less on growth. This is especially true for Japanese banks.

Japanese International Bank Expansion

Perhaps the most significant phenomenon in recent years has been the aggressive international expansion of Japanese banks. Since the mid-1980s, Japanese banks—flush with the proceeds of Japan's trading surpluses—set out to gain market share worldwide through low-cost loans.[2] With more cash than caution, Japanese banks tripled their overseas loan portfolio by 1989, accounting for 38% of international banking assets and over 12% of total lending in the United States.

However, financial adversity at home is now changing the way Japanese banks do business abroad. No longer can they push for market share at the expense of profits. Instead, Japanese banks are making fewer overseas loans, and on those fewer loans they are demanding higher returns. In part, this change is a response to financial market deregulation in Japan, which combined with the recent jump in Japanese interest rates, raised the cost of funds to the banks. The new focus on profit is also affected by the BIS capital requirements.

Like all banks, Japanese banks are trying to meet the new BIS standards. But the Tokyo stock market's collapse during 1990 has made that harder in two ways. For Japanese banks, Tier 2 capital consisted mainly of 45% of the unrealized gains on their huge equity stakes in other companies. The sharp drop in Japanese equity values means that the value of these "hidden reserves" has plunged.

The stock market fall also hurt the ability of Japanese banks to issue equity-linked securities. These issues have been crucial sources of capital, providing Japanese banks with ¥6 trillion ($40 billion) of fresh money between 1987 and 1989.

Moreover, the sharp rise in Japanese interest rates inflicted huge losses on the banks' bond portfolios and lowered their capital ratios still further. By the end of 1990, all the large Japanese banks had slipped below the 8% capital adequacy ratio that they must meet by 1993. To meet this standard, banks must either reduce lending growth, which reduces the amount of equity capital they must hold, or boost profits, which adds to equity. The possibility of a plunge in Japanese real estate prices puts further pressure on Japanese banks to shrink their lending, given their enormous real estate exposure.

---

[2]One indication of the Japanese drive for market share is reflected in the fact that overseas assets account for nearly half of the major banks' total assets, but the margins on these assets are less than one-tenth of those achieved in Japan.

In response to these pressures, Japanese banks are pulling back from "commodity" lending, the business of lending large volumes of money at low margins that fueled their expansion during the 1980s. In so doing, Japanese banks are no longer as dominant a force in international finance. For example, the number of Japanese banks leading syndicated loans in the low-margin Eurocurrency market dropped to just four out of the top 20 in the first six months of 1990. In 1989, they led seven of the top 20 syndicates. After accounting for a peak of 39.4% of all cross-border bank transactions by March 1989, Japanese banks' market share shrank in 1990 for the first time since 1984 to 36%. That compares with 12% for U.S. banks and 9.6% for German banks. The days of lending money at cheap rates just to grab market share are gone for Japanese banks.

■ 25.2 ■
ORGANIZATIONAL FORMS AND STRATEGIES IN BANK EXPANSION OVERSEAS

Decisions by banks as to how to approach foreign markets are influenced by a number of variables, such as overall financial resources, level of experience with the markets, knowledge of the markets, volume of international business, and the strategic plans of the bank—as well as the banking structure of the foreign countries in which business is done. Possible entry strategies include branching, local bank acquisitions, and representative offices. However, until the volume of business in another country is substantial, most banks will choose to rely on correspondent banking relationships to handle their needs in that country. U.S. banks also make use of domestic organizational forms for carrying on international banking activities, including Edge Act and Agreement corporations and international banking facilities. Each of these forms and strategies is described in more detail in this section.

Correspondent Banking

A *correspondent bank* is a bank located elsewhere that provides a service for another bank. U.S. banks without branches abroad have relied on their foreign correspondents to help finance their multinational corporate clients' local foreign subsidiaries that need local currency funding. Foreign correspondents can also provide other services, such as foreign exchange conversions and letters of credit.

Advantages. The major advantage of taking the correspondent route is that the cost of market entry is minimal and can be adjusted to the scale of service required in a given locale; no investment in staff or facilities is required. Yet the bank can still enjoy the benefits derived from having multiple sources of business given and received, as well as referrals of local banking opportunities. Moreover, correspondents' local knowledge and contacts may be extensive and highly useful in rendering services to the bank's clients doing business in that country.

Disadvantages. One problem with relying on correspondent banks to provide all necessary services is that correspondents may assign low priority to the needs of the U.S.

bank's customers. In addition, due to legal restrictions on traditional banking policies, certain types of credits may be difficult to arrange. Correspondents may also be reluctant to provide credits on a more regular and extensive basis.

Representative Offices

Representative offices are small offices opened up to provide advisory services to banks and customers and to expedite the services of correspondent banks. They also serve as foreign loan production offices able to negotiate various business transactions. Representative offices are not authorized to obtain and transfer deposits and do not provide on-site operating services. The assets and liabilities attributable to a representative office are booked elsewhere in the parent bank's system.

Such offices are regarded as excellent sources of economic and political intelligence on the host country and the local market. They also provide financial contacts with local institutions, commercial contacts for the bank's domestic customers, and assistance to customers in obtaining government approvals or understanding government regulations. Representative offices are especially appropriate when the expected business volume in a market is too small to justify the investment required to establish a branch, or local opportunities are uncertain, and the bank wants to learn more about the market at minimal cost before deciding whether further expansion is warranted.

Advantages.   As with exporting, representative offices provide a low-cost means of scouting out the local market. They can deliver certain services more efficiently than can a branch, especially if the required volume is small. They can help the bank attract additional business or prevent the loss of current business.

Disadvantages.   Taking the analogy to exporting further, the benefits may at times be outweighed by the inability to effect more substantial market penetration. And despite the fact that they are not capital intensive when compared with branches or local acquisitions, representative offices can be expensive nonetheless. Moreover, it is more difficult to attract qualified personnel to work in a representative office overseas than in a foreign branch.

Foreign Branches

The principal service offered by *foreign bank branches,* as with commercial banking anywhere, is the extension of credit, primarily in the form of lending money. The major portion of the lending done by branches in important international money centers such as London and Singapore involves cross-border loans, primarily because these locations are the major trading and booking centers for the Eurocurrency and Asiacurrency markets. These branches also serve as deposit-taking institutions.

Despite government regulations that have held down bank branching in foreign markets, the phenomenal growth of international banking over the past 25 years has been paralleled by an explosive expansion in overseas branching. Prior to 1960, only seven U.S. banks maintained a total of 132 branches abroad. By the end of 1979, those numbers had grown to 130 banks with just under 800 foreign branches. Major banks from Canada, Japan, and the Western European countries have also jumped on the branching bandwagon.

There are several reasons for this massive proliferation of overseas branching. First, there is the "follow the customer" rationale. Unless domestic customers that expand abroad are serviced overseas, the bank is likely to lose its clients' domestic, as well as foreign, business. Yet, it turns out that only a minor share of foreign branch business is with head-office customers. Increasingly, the business of overseas branches is with purely local, indigenous enterprises.

This trend relates to the second reason for having foreign branches: the direct contribution to bank earnings that the branches provide, quite aside from any indirect contribution associated with protecting the domestic customer base. Specifically, business with local companies has turned out to be profitable on a stand-alone basis. Moreover, foreign earnings help to diversify the bank's earnings base, thereby moderating swings in domestic earnings.

The third reason for establishing foreign branches is the access these branches provide to overseas money markets. Large international banks have a need for branches located in international money markets abroad, such as London and Singapore, to fund their international assets. At the same time, these international money markets often offer opportunities to invest funds at more attractive rates than can be done in a bank's own domestic money markets.

Advantages. In addition to the above-mentioned advantages, a bank can exert maximum control over its foreign operations through a branch. For one thing, operating and credit policies can be closely integrated. More importantly, a foreign branch network allows the parent to offer its customers—both domestic and foreign—direct and integrated service, such as the rapid collection and transfer of funds internationally in a number of countries on a consistent policy basis. Thus, Citibank may require a branch in France as much to accommodate Siemens and Sony as Coca-Cola. Foreign branches also allow a bank to better manage its customer relationships, providing services to a customer based on the value of its worldwide relationship rather than its relationship in a specific country.

Disadvantages. The cost of establishing a branch can be quite high, running to several hundred thousand dollars annually for a typical European branch, plus the fixed cost of remodeling the new facilities. An indirect cost is the possibility of alienating correspondent banks when a new branch is opened. Developing and training management to staff these branches is also difficult and expensive. On the plus side, having foreign branches offers the chance for junior officers to gain valuable overseas experience, as well as making it easier to attract good personnel eager for that type of experience.

Acquisitions

The alternative to expanding by opening new branches is to grow through acquisitions. This approach is followed by most foreign banks trying to penetrate the U.S. market.

Advantages. Acquiring a local bank has two main advantages. First, buying an existing retail bank will afford immediate access to the local deposit market, eliminating the problem of funding local loans. Second, the existing management will have an established network of local contacts and clients that would be difficult (if not impossible) to duplicate.

Disadvantages.   Despite these advantages, the history of bank acquisitions abroad is littered with examples of ill-fated investments—particularly in the United States. The acquisition by Britain's Midland Bank of a 57% interest in Crocker National, a California bank, must rank as one of the most expensive entrance tickets to a market; Midland's stake, which cost it $820 million in 1981, was worth about $300 million in early 1985. At that time, Midland agreed to buy the remaining 43% of Crocker for about $250 million. In the interim, however, Crocker's continued troubles (it lost $325 million in 1984 alone) forced Midland to invest an additional $250 million in Crocker at the end of 1983 and to lend it $125 million more. In 1986, Midland sold Crocker to Wells Fargo. The other big British banks (National Westminster, Lloyds, and Barclays) have also had their share of troubles in the United States.

These troubles are not confined to British banks entering the U.S. market. In August 1983, Bank of America paid $147 million for Banco Internacional in Argentina—just before the Argentine peso dropped through the floor and the country's seemingly intractable debt problems blew up. France's Credit Lyonnais has been obliged to pump large amounts of fresh capital into its Dutch subsidiary. Sweden's Skandinaviska Enskilda Banken's 24% stake in Banque Scandinaive of Switzerland was followed by two years of large losses.

The basic problem with these troubled investments seems to be that the acquiring banks spent too much energy on making the deal, often to the exclusion of developing future strategy. The usual rationale for the acquisition—synergy—is overworked. In the case of its acquisition of Crocker, for example, Midland brought little more to the deal than new money. The absence of any other contribution by the acquirer is usually a warning sign, for if the business being acquired is healthy apart from needing more capital, why is it choosing to sacrifice its independence rather than to go to the capital markets for additional funds?

The message seems to be that banking acquisitions are expensive, highly risky, and difficult to make work effectively, especially if all the acquirer brings to the deal is money. Unfortunately, most acquirers don't bring more than money to the deal. Not surprisingly, acquirers typically lose in such deals.

Edge Act and Agreement Corporations

Edge Act and Agreement corporations are subsidiaries of U.S. banks that are permitted to carry on international banking and investment activities. The practical effect of the various restrictions they operate under is to limit Edge Act institutions to handling foreign customers and to handling the international business of domestic customers. The list of permissible international activities for an Edge Act corporation includes deposit taking from outside the United States, lending money to international businesses, and making equity investments in foreign corporations, a power denied to its U.S. parent. An Agreement corporation is functionally similar to an Edge Act corporation. Usually it is a state-chartered corporation that enters into an agreement with the Federal Reserve to limit its activities to those of an Edge Act corporation.

Edge Act corporations are physically located in the United States, usually in a state other than where the head office is located to get around the prohibition on interstate branch banking. For example, a California bank can set up an Edge Act subsidiary in New York City to compete with New York banks for corporate business related to international activities—foreign exchange trading, export and import financing, accepting deposits associated with such operations, international fund remittances, and buying and selling domestic securities for foreign customers or foreign securities for domestic customers. Since June 1979, when the Federal Reserve permitted interstate branching by Edge Act corporations, these corporations have rivaled loan production offices in giving money-center banks and major regional banks on-site access to otherwise restricted markets.

A growing share of Edge Act business involves maintaining individual accounts for U.S. citizens living abroad and foreign citizens wanting their deposits in New York, Miami, Los Angeles, or some other U.S. city. Although they don't openly acknowledge the fact, an important source of relatively low cost deposits for Edge Act corporations is in the form of "flight capital" from wealthy Central and South American depositors concerned with the lack of political stability in their own countries.

International Banking Facilities

As we saw in Chapter 22, because of the unfavorable regulatory and tax environment in the United States, many domestic banks conduct their international operations through offshore branches. Frequently, these offices are simply "shell" operations used solely for booking purposes. By using foreign offices, banks are able to avoid state and local taxes on their foreign business profits, as well as costly reserve requirements and interest rate ceilings that would apply if the deposits were placed in the United States.

As a result of these advantages, London became the center of international banking activities. In addition, the number of branches in such places as the Cayman Islands and the Bahamas has grown significantly. Late in 1981, in an attempt to attract Eurodollar business back to the United States from these offshore locations, the Federal Reserve authorized U.S. financial institutions, including U.S. branches and agencies of foreign banks, to establish *international banking facilities* (IBFs). IBFs are permitted to conduct international banking business (such as receiving foreign deposits and making foreign loans) largely exempt from domestic regulatory constraints.

IBFs are merely bookkeeping entities that represent a separate set of asset and liability accounts of their establishing offices. The only requirement to establish an IBF is that the establishing institution must give the Federal Reserve two weeks' notice. The major activities of an IBF are deposit taking and lending to statutorily defined foreign persons, subject to certain restrictions. The major restrictions are (1) engaging only in foreign deposit taking and lending, (2) a minimum transaction size of $100,000, and (3) prohibition from issuing negotiable instruments, such as certificates of deposit (CDs).

Despite these restrictions, IBFs are popular because they are accorded most of the advantages of offshore banking without the need to be physically offshore. Most important is waiver of the regulation requiring that banks keep a percentage of their deposits in noninterest-earning accounts at the Federal Reserve. In addition, deposits in IBFs are not subject to interest rate ceilings or deposit insurance assessment.

IBFs are located mainly in the major financial centers; almost half of the nearly 500 IBFs are in New York, with the remainder being primarily in California, Florida, and Illinois.

Although the geographical distribution of IBFs largely reflects the preexisting distribution of international banking business, differences in tax treatment has had some effect on the location decision. Florida, for example, exempts IBFs from state taxes and also ranks first in the number of Edge Act IBFs and second (next to New York) in the number of IBFs set up by U.S.-chartered banks.

IBFs appear to have a very high proportion of both assets and liabilities due to other banking institutions. This interbank activity reinforces the belief that IBFs are now an integral part of the Eurodollar market. As we saw in Chapter 22, a high proportion of interbank business is one of the characteristics of the Eurocurrency markets since there may be several interbank transactions between ultimate borrowers and ultimate lenders. Thus far, IBFs seem to have had the intended effect of shifting international banking business from offshore locations back to the United States; they have not expanded the total volume of international banking business.

Foreign Banks in the United States

Foreign bank activity in the United States has grown dramatically in recent years. This expansion reflects several key factors, including: (1) the rapid growth of U.S. international trade, (2) the size and importance of U.S. financial markets, (3) the growth of foreign direct investment in the United States, and (4) the role of the U.S. dollar as an international medium of exchange.

Foreign banks operating in the U.S. market typically concentrate their activities heavily on the wholesale market; they are generally not major factors in retail banking markets. In addition, most of the foreign banks that have a sizable presence in the United States are affiliated with well-known major banks abroad (for example, Barclays, Mitsubishi Bank, Swiss Bank Corporation, and Bank of Montreal).

As of year-end 1990, there were more than 250 foreign banks that had some kind of presence in the United States. In the aggregate, the assets of such foreign banks equaled an estimated $868 billion at year-end 1990 and constituted nearly 22% of total U.S. banking assets (see Exhibit 25.5). Foreign banks also account for more than 21% of all commercial and industrial loans outstanding to U.S. companies. Most of the foreign-bank expansion in the United States has been by Japanese banks (as Exhibit 25.5 shows, other foreign banks actually lost U.S. market share), which now account for almost half of the total assets and commercial loans outstanding at foreign banks in the United States. Japanese-owned banks now control about 25% of the banking market in California, largely owing to pricing so razor-thin that American banks have formally ceded certain types of lending. In certain markets, such as standby letters of credit associated with municipal bond offerings, Japanese banks now account for up to 70% of the total U.S. market.

All this is changing, however, as the push for profits over growth appears to be at an end. More stringent international capital standards and risk-based capital requirements are constraining the growth prospects of foreign and domestic banks alike. These tightened standards, added to the reduction in the value of Japanese banks' "hidden reserves," mean that Japanese banks no longer make cheap loans to corporate borrowers to build market share. And they no longer seek to issue every letter of credit written in America. These developments signal slower growth ahead for foreign banks in the United States.

■ **EXHIBIT 25.5** Foreign-Owned Bank Market Share in the United States

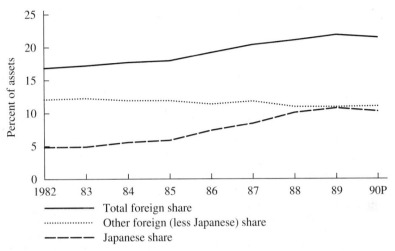

SOURCE: Gary C. Zimmerman, "Slower Growth for Foreign Banks?" *FRBSF Weekly Letter,* Federal Reserve Bank of San Francisco, January 25, 1991, p. 1.

Implications of Europe 1992 for Banks

With the completion of a single European market by the end of 1992, banks will be able to branch throughout the European Community while providing a greater range of financial services.[3] The single license will enable all banks in Europe to realize a number of cost benefits, primarily by being able to operate throughout the EC using common distribution networks, managers, and support systems. A single banking license will also lower bank costs in Europe by eliminating overlapping or conflicting standards and regulatory procedures.

Despite the potential cost advantages of establishing an EC-wide bank network, however, the empirical evidence suggests that the scope for economies of scale in banking is rather limited. Indeed, the correlation between size and profitability for the largest EC banks is either negative or minimal. Economies of scale in banking appear limited to instances where the bank's strategy involves common customers, information systems, skills, or processing facilities. One such business is credit cards, which benefits from economies of scale in issuance, centralized data processing, and design standardization.

Absent these commonalities, it appears unlikely that cross-border mergers between large institutions will create value: The cost of merging operations will probably exceed any economies of scale or scope they might achieve. Moreover, the ever-present danger is that as entry barriers start falling, new entrants might overpay in trying to get established and

---

[3]This section is based on Alan C. Shapiro, "Economic Import of Europe 1992," *Journal of Applied Corporate Finance,* Winter 1991, pp. 25–36.

gain market share. Value-creating mergers are most likely to be between relatively small local banks in countries characterized by relatively low concentration ratios.

Banks seeking to benefit from 1992 should focus on pursuing businesses in which they have a sustainable competitive advantage rather than competing directly against dominant local banks that have strongly entrenched positions in delivering basic banking services.

■ ───

ILLUSTRATION ■

Citicorp's Strategy for Europe 1992. Citicorp's EC strategy has been to utilize a cadre of experienced professionals, with expertise in a number of product categories and management techniques, to develop and deliver products in multiple markets. Although each market presents a unique set of challenges, Citicorp employees have already experienced most, if not all, of these situations elsewhere in the world and, thus, have ideas and procedures for dealing with them. Citicorp's large EC credit-card operation, for example, relies heavily on its extensive U.S. experience. It has also employed its experience in circumventing U.S. restrictions on interstate banking to build a 700-branch network throughout Europe. ■

■ 25.3 ■
VALUE CREATION IN INTERNATIONAL BANKING

This section examines some of the strategies that international banks can use to create value in their marketplace. It also examines the likely shape of future international banking competition.

Capital Adequacy

Banks with a large capital base can gain competitive advantage in underwriting securities and reducing the cost of funding loans. They can also develop more profitable business relations since companies today are paying added attention to the financial strength of the banks they deal with. Given the protracted investment of time and money in building a relationship with a bank, many chief financial officers will only deal with well-capitalized banks, whom they naturally regard as being more reliable financial partners. Such banks can also serve as a credible counterparty where customers assume bank counterparty risk, including L/Cs, swaps, and forwards.

Human Resources and the Banking Organization

International banking is a fiercely competitive business. A corrollary is that it contains no obvious, unexploited profitable niches. Any new insight in developing competitive advantage, such as a novel product or service, is quickly imitated and the extra profits competed away. The real source of competitive advantage is having the organization that can exploit information to learn and to innovate more quickly than competitors. Unfortunately, the advice to be continually innovative and creative is easier said than done.

For a bank to be a successful innovator, its front line people must have—in addition to the necessary information and skills—the authority, accountability, and motivation to use their minds to exploit that information. That means that career systems—promotions, reward, and development—have to be geared to creating and sustaining a learning environment. In the competitive world of international banking, the returns will come not by lending money but by selling companies on the belief that the bank knows how to solve their corporate finance problems and can do so quickly. That is, CFOs expect their bankers to do more than evaluate loan requests. They expect bankers to create tailor-made solutions to corporate financial problems. The demand by large companies for their banks to serve as consultants and problem solvers offers banks the opportunity to perform higher margin, fee-generating services. A bank will succeed in this world only if the people meeting the customers can identify their problems and willingly share that information with others who can develop profitable solutions to those problems.

Bank officers require a lot of training in order to offer such high quality service. This training must emphasize recognizing market opportunities, understanding the corporate environment, and clearly communicating to customers the often complex options available to solve problems.

This view of value creation in international banking suggests that bank strategies should not rely on hardware or expensive acquisitions. Rather, banks should invest in preparing and enabling people to recognize and respond to customer problems. This process is ongoing because today's creative solution to a problem—such as currency swaps—is tomorrow's commodity product. Banks must also invest in the information technology necessary to identify customer problems and create new services and products to solve them.

Information Systems

Perhaps the most pervasive challenge facing the banker in the international market is the requirement for investment in technology. The value of good information is as important today as it was in Baron Rothschild's day when he used carrier pigeons to bring him the news that Wellington had triumphed at Waterloo. Rothschild made his fortune on state-of-the-art communications. Today, bankers rely on computers and telecommunications, not carrier pigeons, but the quest is much the same—seeking tools to carry out banking faster and better than the competition.

Thus, merely to compete in complex global markets requires substantial investment in information systems. A bank can gain by being a purveyor of information transfer systems, either because it has better information to influence business decisions or because it is able to sell information to others. However, the scale of investment in technology to fully exploit the benefits of information acquisition and transfer is bound to be so great that only those banks with a firm commitment to the concept of providing a global service are likely to undertake it.

Transaction Processing Services

Companies that are globalizing their operations are demanding seamless service around the world, including a transfer agent who can pull together all transactions on a global, integrated basis. Thus, transaction processing services, such as funds movement, foreign exchange, international cash management, lockboxes, disbursements, and global custody can be very profitable bank services. However, banks must invest huge amounts of money in a state-of-the-art information system to be a credible player in these businesses. Given the significant economies of scale, market share is critical.

Instead of trying to provide global cash management services, a bank could focus on particular niches. An example would be PC-based treasury workstations that integrated foreign exchange, funds movements, and cash management, instead of mainframe-based bank systems with dumb terminals. Banks are starting to sell the same cross-border payments services to smaller companies that larger companies are now using. With an increasing number of smaller companies doing international business, this is a growing market.

Global Competition in International Banking

The 1990s promises to be an era of intensified global competition in international banking. Already, big banks are battling each other on many fronts: lending, underwriting, leasing, financial advice and risk-management services, currency and securities trading, insurance, money management, and consumer banking. Some experts predict that of some 40 to 50 banks now aspiring to be global banking powerhouses, only six to ten will actually make the grade by the end of the 1990s. Survival will demand an ability to serve the financing and risk-management needs of corporations, big and small, anywhere in the world. They must also be able to intermediate a large share of the growing cross-border flow of capital and be flexible enough to shift resources quickly to fast-growing areas and high-return businesses. At the same time, they must cope with deregulation and the industry's overcapacity—too many banks chasing too few customers.

The major competitors include European, Japanese, and American banks. Each has important competitive strengths and weaknesses.

European Banks. Some of the strongest contenders for global dominance are European banks. Their strengths include solid capital bases, strong balance sheets, and dominant shares of home markets expected to grow quickly with the advent of Europe 1992. But they have little experience with head-to-head competition. Moreover, European banking's profit sanctuaries—local markets protected from price-cutting competition by collusive arrangements—will be invaded in the post-1992 world. The resulting shakeout could leave the strongest European banks—Germany's Deutsche Bank, Union Bank of Switzerland, Credit Suisse, Swiss Bank Corporation, and England's Barclays—stronger than ever. Domestic market dominance will enable them to subsidize forays abroad, but as we saw earlier they will be able to capitalize on their financial strength only if they can bring more to the table than money. So far they have not demonstrated transferable skills that will confer on them a competitive advantage abroad.

Japanese Banks. The giant Japanese banks, backed by a strong economy and powerful corporate customers, are rich in assets. But they are poor in capital and innovativeness and are learning that size does not necessarily translate into competitive advantage. Now, as noted earlier, Japanese financial deregulation threatens many of them by narrowing spreads between borrowing and lending money.

U.S. Banks.   Most large American banks are plagued with weak capital bases and the threat of huge write-downs on their loans to LDCs, real estate developers, and leveraged buyouts. But after two decades of competing domestically and internationally against each other, as well as against insurers, investment banks, and money managers, U.S. banks have developed superior creative skills. By investing heavily in computers, information systems, and personnel training, banks such as Citicorp, Bankers Trust, and J.P. Morgan have effectively managed to institutionalize the process of innovation. Their innovativeness and advanced technology give them the edge in currency and securities trading and in designing and distributing myriad new products—capabilities widely expected to enable them to seize profitable opportunities in the deregulating European and Japanese markets.

■ 25.4 ■
SUMMARY AND CONCLUSIONS

This chapter has examined the various means and reasons whereby banks have expanded their international operations and loan portfolios in the post–World War II period. Banks have several options in their overseas expansion, including foreign branches, correspondent banking, representative offices, acquisitions of local banks, Edge Act and Agreement corporations, and international banking facilities. We have explored the advantages and disadvantages of each of these vehicles for international expansion. In general, those banks that only brought money to the international marketplace have not earned sufficient profits to justify their presence there.

The pattern of bank lending overseas has been one of rapid expansion, beginning in the early 1960s and sharply accelerating after the first OPEC oil price shock in late 1973. This expansion has been followed by a sharp contraction in international bank lending on the heels of the great debt crisis of 1982. More recently, Japanese banks greatly expanded their overseas loan portfolios but are now in the process of retrenching. One reason for this pull-back is the new international agreement setting minimum risk-based capital standards for banks that will take effect by 1993. Marginal banks will find international lending to be uneconomical under these standards.

■ QUESTIONS ■

1. What are the relative advantages and disadvantages of expanding overseas via

   a. Foreign branches?

   b. Representative offices?

   c. Acquisitions?

   d. Correspondent banking?

2. What impact will the new capital requirements have on international bank expansion? On the Eurocurrency market?

3. Japanese banks' share of total bank assets in Los Angeles jumped from 11% to 24% between 1983 and 1988.

   a. What factors might account for the large increase in Japanese bank activity in Southern California?

   b. How will the new capital requirements likely affect Japanese bank expansion in the United States?

4. According to John Reed, Citicorp's chairman, money is "information on the move." Explain what Mr. Reed might mean by this statement.

5. Why have international bank mergers generally been failures?

6. Assess the competitive strengths and weaknesses of European, U.S., and Japanese banks. How is financial deregulation in Japan and Europe likely to affect the competitive balance in international banking?

■ BIBLIOGRAPHY ■

Baughn, William H., and Donald R. Mandich, eds. *The International Banking Handbook.* Homewood, Ill.: Dow Jones-Irwin, 1983.

Chrystal, K. Alec. "International Banking Facilities." *Federal Reserve Bank of St. Louis Review,* April 1984, pp. 5–11.

International Letter. Federal Reserve Bank of Chicago, various issues.

Maidment, Paul. "A Survey of International Banking." *The Economist,* April 7, 1990, special report.

◼ 26 ◼

The International Debt Crisis and Country Risk Analysis

In 1555, the French government issued the "Grand Parti," a ten-year loan consolidating outstanding loans plus a certain amount of new money at a relatively high 16 percent; the large number of individuals who rushed to participate in the loan were disappointed when the loan defaulted two years later.

—Steven I. Davies—

◼ The big money-center banks, as well as many regional banks, rechanneled billions of petrodollars during the 1970s to less-developed countries and Communist countries. Major banks earned fat fees for arranging loans to Poland, Mexico, Brazil, and other such borrowers. The regional banks earned the spreads between what they borrowed Eurodollars at and the rates at which these loans were syndicated. These spreads were minimal, usually on the order of 0.5% to 0.75%.

All this made sense, however, only as long as banks and their depositors were willing to suspend their disbelief about the risks of international lending. By now, the risks are big and obvious. The purpose of this chapter is to explore some of the factors that led to the international debt crisis and that, more generally, determine a country's ability to repay its foreign debts. This is the subject called *country risk analysis*—clearly not a new phenomenon, according to this chapter's opening observation.

The focus here is on *country risk* from a bank's standpoint, the possibility that borrowers in a country will be unable to service or repay their debts to foreign lenders in a timely manner. The essence of country risk analysis at commercial banks, therefore, is an assessment of factors that affect the likelihood that a country, such as Mexico, will be able to generate sufficient dollars to repay foreign debts as these debts come due.

We saw in Chapter 20 that these factors are both economic and political. Among economic factors are the quality and effectiveness of a country's economic and financial management policies, the country's resource base, and the country's external financial position. Political factors include the degree of political stability of a country and the extent to which a foreign entity, such as the United States, is willing to implicitly stand behind the country's external obligations. Lending to a private-sector borrower also exposes a bank to commercial risks, in addition to country risk. Because these commercial risks are generally similar to those encountered in domestic lending, they are not treated separately.

■ 26.1 ■
THE INTERNATIONAL BANKING CRISIS OF 1982

The events that culminated in the *international banking crisis of 1982* began to gather force in 1979. Several developments set the stage. One of these was the growing trend in overseas lending to set interest rates on a floating basis—that is, at a rate that would be periodically adjusted based on the rates prevailing in the market. Floating-rate loans made borrowers vulnerable to increases in real interest rates as well as to increases in the real value of the dollar because most of these loans were in dollars. Because of high U.S. inflation and a declining dollar during most of the 1970s, borrowers were not concerned with these possibilities. Borrowers seemed to believe that inflation would bail them out by reducing the real cost of loan repayment. (Note the inconsistency of this belief with the Fisher effect.) A second development was the second jump in oil prices, in 1979. In the absence of policies that promoted rapid adjustment to this new shock, the LDCs' balance-of-payments deficits soared to $62 billion in 1980 and $67 billion in 1981 and increased the LDCs' need for external financing; the banks responded by increasing the flow of loans to LDCs to $39 billion in 1980 (from $22 billion in 1978 and $35 billion in 1979) and to $40 billion in 1981.

The catalyst of the crisis was provided by the economic policies pursued by the industrial countries in general, and by the United States in particular, in their efforts to deal with rising domestic inflation. The combination of an expansionary fiscal policy and tight monetary policy led to sharply rising real interest rates in the United States—and in the Euromarkets where the banks funded most of their international loans. The variable rate feature of the loans combined with rising indebtedness boosted the LDCs' net interest payments to banks from $11 billion in 1978 to $44 billion in 1982. Furthermore, the dollar's sharp rise in the early 1980s increased the real cost to the borrowers of meeting their debt payments.

The final element setting the stage for the crisis was the onset of a recession in industrial countries. The recession reduced the demand for the LDCs' products and, thus, the export earnings needed to service their bank debt. The interest payments/export ratio reached 50% for some of these countries in 1982. This ratio meant that more than half of these countries' exports were needed to maintain up-to-date interest payments, leaving less than half of the export earnings to finance essential imports and to repay principal on their bank loans. These trends made the LDCs highly vulnerable.

Onset of the Crisis

The first major blow to the international banking system came in August 1982, when Mexico announced that it was unable to meet its regularly scheduled payments to international creditors. Shortly thereafter, Brazil and Argentina—the second- and third-largest debtor nations—found themselves in a similar situation. By the spring of 1983, about 25 LDCs—accounting for two-thirds of the international banks' claims on this group of countries—were unable to meet their debt payments as scheduled and had entered into loan-rescheduling negotiations with the creditor banks.

Compounding the problems for the international banks was a sudden drying up of funds from OPEC. A worldwide recession that reduced the demand for oil put downward pressure on oil prices and on OPEC's revenues. In 1980, OPEC contributed about $42 billion to the loanable funds of the BIS-reporting banks. By 1982, the flow had reversed, as OPEC nations became a net drain of $26 billion in funds. At the same time, banks cut back sharply on their lending to LDCs.

The Baker Plan

In October 1985, U.S. Treasury Secretary (now Secretary of State) James Baker called on 15 principal middle-income debtor LDCs—the *"Baker 15 countries"*—to undertake growth-oriented structural reforms that would be supported by increased financing from the World Bank, continued modest lending from commercial banks, and a pledge by industrial nations to open their markets to LDC exports. The goal of the *Baker Plan* was to buttress LDC economic growth, making these countries more desirable borrowers and restoring their access to international capital markets.

By 1991, achievement stands far short of these objectives. Most of the Baker 15 have lagged in delivering on promised policy changes and economic performance. This recognition has dimmed assessments of the debtors' prospects. Instead of getting their economic house in order, many of the LDCs—feeling they had the big banks on the hook—sought to force the banks to make more and more lending concessions. The implied threat was that the banks would otherwise be forced to take large write-offs on their existing loans.

In May 1987, Citicorp's new chairman, John Reed, threw down the gauntlet to big debtor countries by adding $3 billion to the bank's loan-loss reserves. Citicorp's action was quickly followed by large additions to loss reserves by most other big U.S. and British banks. The banks who boosted their loan-loss reserves have become tougher negotiators, arguing against easing further the terms for developing countries' debt settlements. The decisions of these banks to boost their reserves—plus the announcement by some of their intention, one way or another, to dispose of a portion of their existing LDC loans—have precipitated fresh questioning of the LDC debt strategy, in particular of the Baker initiative. The problem, however, is not with the Baker initiative, but rather with its implementation. By adding to their loan-loss reserves, Citicorp and the other banks that followed suit put themselves in a stronger position to demand reforms in countries to which they lend—a key feature of the Baker Plan.

The Brady Plan

Faced with the Baker Plan's failure to resolve the ongoing debt crisis, Nicholas Brady, James Baker's successor as U.S. Treasury Secretary, put forth a new plan in 1989 that emphasized debt relief through forgiveness instead of new lending. Under the *Brady Plan,* banks have a choice: They either could make new loans or they could write off portions of their existing loans in exchange for new government securities whose interest payments were backed with money from the International Monetary Fund. The problem with the Brady Plan is that, for it to work, commercial banks will have to do both: make new loans at the same time that they are writing off existing loans. Instead, many banks have used the Brady Plan as an opportunity to exit the LDC debt market. They added billions to their loan-loss reserves to absorb the necessary loan writedowns, virtually guaranteeing that they will slash new LDC lending to the bone.

■ ───

ILLUSTRATION ■

Mexico Implements the Brady Plan. Mexico's Brady Plan agreement in February 1990 offered three options to the banks: (1) convert their loans into salable bonds with guarantees attached, but worth only 65% of the face value of the old debt; (2) convert their debt into new guaranteed bonds whose yield was just 6.5%; or (3) keep their old loans but provide new money worth 25% of their exposure's value. Only 10% of the banks risked the new money option, while 41% agreed to debt reduction and 49% chose a lower interest rate. This agreement saved Mexico $3.8 billion a year in debt-servicing costs, but it is unlikely to receive new money in the foreseeable future.

As part of this restructuring, the U.S. government agreed to sell Mexico 30-year, zero-coupon Treasury bonds in a face amount of $33 billion. Mexico bought the zeros to serve as collateral for the bonds it planned to issue as a substitute for the bank loans. When the Mexican deal was struck, 30-year Treasury zeros were selling in the open market to yield 7.75%. But the U.S. Treasury priced the zeros it sold to Mexico to yield 8.05%, reflecting the price not of zeros but of conventional 30-year Treasury bonds. The Treasury also charged Mexico a service fee of 0.125% per annum, as is customary in such special Treasury sales. As a result, Mexico received an effective annual interest yield of 7.925% (8.05% − 0.125%).

The sale of zero-coupon bonds to Mexico at a cut-rate price brought criticism from Congress and Wall Street. Many argued that any U.S. aid to Mexico ought to flow through normal channels, and not be done in a back-door financing scheme. Without taking sides in this dispute, what is the value of the subsidy the Treasury provided to Mexico?

Solution.   If the Treasury had priced the zeros to yield 7.75% less the 0.125% service fee, or 7.625%, the $33 billion face value of bonds would have cost Mexico

$$\$33 \text{ billion}/(1.07625)^{30} = \$3.64 \text{ billion}$$

By pricing the bonds to yield 7.925%, the Treasury sold the bonds to Mexico at a price of

$$\$33 \text{ billion}/(1.07925)^{30} = \$3.35 \text{ billion}$$

The result is a savings to Mexico of about $290 million.

─── ■

The market clearly recognized the deteriorating condition of the LDC debt held by the large U.S. money-center banks. This recognition is reflected in the bond market's increasingly grim view during this period of the creditworthiness of these banks. Yields on money-center bank debt securities approached the levels associated with junk bonds (see Exhibit 26.1). Banks have responded to the decline in the market values of their portfolios by raising additional capital and curtailing asset growth in general and LDC loan growth in particular. The Brady Plan has only hastened their move out of LDC lending.

The pressure from the financial marketplace makes it more difficult for banks to lend money to Brazil and other LDCs. Indeed, the flow of capital is going in the opposite direction: As of February 1990, U.S. bank claims on the 15 most heavily indebted LDCs totaled about $59 billion, down 34% from $90 billion in June 1982. Although much of that reduction is accounted for by loan sales and write-offs, the total bank credit available to the LDCs has also dropped. Simply put, the banks have washed their hands of the LDC debt mess. They are saying, in effect, that there are few good loans to be made in Latin America or Africa, because the politics and systems are so bad that no loan would be good even if the old debts were all canceled.

■ **EXHIBIT 26.1**   Deterioration in Creditworthiness of Major U.S. Banks

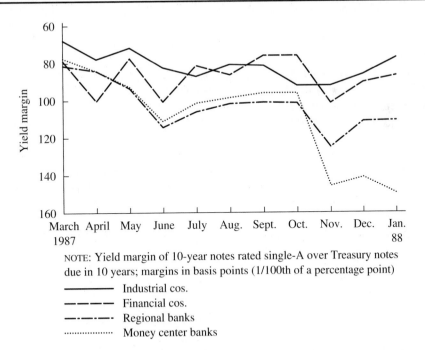

NOTE: Yield margin of 10-year notes rated single-A over Treasury notes due in 10 years; margins in basis points (1/100th of a percentage point)

——————   Industrial cos.
— — — —   Financial cos.
—·—·—·   Regional banks
················   Money center banks

Particularly worrying about the debt crisis is that an eight-year economic boom by industrial countries has failed to pull the debtor nations along with it. If adjustment has proved so difficult in a record period of expansion for industrial countries, what will be the chances for a solution during the current recession?

Debt Renegotiations

Since the early 1980s, there has been a seemingly endless series of *debt renegotiations*. In order to grow, the LDCs require added capital formation. But servicing their foreign debts requires the use of scarce capital, thereby constraining growth. Thus, the debtor LDCs are determined to reduce their net financial transfers—by limiting interest payments and increasing net capital inflows—to levels consistent with desired economic growth. In short, they want more money from their banks. However, the banks first want to see economic reforms that will improve the odds that the LDCs will be able to service their debts. The principal hindrance to bank willingness to supply more funds is skepticism about the ability and willingness of the debtor nations to make sound economic policy.

The predicament facing the LDCs can best be understood by dividing the current-account surplus into two components: the noninterest surplus and interest payments. In order to service their debts without added funding, the LDCs must run a noninterest surplus large enough to pay interest expenses as well as any principal payments that come due. Without economic growth—there has been virtually none since the debt crisis began—either consumption must contract to boost savings or investment must fall. The object is to increase net savings so as to finance the added capital outflow.

Exhibit 26.2 shows how the Latin American debtor nations financed their debt service charges. For the period from 1977 through 1982, these countries ran a noninterest deficit. Consequently, debts increased to finance the noninterest deficit, to finance interest payments, and to finance the flight of capital. The rise in external debt led to an increase in the fraction of gross domestic product (GDP) required to service interest payments. In the period between 1983 and 1985, the noninterest deficit turned into a large surplus, around 5% of GDP. Because the noninterest surplus was almost equal to the interest payments due, very little new money was needed to finance interest payments. The bottom line, however, shows that

■ **EXHIBIT 26.2**   Latin America's Adjustment to the International Debt Crisis (Percent of GDP)

	1977–1982	1983–1985
External debt	34.3	47.2
Interest payments	3.2	5.6
Noninterest surplus	−0.8	4.7
Net investment	11.3	5.5

SOURCE: Rudiger Dornbusch, "International Debt and Economic Instability," *Economic Review*, Federal Reserve Bank of Kansas City, January 1987, p. 19. The original data are from the IMF.

■ **EXHIBIT 26.3**   Results of Cuts in Investment Instead of Public Consumption in Baker
15 Countries

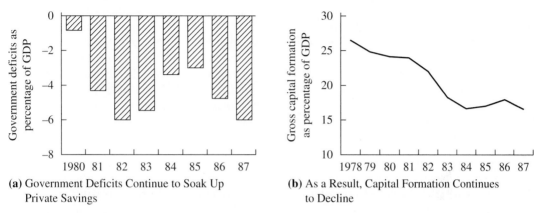

(a) Government Deficits Continue to Soak Up
Private Savings

(b) As a Result, Capital Formation Continues
to Decline

SOURCE: Data from IMF and Federal Reserve Bank of New York.

rather than interest payments coming out of consumption, they were financed by a dramatic
cut in domestic investment. That is, the 5.5% turnaround in the noninterest surplus (4.7 +
0.8) was matched by a 5.8% drop in net investment (calculated as a percent of GDP).

The same story can be told for the Baker 15 in the aggregate. As shown in Exhibit 26.3,
rather than financing interest payments by cutting their deficit-ridden public sectors (Exhibit
26.3a), the Baker 15 cut capital formation (Exhibit 26.3b). The low rate of investment is
ominous for the debtors' economic growth prospects.

One response to this hard arithmetic is seen in Peru's unilateral limit on debt service
payments, in effect since 1985. The result is no new money for Peru. Virtually cut off from
credit, Peru now conducts some of its external trade by barter. Further, Peru has experienced
foreign-direct-investment withdrawals and capital flight.

Another approach is *debt relief*—that is, reducing the principal and/or interest payments
on loans. Yet, the middle-income debtor nations addressed by the Baker and Brady Plans
are neither very poor nor insolvent. They possess considerable human and natural resource,
reasonably well developed infrastructures and productive capacities, and the potential for
substantial growth in output and exports given sound economic policies. In addition, many
of these countries possess considerable wealth—much of it invested abroad.

Although debt burdens have exacerbated the economic problems faced by these
countries, all too often the underlying causes are to be found in patronage-bloated bureaucracies, overvalued currencies, massive corruption, and politically motivated government
investments in money-losing ventures. The Baker countries suffer too from markets that are
distorted by import protection for inefficient domestic producers and government favors for
politically influential groups. For these countries, debt relief is at best an ineffectual
substitute for sound macroeconomic policy and major structural reform; relief would only
weaken discipline over economic policy and undermine support for structural reform.

It is also questionable whether debt relief would significantly reduce net financial transfers by the Baker countries. Most of their debt has been restructured with extended grace periods (the time before they have to repay any principal) and lengthy maturities. Thus, for many years to come, the cash-flow benefit of principal forgiveness would be limited to the interest savings on the forgiven amount. Moreover, debt relief would certainly cause banks and others to cease lending and investing and provoke more capital flight. The loss of new loans and investments for an indefinite period, plus capital flight, could substantially reduce or entirely wipe out, any near-term cash-flow gains from debt relief. Besides, for the Baker countries, debt relief would run directly counter to the objective of restoring access to credit markets. The more concessions these countries get, the further away their reentry to the capital markets becomes. Indeed, the response of banks to the Brady Plan, whose centerpiece is debt forgiveness, has been to cut their LDC lending.

■ 26.2 ■
COUNTRY RISK ANALYSIS IN INTERNATIONAL BANKING

It is worthwhile to note some differences between international loans and domestic loans because these difference have a lot to do with the nature of country risk. Ordinarily banks can control borrowers by means of loan covenants on their dividend and financing decisions. Quite often, however, the borrowers in international loan agreements are sovereign states, or their ability to repay depends on the actions of a sovereign state. The unique characteristics of a sovereign borrower render irrelevant many of the loan covenants—such as dividend or merger restrictions—normally imposed on borrowers. Moreover, sovereign states ordinarily refuse to accept economic or financial policy restrictions imposed by foreign banks.

The key issue posed by international loans, therefore, is how do banks ensure the enforceability of these debt contracts? What keeps borrowers from incurring debts and then defaulting voluntarily? In general, seizure of assets is not useful unless the debtor has substantial external assets, as in the case of Iran. Ordinarily, though, the borrower has few external assets.

One answer to the question of enforceability is that it is difficult for borrowers that repudiate their debts to reenter private capital markets.[1] That is, banks find it in their best interest, ex post, to deny further credit to a borrower that defaults on its bank loans. If the bank fails to adhere to its announced policy of denying credit to its defaulters, some of its other borrowers may now decide to default on their debts because they realize that default carries no penalty. Having a reputation for being a tough bank is a valuable commodity in a hard world that has no love for moneylenders.

The presence of *loan syndications*—in which several banks share a loan—and *cross-default clauses*—which ensure that a default to one bank is a default to all banks—means that if the borrower repudiates its debt to one bank, it must repudiate its debt to *all* the banks. This constraint makes the penalty for repudiation much stiffer because a large number of banks will now deny credit to the borrower in the future. After a few defaults, the borrower will exhaust most of the potential sources of credit in the international financial markets.

---

[1]The discussion of debt repudiation and the nature of international loans comes from Bhagwan Chowdry, "What Is Different about International Lending?" working paper, University of Chicago, November 1987.

For many borrowers, this penalty is severe enough that they do not voluntarily default on their bank loans. Thus, countries will sometimes go to extraordinary lengths to continue servicing their debts. Bank country risk analysis can, therefore, focus largely on ability to repay rather than willingness to repay.

Notice, however, that the threat to cut off credit to borrowers who default is meaningful only so long as the banks have sufficient resources to reward with further credit those who do not default. But if several countries default simultaneously, then the banks' promise to provide further credit to borrowers who repay their debts is no longer credible; the erosion in their capital bases caused by the defaults will force the banks to curtail their loans. Under these circumstances, even those borrowers who did not default on their loans will suffer a reduction of credit. The lesser penalty for defaulting may induce borrowers to default en masse. The possibility of mass defaults is the real *international debt crisis.*

Country Risk and the Terms of Trade

What ultimately determines a nation's ability to repay foreign loans is that nation's ability to generate U.S. dollars and other hard currencies. This ability, in turn, is based on the nation's *terms of trade,* the weighted average of the nation's export prices relative to its import prices—that is, the exchange rate between exports and imports. Most economists would agree that these terms of trade are largely independent of the nominal exchange rate, unless the observed exchange rate has been affected by government intervention in the foreign exchange market.

In general, if its terms of trade increase, a nation will be a better credit risk. Alternatively, if its terms of trade decrease, a nation will be a poorer credit risk. This *terms-of-trade risk,* however, can be exacerbated by political decisions. When a nation's terms of trade improve, foreign goods become relatively less expensive, the nation's standard of living rises, and consumers and businesses become more dependent on imports. But since there is a large element of unpredictability to relative price changes, shifts in the terms of trade will also be unpredictable. When the nation's terms of trade decline, as must inevitably happen when prices fluctuate randomly, the government will face political pressure to maintain the nation's standard of living.

As we saw in Chapter 20, a typical response is for the government to fix the exchange rate at its former (and now overvalued) level—that is, to subsidize the price of dollars. Loans made when the terms of trade improved are now doubly risky: first, because the terms of trade have declined and, second, because the government is maintaining an *overvalued currency,* further reducing the nation's net inflow of dollars. The deterioration in the trade balance usually results in added government borrowing. This was the response of the Baker 15 countries to the sharp decline in their terms of trade shown in Exhibit 26.4. Capital flight exacerbates this problem, as residents recognize the country's deteriorating economic situation.

To summarize, a terms-of-trade risk can be exacerbated if the government attempts to avoid the necessary drop in the standard of living when the terms of trade decline by maintaining the old and now overvalued exchange rate. In reality, of course, this element of country risk is a political risk. The government is attempting by political means to hold off the necessary economic adjustments to the country's changed wealth position.

■ **EXHIBIT 26.4**   Decline in Terms of Trade in Baker 15 Countries

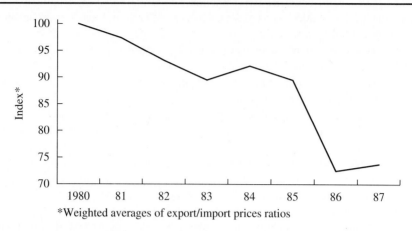

*Weighted averages of export/import prices ratios

SOURCE: Data from OECD, IMF, and Federal Reserve Bank of New York.

A key issue, therefore, in assessing country risk is the speed with which a country adjusts to its new wealth position. In other words, how fast will the necessary austerity policy be implemented? The speed of adjustment will be determined in part by the government's perception of the costs and benefits associated with austerity versus default.

The Government's Cost/Benefit Calculus

The cost of austerity is determined primarily by the nation's external debts relative to its wealth, as measured by its gross national product (GNP). The lower this ratio, the lower the relative amount of consumption that must be sacrificed to meet a nation's foreign debts.

The cost of default is the likelihood of being cut off from international credit. This possibility brings with it its own form of austerity. Most nations will follow this path only as a last resort, preferring to stall for time in the hope that something will happen in the interim. That something could be a bailout by the IMF, the Bank for International Settlements, the Federal Reserve, or some other major central bank. The bailout decision is largely a political decision. It depends on the willingness of citizens of another nation, usually the United States, to tax themselves on behalf of the country involved.[2] This willingness is a function of two factors: (1) the nation's geopolitical importance to the United States and (2) the probability that the necessary economic adjustments will result in unacceptable political turmoil.

The more a nation's terms of trade fluctuate and the less stable its political system, the greater the odds the government will face a situation that will tempt it to hold off on the

[2]See Tamir Agmon and J.K. Dietrich, "International Lending and Income Redistribution: An Alternative View of Country Risk," *Journal of Banking and Finance,* December 1983, pp. 483–495, for a discussion of this point.

necessary adjustments. Terms-of-trade variability will probably be inversely correlated with the degree of product diversification in the nation's trade flows. With limited diversification—for example, dependence on the export of one or two primary products or on imports heavily weighted toward a few commodities—the nation's terms of trade are likely to be highly variable. This characterizes the situation facing many Third World countries. It also describes, in part, the situation of those OECD (Organization for Economic Cooperation and Development) nations heavily dependent on oil imports.

Debt Service Measures

Two measures of the risk associated with a nation's debt burden are the debt service/exports and debt service/GNP ratios, where debt service includes both interest charges and loan repayments. Exhibit 26.5 contains 1982 year-end statistics on these debt service measures for both individual countries and groupings of OPEC and non-OPEC developing countries. To put these figures in perspective, most bankers consider a debt service/exports ratio of 0.25 or higher to be dangerous. In recent years, however, debt reschedulings have steadied the debt service/exports ratio for the Baker 15 (see Exhibit 26.6a). Moreover, their interest/exports ratio is actually improving (see Exhibit 26.6b).

Ex ante what matters is not just the coverage ratio but also the variability of the difference between export revenues, X, and import costs, M, relative to the nation's debt-service requirements (i.e., c.v.$[(X - M)/D]$ where c.v. is the coefficient of variation and D is the debt service requirement). In calculating this measure of risk, it is important to recognize that export volume is likely to be positively correlated—and import volume negatively correlated—with price. In addition, import expenditures are usually positively related to export revenues.

■ **EXHIBIT 26.5**   Debt/Burden Ratios as of Year-End 1982

Country	Debt Service/ Exports	Debt Service/ GNP
Mexico	0.70	0.080
Brazil	0.56	0.063
Argentina	0.41	0.024
Chile	0.54	0.099
Venezuela	0.32	0.090
Spain	0.28	—
Philippines	0.25	0.040
South Korea	0.17	0.063
Non-OPEC LDCs	0.24	0.056
OPEC countries	0.11	0.054

SOURCE: Robert E. Weintraub, *International Debt: Crisis and Challenge* (Fairfax, Va: George Mason University, Department of Economics monograph, April 1983), pp. 17, 19. Used with permission.

■ **EXHIBIT 26.6**   Progress of Baker 15 Countries in Coping with Their Foreign Debts

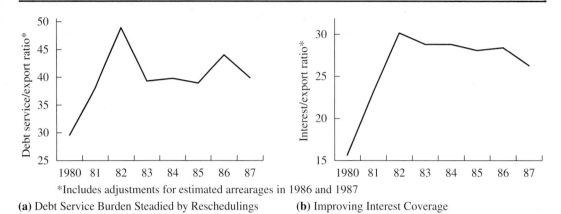

*Includes adjustments for estimated arrearages in 1986 and 1987

(a) Debt Service Burden Steadied by Reschedulings   **(b)** Improving Interest Coverage

SOURCE: Data from IMF and Federal Reserve Bank of New York.

■ 26.3 ■
SUMMARY AND CONCLUSIONS

The end of "let's pretend" in international banking has led to a new emphasis on country risk analysis. From the bank's standpoint, country risk—the credit risk on loans to a nation—is largely determined by the real cost of repaying the loan versus the real wealth that the country has to draw on. These parameters, in turn, depend on the variability of the nation's terms of trade and the government's willingness to allow the nation's standard of living to adjust rapidly to changing economic fortunes.

The countries at the center of the international debt crisis can only get out if they institute broad systemic reforms. Their problems are caused by governments spending too much money they don't have to meet promises they should not make. They create public sector jobs for people to do things they shouldn't do and subsidize companies to produce high priced goods and services. These countries need less government and fewer bureaucratic rules. Debt forgiveness or further capital inflows would just tempt these nations to postpone economic adjustment further.

■ QUESTIONS ■

1. What were the key contributing factors to the international debt crisis that began in 1982?

2. What economic and political factors account for the fact that the foreign loans of major banks are in such bad shape?

3. How are U.S. international banking practices likely to be influenced by the belief that the Federal Reserve would not permit a major U.S. bank to fail?

4. Prior to 1983, U.S. banks did not have to, and generally did not, provide data to the public on the geographical distribution of their loan portfolios. If the stock market is strongly efficient, how would you predict it responded to the public release of information in early 1983 that concerned the extent of bank loans to various Latin American countries? Recall that the international debt crisis struck in mid-1982.

5. Why is it crucial for banks to prevent several defaults at once?

6. What incentive do borrowers have to form a debtors' cartel and simultaneously default? Who would choose not to belong to such a cartel?

7. In the week following Citicorp's $3 billion writedown of its Latin American debt, its stock price rose by 10%. What might explain this rise in Citicorp's stock price?

8. How does capital flight contribute to the international debt crisis?

■ PROBLEMS ■

1. In the Mexican debt restructuring discussed in the chapter, suppose that when the deal was struck 30-year Treasury zeros were selling in the open market at a yield of about 7.62%. But the U.S. Treasury priced the zeros that it sold to Mexico to yield 8.15%. The Treasury also charged Mexico its customary service fee of 0.125% per annum, giving Mexico an effective annual interest yield of 8.025%.

   a. Under these circumstances, what would have been the amount of the subsidy provided by the Treasury (relative to the cost to Mexico of buying the zeros to yield 7.62% less 0.125%)?

   b. What does this complicated deal accomplish? Who benefits? Who loses?

2. In early 1988, the Mexican government sought to swap about $15 billion of its outstanding bank debt for $10 billion in bonds. The principal amount of the Mexican bonds would be secured by 20-year, zero-coupon U.S. Treasury bonds having a face value of $10 billion. Because of doubts about Mexico's creditworthiness, Mexican bank debt was then valued by the market at about 50 cents on the dollar.

   a. How should Mexico's offer be evaluated?

   b. Suppose the bond interest payments are more certain than bank debt payments. Before the bond swap is worthwhile, how much would a Mexican promise to pay $1 in bond interest have to be worth relative to a Mexican promise to pay $1 in bank debt?

■ BIBLIOGRAPHY ■

Lessard, Donald R. "North-South: The Implications for Multinational Banking." *Journal of Banking and Finance,* 1983, pp. 521–536.

————, and John Williamson, eds. *Capital Flight and Third World Debt.* Washington, D.C.: Institute for International Economics, 1987.

Shapiro, Alan C. "Risk in International Banking." *Journal of Financial and Quantitative Analysis,* December 1982, pp. 727–739.

————. "Currency Risk and Country Risk in International Banking." *Journal of Finance,* July 1985, pp. 881–891.

————. "Risk in International Banking." *Journal of Financial and Quantitative Analysis,* December 1982, pp. 727–739.

Wihlborg, Clas. "Currency Risks in International Financial Markets." *Princeton Studies in International Finance,* No. 44, December 1978.

■ PART VI ■
■ Case Study ■

■ Case V1.1
Plano Cruzado

On February 28, 1986, President Jose Sarnay of Brazil announced the Plano Cruzado. At the time, Brazilian inflation was running at an annualized rate of more than 400%. The Plan slashed inflation by freezing prices and wages. The purpose of the Plan was to impose "shock treatment" on the economy and break the cycle of "inertial inflation" caused by high inflationary expectations. However, in a move that foreshadowed the splits that bedeviled the Plan, workers were granted pay hikes of 8% and 15%, just before the freeze. At the same time, government spending went largely unchecked, and the public-sector deficit—financed largely by printing more cruzados—grew to 4.5% of gross national product.

In November, the Plan achieved its first incontrovertible success: Government parties swept the congressional and gubernatorial races. Price controls were eased just after the election. However, the government found it politically impossible to remove subsidies to state industries because these industries formed the base for political power. Instead, large price hikes for state companies were granted by imposing huge increases in indirect taxes and tariffs on their products, and an attempt was made to disguise the effect of these increases on inflation by altering the basket of goods on which inflation was calculated. "They wanted me to tamper with inflation—simple as that," commented the head of the National Statistics Office, who immediately resigned.

QUESTIONS

1. What were the likely consequences for Brazil of controlling prices while gunning the money supply? Consider the effect on production and the availability of products in the stores.

2. How did the Plano Cruzado affect Brazil's huge trade surplus?

3. What would be your forecast of the Plan's effect on Brazil's ability to service its foreign debts?

4. President Sarnay terminated Plano Cruzado in February 1987, one year after it began. What impact do you think the Plan had in reducing inflation and inflation expectations? How would you go about measuring the effect of the Plan on inflation expectations?

5. What was the likely price response to the removal of price controls?

6. If you were a banker, how would seeing such a Plan put into effect affect your willingness to lend money to Brazil? Explain.

SOURCE: Based on a report in *The Wall Street Journal,* February 13, 1987, p.27.

■ GLOSSARY ■
■ Key Words and Terms in International Finance ■

Accounting exposure   The change in the value of a firm's foreign-currency-denominated accounts due to a change in exchange rates.

Act of state doctrine   This doctrine says that a nation is sovereign within its own borders and its domestic actions may not be questioned in the courts of another nation.

Adjusted present value   The net present value of a project using the all-equity rate as a discount rate. The effects of financing are incorporated in separate terms.

Administrative pricing rule   IRS rules used to allocate income on export sales to a foreign sales corporation.

Agency costs   Costs that stem from conflicts between managers and stockholders and between stockholders and bondholders.

All-equity rate   The discount rate that reflects only the business risks of a project and abstracts from the effects of financing.

American Depository Receipt (ADR)   A certificate of ownership issued by a U.S. bank as a convenience to investors in lieu of the underlying foreign corporate shares it holds in custody.

American shares   Securities certificates issued in the United States by a transfer agent acting on behalf of the foreign issuer. The certificates represent claims to foreign equities.

Appreciation   *See* Revaluation.

Arbitrage   Purchase of securities or commodities on one market for immediate resale on another in order to profit from a price discrepancy.

Arm's-length price   Price at which a willing buyer and a willing unrelated seller would freely agree to transact (i.e., a market price).

Back-to-back financing   An intercompany loan channeled through a bank.

Baker Plan   A plan by U.S. Treasury Secretary James Baker under which 15 principal middle-income debtor countries (the "Baker countries") would undertake growth-oriented structural reforms, to be supported by increased financing from the World Bank and continued lending from commercial banks.

Balance of Payments   Net value of all economic transactions—including trade in goods and services, transfer payments, loans, and investments—between residents of the same country and those of all other countries.

Balance of trade   Net flow of goods (exports minus imports) between countries.

Balance-sheet exposure   *See* Accounting exposure.

Bank draft   A draft addressed to a bank; *See* Draft.

Banker's acceptance   Draft accepted by a bank; *See* Draft.

Bank loan swap   *See* Debt swap.

Bearer securities   Securities that are unregistered.

Beta   A measure of the systematic risk faced by an asset or project. Beta is calculated as the covariance between returns on the asset and returns on the market portfolio divided by the variance of returns on the market portfolio.

Bill of exchange   *See* Bank draft.

Bill of lading   A contract between a carrier and an exporter in which the former agrees to carry the latter's goods from port of shipment to port of destination. It is also the exporter's receipt for the goods.

Black market   An illegal market that often arises when price controls or official rationing lead to shortages of goods, services, or assets.

Blocked currency   A currency that is not freely convertible to other currencies due to exchange controls.

Brady Plan   A plan by Nicholas Brady, James Baker's successor as U.S. Treasury Secretary, that emphasized debt relief through forgiveness, instead of new lending. Under this plan, banks have a choice: They either could make new loans or they could write off portions of their existing loans in exchange for government securities whose interest payments were backed with money from the International Monetary Fund.

Branch A foreign operation incorporated in the home country.

Bretton Woods Agreement An agreement, implemented in 1946, whereby each member government pledged to maintain a fixed, or pegged, exchange rate for its currency vis-à-vis the dollar or gold. These fixed exchange rates were supposed to reduce the riskiness of international transactions, thus promoting growth in world trade.

Capital account Net results of public and private international investment and lending activities.

Capital asset pricing model (CAPM) A model for pricing risk. The CAPM assumes that investors must be compensated for the time value of money plus systematic risk, as measured by an asset's beta.

Capital flight The transfer of capital abroad in response to fears of political risk.

Cash pooling *See* Pooling.

CHIPS *See* Clearing House Interbank Payments System.

Clean float *See* Free float.

Clearing House Interbank Payments System (CHIPS) A computerized network for transfer of international dollar payments, linking about 140 depository institutions that have offices or affiliates in New York City.

Concession agreement An understanding between a company and the host government that specifies the rules under which the company can operate locally.

Controlled foreign corporation (CFC) A foreign corporation whose voting stock is more than 50% owned by U.S. stockholders, each of whom owns at least 10% of the voting power.

Correspondent bank A bank located in any other city, state, or country that provides a service for another bank.

Countertrade A sophisticated form of barter in which the exporting firm is required to take the countervalue of its sale in local goods or services instead of in cash.

Country risk General level of political and economic uncertainty in a country affecting the value of loans or investments in that country.

Covered-interest arbitrage Movement of short-term funds between two currencies to take advantage of interest differentials with exchange risk eliminated by means of forward contracts.

Cross-default clauses Clause in a loan agreement that says that a default by a borrower to one lender is a default to all lenders.

Cross-rate The exchange rate between two currencies, neither or which is the U.S. dollar, calculated by using the dollar rates for both currencies.

Currency arbitrate Taking advantage of divergencies in exchange rates in different money markets by buying a currency in one market and selling it in another.

Currency call option A financial contract that gives the buyer the right, but not the obligation, to buy a specified number of units of foreign currency from the option seller at a fixed dollar price, up to the option's expiration date.

Currency futures contract Contract for future delivery of a specific quantity of a given currency, with the exchange rate fixed at the time the contract is entered. Futures contracts are similar to forward contracts except that they are traded on organized futures exchanges and the gains and losses on the contracts are settled each day.

Currency of denomination Currency in which a transaction is stated.

Currency of determination Currency whose value determines a given price.

Currency put option A financial contract that gives the buyer the right, but not the obligation, to sell a specified number of foreign currency units to the option seller at a fixed dollar price, up to the option's expiration date.

Currency risk sharing An agreement by the parties to a transaction to share the currency risk associated with the transaction. The arrangement involves a customized hedge contract imbedded in the underlying transaction.

Currency swap A simultaneous borrowing and lending operation whereby two parties exchange specific amounts of two currencies at the outset at the spot rate. They also exchange interest rate payments in the two currencies. The parties undertake to reverse the exchange after a fixed term at a fixed exchange rate.

Current account Net flow of goods, services, and unilateral transactions (gifts) between countries.

Debt relief Reducing the principal and/or interest payments on LDC loans.

Debt swap A set of transactions (also called a debt-equity swap) in which a firm buys a country's dollar bank debt at a discount and swaps this debt with the central bank for local currency that it can use to acquire local equity.

Depreciation *See* Devaluation.

Depreciation tax shield The value of the tax write-off on depreciation of plant and equipment.

Devaluation A decrease in the spot value of a currency.

"Dirty" float *See* Managed float.

Doctrine of sovereign immunity Doctrine that says a nation may not be tried in the courts of another country without its consent.

Domestic International Sales Corporation (DISC) A domestic U.S. corporation that receives a tax incentive for export activities.

Double dip lease A cross-border lease in which the disparate rules of the lessor's and lessee's countries let both parties be treated as the owner of the leased equipment for tax purposes.

Draft An unconditional order in writing—signed by a person, usually the exporter, and addressed to the importer—ordering the importer or the importer's agent to pay, on demand (sight draft) or at a fixed future date (time draft), the amount specified on its face.

Dual syndicate equity offering An international equity placement where the offering is split into two tranches—domestic and foreign—and each tranche is handled by a separate lead manager.

EAFE Index The Morgan Stanley Capital International Europe, Australia, Far East Index, which reflects the performance of all major stock markets outside of North America.

Economic exposure The extent to which the value of the firm will change due to an exchange rate change.

Economies of scale Situation in which increasing production leads to a less-than-proportionate increase in cost.

Economies of scope Scope economies exist whenever the same investment can support multiple profitable activities less expensively in combination than separately.

Edge Act corporation A subsidiary, located in the United States, of a U.S. bank that is permitted to carry on international banking and investment activities.

Efficient market A market in which new information is readily incorporated into the prices of traded securities.

Eurobond A bond sold outside the country in whose currency it is denominated.

Eurocommercial paper (Euro-CP) Euronotes that are not underwritten.

Eurocurrency A currency deposited in a bank outside the country of its origin.

Euroequity issue A syndicated equity offering placed throughout Europe and handled by one lead manager.

Euronote A short-term note issued outside the country of the currency it is denominated in.

European Community A group of 11 European nations whose purpose is to reduce trade barriers among member states.

European Currency Unit (ECU) A composite currency, consisting of fixed amounts of 10 European currencies.

European Monetary System (EMS) Monetary system formed by the major European countries under which the members agree to maintain their exchange rates within a specific margin around agreed-upon, fixed central exchange rates. These central exchange rates are denominated in currency units per ECU.

Europe 1992 An agreement among the members of the European Community to create a single European market for goods and services by December 1992. The objective of Europe 1992 is to tear down barriers to trade and commerce within Europe so that European nations can achieve economic prosperity.

Exchange-rate mechanism (ERM) A process whereby each member of the European Monetary System determines a mutually agreed upon central exchange rate for its currency; each rate is denominated in currency units per ECU.

Exchange risk The variability of a firm's value that is due to uncertain exchange rate changes.

Export-Import Bank (Eximbank) U.S. government agency dedicated to facilitating U.S. exports, primarily through subsidized export financing.

Exposure netting Offsetting exposures in one currency with exposures in the same or another currency, where exchange rates are expected to move in such a way that losses (gains) on the first exposed position should be offset by gains (losses) on the second currency exposure.

Factor Specialized buyer, at a discount, of company receivables.

FASB No. 8 *See* Statement of Financial Accounting Standards no. 8.

FASB No. 52 *See* Statement of Financial Accounting Standards no. 52.

Fiat money Nonconvertible paper money.

Fisher effect States that the nominal interest differential between two countries should equal the inflation differential between those countries.

Fixed exchange rate An exchange rate whose value is fixed by the governments involved.

Floating exchange rate An exchange rate whose value is determined in the foreign exchange market.

Foreign banking market That portion of domestic bank loans supplied to foreigners for use abroad.

Foreign bond market That portion of the domestic bond market that represents issues floated by foreign companies or governments.

Foreign equity market That portion of the domestic equity market that represents issues floated by foreign companies.

Foreign direct investment The acquisition abroad of physical assets such as plant and equipment, with operating control residing in the parent corporation.

Foreign market beta A measure of foreign market risk that is derived from the capital asset pricing model.

Foreign Sales Corporation (FSC) A special type of corporation created by the Tax Reform Act of 1984 that is designed to provide a tax incentive for exporting U.S.-produced goods.

Foreign tax credit Home country credit against domestic income tax for foreign taxes already paid on foreign-source earnings.

Forward differential Annualized percentage difference between spot and forward rates.

Forward rate The rate quoted today for delivery at a fixed future date of a specified amount of one currency against dollar payment.

Free float An exchange rate system characterized by the absence of government intervention. Also known as a clean float.

Functional currency As defined in FASB No. 52, an affiliate's functional currency is the currency of the primary economic environment in which the affiliate generates and expends cash.

G–5 nations A group of five large nations—the United States, France, Japan, Great Britain, and Germany—that meets periodically to coordinate economic policies. Also known as the Group of Five.

G–7 nations The G–5 plus Canada and Italy. Also known as the Group of Seven.

Global fund A mutual fund that can invest anywhere in the world, including the United States.

Gold standard A system of setting currency values whereby the participating countries commit to fix the prices of their domestic currencies in terms of a specified amount of gold.

Growth options The opportunities a company may have to invest capital so as to increase the profitability of its existing product lines and benefit from expanding into new products or markets.

Hedge To enter into a forward contract in order to protect the home currency value of foreign-currency-denominated assets or liabilities.

Import-substitution development strategy A development strategy followed by many Latin American countries and other LDCs that emphasized import substitution—accomplished through protectionism—as the route to economic growth.

Intercompany loan Loan made by one unit of a corporation to another unit of the same corporation.

Intercompany transaction Transaction carried out between two units of the same corporation.

Interest rate parity A condition where the interest differential is (approximately) equal to the forward differential between two currencies.

Interest rate swap An agreement between two parties to exchange interest payments for a specific maturity on an agreed upon principal amount. The most common interest rate swap involves exchanging fixed interest payments for floating interest payments.

Interest tax shield The value of the tax write-off on interest payments (analogous to the depreciation tax shield).

International Bank for Reconstruction and Development (IBRD) Also known as the World Bank, the IBRD is owned by its member nations and makes loans at nearly conventional terms to countries for projects of high economic priority.

International Banking Facility (IBF) A bookkeeping entity of a U.S. financial institution that is permitted to conduct international banking business (such as receiving foreign deposits and making foreign loans) largely exempt from domestic regulatory constraints.

International diversification   The attempt to reduce risk by investing in more than one nation. By diversifying across nations whose economic cycles are not perfectly in phase, investors can typically reduce the variability of their returns.

International finance subsidiary   A subsidiary incorporated in the United States (usually in Delaware) whose sole purpose was to issue debentures overseas and invest the proceeds in foreign operations, with the interest paid to foreign bondholders not subject to U.S. withholding tax. The elimination of the corporate withholding tax has ended the need for this type of subsidiary.

International Fisher effect   States that the interest differential between two countries should be an unbiased predictor of the future change in the spot rate.

International fund   A mutual fund that can invest only outside the United States.

International Monetary Fund (IMF)   International organization created at Bretton Woods, N.H., in 1944 to promote exchange rate stability, including the provision of temporary assistance to member nations trying to defend their currencies against transitory phenomena.

International monetary system   The set of policies, institutions, practices, regulations, and mechanisms that determine the rate at which one currency is exchanged for another.

J-curve theory   Theory that says a country's trade deficit will initially worsen after its currency depreciates because higher prices on foreign imports will more than offset the reduced volume of imports in the short run.

Law of one price   The theory that exchange-adjusted prices identical tradeable goods and financial assets must be within transaction costs of equality worldwide.

LDC debt swap   *See* Debt swap.

Leading and lagging   Accelerating (leading) and delaying (lagging) international payments by modifying credit terms, normally on trade between affiliates.

Letter of credit   A letter addressed to the seller, written and signed by a bank acting on behalf of the buyer, in which the bank promises to honor drafts drawn on itself if the seller conforms to the specific conditions contained in the letter.

Link financing   *See* Back-to-back financing.

Loan syndication   Group of banks sharing a loan.

London interbank offer rate (LIBOR)   The deposit rate on interbank transactions in the Eurocurrency market.

Look-thru   A method for calculating U.S. taxes owed on income from controlled foreign corporations that was introduced by the Tax Reform Act of 1986.

Louvre Accord   An agreement, named for the Paris landmark where it was negotiated, that called for the G–7 nations to support the falling dollar by pegging exchange rates within a narrow, undisclosed range, while they also moved to bring their economic policies into line.

Managed float   Also known as a "dirty" float, this is a system of floating exchange rates with central bank intervention to reduce currency fluctuations.

Monetary union   Agreement among several economic units to establish one central bank with the sole power to issue a single currency. The European Community is currently talking about monetary union.

Money market hedge   The use of borrowing and lending transactions in foreign currencies to lock in the home currency value of a foreign currency transaction.

Multicurrency clause   This clause gives a Eurocurrency borrower the right to switch from one currency to another when the loan is rolled over.

Netting   *See* Exposure netting or Payments netting.

Nominal exchange rate   Actual spot rate.

Note issuance facility (NIF)   A facility provided by a syndicate of banks that allows borrowers to issue short-term notes, which are then placed by the syndicate providing the NIF. Borrowers usually have the right to sell their notes to the bank syndicate at a price that yields a prearranged spread over LIBOR.

Official reserves   Holdings of gold and foreign currencies by official monetary institutions.

Offshore finance subsidiary   A wholly owned affiliate incorporated overseas, usually in a tax-haven country, whose function is to issue securities abroad for use in either the parent's domestic or foreign business.

Open-market operation Purchase or sale of government securities by the monetary authorities to increase or decrease the domestic money supply.

Operating exposure Degree to which an exchange rate change, in combination with price changes, will alter a company's future operating cash flows.

Optimum currency area The largest economic unit that should have the same currency. This is the area that trades off the benefits of a single currency (reduced risk and lower transactions costs) against its costs (loss of pricing flexibility).

Outright rate Actual forward rate expressed in dollars per currency unit, or vice versa.

Outsourcing The practice of purchasing a significant percentage of intermediate components from outside suppliers.

Parallel loan Simultaneous borrowing and lending operation usually involving four related parties in two different countries.

Payments netting Reducing fund transfers between affiliates to only a netted amount. Netting can be done on a bilateral basis (between pairs of affiliates) or on a multilateral basis (taking all affiliates together).

Plaza Agreement A program launched in September 1985 by the G–5 nations that was designed to force down the dollar against other major currencies and, thereby, improve American competitiveness.

Political risk Uncertain government action that affects the value of a firm.

Pooling Transfer of excess affiliate cash into a central account (pool), usually located in a low-tax nation, where all corporate funds are managed by corporate staff.

Possession Corporation A U.S. corporation operating in a U.S. possession. Such companies are entitled to certain tax breaks.

Price-specie-flow mechanism An automatic balance-of-payments adjustment mechanism under the classical gold standard whereby disturbances in the price level in one country would be wholly or partly offset by the flow of gold coins (also called specie).

Private Export Funding Corporation (PEFCO) Company that mobilizes private capital for financing the export of big-ticket items by U.S. firms by purchasing at fixed interest rates the medium- to long-term debt obligations of importers of U.S. products.

Privatization The act of returning state-owned or state-run companies back to the private sector, usually by selling them off.

Product cycle The time it takes to bring new and improved products to market. Japanese companies have excelled in compressing product cycles.

Property rights Rights of individuals and companies to own and utilize property as they see fit and to receive the stream of income that their property generates.

Protectionism Protecting domestic industry from import competition by means of tariffs, quotas, and other trade barriers.

Purchasing power parity The notion that the ratio between domestic and foreign price levels should equal the equilibrium exchange rate between domestic and foreign currencies.

Rational expectations The idea that people rationally anticipate the future and respond to what they see ahead.

Real exchange rate The spot rate adjusted for relative price level changes since a base period.

Regional fund A mutual fund that invests in a specific geographic area overseas, such as Asia or Europe.

Reinvoicing center A subsidiary that takes title to all goods sold by one corporate unit to another affiliate or to a third-party customer. The center pays the seller and in turn is paid by the buyer.

Reporting currency The currency in which the parent firm prepares its own financial statements; that is, U.S. dollars for a U.S. company.

Revaluation An increase in the spot value of a currency.

Section 482 United States Department of Treasury regulations governing transfer prices.

Securitization The matching up of borrowers and lenders wholly or partly by way of the financial markets. This process usually refers to the replacement of nonmarketable loans provided by financial intermediaries with negotiable securities issued in the public capital markets.

Single-country fund A mutual fund that invests in individual countries outside the United States, such as Germany or Thailand.

Society for Worldwide Interbank Financial Telecommunications (SWIFT) A dedicated computer network to support funds transfer messages internationally between over 900 member banks worldwide.

Sovereign risk   The risk that the country or origin of the currency a bank is buying or selling will impose foreign exchange regulations that will reduce or negate the value of the contract; also refers to the risk of government default on a loan made to it or guaranteed by it.

Special Drawing Rights (SDR)   A new form of international reserve assets, created by the IMF in 1967, whose value is based on a portfolio of widely used currencies.

Spot rate   The price at which foreign exchange can be bought or sold with payment set for the same day.

Statement of Financial Accounting Standards No. 8   This is the currency translation standard previously in use by U.S. firms.

Statement of Financial Accounting Standards No. 52   This is the currency translation standard currently in use by U.S. firms.

Sterilized intervention   Foreign exchange market intervention in which the monetary authorities have insulated their domestic money supplies from the foreign exchange transactions with offsetting sales or purchases or domestic assets.

Subpart F   Special category of foreign-source "unearned" income that is currently taxed by the IRS whether or not it is remitted back to the United States.

Subsidiary   A foreign-based affiliate that is a separately incorporated entity under the host country's law.

Swap rate   The difference between spot and forward rates expressed in points (e.g., $.0001 per pound sterling or DM .0001 per dollar).

SWIFT   *See* Society for Worldwide Interbank Financial Telecommunications.

Systematic risk   That element of an asset's risk that cannot be eliminated no matter how diversified an investor's portfolio.

Target-zone arrangement   A monetary system under which countries pledge to maintain their exchange rates within a specific margin around agreed-upon, fixed central exchange rates.

Tax haven   A nation with a moderate level of taxation and/or liberal tax incentives for undertaking specific activities such as exporting.

Tax Reform Act of 1986   A 1986 law involving a major overhaul of the U.S. tax system.

Terms of trade   The weighted average of a nation's export prices relative to its import prices.

Total dollar return   The dollar return on a nondollar investment, which includes the sum of an dividend/interest income, capital gains (losses), and currency gains (losses) on the investment.

Trade acceptance   A draft accepted by a commercial enterprise; *see* Draft.

Trade draft   A draft addressed to a commercial enterprise; *see* Draft.

Transaction exposure   The extent to which a given exchange rate change will change the value of foreign-currency-denominated transactions already entered into.

Transfer price   The price at which one unit of a firm sells goods or services to an affiliated unit.

Translation exposure   *See* Accounting exposure.

Two-tier foreign exchange market   This arrangement involves an official market (at the official rate) for certain transactions and a free market for remaining transactions.

Unsterilized intervention   Foreign exchange market intervention in which the monetary authorities have not insulated their domestic money supplies from the foreign exchange transactions.

Value-added tax   Method of indirect taxation whereby a tax is levied at each stage of production on the value added at that specific stage.

Value additivity principle   The principle that the net present value of a set of independent projects is just the sum of the NPVs of the individual projects.

Value-dating   Refers to when value (credit) is given for funds transferred between banks.

World Bank   *See* International Bank for Reconstruction and Development.

■ ANSWERS ■
■ Selected Problems ■

CHAPTER 2

1. FF 1 = DM 0.31 × 0.35 = $0.1085.

3. a. The bid-ask quote on the franc in Frankfurt is DM 0.3565–604.

   b. DM bid-ask spread = (0.3310 – 0.3302)/0.3310 = 0.24%. FF bid-ask spread = (0.1190 – 0.1180)/0.1190 = 0.84%.

5. The bid-ask rates for the Canadian dollar are U.S. $0.7692–0.8000. Hence, there is no arbitrage opportunity.

7. Sell pounds in New York for $2.4110 apiece. Sell the dollars in Paris for FF 3.997, and sell the francs in London for £0.1088. This sequence of transactions yields 2.4110 × 3.997 × 0.1088 pounds or £1.0485 per pound initially traded.

9. a. A premium of 6 points.

   b. The 180-day premium is (0.1086 – 0.1080)/0.1080 × 2 = 1.11%.

11. If the trader's expectations are realized, her net profit on a $1 million forward sale would be 1,000,000(205 × 1/195 - 1) = $51,282.

13. According to interest rate parity, if P is the forward premium on the dollar, then $(1.115)(1 + P) = 1.15$, or $P = 3.14\%$.

15. According to the IRPT, the 90-day forward rate on the yen should equal $0.007692[(1 + 0.08/4)/(1 + 0.02/4)] = $0.0078.

17. If interest parity holds, the 90-day forward rate on an ACU must equal $1.1191 + $0.3231 + $0.3875 = $1.8297.

CHAPTER 3

1. See Table 1.
Net profit is $1,250 – 937.50 = $312.50.

3. Sell futures contracts at $0.7145 and buy DM forward in the same amount at $0.7127. The arbitrageur will earn 125,000(0.7145 – 0.7127) = $225 per DM futures contract arbitraged.

5. Citicorp has a net loss of 2 per DM on the call option for a total loss of 0.02 × 500,000 = $10,000.

7. a. If the yen settles at $0.007500, Apex will not exercise the option and will lose the call premium of $18,750. If the yen settles at $0.008400, Apex will exercise the option and earn a net gain of $31,250.

With a futures contract, if the yen settles at $0.007500, Apex will lose $55,000. But if the yen appreciates to $0.008400, Apex will earn $57,500.

   b. If the yen settles at $0.007900, Apex will lose the call premium of $18,750. If Apex hedges with futures contracts, it will lose $5,000.

   c. On the option contract, break-even occurs at $0.008150. In the case of the futures contract, break-even occurs when the spot rate equals the futures rate, or $0.007940.

   d. The sellers' profit and loss and break-even positions on the futures and options contracts will be the mirror image of Apex's position on these contracts.

9. According to put-call option interest rate parity,
$$C - P = (f_1 - E)/(1 + r_h)$$
where C is the call premium and P is the put premium. In this case, $C = 0.000514 + (0.00787 - 0.0077)/1.02 = $0.0007.

CHAPTER 4

1. 300% (the first 100% is its previous value).

3. a. 66.2%.

   b. The lira's dollar value has appreciated by 21.1%.

CHAPTER 6

1. U.S. balance of payments accounts. See Table 2.

CHAPTER 7

1. According to purchasing power parity, $e_{1981} = 0.31 \times 219/163 = $0.4165. The discrepancy between the predicted and actual rates could stem from mismeasuring the relevant price indices. Alternatively, it could be due to a switch in investors' preferences from dollar to nondollar assets.

■ **TABLE 1**

Time	Action	Cash Flow
Monday morning	Investor buys pound futures contract that matures in two days. Price is $1.78.	None.
Monday close	Futures price rises to $1.79. Contract is marked-to-market.	Investor receives $62,500 \times (1.79 - 1.78)$ $= \$625$.
Tuesday close	Futures price rises to $1.80. Contract is marked-to-market.	Investor receives $62,500 \times (1.80 - 1.79)$ $= \$625$.
Wednesday Close	Futures price falls to $1.785. (1) Contract is marked-to-market. (2) Investor takes delivery of £62,500.	(1) Investor pays $62,500 \times (1.80 - 1.785)$ $= \$937.50$. (2) Investor pays $62,500 \times 1.785$ $= \$111,562.50$.

3. According to the international Fisher effect, the spot exchange rate expected in one year equals $1.63 \times 1.09/1.12 = \$1.5863$.
   b. If r_{us} is the unknown U.S. interest rate, and assuming that the British interest rate stayed at 12% (because there has been no change in expectations of British inflation), then according to the IFE, $1.52/1.63 = (1 + r_{us})/1.12$ or $r_{us} = 4.44\%$.

5. Japan's real interest rate is about 5% (8% − 3%). From that, we can calculate France's nominal interest rate as about 17% (12% + 5%), assuming

■ **TABLE 2**

Exports	Imports
a. Merchandise: $300 in goods Services:	b. $225 in goods c. 15 payment of dividends d. 30 in tourist services

Balance on current account: +$30

Capital Outflows	Capital Inflows
a. $300 increase in foreign deposits e. 60 increase in U.S. holdings of foreign stocks g. 8 decrease in foreign-owned U.S. demand deposits	b. $225 decrease in foreign demand deposits c. 15 increase in foreign-owned U.S. demand deposits e. 60 decrease in foreign demand deposits d. 30 in crease in foreign-owned travelers checks drawn on U.S. banks

Balance on capital account: −$38

Reserve Inflows	Reserve Outflows
f. $45 in gold sales	f. $45 increase in foreign demand deposits g. 8 decrease in foreign demand deposits

Balance on official reserves: +$8

that arbitrage will equate real interest rates across countries and currencies. Since England's nominal interest rate is 14%, for interest rate parity to hold, the pound should sell at around a 3% forward premium relative to the French franc.

8. Based on PPP, the expected value of the pound in two years is $12.5 \times (1.06/1.04)^2 = FF\ 12.99$.

10. A 10% appreciation of the dollar relative to the DM is equivalent to a DM depreciation relative to the dollar of $1/1.1 - 1 = 9.1\%$. Therefore, the DM's nominal value at the end of the year relative to its nominal value at the beginning of the year is 0.909. Then the DM's real value at the end of the year, relative to the start of the year, is $0.909 \times 1.04/1.07 = 0.884$. Thus, the DM has depreciated in real terms by 11.6%.

12. During the year, the French franc devalued by $(0.15 - 0.10)/0.15 = 33.33\%$. The nominal dollar cost of borrowing French francs, therefore, was $0.18(1 - 0.3333) - 0.3333 = -21.33\%$ (see Chapter 12 for a detailed explanation of the formula). For each dollar's worth of francs borrowed at the start of the year, it cost only $0.7867 to repay the principal plus interest. With U.S. inflation of 5% during the year, the real dollar cost of repaying the principal and interest is $\$0.7867/1.05 = \$0.7492$. Subtracting the original $1 borrowed, we see that the real dollar cost of repaying the franc loan is −$0.2508 or a real dollar interest rate of −25.08%.

CHAPTER 8

1. According to FASB–52, all assets and all liabilities must be translated at the current rate. Golf du France's net foreign currency translation exposure, therefore, is FF 2,500,000 − FF 900,000 or FF 1,600,000. At the original rate of $0.1270, the value of the franc net exposure was $203,200. By the end of the year, this net exposure equals $188,800. This involves a translation loss for American Golf of $14,400 ($203,200 − $188,800).

If the current assets are all monetary or if inventory is carried at market value, Golf du France's exposure if the dollar is the functional currency would be current assets minus current liabilities or FF 1,000,000 − FF 900,000 = FF 100,000. In this case, American Golf's translation loss would equal $900. This loss must be included in the income statement.

3. a. Zapata's translation exposure depends on the functional currency used. If, over the past three years, Mexico's rate of inflation has exceeded 100%, Zapata must use the dollar as its functional currency. This means that translation exposure is measured using the temporal method. In this case, Zapata's FASB–52 translation exposure will be (in peso millions) Ps 83,000 − Ps 59,000 = Ps 24,000, or $3 million. This calculation treats cash, receivables, inventory, current liabilities, and long-term debt as exposed, and equity and net fixed assets as unexposed. It also assumes that all these assets and liabilities are in pesos.

If the peso is the functional currency, then translation exposure equals Zapata's net worth of Ps 135,000, or $16.875 million. The difference between the two translation exposure figures of Ps 111,000 = $13.875 million equals Zapata's net fixed assets, which are exposed under the current rate method but not under the temporal method.

b. The peso has lost one-third of its dollar value during the year. Hence, Zapata's translation loss equals one-third of its initial exposure. If the dollar is the functional currency, and assuming no change in assets and liabilities, Zapata's translation loss for the year will be $3,000,000/3 = $1 million. Alternatively, if the peso is the functional currency, Zapata's translation loss equals $16,875,000/3 = $5.625 million.

c. If Zapata uses the Ps 15,000 borrowing to pay a dividend to its parent, then its exposure will fall by Ps 15,000 or $1.875 million regardless of the functional currency. If the dollar is the functional currency, its new translation exposure becomes $1.125 million; if the peso is the functional currency, new translation exposure becomes $15 million. If Zapata uses the Ps 15,000 to increase its cash position, then its translation exposure stays the same.

CHAPTER 9

1. a. The expected future spot rate is $1.30(0.15) + 1.35(0.2) + 1.40(0.25) + 1.45(0.20) + 1.50(0.20) = \$1.41$.

b. If the firm wants to maximize expected profits, it should retain its pound receivables and sell the proceeds in the spot market.

c. Risk aversion could lead the firm to sell its receivables forward to hedge their dollar value. However, if the firm has pound liabilities, they could provide a natural hedge. The existence of a cheaper hedging alternative, such as borrowing pounds and converting them to dollars for the duration of the receivables, would also argue against the use of a forward contract. This latter situation assumes that interest rate parity is violated. The tax treatment of foreign exchange gains and losses on forward contracts could also affect the hedging decision.

3. a. The expected future spot exchange rate is $0.13 ($0.11 × 0.25 + $0.13 × 0.50 + $0.15 × 0.25). Because this exceeds the forward rate of $0.12, the trader will buy French francs forward against the dollar. She should buy an infinite amount of francs. This absurd result is due to the assumption of a linear utility function.

b. Regardless of her utility function, she will be restrained by bank policies designed to guard against excessive currency speculation.

c. The expected future spot rate remains at $0.13. But the variance of the expected spot rate has now risen. If the trader is concerned solely with expected values, this will not affect her speculative activities. But if she is concerned with risk in addition to expected return, the greater variance should lead her to reduce her speculative activities.

5. Arco has a contingent pound liability (the cost of its possible purchase of Britoil) offset by a fixed pound asset (the deposit). Hedging that deposit doesn't eliminate exchange risk because, if the deal goes through, Arco will not know at the time of its offer how many dollars it will take to buy $1 billion worth of shares at today's exchange rate. The solution for Arco is to buy a call option on $1 billion worth of pounds at the current spot rate. This limits Arco's downside risk to the call premium, while enabling it to capitalize on an appreciation in the pound's value.

7. Yes. Even though hedging enables K&B to lock in a dollar price for its cost of goods, the price at which it can sell its products depends on the replacement cost of these items, which varies with the exchange rate.

9. The Expos have currency risk since they pay their players in U.S. dollars while their principal source of income, from home game ticket sales, is in Canadian dollars. Most importantly, salaries for Expo ballplayers are based on the salaries they would earn in the United States; they are not based on Canadian salaries. The Expos might protect themselves by doing what the Blue Jays do: Buy U.S. dollars forward. The larger the purchase, the greater the amount of protection. Buying enough U.S. dollars to cover projected currency needs for the coming year will protect them for next year, but it does nothing to hedge their longer-term exposure.

11. Metalgesselschaft confronts two types of risk: (1) relative price risk stemming from fluctuations in the price of copper on the LME and (2) currency risk resulting from fluctuations in the DM/pound exchange rate. Here are calculations for the present values of the alternatives.

a. DM cost = number of tons needed × [sterling price per ton for immediate delivery + pound storage cost in London per ton for a six-month period] × DM spot price of one pound on April 1
= 20,000 × (562 + 60) × 3.61
= DM 44,908,400

b. DM cost = number of tons needed × sterling price per ton of copper for delivery on October 1 × forward DM price per pound on April 1 for delivery on October 1/(1 + opportunity cost of funds)
= 20,000 × 605 × 3.61(1 − 0.063/2)/(1 + 0.08/2)
= DM 40,677,931

c. The DM cost of this option cannot be computed since no information is given as to the projected price of copper or the projected DM value of the pound six months hence.

An additional option would consist of buying the copper on April 1 and storing it in Hamburg. Of the options we can price, the second one, which involves hedging both commodity price risk and currency risk, is the least expensive. Whether Metalgesselschaft should, in fact, hedge depends on how its DM revenues vary with the spot cost of copper expressed in DM. If its DM revenues don't vary with the current DM spot price of copper, the firm is probably better off hedging its copper purchases. On the other hand, if DM revenues vary directly with the spot price of copper, then hedging one end of the profit equation (costs) without hedging the other end (revenues) could subject the firm to more risk than if it didn't hedge at all.

CHAPTER 10

1. Under this scenario the postdevaluation operating cash flow will be $1,268,000 annually, a net gain from devaluation of $368,000 ($1,268,000 − $900,000). In year 3, the postdevaluation cash flow will rise to $1,418,000, which includes a $150,000 gain on repayment of the krona loan. The present value of the economic gain associated with a krona devaluation, based on a three-year adjustment period, is $939,212.

3. **a.** The real dollar value of Hilton's future cash flows from its Swiss hotel investment equals $3,880,000e_{10}/[(1 + k)(1 + i_{us})]^{10}$, where e_{10} is the nominal dollar value of the Swiss franc in ten years, i_{us} is the average annual rate of U.S. inflation over the next ten years, and k is Hilton's real required return for this project. This number should be compared to $1.5 million, the current cost of the investment.

   b. Only fluctuations in the real value of the Swiss franc matter. If the real value of the Swiss franc rises, the real dollar price of the hotel services being sold by Hilton will also rise. If demand for these services is elastic, which it seems to be given the heavy dependence of the Swiss hotel industry on tourists, real dollar revenues will decline. Inelastic demand will lead to an increase in real dollar revenues. The hotel's real dollar cost of Swiss labor and services will rise. Thus, if PPP holds, nominal currency changes shouldn't affect Hilton's Swiss investment; if PPP does not hold, an increase in the real exchange rate is likely to cause a decrease in the real value of Hilton's investment.

   c. There are several ways to forecast the nominal Swiss exchange rate ten years out: (1) Rely on the international Fisher effect, using nominal interest differentials between U.S. and Swiss bonds with maturities of ten years; (2) project relative price levels changes in Switzerland and the U.S. over the next ten years and then use PPP to forecast the rate change; and (3) use the forward rate if a ten-year swap can be found. But what really matters is what happens to the real exchange rate. The best forecast of the real rate ten years out is the current spot rate. Over the long run, PPP tends to hold, leading to a relatively constant real exchange rate.

5. The real value of the yen rose from $0.004000 (1/250) at the start of the year to $0.004339 (1/235 × 1.04/1.02) at the end of the year. Caterpillar should benefit from this 8.47% increase in the real value of the yen since Komatsu does most of its manufacturing in Japan. The inflation-adjusted dollar cost of Japanese-supplied components and labor will rise in line with the yen's real increase. Komatsu's raw materials and energy prices should not rise in dollar terms because these resources are imported.

7. E&J Gallo faces exchange risk because its wines are competing against foreign wines and changes in the value of the dollar affect its competitiveness with wines from Germany, France, Italy, and elsewhere.

9. A grower who sells only in the U.S. still bears exchange risk because the price at which he can sell his almonds varies with the exchange rate.

11. Fluor will benefit from a falling dollar since it will be more cost competitive vis-à-vis foreign contractors both at home and abroad. Its costs are primarily *denominated* and *determined* in dollars. Thus, when the dollar declines, these costs fall relative to those of its foreign competitors. Although many of the costs incurred on foreign projects are set in the local currency, these costs are the same for all potential competitors. Hence, in competing against foreign firms, Fluor will find that some of its costs are the same while other of its costs, particularly for the labor involved in design, engineering, and construction management services, are now lower.

13. As a supplier to industrial customers who compete against imports and that sell overseas, Coo-

per Industries benefits from a weaker dollar and is hurt by a stronger dollar. Customer sales rise with a weak dollar and fall with a strong dollar and these changes translate into more or less sales for Cooper.

15. These firms have benefitted greatly from the yen's appreciation against the U.S. dollar because the won has not risen by nearly the same extent against the dollar. They have used their cost advantage vis-à-vis Japanese competitors to boost sales of low-end consumer electronics products by cutting prices below the level at which the Japanese could make money. Yen depreciation or won appreciation would reduce their cost advantage. Similarly, they face currency risk because competitors in other nations, such as Taiwan or Thailand, might devalue their currencies against the won.

17. Monsanto will be hurt by dollar appreciation and helped by dollar depreciation. However, because it sells brand name products, the demand for its products is less price elastic than if it sold commodities. Thus, Monsanto will not be affected as much by currency changes as it would be if it were in a pure commodity business. The impact of currency changes will be greater on those of its product lines that are commodities.

19. The statement that "Japanese shipyards are extraordinarily productive" tells you that there is not much room for cost cutting by Japanese shipyards. Hence, Japanese shipyards will be devastated by a rise in the yen, as they were. As the yen appreciates against the won, South Korean shipyards gained a substantial cost advantage vis-à-vis the Japanese. The only degree of freedom to adjust Japanese shipbuilder costs takes place on the wage side. Japanese firms typically pay a substantial fraction of workers' wages in the form of a semi-annual bonus that is tied to corporate profits. Thus, during hard times, labor costs fall automatically. However, this decrease in labor costs was not nearly enough and many Japanese shipyards went bankrupt. Japanese shipyards have responded by designing innovative ships for which demand is price inelastic. They are no longer competitive in the commodity ship business.

21. Thomasville bears exchange risk because a falling dollar might push up spare parts prices if these parts cannot be gotten from domestic producers. It will also have to pay higher prices when it goes to replace machines that wear out if it doesn't want to mix and match machines from different manufacturers.

CHAPTER 11

1. a. A relative increase in the U.S. money supply (or velocity); a jump in U.S. inflation; a relative decrease in U.S. income, *or* the expectation of these events in future periods; intervention by the Japanese and/or U.S. governments to push down the dollar's value; or the cessation of government intervention that was previously maintaining an overvalued dollar.

b. Alternatives are (1) raise prices in the U.S. market, (2) do nothing in the short run, (3) invest in the U.S. and build the cars there, (4) try to reduce production costs in Japan, (5) exit the U.S. market, (6) switch production to higher quality, less price-elastic and more income-elastic cars.

c. The appropriate response by Nissan depends on its view of the nature of the economic disturbance that caused the exchange rate change. If the shock is nominal (PPP holds), it can probably pass along all of the exchange rate change to its U.S. customers. If the exchange rate change is real, which it almost surely is, Nissan must make some real changes in response to stay competitive with U.S. automakers.

These changes depend on whether the increase in the real exchange rate is expected to be temporary or permanent. If the increase is due to intervention by the U.S. or Japanese central banks, the change is likely to be temporary because it is a movement away from equilibrium. Alternatively, a real exchange rate change that is due to market forces or to the *cessation* of intervention by the Japanese or U.S. central banks can be assumed permanent. *Permanent* in this context means that the best predictor of tomorrow's real exchange rate is today's rate.

If the real exchange rate increase is expected to be temporary, it may not pay Nissan to raise dollar prices and lose U.S. market share, because of the cost of buying back market share at a later date. But if the increase in the real exchange rate is expected to be permanent, then Nissan should consider raising its prices and making more basic changes in its production and marketing strategy.

d. Here, the tables are reversed from part c. Nissan is "enjoying" an increase of 10% in its yen receipts from U.S. auto sales. Whether its "enjoyment" is real depends again on the nature of the economic disturbance associated with the exchange rate change. If Japanese production costs are rising because of inflation (associated with the yen devaluation), Nissan need not be better off in real terms. Its opportunities still depend on the "real/nominal" and "permanent/temporary" nature of the shock.

3. a. If the international Fisher effect holds, then the expected cost of each loan is the same. If Gizmo is unwilling to assume the IFE holds, then it needs to forecast the DM and Swiss franc exchange rates to calculate the loan whose *expected* U.S. dollar cost is the lowest. But even if the expected cost of each loan is the same, the risk associated with each loan may be different for Gizmo. This risk will depend on the currency denomination of assets that Gizmo holds as well as on the markets in which Gizmo buys its inputs and sells it outputs.

b. If the factory in Geneva sells in Switzerland, then Gizmo has an asset that is essentially denominated in Swiss francs. This may establish a natural hedge against a Swiss franc loan and reduce the risk of this particular alternative. If the expected cost of each loan alternative if the same, and if Gizmo seeks to reduce total risk, then this information would suggest a Swiss franc loan. But if the Swiss factory is exporting to the U.S., or is selling in the Swiss market and facing import competition, then some dollar financing or financing in the currency of the country in which its main competitors are located might be appropriate if Gizmo wants to reduce risk.

5. Boeing would have currency risk even in the absence of foreign competition since currency fluctuations will translate its dollar prices into varying amounts of foreign currency to its foreign customers. Since foreign demand is somewhat responsive to price, and Boeing prices in dollars, dollar appreciation will reduce foreign demand. Alternatively, to maintain sales volume, Boeing will have to cut its dollar price. Dollar depreciation benefits Boeing since it can either raise its dollar price, while keeping its foreign currency prices constant, or keep its dollar price constant and thereby cut its foreign currency prices and boost sales overseas. In reality, Boeing does face a major foreign competitor—Airbus Industrie, a European consortium. The existence of Airbus increases Boeing's price elasticity of demand and, hence, its exchange risk. This means that Boeing is hurt more by dollar appreciation and helped more by dollar depreciation.

7. A company such as Cost Plus will typically negotiate purchase contracts with the suppliers of its catalogue merchandise in advance. Cost Plus (CP) could hedge these purchases using forward contracts. But if the foreign currencies devalue during the life of the catalogue, prices of substitute products for the catalogue items will likely come down somewhat. In this case, some customers who might have bought from CP will decide to buy the cheaper substitutes. This is particularly likely here given the nature of Cost Plus products: low-cost goods presumably bought by a price-sensitive clientele. The existence of quantity risk in addition to price risk suggests that Cost Plus should hedge less than 100% of its projected sales. Alternatively, CP could buy call options to cover its foreign purchases.

9. Since Lyle has chartered out its ships in dollars, it has fixed dollar revenues. By financing its ship purchases with dollars, Lyle can offset these contractual dollar inflows with contractual dollar outflows. Lyle bears significant translation exposure. As the dollar rises against the pound, Lyle will show losses on its dollar debt and vice versa when the dollar falls. But gains or losses on the debts will be canceled out over time by changes in its operating cash flows.

11. Caterpillar now has a diversified cost structure. This means it won't be hurt as much when the dollar rises again, but it also will not benefit as much when the dollar falls. Its main competitors, Deere & Co. and J.I. Case, now have a competitive advantage vis-à-vis Caterpillar by producing most of their small construction equipment in the United States.

13. **a and b.** Since TI's main competitors worldwide are Japanese companies, one critical factor affecting its exposure is the dollar/yen exchange rate. If the dollar appreciates relative to, say, the DM, but the $/¥ exchange rate remains constant, then TI should be able to raise its DM prices without suffering a loss of competitive advantage. However, changes in the dollar value of the DM that are not offset by changes in the dollar value of the yen, *or* changes in the $/¥ rate (even if the dollar value of the DM has not changed), expose TI to currency risk. The more price sensitive the European demand for chips, the more currency risk TI faces. Memory chips, being commodities, are likely to be more price-sensitive than microprocessors. TI's currency risk also depends on the value-added work performed in Europe. The more value-added work done in Europe, or that *can* be done in Europe, the less currency risk TI faces since its local currency inflows will be offset by local currency outflows.

    c. TI should finance itself to a significant degree with Japanese yen, so a yen depreciation that reduces TI's dollar cash inflows will at the same time reduce the dollar amount of its yen debt servicing costs.

CHAPTER 12

1. Since Apex receives only FF 800,000 net of the compensating balance requirement, the effective interest rate is FF 120,000/FF 800,000 = 15%.

3. **a.** The effective interest rate is HK$1.25 × 0.09/HK$1.25 × 0.9 = 10%.

    b. The effective interest rate now is HK$1.25 × 0.09/HK$1.25 × 0.8 = 11.25%.

    c. The effective interest rate here equals HK$1.25 × 0.09/(HK$1.25 × 0.9 − HK$1.25 × 0.09) = 11.11%.

    d. Let L be the size of Top Gum's loan. The amount it winds up with is 0.9L − 0.09L = 0.81L. Hence, the amount TG needs to borrow to receive HK$1.25 million can be found by solving 0.81L = HK$1,250,000, or L = HK$1,543,210.

5. **a.** No. According to the international Fisher effect, the 5% interest differential reflects the market's expectations that the yen will appreciate by approximately 5% relative to the dollar over the coming year.

    b. The breakeven exchange rate is found as the solution to $S = 140 \times 1.05/1.10 = ¥133.64$.

7. The breakeven exchange rate change is $d = (0.12 − 0.078)/1.12 = 3.75\%$.

CHAPTER 14

1. Several techniques are (1) define and analyze the different available payment channels, (2) select the most efficient method, (3) give specific instructions regarding payment procedures to the firm's customers and banks, (4) use multilateral netting, (5) determine the currency of invoice and payment by reference to what is available and what is needed for the system as a whole, and (6) use treasury workstations to keep track of liquidity world wide.

3. SKB identified six major benefits from centralizing international cash management and foreign exchange management: (1) systems expertise centralized at headquarters, (2) speedy communications and processing, (3) better overall picture of where the affiliates stand, (4) help to local managers to better manage their financial positions, (5) lower bank costs, and (6) reduced interest expenses.

7. RJR created a centralized approach to international treasury management. By balancing cash among its operating companies on a daily basis, RJR was able to prevent some of the companies from investing surplus cash while other companies were borrowing at a higher interest rate. Centralization also ensured that accumulated excess funds were invested quickly and at the best available yield.

9. The net benefit to Tiger Car of shifting production to Tennessee equals the reduction in its inventory

carrying costs less its higher labor costs. The inventory carrying cost savings per car equal

$$\frac{\text{interest}}{\text{savings}} = \frac{\text{opportunity cost of funds} \times \text{reduced}}{\text{time in transit} \times \text{cost per car}}$$

$$= 12.5\% \times 65/365 \times ¥825{,}000 = ¥18{,}365$$

Since Tiger's costs will actually rise by ¥33,000 −¥18,365 = ¥14,635, it should not switch production to Tennessee.

CHAPTER 15

1. **a.** Switching from a transfer price of $27,000 to a new transfer price P will lead to a monthly tax savings of $1{,}500(27{,}000 - P)(0.45 - 0.50)$. Tax savings are maximized when P is set equal to $30,000.

   b. If the *ad valorem* tariff is paid by the French affiliate and is tax deductible, a change in the transfer price from $27,000 to P will lead to monthly tax savings of $1{,}500(27{,}000 - P)[0.45 + 0.15 - 0.50(1.15)] = 1{,}500(27{,}000 - P)(0.025)$. In order to maximize the tax savings, P should now be set at its minimum level of $25,000.

   c. A 5% French franc revaluation will increase the dollar value of the transfer price to $28,350. In the absence of a tariff, total taxes paid monthly will decline by $1{,}500(27{,}000 - 28{,}350)(0.45 - 0.50) = \$101{,}250$. With a 15% tariff, monthly taxes will increase by $1{,}500(28{,}350 - 27{,}000)[0.45 + 0.15 - 0.50(1.15)] = \$50{,}625$.

3. **a.** Both subs should speed up their payments to the parent while the German unit should lag its payments to the French firm.

   b. The net effect of these adjustments is that Kodak U.S. reduces its borrowings by $5,000,000, the German unit has $2,000,000 less in cash, and the French affiliate winds up with a decrease in its cash balances of $3,000,000, all for 90 days. U.S. interest expense is pared by $48,750 while German and French interest income are reduced by $16,000 and $22,500, respectively, for a net savings of $10,250.

   c. If Kodak U.S. has excess cash, then the prevailing interest differentials indicate that the French affiliate should lag its payments to both the U.S. and French units.

5. For each $1 increase in income shifted from B to A, A's taxes rise by $0.45. At the same time, B must pay an extra $0.12 in tariffs. The before-tax increase of $1.12 in B's cost gives it a tax write-off worth $1.12 × 0.55 = $0.616. By shifting $1 in income from B to A, the effect is to lower B's tax payments by $0.616 and raise its tariffs by $0.12, a net decrease in tax plus tariff payments of $0.496. The net effect of switching $1 in income from B to A is to lower tax plus tariff payments to the world by $0.496 − 0.45 = $0.046. Thus, the transfer price should be set as high as possible in order to shift as much income to A from B as possible, or $18. The resulting increase in monthly cash flow is $0.046 × 3 × 10,000 = $1,380.

7. **a.** The net effect during the first 90 days of simultaneously switching credit terms and changing the transfer price is to shift $700,000 from the Swiss affiliate to the German affiliate.

   b. The net result of the simultaneous change in credit terms and transfer price is that for the first 90 days the Swiss unit's after-tax cash inflow drops by $925,000 and the German unit's after-tax cash outflow falls by $1,150,000. The $225,000 gain in net cash flow is attributable to a cut in taxes owing to the fact that income in Switzerland is taxed at a rate of 25%, while German income is taxed at 50%.

9. If the full FTC can be used, then the parent's effective tax rate declines to 34%. If the FTC is unusable, the parent's effective tax rate on the affiliate's earnings is 55%. If part, but not all, of the tax credit is usable, the parent's effective tax rate on its French unit's earnings will lie between 34% and 55%.

11. The reinvoicing center can (1) shift liquidity from surplus to deficit affiliates, (2) decentralize management of transaction exposure, (3) reduce taxes by transfer price adjustments, (4) assure consistent pricing to customers placing orders with more than one unit, (5) net intercompany transfers, (6) take advantage of economies of scale in financing and investing, (7) concentrate trading expertise, (8) reduce FX trading costs by dealing in larger volumes, and (8) centralize control over finance functions.

CHAPTER 16

1. 3.78%.

3. 51.17%.

5. a–d

%US	%UK	Exp. Return	Std. Dev.
25	75	12.75	7.93
50	50	13.50	7.75
75	25	14.25	8.51

%US	%SP	Exp. Return	Std. Dev.
25	75	7.50	4.02
50	50	10.00	5.50
75	25	12.50	7.63

   e. Spain offers better diversification opportunities because its fund returns are less correlated with the U.S. market ($r = 0.06$) than U.K. funds ($r = 0.33$).

   f. An investor can improve on the risk-return combination selected in the answer to part d by including the U.K. fund in the portfolio. The appropriate percent to invest in the U.K. fund depends on the correlation between the U.K. fund and the Spain fund, which we don't know.

CHAPTER 17

1. a. Even if GM manages to get its costs down to the level of its Japanese competitors, it will still face a competitive disadvantage because of asymmetrical market shares. Suppose the Japanese cut their prices in order to gain market share in the United States. If GM responds with its own price cuts, it will lose profit on 85% of its sales. By contrast, the Japanese will lose profit on only 25% of their sales. This puts GM in a bind: If it responds to this competitive intrusion with a price cut of its own, the response will hurt GM more than the Japanese.

   b. GM could reduce its costs still further through some major technological breakthroughs, by cutting wages and benefits, or by sourcing more parts and components abroad. It could also improve its product differentiation in ways that are valued by auto buyers. Alternatively, GM could cut price in Japan.

   c. GM is actively engaged in various cost cutting activities and this activity should continue regardless of what the Japanese do. The second response—better product differentiation—is problematic given GM's past history. The third alternative is the one to focus on. The correct place for GM to retaliate against a Japanese competitive intrusion in the U.S. is Japan, where their competitors earn 40% of their profits. This response would hurt the Japanese more than GM. But in order to make this retaliatory threat credible, GM must build up its Japanese market position, a tall order for any U.S. firm.

3. Since the cost of engines, when measured in the same currency, is the same for both Boeing and Airbus, currency changes have no effect here. But other costs measured in the same currency will now be lower for Boeing than for Airbus. Therefore, a falling dollar will place Airbus at a competitive *disadvantage* relative to Boeing. Hence, the story is misleading.

5. If Tandem Computer shifts virtually all the labor-intensive portion of its production to Mexico it will face several risks: (1) quality control, (2) on time delivery, (3) production disruptions, (4) exchange risk, and (5) political risk.

7. a. P&G can use its Japanese affiliate to copy Kao's innovations and then diffuse these innovations through the global distribution network provided by its foreign subsidiaries. In general, P&G can take innovations in process or product technology developed anywhere in the world and then apply them throughout the world. In this way, P&G can achieve the economies of scale and scope associated with investing in a global distribution network. It can also amortize its investments in technology across a global sales base, giving it a higher return for each dollar invested in R&D and enabling it to invest more money profitably in R&D.

   b. If Kao can't replicate P&G's market-sensitive global network of affiliates, it won't be able to exploit its own innovations outside Japan. The inability to capture the full rents associated with its innovations means that Kao's investment in new product and process technologies or in a global distribution system will be less profitable than equivalent P&G investments, placing Kao at a competitive disadvantage relative to P&G.

CHAPTER 18

1. The probability of expropriation has to be 34.1% before the investment no longer has a positive NPV.

3. **a.** Short-run benefits include better quality control, better communication with customers, and the ability to adapt quickly to changing markets. Longer term, a domestic manufacturing facility would give Xebec a laboratory in which to apply the latest thinking about automated production.

   b. The intangible strategic benefits of domestic manufacturing can be factored into the factory location decision by using the option pricing framework. By investing in domestic manufacturing, Xebec creates for itself a series of opportunities to invest capital in the future so as to increase the profitability of its existing product lines and benefit from expanding into new products or markets or new process technologies. Whether Xebec will exercise these growth options depends on what happens in the future, which is unknowable today.

   c. The possibility of radical shifts in manufacturing technology would increase the benefits from investing in factory automation in the U.S. The phrase "radical shifts" implies that the project is high risk, which increases the option component of value.

   d. The more customization is required, the more important it is to work closely with the customer. It is also difficult to coordinate the efforts of the marketing, engineering, design, and manufacturing people when they are spread around the globe. The need for coordination increases the value of domestic production facilities.

   e. The before-tax value of the five-year interest subsidy, discounted at 14%, is $2,014,668.

   f. Assuming that Xebec has no use for excess foreign tax credits, the value of the tax holiday to it is only about $60,000 annually.

CHAPTER 19

1. **a.** The weighted average cost of capital for the project is $k_I = 1/3 \times 12\% + 2/3 \times 7\% = 8.67\%$.

   b. Assuming that the marginal tax rate is about 40%, the unlevered beta is $1.21/[1 + (1 - 0.4)1/2] = 0.93$.

CHAPTER 20

1. Whether privatization benefits Mexico's ruling class depends on how prices are set and the terms of the sale. Even if privatization takes places at unrealistically low prices, it will benefit all Mexicans, provided that (1) no laws restrict the ability of domestic or foreign firms to compete with privatized firms and (2) the government ends its subsidies to them. Competition will force privatized firms to be more efficient, while cutting subsidies will end a major drain on the Mexican treasury.

3. **a.** The system as described completely destroys all incentive to be efficient and profitable. In effect, it penalizes success and rewards failure. At the same time, the ability to borrow unlimited amounts of money at a zero interest rate encourages firms to squander capital without penalty and reduces the incentive to cut costs. Moreover, the absence of any constraints on the ability of state banks to print money to cover shortfalls guarantees rapid expansion of the money supply and inflation.

   b. By printing money while controlling prices, the government is assuring that there will be massive shortages of goods and services throughout the Soviet Union. At the same time, black markets will arise in controlled goods and services while prices of uncontrolled products will skyrocket.

   c. This system of foreign exchange allocation destroys any incentive to conserve on foreign exchange, and allows bureaucrats to decide what amount of foreign exchange is needed to accomplish the state plan. It also discourages Soviet exports since the government imposes what is, in effect, a 100% tax on foreign exchange earnings.

d. The basic problem with this system is that without the possibility of competition, the state enterprises become unregulated monopolies. Since their goods are already underpriced, deregulated enterprises can reach their profit target by raising their prices rather than by cutting costs or producing higher quality goods. In fact, they appear to have not only raised prices but also cut production, thereby simplifying their lives.

e. Although the Western nations are well-intentioned (we think; they may be using this as a means of dumping the agricultural surpluses they have accumulated by subsidizing their farmers), the effect of food aid will be to drive down the price of food in the Soviet Union, thereby reducing the incentive of Soviet farmers to produce food.

f. Massive loans to these nations will alleviate their economic crisis, reducing the governments' incentive to institute real economic and political reform. They also boost the power of the bureaucrats at the expense of the private sector.

g. This policy destroys faith in the monetary system, discourages savings, and will put out of business the entrepreneurs that the Soviet Union so desperately needs.

5. a. Ending monetization of the deficit will reduce the growth in the money supply. This change in policy will actually lower nominal interest rates by reducing inflation expectations. It should also lead to lower real interest rates by reducing the inflation risk premium imbedded in nominal rates. The key question is how the government will deal with the deficit. If it cuts spending, the result will be a healthier economy and stronger growth. Alternatively, the government can sell bonds to the market. This will probably boost real interest rates, but the nominal interest rate will still be lower than it was before. Borrowing from the private sector to finance large deficits, however, is not a sustainable policy. Sooner or later, the government will have to face the issue once again of whether to raise taxes, monetize the deficit, or cut spending.

b. Privatization is probably the single most valuable step that Brazil can take to deal with its economic crisis. Most state-owned enterprises are way overmanned and incredibly inefficient. They should be forced to reduce their employment. But to argue that this will lead to massive unemployment ignores the fact that these enterprises are squandering vast resources—including people and capital—that could be used more efficiently elsewhere in the economy and lead to higher economic growth. Moreover, bankruptcy doesn't destroy assets; it simply transfers them to those who are able to use them more efficiently. It also ends the possibility of cross-subsidization by the private sector through the tax collection mechanism.

c. The more protected an economy is, the greater the disruption when it opens its borders, but also the greater the economic benefit that it reaps. Similarly, the implicit argument that Brazil would wind up running a huge trade deficit ignores the fact that a country can run such a deficit only if other nations are willing to finance it. Given Brazil's travails, it is highly unlikely that it will find many eager foreign investors. If Brazilians demand a lot more imports than foreigners demand Brazilian exports, the value of the cruzeiro will fall until equilibrium is once again established in trade. The net result from free trade, therefore, will be a more competitive Brazil and happier Brazilian consumers.

d. Lowering income tax rates while raising taxes on consumption should stimulate economic activity and savings. The problem facing Brazil is not a lack of consumption. Indeed Brazil is consuming too much relative to its income; otherwise, it would never have run such huge trade deficits. The main effect of higher savings should be to reduce imports and free up resources to service the export market, resulting in a lower current-account deficit. It should also lead to lower interest rates and more investment. Regressivity can be addressed through tax rebates to the poorest segments of society. But increased savings will not lead to less inflation, *unless* the government uses these savings to substitute for newly printed money as a means of financing its deficit.

e. Raising the minimum wage will boost incomes for those workers who retain their jobs. However, it will also cause higher unemployment among unskilled workers and make Brazilian industry less competitive.

f. The argument that floating the cruzeiro will lead to currency devaluation implies that the cruzeiro is currently overvalued. Although devaluation will raise the cost of imported goods, it will also end the subsidies used to maintain cruzeiro overvaluation. These subsidies can be given directly to Brazilians instead of only to those who buy imported products. At the same time, devaluation will make Brazilian industry more competitive internationally and boost Brazil's GNP, benefiting all.

g. Brazil tried this in early 1990. The result was economic chaos. The message such an action sends is that work and saving aren't the ways to get ahead. Citizens figure that such an action is likely to reoccur and respond with capital flight, increased consumption, and less investment.

CHAPTER 22

1. If next period's annualized LIBOR is 13%, then the Eurocurrency loan will be at 14% (13% + 1%) on an annualized basis.

3. a. The taxable proceeds are 1 − 0.10 = 90% of the bearer proceeds. Hence, the taxable shares will sell for 90% of the bearer shares. Bearer shares should be sold.

b. The taxable proceeds are (1 − 0.10)(1 − 0.10) = 81% of gross bearer proceeds, and net bearer proceeds are 1 − 0.20 = 80% of gross bearer proceeds. The firm will now prefer to issue taxable equity.

c. Both issues now yield 90% of gross bearer proceeds. Both types of shares will, therefore, sell for the same price and the firm will be indifferent between the two.

CHAPTER 23

1. a. There is an anomaly between the two markets: One judges that the difference in credit quality between the two firms is worth 200 basis points, whereas the other determines that this difference is worth only 100 basis points. The parties can share among themselves the difference of 100 basis points by engaging in a currency swap. This transaction would involve A borrowing floating-rate funds and B borrowing fixed-rate funds and then swapping the proceeds.

b. If they split the cost savings, the resulting costs to the two parties would be 12.5% for A and LIBOR for B.

3. a. At a forward rate of A$1 = U.S. $0.49, Merrill Lynch would have paid out U.S. $34.3 million for A$70 million, instead of U.S. $37 million. The net savings of $2.7 million would have reduced its net outflow on May 12, 1992 to $7.3 million. The new net present value of the swap to Merrill Lynch, using a 7% discount rate, compounded semiannually, would be $2,877,453.

b. The simplest approach is to assume that Merrill Lynch uses the $2.7 million cost savings to buy a five-year annuity, paid semiannually, which is then subtracted from Kodak's semiannual interest payments. To begin, we find the present value of the $2.7 million cost savings on May 12, 1992, which is $1,914,081 (assuming a 7% discount rate, compounded semiannually). Using the same discount rate assumption, this amount will buy a five-year annuity, paid at the rate of $230,152 every 6 months. This inflow will lower Kodak's semiannual interest payments to $2,526,098, which yields an interest rate of 6.74% compounded semiannually.

c. At LIBOR − 20 basis points, Merrill Lynch would have had to pay another 20 basis points on the U.S. $48 million principal. This would raise the semiannual dollar cost by U.S. $48,000,000 × 0.002 × 180/360 = $48,000. If this amount were added to Kodak's semiannual interest payment, Kodak's annualized interest expense would rise by 2 × 48,000/75,000,000 = 0.128% or 12.8 basis points to 7.478%.

CHAPTER 24

1. The annual interest savings on FF 10 million of restricted funds at 7% when the market rate is 12% equals FF 10,000,000(0.12 − 0.07) or FF 500,000.

3. To begin, it is necessary to recognize that 75% in pesos is not the same as 9% in dollars. In the absence of government controls or access to subsidized financing, the expected before-tax cost of the two loans should be about the same. If there is some tax asymmetry (e.g., foreign exchange losses are not tax deductible), then the expected after-tax costs of the two loans could diverge.

Regardless of the expected costs of the two loans, the risks for Compania Troquelados ARDA are quite different. The dollar loan entails foreign exchange risk, while the peso loan entails inflation risk. A key question, therefore, is how does the return on the firm's assets respond to inflation and changes in the dollar/peso exchange rate. The answer to this question depends on where the company sells (domestic or abroad) and whether it faces import competition on domestic sales. If the company is selling in the United States, the dollar loan will probably lower its exchange risk. If it is selling in Mexico without much import competition (because of trade barriers), then the company's nominal operating profits will likely increase in line with inflation, making the peso loan the low-risk loan. This assumes that the interest rate on the peso loan will adjust periodically. If the peso interest rate is fixed, then the peso loan is the low-risk funding technique only if the firm's real operating profits move inversely with Mexican inflation. Otherwise, the dollar loan is probably a lower-risk bet.

5. Because All-Nippon Airways' yen cash flow will not vary in line with the dollar/yen exchange rate, using dollar financing will expose it to exchange risk. The implicit argument for using dollar financing is that yen appreciation will make it cheaper to repay. But this argument ignores the international Fisher effect, which says that a borrower should expect that any gain on loan repay-

ment will be offset by the higher interest rate on a dollar loan. The key question to ask here is: "What's your business? Is it speculating on the future course of the $/yen exchange rate or is it providing aviation service at a reasonable price?"

7. Good advice would be "Don't speculate." The international Fisher effect says that the expected costs of dollar and yen financing should be the same. Unless Kodak needs yen financing to offset a yen transaction or operating exposure, it should stick to dollar financing.

9. a. The three principal risks faced by Nord Resource's Ramu River project are the following: (1) *Reserve risk.* There may be too few copper reserves or the ore may be too expensive to profitably mine; (2) *Price risk.* The price at which Nord can sell the ore may be too low; (3) *Political risk.* The government of Papua New Guinea may seize the mine if it turns out to be highly profitable. The government may also block repatriation of profits. Exchange risk is unlikely to be a major risk. The price at which the copper can be sold is set in dollars. In addition, Nord's biggest cost is the cost of developing the mine, which is largely set in dollar terms.

b. Nord can use financing to reduce these risks as follows: (1) *Reserve risk.* Use nonrecourse financing with a minimal amount of equity. In this way, the lenders bear the risk of the mine being uneconomical; (2) *Price risk.* Sell the ore in advance at a fixed price. Even if the price varies with the world market price, in the typical take-or-pay contract Nord will have a guaranteed outlet for its ore and will not have to engage in price cutting to sell more output; (3) *Political risk.* Finance the project to the extent possible with funds from the host and other governments, from international development agencies, from overseas banks, and from customers—with payment to be provided out of production—rather than supplying parent company-raised or parent-guaranteed capital.

c. To the extent that Nord can access subsidized financing for the purchase of equipment and contractor services to develop the mine, it

should do so. In addition, Nord can add value
to the project by using financing to reduce the
various operating risks it faces.

CHAPTER 26

1. **a.** If the Treasury had priced the zeros to yield
   7.62% less 0.125%, or 7.495%, the $33 billion
   face value of bonds would have cost Mexico
   $33 billion/$(1.07495)^{30}$ = $3.77 billion. By
   pricing the bonds to yield 8.025%, the Treasury would sell the bonds to Mexico at a price

of $33 billion/$(1.08025)^{30}$ = $3.26 billion. The
result would be a savings to Mexico of about
$510 million.

b. The Treasury proposal was designed to fill the
roughly $500 million financing shortage that
was stalling completion of the agreement. By
selling zero-coupon bonds at a cut-rate price,
the Treasury filled that financing gap with U.S.
taxpayers' money. Under this backdoor financing scheme, the banks and the Mexicans
gain, and the U.S. taxpayer loses.

■ INDEX ■

Association of International Bond
    Dealers, 584
AT&T, 481, 483
Atari, 6, 446
Atlantic Development Group for
    Latin America (ADELA), 596
Atlantic Richfield, 5
At-the-money option, 64
Audits, 341, 424
Austerity programs, 107, 680
Australia, 16, 575
Australian dollar interest rate/
    currency swap, 610–613
Automobile industry:
    corporate strategy in, 415
    growth options and, 473
    importance of foreign
        operations to, 12
    outsourcing in, 257
    pricing strategy in, 254, 255
    product cycles in, 262
    production shifting in, 259
Avis, 434
Avon, 254

Back-to-back loans, 365–367
Bahamas, 555, 663
Baker, James, 116, 597, 673
Baker countries, 116, 673, 677
Baker Plan, 116, 597, 673, 677,
    678
Balance-of-payments:
    categories of, 127–131
    in exchange rate forecasting,
        173
    measures of, 131
    in post-Bretton Woods system,
        115–118
    price-specie-flow mechanism,
        111–112
    statistical discrepancy in, 131
Balance targeting, 349
Ball-bearings industry, 8
Banco do Brazil, 630
Banco Internacional (Arg.), 662
Bank(s):
    central, 89–91, 91–95
    commercial, 34–35
    correspondent, 659–660

development, 594–597, 631
trade financing and, 312
Bank branches, 660–661
Bank capital risk-based, 657
Bankers' acceptances, 287, 308,
    314–315
Bankers' Association for Foreign
    Trade, 319
Bankers Trust, 669
Bank for International Settlements
    (BIS), 654, 656, 680
Banking:
    acquisitions, 661–662
    correspondent, 659–660
    country risk analysis for,
        678–682
    Edge Act and Agreement
        corporations, 662–663
    Europe 1992 and, 665–666
    foreign branches, 660–661
    international banking facilities,
        663–664
    organizational forms and
        strategies in, 659–666
    recent patterns of, 653–659
    representative offices, 660
    value creation in, 666–669
Banking Crisis of 1982, 28,
    655–656, 672–678
Banking relationship, 341–342
Bank loans, 286–289
Bank loan swaps, 671–621
Bank market, foreign, 573
Bank of America, 662
Bank of Montreal, 664
Bank relations, 341–342
Bankruptcy, 638, 642, 678
Banque Scandinaive (Switz.), 662
Barclays (Brit.), 662, 664, 668
Barnet, G., 405
Barriers to entry, 427
Barriers to imitation, 427
Barter, 322
Basel agreement, 656–658
Basic balance, 131
Basic swap, 605
Basket limitations, on tax credit,
    541
Baxter Laboratories, 331

Bayer (Germ.), 494
Bearer form, 588
Beecham (Brit.), 420
Beehive International, 558–559
Beijing Automotive Works,
    524–525
Belgium, 105
Bell & Howell, 434
Bell Atlantic, 577, 578
Below-market financing, 626
Beneficial Corporation, 567
Benefit/cost ratio, 525
BERI (Business Environment Risk
    Index), 506, 510
Bermuda, 557
B.F. Goodrich, 207, 418
BIC (Business income coverage),
    518
Bid price, 38
Bilateral netting, 331
Bill of exchange, 306–309
Bill of lading (B/L), 312–313
Biogen, 433
BIS (Bank for International
    Settlements), 654, 656, 680
BL (Brit.), 432
B/L (bill of lading), 312–313
Black & Decker, 445, 575, 577
Black-market exchange rates,
    174–175
Blocked funds, 367, 383–386,
    468–469
BMC (British Materials
    Corporation), 269–273
Boeing, Co., 473
Bolivia, 151
Bond(s):
    floating rate, 169
    indexed, 170
    in international financing,
        584–592
    measuring total return on,
        395–396
    zero-coupon, 628
Bond market, foriegn, 573
Bond prices, inflation and, 169
Borrowing (see also Loan(s):
    excessive, 636–637
    foreign, 107

■SYMBOLS AND ACRONYMS■

a_h	Expected real return on home currency loan
a_f	Expected real return on a foreign currency loan
ADR	American depository receipt
APV	Adjusted present value
B/L	Bill of lading
β	Beta coefficient, a measure of an asset's riskiness
β^*	All-equity beta
β_e	Levered β
C_t	Local currency cash flows in period t
C	Cost
$C(E)$	Price of a foreign currency call option
d	Amount of currency devaluation
D	Forward discount
D_f	Amount of foreign currency debt
e_t	Nominal exchange rate at time t
e'_t	Real exchange rate at time t
E	(a) Exercise price on a call option or (b) Amount of equity
E_f	Foreign subsidiary retained earnings
f_t	t-period forward exchange rate
g	(a) Expected dividend growth rate or (b) Expected rate of foreign currency appreciation against the dollar
HC	Home currency
i_f	(a) Expected rate of foreign inflation per period or (b) Before-tax cost of foreign debt
i_h	Expected rate of home country inflation per period
i_d	Before-tax cost of domestic debt
I_0	Initial investment
IRPT	Interest rate parity theorem
k	Cost of capital
k_0	Weighted cost of capital